Museum 6
Cabinet War Rooms
Museum of Mankind

Y0-BZJ-271

Time Out

London Guide

Coffee Gallery
139

Chelsea + Kings Road?
W Science B Museum. S. Kensings
C British Museum
W Notting Hill - W. Indian
S Brixton Market
E Brick Lane Mkt - Indian Food (111)
↳ Freedom Press

Pubs
Restaurant
X

Movine lees. E Wood Buildings alley 111
N Camden Town - Brixton
N Vortex - Stoke - Newington
Books
Islington - 2nd hand?

eabs - 124, 127, 137
Bar D?

Penguin Books

PENGUIN BOOKS

Published by the Penguin Group
Penguin Books Ltd, 27 Wrights Lane, London W8 5TZ, England
Penguin Books USA Inc., 375 Hudson Street, New York, New York 10014, USA
Penguin Books Australia Ltd, Ringwood, Victoria, Australia
Penguin Books Canada Ltd, 10 Alcorn Avenue, Toronto, Ontario, Canada M4V 3B2
Penguin Books (NZ) Ltd, 182-190 Wairau Road, Auckland 10, New Zealand

Penguin Books Ltd, Registered Offices: Harmondsworth, Middlesex, England

First published 1989
First Penguin edition 1990
Second edition 1992
Third edition 1994
Fourth edition 1995
10 9 8 7 6 5 4 3 2 1

Colour reprographics by Precise Litho, 34-35 Great Sutton Street, London EC1
Mono reprographics, printed and bound by William Clowes Ltd, Beccles, Suffolk NR34 9QE

Edited and designed by

Time Out Magazine Limited
Universal House
251 Tottenham Court Road
London W1P 0AB
Tel: 0171 813 3000
Fax: 0171 813 6001

Editorial

Managing Editor
Peter Fiennes
Editor
Nicholas Royle
Indexer
Jackie Brind

Design

Art Director
Warren Beeby
Art Editor
John Oakey
Designers
Paul Tansley, James Pretty
Picture Editor
Catherine Hardcastle

Advertising

Group Advertisement Director
Lesley Gill
Sales Director
Mark Phillips
Advertisement Sales
Steve Barker, Darren Loughnane
Copy Controller
Philippa Bowes

Administration

Publisher
Tony Elliott
Managing Director
Mike Hardwick
Financial Director
Kevin Ellis
Marketing Director
Gillian Auld
Production Manager
Mark Lamond

Features in this Guide were written and researched by:
Introduction Nicholas Royle. **Essential Information** Nicholas Royle. **Getting Around** Guy Dimond, Nicholas Royle. **Accommodation** Jonathan Cox. **London By Season** Kathy Sweeney. **Sightseeing** Sarah McAlister (*Hayward Gallery Neon Tower* Nicholas Royle). **Parks & Gardens** Sarah McAlister (*Wild at Heart* Bill Oddie). **Architecture** Sarah McAlister. **River & Canal** Sarah McAlister, Nicholas Royle. **History** Sarah McAlister (*Bedlam* Nicholas Royle). **London Today** Nicholas Royle. **London by Area: Central London** Conrad Williams (*Java jive* Christopher Hemblade; *The Brain of London* Jonathan Coe). **West London** Conrad Williams (*Montparnasse, SW10* Alan Ross; *Way-out Westway* Will Self © *ES Magazine*). **South London** Ian Cunningham (*The Course of the Heart* M John Harrison). **East London** Ian Cunningham. **North London** Conrad Williams (*The Books of Blood* Kim Newman). **Restaurants** Sarah Guy (*The Curry Trail* Guy Dimond). **Cafés & Brasseries** Sarah Guy. **Pubs & Bars** Sarah Guy. **Shopping & Services** adapted from *Time Out Shopping & Services Guide*. **Museums** Charlie Godfrey-Faussett. **Media** Simon Read. **Comedy** Malcolm Hay. **Clubs** Ben Bellman. **Dance** Milu Chatterjee. **Film** Nicholas Royle. **Music: Classical & Opera** Martin Hoyle, Rick Jones. **Music: Rock, Folk & Jazz** Simon Read (*Music Festivals* Kathy Sweeney). **Sport & Fitness** Graham Snowdon. **Theatre** James Christopher. **After Hours** Nicholas Royle. **Business** Tim Robinson. **Children** Peter Fiennes. **Gay & Lesbian** Caroline Roux. **Students** Emma Perry. **Women's London** Emma Perry. **Trips Out of Town** Julie Meech (*Intro* Guy Dimond, Nicholas Royle; *Brighton* Nicholas Royle; *Windsor* Julie Emery; *Country House Gardens* Jennifer Alexander). **Survival** Nicholas Royle, Conrad Williams.

The Editor would like to thank the following for help and information:
Liz Aram (Maudsley Hospital), Dr Jim Brock (Horniman Museum), Jan Brookhouse, Malcolm Brooks (Met Office), Laura Craik, Ian Cunningham, Fiona Greenway, Ciara Hedgecock, John Hegley, Susannah Hickling, Kathryn Johnson (Capital Transport Campaign), Vince Lyons, Caroline North, Jessie O'Connell, Trisha O'Reilly (LDDC), Christopher Petit, Simon Pitts, Dill Roberts, Tim Robinson, Kate Ryan, Nigel Semmens (Hayward Gallery), Mark Sherwood, Iain Sinclair, Nick Summers, Kathy Sweeney, Peggy Tout, Mark Walker (Rail, Maritime & Transport Workers' Union).

Photography by Jon Perugia except for:
Ardea page 64; **British Museum** page 195; **Cameraworks** page 184; **Michael Carter** page 152; **Channel 4** page 208; **Julia Claxton** page 285; **Dominic Dibbs** page 27; **Mary Evans Picture Library** page 67; **Flamingo** page 289; **Flowers East** page 187; **Alex Fraser** page 243; **Guildhall Library/Bridgeman Art Library** page 73; **Hayward Gallery** pages 39, 183; **Barry J Holmes** pages 29, 148, 179, 193, 198; **Hulton Deutsch Collection** pages 68, 70, 77, 80, 81, 83, 85; **Walter Hussey Bequest, Pallant House, Chichester/Bridgeman Art Library** with permission of Henry Moore Foundation page 82; **Imperial War Museum** page 192; **Jewish Museum** page 201; **Geraint Lewis** page 25; **Logic Records** page 235; **Julie Meech** pages 294, 295, 296, 298, 299, 300, 305; **National Theatre** page 253; **Petrie Museum** page 197; **Donna Francesca/Polydor** page 242; **Nicholas Royle** pages 112, 113, 223 (r); **Saatchi Collection** page 181; **Sir John Soane Museum/Bridgeman Art Library** page 76; **Sportsphoto** page 84; **Dave Swindells** 213, 214, 216; **Tate Gallery** page 78; **V&A** pages 177, 190; **Waddington's** page 185; **John Williamson** page 219.

Contents

About the Guide

This edition of the *Time Out London Guide* has been completely rewritten by a team including new writers and tried and trusted experts.

For over 25 years *Time Out* magazine has worked so hard to be London's looking-glass, it's ended up becoming an essential part of the city it has been reflecting week after week. The *Time Out London Guide* in turn reflects that degree of inside information, that level of metropolitan knowledge. It's the cutting edge of insider dealing. You buy the book, we tell you what happens.

What happens is this.

London is packed full of sights and sounds, restaurants, cafés, pubs and bars, art galleries, museums, cinemas, theatres and clubs. More classical music is played in London than in any other city. Where would pop and fashion be today, were it not for Malcolm McLaren, Vivienne Westwood and the 100 Club? *Time Out*'s reputation for incisive criticism of all the arts, and its readiness to enthuse over new forms and exponents, are world-renowned. The *Time Out London Guide* casts a critical eye over the very best of the city's arts and entertainments, its vast array of historical sites. We won't send you somewhere if it's not worth going. And if it is worth your time and effort, we make sure you know about it.

THE DATA

All the listings information was fully checked and correct at time of going to press, but owners and managers can change their arrangements at any time. So it's always best to telephone before you set out to check opening times, dates of exhibitions, admission fees and other details. We have made every effort to include information on access for the disabled, but again, you're advised to telephone first to check your needs can be met.

The prices listed throughout should be used as guidelines. Exchange rates and inflation can cause sudden changes – even, occasionally, in the consumer's favour. But if a particular set of prices or services vary greatly from those we have listed, ask why. (You can always go elsewhere. There are plenty of alternatives.) But do please let us know. We always aim to give the best, up-to-date advice, so we want to hear if you've been ripped off.

TELEPHONES

All London numbers are prefixed by either 0171 or 0181: 0171 for central London and 0181 for outer London. If you're in an 0171 area, you'll have to dial 0181 and then the phone number to reach

someone in the suburbs; in an 0181 area dial 0171 for central London. If you're phoning to someone in the same band, no prefix is required.

CREDIT CARDS

The following abbreviations have been used for credit cards: A: Access/Mastercard; AmEx: American Express; DC: Diners' Club; EC: Eurocheque card; JCB: Japanese credit card; LV: Luncheon vouchers; SC: store's own card; TC: travellers' cheques in any currency; $TC, £TC, and so on: travellers' cheques in US dollars, sterling or other specified currencies; V: Visa/Barclaycard.

BOLD

Within any chapter we may mention places or events that are listed elsewhere in the guide. In these cases, we have highlighted the place, event or thing by printing it in **bold**. This means you can find it in the index and locate its full listing.

FAIR EXCHANGE

In all cases the information we give is impartial. No organisation or enterprise has been included because its owner or manager has advertised in our publications. We hope you enjoy the *Time Out London Guide*, but if you take exception to any of our reviews, feel free to let us know. Readers' comments are always welcome and are taken into account when compiling later editions. There's a reader's reply card in the book.

Introduction

A friend of mine was working at Liberty department store a few years ago and had to deal with a difficult customer. You know the sort. Constantly complaining about perfectly reasonable things, endlessly questioning whatever anybody told him. Normally, you turn the other cheek or give some back, but when you're serving in Liberty you keep your cool. So when the awkward customer, who also happened to be a tourist, asked my friend the way to Buckingham Palace, my friend advised him to leave the store and go directly to Oxford Circus tube. Thence to take the Central Line to West Ruislip (a 15-mile trip) and when he emerged from the station to turn left and walk for 15 minutes.

It was tagging that 15-minute walk on the end that got me. Brilliant.

This guide isn't going to send you off to West Ruislip in search of the royal family, though it does make an effort to reach parts of London other guide books don't reach. The brightest spotlights may constantly be trained on Westminster Abbey, the Tower of London and St Paul's Cathedral – and rightly so – but that dooesn't mean there aren't many fascinating hidden corners that will more than repay the time and effort taken to get to them.

Indeed, this guide is aimed just as much at Londoners themselves as at tourists. If Dickens were alive today, I like to think he might pick up a copy and, shaking his head, be heard to murmur 'Well, I never knew that'.

London is a richly varied, endlessly exciting city. So it rains a bit and could be a tad cleaner and have fewer cars choking up its streets. So what. You go to the wide open spaces of Western Australia and talk to Londoners who've emigrated there. Yes, the sun shines all day and you can drive for hours and not see another car, but as they go on and on about how they don't miss London, you soon realise how untrue that is. Tell us about London, they're saying by the end of the evening. Is it still the same? Well, no it isn't. It's better. There are as many nationalities of cuisine as there are stops on the Northern Line. London no longer goes to sleep at midnight: you can drink coffee round the clock in Soho, breakfast on fresh steak in Smithfield. There are as many different shops as there are grains of sand on the beach at the bottom of your Australian friends' garden.

I conducted a straw poll among friends who do still live here, to find out about people's favourite things in the city. Escaping reality in the Clapham Picture House came up; so did mooching round HMV on Oxford Street. Kite-flying on Hampstead Heath takes some beating, but then so does a visit to Nunhead Cemetery. Most frequently, though, it was the River and its bridges. The view of St Paul's from Waterloo Bridge. Strolling over Westminster Bridge. A late drive down Chelsea Embankment to see Albert Bridge lit up like a cake.

What's really great about London, apart from the dizzying amount of things going on, the arts and entertainments, the possibilities for meeting people and making friends, is the fact that even in a city of this size you can lay down a few emotional routes – you can drive round town at night and watch the winking lights of the BT Tower and Canary Wharf, the beating at the heart of the city. You can rise early and watch the sun rise over the River. You can be a regular in a local in the centre of town where the bartender knows your name and what you like to drink. Stay here a few years and you can't go out on the streets in the centre of town without seeing people you know. Even if it's only a few celebrities.

There will always be questions. Newspaper vendors – do they have to sign a clause saying they'll be unpleasant to anyone asking for directions? When will British Telecom re-open the revolving restaurant at the top of the BT Tower? And why oh why do tourists use camcorders on still objects?

Some answers: if you stop a black cab and state your destination, the driver is obliged to take you, as long as it is six miles away or less. If they drive off, take down their number and complain. Cars have to stop if you have your foot on the zebra – standing on the edge of the pavement is no good to anyone, so get that foot on the zebra. And if the Scientologists stop you on Tottenham Court Road and suggest you take a personality test, just say no. You can be ruder if you like. I always am. I tell them where to go. I tell them to go to West Ruislip. *Nicholas Royle*

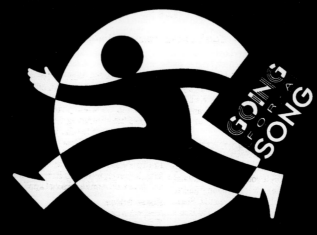

Essential Information

The facts, the figures – don't leave home without reading this first.

If you're visiting London there's some advice you need before you get here, and there are things you need to know right at the start of your visit. For other key facts, *see chapter* **Survival**. Transport gets a *chapter* to itself in **Getting Around**.

Visas

A valid passport is all you require for a visit of up to six months in the UK if you are an EC national, or if you live in a Commonwealth country (unless you come from Nigeria, Ghana, Uganda, Sierra Leone, India, Bangladesh, Sri Lanka or Pakistan).

Residents of the USA, Japan, Iceland, Mexico and Switzerland may also visit Britain without a visa. If you do need a visa, apply to the British Embassy, High Commission or Consulate in your own country before leaving. The visa allows you to seek entry for a maximum of six months. *See chapter* **Survival: Working in London** for information on work permits, which must be arranged before entering the UK.

To obtain visas to other countries, contact the embassies concerned (*see chapter* **Survival**), or have the paperwork handled for you, for a fee, by **Rapid Visa** or **Worldwide Visas**. Certain countries, however, including Italy, Canada, Guyana and Japan, do require personal applications.

Home Office

Immigration and Nationality Department, Lunar House, Wellesley Road, Croydon CR9 2BY (0181 686 0688). East Croydon BR. **Open** 8.30am-4pm Mon-Fri.
The immigration department of the Home Office deals with queries about immigration matters, visas and work permits for citizens from Commonwealth and a few other countries.

British Summer Time, from April to October, is one hour ahead of **Greenwich Mean Time**.

The famous red telephone boxes, superseded by smoked-glass booths, are now very rare.

Rapid Visa

*Top Deck House, 131-135 Earl's Court Road, SW5
(0171 373 3026). Earl's Court tube.* **Open** 9am-5.30pm
Mon-Fri; 9.30am-12.30pm Sat. **Credit** £TC.
Rapid Visa will sort out your visa requirements for £11.

Worldwide Visas

*194 Kensington High Street, W8 7RG (0171 938 3939).
High Street Kensington tube.* **Open** 9am-6pm Mon-Sat.
Credit A, AmEx, DC, V.
If you want an extension to your UK visa for up to six
months, Worldwide will sort out the red tape, for about £150.
They also arrange visas for other countries.

Customs

For citizens of non-EC countries and for anyone
buying duty-free goods, the following import
limits apply, when entering the UK:
• 200 cigarettes **or** 100 cigarillos **or** 50 cigars **or**
250 grams (8.82 ounces) of tobacco
• 2 litres still table wine **plus either** 1 litre spirits
or strong liqueurs (over 22 per cent alcohol), **or** 2
litres fortified wine (under 22 per cent alcohol),
sparkling wine or other liqueurs
• 60cc/ml perfume
• 250cc/ml toilet water
• other goods to the value of £136 for non-com-
mercial use
• the import of meat, meat products, fruit, plants,
flowers and protected animals is restricted or
forbidden
• no restrictions on import and export of currency.

Since the Single European Market agreement
came into force at the beginning of 1993, people
over the age of 17 arriving from an EC country
have been able to import limitless goods for their
own personal use, if bought tax-paid (not duty-
free). But Customs officials may need convincing
that you do not intend to sell any of the goods.

Insurance

It's advisable to take out insurance for your
personal belongings. Medical insurance is often
included in travel insurance packages, and it's
important to have it unless your country has a
reciprocal medical treatment arrangement with
Britain (*see chapter* **Survival**). All EC citizens will
need to produce one of forms E110, E111 or E112.

Make sure you're insured before you leave
home, since it's almost impossible to arrange once
you've arrived in London.

Money

The currency in Britain is pounds sterling (£). One
pound equals 100 pence (p). 1p and 2p coins are
copper; 5p, 10p, 20p and 50p coins are silver; £1 is
a yellow coin. Paper notes are as follows: blue £5,
orange £10, purple £20 and green £50.

You can exchange foreign currency at banks
or bureaux de change. If you're here for a long stay,
you may need to open a bank or building society

account. To do this, you'll probably need to present a reference from your bank back home, and certainly a passport as identification.

Banks

Opening hours vary considerably. Minimum hours are 9.30am-3.30pm Mon-Fri, but some branches are open until 5pm. Nat West branches which stay open until 5.30pm include the following: 94 Kensington High Street, W8; South Kensington tube station; Regent Street, W1; and the Strand, WC2. Cashpoint machines are outside most branches; they're usually open 24 hours daily.

Banks generally offer the best exchange rates. Commission is sometimes charged for cashing travellers' cheques in foreign currencies, but not for sterling travellers' cheques, provided you cash the cheques at a bank affiliated to the issuing bank (obtain a list when you buy your cheques). Commission is charged if you change cash into another currency. You always need identification, such as a passport, when exchanging money.

Bureaux de Change

If you cash travellers' cheques or buy and sell foreign currency at a bureau de change, you'll be charged for it. Commission rates, which should be clearly displayed, vary. **Chequepoint** (25 London branches) and Lenlyn (20 London branches) are reputable bureaux.

The major rail and tube stations in central London have bureaux de change, and there are many in tourist areas. Most are open 8am-9pm, but those listed below are open 24 hours daily.

Chequepoint
Branches at:
548 Oxford Street, W1 (0171 723 2646). Marble Arch tube.
222 Earl's Court Road, SW5 (0171 370 3238). Earl's Court tube.
2 Queensway, W2 (0171 229 0093). Queensway tube.
Victoria Station, SW1 (0171 828 0053). Victoria tube.

Opening Times

For the listings in this guide we give full opening times, but generally shops open 9am-6pm Monday to Saturday. Many stores stay open later, particularly on Thursdays (*see chapter* **After Hours**).

The laws regarding the so-called day of rest finally changed in August 1994 when Sunday trading was deregulated. There are now no restrictions on most shops. Large shops such as supermarkets and out-of-town superstores may open for six hours on Sunday, opening times being decided by the stores themselves. The deregulation also affected sport: punters may now go to horse races and greyhound races, and place bets, formerly prohibited activities. As we write, a bill is being prepared for parliament further to relax the Sunday

You can't miss the large, red post boxes.

licensing laws, allowing the sale of alcohol in pubs and off-licences to continue throughout Sunday up to 10.30pm, thereby doing away with the gap between 3-7pm. Most West End pubs open from 11am-11pm Monday to Saturday.

Post Restante

If you intend to travel around Britain, you can ask friends from home to write to you care of a post office for up to one month. Your name and 'Poste Restante' must be clearly marked on the letter above the following address: Post Office, 24-28 William IV Street, London WC2N 4DL. For other post office services, *see chapter* **Survival**.

Public Holidays

On public holidays (known as Bank Holidays) many shops remain open, but the public transport service is less frequent. The exception is Christmas Day: apart from a few restaurants (booked weeks in advance), and shops run by non-Christians, almost everything closes down.

Christmas Day Monday 25 December 1995; Wednesday 25 December 1996; Thursday 25 December 1997.

Boxing Day Tuesday 26 December 1995; Thursday 26 December 1996; Friday 26 December 1997.

New Year's Day Monday 1 January 1996; Wednesday 1 January 1997; Thursday 1 January 1998.
Good Friday Friday 5 April 1996; Friday 4 April 1997.
Easter Monday Monday 8 April 1996; Monday 7 April 1997.
May Day Holiday Monday 6 May 1996; Monday 5 May 1997.
Spring Bank Holiday Monday 3 June 1996; Monday 2 June 1997.
Summer Bank Holiday Monday 26 August 1996; Monday 25 August 1997.

Telephone

To phone London from outside the UK, you must first dial the international code (it varies from country to country), followed by 44 (the code for Britain), then the ten-digit number starting with 171 or 181 (omitting the first 0). For phone calls made from London *see chapter* **Survival**.

Time & The Seasons

Every year in spring (31 March 1996, 30 March 1997) we put our clocks forward by one hour to give British Summer Time (BST). In autumn (27 October 1996, 26 October 1997) the clocks go back by one hour to Greenwich Mean Time (GMT).

The British climate is predictable only in so far as it is unpredictable. This makes the meteorologist's job a nightmare and puts visitors and commuters in a quandary. If you want some guidance, try Weathercall on 0891 500 401 (calls cost 39p per minute cheap rate and 49p per minute at all other times). The following figures have been kindly provided by the Met Office. Temperatures show the seasonal range from the *average minimum* temperature to the *average maximum* temperature.
Spring *Average temperatures 6.8-13.5°C (35.8-39.5°F). Rainfall 124.5mm. Sunshine 455.1 hours.* Spring is March, April and May, though winter often seems to drag on until after February. March winds and April showers may turn up either a month early or a month late; there's just no telling. May is generally very pleasant.
Summer *Average temperatures 13.6-21.3°C (39.6-43.8°F). Rainfall 139.9mm. Sunshine 585.7 hours.* In the summer months of June, July and August, London's weather can still be changeable. Searing heat one day followed by sultry overcast and thunderstorms the next. The hotter it gets, the fuller the parks become. The combination of high temperatures and concentrated car exhaust fumes can create problems for anyone with breathing difficulties – so head for the open spaces.
Autumn *Average temperatures 9.6-15.1°C (37.3-40.4°F). Rainfall 146.5mm. Sunshine 326.2 hours.* Summer weather may extend into September,

while October is usually mellow, fruitful and beginning to get chilly in the evenings, then along comes November just to remind us that London is actually situated on a fairly northerly latitude.
Winter *Average temperatures 4-7.8°C (34.2-36.3°F). Rainfall 121.7mm. Sunshine 165.5 hours.* While you may get the odd mild day, don't bank on it. December, January and February are generally pretty chilly in London. It could snow, hail or sleet at any time so wrap up warm – although you can be sure that if you've put money on a white Christmas, there won't be so much as a frost.

Tipping

In Britain it's accepted that you tip in taxis, minicabs, restaurants, hairdressers, hotels and some bars (not pubs) – anything up to 15 per cent.

Tourist Information

The London Tourist Board runs the information centres listed below; the information centres will also supply a free map of central London. You can also ring Visitorcall on 0839 123456, which is a recorded information service with different lines providing information on events and entertainment. NB: hotlines cost 39p per minute cheap rate, 49p per minute all other times. Phone 0171 971 0026 to order a card listing the services.

Heathrow Terminals 1, 2, 3
Tube station concourse, Heathrow Airport. **Open** 8.30am-6pm daily.

Liverpool Street Station
Tube station, EC2. **Open** 8.15am-7pm Mon; 8.15am-6pm Tue-Sat; 8.30am-4.45pm Sun.

Selfridges
Basement Services Arcade, Selfridges, Oxford Street, W1. Bond Street tube. **Open** (shop hours) 9.30am-7pm Mon-Wed, Fri, Sat; 9.30am-8pm Thur.

Victoria Station Forecourt
Victoria Station, SW1. **Open** 8am-7pm daily (reduced hours in winter).

Waterloo International Terminal
Arrivals Hall, SE1. **Open** for train arrivals.

Getting Around

It would be nice if we could lay turf over major thoroughfares and walk everywhere we want to go, but until that day arrives, the following remains useful.

'Cars are extraordinarily convenient. You have your own company, your own temperature control, your own music – and you don't have to put up with dreadful human beings sitting alongside you.' The words of Steven Norris MP, Transport Minister for London, delivered to the Commons environment committee on 8 February 1995. The media had a field day as they duly strung him up and irate commuters suggested Norris be obliged to ride the Circle Line for a day. One harassed passenger on the Northern (aka Misery) Line was quoted as saying, 'I feel sorry for veal calves in crates, but at least there is a protest movement trying to improve their conditions.'

Compared to other European capitals, the level of subsidies for public transport in London is very low. Consequently you can be dogged by delays, but take time to get to know the system and travelling by bus and rail can be an excellent insight into London life.

Arriving & Leaving

Airports

Heathrow

Heathrow Airport (0181 759 4321) is about 15 miles/24 km west of central London, just off the M4.
The quickest, cheapest and most reliable way of travelling between Heathrow and central London is by the **Piccadilly Line** tube (50-60 minutes from Piccadilly Circus). Tickets from central London cost £3.10 one way (£1.40 under-16s). Trains run from about 5.30am to 11.30pm. There's a stop for Terminal 4 and a stop for Terminals 1, 2 and 3; check which Terminal you want.

Airbuses A1 and A2 (*0171 222 1234/0181 897 3305*) also offer a direct service to all four terminals at Heathrow (60-80 minutes from central London). These special double-deckers have ample room for luggage and most of them are accessible by wheelchair (*0181 897 3305*). The A1 runs to and from Victoria Coach Station (*see below*) with stops at Victoria Station, Hyde Park Corner, Harrods and Earl's Court tube. The A2 runs to and from Russell Square/Woburn Place, WC1 (Russell Square tube), with stops at Euston Station and Great Portland Street, Baker Street and Marble Arch tubes, Albion Street, Paddington Station, Queensway tube, Notting Hill Gate tube and Kensington Hilton Hotel (Holland Park Avenue). Buses run about every 20-30 minutes from approximately 6am to 8.30pm daily. Tickets cost £6 single, £10 return (£4 single, £6 return under-16s, free under-5s).

Taxi fares are high (£30 or more) and the journey time is about 45-60 minutes, except during the rush hour (8-9.30am and 5-6.30pm), when road travel is best avoided.

Gatwick

Gatwick Airport (01293 535353) is about 30 miles/50 km south of London, off the M23.
The **Gatwick Express** train from Victoria Station (BR) is the fastest and easiest service; the journey takes about 35 minutes. Trains run every 15 minutes from 5.30am-8pm, every 30 minutes from 8pm-1am, and every hour (on the hour) from 1-4am. Tickets cost £8.90 single, £16.80 return (£4.45/£8.90 under-15s).

The **Flightline 777** bus (*0181 668 7261/01737 242411*; you may wait a long time for the phone to be answered) from Victoria Coach Station (*see below*) is cheaper than the Gatwick Express but the journey time is about 75 minutes. Buses run from 6.35am-11.25pm daily, about one an hour during the day (phone to check). Tickets cost £7.50 single, £11 period return (half-price under-15s; free under-5s).

London City Airport

The small City Airport (0171 474 5555) is situated about nine miles east of central London, in Docklands.
Silvertown BR station, on British Rail North London Line (*see below*), is about five minutes' walk away. An alternative way to get there is by the blue-and-white **Airbus** service from Liverpool Street Station, or from Canary Wharf station on the Docklands Light Railway (*see below*). From Liverpool Street, the airport shuttle bus leaves from Bus Stop A every 20 minutes from 7.10am to 8.10pm; tickets cost £3. From Canary Wharf, airbuses leave about every ten minutes at peak times, or every 30 minutes at off-peak times; tickets cost £1. The journey by taxi to Silvertown takes about 45 minutes from the City, and costs around £12.

Stansted Airport

Stansted (01279 680500), London's newest airport, lies about 35 miles/60 km north-east of central London.
The quickest way to get there is by the **Stansted Express** train (*0171 928 5100*) from Liverpool Street Station. The journey time is 45 minutes. Trains leave every half hour from 5.30am-11pm Monday to Friday; 6.30am-11pm Saturdays, and 7am-11pm Sundays. Tickets cost £10.40 single, £21.60 return for adults (under-15s half-price). The journey by road from London takes about one hour on the M11 (junction 8).

Channel Tunnel

Eurostar

Waterloo International Terminal, SE1 (01233 617575). Waterloo tube/BR.
There are two routes – Paris or Brussels. First class Discovery Gold (£195 return) compares favourably against first class air fares, but the standard Discovery fares work out more expensive than standard class flights: £155 return, unless you book 14 days in advance for the Discovery Special £95 fare. Journey time to Paris is three hours, Brussels three hours, 15 minutes, with the tunnel section taking under 25 minutes. There are currently four trains a day to Paris and three from Brussels. Single fares cost half the price of returns, there are children's concessions, and it's worth asking about offers such as the weekend Apex fare (currently £84 return).

Coaches

Victoria Coach Station
*164 Buckingham Palace Road, SW1 (0171 730 0202).
Victoria tube/BR.*
The main terminus for coach services to and from all parts
of the British Isles and the Continent. The Coach Station is
about ten minutes' walk from Victoria Station. The biggest
coach company is National Express (*0171 730 0202*) which
runs services to destinations all over England, Scotland and
Wales. Many other coach companies also operate from this
terminus, including Eurolines (*0171 730 0202/8235*).

Railway Stations

Charing Cross *Strand, WC2 (0171 928 5100)*. For fast
trains to and from south-east England (including Dover,
Folkestone and Ramsgate).
Euston *Euston Road, NW1 (0171 387 7070)*. For trains
to and from the north and north-west of England, and a
suburban line to and from Watford (via Kilburn).
King's Cross *Euston Road, N1 (0171 278 2477)*. For
trains to and from the north and north-east of England
and Scotland, and suburban lines to north London and
Hertfordshire.
Liverpool Street *Liverpool Street, EC2 (0171 928
5100)*. For fast trains to and from the east coast (including
Harwich) and Stansted Airport; also trains to East Anglia
and suburban services to east and north-east London.
Paddington *Praed Street, W2 (0171 262 6767)*. For
trains to and from the south-west, west, south Wales and
the Midlands.
Victoria *Terminus Place, SW1 (0171 928 5100)*. For
fast trains to and from the Channel ports (Dover, Folkestone,
Newhaven); also trains to and from Gatwick Airport, plus
suburban services to south and south-east London.
Waterloo *York Road, SE1 (0171 928 5100)*. For fast
trains to and from the south and south-west of England
(Portsmouth, Southampton, Dorset, Devon), plus
suburban services to south-west London (Hampton Court,
Richmond, Twickenham).

Stationlink Bus
(Information 0171 222 1234)
The red-and-yellow Stationlink bus is convenient for the disabled, the elderly or people laden with luggage or small children. It connects all the main London rail termini on a round
trip. Buses run from about 9am to 8pm (phone for details).
Fares cost £1 (50p 5-15s).

Hitching

Single women should not hitch: the risk is not
worth it. You're unlikely to get a lift within London
except at the start of major roads and motorways.

M1 for the north ('change' at Watford Gap Services for
the north-west and Scotland, via M6): Staples Corner
(Brent Cross tube).
M2 for Dover: Rochester Way, A2 (Blackheath BR).
M3 for the south and south-west: Chertsey Road at
junction with Whitton Road (Twickenham BR).
M4 for the west and south Wales: ('change' before
Bristol for M5 and the south-west): Great West Road, A4,
at Hammersmith Flyover (Hammersmith tube); or at
Chiswick (Gunnersbury tube/BR).
M11 for Cambridge and East Anglia: M11 junction
with Eastern Avenue (Redbridge tube).
M20 for Folkestone: Sidcup Road junction with Court
Road (Mottingham BR).
M23 for Brighton: Purley Way junction with Stafford
Road (Waddon BR).

M40 for Oxford and the Midlands: Gipsy Corner,
junction Western Avenue/Horn Lane (North Acton tube).
A1 for A1(M) and the north: Watford Way at
junction 2 with M1 (Hendon Central tube).
A12 for Harwich and East Anglia: Gants Hill Cross
(Gants Hill tube).

Public Transport

The tube system and buses within the Greater
London area are both run by London Regional
Transport (LRT), which has a 24-hour, seven-day
enquiry telephone service on 0171 222 1234 (24-
hour recorded information service 0171 222 1200).

LRT Travel Information Centres

Centres provide free maps and information about
the tube, buses and airbuses, night-bus timetables,
and the Docklands Light Railway. You can find
them in the following stations:

Euston (7.15am-6pm Mon-Sat; 8.30am-5pm Sun).
Hammersmith Bus Station (7.15am-6pm Mon-Fri;
8.15am-6pm Sat).
Heathrow Terminals 1, 2 & 3 (*tube station* 7.15am-
6pm Mon-Sat; 8.15am-6pm Sun); **Terminal 1** (7.15am-
10pm Mon-Sat; 8.15am-10pm Sun); **Terminal 2**
(7.15am-5pm Mon-Sat; 8.15am-5pm Sun); **Terminal 4**
(6am-3pm Mon-Sat; 7.15am-3pm Sun).
King's Cross (8.15am-6pm Mon-Sat; 8.30am-5pm Sun).
Liverpool Street (8.15am-7pm Mon; 8.15am-6pm Tue-
Sat; 8.30am-4.40pm Sun).
Oxford Circus (9am-6pm Mon-Sat).
Piccadilly Circus (9am-6pm daily).
St James's Park (8.30am-5.30pm Mon-Fri).
Victoria (8.15am-7.30pm Mon-Sat; 8.45am-7.30pm Sun).

Fares & Travelcards

LRT bus and tube fares are based on a zone system. There are six zones which stretch 12 miles/20
km out from the centre of London (*see* **Maps**). LRT
has introduced an on-the-spot £10 fine for anyone
caught travelling without a valid ticket.

Adult Fares
The single underground fare for adults in Zone 1 is £1; for
Zones 1 and 2, £1.30; rising to £3.10 for an all-Zone single
fare. Single bus fares are cheaper. Buying individual tickets
is the most expensive way to travel. If you are likely to make
three or more journeys in one day, or if you are staying in
London for more than one day, it's always better value to
buy a Travelcard (*see below*).

Child Fares
On all buses, tubes and BR's Network SouthEast trains, children are classified as under 16 years of age. Under-fives travel free. Under-16s pay a child's fare until 10pm; after 10pm
(buses only) they pay an adult fare. Fourteen and 15-year-
olds must carry Child Rate Photocards, available free from
any post office in the London area: take a passport-size photo
and proof of age (passport or birth certificate) with you. The
single underground fare for children in Zone 1 is 50p; for
Zones 1 and 2, 70p; rising to £1.40 for an all-Zone ticket.

Travelcards
The most economical way to travel is to buy a Travelcard,
which you can use on the tube, buses (except night buses),
Network SouthEast trains, the Docklands Light Railway and

some Green Line bus services. Travelcards are sold at all tube and BR stations and also at appointed newsagents. The most convenient cards for visitors are the One-Day or One-Week Travelcards; monthly tickets are available on request.

One-Day Travelcards can be used after 9.30am Mon-Fri, all day at weekends. Make unlimited journeys within the Zones you select. These tickets are not valid on night buses. Tickets cost £2.80 for Zones 1 & 2; £3.30 for Zones 1, 2, 3 and 4; £3.80 for all Zones (child £1.50 for an all-Zone ticket).

One-Week Travelcards offer unlimited journeys throughout the selected Zones for seven days, including use of night buses. You must get a Photocard: take a passport-size photo with you when you buy your first ticket, available at any tube station, Network SouthEast station or appointed newsagents. Weekly tickets cost £11 for Zone 1; £13.80 for Zones 1 and 2; £18.30 for Zones 1, 2 and 3; £23.30 for Zones 1-4; £31.20 for all Zones (child £4.20 for Zone 1; £4.50 for Zones 1 and 2; £6.40 for Zones 1, 2 and 3; £9.40 all Zones).

Disabled Travellers

For people with disabilities, LRT publishes a booklet called *Access to the Underground*, which gives information on lifts and ramps at individual underground stations. It's available free from LRT ticket offices or from London Regional Transport, Unit for Disabled Passengers, 55 Broadway, SW1H 0BD (phone/minicom 0171 918 3312) and at Travel Information Centres (*see above*). The unit also provides details on buses and Braille maps for the visually impaired. The Docklands Light Railway has wheelchair access at all its stations.

The Underground

The tube is the fastest way to get about in London. However, lines do suffer from delays, escalators out of action and, occasionally, station closures. Smoking is illegal anywhere on the underground system. Everyone has a different and strongly held opinion about which line is most dangerous, but generally there's a lot less crime than on the New York subway. Minor harassment (mostly begging) does go on. Be careful about getting into an empty carriage on your own and beware of pickpockets.

Using the System

If you haven't bought a Travelcard, tickets can be bought from a station ticket office or from self-service machines, now in most stations. Put your ticket through the automatic checking gates or show it as you pass through the barriers. Keep your ticket until you have passed the barriers at your destination. There are 11 underground lines, colour-coded on the tube map (*see* **Maps**). The £1.9 billion Jubilee Line extension, due to open in 1998, will link Green Park to Stratford via Waterloo, Bermondsey and Canary Wharf.

Underground Timetable

Trains run daily, starting at around 5.30am Mon-Sat, 7am Sun. The only exception is Christmas Day, when there's no service. You won't usually have to wait more than ten minutes for a train; during peak times the service should run every couple of minutes. Times of last trains vary: usually 11.30pm-1am on week nights, and 11.30pm Sun. The only all-night transport is by night bus (*see below* **Buses**) or taxi.

Docklands Light Railway (DLR)

(0171 538 9400)

The DLR is administered as part of the tube system. It's a hi-tech service that runs on a raised track from Bank station (Central Line tube) or Tower Gateway (a short walk from Tower Hill tube). Trains run from 5.30am to around 12.30am Mon-Sat, 7.30am-11.30pm Sun.

Buses

Many of the new buses, more ungainly than the 30-year-old red Routemasters and operated by a single driver/conductor, are slower. But travelling by bus is still a pleasurable way of getting about. If you don't know where to get off, just ask.

Night Buses

Night buses run through central London from midnight to 6am, about once an hour on most routes. Most pass through Trafalgar Square, which is the best place to head for if you're unsure which bus to get. Night buses have the letter N before their number. Pick up a free map and timetable from one of the Travel Information Centres (*see above*).

Green Line Buses

Green Line buses (*0181 668 7261*) serve the suburbs and towns within a 40-mile (64 km) radius of London. Main departure point is Eccleston Bridge, SW1 (Colonnades Coach Station, behind Victoria).

British Rail

Network SouthEast (*0171 928 5100*, 6.45am-10.25pm daily) is run by British Rail and crisscrosses London and the suburbs. Most routes interchange with at least one main tube line and you don't have to buy a separate ticket if you have an LRT Travelcard. The North London Line (*0923 245001*, 7am-10pm Mon-Sat; 7.15am-9pm Sun) is a useful overground service which runs from Richmond (in the south-west) to North Woolwich (in the east). It connects with the tube at several stations. Trains run about every 20 minutes Mon-Sat, with a restricted service on Sundays. Travelcards can be used on this line, and it's worth it for a great view of London's back gardens.

Taxis

Black Cabs

The traditional London taxis are called black cabs (even though they may be other colours). Every licensed black cab has a For Hire sign and a white licence plate on the back of the vehicle stating how many passengers it is permitted to carry. Drivers of black cabs must pass 'The Knowledge' to prove they know where every street is and the shortest route to it. Any complaints or enquiries should be made to the Public Carriage Office (*0171 230 1631/1632/lost property 0171 833 0996*; 9am-4pm Monday-Friday). In case of complaint, note the number of the cab. You can hail a taxi

*Environmentally hostile but beautiful, the **Westway** or A40(M) takes you out of town fast.*

in the street if the For Hire light is switched on.
Radio Taxis *(0171 272 0272)*. Round-the-clock service
for black cabs. Maximum call-out fee is £2.

Minicabs

Over long distances, minicabs (saloon cars) are
cheaper than black cabs, especially at night and
weekends. However, the drivers are unlicensed,
untrained, frequently uninsured and not always
reliable. Always ask the price when you book and
confirm it with the driver. Minicabs can't be hailed
in the street: avoid drivers touting for business
(common at night) as it's illegal. Consult the *Yellow
Pages* for a local firm. Single women may prefer to
use Lady Cabs *(0171 272 3019/254 3314)* which
employs only women drivers.

Car Hire

To hire a car you must have at least one year's driving experience with a full current driving licence.
If you are an overseas visitor your current driving
licence is valid in Britain for a year. Prices for car
hire vary; always ring several competitors for a
quote. We list a couple of reputable places below.

Avis *(Central reservations 0181 848 8733)*. **Open** 8am-
8pm Mon-Fri; 9am-5.30pm Sat. **Credit** A, AmEx, DC,
£TC, V.
You must be over 23 to hire a car here. Chauffeur-driven cars
are also available. Cheapest rental is £45.50 per day inclusive (no deposit). Consult the phone book for branches.
British Car Rental *30 Woburn Place, WC1 (0171 255
2339)*. *Russell Square tube*. **Open** 8am-6pm Mon-Fri.
Credit A, AmEx, DC, £TC, V.
You must be over 21 to hire a car here, with at least two
years' driving experience. Cheapest rental is £26.78 per day
inclusive (no deposit for credit card payment).

Cycle Hire & Storage

The *Guardian* noted in April 1995 that the 1,200-
mile cycle road network proposed for London
would cost the same as 400 yards of the Jubilee
Line tube extension. With the latter due to open in
1998, the former remains a dream. Hazardous
though it may be in the meantime, cycling is faster
than going by car (motor traffic moves at an average of 11 miles/17.7 km per hour). Cycle route
maps published by the London Cycling Campaign
(0171 928 7220) are available from bike shops.

Bikepark *14½ Stukeley Street, WC2 (0171 430 0083)*.
Covent Garden tube. **Open** 7.30am-10pm Mon-Fri;
8.30am-9.30pm Sat, Sun. **Hire** £10 first day; £5 second
day; £3 per day thereafter. **Deposit** £175. **Credit** A, V.
Leave your bike in secure parking (50p for 6 hrs, £1 for 12
hrs), use the showers, change; or hire a hybrid or mountain
bike and accessories for commuting or touring.
London Bicycle Tour Company *11 Gabriels Wharf,
56 Upper Ground, SE1 (0171 928 6838)*. *Blackfriars
tube/BR*. **Open** *Easter-Oct* 10am-6pm daily. **Hire** £9.95
first day; £5 per day thereafter. **Deposit** £100. **Credit** A,
AmEx, V.
There's a cycle hire service in addition to sightseeing tours.

Motorbike Hire

Scootabout *59 Albert Embankment, SE1 (0171 582
0055)*. *Vauxhall tube/BR*. **Open** 9am-6pm Mon-Fri; 9am-
1pm Sat. **Credit** A, AmEx, DC, £TC, V.
Any British driver's licence or foreign motorbike licence
qualifies you to drive a 50cc moped. The hire charge for a
Honda 100 goes from £30.40 per day including unlimited
mileage and helmet, and from £117 per week. A Honda CBR
1000 can be hired for £70.50 per day, or £305 per week. No
deposit is needed for credit card users, but if you pay by
cheque or cash you will have to pay £500 deposit.

For sightseeing tours, *see chapter* **River & Canal**.

Accommodation

From the Ritz to the pits, we guide you through the London hotel jungle.

Humorist Gerard Hoffnung said: 'Standing among savage scenery, the hotel offers stupendous revelations.' Alas, the revelations offered by hotels standing among the savage scenery of the capital are likely to be of the 'How much?!' variety.

There is no getting around the fact. This is an expensive city. A further difficulty for visitors is that, while there is no shortage of accommodation on offer, much of it ranges from the clean but characterless to the distinctly shoddy. If all you want from life is a trouser press, a minibar and 300 cable channels then there are plenty of chains to cater to your needs. If, however, facilities are less important to you than character, value for money and the warmth of the reception you receive, then we hope you will find somewhere to suit your pocket and taste in the selection that follows.

Information & Booking

If you have not booked ahead, London Tourist Board (LTB) information centres will help. A fee of £5 is charged and a deposit is required for reservations. *See chapter* **Essential Information** for centres. *Where to Stay in London* (£2.95) is published annually by the LTB and can be found in information centres and large bookshops.

Telephone Bookings

London Tourist Board (LTB)
(0171 824 8844). Credit card bookings (A, EC, V only) for all classes of accommodation. Booking fee charged £5.

Forte Hotels Reservations Line
(01345 404040). **Open** 8am-9pm Mon-Fri; 9am-9pm Sat, Sun. You can book Forte hotels anywhere in the world on this line including 16 in London. These range in price from £43-£215 per night for a single room.

Visitors With Disabilities

Holiday Care Service
2 Old Bank Chambers, Station Road, Horley, Surrey (01293 774535). This advisory service can help disabled visitors to find suitable accommodation.

Complaints

If you have a complaint about anywhere you stay in London, you should inform the management at the time of the incident. In some circumstances, the LTB may look into complaints. Please let us know if any of the hotels listed do not come up to scratch.

Hotels

Hotels in the UK are rated according to the star or crown systems. This relates only to the facilities on offer and not to any consideration of style, atmosphere or friendliness. For instance, a one-crown hotel is guaranteed to have washbasins in every room, a lounge and use of a telephone, while rooms in a five-crown establishment will have en suite bathroom and toilet, plus many additional services such as room service and a restaurant.

You will find most of London's best known hotels in Mayfair, while budget accommodation is often clustered around rail stations. The latter can be rather seedy but Ebury Street (near Victoria), Sussex Gardens (near Paddington) and Gower Street (near Euston) also have good-quality, cheap hotels. There are also large numbers of hotels in the Earl's Court area and around Queensway, W2.

Hotels are classified below on the price of the cheapest single room for one night, inclusive of 17.5 per cent VAT. Many large hotels quote prices *exclusive* of VAT so do ask. All *Deluxe* and *Expensive* hotels will have en suite bath and/or shower and toilet. Most *Cheap* hotels have shared facilities. *'Including breakfast'* means Continental breakfast which may consist of little more than coffee and toast. *'English breakfast'* will involve some of the following: egg, bacon, sausage, tomato, baked beans, mushrooms, black pudding and fried bread.

Deluxe (£140 and over)

Even if you are unable to afford to stay in London's most famous hotels, their restaurants and bars are open to the public, and they all serve afternoon tea.

Brown's
Albermarle Street (entrance Dover Street), W1A 4SW (0171 493 6020/fax 0171 493 9381). Green Park tube. **Rooms** 116. **Rates** *single* £217-£241; *double* £241-£300; *suite* £376-£676. **Credit** A, AmEx, DC, EC, JCB, TC, V. Brown's epitomises an almost mythical ideal of Englishness: restraint, impeccable manners and discreet good taste. Converted from 14 nineteenth-century townhouses, the Dover Street side was refurbished in early 1995, and all rooms are different shapes and sizes. Afternoon teas at Brown's are no longer the event they once were, though legend has it that a gentleman, when asked which hotel he stayed at when in London, responded: 'I don't stay at a hotel, I go to Brown's.' **Hotel services** *Baby-sitting. Bar. Conference facilities. Currency exchange. Fax. Laundry. Multi-lingual staff. Non-smoking rooms. Restaurant.* **Room services** *24-hour room service. Air-conditioning. Minibar. Radio. Safe. Telephone. TV.*

Claridge's

Brook Street, W1A 2JQ (0171 629 8860/fax 0171 499 2210). Bond Street tube. **Rooms** 192. **Rates** *single £217-£258; double £270-£347; suite £646-£1,410.* **Credit** A, AmEx, DC, EC, JCB, TC, V.

Claridge's has class and it knows it. A favourite haunt of royalty for a century, it remains remarkably relaxed. Art deco is the dominant style although the size, shape and décor of every room is different. One suspects that the tartan suite is probably more popular with Americans than Scots. There is no bar but drinks are served in the lavish foyer; the idea being to make Claridge's feel more like a 'home away from home' than a hotel. The smorgasbord in the Causerie restaurant is renowned, while the main restaurant serves international cuisine, with dinner dances on Fridays and Saturdays. **Hotel services** *Baby-sitting. Banqueting rooms. Beauty salon. Conference facilities. Currency exchange. Disabled: access. Fax. Free membership of Bath & Racquets Club for men. Hairdressing. Laundry. Multi-lingual staff. Restaurants (2).* **Room services** *24-hour floor service. Air-conditioning. Maid. Minibar. Radio. Telephone. TV. Valet.*

The Connaught

Carlos Place, W1Y 6AL (0171 499 7070/fax 0171 495 3262). Bond Street tube. **Rooms** 90. **Rates** *single £217; double £276-£305; suite £511-£670.* **Credit** A, AmEx, DC, EC, TC, V.

Staying at the Connaught is akin to starring in your own Merchant-Ivory production. It has the atmosphere of a country house, all mahogany and restrained colours. And it offers the ultimate in personal service. Over 80 per cent of guests return and staff pride themselves on their encyclopaedic knowledge of each regular's idiosyncrasies. This even goes as far as decorating the rooms to suit the wishes of their most valued guests. You won't find minibars in the rooms. Tell the staff what you like beforehand and your favourite drinks will be awaiting you on your arrival. The French and British cuisine of the Connaught's two restaurants (both serve the same food) is superb. Gentlemen are required to wear a jacket and tie to dine, naturally. **Hotel services** *Baby-sitting. Bar. Currency exchange. Fax. Laundry. Multi-lingual staff. Restaurants (2).* **Room services** *24-hour room service. Air-conditioning. Drinks cabinet. Radio. Telephone. TV.*

The Dorchester

53 Park Lane, W1A 2HJ (0171 629 8888/fax 0171 409 0114). Hyde Park Corner tube. **Rooms** 247. **Rates** *single £229-£264; double £264-£300; suite £440-£1,469.* **Credit** A, AmEx, DC, EC, JCB, TC, V.

Within weeks of its opening in 1931, the Dorchester had established itself as a benchmark in hotel luxury and style. It's particularly favoured by stars of screen and CD. The outrageously camp Oliver Messel suite (£1,000 a night) has played host to Elizabeth Taylor, Michael Jackson and Peter Sellers amongst others. Charlton Heston said that the enormous baths were the only ones in which he could get his knees underwater. Food is also taken seriously here. There are three excellent restaurants including the Michelin-starred Oriental which serves Cantonese cuisine. You can also get good Italian food at the bar, and the collonaded promenade is a wonderfully glamorous place to take afternoon tea. **Hotel services** *Baby-sitting. Banqueting rooms. Bar. Conference facilities. Currency exchange. Disabled: access. Fax. Hairdressing. Health spa. Laundry. Multi-lingual staff. Non-smoking rooms. Restaurants (3).* **Room services** *24-hour room service. Air-conditioning. Disabled: room. Maid. Minibar. Radio. Telephone. TV. Valet.*

The Lanesborough

Hyde Park Corner, SW1X 7TA (0171 259 5599/fax 0171 259 5606). Hyde Park Corner tube. **Rooms** 95. **Rates** *single £206-£241; double £288-£364; suite £452-£3,525.* **Credit** A, AmEx, DC, EC, JCB, TC, V.

The Lanesborough, *née St George's Hospital.*

There are few hotels that actually take the breath away: the Lanesborough is one of them. Built at a cost of £95 million behind the façade of the old St George's Hospital, it offers the ultimate in luxury. The sumptuous Regency décor by Ezra Attia has a rich, almost masculine, solidity which has proved popular with the wealthier businessman. The Conservatory restaurant is lighter in style though no less opulent. It serves international cuisine including a vegetarian menu and hosts dinner dances on Fridays and Saturdays. Modelled on Brighton Pavilion, the Lanesborough is certainly an interesting place to take afternoon tea. Room prices are heart-stoppingly high. The Royal suite is easily the most expensive suite in London at an astonishing £3,525. **Hotel services** *Baby-sitting. Banqueting rooms. Bar. Car park. Conference facilities. Complimentary first suit or dress pressing. Currency exchange. Disabled: access. Exercise room. Fax. Laundry. Multi-lingual staff. Non-smoking rooms. Restaurants.* **Room services** *24-hour room service. Air-conditioning. Butler. CD. Decanter bar. Direct line telephone. Fax. Minibar. Personalised stationery and business cards. Radio. TV/VCR.*

The Ritz

150 Piccadilly, W1V 9DG (0171 493 8181/fax 0171 493 2687). Green Park tube. **Rooms** 130. **Rates** *single £223; double £270-£305; suite £582-£1,016.* **Credit** A, AmEx, DC, EC, JCB, TC, V.

Although the Ritz undeniably has glitz, its scale is surprisingly human. Louis XVI décor, all gold leaf and mirrors, prevails throughout but the opulence is never overwhelming. History permeates the place. It is alive with the ghosts of more glamorous and innocent days, of the glitterati and their lavish balls, when this was *the* place in London to be seen. Book a week ahead for afternoon tea in the Palm Court. **Hotel services** *Baby-sitting. Bars (2). Conference facilities. Currency exchange. Disabled: access. Fax. Hairdressing. Laundry. Multi-lingual staff. Non-smoking rooms. Restaurants (2).* **Room services** *24-hour room service. Air-conditioning. Minibar. Radio. Telephone. TV.*

The Savoy

Strand, WC2R 0EU (0171 836 4343/fax 0171 240 6040). Charing Cross tube/BR. **Rooms** 202. **Rates** *single* £211; *double* £241-£323; *suite* £294-£693. **Credit** A, AmEx, DC, EC, JCB, TC, V.

Ever since the great French chef Escoffier worked at the Savoy the culinary reputation of the hotel has been exemplary. There are three restaurants, including MPs' favourite the Savoy Grill, serving French, British and fish dishes. Pre- and post-theatre dining is possible. The hotel is blessed with a rare commodity in London: space. All rooms are large and most are art deco. The Savoy has London's finest set of hotel banqueting rooms and an excellent fitness centre and pool. **Hotel services** *Baby-sitting. Banqueting rooms. Bars (2). Beauty salon. Car park. Conference facilities. Currency exchange. Disabled: access. Fax. Fitness centre and pool. Hairdressing. Laundry. Multi-lingual staff. Non-smoking rooms. Restaurants (3).* **Room services** *24-hour floor service. Air-conditioning. Minibar. Radio. Safe. Telephone. TV.*

The Stafford

St James's Place, SW1A 1NJ (0171 493 0111/fax 0171 493 7121). Green Park tube. **Rooms** 74. **Rates** *single* £184; *double* £200-£215; *suite* £360-£430; *carriage house* £244-£290. **Credit** A, AmEx, DC, EC, JCB, TC, V.

The Stafford is an oasis of calm just off Piccadilly. It was converted from a series of Victorian townhouses in 1922 but its intimate yet airy atmosphere and pastel yellow and white décor are more redolent of the eighteenth than the nineteenth century. Rooms in the carriage house with their own front doors overlook a cobbled courtyard. The American bar, with memorabilia donated by customers, is recommended. **Hotel services** *Baby-sitting. Bar. Conference facilities. Currency exchange. Disabled: access. Fax. Laundry. Multi-lingual staff. Non-smoking rooms. Restaurant.* **Room services** *24-hour room service. Radio. Telephone. TV.*

The Waldorf

Aldwych, WC2B 4DD (0171 836 2400/fax 0171 836 7244). Temple tube. **Rooms** 292. **Rates** *single* £165; *double* £185; *suite* £340. **Credit** A, AmEx, DC, EC, JCB, TC, V.

The elegant Edwardian Waldorf was given a £20 million facelift in 1992 and, although it is no longer as exclusive as it once was, it still has a certain raffish class. It is perhaps most famous for its weekend tea dances (£20.50 per person including afternoon tea) held in the Palm Court. Booking is advisable and men should wear a jacket and tie. The Aldwych Brasserie and Footlights bar open on to the street. **Hotel services** *Baby-sitting. Bars (2). Beauty salon. Conference facilities. Currency exchange. Fax. Hairdressing. Laundry. Multi-lingual staff. Non-smoking rooms. Restaurants (3).* **Room services** *24-hour room service. Air-conditioning. Minibar. Radio. Telephone. TV.*

Expensive (£90-£140)

11 Cadogan Gardens

11 Cadogan Gardens, SW3 2RJ (0171 730 3426/fax 0171 881 3318). Sloane Square tube. **Rooms** 60. **Rates** *single* £98-£128; *double* £148-£188; *suite* £225-£350. **Credit** A, AmEx, DC, EC, TC, V.

Privacy is paramount at 11 Cadogan Gardens: there is nothing outside to indicate that it is a hotel. It's favoured by the wealthy and famous who wish to retire into peaceful anonymity after a tough day in the bustle of the city. Wood panelling and William Morris print wallpaper, hung with nineteenth-century oils, lend the place the atmosphere of a luxurious townhouse rather than a hotel. Breakfast is usually served in guests' bedrooms. **Hotel services** *Baby-sitting. Drawing room. Fax. Gym. Laundry. Library. Multi-lingual staff. Restaurant.* **Room services** *24-hour room service. Telephone. TV.*

*Mid-range **Academy** – panache and a patio.*

The Beaufort

33 Beaufort Gardens, SW3 1PP (0171 584 5252/fax 0171 5849 2834). Knightsbridge tube. **Rooms** 28. **Rates** *single* £129-£153; *double* £176-£253; *suite* £282. **Credit** A, AmEx, DC, EC, JCB, £TC, V.

Prices are steep but the hotel undoubtedly has style and the service is first class. America's most prestigious hotel guide, *Zagat*, rates the Beaufort in the top five hotels in London for quality of room and service and value for money. Rooms are light, airy and unfussily modern. You will find Champagne, chocolates and flowers awaiting you on your arrival. **Hotel services** *Babysitting. Bar. Drawing room. Fax. Laundry. Library.* **Room services** *Air-conditioning. Radio. Room service. TV/VCR. Walkman.*

Blakes

33 Roland Gardens, SW7 3PF (0171 370 6701/fax 0171 373 0442). Gloucester Road or South Kensington tube. **Rooms** 52. **Rates** *single* £125; *double* £235; *suite* £235-£590. **Credit** A, AmEx, DC, EC, JCB, TC, V.

Anouska Hempel's luxuriant designs have, in 15 years, made this small hotel one of the most individual and desirable in the world. The sumptuous colours and fabrics, different in every room, create a feeling of comfort and security. This is much appreciated by the shyer breed of celebrity such as Robert De Niro who would not stay anywhere else in London. The restaurant is top notch and always full in the evenings. **Hotel services** *Baby-sitting. Bar. Currency exchange. Fax. Laundry. Multi-lingual staff. Restaurant.* **Room services** *24-hour room service. Minibar. Radio. Safe. Telephone. TV.*

Hazlitt's

6 Frith Street, W1V 5TZ (0171 434 1771/fax 0171 439 1524). Tottenham Court Road tube. **Rooms** 23. **Rates** *single* £121; *double* £150; *suite* £197. **Credit** A, AmEx, DC, EC, JCB, £TC, V.

Hazlitt's is one of a kind. Peter McKay converted the former home of the essayist William Hazlitt into a wonderfully unobtrusive hotel eight years ago. Only a short stagger from the Groucho Club, it has been a favourite of arts and media luminaries ever since. The buildings date from 1718 and the

décor is true to the period. Rooms are furnished in mahogany, oak and pine and have free-standing Victorian baths. **Hotel services** *Fax. Laundry. Lounge. Multi-lingual staff.* **Room services** *Telephone. TV.*

Petersham Hotel

Nightingale Lane, Richmond, Surrey (0181 940 7471/fax 0181 940 9998). Richmond tube/BR then 65 or 371 bus. **Rooms** 54 (all en suite). **Rates** *single £103-£115; double £130-£160, including English breakfast.* **Credit** A, AmEx, DC, EC, TC, V.

The Petersham commands magnificent views over the Thames and greater Surrey and yet is only eight miles (13 km) from the centre of London. It was purpose-built in 1865 in the French/Gothic style popular at the time and offers traditional elegance and comfort. Rooms are spacious with furnishings varying slightly in each. Five minutes' walk away is beautiful **Richmond Park**, the largest and wildest city park in Europe.

Hotel services *Babysitting. Bar. Car park. Conference facilities. Currency exchange. Laundry. Library. Multi-lingual staff. Restaurant.* **Room services** *24-hour room service. Radio. Telephone. TV.*

Moderate (£40-£90)

Academy Hotel

17-21 Gower Street, WC1E 6HG (0171 631 4115/fax 0171 636 3442). Goodge Street tube. **Rooms** 33 (all en suite). **Rates** *single £86; double £103; suite £145.* **Credit** A, AmEx, DC, EC, JCB, TC, V.

The Academy is a rare find in London: a mid-range hotel with genuine panache. The manager and some of her staff are Danish, and Scandinavian standards of cleanliness, efficiency and style are evident throughout. The patio garden is a haven in summer and chef John O'Riordan cooks up top-class international cuisine in the GHQ Dining Club.

Hotel services *Babysitting. Bar. Conference facilities. Currency exchange. Fax. Laundry. Library. Multi-lingual staff. Non-smoking rooms. Patio. Restaurant.* **Room services** *Radio. Room service. Telephone. TV.*

Amber Hotel

101 Lexham Gardens, W8 6JN (0171 373 8666/fax 0171 835 1194). Earl's Court tube. **Rooms** 40 (all en suite). **Rates** *single £70; double £80, including breakfast.* **Credit** A, AmEx, DC, EC, JCB, £TC, V.

This hotel is smarter than most in the area but has a relaxed feel. It caters particularly for businessmen and has a unusually large number of single rooms.

Hotel services *Bar. Currency exchange. Fax. Lift. Multi-lingual staff.* **Room services** *Radio. Room service. Tea/coffee. Telephone. Trouser press. TV.*

Fielding

4 Broad Court, WC2B 5QZ (0171 836 8305/fax 0171 497 0064). Covent Garden or Holborn tube. **Rooms** 26 (24 en suite). **Rates** *single £47; double £78.* **Credit** A, AmEx, DC, EC, £TC, V.

Rooms at the Fielding are nothing special considering the price. What you are paying for is the location, on a pedestrianised street near to Covent Garden. There's a wonderful prize-winning floral display outside and you are assured a warm welcome from the staff and Smoky the parrot.

Hotel services *Bar. Fax. Multi-lingual staff.* **Room services** *Radio. Room service. Telephone. TV.*

Five Sumner Place

5 Sumner Place, SW7 3EE (0171 584 7586/fax 0171 823 9962). South Kensington tube. **Rooms** 13 (all en suite). **Rates** *single £73-93; double £100-112, including breakfast.* **Credit** A, EC, JCB, £TC, V.

Five Sumner Place won the British Tourist Authority award for best small hotel in London in 1991 and 1993. Situated in

fashionable South Kensington, it is spotless and tastefully decorated but not cheap for the facilities on offer.

Hotel services *Fax. Lift.* **Room services** *Refrigerator. Telephone. Trouser press. TV.*

La Gaffe

107-111 Heath Street, NW3 6SS (0171 435 4941/fax 0171 794 7592). Hampstead tube. **Rooms** 18 (all en suite). **Rates** *single £42.50; double £65, including breakfast.* **Credit** A, AmEx, DC, EC, £TC, V.

Rooms at La Gaffe are small but pretty and the location is superb – in Hampstead village near the Heath. The Italian owners also run the restaurant and wine bar below. All rooms are non-smoking and some have four-poster beds.

Hotel services *Fax. Non-smoking rooms. Terrace garden.* **Room services** *Telephone. TV.*

La Reserve

422-428 Fulham Road, SW6 1DU (0171 385 8561/fax 0171 385 7662). Fulham Broadway tube. **Rooms** 37 (all en suite). **Rates** *single £75; double £90, including breakfast.* **Credit** A, AmEx, DC, EC, JCB, £TC, V.

Lying in the shadow of Chelsea football ground, La Reserve is one of London's few stylish modern hotels. It has a minimalist feel with lots of black and solid blocks of colour, but in the evening the bar and restaurant have a warm, intimate atmosphere. Most of its customers are businessmen.

Hotel services *Babysitting. Bar. Car park. Fax. Laundry. Lifts. Lounge. Multi-lingual staff. Non-smoking rooms. Restaurant.* **Room services** *Minibar. Room service. Tea/coffee. Telephone. Trouser press. TV.*

Number Sixteen

16 Sumner Place, SW7 3EG (0171 589 5232/fax 0171 584 8615). South Kensington tube. **Rooms** 36 (34 en suite). **Rates** *single £78-£99; double £130-£155, including breakfast.* **Credit** A, AmEx, DC, EC, £TC, V.

Number Sixteen is actually four townhouses in this smart street near to the museums. The staff are relaxed, friendly and eager to please. Décor is somewhat eccentric – rooms are themed – and ranges from modern to traditional, from tasteful to decidedly curious. There is a pretty patio with a pond and a conservatory where drinks and snacks can be taken.

Hotel services *Conservatory. Drawing room. Fax. Honour bar. Laundry. Lift. Multi-lingual staff. Patio garden.* **Room services** *Minibar. Radio. Telephone. TV.*

The Plough

42 Christchurch Road, SW14 7AF (0181 876 7833/fax as phone). Richmond tube/Mortlake BR. **Rooms** 7 (all en suite). **Rates** *single £47-£50; double £60-£65, including English breakfast.* **Credit** A, AmEx, EC, V.

The Plough is probably the nearest thing to a traditional English country inn within the M25. Flowers bedeck the outside, while thick walls and low beams inside create a cosy atmosphere. Rooms are pretty and the home-cooked pub food excellent.

Hotel services *Telephone.* **Room services** *Tea/coffee. TV.*

Portobello Hotel

22 Stanley Gardens, W11 2NG (0171 727 2777/fax 0171 792 9641). Holland Park or Notting Hill Gate tube. **Rooms** 24 (all en suite). **Rates** *single £75-£90; double £110-130; special rooms £170-£190, including English breakfast.* **Credit** A, AmEx, DC, EC, £TC, V.

This low-key hotel in fashionable Notting Hill, just off Ladbroke Grove, is full of antiques and off-beat charm. All the rooms are different and the 'special rooms' have unusual features. One has a round bed, an extraordinary Heath Robinson-like bath/shower and an attractive garden view. There's also a 24-hour bar and restaurant.

Hotel services *Bar. Lounge. Fax. Laundry. Lifts. Multi-lingual staff. Restaurant.* **Room services** *Minibar. Room service. Telephone. TV.*

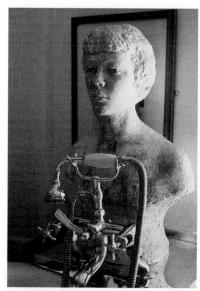

*Free-standing Victorian baths at **Hazlitt's**.*

Windermere Hotel

142-144 Warwick Way, SW1V 4JE (0171 834 5163/ 5480/fax 0171 630 8831). Sloane Square tube or Victoria tube/BR. **Rooms** 23 (19 en suite). **Rates** *single £46-£76; double £54-£82, including breakfast.* **Credit** A, AmEx, EC, JCB, £TC, V.
A gem. Located near Victoria BR and coach stations, the hotel has the atmosphere of a civilised townhouse but at very reasonable prices. It has been commended by the English Tourist Board, recommended by the AA and highly acclaimed by the RAC. You will find only bone china in the fully licensed restaurant and the rooms are spotless and airy. **Hotel services** *Fax. Lounge. Multi-lingual staff. Restaurant.* **Room services** *Room service. Tea/coffee. Telephone. TV.*

Cheap (under £40)

Annandale House

39 Sloane Gardens, SW1W 8EB (0171 730 5051). Sloane Square tube. **Rooms** 12 (9 en suite). **Rates** *single £38; double £70, including vegetarian English breakfast.* **Credit** A, EC, £TC, V.
In a highly fashionable area, the Morrises' warm welcome and the airy comfort of their high-ceilinged rooms will make you feel at home immediately. A hallmark of the hotel is that a different vegetarian breakfast is served every day, from top-notch Welsh rarebit to scrumptious French toast. **Room services** *Radio. Tea/coffee. Telephone. TV.*

Hotel Boka

33-35 Eardley Crescent, SW5 9JT (0171 370 1388/fax 0171 589 6412). Earl's Court tube. **Rooms** 50 (7 en suite). **Rates** *single £15; double £25, including English breakfast.* **Credit** A, AmEx, EC, £TC, V.
As basic as they come. Chief attractions are the prices and the location, one minute's walk from Earl's Court tube. **Hotel services** *TV lounge.*

Cartref House & James House

129 Ebury Street, SW1W 9QU & 108 Ebury Street, SW1W 9QD (0171 730 6176 & 0171 730 7338). Victoria tube/BR. **Rooms** 11 Cartref (8 en suite); 10 James (1 en suite). **Rates** *single £37; double £50-£60, including English breakfast.* **Credit** A, AmEx, EC, JCB, V.
Derek and Sharon James are proprietors of both these guesthouses in this chic Georgian street close to Victoria. The rooms are very clean and often fully booked. **Hotel services** *Fax.* **Room services** *Tea/coffee. TV.*

Curzon House

58 Courtfield Gardens, SW5 0NF (0171 581 2116/fax 0171 835 1319). Gloucester Road tube. **Rooms** 16 (6 en suite). **Rates** *shared room £13; single £26; double £38, including breakfast.* **Credit** A, EC, V.
This is a favourite place with backpackers, chiefly because of the low rates and use of the kitchen. Rooms are basic but the bubbly Kayleen is sure to make you feel welcome. **Hotel services** *Drinks machine. Kitchen. TV lounge.*

Edward Lear Hotel

28-30 Seymour Street, W1H 5WD (0171 402 5401/fax 0171 706 3766). Marble Arch tube. **Rooms** 31 (4 en suite). **Rates** *single £39.50-£55; double £49.50-£67.50, including English breakfast.* **Credit** A, EC, £TC, V.
The king of the limerick once lived in this lovely townhouse. It's now an excellent and surprisingly cheap hotel, only a minute's walk from Oxford Street. Guests get their own front door key and all rooms have TV with free film channel. **Hotel services** *Fax. Library. Multi-lingual staff. TV lounge.* **Room services** *Radio. Tea/coffee. Telephone. TV.*

Europa House Hotel

151 Sussex Gardens, W2 2RY (0171 723 7343 or 402 1923/fax 0171 224 9331). Paddington tube/BR. **Rooms** 18 (all en suite). **Rates** *single £34; double £48, including English breakfast.* **Credit** A, EC, £TC, V.
All rooms have en suite facilities in this clean but unexciting B&B near to Paddington rail station. There is a four per cent charge on credit card payments. **Hotel services** *Fax.* **Room services** *Tea/coffee. Telephone. TV.*

Gower House Hotel

57 Gower Street, WC1E 6HJ (0171 636 4685). Goodge Street tube. **Rates** *single £30; double £40-£60, including English breakfast.* **Credit** A, EC, £TC, V.
Rooms are clean and prices are good for the area. There is a two per cent charge on payments by credit card. **Hotel services** *Fax. Multi-lingual staff.* **Room services** *Coffee and tea facilities. TV.*

Hampstead Village Guesthouse

2 Kemplay Road, NW3 1SY (0171 435 8679/fax 0171 794 0254). Hampstead tube. **Rooms** 5. **Rates** *single £30-£45; double £50-£60.* **Credit** A, AmEx, EC, £TC, V.
This Victorian family home is also a delightful guesthouse. All rooms are different, full of character and clutter. Breakfast is served in the garden in summer. No smoking. **Hotel services** *Fax. Garden.* **Room services** *Iron & ironing board. Refrigerator. Tea/coffee. Telephone. TV.*

Holland Park Hotel

6 Ladbroke Terrace, W11 3PG (0171 792 0216/0171 727 5815/fax 0171 727 8166). Notting Hill Gate tube. **Rooms** 23 (19 en suite). **Rates** *single £37-£49; double £49-£66, including breakfast.* **Credit** A, AmEx, DC, EC, £TC, V.
A superior bed and breakfast hotel in a leafy avenue near to Kensington Palace. The décor is classically simple but of better quality than in many more expensive hotels. There is also a lovely lounge and a private garden for the use of guests. **Hotel services** *Fax. Multi-lingual staff.* **Room services** *Tea/coffee. Telephone. TV.*

Hyde Park House

48 St Petersburgh Place, W2 4LB (0171 229 1687).
Bayswater or Queensway tube. **Rooms** 11 (1 en suite).
Rates *single £25; double £35.* **Credit** EC, £TC.
Basic but cheap accommodation in a pleasant, quiet street.
Hotel services *Lounge. Tea/coffee.* **Room services** *TV.*

Nevern Hotel

31 Nevern Place, SW5 9NP (0171 370 4827/0171 244
8366/fax 0171 370 1541). Earl's Court tube. **Rooms** 35
(21 en suite). **Rates** *single £30; double £40, including*
breakfast. **Credit** A, AmEx, EC, £TC, V.
The charming Mr and Mrs Przybylski offer a warm welcome.
Unusually high percentage of rooms with en suite facilities.
Hotel services *TV lounge.* **Room services** *Telephone. TV.*

Ruskin Hotel

23-24 Montague Street, WC1B 5BN (0171 636 7388/fax
0171 323 1662). Holborn, Russell Square or Tottenham
Court Road tube. **Rooms** 33 (6 en suite). **Rates** *single*
£34; double £49-£60, including English breakfast. **Credit**
A, AmEx, DC, EC, £TC, V.
Tony Barranco has been running the Ruskin for 17 years.
Rooms are spotless and the location is prime.
Hotel services *Lift. Multi-lingual staff. TV lounge.*
Room services *Tea/coffee.*
Branch: Haddon Hall Hotel 39-40 Bedford Place,
WC1B 5JT (0171 636 0026/2474/fax 0171 580 4527).

Swiss House Hotel

171 Old Brompton Road, SW5 0AN (0171 373 2769/fax
0171 373 4983). Gloucester Road tube. **Rooms** 15 (14 en
suite). **Rates** *single £34-£50; double £64, including*
breakfast. **Credit** A, AmEx, DC, EC, £TC, V.
A cut above most B&B hotels. Staff are friendly, bedrooms
clean. There is a 5 per cent charge on credit card payments.
Hotel services *Fax. Multi-lingual staff. Non-smoking*
rooms. **Room services** *Room service. Telephone. TV.*

Vicarage Hotel

10 Vicarage Gate, W8 4AG (0171 229 4030). Notting
Hill Gate tube. **Rooms** 18 (0 en suite). **Rates** *single £34;*
double £55, including English breakfast. **Credit** EC, £TC.
Excellent B&B hotel in a handsome Victorian terrace. Rooms
are large and tastefully decorated. Book well in advance.
Hotel services *Fax. Payphone. Tea/coffee. TV lounge.*

Woodville House

107 Ebury Street, SW1W 9QU (0171 730 1048/fax
0171 730 2574). Victoria tube/BR. **Rooms** 12. **Rates**
single £36; double £54, including English breakfast.
Credit EC, £TC.
Ian Berry and Rachel Joplin will give you plenty of helpful
advice on avoiding the pitfalls of visiting London. Rooms are
small but clean, breakfasts hearty and the patio a delight.
Hotel services *Fax. Kitchenette. Library. Multi-lingual*
staff. Patio. **Room services** *Tea/coffee. TV.*

Children's Hotel

Pippa's Pop-Ins

430 Fulham Road, SW6 1PU (0171 385 2458). Fulham
Broadway tube. **Rates** £25 Mon-Thur; £30 Fri-Sun.
Credit A, AmEx, V.
Children aged two-12 can be left at Pippa's for up to 24 hours.

Youth Hostels & YMCAs

Youth Hostels

You don't get much privacy in youth hostels as
most beds are in dormitories, but the atmosphere

is usually friendly and they are great value. If
you are not a member of the International Youth
Hostel Federation (IYHF) you will have to pay
an extra £1.50 to stay at their hostels. Alternatively, you can join IYHF (the charge is £9
in 1995) at any of the hostels or at the YHA
Adventure Shop, 14 Southampton Street, WC2
(0171 836 1036). There are seven hostels in
London and it is always wise to phone first to
check availability of beds.

City of London Youth Hostel

36-38 Carter Lane, EC4 5AD (0171 236 4965/fax
0171 236 7681). St Paul's tube. **Beds** 190.
Reception open 7am-11.30pm daily; 24-hour access.
Rates £14.20-£22.20; £11.10-£18.70 under-18s. **Credit**
A, TC, V.
Hostel services *Bureau de change. Full canteen*
facilities. Hostel booking service. Public telephone. Shop.
TV lounge. TVs in some rooms.

Earl's Court Youth Hostel

38 Bolton Gardens, SW5 0AQ (0171 373 7083/fax 0171
835 2034). Earl's Court tube. **Beds** 154. **Reception**
open 7am-11pm daily; 24-hour access. **Rates** £17.10; £15
under-18s, *including breakfast.* **Credit** A, TC, V.
Hostel services *Bureau de change. Coach and hostel*
booking service. Full canteen and kitchen facilities.

Hampstead Heath Youth Hostel

4 Wellgarth Road, NW11 7HR (0181 458 9054/fax
0181 209 0546). Golders Green tube. **Beds** 200.
Reception open 7am-11.30pm daily; 24 hour access.
Rates £14; £11.90 under-18s. **Credit** A, TC, V.
Hostel services *Bureau de change. Canteen: breakfast*
& dinner. Hostel booking service. Kitchen facilities.
Laundrette. Public telephones. TV.

Highgate Village Youth Hostel

84 Highgate West Hill, N6 6LU (0181 340 1831/fax
0181 341 0376). Archway or Highgate tube. **Beds** 72.
Reception open 7am-midnight daily; no access after
midnight. **Rates** £11.85; £7.90 under-18s.
Hostel services *Canteen: breakfast only. Food shop.*
Kitchen facilities. Public telephone. TV.

Holland House Youth Hostel

Holland House, Holland Park, W8 7QU (0171 937
0748/fax 0171 376 0667). High Street Kensington or
Holland Park tube. **Beds** 201. **Reception open** 6.45am-
11.30pm daily; 24-hour access. **Rates** £17.10; £15 under-
18s, *including breakfast.* **Credit** A, TC, V.
Hostel services *Bureau de change. Coach, theatre and*
hostel bookings. Kitchen facilities. Laundrette. Public
telephone. TV.

Oxford Street Youth Hostel

14 Noel Street, W1V 3PD (0171 734 1618/fax 0171 734
1657). Oxford Circus tube. **Beds** 89. **Reception open**
6.45am-11pm daily; 24-hour access. **Rates** £16.70; £13.60
under-18s. **Credit** A, TC, V.
Hostel services *Bureau de change. Hostel booking*
service. Kitchen facilities. Public telephones. TV.

Rotherhithe Youth Hostel

Island Yard, Salter Road, SE16 1PP (0171 232
2114/fax 0171 237 2919). Rotherhithe tube. **Beds**
320. **Reception open** 7am-11pm; 24-hour access.
Rates £19.10; £16 under-18s, *including breakfast.*
Credit A, TC, V.
Hostel services *Bureau de change. Hostel booking*
service. Kitchen facilities. Public telephones, TV.

Bargain-basement prices at the Hotel Boka.

YMCAs

You often need to book at least two months in advance. Many YMCAs specialise in long-term accommodation. A few of the larger hostels are listed below (all unisex) but the National Council for YMCAs (*0181 520 5599*) will supply you with a full list. Prices are from £20 per night for a single room and £35 for a double with special prices for long stay.

Barbican YMCA

2 Fann Street, EC2Y 8BR (0171 628 0697/fax 0171 638 2420). Barbican tube. **Beds** 240.

Central Club

16-22 Great Russell Street, WC1B 3LR (0171 636 7512/fax 0171 636 5278). Tottenham Court Road tube. **Rooms** 105.

London City YMCA

8 Errol Street, EC1Y 8SE (0171 628 8832/fax 0171 628 4080). Barbican tube. **Beds** 111.

Wimbledon YMCA

200 The Broadway, SW19 1RY (0181 542 9055/fax 0181 542 1086). Wimbledon tube/BR. **Beds** 110.

YWCA

Elizabeth House, 118 Warwick Way, SW1V 1SD (0171 630 0741). Victoria tube/BR. **Beds** 54.

Staying With Families

If you find hotels impersonal then staying in someone's home can be a good way to make your visit more companionable. Rates include breakfast.

Central London Accommodations

83 Addison Gardens, W14 0DT (0171 602 9668/fax 0171 602 5609). Goldhawk Road or Shepherd's Bush tube. **Open** 10am-5pm Mon-Fri. **Rates** from *single* £23; *double* £36. **Credit** A, EC, £TC, V. Minimum stay: three nights.

Host and Guest Service

Harwood House, 27 Effie Road, SW6 1EN (0171 731 5340/fax 0171 736 7230). Fulham Broadway tube. **Open** 9am-5.30pm Mon-Fri. **Rates** from £16.50 per person; students from £75 per week. **Credit** A, EC, £TC, V. Minimum stay: two nights.

London Homestead Services

Coombe Road, Kingston-upon-Thames, Surrey (0181 949 4455/fax 0181 549 5492). Norbiton BR. **Open** 9am-5pm Mon-Fri. **Rates** from *single* £16; *double* £28. **Credit** A, EC, £TC, V. Minimum stay: three nights.

Self-catering Apartments

It can be very expensive to rent accommodation in London, but if you are in a group then you may actually be able to save money by renting a flat. The following specialise in holiday lettings. See also *Yellow Pages*.

Aston's

39 Rosary Gardens, SW7 4NQ (0171 370 0737/fax 0171 835 1419). Gloucester Road tube. **Open** 9.30am-5.30pm Mon-Sat. **Rates** *single studio* £37 per night; *double studio* £49 per night. **Credit** EC, £TC. Aston's have 60 flats in South Kensington. Minimum stay: three nights. Special weekly rates.

Holiday Flats Services

2nd floor, 140 Cromwell Road, SW7 4HA (0171 373 4477/fax 0171 373 4282). Gloucester Road tube. **Open** 9.30am-6pm Mon-Fri. **Rates** *from £80 per night for a studio flat (1-2 people).* **Credit** A, AmEx, EC, £TC, V. This agency has properties all over central London.

Palace Court Holiday Apartments

1 Palace Court, Bayswater Road, W2 4LP (0171 727 3467/fax 0171 221 7824). Bayswater, Notting Hill Gate or Queensway tube. **Open** 8.30am-11pm Mon-Fri. **Rates** *single studio* £42 per night; *double* £56 per night; *treble* £66 per night. **No credit cards**. Palace Court have 37 apartments in Bayswater. Minimum stay: two nights. Special rates for stays over two weeks.

University Residences

During university vacations much of London's student accommodation is opened to visitors and can be very good value.

Butler's Wharf LSE Residence

11 Gainsford Street, SE1 2NE (0171 407 7164/fax 0171 403 0847). Tower Hill or London Bridge tube/BR. **Rooms** *self-contained flats sleeping 7 max* 48. **Rates** £18 per person; under-12s half price. **Available** Aug-Sept.

Carr-Saunders Hall

18-24 Fitzroy Street, W1P 5AE (0171 323 9712/0171 580 6338/fax 0171 580 4718). Warren Street tube. **Rooms** *single* 133; *twin* 12; *self-contained flats* 72 *(sleeping 2-5).* **Rates** £18.50-£21.50 per person; *flats* £238-£539 per week. **Available** Apr (rooms only), July-Sept.

Cartwright University Halls
36 Cartwright Gardens, WC1H 9BZ (0171 388 3757/fax 0171 388 2552). Russell Square tube or Euston tube/BR. **Rooms** *single* 153; *twin* 49. **Rates** *single* £25; *twin* £45. **Available** Apr, July-Sept.

Goldsmid House
36 North Row, W1R 1DH (0171 493 8911/6097). Marble Arch tube. **Rooms** *single* 10; *double* 120. **Rates** *single* £15-£25; *double* £30-£40.* **Available** June-Sept.

High Holborn Residence
178 High Holborn, WC1V 7AA (0171 955 7532/fax 0171 955 7717). Holborn tube. **Rooms** *single* 400; *twin* 48. **Rates** *single* from £15.50. **Available** Easter, June-Sept. Due to open in September 1995, this new London School of Economics hall is centrally located. Its name is set to change.

Hughes Parry Hall
19-26 Cartwright Gardens, WC1H 9EF (0171 387 1477/fax 0171 383 4328). Russell Square tube or Euston tube/BR. **Rooms** *single* 290; *twin* 5. **Rates** *single* £18.50; *twin* £37.* **Available** Mar-Apr, June-Sept.

John Adams Hall
15-23 Endsleigh Street, WC1H 0DP (0171 387 4086/fax 0171 383 0164). Euston tube/BR. **Rooms** *single* 127; *twin* 22. **Rates** *single* £19-£21; *twin* £33-£37.* **Available** Apr, July-Sept.

Ifor Evans Hall/Max Rayne House
109 Camden Road, NW1 9HA (0171 485 9377/fax 0171 284 3328). Camden Town tube. **Rooms** *single* 278; *twin* 50. **Rates** £10 per person. **Available** Apr, June-Sept.

International Student House
229 Great Portland Street, W1N 5HD (0171 631 8300/fax 0171 631 8315). Great Portland Street tube. **Rooms** *single* 159; *double* 107. **Rates** *single* £23.40; *double* £39.50; *dormitory* £14. **Available** all year.

A lofty, leafy view at the **Holland Park Hotel.**

King's College Campus Vacation Bureau
552 King's Road, SW10 0UA (0171 351 6011/fax 0171 352 7376). Fulham Broadway tube. **Rates** *single* £16.50-£22; *double* £24-£33.50.* **Available** Easter, June-Sept. King's College has seven halls of residence offering approximately 1,600 beds to visitors.

Passfield Hall
1-7 Endsleigh Place, WC1H 0PW (0171 387 7743/3584/fax 0171 387 0419). Euston tube/BR. **Rooms** *single* 100; *twin* 34. **Rates** *single* £18.50-£21.50; *twin* £37-£42.* **Available** Easter, July-Sept.

Ramsay Hall
20 Maple Street, W1P 5GB (0171 387 4537). Warren Street tube. **Rooms** *single* 364; *twin* 20. **Rates** £18.50-£19.50 per person.* **Available** Apr, June-Sept.

Regent's College
Inner Circle, Regent's Park, NW1 4NS (0171 487 7483). Regent's Park tube. **Rooms** *single* 26; *twin* 36; *triple* 42. **Rates** *single* £26; *twin* £38; *triple* £42.* **Available** Jan, May-Aug.

Rosebery Hall
90 Rosebery Avenue, EC1R 4TY (0171 278 3251/fax 0171 278 2068). Angel tube or King's Cross tube/BR. **Rooms** *single* 250; *double* 33. **Rates** *single* £19; *double* £31.50-£42.* **Available** Apr, July-Sept.

Sir John Cass Hall
150 Well Street, E9 7LQ (0181 533 2529/fax 0181 525 0633). Bethnal Green tube. **Rooms** *single* 100. **Rates** *single* £10-£16.* **Available** June-Sept.

University of North London
Accommodation Office, Tower Building, 166-220 Holloway Road, N7 8DB (0171 607 2789/fax 0171 753 5761). Holloway Road tube. **Available** June-Sept.

Walter Sickert Hall
29 Graham Street, N1 8LA (0171 477 8822/fax 0171 477 8823). Angel tube. **Rooms** *single* 210; *twin* 5. **Rates** *single* £30; *twin* £48.* **Available** July-Sept.

Camping & Caravanning

Abbey Wood Caravan Club
Federation Road, SE2 0LS (0181 310 2233). Abbey Wood BR. **Open** *all year* office 8am-8pm daily. **Rates** £3.20-£3.50; £1.20 children; plus *caravan pitch* £4-£6.50; *car and tent pitch* £5.50; *motorbike and tent pitch* £2.50; *bicycle/walker and tent pitch* £2; *electricity hook-up* £1.25-£2. **Credit** A, EC, £TC, V.
You pay a fee per person and then a pitch fee at the Club but there are facilities galore: laundry, showers, hot water, toilets, washing-up area, mini-market, children's play area.

Crystal Palace Camping
Crystal Palace Parade, SE19 1UF (0181 778 7155). Crystal Palace BR/3 bus. **Open** *all year* office 8am-8pm daily. **Rates** £3.20, plus *caravan pitch* £7; *car and tent pitch* £3; *motorbike and tent pitch* £2.50; *bicycle/walker and tent pitch* £1; *electricity hook-up* £1.25. **Credit** A, EC, £TC, V.
This big site has room for 200 tent and 84 caravan pitches. There are all the facilities you'd expect plus fresh bread in the summer and 33 restaurants within two minutes' walk.

Hackney Camping
Millfields Road, E5 0AR (0181 985 7656). Bus 38. **Open** *early June-late Aug.* **Rates** £4.50 per person; £2.25 under-15s; under-5s free. **Credit** EC, £TC.

A moment's reflection at **Number Sixteen**.

This site is run by Tent City and offers similar facilities but no hostel beds. It is the closest campsite to the City of London yet is within the Lea Valley Nature Reserve.

Lee Valley Campsite

Sewardstone Road, E4 7RA (0181 529 5689).
Walthamstow Central tube/BR then 215 bus. **Open** *Apr-Oct* 8am-10pm daily. **Rates** £4.50; £1.75 under-16s; *electricity hook-up* £1.75 per day. **Credit** A, V.
Although this big site is 12 miles (20 km) from central London it has good facilities: play areas, washing-areas and a shop. And it's cheap. No single-sex groups are admitted.

Lee Valley Park

Lea Valley Leisure Centre, Pickett's Lock Lane, N9 0AS (0181 345 6666/fax 0181 884 4975). Edmonton Green BR/W8 bus or Tottenham Hale tube/363 bus. **Open** 8.30am-7.30pm Mon-Sat. **Rates** £4.50; £1.80 under-15s; *electricity hook-up* £2.20 per day. **Credit** A, EC, £TC, V.
Located behind a leisure centre, this is the ideal camp site for the sporty. There are 100 touring caravan pitches and 100 tent pitches plus washing facilities, showers and a shop. If you are camping alone the minimum charge is £6.30.

Tent City

Old Oak Common Lane, W3 7DP (0181 743 5708/fax 0181 749 9074). East Acton tube. **Open** *early June-early Sept* 24 hours daily. **Rates** £5.50; £2.75 under-15s; under-5s free. Discounts for groups and extended stay. **Credit** EC, £TC.
Tent City celebrated its twenty-fifth anniversary in 1995. This venerable institution provides 270 beds in a tented hostel as well as 200 tent pitches. Facilities are superb: free showers, toilets, washing and cooking facilities, and baggage and valuables store. There are cheap barbecues every week and free entertainment at weekends. All profits go to charity.

Emergency Accommodation

It is never wise to sleep out in the open. But if the worst happens and you are left stranded, one of the organisations below might be able to help.

Advisory Service for Squatters

2 St Paul's Road, N1 2QN (0171 359 8814). Highbury & Islington tube/BR. **Open** 2pm-6pm Mon-Fri.
Squatting is still legal in the UK. ASS provides legal and practical advice for squatters and homeless people as well as contacts with local groups. They publish *The Squatter's Handbook* (70p or £1 by post).

Shelter Nightline

(Freephone 0800 446441). **Open** 6pm-9am Mon-Fri; 24 hours Sat, Sun.
Although this voluntary organisation primarily helps homeless UK residents, it can offer advice to stranded tourists in emergencies. It can also provide information on free cold-weather shelters which are open in winter from November to the end of March. You could also call **Piccadilly Advice Centre** (*0171 434 3773*, after 2pm) or **Shack** (*0171 404 2614*) if you are homeless or on income support. **Alone In London** (*0171 278 4224*) is specifically for homeless under-21s.

The Tonbridge Club

120 Cromer Street, WC1H 8BS (0171 837 4406). King's Cross tube/BR. **Open** *summer* 10pm-midnight; *winter* 9.30-11pm. **Rates** £3.50.
By day it's a school club, by night it's the cheapest hostel in London. If you are stranded or don't mind roughing it, the Tonbridge Club is a godsend. You'll have to sleep on a mattress on the gym floor but there are hot showers, a TV and use of the games room, all just for £3.50. Only foreign visitors and students are allowed to stay.

Women's Link

1A Snow Hill Court, EC1A 2EJ (0171 248 1200). St Paul's tube. **Open** *phone calls only* 10am-4pm Mon-Thur; 1-4pm Fri.
This general housing advice centre for women can also help find emergency accommodation. Its pamphlet *Hostels In London* costs £2.50 (including postage).

Longer Stay

If you are planning on staying in London for a period of months rather than weeks, then it will usually work out cheaper if you find a flat or a room in a house to rent.

But maybe not that much cheaper. Rented accommodation in the capital is expensive and competition is often fierce. When viewing places you may feel that you are the one being assessed rather than the one doing the assessing. The outlay can be heavy. You will normally be asked to pay a month's rent in advance and another month deposit (although this should be returned to you when you leave).

The best source for places to rent is *Loot*, published daily. Buy it as early in the day as you can and get straight on the phone. Many rooms will be taken by the evening. Capital Radio publishes a flatshare list available from their foyer (Euston Tower, Euston Road, NW1 – Warren Street tube) each Friday afternoon around 3pm. Also worth trying are *Time Out* magazine, which comes out on Tuesday in central London and on Wednesday further out, *Midweek* magazine, free from tube stations on Thursdays, and the 11am edition of the *Evening Standard*.

London
by Season

Celebrate through the year with the capital's spectacular calendar of events.

The **Oxford and Cambridge Boat Race** *goes from Putney to Mortlake, four miles 374 yards.*

London has an amazing range of seasonal events, covering exhibitions, fairs, music festivals, sporting events and, of course, a great welter of pomp and pageantry. These can include grandiose beanos, such as the **Lord Mayor's Show** and **Trooping The Colour**, but also an extraordinary number of small, quirky events, many of which are free. *See also chapters* **Music: Rock, Folk & Jazz** *and* **Sport & Fitness**.

Frequent Events

Ceremony of the Keys

HM Tower of London, EC3 (0171 709 0765). Tower Hill tube. **Date** 9.35-10.05pm daily (except Christmas Day). **Maximum** in party *Apr-Oct* 8; *Nov-Mar* 15. **Admission** free, by prior arrangement.

'Halt! Who comes there?' 'The keys.' 'Whose keys?' 'Queen Elizabeth II's keys' 'Pass the keys. All's well.' Thus goes the painstaking exchange between the Sentry and Chief Yeoman Warder, and has done so 365 days a year, for the past 700 years, as part of the locking-up routine of the **Tower of London**. Ticket holders should arrive by 9.35pm. The real business begins at 9.53pm exactly, when the Chief Warder leaves the Byward Tower and it's all over before the clock

chimes for 10am and the Last Post is sounded. Apply for tickets, giving alternative dates, at least two months in advance, in writing with a stamped addressed envelope to: The Resident Governor, Queen's House, HM Tower of London, EC3N 4AB.

Druid Ceremonies

(Druid Order 0181 771 0684).
Summer Solstice *Stonehenge, A303, Wiltshire/White Horse Stone, A229, 2 miles east of Aylesford, Kent.* **Date** Dawn (about 4.30am), 21 June 1996, 1997.
Autumn Equinox *Primrose Hill, NW3.* **Date** 1pm, 21 Sept 1995, 22 Sept 1996.
Spring Equinox *Tower Hill (west side of Tower), EC3.* **Date** noon, 20 Mar 1996, 1997. **Admission** free.

By day the Druids are probably bank clerks, but come a solstice or equinox, they don white, hooded gowns and worship the seasons of renewal (spring) and harvest (autumn). Their gowns have not changed since the eighteenth century, when there was a resurgence of interest in this order. Before this, the ancient Druids used to be naked. Any virgins out there can relax, as ritual sacrifice is also a thing of the past.

Funfairs

Alexandra Park *Muswell Hill, N22 (0181 365 2121). Wood Green tube/Alexandra Palace BR/W3 bus.*
Battersea Park *Albert Bridge Road, SW11 (0181 871 7530). Sloane Square tube/Battersea Park or Queenstown Road BR/97, 137 bus.*

Hampstead Heath *NW3 (0171 485 4491 for a leaflet detailing events in the park throughout the year). Belsize Park or Hampstead tube/Gospel Oak or Hampstead Heath BR/24 bus.*
Dates *Easter 5-8 Apr 1996; 28-31 Mar 1997. Spring Bank Holiday 24-27 May 1996; 23-26 May 1997. August Bank Holiday 23-26 Aug 1996; 22-25 Aug 1997.*
Admission free.

Gun Salutes
Hyde Park, W2 and the Tower of London, EC3. **Dates** 2 June (Coronation Day); 10 June (Duke of Edinburgh's birthday); 16 June (Trooping the Colour, *see below* **Summer**); 4 Aug (Queen Mother's birthday); 6 Feb (Accession Day); 21 Apr (the Queen's birthday); the State Opening of Parliament (*see below* **Autumn**). If the date falls on a Sunday, salutes are fired on following Monday. **Admission** free.
The cannons are primed on important royal occasions for gun salutes. The King's Troop of the Royal Horse Artillery makes a mounted charge through **Hyde Park**, sets up the guns and fires a 41-gun salute (noon, except for Opening of Parliament); then, not to be outdone, at the **Tower of London**, the Honourable Artillery Company fires a 62-gun salute at 1pm.

Spring

St Patrick's Day
Date 17 March.
London is the third largest Irish city, after New York and Dublin. There are no big parades, but head for Kilburn, NW6 for the craic.

London Harness Horse Parade
Battersea Park, Albert Bridge Road, SW11 (0181 871 7530). Sloane Square tube/Battersea Park or Queenstown Road BR. **Date** 9am-1.30pm Easter Monday (14 Apr 1996; 31 Mar 1997). **Admission** free.
Working horses, traditional brewers drays, carts and carriages tour **Battersea Park** competing for Rosettes. The public are welcome to inspect the horses. The spectacle provides some indication of what London was like before the advent of the motor car.

Oxford and Cambridge Race
On the Thames from Putney to Mortlake (0171 730 3488). **Date** 6 April 1996. **Admission** free.
This highly competitive boat race between the universities of Oxford and Cambridge has been waged for over 150 years. Starting from Putney, SW6 and finishing at Mortlake, SW14, the course is four miles and 374 yards long. Large crowds gather on the banks of the Thames, especially at bridges and pubs, such as The Swan at Mortlake.

London Marathon
Greenwich Park, Blackheath to Westminster Bridge via the Isle of Dogs, Victoria Embankment and St James's Park (0171 620 4117). **Date** 21 April 1996, phone to confirm 1997 date. **Admission** free to spectators.
The London Marathon is the world's biggest road race, with around 30,000 starters (out of about 75,000 applicants). Competitors include athletes, joggers, celebrities, wheelchair racers and fundraisers from all over the world. The course is a real test of stamina, and some of those in fancy dress must surely regret dressing up as a rabbit after the first few hundred yards of the course's 26 miles and 385 yards.

May Fayre and Puppet Festival
St Paul's Church Garden, Covent Garden, WC2 (0171 375 0441). Covent Garden tube. **Date** Second Sunday in May. **Admission** free.

A free festival of puppetry and Punch & Judy, along with a procession and other entertainment.

Chelsea Flower Show
Royal Hospital, SW3 (0171 834 4333). Sloane Square tube. **Dates** 21-24 May 1996. **Open** 8am-8pm Thur; 8am-5pm Fri. **Admission** £23.
The world-renowned gardening extravaganza and society event, laid on by the Royal Horticultural Society, featuring plants, flowers of all seasons, garden furniture, tools, theme gardens and greenhouses. Book your tickets early.

Summer

Kenwood Lakeside Concerts
Kenwood House, Hampstead Lane, NW3 (concert information 0171 973 3427). Archway, Hampstead or Highgate tube. **Dates** every Sat June-Sept. **Tickets** book on 0171 379 4444, or on the night two hours before the concert begins. **Admission** £5.50-£25.
A picnic at one of these outdoor concerts of popular classics can make an idyllic summer evening (weather permitting). Prices have rocketed in recent years, but you can still hear the music if you sit on the grassy slopes just outside the barrier. *See chapter* **Music: Classical & Opera**.

Beating Retreat
Horse Guards Parade, Whitehall, SW1 (0171 930 4466). Westminster tube or Charing Cross tube/BR. **Dates** early June. **Admission** £3-£10.
The 'Retreat' is beaten on drums by the Mounted Bands of the Household Cavalry and The Massed Bands of the Guards Division. It refers to the setting of the sun, not of the British Empire. It's a colourful musical ceremony, performed by a different regimental band each year. Tickets from Premier Box Office (*0171 930 0292*). There are often tickets left on the day of performance.

Derby Day
Epsom Racecourse, Epsom, Surrey (01372 470047). Epsom BR. **Date** first Wed in June. **Open** 10am. **Race** 3.45pm. **Admission** £4-£50.
This world-famous horse race over the flat is responsible for millions of bets and a few heart attacks. A frightfully British affair where the poorer classes are herded into one enclosure, while those with fat wallets and braying voices strut about in another.

Royal Academy Summer Exhibition
Royal Academy, Burlington House, Piccadilly, W1 (0171 439 7438). Green Park or Piccadilly Circus tube. **Dates** June-Aug. **Open** 10am-6pm (last admission 5.30pm) daily. **Admission** £4.80; £3.50 OAPs, students, UB40s; £1.80 under-18s.
Something of an artistic hotchpotch with loose criteria for determining what's exhibited. It's mostly an amateur event, with some professional exhibits, but it's tremendous fun.

Trooping the Colour
Horse Guards Parade, Whitehall, SW1 (information 0171 414 2279). Westminster tube or Charing Cross tube/BR. **Date** 15 June 1996. **Starts** 10.40am Buckingham Palace. **Tickets** write by end Feb to *The Brigade Major (Trooping the Colour), HQ, Household Division, Horse Guards, Chelsea Barracks, SW3.* **Admission** about £12.50 – limit of two tickets per person. **No credit cards.**
Trooping the Colour is the Queen's official birthday party – her real one is in April. The ceremony originates in the battlefield tradition of raising a regiment's colours for identification. The Queen leaves **Buckingham Palace** at 10.40am and travels down The Mall to Horseguards Parade, arriving at 11am. The route is always packed but you may

Festivals

London's multicultural history has spawned a multitude of varied festivals, such as the **Notting Hill Carnival** and **Chinese New Year** celebrations.

Specialist festivals are often spread over several venues: the **Greenwich Festival** in June *(0181 305 1818)*; the **July City of London Festival** *(0171 638 8891)*; and the **Soho Jazz Festival** (late Sept-early Oct, *0891 774774*).

The **Capital Radio Music Festival** (mid June-mid July, *0171 608 6080*) is now Europe's biggest music festival.

The **August International Street Performers Festival** is held in the Covent Garden Piazza; and the **Gran Gran Fiesta** *(0171 620 0544)* is a two-week festival of Latin American music and dance which hits Bernie Spain Gardens and Gabriel's Wharf on the South Bank as part of the **Coin Street Festival**, which runs July-Aug.

Festival of Mind, Body, Spirit
Royal Horticultural Halls, Greycoat Street, SW1 (0171 938 3788). St James's Park tube. **Date** last ten days of May.
A New Age festival featuring an astonishing array of different approaches to health, healing, spiritualism and the environment.

Glastonbury Festival
Worthy Farm, Pilton, Somerset (01749 890470/info line 01839 668899). **Date** last weekend in June.
The largest and most expensive of the UK's festivals – in 1995 the tickets cost £65 – but still probably the best. For three days, Michael Eavis's farm becomes a bustling city of music (with over 17 stages), alternative arts performances and exotic food stalls, all in aid of Greenpeace. Recently, tickets for the festival have been selling out well in advance, so book early.

City of London Festival
Venues in and around the City, EC2 (festival box office 0171 377 0540/information 0171 377 0540). **Date** 25 June-12 July 1996; phone for 1997 dates.
The City of London Festival is an international line-up of soloists, string quartets, orchestras and choirs, along with poetry and theatre events in the City's churches, Livery Halls, **Guildhall**, **St Paul's Cathedral**, the **Barbican** and other venues.

Great British Beer Festival
Olympia, Hammersmith Road, W4 (provisional venue, phone to check 01727 867201). Kensington Olympia Tube. **Date** 6-10 Aug 1996; phone for 1997 dates. **Admission** £1-£3.
Organised by the Campaign for Real Ale (CAMRA), the Great British Beer Festival has around 300 real ales to sample, a foreign beer bar with speciality beers from around the world, and an assortment of traditional ciders. All in the interests of research, of course.

Edinburgh International and Fringe Festivals
International Festival 21 Market Street, Edinburgh EH1 (0131 226 4001). **Fringe Festival** *180 High Street, Edinburgh (0131 226 5257).* **Jazz Festival** *116 Canongate, Edinburgh EH8 8DD (0131 557 1642).* **Film Festival** *88 Lothian Road, Edinburgh, EH7 5JW (0131 228 4051).* **Date** last three weeks of Aug & first week of Sept.
Well, it's not in London, but it is the world's largest arts festival. The scale of the thing necessitates it being divided into individual mini-festivals: the most impressive is perhaps the **Fringe Festival**, with hundreds of visiting companies occupying every available yard of performance space. It encompasses the high-profile **Comedy Festival**, which can make or break an act. The **International Festival** has visiting orchestras and opera, ballet and theatre companies. The **Film Festival** is the longest continually running film festival in the world, with previews of blockbusters and art-house movies. The **Jazz Festival** attracts musicians from around the world. The **Military Tattoo** is performed in Edinburgh Castle.

Latin American Festival
The Calthorpe Project Community Garden, 258-274 Gray's Inn Road, WC1 (0171 837 8019). **Date** last weekend in August.
A carnival of Latin American bands, dancing and food.

Festival of Mind, Body & Spirit – *in May.*

find space on the **Green Park** side of the Mall. Back home in the Palace by 12.30pm, the Queen takes to the balcony to watch a Royal Air Force jet zoom past at about 1pm, and there is a gun salute at the **Tower of London**.

Royal Ascot

Ascot Racecourse, Ascot, Berkshire (01344 22211). Ascot BR. **Dates** mid June, phone for details. **Open** 11am until last race. **Admission** £23.

The Queen and her chums, plus assorted royals, travel down the racecourse in open pram-like carriages on Ladies' Day. The ladies' outrageous headwear jockeys for attention with the racing results.

Chaucer Festival

Hay's Galleria, Tooley Street, SE1 (information on 01227 470379). London Bridge tube/BR. **Date** mid June. **Admission** free.

A costumed cavalcade proceeds from **Southwark Cathedral** to the **Tower of London** for this annual celebration of Chaucer's *Canterbury Tales*. The 'pilgrims' then join a medieval fair at the Tower, with sideshows, food stalls and much merry-making.

Kite Festival

Hackney Marshes, Homerton Road, E9. Leyton tube/Hackney Wick BR. **Date** mid June. **Admission** free.

An extravaganza of kite displays, including quadline kite football, stunt flyers and urban kite buggy races. Later there are PyroKiteNics (launching fireworks from kites), along with juggling and live music.

Middlesex Show

Showground, Park Road, Uxbridge, Middlesex (0181 866 1367). Uxbridge tube, then free bus to ground. **Dates** 22, 23 June 1996. **Open** 9am-6.30pm. **Admission** £5; £2.50 under-16s, OAPs; free under-5s. **No credit cards.**

County shows are a British institution, harking back to when ye olde British yeomen chewed straw at farm gates. This major show is a great family day out with Morris dancing, falconry, shire horses, veteran cars and the unmissable dog agility trials.

Wimbledon Lawn Tennis Championships

All England Club Lawn Tennis and Croquet Club, PO Box 98, Church Road, SW19 (0181 944 1066/recorded information 0181 946 2244). Southfields tube/Wimbledon tube/BR. **Dates** last week of June, first week of July. **Open** 11am; *play on outside courts* 12.30pm; *play on show courts* 2pm. **Admission** tickets by ballot of entries between Sept and Dec previous year; send SAE to above address for application form. **No credit cards.**

As much society event as ball-game, Wimbledon's international reputation cannot be disputed. If you haven't ordered tickets or blagged free seats at a company marquee, you'll have to queue from early morning. Go early evening, when you can sometimes get a seat for an evening match for as little as a fiver, after the people who have been guzzling free Champagne all day have had to go home. Prohibitively expensive refreshments.

National Music Day

Over 1,000 venues throughout the UK. Information (0171 491 0044). **Dates** end of June. **Admission** free.

NMD began in 1992, after Mick Jagger put forward an idea based on similar events in France and Australia. There are over 50 shows in London. The aim is to generate more live music events in the UK and explore new musical genres.

Royal Tournament

Earl's Court Exhibition Centre, Warwick Road, SW5 (tickets 0171 373 8141/information 0171 244 0371). Earl's Court tube. **Dates** July, phone to confirm. **Admission** £5-£24. **Credit** A, AmEx, V.

Presented by the Army, Navy and RAF, who pit themselves physically and mentally against each other in larger-than-life displays of bravery and courage. There are also deafening military bands, pageantry and lots of running about with gun carriages.
Disabled: access. Group discount.

BBC Henry Wood Promenade Concerts

Royal Albert Hall, Kensington Gore, SW7 (0171 927 4296). South Kensington tube. **Dates** 21 July-16 Sept 1995; similar dates in 1996, 1997. **Admission** £3.50-£15. **Credit** A, AmEx, V.

Possibly the world's greatest classical music festival. The atmosphere is informal: the **Royal Albert Hall** has standing-room for up to 1,600. The Last Night of the Proms is famous for its overdose of patriotism and bombast, culminating in a tumultuous rendition of 'Land of Hope and Glory'.

Swan Upping on the Thames

from Sunbury, Surrey to Pangbourne, Berkshire, and back (0171 236 1863). **Dates** 9.30am-5pm Mon-Fri, third week in July. **Admission** free.

This 300-year-old tradition is a bizarre spectator event. All the swans on the Thames belong to either the Queen or the Vintners' or Dyers' livery companies. For five days herdsmen paddle about trying to count and mark the cygnets. A Dyers' company swan gets one nick on the beak, a Vintners' two and the Queen's are left unmarked. When the boats are in sight of Windsor Castle, all the Swan Uppers stand to attention in their boats and, raising their oars, salute 'Her Majesty the Queen, Seigneur of the Swans!'.

Cart Marking

Guildhall Yard, EC2 (information 0171 489 8287). Bank tube or Moorgate tube/BR. **Date** end of July to early Aug, phone to confirm. **Starts** 11.30am. **Admission** free.

Traffic jams in 1681 forced the city authorities to pass an Act of Common Council limiting the number of carts on the road to 421. With traffic today back to horse-and-cart speeds, there's a lesson here. The keeper of the **Guildhall** marks each cart with the City Arms on the shafts, giving each one a number on a brass plate in a ceremony lasting three hours.

Notting Hill Carnival

North Kensington (0181 964 0544). Ladbroke Grove, Notting Hill or Westbourne Park tube. **Date** noon-9pm last Sun, Mon in Aug. **Admission** free.

The largest street festival in Eurpope, the Notting Hill Carnival is a vast, open-air party, featuring steel bands, sound systems, a procession of colourful floats and plentiful Caribbean food. It can be a bit of a crush, but it is an uplifting experience and an exciting day out. For families there's the children's carnival on Sunday.

Autumn

Chinatown Mid-Autumn Festival

Chinese Community Centre, Gerrard Street & Newport Place, WC1 (0171 439 3822). Leicester Square or Piccadilly Circus tube. **Date** Sept (phone to confirm). **Admission** free.

Similar to the Chinese New Year but on a smaller scale (*see below* **Winter**). Colourful lanterns of every shape and size are made by and for children, and there's plenty of entertainment and stalls. A stage is set up in Gerrard Street and dragons dance about outside Chinese restaurants and shops. Much of the food on sale is specially for this festival.

The **Remembrance Sunday Ceremony** *takes place at the Cenotaph on the Sunday nearest to Armistice Day (11 November).*

Horseman's Sunday

*Church of St John & St Michael, Hyde Park Crescent, W2
(0171 262 1732). Marble Arch tube/Paddington tube/BR.*
Dates third Sunday in Sept, phone to confirm. **Service**
11.30am. **Admission** free.

A relatively new tradition, dating from 1969 when local riding stables feared closure and held an open-air service to protest. From horseback the vicar blesses over 100 horses. Afterwards, the blessed animals trot around the surrounding streets and then through **Hyde Park**. Later (1.30-5.30pm) you can watch show-jumping at nearby Kensington paddock, at the northern part of **Kensington Gardens**. Early arrivals can catch the Morris dancing at 11am.

Horse of the Year Show

*Wembley Arena, Wembley, Middlesex (0181 900 1234).
Wembley Central tube.* **Date** first week in Oct.
Admission £9-£30, bookable in advance.

Dressage, show-jumping and pony club trials.

Costermonger's Pearly Harvest Festival

*St Martin-in-the-Fields, Trafalgar Square, WC2 (0171
930 0089). Leicester Square tube/Charing Cross tube/BR.*
Dates first Sun in Oct. **Service** 2pm. **Admission** free.

A barrowload of be-buttoned cockneys: Pearly Kings, Queens and Princesses from all the London boroughs. Dressed in their traditional costumes, they gather here for a harvest thanksgiving. The 'Pearlies' or Costermongers, to give them their proper title, were originally apple sellers, but because of their flamboyant dress, became popular local figures and began to raise money for charity.

Punch and Judy Festival

*Covent Garden Piazza, WC2 (0171 240 0930). Covent
Garden tube.* **Date** first Sun in Oct. **Admission** free.

The pugnacious puppets' own festival. Diarist Samuel Pepys watched the first Punch and Judy show on 9 May 1662.

Bonfire Night

*All over England, Scotland and Wales (phone London
Tourist Board 0171 971 0026, 9am-6pm, Mon-Fri for
details of major firework displays).* **Date** 5 Nov; firework
displays on nearest weekend.

There are bonfires and firework displays all over London's parks to commemorate the failure of the Gunpowder Plot of 1605, when Guy Fawkes attempted to blow up James I and his Protestant Parliament. Not taking any chances, it is now a tradition that before the State Opening of Parliament, the vaults beneath are searched by the Yeoman of the Guard.

State Opening of Parliament

*House of Lords, Palace of Westminster, SW1 (0171 219
4272). Westminster tube.* **Date** usually first week in Nov,
phone for details. **Admission** free.

Members of Parliament are welcomed back from their summer hols by the Queen at the State Opening of Parliament. The public get a good chance to see the Queen as she arrives and departs in her Irish or Australian State Coach, attended by the Household Cavalry. As she enters the House of Lords, a gun salute is fired. Inside she reads a speech outlining the Government's legislative plans. There is a very slim chance of getting a ticket if you contact your MP.

London to Brighton Veteran Car Run

*Starting point: Serpentine Road, Hyde Park, W2 (01753
681736 for details). Hyde Park Corner tube.* **Date** first
Sun in Nov. **Start** 7.30am. **Admission** free.

The rally commemorates 'Emancipation Day' when it was no longer necessary for a man with a red flag to walk in front of the new 'horseless carriages'. The motors, limited to an average of 20 mph (32 kmph), aim to reach Brighton before 4pm. The start at **Hyde Park** has a great sense of occasion, but crowds line the whole route (via **Westminster Bridge** and Croydon, along the A23).

Lord Mayor's Show

Various streets in the City of London (0171 606 3030).
Date usually second Sat in Nov. **Show** 9am-5pm.
Admission free.

The City gets a facelift for one day a year with a procession of 140 floats, as the plume-hatted new Lord Mayor travels from Westminster in a gilded coach, leaving at 9am. From 11.10am at the **Guildhall**, the procession snakes through the City to the **Royal Courts of Justice** at 11.50am. There the new mayor swears solemn vows before returning to the Guildhall by 2.20pm. Later the merriment continues with fireworks launched from a barge moored on the Thames between bridges Waterloo and Blackfriars.

Remembrance Sunday Ceremony

*Cenotaph, Whitehall, SW1 (0171 730 3488).
Westminster tube/Charing Cross tube/BR.* **Date** 10.30-11.30am, nearest Sun to Armistice Day (11 Nov).
Admission free.

The Queen, the PM and other dignitaries lay wreaths and observe a minute's silence at the Cenotaph to commemorate the people who gave their lives for their country in both world wars. Afterwards, the Bishop of London takes a short service of Remembrance.

Winter

Christmas Lights

*Covent Garden, WC2 (0171 836 9136); Oxford Street,
W1 (0171 629 1234); Regent Street & Bond Street, W1
(0171 629 1682); Trafalgar Square, SW1.* **Dates** *lights
on early Nov; Trafalgar Square Christmas Tree early Dec.*

It's a truism that Christmas seems to come earlier each year and, going by our schedule, this should have appeared under **Autumn**, since the lights are switched on in early November. However, Christmas is Christmas. Each year the citizens of Oslo, Norway give the citizens of London a fir tree to thank Britain for liberation from the Nazis, even though acid rain damage to Norwegian firs by British pollution has put the tradition in doubt. Regent Street has London's best decorations. If you fancy seeing the lights switched on by a celebrity, be aware of the nightmarish congestion. Other lights at which to gawp hang across St Christopher's Place, W1; Bond Street, W1; and Kensington High Street, W8. 'Alternative' lights twinkle around Carnaby Street, W1.

New Year's Eve Celebrations

*Trafalgar Square, W1. Leicester Square tube/Charing
Cross tube/BR.* **Date** 31 Dec-1 Jan. **Admission** free.

Trafalgar Square is the venue for this truly grisly, joyless 'celebration'. In recent years, police have banned alcohol, resulting in near-riots as revellers, having spent all night canning it, pour into Trafalgar Square in a great, moronic, stampede and try to jump in the fountain. Choose any pub or club and have a far better time. Lager companies have done the one thing to stop drunk-driving the Government won't admit works: sponsoring free public transport all night. On New Year's Day a procession of bands marches through town from the West End to Hyde Park at lunchtime.

Chinese New Year Festival

*Chinatown, around Gerrard Street, W1 (Chinatown
Chinese Association 0171 437 5256). Leicester Square,
Piccadilly Circus or Tottenham Court Road tube.* **Date**
first Sun after Chinese New Year, phone to confirm;
11am-5pm. **Admission** free.

The high-spot of the Chinese calender. The atmosphere is electric as lions and dragons snake their way through the streets, gathering gifts of money and food along the way. There's a stage for performers in Leicester Square and early Chinese history is told to anyone who'll listen. Afterwards, eat from the special dim sum menus offered by many local Chinese restaurants (*see also* chapter **Restaurants**).

Sightseeing

From the top of Canary Wharf to the Crypt of St Paul's, there's so much to see you'll have to come back. And back and back again.

For guided bus, coach and walking tours, *see page 46* **Trips & Tours**.

Focal Points

Covent Garden Piazza
WC2 (Market office 0171 836 9136). Covent Garden tube.
Covent Garden Piazza was *the* fashionable place to be in the seventeenth century, with coffee houses and street entertainment, but as the fruit and vegetable market took over the area, the in-crowd moved west. In 1974, when the market moved out, the covered marketplace (1831) was saved from demolition and soon emerged as a focus for London's new café society: back came the street entertainers, pavement cafés and boutiques. Sadly it's gone downhill since; prices are high and chains are creeping in. Still, the Piazza is one of the few places where you can stroll, browse and watch street shows without having to fight with the traffic.

Piccadilly Circus
SW1. Piccadilly Circus tube.
The bustling, noisy Circus with its blaze of neon signs is a famous meeting place. It's not actually a circus any more, but it's still a hub of activity at the junction of six main roads. The statue of **Eros**, once surrounded by traffic, has been moved to one side, making it a less perilous rendezvous for the backpackers who gather on the steps during the day; it has a less salubrious reputation after dark. Nearby Leicester Square, home of several cinemas and the Half-Price Ticket Booth (*see chapter* **Theatre**) is also a popular meeting point.

Trafalgar Square
WC2. Charing Cross tube/BR.
The **National Gallery** overlooks the square on the north; Canada House and South Africa House stand on sides west and east, but the oldest building is the church of **St Martin-in-the-Fields**. The square was laid out in 1830-40 on the site of the old Royal Mews to commemorate Admiral Nelson who defeated the French and Spanish at the Battle of Trafalgar (1805); **Nelson's Column** towers over the fountains and Landseer's lions. On the south side, a brass plaque tells that distances to London are measured from here.

Major Sights

Big Ben
St Stephen's Clock Tower, Houses of Parliament, SW1. Westminster tube. **Not open** to the public.
The Clock Tower at the Houses of Parliament stands beside **Westminster Bridge**. Big Ben is the bell which chimes the hours. The clock face is 22ft 6in (6.86m) across, and the minute hand is 14ft (4.27m) long. A light shines from the top of the tower at night when the House of Commons is sitting.

Buckingham Palace
SW1 (0171 930 4832/recorded information 0171 799 2331/disabled 0171 839 1377 ext 4204). Green Park or St James's Park tube. **Open** early Aug-end Sept 9am-4.15pm daily. **Admission** £8.50; £6 OAPs; £4.50 under-17s.

Trafalgar Square – *heart of modern London.*

Built in 1703 for the wealthy Duke of Buckingham, the original Buckingham House was bought by George III and converted into a palace by his son George IV. In 1837, the young Queen Victoria decided to make Buckingham Palace her home, and it's been the London residence of the Royal Family ever since. The Royal Standard flies above the Palace when the Queen is in London. For a price, you may visit the State Apartments, used for banquets and investitures, while the Royals are away. The 18 rooms on view include the Throne Room, State Dining Room, the Green, Blue and White drawing rooms and the Music Room. Tickets are only available on the day, on sale from 9am at the Ticket Office in Constitution Hill; average queuing time is about 40 minutes. No cameras or videos are allowed inside the Palace gates. (*See also* **Queen's Gallery** and **Royal Mews**.)

Changing the Guard
Buckingham Palace, Horse Guards and St James's Palace, SW1 (recorded information 0839 123411/0891 505452). St James's Park or Green Park tube.
Ceremonies *Buckingham Palace* mid April-end July 11.30am daily; Aug-Apr 11.30am alternate days (phone for dates). *St James's Palace* 11.15am (dates as for Buckingham Palace). *Horse Guards* 11am Mon-Sat; 10am Sun.

Tower Bridge – designed in flamboyant Victorian Gothic style by Horace Jones, opened 1894.

The most spectacular ceremony is at **Buckingham Palace**. On Guard Changing days the new Guard and its regimental band lines up in the forecourt of Wellington Barracks, Birdcage Walk, from 10.45am. It's usually one of the five regiments of Foot Guards in their scarlet coats and bearskin hats. At 11.27am they march to the Palace for the changing of the sentries, who stand guard in the Palace forecourt. At **St James's Palace**, a detachment of the old guard marches off at 11.15am and back at 12.05pm. At Horse Guards in Whitehall, it's the Household Cavalry who mount the guard (10am-4pm daily); they ride along the Mall before and after.

Houses of Parliament

Parliament Square, SW1 (Commons information 0171 219 4272/Lords information 0171 219 3107). Westminster tube. **Open** *when the Houses of Parliament are in session. House of Commons Visitors' Gallery 2.30-10.30pm (or later) Mon, Tue, Thur; 10am-2pm, 2.30pm-10pm (or later) Wed; 9.30am-3pm Fri. House of Lords Visitors' Gallery phone for details. Victoria Tower Gardens 7am-dusk daily.* **Admission** *free.*

The first Parliament was held here in 1275, in Edward I's reign, and it became Parliament's permanent home in 1532, when Henry VIII moved to Whitehall. Parliament was originally housed in the choir stalls of St Stephen's Chapel, where members sat facing each other from opposite sides; they use the same tradition today. The only remaining parts of the original Palace are Westminster Hall, with its hammer-beam roof, and the **Jewel Tower**; all the rest was burned down in a great fire (1834) and rebuilt in the neo-Gothic style by Charles Barry and Augustus Pugin (1852). There are 1,000 rooms, 100 staircases and 11 courtyards. Anyone can watch the House of Commons or the House of Lords in session from the Visitors' Gallery. There's no minimum age but children should be able to sign their name in the visitors' book. *Disabled: access (by prior arrangement, phone 0171 219 3060). Educational facilities/worksheets. Guided tour (Mon-Thur only) or a seat at Question Time (2.30pm Mon-Thur) by prior arrangement with your MP or embassy. Post Office. Shop. Toilets for the disabled.*

St Paul's Cathedral

EC4 (0171 248 2705). St Paul's tube. **Open** *doors open 8.30am-4pm Mon-Sat. Galleries, crypt and ambulatory 10am-4pm Mon-Sat.* **Admission** *cathedral, crypt and ambulatory (except services) £3; £2.50 students; £1.50 under-16s. Galleries £2.50; £2 students; £1.50 under-16s. Combined tickets (access all areas) £5; £4 students; £3 under-16s.* **Credit** *shop* A, £TC, V.

Once dominating London's skyline, St Paul's is Wren's masterpiece. Replacing Old St Paul's which burned down in the Great Fire of 1666, it's one of the few cathedrals ever to be designed by one architect and built in his lifetime (*see chapter* **Architecture**). His epitaph on the floor below the dome states, 'If you seek his monument, look around'. It's a sign of the times that you now have to pay to look around. High up in the Dome, people in the Whispering Gallery strain to hear reverberating voices above the muffled din. Beyond that are the viewing galleries: the Stone Gallery (at the base of the Dome) and the Golden Gallery (at the top). It's a long hard climb (no lift) but worth it for the view. In the Crypt are the tombs of the Duke of Wellington and Admiral Nelson, and Wren's simple slab. St Paul's survived the bombs of WWII, which laid waste the streets all around. Some of the post-war buildings on the north side in Paternoster Square are awaiting demolition; Prince Charles has fought for the replacements to be in keeping with the scale and style of St Paul's. *Disabled: access to main body & crypt. Guided tours. Shop.*

Tower Bridge

SE1 (0171 407 0922). Tower Hill or London Bridge tube/BR. **Open** *Apr-Oct 10am-6.30pm daily; Nov-Mar 10am-5.15 pm daily (last admission 75 mins before closing).* **Closed** *Good Friday, Christmas Eve, Christmas Day, Boxing Day, New Year's Day.* **Admission** *£5; £3.50 under-15s, OAPs, students, UB40s.* **Credit** *(shop only, but shop sells tickets)* A, £TC, V.

Tower Bridge, designed in Victorian Gothic style by the City's architect Horace Jones, opened with flags and fanfares on 30 June 1894. It was a triumph of engineering; the steam engines which raised the bridge to allow ships through can

still be seen, and were in continuous use until 1976. The centenary exhibition charts the bridge's history with 'Harry' and other animatronic characters taking you back to the 1890s.
Disabled: access. Group discount. Shop.

Tower of London

Tower Hill, EC3 (0171 709 0765). Tower Hill tube/ Fenchurch Street BR. **Open** *Mar-Oct* 9am-6pm Mon-Sat; 10am-6pm Sun. *Nov-Feb* 9am-5pm Mon-Sat; 10am-5pm Sun. **Admission** £8.30; £6.25 OAPs, students, UB40s, disabled; £5.50 children; free under 5s; £21.95 family (2 adults, 3 children). **Credit** A, £TC, V.

The Tower has been a castle, a palace and a prison during its long history and it remains one of the capital's most important sights. It's expensive, but not a rip-off. It's worth taking hours to see it all, from William the Conqueror's White Tower, the ravens and polite Beefeaters, who give free tours, to the recently opened medieval palace of Edward I. Traitor's Gate and the Bloody Tower allow a glimpse into our macabre history; torture, murder and executions were an accepted part of medieval life. Of the many armour museums, the oriental display is the one you shouldn't miss. The Crown Jewels are now on display in the brand new, much larger **Jewel House**, opened in 1994, a great improvement on the previous one; on very busy days though, you may find yourself ferried through on a non-stop moving walkway.
Disabled: access with assistance (one adult admitted free if assisting disabled person). Gift shops. Group discount. Guided tours (free, every half hour for one hour).

Westminster Abbey

Dean's Yard, SW1 (0171 222 5152/222 7110). St James's Park or Westminster tube/ 3, 11, 12 bus. **Open** *nave* 7.30am-6pm Mon, Tue, Thur-Sat; 7.30am-7.45pm Wed; between services on Sunday. *Royal Chapels* 9am-4pm Mon-Fri; 9am-2pm, 3.45-5pm Sat; also 6-7.45pm Weds eve. *Chapter House, Pyx Chamber & Abbey Museum* 10.30am-4pm daily. *College Garden Apr-Sept* 10am-6pm Tue, Thur; *Oct-Mar* 10am-4pm Tue, Thur. *Brass Rubbing Centre (0171 222 2085)* 9am-5pm Mon-Sat. **Admission** *nave* Royal Chapels £4; £2 OAPs, students, UB40s; £1 under-16s; £2, £1 concs Weds eve (6-7.45pm). *Chapter House, Pyx Chamber & Abbey Museum* combined ticket £2.50; £1.90 OAPs, students, UB40s; £1.30 under-16s. *Sound guides (in several languages)* £6 (including admission).

Since Edward the Confessor built his huge Norman church, consecrated in 1065, the Abbey has been inextricably bound with British royalty. Every king and queen of England since William the Conqueror (in 1066) has been crowned here, and many are buried here too – the Royal chapels and tombs beyond the nave include Edward the Confessor's shrine and the Coronation Chair (1296). Of the original Abbey, only the Pyx Chamber and Norman undercroft remain; the Gothic nave and choir were rebuilt by Henry III in the thirteenth century; the Henry VII Chapel, with its fan vaulting, was added 1503-12; the west towers (by Hawksmoor) completed the building in 1745. The interior is cluttered with monuments to statesmen, politicians and poets. The octagonal Chapter House (1253) is well worth seeing. It's difficult to enjoy the Abbey among great crowds; the best time is around 8am, when the nave and cloisters are usually empty.
Disabled: access.

Royal London

For **Buckingham Palace** and the **Tower of London**, *see above* **Major Sights**.

Banqueting House

Whitehall, SW1 (0171 930 4179). Westminster tube or Charing Cross tube/BR. **Open** 10am-5pm Mon-Sat (can be shut at short notice for government receptions).

Tower of London *– glimpse into the macabre.*

Admission £2.90; £2.25 OAPs, students, UB40s; £1.90 under-16s. **Credit** *shop* A, AmEx, £TC, V.
The Banqueting House is the only surviving part of the former Whitehall Palace. Completed in 1622 for James I, it was designed by Inigo Jones, and was the first building in central London to introduce the Classical Renaissance style. James's son, Charles I, commissioned Peter Paul Rubens to decorate the ceiling of the great saloon room with allegorical paintings celebrating the divine right of the Stuart kings. A bust over the entrance reminds us that Charles was beheaded outside this building on 30 January 1649.
Shop. Group discount. Video tours.

Hampton Court Palace

East Molesey, Surrey (0181 781 9500). Hampton Court BR/riverboat from Westminster or Richmond to Hampton Court Pier (Apr-Oct). **Open** *Apr-Oct* 10.15am-6pm Mon; 9.30am-6pm Tue-Sun. *Oct-Mar* 10.15am-4.30pm Mon; 9.30am-4.30pm Tue-Sun (last admission 45mins before closing). **Park** open dawn to dusk daily. **Admission** inclusive ticket to palace, courtyard, cloister and maze £7.50; £5.60 OAPs; £4.90 under-5s; under-5s free; £19.30 family. **Maze only** £1.70; £1 under-16s, OAPs. **Credit** A, AmEx, £TC, V.
The grandest Tudor residence in England, Hampton Court was built as a country seat by the powerful Cardinal Wolsey in 1514, and taken over by Henry VIII in 1529 when Wolsey fell from favour. Henry's additions to the Palace include the magnificent roof of the Chapel Royal, which took 100 men nine months to complete. In the 1690s, William and Mary commissioned Wren to rebuild the State Apartments in the classical renaissance style (the King's Apartments, badly damaged by fire in 1986, have been painstakingly restored). You need half a day to stroll round; don't miss the huge old kitchens, the Great Vine (planted in 1769), the Tudor tennis court and the Astronomical Clock (1540) on which the sun

still revolves round the earth. Choose a fine day to see the spacious riverside gardens, including the famous Maze, laid out in 1714; nearby Bushy Park has herds of deer, ornamental ponds and a mile-long avenue of horse chestnuts, covered with pink and white flowers in May.

Car park (£1.60, free for disabled). Disabled: access; toilets. Guided tours (phone for details). Shop.

Jewel Tower

Abingdon Street, SW1 (0171 222 2219). Westminster tube. **Open** *Apr-Jun* 10am-1pm, 2-6pm, daily; *Oct-Mar* 10am-1pm, 2-4pm, daily. **Admission** £1.50; £1.10 OAPs, students; 80p under-15s. **Credit** A, £TC, V.

Along with Westminster Hall, the moated Jewel Tower is a survivor from the medieval Palace of Westminster. It was built (1365-66) to house Edward III's gold and jewels. From 1621-1864, the tower stored records of the House of Lords. Beautifully restored, it now has an exhibition of Parliament past and present, with a series of panels and a video.

Kensington Palace

Kensington Gardens, W8 (0171 937 9561). Queensway or High Street Kensington tube. **Open** 9am-5pm Mon-Sat; 11am-5pm Sun. **Admission** £4.50; £3.40 OAPs, students, UB40s; £3 under-15s; £12.50 family (2 adults, 2 children). **Credit** £TC.

William and Mary made this the royal residence in 1689 because living near the river at Whitehall disagreed with William's asthma. Wren and Hawksmoor were brought in to redesign the building. Princess Victoria lived here until she became Queen at the age of 18 and moved to **Buckingham Palace**. The State Apartments and Court Dress Collection will be closed from September 1995 for a £2.8 million refurbishment; not due to reopen until spring 1997, they may possibly reopen for summer 1996 (phone to check).

Café. Disabled: access to ground floor only. Group discount. Shop.

Kew Palace

Kew Gardens, Richmond (0181 332 5189). Kew Gardens tube/Kew Gardens or Kew Bridge BR/boat to Kew Pier/7, 22, 65, 90B, 237, 267, 391 bus. **Open** *Apr-Sept* 11am-5.30pm daily (last admission 5.15pm). **Admission** *Palace only* 80p. *Palace & Gardens* combined ticket £4.80 adults; £2.80 OAPs, students, under-16s. **Credit** £TC.

The former name for this Jacobean mansion was the Dutch House, because of its distinctive gables. Built in 1631, it was purchased by George III in 1781 and used as a country retreat by the royal family until about 1820. It's the smallest and most intimate of the royal homes, but was modernised several times by its Georgian residents. Two floors are open to the public, decorated in eighteenth-century style. There's a small museum and a beautiful herb garden.

Cafés in gardens. Disabled: access to ground floor only. Group discount. Shop.

Queen's House

Romney Road, SE10 (0181 858 4422). Greenwich or Maze Hill BR/Island Gardens DLR then Greenwich foot tunnel/53, 54, 75, 89, 108, 177, 180, 188 bus. **Open** *May-Sept* 10am-5pm daily. *Oct-Apr* 10.30am-3.30pm daily. **Tours** every 15 mins. **Admission** £5.50; £4.50 students, OAPs, UB40s; £3 under-16s. Price includes entry to Old Royal Observatory and National Maritime Museum plus a free repeat visit in the next 12 months. **Credit** A, AmEx, DC, JCB, £TC, V.

Restored and furnished as it would have been in the seventeenth century, this was the first Palladian-style villa in Britain, designed by Inigo Jones in 1616 for James I's wife, Anne of Denmark, who died before it was finished. It was completed for Charles I's queen, Henrietta Maria. From October 1995, there will be a new permanent exhibition, the New Nelson Gallery. Go to Island Gardens on the Isle of Dogs for a wonderful view of Greenwich and the Queen's House.

Royal Mews

Buckingham Palace Road, SW1 (0171 930 4832). St James's Park or Victoria tube/BR. **Open** *Oct-Dec* noon-4pm Wed; *Apr-Oct* noon-4pm Tue-Thur (last admission 3.30pm). **Admission** £3.50; £2 OAPs; £1.50 under-16s; free for disabled. **Credit** A, AmEx, £TC, V.

The Mews houses the royals' coaches and carriages. The gilt palm-wood of the Coronation Coach, the elegant Glass Coach, the immaculately groomed horses and the craftsmanship of the sleek black landaus make the Mews one of the capital's better value collections. The Mews is closed during Royal Ascot week (June) and on State occasions.

Disabled: access. Shop.

St James's Palace

Junction of Pall Mall and St James's Street, SW1. Green Park tube. **Not open** to the public.

The redbrick Tudor palace and gatehouse, built by Henry VIII in the 1530s on the site of a leper hospital, was used as the main royal residence from 1702-1837, after Whitehall Palace had been destroyed by fire. It is still used as a royal residence and as the official Court for the reception of foreign ambassadors. **Changing the Guard** here is linked with the ceremony at **Buckingham Palace**.

Attractions

Britain at War Experience

64-66 Tooley Street, SE1 (0171 403 3171). London Bridge tube/BR. **Open** *Apr-Sept* 10am-5.30pm (last admission); *Oct-Mar* 10am-4.30pm (last admission). **Admission** £4.95; £3.75 students, OAPs; £2.75 under-14s; £13 family (2 adults, 3 children).

The latest of London's 'real life' experiences: this one transports you back to London in the Blitz, a time of air raids, gas masks, black-outs, ration books and propaganda.

Guinness World of Records

The Trocadero, Piccadilly Circus, W1 (0171 439 7331). Piccadilly Circus tube. **Open** 10am-10pm daily. **Admission** £5.95; £4.20 OAPs, students; £3.95 under-16s; under-4s free; £15 family (2 adults, 2 children). **Credit** A, AmEx, DC, £TC, V.

The exhibits, illustrating feats, facts and record-breakers from the best-selling *Guinness Book of Records*, use scale models, films, recordings and lots of push-button machines. The place is definitely showing signs of wear and tear – not surprising given the number of visitors over the last ten years. Even so, it's better value than most tourist traps because there's enough here to keep adults and children entertained for a good couple of hours; plus it's open (and quietest) in the evening.

Disabled: access; toilets. Group discounts. Shop.

London Dungeon

28-34 Tooley Street, SE1 (0171 403 0606). London Bridge tube/BR. **Open** *Apr-Sept* 10am-6.30pm daily; *Oct-Mar* 10am-5.30pm daily (last admission 1 hour before closing). **Admission** £7.50; £6 students; £4.50 OAPs, under-14s; disabled in wheelchairs and under-5s free. **Credit** A, AmEx, £TC, V.

Peer through corroded railings in a dank, dark, musty-smelling maze of gloomy arches and eerie nooks, with the railway rumbling overhead. You'll see medieval torture scenes and hear the screams as the rack tightens. The location, artefacts, atmosphere and basic idea of presenting the grizzliest moments of British history are successful and most people enjoy their visit. A recent addition is the Jack the Ripper experience, which has provoked protests for its glorification of a rapist and murderer. Still, the coach parties pile through, and the shop does a roaring trade. The Dungeon is least busy Monday to Wednesday mornings.

Café. Disabled: access; toilets. Group discount. Shop.

The **Changing of the Guard** *takes half an hour with lots of shouting and stamping of feet.*

London Planetarium

Marylebone Road, NW1 (0171 486 1121). Baker Street tube. **Open** *June-Aug* 10.20am-5pm daily. *Sept-May* 12.20-5pm Mon-Fri; 10.20am-5pm Sat, Sun. **Admission** £4.75; £3.10 OAPs; £2.50 under-16s (no children under 5). *Combined ticket with Madame Tussaud's* £11.25; £8.50 OAPs, students; £6.95 under-16s; £29.45 family (2 adults, 2 children). **Credit** A, AmEx, £TC, V.

Following a £4.5 million refit there's a new entrance, bigger exhibition area and new auditorium with uni-directional seating (not so much fun as sitting round under the huge dome, as before, but the view is supposed to be better). The Zeiss projector has been replaced with the Digistar Mark 2 – the most advanced star projector in the world.
Café. Foreign-language translation. Group discount. Induction loop facilities. Shop.

London Zoo

Regent's Park, NW1 (0171 722 3333). Camden Town tube/Baker Street tube then 74 bus. **Open** 10am-5.30pm daily. **Admission** £7; £6 OAPs; £4 under-15s; free under-4s; £20 family (2 adults, 2 children). **Credit** A, AmEx, £$TC, V.

The British obsession with pets gets serious: you can adopt an octopus for £15 or an elephant for £6,000. The money goes towards looking after the beast for a year and your name will go on a plaque by its enclosure. It's a marvellous place for kids: feeding times and special events are posted on noticeboards, and the new Children's Zoo is much larger than before (*see chapter* **Children**). The gardens are beautifully landscaped and the Zoo buildings include some gems of modern architecture: look out for the Penguin Pool (1934) by Lubetkin, Hugh Casson's Elephant House (1965) and Lord Snowdon's Aviary (1965).
Disabled: access; toilets. Education centre. Films. Group discount. Lectures. Restaurant. Shop.

Madame Tussaud's

Marylebone Road, NW1 (0171 935 6861). Baker Street tube. **Open** *May-Sept* 9am-5.30pm daily. *Oct-Jun* 10am-5.30pm Mon-Fri; 9.30am-5.30pm Sat, Sun. **Admission** £8.35; £6.25 OAPs; £5.25 under-16s; £21.95 family (2 adults, 2 children). *Combined ticket with. Planetarium* £11.25; £8.50 OAPs, students; £6.95 under-16s; £29.45 family (2 adults, 2 children). **Credit** A, AmEx, £$TC, V.

Madame Tussaud lived in Paris during the French Revolution and learnt the art of waxworks from her uncle; in 1802 she brought her collection to London, and it's been pulling the crowds ever since. One of the oldest and most gruesome exhibits (in the Chamber of Horrors) is the guillotine blade which beheaded Marie Antoinette. To be measured up for a wax model here is proof of fame: ideas for new figures come from a poll of visitors. Latest additions to the ranks of royalty, politicians, sports stars and celebrities include David Copperfield, Joanna Lumley, Hugh Grant and Linford Christie. It's recently been reorganised into themed

St Paul's Cathedral – *Wren's masterpiece.*

areas with a dark-ride finale, The Spirit of London, taking you on a journey through history in a 'time-taxi'. There's nearly always a queue (not surprising with 2.3 million visitors a year), but you can avoid it by booking the day before. *Café. Group discount. Disabled: access by prior arrangement; toilets.*

Rock Circus

London Pavilion, Piccadilly Circus, W1 (0171 734 7203). Piccadilly Circus tube. **Open** 11am-9pm Mon, Wed, Thur, Sun; noon-9pm Tue; 11am-10pm Fri, Sat. **Admission** £7.50; £6.50 OAPs, students; £5.50 under-16s; disabled and under-5s free; £19.95 family (2 adults, 2 children). **Credit** £$TC.
The first part has static tableaux of wax pop stars – George Michael, Status Quo and the late Jim Morrison are all present. Headphones pick up infra-red signals and play a song for the display you're looking at. There's a 20-minute 'concert': seeing bionic wax models of the Beatles in a revolving theatre can be unnerving, especially when sound and motion are synched, or when Bruce Springsteen gives it some on the guitar. The use of video backing, however, rather undermines the whole concept. It's all good fun, for a hefty fee. *Disabled: access; toilets. Group discount. Shop.*

Sherlock Holmes Museum

221B Baker Street, NW1 (0171 935 8866). Baker Street tube. **Open** 9.30am-6pm daily. **Admission** £5; £3 under-16s. **Credit** A, AmEx, JCB, £TC, V.
Not strictly a museum as there are no genuine artefacts on show and no information about Conan Doyle (who created Holmes) or the Edinburgh surgeon who was the inspiration for the fictional character. Instead, the admission price allows the visitor to trot up and down four floors of Victorian bric-à-brac which recreates the lodgings of Sherlock Holmes and Dr Watson. In the cosy living room you can pose in Holmes' armchair with his pipe and Stradivarius. The room upstairs is lined with lookalike 'artefacts' such as the club used to murder Colonel Barclay in *The Crooked Man* and Dr Mortimer's stick from *The Hound Of The Baskervilles*. One room is taken up by a souvenir shop; clearly profit is the driving force. The recreation of the rooms is done well but a fiver is steep for a bit of atmosphere. *Shop. Restaurant.*

Tower Hill Pageant

1 Tower Hill Terrace, EC3 (0171 709 0081). Tower Hill tube. **Open** 9.30am-4.30pm daily. **Admission** £5.95; £3.95 4-15s; £14.95 family (2 adults, 2 children).
A dark-ride museum in which you sit in a time car and glide past 26 illuminated tableaux of old London, with appropriate sounds and smells provided along the way. The trip takes about 15 minutes (you can ride more than once if you want to) and there's an excellent display of the latest archaeological finds from Roman times.

The Trocadero

13 Coventry Street, Piccadilly, W1 (0171 439 1791/Food Street 0171 287 2681). Piccadilly Circus tube. **Open** 10am-midnight daily; *Food Street* noon-1am daily.
Admission *Trocadero Passport* Mon-Fri, valid 5 days to all 4 attractions £14.95; £12.95 under-16s.
The choking, road-doomed area around Piccadilly Circus must prove a sorry disappointment to the thousands of tourists who've no doubt traipsed there in the mistaken belief that it's the pulsing heart of London. Well it's not, of course, but once they're in the area there's no avoiding the screaming posters for this self-consciously space-age centre. The headline act is arguably the **Guinness World of Records** (*see above*), but it's by no means the most fun. You can join in the shrieking office parties at **Quasar** (*0171 434 0795*), an action Laser Gun Game, which involves blasting everyone in sight in a darkened arena throbbing with brain-shattering music (10am-11pm Mon-Thur, Sun; 10am-midnight Fri,

*The **Lloyd's** building – City beacon at night.*

Sat; £6 per adult for a 20-minute off-peak session, £4.50 children; £7 and £5.50 at weekends). **Alien War** (*0171 437 2678*) offers the chance to be devoured by a seven-foot monster with acid for blood (£7.95 for 20 minutes, £5.95 children, family ticket £23, under-12s must be accompanied by an adult); while **Emaginator** (*0171 734 3271*) has a choice of four thunderous, white-knuckle rides (open 11am-midnight daily, £3.50 per ride, £5.50 for two rides, £15 for six). If you still have the stomach for it, **Food Street** serves Oriental food, including some good dim sum and satay (the *real* **Chinatown** is just round the corner in Gerrard Street). The Trocadero Passport allows you five days' access to this temple of Mammon, plus entry to the the seven-screen MGM cinemas for £2 before 6pm (*see chapter* **Film**). It's worth a blast.

Business London

Bank of England

Bartholomew Lane, EC2 (0171 601 5545). Bank tube. **Open** *Bank of England Museum* 10am-5pm Mon-Fri. **Admission** *Museum* free.
The Bank was founded in 1694. Only the outside curtain walls remain of Sir John Soane's elegant design for the first Bank; the rest was demolished in an enlargement carried out between the wars. The modern bank covers three acres; the underground vaults store Britain's gold reserves. The only part open to the public is the excellent Bank of England Museum, which includes a faithful restoration of Soane's Bank Stock Office from 1793. Original artwork for banknotes is also displayed inside closely monitored cabinets that check humidity and thieving hands. The Bank Today section has interactive videos and a dealing desk.
Disabled: access by prior arrangement. Educational films. Lectures by prior arrangement. Shop. Tour and touch sessions for the visually impaired by prior arrangement.

Guildhall

off Gresham Street, EC2 (0171 606 3030). Bank tube.
Open *Guildhall* 9am-5pm daily; *clock museum* 9.30am-4.45pm Mon-Fri. **Admission** free.
Guildhall has been the centre of the City's local government for over 800 years. The fifteenth-century Great Hall, twice gutted by fire, has been beautifully restored. It's decorated with the banners and shields of the 100 Livery Companies and the windows record the names of every Lord Mayor since 1189; there are monuments to Wellington, Nelson and Churchill. Meetings of the Court of Common Council (the governing body for the Corporation of London, presided over by the Lord Mayor) are held here monthly on Thursdays at 1pm, except during August (visitors welcome; phone for dates). It's also used for banquets and ceremonial events. The buildings alongside house the Corporation offices, the Guildhall Library and the **Clockmakers' Company Museum**. *Disabled: access; toilets. Free guided tours (write in advance to: The Keeper of Guildhall, Guildhall, EC2). Shop.*

Lloyd's of London

Lime Street, EC3 (0171 327 6210). Bank or Monument tube. **Not open** to the public except by advance booking from recognised groups.
The world's most famous insurance market started life in Edward Lloyd's coffee shop in 1688, where ship's captains, owners and merchants gathered to exchange news; it now operates in one of the City's most controversial high-tech buildings by Richard Rogers (*see chapter* **Architecture**). Lloyd's is a society of underwriters (Names) who pledge personal fortunes to insure everything from oil rigs to Elton John's fingers. Marine insurance forms the bulk of the business. The bell of HMS *Lutine* is tolled once for bad news, twice for

St Anne's, Limehouse – *under restoration.*

Hayward Gallery Neon Tower

'The idea of an external sculpture for the Hayward Gallery aroused my interest as it seemed to offer an alternative to the showing of work in a gallery where the clientèle represents only a small section of this society.' Philip Vaughan could little have suspected, when he and collaborator Roger Dainton were approached by the Arts Council in 1969, that they were about to effect a change in the London skyline that would remain in place for at least 25 years.

The Neon Tower is a 48-foot (14.6m) construction of 108 tubes (36 yellow, 36 magenta, 12 each of blue, green and red). Six octahedrons (two square-based pyramids back-to-back) are stacked vertically to make up the structure, resulting in a secondary pattern of three spiralling helixes clockwise and three anti-clockwise. The structure is then completed with seven alternately opposed triangles forming the horizontal planes.

Roger Dainton, responsible for the kinetics, decided to use sequences of moving shapes as a visual display of the wind. 'Casual passers-by can feel changes in the strength and direction of the wind and also relate this immediately to the changing appearance of the tower.' There are eight different sequences of moving shapes, one for each point of the compass. The eight sets are selected by the movement of the weather vane on top of the tower. 'The speed at which the shapes appear to move is controlled by the speed of the wind, which is measured by an anemometer, also at the top of the tower.'

Walk south over Waterloo Bridge at dusk to see the Neon Tower at its most beautiful and mysterious. With a sweep of the head you can see St Paul's, Canary Wharf, the National Theatre, Royal Festival Hall and the Houses of Parliament. And at the heart of that extraordinary panorama is the Neon Tower.

City Churches

Before the Great Fire, nearly 100 churches stood within the City wall; 87 were destroyed. Sir Christopher Wren was responsible for 51 of the 54 churches which were rebuilt. His interiors are light and uplifting, painted in white and gold (considered pagan by the Victorians, who preferred the dim light and stained glass of the old Gothic style). Wren used clear glass windows to show the fine wood carving, painted altar pieces and ironwork. WWII saw many of these churches bombed; 11 were destroyed. Only 38 remain; St Ethelburga's in Bishopsgate – one of the few medieval churches which had survived both the Great Fire and the Blitz – was destroyed by an IRA bomb in 1993.

All Hallows by the Tower
Byward Street, EC3 (0171 481 2928). Tower Hill tube. **Open** 9am-5.45pm Mon-Wed, Fri; 9am-7pm Thur; 11am-5pm Sat; 10am-5pm Sun.
This church, partly rebuilt since WWII, is full of relics – the remains of a seventh-century Saxon arch, from the original church on this site, ancient Saxon crosses and a Roman tessellated pavement, Tudor monuments, sword-rests and brasses, a carved limewood font cover (1682) by Grinling Gibbons and a collection of model ships.

St Bartholomew-the-Great
West Smithfield, EC1 (0171 606 5171). Farringdon tube/BR. **Open** 10am-3pm Mon-Fri; 10am-4.30pm Sat; noon-6pm Sun.
Part of a twelfth-century Norman priory, St Bart's is now the oldest parish church in London. Built in 1123 by Rahere, a courtier of Henry I, who also founded St Bartholomew's Hospital, the nave once extended to the thirteenth-century gateway, topped by a half-timbered Tudor gatehouse, which is now the entrance from Smithfield.

St Bride's Church
Fleet Street, EC4 (0171 353 1301). Blackfriars tube/BR. **Open** 8.30am-5pm Mon-Sat; 10am-7.30pm Sun.
Wren completed St Bride's in 1703. The spire is his tallest at 226 feet/69m. The church was gutted in the Blitz, revealing Roman and Saxon remains, now displayed in the crypt. The press may have deserted Fleet Street but St Bride's is still known as the Journalists' Church. It also organises free lunchtime concerts.

St Helen's Bishopsgate
Great St Helen's, EC3 (0171 283 2231). Liverpool Street tube/BR. **Closed for repairs**.
This thirteenth-century church (damaged by an IRA bomb in 1992, expected to reopen in early 1996) is one of the few remaining pre-fire churches. The unusual double nave shows that this was once two churches side by side, one belonging to a Benedictine nunnery; you can still see, on the north side, the small staircase which led to the nuns' dormitory, and the 'squint' where nuns not admitted could look through to the altar. St Helen's is known as the 'Westminster Abbey of the City' because of its splendid collection of medieval and Tudor monuments to City dignitaries. St Andrew Undershaft, nearby, and St Olave's, Hart Street, are also pre-fire churches.

St Magnus Martyr
Lower Thames Street, EC3 (0171 626 4481). Monument tube. **Open** 10am-4pm Tue-Fri; 10.30am-1pm Sun.
The splendid interior was described by TS Eliot as an 'inexplicable splendour of Ionian white and gold'. The stones in the churchyard were part of Old London Bridge.

St Mary-le-Bow
Cheapside, EC2 (0171 248 5139). Bank or St Paul's tube. **Open** 6.30am-6pm Mon-Thur; 6.30am-4pm Fri.
Wren's elegant white tower and spire, topped with a nine-foot winged dragon, rises above busy, modern Cheapside. True Londoners, or 'cockneys', had to be born within the sound of Bow bells. The interior was destroyed in 1941, but has been restored in their original style. The Tuesday dialogue (at 1.05pm during University term-time) is a regular event, with guest speakers. The Norman crypt is occupied by a vegetarian restaurant, The Place Below.

St Mary Woolnoth
Lombard Street, EC3 (0171 626 9701). Bank tube. **Open** 7.30am-5.15pm Mon-Fri.
John Newton, who wrote the hymns 'Amazing Grace' and 'Glorious Things of Thee Are Spoken', was incumbent at Hawksmoor's only City church from 1780 until his death in 1807. When Bank tube station was constructed in 1897-1900, the dead had to be removed from the vaults. Completely undermined, the church was supported on steel girders, and lift shafts were sunk directly beneath it.

St Stephen Walbrook
Walbrook, EC4 (0171 283 4444). Mansion House tube. **Open** 10am-4pm Mon-Thur; 10am-3pm Fri.
The dome rests on a ring of circular arches, supported by eight Corinthian columns, giving a feeling of space and light. Perhaps Wren's finest parish church (*pictured below*), it has been beautifully restored. The Reverend Chad Varah founded the **Samaritans** here in 1953.

good. In the early '90s, most of the news was bad, and many Names, if not Lloyd's itself, are on the brink of bankruptcy. *Disabled: access. Exhibitions. Shop.*

Royal Exchange
Cornhill, EC4 (0171 623 0444). Bank tube. **Open** group visits by appointment only. **Admission** free.
In 1567 London's first covered marketplace for financial traders opened here, contributing enormously to the city's prosperity. It was twice destroyed by fire but the present building by William Tite (1844) still honours its founder, Sir Thomas Gresham, with a statue over the entrance in Exchange Buildings and his golden grasshopper emblem on the bell tower. Recently renovated, Richard Westmacott's pediment sculptures show the central figure of Commerce with the Lord Mayor and groups of merchants. The dealers have moved on but among the restaurants below is the **Imperial City**, one of London's finest Chinese restaurants.

Cathedrals & Churches

For **St Paul's Cathedral** *see above* **Major Sights**.

Brompton Oratory
Thurloe Place, Brompton Road, SW3 (0171 589 4811). South Kensington tube. **Open** 6.30am-8pm daily.
Services 6 masses daily Mon-Sat (phone to check); 7am, 8am, 9am, 10am, 11am (Sung Latin mass), 12.30pm, 4.30pm, 7pm, Sun.
Brompton Oratory, built in 1884 after little-known young architect Herbert Gribble won an open competition, was the leading Catholic church in London until Westminster Cathedral opened its doors in 1903. The apostles lining the church are by Mazzuoli; they stood for 200 years in Siena Cathedral.

Chelsea Old Church
Cheyne Walk, SW3 (0171 352 5627). Sloane Square tube/19, 39, 45, 49, 219 bus. **Services** 8am Thur; noon Fri; 8am, 10am, 11am (matins), noon, 6pm, Sun.
Most of this riverside church was destroyed in WWII, but the original structure dated back to 1157. Henry VIII reputedly married his third wife Jane Seymour here before their state wedding, and Sir Thomas More had a private chapel built on to the church in 1528. Look for the memorials to author Henry James and the architect Sir Hans Sloane.

Christchurch Spitalfields
Commercial Street, E1 (0171 247 7202). **Open** for concerts, otherwise apply at the crypt door.
The largest of Hawksmoor's six churches, its triangular spire towers above Spitalfields' splendid Georgian houses. The crypt is used as a rehabilitation centre for alcoholics. A Festival of Early Music is held here in July (*see chapter* **Music: Classical & Opera**).

Church of the Immaculate Conception
Farm Street, W1 (0171 493 7811). Green Park or Bond Street tube. **Services** 7.30am, 8.30am, 12.05pm, 1.05pm, 6pm, Mon-Fri; 7.30am, 8.30am, 11am, 6pm, Sat; 7.30am, 8.30am, 10am, 11am (sung Latin), 12.15pm, 4.15pm, 6.15pm, Sun.
One of London's few Catholic churches where a sung Latin mass is celebrated, this splendid Gothic Revival building is the British Province headquarters of the Jesuit Fathers.

St Alfege Greenwich
Greenwich High Road, SE10 (0181 858 3458). Greenwich BR. **Open** 11am-3pm Tue-Fri; 2-4pm Sat, Sun.
This church, which Hawksmoor started building in 1714, was gutted in May 1941 and carefully restored by Sir Albert Richardson. A little of Grinling Gibbons' original wood-carving remains in the posts under the galleries and the Beasts on the Royal Pew.

Marble Hill House – *a fine Palladian villa.*

St Anne's, Limehouse
Three Colt Street, E14 (0171 987 1502). Westferry DLR. **Open** 2-4pm Mon-Fri; 2-5pm Sat, 2.30-5.30pm Sun; 11am-4pm Bank Holidays.* **Services** 10.30am, 6pm, Sun.
Another Hawksmoor building currently in the middle of a longterm restoration project, St Anne's boasts a backwards-leaning tower and an odd pyramidal tomb which is thought to contain the remains of a number of old sea captains.

St Etheldreda's
Ely Place, EC1 (0171 405 1061). Chancery Lane tube. **Open** 7.30am-7pm daily. **Services** 8am, 1pm, Mon-Fri; 9am, 11am (choral), Sun.
This thirteenth-century church (Britain's oldest Catholic church) is one of the finest examples of Decorated Gothic architecture. Built in the reign of Edward I, it was once the private chapel for the Bishop of Ely's London residence. The gardens at Ely Place were famous for their strawberries; the street still hosts an annual Strawberrie Fayre in June. Nearby in Ely Court, visit the tiny Olde Mitre Tavern, built in 1546.

St George's, Bloomsbury
Bloomsbury Way, WC1 (0171 405 3044). Holborn or Tottenham Court Road tube. **Open** 10am-3pm Mon-Fri. **Services** 1.10pm Wed, Fri; 10am, 6.30pm, Sun.
This Hawksmoor church is unusual in that it can work along either an east/west or a north/south axis. Its northern face is surprisingly light for the celebrated, prolific architect.

St George-in-the-East
The Highway, E1 (0171 481 1345). Shadwell tube/DLR. **Open** 8am-5pm Tue-Sun. **Service** 1.05pm Wed; 7pm Thur; 10.15am, 6.30pm, Sun.
St George's was gutted in WWII and a new church opened inside the ruins in 1963, but the majestic exterior with its monumental tower remains characteristically Hawksmoor.

St James's Church Piccadilly

197 Piccadilly, W1 (0171 734 4511). Piccadilly Circus tube. **Open** 8.30am-7pm daily (phone for details of evening events). *Café* 8am-7pm Mon-Sat; 10am-5pm Sun. **Services** 8.30am, 5.45pm, Tue; 8.30am Wed-Fri; 8.30am, 11am, 5.45pm, Sun.

This Wren church, the only one in London which he built on a new site, was damaged in WWII and restored by Sir Albert Richardson. Grinling Gibbons' marble font has been saved. The Wren Café next door has inexpensive vegetarian food.

St Margaret's Westminster

Parliament Square, SW1 (0171 222 5152). Westminster tube. **Open** 9.30am-4pm daily. **Services** 11am Sun.

It's easy to overlook this historic medieval church, dwarfed by the adjacent Abbey. The stained glass is among the best in London. The impressive east window, in richly coloured Flemish glass, commemorates the marriage of Henry VIII and his first wife Catherine of Aragon (1509). Later windows celebrate Britain's first printer, William Caxton, buried here in 1491; the explorer Sir Walter Ralegh, who was executed over the road in Old Palace Yard; and the writer John Milton (1608-74) who worshipped here.
Disabled: access.

St Martin-in-the-Fields

Trafalgar Square, WC2 (0171 930 1862). Charing Cross tube/BR. **Open** 8am-6.30pm daily. **Services** 7pm Mon (taize prayers); 8am, 8.30am, 5.30pm, Mon-Fri; 6pm Wed; 1.05pm Thur; 9am Sat; 8am, 9.45am (choral), 11.30am, 12.30pm, 2.45pm (service in Cantonese), 5pm (evensong), 6.30pm, Sun.

A church has stood here since the thirteenth century, when it really was 'in the fields' between the City and Westminster. The present church (1726), with its wide, welcoming portico, was designed by James Gibbs (*see chapter* **Architecture**). The interior is embellished with dark woodwork and ornate Italian plasterwork; note the Royal Box to the left of the gallery because this is officially the parish church for Buckingham Palace. The free lunchtime concerts (*see chapter* **Music: Classical & Opera**) provide an excellent opportunity to relax and admire the interior.

St Mary's Battersea

Battersea Church Road, SW11 (0171 228 9648). Bus 19, 219. **Open** Fri pm, phone first. **Services** 11am Sun.

The present church was built by churchwarden Joseph Dixon in the 1770s, the old building having become too small. Painter and visionary William Blake married the daughter of a local market gardener here, and the artist JMW Turner would come to watch sunsets from the vestry window.

St Paul's Church

Bedford Street, WC2 (0171 836 5221). Covent Garden tube. **Open** 9.30am-2.30pm Mon; 9.30am-4.30pm Tue-Fri. **Services** 1.10pm Wed; 8.30am Mon, Tue, Wed; 11am Sun.

Known as the Actors' Church, the St Paul's interior is filled with memorials dedicated to actors and actresses. Designed by Inigo Jones in 1633, this was the first church to be built in the simple classical style (*see chapter* **Architecture**). The splendid portico on the Piazza, famously featured in *My Fair Lady*, is in fact at the back of the church. The entrance is from the secluded churchyard garden at the front (gates in Bedford Street, King Street and Henrietta Street).

Southwark Cathedral

Montague Close, SE1 (0171 407 2939). London Bridge tube/BR/Riverbus to London Bridge City Pier. **Open** 8am-6pm daily. Closing times vary on religious holidays. **Services** 12.45pm, 5.30pm, Mon-Fri; 9am (morning prayer), 9.15am, noon, 4pm, Sat; 9am, 11am, 3pm, Sun. **Admission** free. **Credit** *café* A, AmEx, DC, £TC, V.

Southwark Cathedral was a monastic church which became an Anglican cathedral in 1905. Parts of the building date back to 1220, when the church was known as St Mary Overy. After the Reformation it fell into disrepair, and sections of it became a bakery and a pig-sty. It was much restored during the nineteenth century. The cathedral possesses a fascinating mixture of architecture, including a fine Gothic choir.
Café (0171 378 6446; open 10am-4.30pm Mon-Fri). Crèche (Sun 11am service only). Disabled: access. Shop. Tour by prior arrangement.

Temple Church

Inner Temple, King's Bench Walk, EC4 (0171 353 1736). Temple tube. **Open** 10am-4pm Mon-Sat. **Services** 8.30am (Holy Communion), 11.15am (morning service), Sun. **Admission** free.

Built by the Knights Templars between 1170 and 1240, the beautiful Temple Church is based on the Church of the Holy Sepulchre in Jerusalem. Although it has been rebuilt after WWII, it still has the ground plan of the original church and marble effigies of thirteenth-century knights.
Disabled: access.

Westminster Cathedral

Victoria Street, SW1 (0171 798 9055). Victoria tube/BR. **Open** 7am-8pm daily. **Services** 7am, 8am, 8.30am, 9am, 10.30am, 12.30pm, 1.05pm, 5.30pm (sung Mass), Mon-Fri; 7am, 8am, 8.30am, 9am, 10.30am (sung Mass), 12.30pm, 6pm, Sat; 7am, 8am, 9am, 10.30am (sung Mass), noon, 5.30pm, 7pm, Sun.

The headquarters of the Catholic Church in Britain. Candy-like bands of red brick and stone in Christian Byzantine style make this 1903 cathedral an imposing sight. Inside, the decoration still isn't complete, and the domes are bare. But the columns and mosaics (made from over a hundred kinds of marble) are magnificent, the nave is the widest in Britain, Eric Gill's sculptures of the Stations of the Cross (1914-18) are especially fine and the view from the campanile is superb.

Famous Residences

See chapter **Museums** for **Carlyle's House, Freud's House** *and* **Keats' House**.

Darwin's House

Downe House, Luxted Road, Downe, Orpington, Kent (06898 59119). Bromley South BR, then 146 bus. **Open** 1-6pm Wed-Sun (last adm 5.30pm). **Admission** £2.50; £1.50 OAPs, students; £1 under-15s. **No credit cards.**

The naturalist Charles Darwin's radical 'survival of the fittest' theory of evolution was partly written in this large house, where he lived for 40 years. The house has been restored as closely as possible to its state in Darwin's lifetime and contains the original drawing room and study.
Disabled: access. Shop.

Dickens' House

49 Doughty Street, WC1 (0171 405 2127). Russell Square or Chancery Lane tube. **Open** 10am-5pm Mon-Sat. **Admission** £3; £2 OAPs, students, UB40s; £1 under-16s; £5 family (2 adults, 3 children). **Credit** *shop* A, AmEx, V.

This Georgian terrace house is where the novelist Charles Dickens lived from April 1837-December 1839. It is the only one of his London residences to have survived. The house is full of Dickens memorabilia, including portraits of himself and his family, his desk and chair, and the room in which his sister-in-law, 16-year-old Mary Hogarth (with whom he had fallen in love), died. Although the novelist lived here for just two and a half years, this is where he wrote *Oliver Twist*, *Nicholas Nickleby* and the last five chapters of *The Pickwick Papers*.
Bookshop (sells first and early editions of Dickens). Research facilities.

Hogarth's House

Hogarth Lane, Great West Road, W4 (0181 994 6757).
Turnham Green tube/Chiswick BR. **Open** *Apr-Sept* 11am-
6pm Mon, Wed-Sat; 2-6pm Sun. *Oct-Mar* 11am-4pm Mon,
Wed-Sat; 2-4pm Sun (closed first two weeks in Sept and
last three weeks in Dec). **Admission** free.
Hogarth's country retreat has been restored to its eighteenth-
century condition and provides wall space for 200 of the
social commentator's prints, though his most famous work,
The Rake's Progress, is present only in copied form. An orig-
inal is in **Sir John Soane's Museum**.
*Car park. Disabled: access to ground floor only. Gift shop.
Tour by prior arrangement.*

Dr Johnson's House

17 Gough Square, Fleet Street, EC4 (0171 353 3745).
Chancery Lane or Temple tube or Blackfriars tube/BR.
Open *May-Sept* 11am-5.30pm Mon-Sat; *Oct-Apr* 11am-
5pm Mon-Sat. **Admission** £3; £2 children, OAPs,
students; £1 10-16s; free under-10s. **No credit cards.**
Dr Samuel Johnson lived in this splendid example of a
Georgian townhouse from 1748 to 1759, while working on
the first comprehensive English dictionary. You can meander through the spacious rooms guided by descriptions and
quotes on handheld boards, but furnishings are few and
barest of all is the long garret where all his wordy toiling
took place. An authentic setting but sparse presentation.
Shop.

Historic Houses

Chiswick House

Burlington Lane, W4 (0181 995 0508). Turnham
Green tube/Chiswick BR. **Open** *Apr-Sept* 10am-1pm, 2-
6pm, daily; *Oct-Mar* 10am-1pm, 2-4pm, Wed-Sun.
Admission £2.50; £1.90 OAPs, students, UB40s; £1.30
under-16s. **Credit** A, V.
The Italian architect Andrea Palladio's architectural studies
of ancient buildings influenced designers more than any
other in the eighteenth century. Lord Burlington's 1729
design for this mansion is based on Palladio's Villa Capra
(the Rotonda) in Vicenza and was realised by William Kent.
Group discount.

Ham House

Ham, Richmond, Surrey (0181 940 1950). Richmond
tube/BR then 71 bus. **Open** *house* 1-5pm Mon-Wed; 1-
5.30pm Sat; 11.30am-5.30pm Sun. *Gardens* 10.30am-6pm
(or dusk) daily. **Admission** *house* £4; £2 OAPs, under-
16s. **No credit cards.**
This handsome, redbrick seventeenth-century riverside mansion, now owned by the National Trust, has recently been
restored with all its magnificently over-the-top furnishings
and decorations. Surrounded by water meadows, the formal
garden and 'wildderness' looks much as it did 300 years
ago. The most romantic way to get there is by ferry from the
towpath near Marble Hill House (*see below*).

Hatfield House

Hatfield, Hertfordshire (01707 262823). Hatfield BR.
Open *Mar-Oct* noon-4pm Tue-Sat; 1.30-5pm Sun; 11am-
5pm Bank Holidays. **Admission** *house and gardens*
£4.70; £3.90 OAPs; £3.20 under-16s. *Gardens only* £2.60;
£2.40 OAPs; £2 under-16s. **Credit** *shop* A, £$TC, V.
A splendid, fully furnished Jacobean house with paintings,
tapestries and armour, as well as exhibitions of model soldiers and Jacobean kitchens. Look round the late-fifteenth-
century gardens and see the ruins of the Royal Palace of
Hatfield where Elizabeth I spent much of her childhood.
Café. Children's playground. Disabled: access; toilets.
Elizabethan banquets (01707 2 62055). Garden festival
(June). Group discount. Guided tours. Multi-lingual tours
by prior arrangement. Restaurant. Shop.

Kenwood House

Hampstead Lane, NW3 (0181 348 1286). Archway,
Golders Green or Highgate tube/210 bus. **Open**
Apr-Sept 10am-6pm daily; *Oct-Mar* 10am-4pm daily.
Admission free.
This elegant mansion overlooking Hampstead Heath was
rebuilt in classical style for the Earl of Mansfield by Robert
Adam in 1767-69 and bequeathed to the nation in 1927. A
stroll across the Heath and through the house, with its paint-
ings, furniture and beautiful oval-shaped Library, is one of
the great pleasures of living in London. The small but superb
collection of Old Masters includes a famous Rembrandt
self-portrait, Vermeer's *Lute Player*, and works by Turner,
Hals, Gainsborough and Reynolds. The Kenwood Lakeside
Concerts are held near here on Saturday evenings during the
summer (*see chapter* **Music: Classical & Opera**).
Coach House Café. Disabled: access. Gift shop.

Marble Hill House

Richmond Road, Twickenham, Middlesex (0181 892
5115). Richmond tube/BR/33, 90, 270, 290, H22, R70
bus. **Open** *Apr-Sept* 10am-1pm, 2-6pm, daily; *Oct-Mar*
10am-1pm, 2-4pm, Wed-Sun. **Admission** £2; £1.50
OAPs, students, UB40s, under-16s.
Marble Hill House, overlooking the Thames in Marble Hill
Park, is a fine example of a Palladian villa, built for Henrietta
Howard, the mistress of George II, and later occupied by Mrs
Fitzherbert, George IV's secret wife. The interior Cube Hall
has beautiful moulded decoration, and the house has been
immaculately restored with original Georgian furnishings
and paintings. On Sunday evenings in summer there are con-
certs in the park (*see chapter* **Music: Classical & Opera**).
Café (Apr-Sept). Disabled: access to ground floor only.

Osterley Park

Osterley, Isleworth, Middlesex (0181 560 3918).
Osterley tube. **Open** *Apr-Oct* 1-5pm Wed-Sat; 11am-5pm
Sun. **Admission** £3.60; £1.80 under-16s; £9 family
(2 adults, 2 children).
The Elizabethan house built for Sir Thomas Gresham
(founder of the **Royal Exchange**) was transformed in the
eighteenth century by the architect Robert Adam (who redesigned **Kenwood House** and **Syon House**). The rooms
'below stairs' (the kitchens, the housekeeper's rooms and the
head butler's offices) are fascinating; look for the list of wage
payments on the wall. The gardens are extensive and magnificent with huge cedars and oaks, an ancient mulberry tree,
and an artificial lake with a small floating pagoda.
Café (Apr-Dec). Group discount. National Trust Shop
(Apr-Dec).

Spencer House

27 St James's Place, SW1 (0171 499 8620). Green Park
tube. **Open** 11.45am-4.45pm Sun (closed Aug and Jan).
Admission £6; £5 OAPs, students, under-16s (no
children under 10). **No credit cards.**
Restored at a cost of £1.6 million, Spencer House was built
between 1756-66 by John Vardy for the first Earl Spencer
(ancestor of Princess Diana). The nine state rooms were the
first in the neo-classical style to be designed in England.
Guided tours, for maximum 15, start at 11.45am and continue at 15-minute intervals. Larger groups may pre-book.
Guided tours.

Sutton House

2 & 4 Homerton High Street, E9 (0181 986 2264).
Hackney Central BR/Bethnal Green tube, then 253 bus.
Open *Historic rooms* 11.30am-5pm Wed, Sun, Bank
Holidays; 2-5pm Sat. **Admission** £1.60; 50p under-17s.
The redbrick Tudor mansion, built in 1535 for Henry VIII's
First Secretary of State, is the oldest house in east London.
Now owned by the National Trust, it recently opened as a
community arts centre after restoration, and is also the home
of the Early Music Centre. Tudor, Jacobean and Georgian

interiors are on show, as well as the Edwardian chapel, medieval foundations in the cellar and '80s graffiti under the roof. It also boasts what is possibly London's oldest loo: a sixteenth-century 'garderobe' boarded up in the 1700s. *Café, bar, shop and gallery open Wed-Sun inclusive. Concerts, workshops and performances take place regularly (booking details 0181 986 0221).*

Syon House

Syon Park, Brentford, Middlesex (0181 560 0881). Gunnersbury tube/Syon Lane BR/237, 267 bus. **Open** *house Apr-Sept* 11am-4.15pm Wed-Sun; *Oct* 11am-4.15pm Wed, Sat, Sun, Bank Holidays. *Gardens* 10am-6pm daily. **Admission** *house* £4; £3 OAPs, under-16s. *Gardens* £4; £3 OAPs, under-16s. *Combined ticket* £5.50; £4 OAPs, under-16s.

Arguably Robert Adam's masterpiece, built when the architect was at the height of his fame (1761). His task was to remodel an existing house that had been the home of the Percy family (the Earls of Northumberland) since 1594. The gallery leading to the circular bird-cage room was designed for use by women and decorated in pastel purples, greens, light grey and pinks; the dining room, ante-room, and hall were bastions of masculinity and are adorned with classical heroes. The riverside gardens (opposite Kew), landscaped by Capability Brown, now include the London Butterfly House. *Car Park (free). Disabled: access to gardens only. National Trust shop.*

Law & Order

The Clink Exhibition

1 Clink Street, SE1 (0171 403 6515). London Bridge tube/BR. **Open** *Jan-Nov* 10am-6pm daily. **Admission** £2.50; £1.50 OAPs, students, UB40s, under-16s. Under-16s must be accompanied by an adult. **No credit cards**. The 'oldest profession in the world' came to London with the Romans and during the Middle Ages – prostitution's heyday – it was the clergy who raked in the profits. Successive Bishops of Winchester ran London's red-light district with its brothels, taverns, bull/bear-baiting, theatres and, on Clink Street, its own jail. Thus the inmates of the Clink (a byword for prison) ranged from thieves and actors to priests and prostitutes. Many curious and uncomfortable facts are laid out, especially in the adults-only room, but the exhibition is rather lifeless: mainly text with black and white illustrations plus fuzzy piped medieval music. There are a couple of cell recreations but hands-on exhibits amount to little more than a ball and chain on the floor which you may pick up. Much more could be made of Southwark's ribald past. *Shop.*

House of Detention

Clerkenwell Close, EC1 (0171 253 9494). Farringdon tube. **Open** 10am-6pm daily. **Admission** £3; £2 children, students, OAPs; £8 family. In the nineteenth century you could find yourself clapped in irons here for begging, attempting suicide or even 'stealing two grapes'. There has been a prison on this site since 1616 but it was at its busiest between 1846-78, receiving more than 10,000 inmates a year. Now the underground remains – left after the prison was demolished in 1890 – receive a steady flow of visitors and are open to the public keeps growing. (It can even be hired for private parties but you may consider the charges criminal.) After a lively and informative guided tour, wander around on your own; the piped sound-effects become quite creepy when there are no other visitors around in the dimly lit tunnels and chambers. Also included in the admission is 'Crime of Your Life'; the true story of a prisoner, narrated on tape, guides you through various aspects of the Victorian prison system depicted in several cells, so allow yourself an hour or so for the whole visit. Not a place to be caught during a power cut.

Old Bailey

Corner of Newgate Street and Old Bailey, EC4 (0171 248 3277). St Paul's tube. **Open** 10.30am-1pm, 2-4pm, Mon-Fri. **Admission** free (no under-14s admitted, 14-16s accompanied by adults only). The Old Bailey – or Central Criminal Court – has dealt with some of the most publicised criminal cases in London's history. The court was built on the site of the notorious Newgate prison, and the figure of Justice on the domed roof overlooks the area where convicts were once executed. The tradition of judges carrying bouquets of flowers into court was designed to counteract the foul smells emanating from the prison. The public are admitted to watch trials.

Royal Courts of Justice

Strand, WC2 (0171 936 6000). Aldwych or Temple tube. **Open** 10am-4.30pm Mon-Fri. (No court cases during the August recess). **Admission** free. For centuries these courts were housed in the Palace of Westminster; the current premises were opened by Queen Victoria in 1882. The neo-Gothic building, designed by GE Street, is a fine example of Victorian architecture, with its towers, pillars and great entrance hall. Visitors have access to any of the public galleries at the back of the 58 courts. *Disabled: access.*

Inns of Court

There are four Inns of Court – Gray's Inn, Lincoln's Inn, Middle Temple and Inner Temple – and all London's barristers work from within their walls. Students hoping to become London barristers have to dine 24 times in the imposing halls before being eligible to be called to the bar. *See also* **Middle Temple Hall** and **Temple Church**.

Lincoln's Inn *Lincoln's Inn Fields, WC2 (071 405 1393). Chancery Lane or Holborn tube.* **Open** *grounds* 9am-6pm Mon-Fri; *chapel* noon-2.30pm Mon-Fri.

Gray's Inn *Gray's Inn Road, WC1 (071 405 8164). Chancery Lane or Holborn tube.* **Open** 10am-4pm Mon-Fri.

Inner Temple *King's Bench Walk, EC4 (071 353 8462). Temple tube.* **Open** 10am-4pm Mon-Sat; 12.45-4pm Sun.

Middle Temple *Middle Temple Lane, EC4 (071 353 4355). Temple tube.* **Open** 10am-11.30am, 3-4pm, Mon-Fri. **Admission** free.

Maritime London

HMS Belfast

Morgan's Lane, Tooley Street, SE1 (0171 407 6434). London Bridge tube/BR/riverboat from Tower Pier (Feb-Oct daily; Nov-Jan Sat, Sun; 40p adults, 30p under-16s). **Open** *Mar-Oct* 10am-6pm daily; *Nov-Mar* 10am-4.30pm daily. **Admission** £4; £3 OAPs, students; £2 under-16s; under-5s free; £10 family (2 adults, 2 children). **Credit** A, £TC, V. To see the cabins, gun turrets, sick-bay, bridge and boiler-room of this uncompromisingly physical tourist attraction, you must negotiate gangways, airlocks and near-vertical stairways. (*See chapter* **Two World Wars**.) *Café. Disabled: access to main deck only. Group discount. Shop.*

Cutty Sark

King William Walk, SE10 (0181 858 3445). Greenwich or Maze Hill BR/Island Gardens DLR/177, 180, 286 bus/boat to Greenwich Pier. **Open** *May-Sept* 10am-6pm Mon-Sat; noon-6pm Sun. *Oct-Apr* 10am-5pm Mon-Sat; noon-5pm Sun. (Last admission 30 mins before closing).

Trips & Tours

Air Tours

Cabair Helicopters
Elstree Aerodrome, Hertfordshire (0181 953 4411). Elstree BR (free pick-up from station). **Flights** 11.30am Sun. **Fare** £99 per person for 30 mins. **Credit** A, £TC, V.

London Flightseeing Tours
36 Rostella Road, SW17 (0181 767 9055). **Open** 9am-6pm daily. **Fare** £65 per person (for a party of four). **No credit cards.**

Bus Tours

Big Bus Company
(0181 944 7810). **Open-top bus tours** (90 mins) with live commentary. **Departures** every 30 mins Mon-Fri; every 15 mins Sat, Sun. **Pick-up** Green Park (near Ritz); Marble Arch (Speakers' Corner); Trafalgar Square; Tower of London; Victoria (outside Royal Westminster Hotel, Buckingham Palace Road, SW1). **Fares** £8; £5 children.
New Stopper Tour (valid 24 hours) allows you to get on and off to visit 15 different locations. **Departures** *Apr-Sept* every 15 mins, 8.50am-4.50pm daily. **Pick-up** as above. **Fares** £10; £5 under-16s.

Frames Rickards
(0171 837 3111). **Open** 7.30am-7.30pm daily. **Pick-up** 11 Herbrand Street, WC1 (Russell Square tube). **Fares** £13-£49; £9.50-£42 under-16s.

Original London Sightseeing Tour
(0181 877 1722). **Departures** 9.30am-5.30pm daily. **Pick-up** Victoria Station; Marble Arch (Speakers' Corner); Piccadilly Circus tube; Baker Street tube (forecourt). **Fares** £10; £5 under-16s.

Personal Guides

Tour Guides
(0171 495 5504).
Tailor-made tours with Blue Badge guides, for individuals, small or large groups, on foot, by car, coach or boat.

Specialist Tours

Architectural Dialogue
(0181 341 1371). **Departures** 10.15am. **Meeting point** Royal Academy, Piccadilly, W1 (Piccadilly Circus tube). **Fares** £15 adults; £9 students. *Advance booking esssential.*

Beatles Walks
(0171 624 3978). Beatles Magical Mystery Tour **Departure** 11am Thur, Sun. **Pick-up** Dominion Theatre, Tottenham Court Road, W1 (Tottenham Court Road tube).
Beatles In My Life Tour **Departure** 11am Sat, Tues. **Meeting point** Baker Street tube.
Both **Fee** £4; £3 concs.
Two walking tours (roughly 2½ hours).

Bicycle Tours
(0171 928 6838). **Departure** 2pm Sun (approx 3-hour tour). **Meeting point** Gabriel's Wharf, 56 Upper Ground, SE1 (Blackfriars tube/BR). **Fee** £9.95. **Independent hire** from £9.95 per day; £2 per hour. London Bicycle Tour Company tours the East End. *Booking advisable.*

Bus Trip to Murder
(0181 857 1545). **Departure** 7pm daily. **Meeting point** Temple tube (Strand Palace Hotel, The Strand, WC2 on Sundays). **Fare** £12.50; £8.50 children. Three-and-a-half-hour trip with Tragical History Tours.

Garden Day Tours
(0171 720 4891). **Departure** 8.30am Wed, Thur (return 6pm). **Meeting point** Embankment tube (riverside exit). **Fares** £46 per day (lunch not incl).

National Theatre Tours
(0171 633 0880). **Departures** 10.15am, 12.30pm, 12.45pm, 5.45pm, Mon-Sat. **Fee** £3.50 adults; £3 OAPs, students, children. *Advance booking essential.*

Royal and Celebrity Tour
(01932 854721). **Departures** Wed, Fri, Sat (phone for times). **Pick-up point** Victoria BR (Tourist Information Centre). **Fare** £13.

Wembley Stadium Tours
(0181 902 8833). **Departures** 10am-4pm daily (phone to check). **Meeting point** under the twin towers, Empire Way, Wembley (Wembley Park tube). **Fee** £6.45 adults; £5.25 students; £4.50 OAPs, children; free under-5s; £16.50 family.

Walking Tours

'Walks in London Docklands' comes with maps of nine walks, available from the London Docklands Visitor Centre *(0171 521 1111)*, 3 Limeharbour (Crossharbour DLR).

For more walks, consult the Around Town section of *Time Out*, or contact:

Citisights (0181 806 4325); **Historical Tours** (0181 668 4019); **Original London Walks** (0171 624 3978).

Beatles Walks – *the writing's on the wall.*

Admission £3.25; £2.25 under-15s, OAPs; £8 family (2 adults, 3 children). Children must be accompanied by an adult. **Credit** *shop* A, V.

The world's only surviving tea and wool clipper, this 1869 vessel smashed speed records. You're free to roam about the beautifully restored decks and crew's quarters and gaze up at the masts and rigging. Inside are collections of prints and naval relics, plus the world's largest collection of carved and painted figureheads.

Disabled: access to one deck. English, French & German information point. Shop. Underground car park.

Gipsy Moth IV

King William Walk, Greenwich, SE10 (0181 853 3589). Greenwich or Maze Hill BR/1, 177, 188 bus/boat to Greenwich Pier. **Open** *Easter-Oct* 10am-6pm Mon-Sat; noon-6pm Sun (last admission 5.30pm). **Admission** 50p; 30p under-16s, OAPs.

Beside the **Cutty Sark**, *Gipsy Moth IV* looks like a toy, but it's a record-breaking boat. Francis Chichester deserved his knighthood just for staying on it for 226 days at the age of 66, let alone for using the 54ft (16m) craft to make the first English solo circumnavigation of the world in 1966-67.

Old Royal Observatory

Romney Road, SE10 (0181 858 4422). Greenwich or Maze Hill BR/Island Gardens DLR then Greenwich foot tunnel/1, 177, 188 bus/boat to Greenwich Pier. **Open** 10am-5pm daily. **Admission** *passport to all sections (National Maritime Museum, Queen's House, East Wing Exhibition or Old Royal Observatory)* £5.50; £4.50 disabled, OAPs, students, UB40s; £3 under-16s; £16 family; under-7s free. **Credit** A, AmEx, £TC, V.

The observatory commands a view across **Greenwich Park** to the **National Maritime Museum**, the **Queen's House** and beyond. The Observatory was founded by Charles II in 1675 to find a solution to the problem of determining longitude at sea. It's the home of Greenwich Mean Time and the zero meridian line, dividing the globe into East and West. *Café. Group discount. Shop.*

Royal Naval College

King William Walk, SE10 (0181 858 2154). Greenwich or Maze Hill BR. **Open** 2.30-4.45pm daily. **Admission** free.

Walk through the Greenwich foot tunnel to Island Gardens for a superb view of the College (possibly the least altered view in London). It was founded by William III as a naval hospital, designed by Wren, and built on the site of Greenwich Palace. The College (a working naval college) is split in two because Queen Mary didn't want the view of the River obscured from the Queen's House. Inside, the Chapel ceiling is classically ornate and the Hall lavishly painted. *Disabled: access by prior arrangement. Shop.*

St Katharine's Dock

St Katharine's Way, E1 (0171 488 2400). Tower Hill tube/Tower Gateway DLR/23, 42, 78 bus. **Open** 24 hours daily. **Admission** free.

Originally an unloading point for rum, sugar and wool, in 1973 it became the first of the Docklands redevelopments with its new marina and network of warehouse conversions. The dock is full of visiting yachts and a few historic vessels, including a bright red lightship, the *Nore*, and several huge Thames sailing barges; one of these, *Lady Daphne*, can be hired to take groups on trips to the Thames Barrier and back.

Thames Barrier Visitors' Centre

Unity Way, SE18 (0181 854 1373). Charlton BR/boats to and from Greenwich Pier (0181 305 0300) & Westminster Pier (0171 930 3373)/180 bus. **Open** 10am-5pm Mon-Fri; 10.30am- 5.30pm Sat, Sun. **Admission** £2.50; £1.55 under-16, OAP; £6.80 family (5 people, minimum 2 children). **Credit** *shop* A, V.

The Thames Barrier, the largest flood barrier of its type in the world was completed in 1984. Nine massive, shining piers support the giant steel floodgates which can be raised if the Thames threatens to flood (as it last did in 1953, with 300 people drowned and devastating damage). The Visitors' Centre has scale working models and an audio-visual presentation to show how and why this amazing structure was built. Once a month the Barrier is raised for testing (telephone for dates and times).

Café. Disabled: access; toilets. Shop.

Tobacco Dock

The Highway, E1 (0171 702 9681). Wapping tube/Shadwell tube/DLR. **Open** *shops* 10am-6pm daily.

Only four stores remain in this ailing Docklands shopping centre. The main attractions are two replicas of ships of the type that once delivered tobacco and wine to the dock. *Disabled: access.*

Monuments & Statues

Albert Memorial

Kensington Gardens, SW7. Knightsbridge or Kensington High Street tube, then 9, 33, 49, 52, 73 bus.

Designed by Sir George Gilbert Scott and finished in 1872, the Albert Memorial commemorates the Prince Consort, beloved husband of Queen Victoria. The effigy of the Prince portrays him reading a copy of the catalogue of the Great Exhibition of 1851, which he helped to organise. The life-size figure is dwarfed by the symbolism of spires, pinnacles and bas reliefs. The complexity of the design may hide its inner meaning, for it is in effect nothing more than a vast ciborium, or design intended to be placed over an altar – thereby symbolically raising the Price Consort to the status of a god.

Cenotaph

Whitehall, SW1.

This monument, inscribed 'To the Glorious Dead', was designed by Edwin Lutyens in 1920, and has become the national memorial for the dead of both World Wars. A Remembrance Service is held here every year on the Sunday nearest to 11 November.

Cleopatra's Needle

Victoria Embankment, WC2. Embankment tube.

Nothing to do with Cleopatra, the needle was unearthed from the sand outside Alexandria and was brought to London in 1878. The hieroglyphics tell us it was originally erected by Thothmes III in what we now call the Eighteenth Dynasty, long before Cleopatra's time. Originally one of a pair, its partner stands in New York's Central Park.

Eros

Piccadilly Circus, W1. Piccadilly Circus tube.

Unveiled in 1893, Alfred Gilbert's 'Angel of Christian Charity', symbolising the philanthropy of the Seventh Earl of Shaftesbury, shocked the prudish Victorians who thought it undignified. Since then Eros (London's first aluminium statue) has become a national emblem.

Monument

Monument Street, EC2 (0171 626 2717). Monument tube. **Open** *Apr-Sept* 9am-6pm Mon-Fri; 2-6pm Sun. *Oct-Mar* 9am-4pm Mon-Sat. **Admission** £1; 25p OAPs, under-16s.

London's reminder of the Great Fire of 1666 is 202ft (60.6m) high; equal to its distance from where the five-day blaze started in a Pudding Lane bakery. When built, it was the world's tallest isolated stone column. Office blocks break up the view but the riverscape makes the steep climb (311 steps up a spiral staircase) well worthwhile. **NB** The Monument is closed for refurbishment from September 1995-April 1996.

Nelson's Column

Trafalgar Square, WC2. Charing Cross tube/BR.
London's best-known landmark commemorates Admiral Horatio Nelson, who defeated the French and Spanish at the famous Battle of Trafalgar in 1805. The statue (by Edward Bailey) stands aloft on a 171ft (51m) Corinthian column (by William Railton), gazing out along the Mall. In October 1843, a few days before Nelson's statue was put in place, 14 people ate a steak dinner on top of the column. The bronze friezes at the base show four famous victories, which cost Nelson an eye, an arm and finally his life. The four lions, by Sir Edwin Landseer, were added in 1868.

Victoria Memorial

Queen's Gardens, Buckingham Palace, SW1. St James's Park tube.
Thomas Brock's work commemorates the life of England's longest-reigning monarch. Standing in front of Buckingham Palace, the 13ft (3.9m) queen is surrounded by the female allegories of Victorian virtues – charity, truth and justice must share space with shipbuilding, war, manufacturing and progress. 'Victory' soars over all.

Notable Buildings
Pre-Twelfth Century

Temple of Mithras

On the raised courtyard in front of the Sumitomo Bank, Temple Court, 11 Queen Victoria Street, EC4. Mansion House tube. **Open** 24 hours daily. **Admission** free.
A heap of stones is all that's left of the small pagan temple (built around AD240-250), which once stood on the banks of the River Walbrook, near today's church of **St Stephen Walbrook**, but the outline clearly shows the Roman influence on the later design of churches: rounded apse, central nave and side aisles. The difference is that Christian churches were built in the shape of a cross with the altar facing east. The story of the temple, and the marble sculptures found buried underneath, can be seen in the **Museum of London**.

Pre-Seventeenth Century

Fulham Palace

Bishop's Avenue, Fulham Palace Road, SW6 (0171 736 3233). Putney Bridge tube/220 bus. **Open** 2-5pm Wed-Sun. **Admission** 50p; 25p children, OAPs, students, UB40s.
From the eighth century until 1973, Fulham Palace was the official residence of the Bishops of London. The present building dates from Tudor times and part of it is now open as a museum, detailing the history of the palace, the bishopric and the archaeology of the site. There are free tours of the palace and grounds once a month. Stroll through the surrounding **Bishop's Park** which contains many plants brought from the Americas in the seventeenth century.

Globe Theatre

New Globe Walk, Bankside, SE1 (0171 928 6406). Mansion House or Cannon Street tube/London Bridge tube/BR. **Open** 10am-5pm daily. **Admission** £4; £3 OAPs, students; £2.50 children; £11 family.
The original Globe Theatre, where many of Shakespeare's plays were first performed, burned down in 1613 during a performance of *Henry VIII*, when a cannon spark set fire to the roof; the only minor casualty was a man whose breeches caught fire. Three hundred and eighty years later the Globe is rising again, thatched roof and all. The opening is planned for summer 1996 when the theatre will start putting on full Shakespeare productions, done Elizabethan style: in natural light, using a simple, unchanging stage set and allowing the audience full and authentic interaction. Until it

officially opens you can take an excellent 40-minute guided tour to see the theatre being built. If you're lucky, the guide will be a member of the Original Shakespeare Company, bringing history to life and making even the finer technical merits of lime plaster an item of interest.
Shop. Tours.

Middle Temple Hall

Middle Temple Lane, EC4 (0171 353 4355). Temple tube. **Open** 10am-noon, 3-4pm, Mon-Fri (the Hall is often in use in the afternoon, so phone first). **Admission** free.
The most impressive feature of the Hall, completed in 1573, is its oak, double hammerbeam roof. The 29ft/9m Bench Table, donated by Elizabeth I, was made from a single Windsor Park oak. The smaller table in front, known as 'the Cupboard', was made from a piece of wood from Sir Francis Drake's *Golden Hinde*. Shakespeare's own company is said to have performed *Twelfth Night* here on 2 February 1602.

Staple Inn

Holborn, WC1 (no phone). Chancery Lane tube. **Open** *courtyard only* 8am-8pm Mon-Fri. **Admission** free.
The only surviving half-timbered Elizabethan terrace in central London, Staple Inn was founded in 1378 as an Inn of Chancery, a type of prep school undertaken before joining the **Inns of Court** to train as a barrister. The present splendid building dates from 1586.

Seventeenth & Eighteenth Centuries

College of Arms

Queen Victoria Street, EC4 (0171 248 2762). Blackfriars tube/BR. **Open** 10am-4pm Mon-Fri. **Admission** free.
The home of heraldry since 1484, the College of Arms grants coats of arms to those who think they are worth having and can afford them. Its seventeenth-century redbrick building has been beautifully restored, the iron gates brought from Herefordshire in 1956. If you want to trace your roots, write for an appointment to the Officer in Waiting.
Tour by prior arrangement.

Dennis Severs' House

18 Folgate Street, E1 (0171 247 4013). Liverpool Street tube/BR. **Open** 2-5pm first Sun of every month; three times per week for theatrical performances, played to an audience of eight people. Phone for details.
Performance 7.30pm. **Admission** *Performance* (book) £30; *house* £5. **No credit cards.**
A beautifully preserved Georgian redbrick terrace house, built 1724, in Spitalfields. The owner, Dennis Severs, invites guests to join in a performance (lasting three hours) in which they become ghosts of an imaginary family, which inhabited the house between the years 1685-1919. It's a great introduction to the flavours and feelings of eighteenth-century life. The house is also open occasionally for tours – phone for details. You should book about three weeks in advance for the shows, although it's always worth phoning to see if there's been a cancellation.

Mansion House

Walbrook, EC4 0171 626 2500). Bank tube. **Open** for group visits by written application, at least two months in advance (min 16, max 40). **Admission** free.
The Lord Mayor's official residence during his year in office was completed in 1753. Designed by George Dance, its imposing portico with six massive Corinthian pillars faces the Bank and **Royal Exchange**; the pediment sculpture depicts Father Thames and the burgeoning commercial City. The splendid state rooms include the Egyptian Hall, scene of many sumptuous banquets. This is the only private house in England with its own Court of Justice (presided over by the Lord Mayor, as the City's Chief Magistrate), complete with 11 cells, including one for women ('the birdcage'), where suffragette Emmeline Pankhurst was once imprisoned.

Prince Henry's Room

17 Fleet Street, EC4 (0181 294 1158). Temple tube.
Open 11am-2pm Mon-Sat. **Admission** free.
Built in 1611 and named in honour of James I's eldest son,
this is one of the few City buildings to survive the Great Fire,
with oak panelling and plaster ceiling intact. It now houses
a collection of Samuel Pepys memorabilia.

Royal Hospital

*Chelsea Royal Hospital Road, SW3 (0171 730 5282).
Sloane Square tube/11, 19, 22, 137 bus.* **Open** *museum,
chapel and great hall* 10am-noon, 2-4pm, Mon-Fri; 2-4pm
Sat. **Services** (in chapel) *Communion* 8.30am Sun;
Parade Service 11am Sun. **Admission** free.
This 1682 Wren building was founded by Charles II for vet-
eran soldiers and is still home for 420 Chelsea Pensioners.

Nineteenth Century

The Athenaeum

107 Pall Mall, SW1. Piccadilly Circus tube.
Named after Hadrian's university in Rome, the Athenaeum
club was designed by Decimus Burton and has been used as
a meeting place and home-from-home by (male) government
ministers, bishops and writers since 1824. Not open to the
public, but visits may be arranged (write to the Secretary).

St Pancras Station

Euston Road, NW1. King's Cross tube/BR.
Sir George Gilbert Scott's 1870s design for the luxury hotel
frontage is inspired by Medieval High Gothic, and the recent
restoration reveals the decoration in all its magnificent detail.
But the train shed – a lofty 100ft/30m high with a 240ft/72m
span – is pure engineering. The glass arch, supported by its
huge iron ribs, was once the largest clear span in the world.

Smithfield Market

*West Smithfield, EC1. Farringdon tube/N21, N76, N85,
N89, N98 bus.* **Open** 5-10.30am Mon-Fri.
From 1150 to 1850 there was a livestock market on this site;
the riotous Bartholomew Fair (described in Ben Jonson's
play) and public executions also took place In the 1850s it
became a 'dead meat market' and the huge building, with its
grand avenue and four trading halls, was designed by the
City architect, Horace Jones. Today Smithfield is the only
wholesale market still trading on its original City site. Local
pubs open from 7am for the meat porters and the **Fox &
Anchor** on Charterhouse Street is famed for its breakfasts.

Twentieth Century

Broadgate Centre

*Eldon Street, EC2 (0171 588 6565). Liverpool Street
tube/BR.*
This huge modern development adjoining Liverpool Street
Station provides as much new office space as five Empire
State buildings. Vast glass atria and cascading foliage sur-
round the Broadgate Arena, which becomes a performance
space in summer and an open-air ice-skating rink in winter.
Bars, shops and restaurants keep visitors and the resident
bankers entertained. Look out for the many sculptures dotted about the complex, including George Segal's *Rush Hour*
and Richard Serra's *Fulcrum* at the Eldon Street entrance.

Broadcasting House

*Langham Place, Regent Street, WC1 (0171 580 4468).
Oxford Circus tube.*
Daily BBC radio programmes first emanated from Savoy
Hill (next to the Savoy Hotel) on 14 November 1922, but by
1932 Broadcasting House was ready, complete with 22
sound-proofed studios. It was designed by G Val Myers and
is decorated with a notable sculpture of Shakespeare's
Prospero and Ariel by Eric Gill.

St Pancras Station – *magnificently detailed.*

Canary Wharf

Isle of Dogs, E14. Canary Wharf DLR/D5 bus.
Cesar Pelli's massively imposing 1991 Canary Wharf tower
now dominates the London cityscape. At 800foot/250m, it's
the tallest building in Europe, but currently, unless you work
there – and the tower is slowly beginning to fill up – you can't
get inside to take in the view.

Daily Express Building

121-128 Fleet Street, EC4. Blackfriars tube/BR.
Owen Williams' Daily Express Building is the most dramatic
piece of art deco in central London. Completed in 1932, the
building is sheathed in a chrome and black glass curtain
wall. Visible behind is an art deco foyer and staircase.
Disabled: access to ground floor only.

Hyde Park Barracks

Knightsbridge, SW1. Knightsbridge tube.
Basil Spence's brutal 1959 building design has been popu-
larly barracked as an eyesore. It is the home of the Household
Cavalry, who can be seen riding through Hyde Park to Horse
Guards Parade every morning at 10.30am (9.30am on Sun-
days) for the **Changing of the Guard**.

Michelin Building

*Michelin House, Fulham Road, SW3 (0171 589
7401/Bibendum restaurant 0171 581 5817). South
Kensington tube.* **Open** 9.30am-6pm Mon, Wed-Sat;
10am-6pm Tue; noon-5pm Sun.
Designed for the tyre manufacturers by François Espinasse
in 1905, the Michelin Building added a note of humour to the
pompous architecture of the Edwardian era. Restored in 1985
by Terence Conran (replacing tiles, stained glass and the
mosaic 'Bibendum' tyre man), it now houses a publishing
company, the Conran shop and the **Bibendum** restaurant.
Disabled: access.

Parks & Gardens

What with Henry VIII's hunting grounds, huge Victorian cemeteries and more gardens than seems feasible for a major modern city, London is practically overrun with flora and fauna.

Hyde Park was the first of the central royal parks to be opened to the public in 1637. New breathing spaces were added as the city expanded to provide an extraordinary variety of greenery around the capital, from open heaths and pockets of ancient woodland, to landscaped parks with lakes and ponds, shady squares, secluded gardens and over-grown cemeteries. Most of the royal parks were once royal hunting grounds teeming with wildlife, enclosed by Henry VIII for his own use. Later monarchs opened up this land to the citizens of London, a legacy which today includes **St James's Park**, **Green Park**, **Hyde Park** and **Kensington Gardens**, **Regent's Park** and **Primrose Hill**, **Greenwich Park** and **Richmond Park**. Even the wildlife is returning (*see page 53*).

Some of the very large open spaces (such as Blackheath, Hampstead Heath and Wimbledon Common) are ancient common land, where local people once had rights to graze their animals and gather firewood. Hard-fought campaigns have preserved the commons that still exist, despite the persistent efforts of property developers to carpet them with concrete.

In the nineteenth century, several municipal parks (such as Battersea Park and Victoria Park) were created, following a Parliamentary Report of 1833 which reached the conclusion that occasional relaxation was 'as necessary to the poor as to the rich'. It recommended the laying out of parks in the rapidly expanding and overcrowded suburbs, in the hope that the 'lower orders' would not only benefit from healthy exercise and contact with nature, but would also be distracted from their usual recreations such as 'drinking houses, dog fights and boxing matches'.

During the eighteenth century, the earlier fashion for formal gardens (which can still be seen at Ham House and in the herb garden at Kew Palace) was replaced by a preference for more natural landscaping. Curved paths and lakes, sweeping lawns and groups of trees were introduced at Kenwood House, Syon Park and other grand houses by landscape architects such as Capability Brown and Humphrey Repton. This style became the hallmark of English parks and gardens.

The English style was apparently highly regarded by others, including the German King Ludwig I, who imagined that the comparative lack

of unrest among the London working class must be the result of an abundance of beautiful parks. He decided to cure his country's ills in 1848 by creating more gardens, such as the Englischer Garten in Berlin. Unfortunately for Ludwig's theory, the English Chartists rioted at about the same time in Victoria Park and Kennington Park.

New London parks were added in the late nineteenth and twentieth century. In 1878 Epping Forest, which was under threat from property developers, was acquired and saved for public use by the City Corporation, who later also purchased Highgate Woods and **Hampstead Heath**. Some parks, including Brockwell Park (1892) and **Holland Park** (1952), were private estates bought by the London County Council and converted to public parks; others (such as **Waterlow Park**) were the gift of philanthropists. The new interest in ecology is encouraging urban nature reserves.

We've selected the pick of London's open spaces, but you can discover many other parks, squares and gardens. Over 3,000 private gardens are also open to the public each year as part of the National Gardens Scheme (*01483 211535*); their annual booklet *Gardens of England and Wales* gives descriptions, dates and admission charges. (*See also* **Museum of Garden History**.)

Central

Green Park
Entrances from Piccadilly and Constitution Hill, SW1 (0171 930 1793). Green Park or Hyde Park Corner tube. **Open** *dawn to dusk daily.*
Green Park was once part of the meadowland surrounding St James's Palace. It's now a large, quiet shady expanse of grass and trees, which links **St James's Park** with **Hyde Park**. Queen's Walk (on the east side) is a delightful walk from Green Park tube to **Buckingham Palace**, in the Mall, with the original gas lamps still in place.
Deckchairs in summer.

Hyde Park
W2 (0171 298 2100). Hyde Park Corner, Knightsbridge, Lancaster Gate, Marble Arch or Queensway tube. **Open** *5am-midnight daily.*
Hyde Park is central London's largest park and a wonderful place to relax. In 1637 it became the first royal park to be opened to the public. Highwaymen once lurked here and duels were fought; in 1851 it was the site of the Great Exhibition and, a hundred years later, a Rolling Stones gig (1969). You can trot a horse down Rotten Row, row on the Serpentine lake or just lie back and sunbathe, gaze at paintings in the

*In 1764, at the age of eight, Mozart gave a concert in Chelsea's **Ranelagh Gardens**.*

Serpentine Gallery or collapse into a deckchair and, on summer Sundays, listen to military bands. Every Sunday, at Speakers' Corner near Marble Arch, soapbox orators revive the flagging British tradition of free speech. On royal anniversaries and special occasions, a 41-gun salute is fired in the park, opposite the Dorchester Hotel in Park Lane (*see chapter* **London By Season: Gun Salutes**). Although it stays open till late, the park should be avoided after dark. *Boats for hire (J&T Maxwell, 0171 262 3751). Dell Restaurant open Apr-Sept 10am-7pm; Oct, Nov & Mar 10am-4pm. Disabled: toilets. Lido swimming pool closed: re-opening Easter1996. Playground. Refreshment kiosks.*

Kensington Gardens

W8 (0171 724 2826). Bayswater, High Street Kensington, Lancaster Gate or Queensway tube. **Open** *dawn-dusk daily.*
These royal gardens merge into Hyde Park, but have a distinct, more formal character; they are still the haunt of English nannies pushing prams. **Kensington Palace** is on the west side. In the grounds you can wander through the sunken garden and the Orangery. The huge Round Pond is a focus for small boys (most of them over 40) sailing their model boats. Near the Long Water, the statue of Peter Pan is modelled on a girl not a boy. Also for children, look out for Elfin Oak, puppet shows in the summer and two playgrounds, one off Broad Walk and one near Black Lion Gate. *Children's playgrounds. Disabled: toilets. Refreshment kiosks. Model boating lake.*

Regent's Park

NW1 (0171 486 7905). Baker Street, Camden Town, Great Portland Street or Regent's Park tube. **Open** *park and Queen Mary's Rose Garden 5am-30 mins before dusk daily; tennis courts 7am-30 mins before park closing time daily; playgrounds 10am to 30 mins before dusk daily.*
Regent's Park was laid out in 1817-28 by John Nash, as part of his master plan for the Prince Regent (*see chapter* **Architecture**). A former hunting ground of Henry VIII, it's lively in summer, with a boating lake (herons live on the islands), three playgrounds, bandstand music, tennis courts and an Open Air Theatre, from May to September. It's bordered on the south by Regent's Crescent, on the west and east by Palladian mansions and on the north by the Regent's Canal. Strolling in Queen Mary's Rose Garden on a summer evening is one of the best reasons for being in London. **London Zoo** is in the north-east corner of the park.

Boats for hire (J&T Maxwell, 0171 486 4759). Boules. Children's boating lake. Disabled: toilets. Football, rugby, softball. Free outdoor gym. Hockey. Rose Garden Buffet & Broadwalk Café (0171 935 5729). Refreshment kiosks. Running track.

St James's Park

The Mall, SW1 (0171 930 1793). St James's Park tube. **Open** *dawn to dusk daily.*
Compact, beautiful and close to the West End, this royal park is the ideal place to take a rest from shopping/sightseeing. Landscaped by John Nash in the early nineteenth century, there's a wonderful view of **Buckingham Palace** from the bridge over the lake (beautiful at night when the Palace is floodlit). The lake has become a sanctuary for wildfowl and there are three pelicans living on the island in the lake (fed at 3pm daily). There's a playground at the Buckingham Palace end, and the Cake House serves refreshments. *Bands in bandstand daily. Deckchairs for hire. Disabled: toilet at Marlborough Gate. Playground. Restaurant.*

Victoria Tower Gardens

Millbank, SW1. Westminster tube. **Open** *7am-dusk daily.*
Beside the Victoria Tower, the tallest part of the **Houses of Parliament**, this riverside garden is a good place to escape to for a picnic, with a view across the Thames to Lambeth Palace. There's a Gothic revival drinking fountain, a children's play area, a cast of Rodin's sculpture *Burghers of Calais* and a bronze statue of Emmeline Pankhurst.

West

Bishop's Park

Bishop's Park Road, SW6 (0171 736 3854). Putney Bridge tube. **Open** *dawn-dusk daily.*
It may only be small, but Bishop's Park in Fulham offers beautiful leafy walks by the side of the Thames on a stretch where the river is at its prettiest. *Adventure playground. Pavilion. Rainbow play house.*

Chelsea Physic Garden

66 Royal Hospital Road, SW3 (0171 352 5646). Sloane Square tube/11, 19, 22, 239 bus. **Open** *Apr-Oct 2-5pm Wed; 2-6pm Sun.* **Admission** *£2.50; £1.30 students, UB40s, under-16s.*
Designed by the Society of Apothecaries in 1673, and developed by the physician Sir Hans Sloane with his gardener

Philip Miller, these herb, plant, water and rock gardens were grown to study the therapeutic properties of plants. Today, it's a vital centre for botanical research and education. The gardens are sheltered by brick walls and the surrounding square, making them warm enough for a Crimson Bengal to flower continually, a nineteenth-century olive tree to fruit, peonies to bloom in spring, and eastern herbs to grow in the oldest rock garden in Europe. (*See also chapter* **Museums**.) *Disabled: access. Guided tours by appointment (£10 incl, up to 25 people). Shop. Tea (3.15-4.45pm).*

Holland Park

Entrances in Holland Park, Abbotsbury Road, Holland Walk and Kensington High Street, W8. High Street Kensington or Holland Park tube. **Open** 7.30am-30 mins before dusk daily.
This is one of the most romantic parks in London, with beautiful woods and formal gardens surrounding the Jacobean-style Holland House, built in 1606 as a country mansion. The House was bombed in World War II and the only remaining wing is used as part of the Youth Hostel. The summer ballroom has been converted into a stylish modern British restaurant, the Belvedere (*see chapter* **Restaurants**). Open-air theatre under an elegant canopy is staged in the park during the summer. For children, there's an adventure playground, with tree walks and rope-swings.
Adventure playground (0171 603 6956). Café (0171 602 2216) open 10am-30 mins before park closes. Cricket nets & pitch. Disabled: access; toilets. Football. Golf nets. One O'Clock Club (0171 603 2838). Sports booking (0171 602 2226). Squash. Tennis. Toilets, changing rooms.

Ranelagh Gardens

Entrance on Royal Hospital Road, SW3, or Chelsea Embankment, SW3. Sloane Square tube. **Open** 10am-1pm, 2pm-sunset, Mon-Sat; 2pm-sunset Sun.
In the eighteenth century the Ranelagh Pleasure Gardens attracted the elite of London society, who promenaded on summer evenings. The eight-year-old Mozart gave a concert here in 1764. Canaletto's painting of the gardens can be seen in the **National Gallery**. On a fine day, the gardens provide a beautiful setting for views of Wren's **Royal Hospital**.

South

Battersea Park

Albert Bridge Road, SW11 (0181 871 7530). Sloane Square tube/Battersea Park or Queenstown Road BR. **Open** 8am-dusk daily.
In the 1850s the once swampy land here was transformed into a riverside park by raising the ground level with earth transferred from the newly dug docks in the East End. The park was opened in 1858 by Queen Victoria and is now one of London's liveliest open spaces. Its most famous feature, the Festival Gardens, was one of the main attractions of the 1951 Festival of Britain. There are sports facilities and play-grounds, a good boating lake and a small children's zoo. Bank Holiday Funfairs are held here and many events take place throughout the year. The Peace Pagoda overlooking the Thames was built by Japanese monks and nuns in 1985.
Boats for hire (£3.50 per hour, £2.50 half hour). Disabled: garden. Lakeside Café. Old English & Herb Gardens. Pumphouse Gallery. Sports: boules, bowling, athletics track, tennis courts (bookings 0181 871 6259).

Greenwich Park

Charlton Way, SE10 (0181 858 2608). Greenwich or Maze Hill BR/177, 180, 286 bus/boat to Greenwich Pier. **Open** *pedestrians* 5am-dusk daily; *traffic* 7am-dusk daily.
The remains of a Roman temple and some 20 Saxon gravemounds have been identified here, but the beautiful riverside park is more famous for its Tudor and Stuart history. Henry VIII was born at Greenwich and it was his favourite palace, surrounded by a magnificent park for hunting and hawking, which had first been enclosed in 1433 by the Duke of Gloucester. In 1616, James I commissioned Inigo Jones to rebuild the Tudor palace; the result was the **Queen's House**, England's first Palladian villa. In the 1660s, the park was redesigned by Le Nôtre, who landscaped Versailles, but Charles II's plan for a new palace was later adapted to become the **Royal Naval College**. Crowning the hill at the top of the park are the **Old Royal Observatory** and Flamsteed House (with the red time-ball which drops each day at 1pm Greenwich Mean Time), both built by Wren; nearby is the Wolfe Monument (commemorating General James Wolfe

A moment's reflection in **Holland Park**, *one of London's most romantic green spaces.*

who helped win Canada for Britain). The view from here, over the Queen's House, Royal Naval College and the river, is one of the best in London. In summer, brass bands perform on Sunday afternoons and there are puppet shows in the playground during August. As we go to press, Greenwich Palace and park are being proposed for declaration as a World Heritage Site. The millennium celebrations for the world will begin at Greenwich Observatory as 2000 dawns. *Bandstand. Café (facing Observatory) open 10am-30 mins before dusk. Children's boating lake (J&T Maxwell, 0171 262 3751). Deck chairs. Playground.*

Richmond Park

Richmond, Surrey (0181 948 3209). Richmond tube/BR.
Open *pedestrians 24 hours daily; traffic Mar-Sept 7am to 30mins before dusk daily; Nov-Feb 7.30am to 30mins before dusk daily.*
The best countryside substitute in London, Richmond Park covers 2,500 acres (820 hectares) and was once a Royal hunting ground. There is a famous view over the Thames from the top of Richmond Hill. It is an ideal place for rambling, cycling and riding, and is also home to wildlife – there are foxes scurrying about at dusk, badgers barging through the

undergrowth and herds of red and fallow deer in the enclosures. There are two culls a year, in August and November, each lasting between two and three weeks when pedestrians are asked to leave the park at the same time as the traffic (30 minutes before dusk).
Café. Horse riding at Roehampton Riding Stables (0181 876 7089). Public golf courses by Roehampton Gate (0181 876 3205) £9.25 Mon-Fri; £13 Sat, Sun.

Royal Botanic Gardens (Kew Gardens)

Kew Road, Richmond, Surrey (0181 332 5622 or 940 1171). Kew Gardens tube/Kew Bridge BR/27, 65 bus.
Open *Nov-Jan* 9.30am-4pm daily; *Feb* 9.30am-5pm daily; *Mar* 9.30am-6pm daily; *Apr-Aug* 9.30am-6.30pm Mon-Sat; 9.30am-8pm Sun, Bank Holidays; *Sept-mid-Oct* 9.30am-6pm daily (glasshouses close 30 mins before closing times, galleries 15 mins before closing times, subject to variation). **Admission** £4; £2 OAPs, students; £1.50 under-16s; under-5s free; £10 family day ticket.
Credit (shop only) A, £TC, V.
The tranquil riverside Kew Gardens were first planted in the seventeenth and eighteenth centuries in the grounds of today's **Kew Palace**, bought and extended by George III,

Wild at Heart

Bill Oddie on the fauna of London.

There's plenty of wildlife in London. Even in the inner city, it would be hard to ignore the birds, and I don't just mean the pigeons. Keep an eye on the skies and you'll soon become aware of avian commuters. Many of them will be water birds travelling between roosting and feeding places: gulls, herons and cormorants. Buildings provide perches for vast winter clouds of starlings, and nesting sites for kestrels.

At migration times – spring and autumn – just about anything can and does fly over.

Best places for enjoying a variety of birdlife are the high points, Alexandra Palace and Hampstead Heath, for visible migration; the parks and their lakes, which often have collections of tame wildfowl; and the many large reservoirs in the suburbs. Some of these require a permit – Barn Elms near Hammersmith Bridge, for example – while others have public access and even hides, nature trails and information boards. The most extensive area of productive habitat is the Lee Valley complex of waterways and marshes, which stretches from the River Thames northwards to beyond the M25.

Although birds tend to get the highest profile – they're easier to see and there are a lot birdwatchers – most of the good bird areas will also be good for insects (such as butterflies, moths,

dragonflies), wildflowers and pond life. Urban nature reserves – such as the long fought-for **Camley Street** at King's Cross (pictured) – provide not only wildlife havens, but also invaluable educational facilities for city children.

Animals tend to be harder to see, though the sight and sounds of urban foxes are becoming increasingly common, and the healthy kestrel and tawny owl populations indicate that there must be plenty of voles and mice for them to feed on.

The fact is, whatever your wild inclination, London will cater for it. The wildlife is there, and so are the experts to guide you: bat group outings, pond-dipping days, wildflower walks, birdwatching field trips. All the information you need is available from the London Wildlife Trust, the London Natural History Society, and from more specialised and local groups.

Get out and enjoy, but please also make sure we protect and preserve what's there.

London Wildlife Trust

80 York Way, N1 9AG (0171 278 6612).
Write or phone for free map of nature reserves, *Leafy London* pack on trees, or membership details.

London Natural History Society

Department of Entomology, Natural History Museum, Cromwell Road, SW7 5DD (0171 938 8905).
Phone or write to Steve Brooks for membership details.

landscaped by William Chambers and Capability Brown, planted with specimens from all continents by Sir Joseph Banks, and donated to the state in 1841; since then Kew has become a world-renowned centre for horticultural research (including the world's largest collection of orchids). The Palm House (Decimus Burton and Richard Turner, 1848) is the finest existing glass and iron structure in England, best seen from the galleries where you look down on a warm, damp jungle of palm and fern; the renovated Temperate House is also by Burton and Turner. Don't miss the steamy Aroid House (John Nash, 1836), where you step into a tropical rainforest. Surrounding the glasshouses are 300 acres of landscaped gardens and woodland walks, filled with every imaginable variety of trees, shrubs and flowers; hidden among the trees are some interesting buildings and sculptures including the Great Pagoda (William Chambers, 1762), a Japanese Gateway and a Thatched Cottage. The Marianne North Gallery, with a collection of paintings of rare plants, and the small Wood Museum, are also open to visit.
Café & restaurant. Disabled: toilets; wheelchairs on free loan. Shop. Tours 11am and 2pm daily, £1 per person.

East

Victoria Park
Old Ford Road, E3 (0181 985 6186). Mile End tube/Cambridge Heath BR/2, 30, 55, 253, 277 bus. Open 8am-dusk daily.
This East End park was opened in 1845, after a Parliamentary Report of 1833 stressed the need for more open spaces in towns. Bordered on the south side by the canal, it has two lakes, a deer herd, playgrounds and sports facilities. The Victoria Park Model Boat Club (the oldest such club in the world, founded 1904) meets here most Sunday mornings.
Animal enclosure. Athletics track. Bowling green. Café. Children's playgrounds. Cricket pitches. Football pitches. One O'Clock Club for under-5s. Tennis courts.

North

Alexandra Park
Muswell Hill, N22 (park 0181 444 7696/general information 0181 365 2121). Wood Green tube/Alexandra Palace BR/84A, 144, 144A, W2, W3, W7 bus. Open 24 hours daily.
The view over London from Alexandra Palace, at the top of this steeply sloping north London park, is impressive on a clear day. The 'Palace' (known to Londoners as Ally Pally) once housed the BBC's first television studio, but it's now an entertainment and exhibition centre with an indoor ice-rink. The park has public gardens, with plenty of children's attractions and sports facilities. There are Bank Holiday funfairs, and a free fireworks display on Bonfire Night (5 November).
Boating lake (0181 889 9089). Garden Centre (0181 444 2555). Ice Rink. Jazz concerts in the Grove (organised by the Actual Workshop 0181 883 7173).

Hampstead Heath
NW3 (Parliament Hill 0171 485 4491/Kenwood House 0181 340 5303/Golders Hill 0181 455 5183). Belsize Park or Hampstead tube/Gospel Oak or Hampstead Heath BR/24 bus. Open 24 hours daily.
A stroll around this huge semi-landscaped heath, with Kenwood at the northern end, rolling grassland and 12 ponds, rejuvenates both the tired Londoner and the visitor. You can jog, stroll, sunbathe, picnic, swim in the ponds, walk the dog, or fly a kite from the top of Parliament Hill (at the south end). Alternatively, sit and admire the views; on a clear day you can take in the whole of central London. At the northern end, visit Kenwood House to see the superb collection of paintings, and look for one of Kenwood's hidden treasures – the Buckland Caravan, a beautifully restored Romany caravan, in a small building near the Coach House

Café (open most Saturday and Sunday afternoons). On fine Saturday evenings in summer, thousands make their way to Kenwood for the Lakeside Concerts (*see* **Music: Classical & Opera**). Funfairs are held on the Heath, at the upper and lower ends, on Easter, May and August Bank Holidays.
Bathing ponds (for men only, women only and mixed bathing) open 7am-sunset daily, free. Children's playgrounds & paddling pool. Disabled: toilets at Parliament Hill Fields Running Track. Fishing. Parliament Hill Lido (open-air pool open from end Apr, 0171 485 3873). Tennis courts (0171 284 3779).

Primrose Hill
NW3 (0171 486 7905). Chalk Farm, Camden Town or St John's Wood tube/31, 74 bus. On a fine day there's a great view of central London landmarks from this hill. In icy winters, the park becomes a venue for scudding toboggans; there are fireworks on Bonfire Night and druids conduct pagan rites at the Autumn Equinox (*see* chapter **London By Season**).

Waterlow Park
Highgate Hill, N6 (0171 272 2825). Archway tube/271, C11 bus. Open 7.30am-dusk daily.
A small, beautiful park near Highgate Cemetery, with steep slopes, ponds, magnificent trees and a small aviary. It was bequeathed by the former owner, Sydney Waterlow, as 'a garden for the gardenless'. There are tennis courts, a putting green, a dog-free play area for under-fives, and a lovely garden café in sixteenth-century **Lauderdale House**.
Lauderdale House (0181 348 8716). Tennis courts.

Cemeteries

Because of the massive increase in population in Victorian times, London's church graveyards began to overflow. In Dickens' words, 'rot and mildew and dead citizens formed the uppermost scent in the City', causing grave concern for health. The 1832 cholera epidemic forced the government to act, and they authorised private companies to establish seven enormous new cemeteries around London. These were to be well-drained, landscaped and managed, providing a more agreeable resting place for those who could afford it.

Famous and infamous, eccentric and ordinary, all lie side by side in these cemeteries, the people

Waterlow Park – *near Highgate Cemetery.*

*Stoke Newington's restful **Abney Park Cemetery** – once overgrown, now being restored.*

who lived and breathed in the London of centuries past. It's often only after death that we find out what really makes people tick: take 'James' Barry (1788-1865), the first woman doctor, who now lies in Kensal Green. She concealed her sex while serving as an army surgeon, became inspector general of hospitals in 1858-59, and was only discovered to be a woman when laid out after death.

Some of these Victorian cemeteries have fallen into disrepair and become overgrown. While in some respects this is regrettable, neglect has produced necropolises groaning with atmosphere and teeming with wildlife, though some have now been rescued from ruin by organisations of dedicated Friends. There are few more peaceful experiences to be had in London than losing yourself for an afternoon in Highgate, Nunhead or Kensal Green.

Abney Park Cemetery
Stoke Newington High Street, N16 (0171 275 9443). Stoke Newington BR/73 bus. **Open** *summer* 9am-7pm; *winter* 9am-3pm.
Once completely overgrown, Abney Park is in the process of being restored thanks to the efforts of the Save Abney Park Cemetery Committee, formed in 1974 after the Chapel was wrecked. The Victorian cemetery, laid out in 1840, took over from Bunhill Fields as the resting place for religious dissenters and nonconformists, and contains the graves of General Booth, founder of the Salvation Army, and the Chartist leader James O'Brien. Guided tours are available.

Brompton Cemetery
Finborough Road, SW10 (0171 352 1201). West Brompton tube. **Open** 8.30am-dusk daily.
The main entrance to this graceful cemetery is surrounded by catacombs and crowned by a triumphal arch. Now closed to burials except where old tombs are reopened, Brompton holds some eminent corpses, including those of suffragette Emmeline Pankhurst (died 1928), Frederick Leyland, patron of the pre-Raphaelites, and auctioneer Samuel Sotheby.

Bunhill Fields
City Road, EC1 (0181 472 3584). Old Street tube. **Open** *Apr-Sept* 7.30am-7pm Mon-Fri; *Oct-Mar* 7.30am-4pm Mon-Fri; 9.30am-4pm Sat, Sun.
Bunhill (or Bonehill) probably got its name in 1549 when bones from the charnel chapel of **St Paul's** were deposited here. From 1665 until 1855 it was the foremost graveyard for religious dissenters. Authors Daniel Defoe and John Bunyan, and the poet and visionary William Blake are buried in these peaceful, shaded gardens just outside the City bounds.

Highgate Cemetery
Swain's Lane, N6 (0181 340 1834). Archway tube/271 bus. **Open** *Apr-Oct* 10am-5pm daily; *Nov-Mar* 10am-4pm daily. **Admission** £1 East Cemetery; £3 tour of West Cemetery, £2 students, OAPs, UB40s. **No credit cards**.
Opened in 1839, this is London's most famous and exotic graveyard. Apart from it being the last resting place of Karl Marx, the east side is rather drab. The west side is a romantic wilderness of tombs and catacombs. Usually, this section can only be visited on a guided tour (phone for details), but on open days (three Sundays a year) you can wander around at will. Eminent Victorians residing here include novelist George Eliot and chemist Michael Faraday.

Kensal Green Cemetery
Harrow Road, W10 (0181 969 0152). Kensal Green tube. **Open** 8.30am-5.30pm Mon-Sat; 10am-5.30pm Sun.
Possibly the most beautiful and distinguished of London's big cemeteries, Kensal Green, running alongside the quiet Grand Union Canal under the looming shadow of the nearby gasworks, boasts an unequalled array of mausolea. Resting here, along with 'James' Barry, are the engineer Isambard Kingdom Brunel, novelists Anthony Trollope and William Thackeray, and the tightrope-walker Blondin.

Nunhead Cemetery
Linden Grove, SE15 (0171 639 3121). Nunhead BR. **Open** 2-4pm Wed; 10am-4pm Sat; noon-4pm Sun.
The easiest of the big Victorian cemeteries in which to get completely lost, Nunhead more than repays a visit to this otherwise unspectacular corner of south-east London. When in 1909 it was curtains for draper Frederick Gorringe, his mourners found themselves drawn to Nunhead.

Architecture

From Norman wisdom to monstrous carbuncles, London's mass of building styles is nothing if not byzantine.

Not since Roman times has London had any coherent city plan; it has simply evolved over the centuries in a rather muddled way. The City and Westminster were the two centres around which medieval London steadily grew, but its breathtaking growth since the eighteenth century has swallowed up the surrounding land for miles around. What we see now is a vast conglomeration of loosely connected 'villages' in a hotch-potch of architectural styles. Here and there we can detect valiant attempts to create order out of the chaos (as in John Nash's master plan for Regent Street and Regent's Park), but there is nothing to compare with the grid system of roads in New York, the *grands boulevards* of Paris, or the Ring Road of Vienna. The skyline of London is constantly changing but nowhere faster than in the financial City and the new Docklands.

*This way for the **Roman Wall** at Tower Hill.*

Roman & Saxon Legacy

The Roman city vanished during the Dark Ages. All that survived was the massive Roman Wall (built around AD 200), of which a few impressive chunks remain standing at Tower Hill and Cooper's Row (near Tower Hill tube), and at Noble Street, St Alphage Gardens and the **Museum of London** (near Barbican tube). There is also a trail, the London Wall Walk (1.8 miles/2.8 km, booklet available from the Museum of London Bookshop, £1.95). Our Roman origins can still be seen in the site and shape of today's City, and in the long, straight roads which lead out of London (Edgware Road, Oxford Street and Bayswater Road, Kingsland Road) along the lines of the old Roman roads.

The Saxons who settled around London in the fifth to eighth centuries built mainly in wood, and little has survived except a stone archway in the crypt of **All Hallows by the Tower**, one of the earliest Christian churches; the arch was built with Roman tiles, no doubt recycled from the ruins.

By the eleventh century, when the Normans invaded, the Saxons had rebuilt London within the Roman Wall, with 25 administrative wards (which still exist), a growing number of parish churches and an irregular street plan of narrow alleys.

English Norman

The Norman (or Romanesque) style came from France and appeared here during the eleventh century. It was modelled on the great stone-vaulted buildings of early Christian Rome, with thick round pillars and rounded arches. Stone was a luxury commodity, used only for churches, monasteries, castles and palaces; the common people built houses of wood and plaster.

Even before the Norman invasion of 1066, this style was used by Edward the Confessor for the first Abbey and Palace of Westminster (1050-65); his splendid building is pictured on the famous Bayeux Tapestry in France. The Norman foundations and undercroft (now the **Westminster Abbey Museum**) still survive, but the Abbey was subsequently rebuilt in Gothic style.

After 1066, William the Conqueror and his barons built imposing strongholds around London and throughout England; stone from Caen (in France) and teams of skilled masons and carpenters were used to build the **Tower of London** and Windsor Castle. The finest examples of Norman architecture to be seen in London today are St John's Chapel (in the Tower) and the church of **St Bartholomew the Great** (1123) at Smithfield. **Temple Church** (1185) is one of only five circular churches in the country. The original Norman crypt also survives at **St Mary-le-Bow**.

Medieval Gothic

In 1245, Henry III embarked on a plan to rebuild **Westminster Abbey** in the Gothic style as a shrine to its founder, Edward the Confessor; the main part of the nave and the octagonal Chapter

House were completed before he died in 1272. Later monarchs completed the nave over the next two centuries. Other examples of the plain, Early English style can be seen in **Southwark Cathedral** (choir and Lady Chapel), and in the chancel of **Temple Church**. The only example of the Decorated Gothic style is the thirteenth-century church **St Etheldreda's** near Holborn.

The ultimate Perpendicular Gothic style produced lace-like fan vaulting, of which the best example in London is the breathtaking ceiling of the Henry VII Chapel in **Westminster Abbey** (1503-09). The most impressive secular building is Westminster Hall (240 feet by almost 68 feet), part of the original Palace of Westminster but rebuilt (1394-1401) by Richard II's court mason Henry Yevele, with an oak hammerbeam roof by Hugh Herland. The **Jewel Tower** nearby (c1380) was also built by Yevele. The City's **Guildhall** (1411-40) is another example of the Gothic style.

Tudor & Jacobean

Under the Tudor monarchs in the sixteenth century London grew and prospered. The new wealth was reflected in the building of numerous palaces (including **Hampton Court** and **St James's Palace**) and town and country mansions (such as **Sutton House**), for which redbrick replaced stone as the fashionable material. Henry VIII's dissolution of the monasteries (*see chapter* **Tudors & Stuarts**) released acres of property and land around the capital, which were snapped up by the nobility and gentry for future development.

It was in the Tudor period that the impact of the Renaissance first began to influence English architecture. Pietro Torregiano (who reputedly broke Michelangelo's nose in a fight, and subsequently sought patronage in a foreign court) was one of the first Italian craftsmen to introduce Renaissance ornamentation in his design for Henry VII's tomb in **Westminster Abbey** (1512), with carvings and mouldings of fruit, flowers and cherubs.

By far the grandest Tudor building is **Hampton Court Palace** (1514-39). Although partially rebuilt in 1689-94 by Christopher Wren, most of the original palace remains intact, including the turreted Great Gatehouse (in warm redbrick faced with stone), wood-panelled rooms, huge kitchens and magnificent Great Hall; the chimney-stacks, decorated with moulded brick patterns, are a distinctive Tudor feature. Italian craftsmen (including Torregiano) were brought in to add terracotta medallions and other ornamentation. Early Tudor redbrick Gatehouses can also be seen at Lambeth Palace (1495) and at **Lincoln's Inn** (1518).

The reign of Elizabeth I (1558-1603) saw the establishment of galleried inns and taverns (of which the rebuilt **George Inn** in Southwark is the only survivor), and the Elizabethan theatres – the

Globe, the Rose and the Swan. The new **Globe Theatre** on Bankside, due to open in the summer of 1996, is a faithful replica of the original circular theatre, built in timber with a thatched roof. But the finest Elizabethan building in London is the splendid **Middle Temple Hall**, built in 1566-73 and still in use daily (*see* **Inns of Court**).

In the Tudor city, most of the dwellings were traditional timber-framed houses, with gables and overhanging upper storeys, which can still be seen (much restored) at **Staple Inn** in Holborn. On a grander scale, the carved front of the wealthy Sir Paul Pindar's House, built in 1599, is preserved in the **Victoria & Albert Museum**.

Jacobean style refers to the reign of James I, in the early seventeenth century. Splendid Jacobean mansions such as Charlton House, **Hatfield House** and the remains of Holland House show some influence of the new Renaissance style. **Prince Henry's Room** in Fleet Street (1611) has a typically elaborate decorated plaster ceiling.

English Renaissance

Two outstanding architects and one momentous event brought about the most profound changes during the seventeenth century. The architects were Inigo Jones and Christopher Wren; the event was the Great Fire of London in 1666.

Lincoln's Inn – *one of four Inns of Court.*

Inigo Jones (1573-1652) was the first British architect in the modern sense, as a creator and designer of buildings; until then, buildings had been produced by skilled craftsmen in the service of the Church and State. Jones, a talented artist, travelled in Italy and was greatly inspired by Andrea Palladio's Renaissance-style buildings. First employed by James I as a stage designer for elaborate court 'masques', he was later appointed Surveyor-General to the King and began work on England's first truly classical buildings: the **Queen's House** in Greenwich (1616) and the **Banqueting House** at Whitehall Palace (1619). When completed in 1622, the **Banqueting House** was the most outstanding sight in London; its elegantly proportioned classical façade, in fine white Portland stone, towered over the surrounding maze of medieval and Tudor buildings. In the 1630s, Jones launched a new project – **Covent Garden Piazza**, London's first residential square. Colonnades and terraces of brick houses were built around a garden, with the porticoed **St Paul's Church** (1633) on the west side. The Duke of Bedford made a handsome profit selling leases, and this established a pattern of speculative development in the West End for the next two centuries.

The Great Fire of London in 1666 (*see chapter* **Tudors & Stuarts**) opened the way for a new-look London, and Christopher Wren (1623-1732) rose to the occasion. Within a week, Wren (a mathematician and astronomer who had turned his talents to designing buildings) presented Charles II with a plan for rebuilding the City, with wide avenues radiating from circular piazzas. His plan was rejected; the pattern of land ownership was too complicated and there was no money to pay for the changes, so the medieval street plan was preserved. New standards were set: houses were to be built in brick or stone, most streets widened and pedestrians given raised pavements for the first time. These standards were applied to the new residential developments around The Strand, Bloomsbury, Soho and St James's, and the terrace house became the new style of residence. Queen Anne's Gate (1704), south of **St James's Park**, is a beautiful example of early terrace housing.

Wren, as newly appointed Surveyor-General, set about the awesome task of rebuilding **St Paul's Cathedral** and 51 of the City churches (*see chapter* **Sightseeing**). He used classical, French and Dutch models, blending them into a style all his own; he employed craftsmen to adorn his buildings with carved stone and wood, and wrought iron. His new churches were airy, lit by big windows with plain glass, and simply decorated with white plasterwork and gold leaf; for each he designed a tower or spire, with vanes or finials. Wren finally began work on his new cathedral in 1675 (the Great Model, in the Crypt, shows his first design, considered too revolutionary). Huge

quantities of white Portland stone were brought by boat from Dorset, money was raised by a tax on coal, and after 35 years St Paul's was complete. Nothing like it had been seen before in England. The great dome dominated the London skyline surrounded by a forest of spires – a sight now seen only in eighteenth-century paintings. Wren left his mark in buildings all over London, including **St James's Church Piccadilly**; the **Royal Hospital** in Chelsea; **Hampton Court Palace** (East Wing); the **Old Royal Observatory** and Royal Naval Hospital (*see* **Royal Naval College**), Greenwich.

In 1710, Parliament passed an Act for the building of 50 new churches in London. Only 12 were actually built, including six monumental buildings by Wren's colleague Nicholas Hawksmoor (the best examples are **Christchurch Spitalfields**, **St Mary Woolnoth** and St George Bloomsbury). Hawksmoor later designed the west towers for **Westminster Abbey** (1734-39).

By the time George I came to the throne in 1714, London had been transformed from a timber-built, ramshackle medieval port into a predominantly classical brick- and stone-built city.

Georgian

The early eighteenth century saw a swing back to the purely classical (or Palladian) style of building, introduced a century earlier by Inigo Jones. This was mainly due to the influence of the wealthy Lord Burlington, who virtually dictated the taste of his time, and disapproved of the exuberant baroque ornamentation associated with some of Wren's and Hawksmoor's work. Burlington's own country villa, **Chiswick House** (1725-29), is the best example of the pure Palladian style in London.

The classical influence persisted all through the Georgian period, but reaction set in against the strict rules of the Palladians (which could produce dull and austere buildings) and new influences began to take root in the mid-eighteenth century, known as 'picturesque' and 'neo-classical' styles.

Robert Adam (1728-92) was considered the most brilliant designer of his day. The son of a Scottish architect, Adam studied in Rome before settling in London. He brought a lightness to the rigid classical style by adding decorative motifs and subtle use of colour, especially in his 1760s remodelling of **Kenwood House**, **Osterley Park** and Syon Park (*see* **Syon House**).

The greatest achievement of John Nash (1752-1835), a versatile architect who became Surveyor-General to the Prince Regent (later George IV), was his transformation of the West End (1811-28). The Regent's plan (intended to outdo Napoleon's for Paris) was to create a 'triumphal way', linking his residence near **St James's Park** (where Carlton House Terrace is now) with a new palace in

Bentley's **Westminster Cathedral** *(1903).*

Regent's Park. Nash's scheme resulted in the laying out of Regent Street (from Waterloo Place to Portland Place, with the church of All Souls, Langham Place as a focal point), and the landscaping of **Regent's Park** with its surrounding terraces of grand houses (Chester Terrace, Cumberland Terrace, Park Crescent); he also built Theatre Royal Haymarket (1831) and planned the layout of **Trafalgar Square**. Regent Street has been altered, but Nash's work remains the boldest piece of town planning in London.

Other notable architects of the time include James Gibbs, whose design for **St Martin-in-the-Fields** (1726), with its classical portico, tower and steeple, became the model for many American churches; George Dance, who beat Gibbs in a competition to design the Mansion House (1753), the Lord Mayor's residence; and Sir John Soane, who built the **Bank of England** (1788-1808) and left his own house to the nation (*see* **Sir John Soane's Museum**). Two extraordinary buildings of the time are Horace Walpole's Strawberry Hill (1749-76), a Gothic-style mansion in Twickenham, and William Chambers' exotic Pagoda in **Kew Gardens** (1761), in contrast to his more sober Somerset House (1775) in the Strand.

One of London's legacies from this period is the Georgian terraced house. Many of these simple, elegant houses (usually of three or four storeys, with evenly spaced sash windows, and decorative iron balconies and railings) survive in Bloomsbury, Marylebone, Camden Town, Greenwich,

Dulwich, Islington, Hampstead and Highgate. The dark red brick of the earlier houses was replaced by yellow London brick, or smooth stucco facing (made popular by Nash) painted in cream or white. Two of the finest examples are Bedford Square, WC1, and Church Row, Hampstead.

Victorian

The nineteenth century was a time of unprecedented growth. Even before Victoria came to the throne in 1837, the Industrial Revolution was already transforming the face of London, with new docks, canals, roads, bridges, railways and prestigious public buildings. Some architects continued in the dignified Neoclassical tradition with buildings such as the **National Gallery** (William Wilkin, 1830) and the **Royal Exchange** (William Tite, 1844); Robert Smirke revived the ancient Greek style for the massive portico of the **British Museum** (begun in 1823). At the same time, the Gothic style re-emerged with the building of the new **Houses of Parliament** by Charles Barry and Augustus Pugin (1834-52), and later in **St Pancras Station** (1868) by Sir George Gilbert Scott (who designed the **Albert Memorial**), and the **Royal Courts of Justice** (1882) by George Street. Churches were built in the new suburbs, nearly all in the High Gothic style (including All Saints, Margaret Street; St Augustine, Kilburn; St Cyprian's, Clarence Gate). Terracotta and other man-made materials were used in place of stone and brick for colourful surface decoration, used to great effect on the **Natural History Museum** by Alfred Waterhouse (1881).

Engineers, as much as architects, changed the face of Victorian London. From the 1830s, new technology and mass production made possible the building of huge iron and glass structures: Decimus Burton's Palm House (1848) and Temperate House (1862) at **Kew Gardens** still survive, but Joseph Paxton's Crystal Palace burned down in 1936. The big covered markets – **Smithfield Market** (1866), old Billingsgate Market (1875) and Leadenhall Market (1881) – and the steel-framed **Tower Bridge** (1894) were all designed by the Corporation architect/engineer Horace Jones.

Railway stations were a new concept: the showy façade, often a hotel, was usually designed by architects, while the covered span – often the most amazing feat of engineering – got less credit. The St Pancras train shed (689 feet by 245), by Barlow and Ordish, was once the widest span in the world.

The engineer who had the greatest impact on Victorian London was Sir Joseph Bazalgette. He masterminded the building of the Victoria, Albert and Chelsea Embankments (1864-70) and the vast sewerage and drainage system running east-west across the capital, two immense projects from which we still benefit today.

London Central Mosque *near Regent's Park.*

As the population grew from one million in 1801 to four million in 1901, bricks and mortar swallowed up fields for miles around. New speculative developments ranged from grand estates, such as Thomas Cubitt's Belgravia, Bloomsbury and Barnsbury, to overcrowded tenement blocks and bleak terraces along the railway lines for the poor.

At the same time, the Arts and Crafts movement, inspired by the work of artist-designer William Morris, came up with a new vernacular style which continued into the next century. Leading architects in this group were Norman Shaw (who laid out Bedford Park in Chiswick, London's first 'garden suburb'), Aston Webb and Edwin Lutyens. Two rare examples of the Art Nouveau style in London, the **Whitechapel Art Gallery** (1899) and the **Horniman Museum** (1901), were designed by C Harrison Townsend.

The **Victorian Society** *(0181 994 1019, 9am-5pm Mon-Fri) organises lectures and visits to Victorian buildings, and will try to answer enquiries about architecture and interiors.*

Edwardian

The late Victorian and Edwardian era, until World War I, produced the last great period of development. Buildings continued to go up on a grand scale, usually in Portland stone. Edward Mountford's **Old Bailey** (1907), Ralph Knott's County Hall (begun 1905) and the first department stores, **Harrods** (1905) and **Selfridges** (1907), are good examples. Sir Edwin Lutyens (who later built the **Cenotaph**) was involved in the design of Hampstead Garden Suburb, the closest to Ebenezer Howard's ideal of the 'garden city'; Aston Webb created London's first royal processional route when he laid out The Mall (1912-13), with the **Victoria Memorial** at one end and Admiralty Arch at the other. John Francis Bentley's **Westminster Cathedral** (1903) is a unique mixture of Byzantine and Romanesque styles.

An exuberant, delightful freak is F Espinasse's Michelin House (1905-11, *see* **Michelin Building**); restored in 1985 by Terence Conran, it houses his **Conran Shop** and **Bibendum** restaurant.

Early Modernism

After 1918, the architectural initiative passed to Paris, Berlin and other European centres; Britain was slow to adopt Modernism. As London's population doubled again (to 8.5 million in 1939), building concentrated on suburban expansion along the Underground ('Metroland'). Charles Holden was responsible for over 30 Underground stations, of which many were modernist gems (notably Bounds Green, 1930, and Arnos Grove, 1932); he also designed London Transport's Broadway House (1927-29) at St James's Park station, with sculptures by Gill, Epstein and Moore, and London University's Senate House (1933).

British Modernism did have its moments, most impressively with the Daily Express Building (1932) by Owen Williams, in black and transparent glass with curved corners. Huge art deco cinemas were built (though few survive). But the new impetus in British architecture came from Gropius, Mendelsohn, Breuer and Lubetkin, refugees from Nazi persecution. They introduced new designs using reinforced concrete, such as Lubetkin's Penguin Pool in **London Zoo** (1934), a playful construction of interlocking concrete spirals.

Freemasons' Hall (1933) was loathed by half the population when it opened, and kept the *Times* letters page filled for months, but the most extraordinary building of the period is the massive Battersea Power Station (1929-33), like a left-over from the film set of Fritz Lang's *Metropolis*.

Waterloo International Terminal *(1993).*

Post War

A period of austerity followed World War II (in which the City and East End suffered worst), but the modern movement finally arrived with London County Council's **Royal Festival Hall**, built for the Festival of Britain in 1951, and still one of the best modern buildings in London. Sadly, the post-war reconstruction of London led to a deterioration in the quality of building. Enthusiasm to improve society led to the sweeping away not only of slums but also of Georgian squares. Councils erected hundreds of concrete tower blocks, and vast City office developments were similarly insensitive, such as the bleak Paternoster Square, near **St Paul's Cathedral** (about to be redeveloped).

One of the more adventurous buildings is the **Commonwealth Institute** (Robert Matthew and P Johnson-Marshall, 1962), with its hyperboloid roof of Zambian copper. The Post Office Tower (Eric Bedford, 1964, now the **BT Tower**) and the **London Central Mosque** (Sir Frederick Gibberd, 1978) were new additions to the skyline. The 'multi-level city' of raised pedestrian decks and terraces began with the South Bank Complex, but the building of the **National Theatre** (Denys Lasdun, 1977) had people describing the new architecture as 'concrete bunkers' or 'brutalism'. The development of the Barbican Estate and **Barbican Centre** (1982) followed the same pattern.

Post-Modernism

Fierce public debates on Modernism versus Classicism were provoked in 1984 when the Prince of Wales denounced the prize-winning entry for the **National Gallery**'s new extension as 'a monstrous carbuncle'; planning permission was refused, and American architects Venturi, Scott-Brown & Associates were commissioned to build the **National Gallery**'s Sainsbury Wing (1988-91) in Post-Modern Classical style. At the same time, a tremendously diverse range of buildings has emerged in the building boom of the last 15 years, mainly in the City and Docklands: vast office developments for computerised trading, new premises for national newspapers relocating from Fleet Street, and luxury housing for City workers.

Architects Norman Foster, Richard Rogers and Nicholas Grimshaw collaborate with engineers to produce space-age constructions of steel and glass. Foster's work includes the light and airy Sackler Galleries (1991) at the **Royal Academy** and the new **Stansted Airport** (1985-91). Rogers, famous for his Pompidou Centre in Paris, designed the controversial **Lloyd's of London** (1986) and the Channel 4 Television building (1994); his stunning internal conversion of the old Billingsgate Market (1988) is sadly not open to visit, but he has recently won a competition to redesign the South Bank

Centre. Grimshaw's work includes the Waterloo International Terminal (1993).

James Stirling and Terry Farrell prefer traditional materials – concrete, brick, marble, stone – and tend to use pattern and colour, with references to Egyptian, ancient Greek, art deco and other styles. Stirling designed the Clore Gallery at the **Tate**, while Farrell is said to be the most prolific London architect since Wren. One of his best known buildings is the canalside MTV HQ (formerly TV-am) at Camden Lock, topped with his famous egg cups. Recent buildings include Embankment Place (1990, above Charing Cross) and the green and white ziggurat Vauxhall Cross (1993, south of Vauxhall Bridge) for MI6.

Other landmarks of recent years include the **Canary Wharf** tower (Cesar Pelli, 1991), the first skyscraper to be clad in stainless steel; the huge Broadgate development (next to **Liverpool Street Station**), worth exploring if only to find works by many well-known contemporary artists; Conran Roche's transformation of the South Bank at Butler's Wharf (near **Tower Bridge**); and the **Thames Barrier**, a remarkable engineering feat described as 'the eighth wonder of the world'.

*Cesar Pelli's **Canary Wharf** tower (1991).*

Projects to keep an eye on include the continuing saga of the grotesque new British Library (next to **St Pancras Station**), long overdue and over-budget; and plans for the South Bank, particularly the development of the derelict Bankside Power Station as the **Tate**'s new Museum of Modern Art.

For more new buildings, see Samantha Hardingham's excellent book *London: A Guide To Recent Architecture* (*see chapter* **Further Reading**).

River & Canal

The last hundred years have seen the taming of the Thames, with the building of embankments, a flood barrier, the redevelopment of the docks and an ongoing clean-up campaign.

River Thames

Taking a trip on the River puts London into a different perspective. The shortest and most popular trip is from Westminster to the Tower. From the Tower towards Greenwich and the sea, the banks are littered with relics of London's sea-faring past. Upstream from Westminster, past the looming hulk of Battersea Power Station, the character changes completely with tree-lined banks and the riverside pubs of Chelsea, Putney and Barnes.

The London Tourist Board booklet *Discover the Thames* has information on attractions, events and trips. Westminster Passenger Services Association *(0171 930 2062)* has further information on return services and evening cruises. Upstream trips run only in the summer. All trips quoted are from Westminster Pier, Victoria Embankment, SW1 (Westminster tube). Journey times vary.

Downriver

To Greenwich *(0171 930 4097)*.
10.30am then every 30 mins until approx 5pm. **Duration** 45 mins. **Fares** *Single* £4.80; £3.80 OAPs; £2.40 under-16s; £12.50 family. *Return* £5.60; £4.60 OAPs; £2.80 under-16s; £14.50 family.
To Tower of London *(0171 930 9033)*.
10.20am-5.20pm every 20 mins; 3pm-6pm every 30 mins. **Duration** 30 mins. **Fares** *Single* £3.80; £2 under-16s; free under-4s. *Return* £5.20; £3 under-16s.
To Thames Barrier *(0171 930 3373)*.
Apr-Oct 10.15am, 11.15am, 12.45pm, 1.45pm, 3.15pm (also

Thames Bridges

Hammersmith Bridge *Hammersmith tube.*
Sir Joseph Bazalgette's 1887 structure (replacing the 1827 bridge) survived an attempt by the IRA to blow it up in 1939, a passerby throwing the bomb into the Thames.

Putney Bridge *Putney Bridge tube.*
A timber bridge was opened in 1729. The present incarnation is a five-span granite bridge designed by Sir Joseph Bazalgette (1886). The University Boat Race between Oxford and Cambridge starts from here.

Wandsworth Bridge *Wandsworth Town BR.*
A five-span lattice-girder bridge (1873) was replaced by a steel-plate girder bridge (1940).

Battersea Bridge *Sloane Square tube/19, 22 bus.*
A wooden bridge (1772) replaced the Chelsea-Battersea ferry. The present bridge (1890) is another Sir Joseph Bazalgette creation.

Albert Bridge *Sloane Square tube/19, 22 bus.*
This lovely triple-arched, cast-iron bridge (1873) is breathtakingly lit at night. Overhauled by Sir Joseph Bazalgette.

Chelsea Bridge *Sloane Square tube.*
A suspension bridge with cast-iron towers (1858) was replaced in 1934. Hot rods, customised Minis and bikers gather on the bridge and in Battersea Park for the Chelsea Cruise at 8.30pm on the last Saturday of the month.

Vauxhall Bridge *Vauxhall tube.*
The first iron bridge (1816) over the Thames in London. The present design (1906) consists of steel arches on granite piers.

Lambeth Bridge *St James's Park tube.*
The 1932 five-span steel-arch bridge replaced the bridge designed by PW Barlow (1862).

Westminster Bridge *Westminster tube.*
In 1750, it became the second bridge in central London. Hawksmoor was among those whose designs were rejected. The present cast-iron bridge dates from 1862.

Hungerford Bridge *Embankment or Waterloo tube.*
Completed in 1864, the railway bridge incorporated a footbridge. Lay-bys are used by buskers and courting couples.

Waterloo Bridge *Temple or Waterloo tube.*
The Prince Regent opened the first bridge in 1817. It was replaced in 1942 by today's construction of cantilevered reinforced concrete box girders. Watch out for motorists slowing down to admire the wonderful views.

Blackfriars Bridge *Blackfriars tube/BR.*
The first bridge was opened in 1769, its successor in 1869. Italian banker Roberto Calvi was found hanging underneath it on 15 June 1982. Two railway bridges were built, the western bridge (1864) is now disused.

Southwark Bridge *Cannon Street tube/BR.*
Casting John Rennie's 1819 three-arch iron bridge bankrupted Walker's of Rotherham. It was replaced in 1921.

Cannon Street Rail Bridge *Cannon Street tube/BR.*
The rail bridge was finished in 1866, widened in 1893 and renovated in 1979.

London Bridge *London Bridge tube/BR.*
Old London Bridge was replaced by a five-arch granite bridge by John Rennie. When the present bridge was built in 1973, Rennie's went to Arizona for £1 million.

Tower Bridge *Tower Hill tube or Tower Gateway DLR.*
Sir Joseph Bazalgette actually had a design turned down and a bascule bridge was built. London's most instantly recognisable symbol was opened in 1894.

*The **Thames** – Iain Sinclair's 'flooded temple'.*

stops at Canary Wharf). **Duration** 75 mins. **Fares** *Single* £4; £2.30 under-16s; £3 OAPs. *Return* £5.70; £2.85 under-16s; £4.70 OAPs.

Upriver

To Hampton Court (*0171 930 4721*).
Apr-Oct 10.30am, 11.15am, noon. **Duration** approx 3-4 hours. **Fares** *Single* £7; £4 4-14s. **Return** £10; £7 4-14s.
To Kew (*0171 930 2062/4721*).
Apr-Oct 10.15am, 10.30am, 11am, 11.15am, noon, 2pm, 2.30pm. **Duration** approx 90 mins. **Fares** *Single* £8; £5 under-14s. *Return* £7; £4 under-14s.
To Putney (*0171 930 2062/4721*).
Apr-Oct 10.15am, 10.30am, 11am, 11.30am, noon, 2pm, 2.30pm, 3pm, 3.30pm. **Duration** approx 40 mins. **Fares** *Single* £3.50; £2.50 under-14s. *Return* £6; £3 under-14s.
To Richmond (*0171 930 2062/4721*).
Apr-Oct 10.30am, 11.15pm, noon. **Duration** approx 2 hrs. **Fares** *Single* £6; £3.50 under-14s. **Return** £9; £6 under-14s.

Grand Union Canal

The Grand Union (or Regent's) Canal (1811-20) snakes across north London from Willesden to Hackney, before turning south to join the Thames at Limehouse. Before the railways, the canal was a crucial link between London and the Midlands. Sea-borne vessels transferred their cargo to barges which set off along the canal towed by horses.

For cruises between Little Venice (Warwick Avenue tube) and Camden Lock (Camden Town tube), contact one of the following companies. Drift past back gardens and old warehouses, through **Regent's Park** and the Maida Hill tunnel. Jason's Trip and Jenny Wren both offer three or four round trips each day on narrowboats (adult fares £4-£5 return). London Waterbus stops at the Zoo, with a combined ticket for Zoo admission.
Jason's Trip *Opposite 60 Blomfield Road, W9 (0171 286 3428). Warwick Avenue tube.*
Jenny Wren Cruises *250 Camden High Street, NW1 (0171 485 4433). Camden Town tube.*
London Waterbus Company *Camden Lock Place, NW1 (0171 482 2550). Camden Town tube.*

Woolwich Horror

It was a tough one for the environmental health officers. They'd never seen anything quite like them. One official mentioned cockroaches, another woodlice. But these hideous creatures were one and a half inches (3.8 cm) long and they'd crawled out of the Thames.

Industrial workers in Woolwich, men hardened by exposure to the eldritch horrors of Grand Depôt Road, fled as the armour-plated bugs surmounted the river wall and crawled towards them in an advancing oily tide. There were hundreds of them, thousands, and men who were too slow to retreat crunched them underfoot, carapaces crackling.

With the bug men of Greenwich dumbfounded, it was down to Dr Jim Brock, an entomologist at the **Horniman Museum**, to make a positive identifcation. '*Ligia oceanica*,' he declared. 'They thrive in salt water conditions. They are very elusive and people hardly ever come into contact with them. When they do they are often frightened out of their skins because they are so big.'

The crustaceans, which must have been washed upstream by a high tide, have now disappeared. Presumably they all died. Or went into hiding….

Ligia oceanica – *thrives in salt water.*

History

Roman to Norman

After its foundation by the Romans, London saw almost four centuries of progress before being plunged into the Dark Ages.

THE ROMAN PROVINCE

London was founded by the Romans almost 2,000 years ago. Long before they arrived, the Thames had been used as a highway by seafaring traders and invaders, and as a line of defence by Celtic tribes. Julius Caesar led two expeditions to Britain to curb the unruly Celts. It was not until AD43 that an invasion under the Emperor Claudius led to the conquest of Britain and the establishment of the Empire's new frontier province.

During the first two centuries, the Romans built roads, towns and forts; trade flourished. Exports were tin, silver, jet, pearls, hides, grain, slaves and hunting-dogs; imports included olive oil, wine, fine pottery, glass and marble. In the fourth century, racked by barbarian invasions and internal strife, the Roman Empire was in decline. Towns fell into disrepair and country villas were abandoned by their owners; some left buried riches, such as the Mildenhall Treasure and Hoxne Hoard, now in the **British Museum**. In AD410 the last troops were withdrawn; London became a ghost city. The Roman way of life – culture, arts, language and politics – vanished when the Romans withdrew. Their only enduring legacies were the roads, early Christianity and new cities such as London.

THE FIRST PORT OF LONDON

The first mention of London (or Londinium), by the Roman historian Tacitus, records that in AD60 it was 'filled with traders and a celebrated centre of commerce'. This thriving settlement probably started to develop around AD50, when the Romans built the first timber bridge across the Thames (near today's **London Bridge**). This became a focus for Roman roads to all parts of the province, and the most convenient landing place for traders from the Continent. Quays and jetties were established and London became a busy trading port.

Progress was brought to a halt in AD61, when Boadicea, the widow of an East Anglian chieftain, rebelled against the Imperial forces who had seized her land, flogged her and raped her daughters. She led the Iceni in a savage revolt which destroyed the Roman colony at Colchester and marched on

London, then unfortified and without a garrison: the inhabitants were massacred and the settlement burnt to the ground. Even today a layer of dark red ash can be found in excavations. A bronze statue of the rebel queen and her daughters in their chariot (by Thomas Thorneycroft, 1902) stands on the north side of **Westminster Bridge**.

CREATION OF A CAPITAL

Order was restored by the new procurator, Julius Alpinus Classicianus, whose tomb, discovered near the Roman Wall at Tower Hill, can be seen in the **British Museum**. London was rebuilt on the north bank, around today's Cornhill; trade boomed and London became the capital of the province.

The ruins of Roman London are still being discovered. The foundations of a huge basilica and forum (which combined town hall and law courts with a temple, shops and arcades) came to light in 1881, when the new Leadenhall Market was built. Excavations at Cannon Street Station revealed the foundations of a villa, thought to be the Governor's Palace, with lavish state rooms, private apartments, baths and ornamental gardens. In 1987, parts of a large amphitheatre were discovered under Guildhall Yard (not yet open to the public).

The ruins of the **Temple of Mithras**, discovered in 1954, show that pagan religions were popular in the third century when it was built. In the

The ruins of the pagan **Temple of Mithras.**

fourth century, when Christianity was recognised by the Romans, pagan temples were destroyed.

The only part of the Roman city to survive was the massive Roman Wall (*see chapter* **Architecture**), nine feet thick and 20 feet high, built of Kentish ragstone (carried up the river in barges) interspersed with layers of red tile. Repaired and rebuilt several times during the Middle Ages, the wall remained almost intact until 1760, when most of it was demolished. Of the original gates, only the names remain: Aldgate, Bishopsgate, Cripplegate, Aldersgate, Newgate and Ludgate.

The most treasured artefacts from Roman London can be seen in the **Museum of London** and the **British Museum**. Recent archaeological finds are on display at **Tower Hill Pageant**.

THE DARK AGES

In the fifth and sixth centuries history gives way to legend. We know that the Saxons crossed the North Sea and established themselves in east and south England, appearing to have avoided the ruins of London; they built farmsteads and small trading settlements outside the walls, including a larger settlement around the Strand. In AD731 the Venerable Bede mentions 'Lundenwic' as 'the mart of many nations resorting to it by land and sea'; this probably refers to the settlement in the Strand, now known as Aldwych. The Germanic speech of the Saxons replaced Latin, and Anglo-Saxon became the primary source of modern English.

THE COMING OF CHRISTIANITY

In AD597 Pope Gregory sent Augustine to convert the English to Christianity. Ethelbert, Saxon King of Kent, proved a willing convert, and Augustine was appointed the first Archbishop of Canterbury. Since then Canterbury (*see chapter* **Trips out of Town**) has remained the centre of the English Christian church. London's first Bishop was Mellitus, one of Augustine's missionaries, who converted the East Saxon King Seebert and, in AD604, founded a wooden cathedral dedicated to St Paul inside the old city walls. On Seebert's death, his followers reverted to paganism, but later generations of Christians rebuilt **St Paul's**.

DANISH INVADERS

In the ninth century, London was sacked by Danes. AD841 was a 'year of great slaughter' and in AD851 the raiders returned with 350 ships, leaving the city in ruins. It was not until AD886 that King Alfred of Wessex (later known as Alfred the Great) regained London, rebuilt its defences and defeated the Danes. He re-established London as an important trading centre, with a merchant navy and new wharfs at Billingsgate and Queenhithe.

During the tenth century, the Saxon City prospered. Churches were built, parishes and wards were established, markets were set up and traders sailed in. Leading citizens were the Port Reeve and

Shire Reeve (or Sheriff – the oldest office still existing in the City), appointed by the King to enforce the law and collect taxes; the Bishop of London, and the ealdormen (or aldermen) who supervised the city's 24 wards. All citizens were summoned to an assembly, the Folk Moot, three times a year at Paul's Cross (the spot is still marked in St Paul's Churchyard). The layout of the City, street names, and many of its institutions date from this time.

In the eleventh century, the Danes again harassed the town, and the English were forced to accept a Danish king Cnut (aka Canute) from 1016-40. During his brief but important reign, London replaced Winchester as the capital of England.

THE BUILDING OF WESTMINSTER

In 1042 the throne reverted to the English king Edward, known as 'the Confessor' because of his piety. He devoted himself to building the grandest church in England in the Norman style (*see chapter* **Architecture**), and chose a site two miles (3 km) west of the City. He replaced the timber church of St Peter's with a huge abbey church known as 'the West Minster' or **Westminster Abbey**, and removed his court to the new Palace of Westminster. The Abbey was consecrated in December 1065. One week later Edward died and was buried in his new church. From then on, London grew

Under **Cnut** *London became the capital city.*

Old London Bridge

Old London Bridge, the only city bridge to span the Thames until 1750, became one of the wonders of the medieval world. Built between 1176-1209, the first stone bridge (the longest in Europe at the time) was the brainchild of a parish priest, Peter de Colechurch. From shore to shore it was nearly 350 yards (318 metres) long, built on 19 piers protected by boat-shaped 'starlings' (wooden stakes driven into the river bed and filled with rubble) which restricted the flow of the River, so that boats passing through the bridge had to shoot the rapids. In hard winters, the river froze solid upstream of the bridge leading to famous Frost Fairs on the ice.

Houses on the bridge were much sought after for their salubrious position: fresh air, a fine view and superior sanitation. By the sixteenth century, the bridge was packed with houses and shops, the small chapel of St Thomas à Becket (in which de Colechurch was buried), a drawbridge and the palatial Nonsuch House, erected in 1577. From the north, the approach to the bridge was from Fish Street Hill (20 yards east of the present **London Bridge**). The church of **St Magnus Martyr** stood at the north end, and at the Southwark end was a stone gatehouse, over which the severed heads of traitors, parboiled and tarred, were displayed on spikes.

Frequent repairs were necessary, the starlings suffering constant erosion, and the cost of maintenance was heavy. Rents from houses and shops on the bridge were put towards this, and tolls were introduced as the thoroughfare became increasingly crowded with stalls, traffic and animals. Merchants left bequests to 'God and the Bridge', and the Bridge House Estates Fund, which has grown over the centuries, now maintains all four City bridges (**Tower Bridge**, **London Bridge**, **Southwark Bridge** and **Blackfriars Bridge**); the interest amounts to an annual income of over £12 million.

By 1760, Old London Bridge was in such bad repair that the houses were pulled down, and the crumbling remains were finally demolished in 1831. A few remnants of the ancient stonework can be seen in the churchyard of **St Magnus Martyr**; some of the original lamps and stone shelters which stood on the bridge now stand in the churchyard of St Botolph Bishopsgate; there are models and old prints in the **Museum of London**, and the famous bridge will always be remembered in the popular nursery rhyme 'London Bridge is Falling Down'.

Old London Bridge (1756) – not long to go.

around two centres: Westminster as the centre for the royal court, government and law, and the City of London as the centre for trade and commerce.

THE NORMAN CONQUEST

On Edward's death, there was a dispute over the succession. William, Duke of Normandy, claimed that the Confessor (his cousin) had promised him the English crown; the English chose Edward's brother-in-law Harold to be king. William gathered a large army and invaded. On 14 October 1066, he defeated Harold at the Battle of Hastings and marched on London. City elders had little option but to offer William the throne; he was crowned in **Westminster Abbey** on Christmas Day, 1066.

William, recognising the need to win over the prosperous community of City merchants by negotiation rather than force, granted the Bishop and burgesses of London a charter (still kept at **Guildhall**) which acknowledged their former rights and independence in return for payments and taxes. He ordered strongholds to be built alongside the City wall, including the White Tower (the tallest building in the **Tower of London**) to the east, and Baynard's Castle (destroyed in the Great Fire) to the west, so that he could keep a wary eye on the powerful and unruly inhabitants.

In 1154 the Norman kings were succeeded by the French-speaking Plantagenet kings. Shortly after, in 1183, we have the first recorded written account of contemporary London by a monk, William Fitz Stephen. He writes a glowing account of the walled city and, outside, describes pastures and woods for hunting, and youths wrestling and fencing in Moorfields, or skating on frozen ponds with 'the shin-bones of beasts' lashed to their feet.

The Middle Ages

London's trade and commerce increased, but so did poverty and squalor – leading to the Black Death, which was to wipe out a third of the population.

The Middle Ages (from the late twelfth century to the late fifteenth century) were turbulent times. There were constant disputes between powerful kings and barons, and wars both at home and abroad (particularly in France); weak kings were murdered or deposed; plague and pestilence devastated the population in the fourteenth century. In spite of all this, the monarchy was generally strong, England was safe from invasion and the foundations for the British parliamentary system, English common law and the jury system were all laid at this time. As government became firmly established, trade boomed and London prospered.

Three groups vied for power and wealth: the King and the aristocracy at Westminster; the bishops and clergy of the Catholic Church; and the Lord Mayor and guilds of the City of London. Tensions frequently arose between (and within) all three groups.

MOTHER OF PARLIAMENTS

In the early middle ages, the king and his court frequently travelled to other parts of the kingdom or abroad, but in the fourteenth and fifteenth centuries, the Palace of Westminster became the principal seat of law and government. The wealthy noblemen and bishops who attended court built themselves palatial houses along the Strand, from the City to Westminster, with gardens which stretched down to the river. It was near here in 1291 that the sorrowful Edward I built his last memorial cross to commemorate his dear queen Eleanor (the 'Chère Reine' or Charing Cross).

The first Model Parliament, which agreed the general principles of government, was held in Westminster Hall in 1295, presided over by Edward I, and attended by barons, clergy and elected representatives of knights and burgesses. But the first step towards establishing personal rights and political liberty, and curbing the power of the king, had been taken in 1215 with the signing of the Magna Carta (or Great Charter) by King John (a copy of which can be seen in the British Library). In the fourteenth century, subsequent assemblies gave rise to the House of Lords (which met at the Palace of Westminster) and the House of Commons (which met in the Chapter House at **Westminster Abbey**).

Successive kings were always in need of money to finance extravagant building projects (such as Henry III's rebuilding of **Westminster Abbey**) or to fund military conflicts at home or abroad. Money for these projects was raised from taxes and hefty loans from the City merchants and foreign money-lenders (the Jews, until they were expelled in 1290, and later the Lombard bankers from north Italy – hence the street names Old Jewry and Lombard Street).

THE MEDIEVAL CITY

The privileges which had been granted to the City merchants under the Norman kings, allowing them independence and self-regulation, were extended by the kings who followed, in return for financial favours. In 1191, during the reign of Richard I (who was trying to raise money for his crusading expeditions), the City of London was given formal recognition as a commune (a self-governing community) and, in 1197, won control of the Thames, including the lucrative fishing rights (which they retained until 1857). In 1215, in return for financial support, King John confirmed the City's right 'to elect every year a mayor', a position of great authority with power over both the Sheriff and the Bishop of London. One month later the Mayor joined the rebel barons in signing the Magna Carta (*see above*).

Over the next two centuries, the power and influence of the trade and craft guilds (which later became the City Livery Companies, *see page 71*) increased rapidly as trade with Europe expanded. The wharfs near **London Bridge** were crowded with imports from abroad: fine cloth, furs, wine, garlic, spices and precious metals. Port dues and taxes were paid to the customs officials, of whom one was the poet Geoffrey Chaucer (*c*1342-1400), whose *Canterbury Tales* became the first published work of English literature.

The City's markets, which were already well established, drew produce from miles around: live meat at **Smithfield** (originally Smooth Field), fish at Billingsgate and poultry at Leadenhall; the street markets or 'cheaps' around Westcheap (now Cheapside) and Eastcheap were crammed with other goods, as their names indicate: Milk Street, Bread Street, Ironmonger Lane, Honey Lane, Fish Street Hill.

As trade and commerce increased, and foreign traders and craftsmen settled in and around the port, the population within the City wall grew from about 18,000 in 1100 to over 50,000 in the 1340s. Lack of hygiene became a serious problem. Water was provided in cisterns at Cheapside and elsewhere, but the supply (which came more or less directly from the Thames) was limited and polluted. Houndsditch was so called because Londoners threw their dead animals into the ditch that formed the City's eastern boundary. There was no proper sewerage system and in the streets around Smithfield (known as the Shambles), the butchers left the entrails of slaughtered animals. These unsanitary conditions provided the breeding ground for the greatest catastrophe of the Middle Ages: the Black Death of 1348-49.

The plague reached London from Europe, carried by rats on cargo ships. During this period, about 30 per cent of England's population died of the disease. When the plague abated, it was to recur in London on several occasions during the next three centuries.

These epidemics left the labour market in short supply, causing unrest among the overworked peasants; the subsequent imposition of a poll tax (one shilling per head) lead to the Peasants' Revolt. In 1381, during the reign of the boy-king Richard II, thousands marched on London led by Jack Straw from Essex and Wat Tyler from Kent. In the rioting and looting that followed, the Savoy Palace in the Strand (home of the king's powerful uncle, John of Gaunt) was destroyed, the Archbishop of Canterbury was executed, and hundreds of prisoners were set free.

When the 14-year-old Richard rode out to Smithfield to face the rioters, the ringleader, Wat Tyler, was fatally stabbed by the Lord Mayor, William Walworth (whose dagger is preserved in Fishmongers' Hall). The other ringleaders were subsequently rounded up and hanged. But no more poll taxes were imposed.

CHURCHES AND MONASTERIES

Like every other medieval city, London had a large number of parish churches and monastic churches, as well as the huge cathedral of **St Paul's**. Although allowed access to the great churches, most Londoners' lives revolved around their own local parish churches, where they were baptised, married and buried. They maintained the clerics, worshipped regularly and frequently gave money to renovate their churches or decorate them with precious objects; many churches were linked with particular craft and trade guilds (*see page 71*).

Huge monasteries and convents were established, all of which owned valuable acres of land just inside and outside the walls of the city: the crusading Knights Templars and Knights

Shambles – *breeding ground for the Plague.*

Hospitallers were two of the earliest religious orders to settle, but the increasingly unruly Templars were disbanded in 1312 by order of the the Pope. Their land, handed over to their rivals the Hospitallers, was leased to the lawyers and their students, who founded the Inns of Court, and are still based at the Inner Temple and Middle Temple (*see* **Temple Church** and **Middle Temple Hall**).

The surviving church of **St Bartholomew-the-Great** (founded in 1123) and the names of **St Helen's Bishopsgate**, Spitalfields and St Martin le Grand, are all reminders of these early monasteries and convents. The Friars, who were active social workers among the poor and destitute living outside the City walls, were known by the colour of their habits: the Blackfriars (Dominicans), the Whitefriars (Carmelites) and the Greyfriars (Franciscans). Their names are still found in the area around Fleet Street and the west of the City.

PRINTING AND PUBLISHING

Towards the end of the fifteenth century, literacy was on the increase among the better off citizens. This was greatly advanced by the setting up of the first printing press by William Caxton in 1476, at Westminster. After Caxton's death, his apprentice Wynkyn de Worde set up his press near St Bride's Church in Fleet Street, which became the focus of the printing and publishing trade for several hundred years.

Tudors & Stuarts

It was a time of peace and war, of circumnavigation and people losing their heads – and ultimately it was a time of fire.

Charles I – *beheaded on 30 January 1649.*

During the reign of the Tudor monarchs (1485 to 1603), with the discovery of America and the ocean routes to Africa and the Orient, London became one of Europe's largest cities. Henry VII brought to an end the Wars of the Roses by defeating Richard III at the Battle of Bosworth, and marrying Elizabeth of York. The resulting Tudor rose can be seen in many of the Tudor palaces. Henry VII's greatest achievements were in establishing peace, building a merchant navy and building the Henry VII Chapel in **Westminster Abbey** as a resting place for himself and his queen. He was succeeded in 1509.

HENRY VIII

Henry's notoriety stems from the fact that he had six wives and beheaded two of them, but his 38-year reign brought profound changes, including the Reformation of the Church and the establishment of the Royal Navy. Born in Greenwich, Henry became king at the age of 18, and was immensely popular in the first years of his reign: well educated, strong, handsome, and an accomplished horseman and archer. His marriage in the same year to his widowed sister-in-law, Catherine of Aragon, forged a diplomatic link with Spain. Of their six children, only Mary survived; Henry longed for a male heir. The turning-point came in 1527, when he determined that his 18-year marriage to Catherine should be annulled, so he could marry Anne Boleyn; his efforts were frustrated by the Pope. Defying the Catholic church, Henry demanded that he himself be recognised as Supreme Head of the Church in England and ordered the execution of anyone who refused to accept this (including his Chancellor Sir Thomas More). The Dissolution of the Monasteries transformed the face of the medieval city with the confiscation of all property owned by the Catholic Church: priories, hospitals, chapels, gold plate, furniture and all church estates were seized by the king, or sold off to courtiers.

Henry married Anne Boleyn, who gave birth to Elizabeth; less than three years later she was executed for infidelity. He then married Jane Seymour (who died in childbirth, leaving a son, Edward), followed by Anne of Cleves (from whom he was divorced), Catherine Howard (who suffered the same fate as Anne Boleyn), and finally Catherine Parr, who survived him. (A mnemonic: divorced, beheaded, died; divorced, beheaded, survived.)

In supporting Spain against France, Henry developed a professional navy, founding the royal dockyards at Woolwich in 1512 and Deptford a year later. He established palaces at **Hampton Court** and Whitehall (having seized both from his disgraced chancellor, Thomas Wolsey), and built a new residence at **St James's Palace**. Much of the land he annexed for hunting has now become the Royal Parks, including **Hyde Park**, **Regent's Park**, **Greenwich Park** and **Richmond Park**.

BLOODY MARY

Henry was succeeded in 1547 by his frail young son, Edward VI, who died six years later at the age of 16. During his reign, the Reformation continued apace and Protestantism was imposed on the kingdom. In parts of England, there had been strong

The Great Fire of London

In 1664-65, at least 70,000 Londoners died in the Great Plague, the worst epidemic to strike the capital. Those who could left the City; the King and his Court moved to Oxford; the plague pits were overflowing and businesses went under.

The following year, the City was struck by a second disaster, not this time in loss of life but in the destruction of the City itself. On the night of 2 September 1666 (almost exactly six hundred years since the day of the Norman conquest), the Great Fire of London started in a baker's shop on Pudding Lane. Fires were a frequent occurrence in London and, when roused from his bed, the Lord Mayor, Sir Thomas Bludworth, is reported to have dismissed the danger with the remark 'A woman might piss it out', words he most certainly lived to regret. An unusually strong east wind fanned the flames and before long neighbouring houses and riverside warehouses, packed with tar and other combustibles, were ablaze.

In the narrow City streets, the only action that could save a fire from spreading was to create a gap by pulling down buildings, but the Lord Mayor failed to act in time. It was only when the king's brother James took charge that the blaze began to be checked. Even so, the fire raged for three days, sweeping west to destroy **Guildhall**, the **Royal Exchange** and **St Paul's Cathedral**, together with almost all that remained of medieval London. The estimated loss was 13,200 houses, 87 churches and 44 Livery Halls. Astonishingly, only eight people are reported to have lost their lives.

These unlucky eight aside, perhaps the greatest loss of all was of the irreplaceable books, pictures and manuscripts which had been hurriedly carried to the crypt and Chapel of St Faith's below **St Paul's** for safety. In the fierce heat of the blaze, the leaden roof of the Cathedral crashed down and the burning floor caved in, destroying everything below.

An eye-witness account of the Fire by Samuel Pepys can be seen and heard at the **Museum of London**. In the short term, it was an unmitigated disaster for the City: thousands were left homeless, businesses were destroyed and the cost of rebuilding was enormous. But in the long term, it paved the way for a new, healthier city, in which outbreaks of plague were rare. The Fire marked the end of medieval London: a new era had begun (*see chapter* **Architecture**).

The Great Fire of London, *Stadler (1799)*.

---

resistance to religious change; most Londoners, however, seem to have been in sympathy with the new religion. The brief Catholic revival under Queen Mary (1553-58), and her marriage to Philip II of Spain, met with much opposition in the capital and over 300 Protestants were brutally persecuted and burned at the stake at Smithfield, after which the queen was known as 'Bloody Mary'.

THE ELIZABETHAN AGE

Elizabeth I came to the throne in 1558, and her 45-year reign is looked upon as a 'golden age'. The founding of the Exchange by Sir Thomas Gresham in 1567 (given the title **Royal Exchange** by the Queen in 1570) gave London its first trading centre. London emerged as Europe's leading commercial and financial centre. The merchant venturers and the first joint-stock companies (the Russia Company and the Levant Company) established new trading

enterprises, and British explorers Drake, Ralegh and Hawkins sailed to the New World and beyond. In 1580, the Queen travelled to Deptford to knight Sir Francis Drake on his return from a three-year circumnavigation. Eight years later, it was Drake and Howard who defeated the Spanish Armada.

As trade grew, so did London. By 1600 there were 200,000 people living here, many in dirty, overcrowded conditions, with plague and fire constant hazards. The most complete picture of Tudor London is in John Stow's *Survey of London* (1598), a fascinating first-hand account by a diligent Londoner whose monument stands in the City church of St Andrew Undershaft.

SHAKESPEARE'S BANKSIDE

The glory of the Elizabethan era was the development of English drama, popular with all social classes but treated with disdain by the Corporation

City Livery Companies

Since the Middle Ages, the government of the City of London has been in the hands of the Guilds or Livery Companies, so called because of the costumes (or 'liveries') which senior members are allowed to wear. The Livery Companies are descendants of the ancient Saxon 'frith guilds'. These mutual aid societies provided support in times of need, in return for a payment ('gild' or 'geld'). In medieval times, the guilds became associated with particular trades and crafts. Members grouped together to promote their trade and to regulate standards, the training of apprentices and pricing of their goods.

Membership of a trade or craft guild, gained by seven years' apprenticeship, was the only way to be granted 'freedom of the City', still a qualification for holding civic office ('freedom' can nowadays be bought, rather than earned). Non-freemen had no say in the government of the City; they could not keep a shop or exercise a craft or trade inside the City walls, and had to pay a fee to sell their goods at market. Apprentices had a terrible reputation, frequently running riot and attacking 'foreigners' (from other parts of Britain) or 'aliens' (anyone from abroad).

The Weavers' Guild was the first craft guild to purchase its royal charter in 1155. The first Livery Company to be incorporated was the Mercers' Company (traders in fine cloth) who received their charter in 1394. By 1423, over 100 Guilds and Livery Companies were registered, and the **Guildhall** (1411-22) became the meeting place for the Corporation's government.

By monopolising trade, the guilds prospered. They bought land and built imposing halls, furnished with gold and silver plate. In keeping with their charitable origins, they established schools, almshouses and other institutions for the benefit of their members and for the poor.

By the eighteenth century, the Livery Companies no longer dominated trade and many of the old crafts (such as the Longbowstring Makers) were defunct. Nevertheless, the Liveries continue to play a key role in the government of the City. Some Companies (such as the Goldsmiths and Fishmongers) still fulfil an active role in supervising their trades; others are more concerned with social and philanthropic activities; new companies are still being formed (the Information Technologists recently became the one hundredth Company), and only officers of the Livery Companies can take part in the election of the Sheriffs (24 June) and the Lord Mayor (29 September), both held at **Guildhall**.

*The splendid **Guildhall** (built 1411-22) became the venue for ceremonial occasions.*

of London, who banned theatres from the City in 1575. Two famous rival theatres, the Rose (1587) and the **Globe** (1599) were erected on the south bank of the Thames at Bankside. These wooden theatres had a large stage and open central area surrounded by tiers of galleries, and it was here that Marlowe and Shakespeare wrote their plays. As well as the theatre, bear- and bull-baiting, cockfighting, taverns and the 'Stewes' (or brothels) all provided diversion for the average citizen.

THE UNITED KINGDOM

Elizabeth I died in 1603 and the Tudor dynasty died with her. Her successor, the Stuart king James VI of Scotland, became James I of England and Scotland, creating the United Kingdom. On 5 November 1605, James escaped death when Guy Fawkes and his gunpowder were discovered hidden underneath the Palace of Westminster. The Gunpowder Plot was in protest at the failure to improve conditions for the persecuted Catholics. The date is commemorated as Bonfire Night.

It was James I who employed Inigo Jones to design court masques, and later new buildings, thus introducing the first classical Renaissance style to London (*see chapter* **Architecture**).

CIVIL WAR

Charles I succeeded his father in 1625, and fell out with both the City of London (from whose citizens he tried to extort taxes) and Parliament. The last straw came in 1642 when he intruded on the **Houses of Parliament** in an attempt to arrest five MPs who had fled to safety in the City. The

The **Royal Exchange** – *founded in 1567.*

result was Civil War (1642-49) between the Parliamentarians (representing landowners, under the Puritan Oliver Cromwell) and the Royalists. The Royalists were eventually defeated. Charles I was taken prisoner and tried in Westminster Hall for treason. He rejected the legitimacy of the court, refusing to plead. He was declared guilty and on 30 January 1649 was beheaded outside the **Banqueting House** in Whitehall. The equestrian statue of Charles I (1633), which stands on a traffic island at the top of Whitehall, was ordered to be destroyed by Cromwell's men, but was buried and re-erected after the Restoration of the Monarchy.

From 1649-60 after Charles's execution England became a Republic. During this period of Puritan rule, theatres were closed and church monuments destroyed. There was relief and rejoicing in May 1660, when the exiled Charles II was restored to the throne. Theatres re-opened, but the old conventions of the open-air Tudor playhouse came to an end with the introduction of Restoration drama. The new theatres were indoors, and actresses were admitted to the stage for the first time.

GLORIOUS REVOLUTION

After the Great Fire of 1666 (*see page 73*), former City residents moved to residential developments in the West End. In the City, the **Royal Exchange** was rebuilt, but merchants increasingly used the new coffee houses (such as Edward Lloyd's, later Lloyd's Insurance) for the exchange of news. With the expansion of the joint-stock companies and the chance to invest capital, the City was emerging as a financial, rather than a manufacturing, centre.

Anti-Catholic feeling still ran high, so the accession of the Catholic James II in 1685 aroused fears of a return to Catholicism, and led to the Dutch Protestant king William of Orange being invited to take the throne with his wife Mary Stuart (James's daughter). James fled to France in what became known as the Glorious Revolution of 1688.

The new Bill of Rights drawn up at this time defined the limitations of the sovereign's power, and the Act of Settlement (1701) barred Catholics (or anyone married to one) from taking the throne, establishing Britain as the first constitutional monarchy. One significant result of William's reign was the founding of the **Bank of England** in 1694, to finance the king's wars with France.

At the turn of the century, in 1700, the capital's population stood at 575,000. London was now the biggest city in western Europe.

The last of the Stuart line was Mary's sister Anne, in whose reign the Act of Union (1707) was signed, combining the parliaments of England and Scotland. Queen Anne died childless in 1714 (in spite of giving birth to 17 children, none of whom survived childhood). Her statue stands outside the West Front of **St Paul's Cathedral** which was completed during her reign, in 1710.

Georgian London

A German speaker on the throne, gin bottles littering Fleet Street slums, organised trips to mock the afflicted in Bedlam – London in the 1700s was crying out for change.

In accordance with the Act of Settlement (1701), after the death of Queen Anne the throne passed to George, the great-grandson of James I, who had been born and brought up in Hanover, Germany. Thus a German-speaking king (who never learned English) became the first of four Georges in the Hanoverian line. During his reign (1714-27), and for several years after, the Whig party (Liberals), led by Sir Robert Walpole, had the monopoly of power in Parliament; their opponents, the Tories, supported the Stuarts and had opposed the exclusion of the Catholic James II. Walpole chaired, on the king's behalf, a group of ministers (the forerunner of today's Cabinet) and thus became the first prime minister; he was also presented with 10 Downing Street as a residence, which became the permanent home of all prime ministers.

During the eighteenth century, London expanded with astonishing acceleration, both in population and built-up area. New squares and new streets of Georgian-style terraced houses (*see chapter* **Architecture**) spread over Bloomsbury, Soho, Mayfair and Marylebone as wealthy landowners and speculative developers took advantage of the demand for leasehold properties. Horse and carriage stabling, built behind the terraces, has become today's fashionable mews housing. South London became more accessible with the opening of the first new bridges – **Westminster Bridge** (1750) and **Blackfriars Bridge** (1763); until then, **London Bridge** had been the only bridge across the Thames. The old City gates, most of the Roman Wall and the remaining houses on old **London Bridge** were demolished, allowing easier access to the City for traffic and people.

In the older districts, however, people lived in terrible squalor and poverty, far worse than that of Victorian times. Some of the worst slums (overcrowded and filthy) were around Fleet Street and St Giles, only a stone's throw from streets of fashionable residences, maintained by large numbers of servants. To make matters worse, gin ('mother's ruin') was readily available at very low prices, and many poor Londoners drank excessive amounts in an attempt to escape from the horrors of daily life. The average per capita consumption of gin (children included) was estimated at two pints a week. This contributed to the appalling death rate: in the years 1725-50, three out of four children aged one to five died. In 1751, Parliament was forced to act, imposing duties which raised the price of gin so that the poor could no longer afford it.

Worse still, the well-off seemed completely complacent. They regularly amused themselves not only at the popular Vauxhall and Ranelagh Pleasure Gardens, but with organised trips to Bedlam (Bethlehem or Bethlem Hospital, *see page 78*) to mock the mental patients. Public executions at Tyburn (close to where Marble Arch now stands) were among the most popular events on the social calendar.

The outrageous imbalance in the distribution of wealth encouraged crime: robberies in the West End often took place in broad daylight. Reformers were few and far between, though there were some notable exceptions. Henry Fielding, the satirical writer and author of the picaresque novel *Tom Jones*, was also an enlightened magistrate at Bow Street Court. In 1751, he established, with his blind brother John, a volunteer force of 'thief-takers' to back up the often ineffective efforts of the parish constables and watchmen who were the only lawkeepers in the city. This group of early cops, known as the Bow Street Runners, were the forerunners of the present day Metropolitan Police (established in 1829).

Some attempt to alleviate the grosser ills of poverty was made by the establishment of five major new hospitals by private philanthropists. St Thomas' and St Bartholomew's had long been established as monastic institutions for the care of the sick, but Westminster (1720), Guy's (1725), St George's (1734), London (1740), and the Middlesex (1745) later became world-famous teaching hospitals. Thomas Coram's Foundling Hospital, for abandoned children, was also one of the remarkable achievements of the time (*see page 76*).

Not only did the indigenous population of London increase in the eighteenth century, but country people (who had lost their own land because of enclosures and were faced with starvation wages or unemployment) drifted into the towns in large numbers. The East End was increasingly the focus for poor immigrant labourers, especially towards the end of the eighteenth

William Hogarth

The painter and engraver William Hogarth (1697-1764), whose satirical works give us the most vivid picture of high life and low life in Georgian London, was a Londoner born and bred. The son of a teacher, he was born in Smithfield, baptised in the church of **St Bartholomew-the-Great**, and apprenticed to an engraver. He studied painting with Sir James Thornhill (whose paintings adorn the dome of **St Paul's Cathedral** and the Painted Hall at Greenwich) and became his son-in-law, after eloping with his daughter.

Hogarth's father, who taught classics, had the extraordinary idea of setting up a coffee house in which everyone had to speak Latin. Not surprisingly, the business failed and Hogarth senior was imprisoned for debt, leaving the young Hogarth with a hatred of poverty and injustice, which was powerfully conveyed in his work.

His favourite pursuit was painting, but his skill as an engraver allowed him to print and publish his own work, giving him a wider audience and more reliable income than painting alone. He took his inspiration entirely from the London characters and scenes which surrounded him, and developed pictures which he called 'modern moral subjects', using sequences of six or more pictures which together tell a story, pin-pointing human foibles, such as *A Rake's Progress* and *The Election*, a wry comment on the political corruption of the times (the original paintings for both of these series can be seen in **Sir John Soane's Museum**). *Industry and Idleness* contrasts the good and bad apprentice, and *Gin Lane* gives some idea of the desperate squalor to which most Londoners were reduced.

As a successful artist, Hogarth lived at 30 Leicester Square from 1733 till his death; he also owned a country cottage in Chiswick (*see*

Hogarth's **The Rake at the Rose Tavern**.

Hogarth's House). His wide circle of friends included Samuel Johnson and James Boswell, Handel, the actor David Garrick and younger artists Thomas Gainsborough and Joshua Reynolds, whom he persuaded to teach at the Artists' Academy in St Martin's Lane, where he had once studied and which he re-established in 1735 as a school of art (later to become part of the **Royal Academy of Art**).

He (and Handel) also befriended and supported Thomas Coram, a retired sea captain, who determined to relieve the shocking plight of London's abandoned children by raising money to build a Foundling Hospital. Hogarth gave paintings, and persuaded his friends to do the same; his large, splendid portrait of the kindly captain still hangs on the staircase at the Coram Foundation in Brunswick Square.

During his lifetime, Hogarth's paintings were less popular than his prints, though he is now accepted as the first of the great English painters. He died at Leicester Square in 1764, and is buried in Chiswick Cemetery.

---

century with the building of the docks. By 1801, when the first census was taken, London's population had grown to almost a million inhabitants, the largest in Europe, and by 1837 (when Queen Victoria came to the throne), five more bridges and the capital's first railway line (from London Bridge to Greenwich, 1836) were further signs of the expansion to follow.

THE GORDON RIOTS

This was the age of the London Mob, when a large band of protesters could gather at short notice. Riots were directed against middle-men charging too high prices, or merchants adulterating their food. In June 1780, London was hit by the Gordon Riots, the worst in its violent history. They started when Lord George Gordon, an MP and anti-Catholic agitator, led a crowd of 50,000 to Parliament with a petition against legislation which allowed Catholics to buy and inherit land. Gordon soon lost control of his mob which, apparently forgetting why it had assembled, spent the next five days looting and pillaging the capital. Newgate Prison was stormed, and thousands of inmates set free; a distillery was broken into; Downing Street and the **Bank of England** were unsuccessfully stormed. The riots were eventually suppressed with the loss of over 300 lives.

The Victorian Era

Darwin derailed the people's train of thought, but the construction of London's underground railway got them back on track.

Victorian London was a city of uncomfortable extremes. As well as being the administrative and financial capital of the British empire, spanning one fifth of the globe, London was also its chief port and the world's largest manufacturing centre, with breweries, distilleries, tanneries, shipyards, engineering works and many other grimy industries lining the south bank of the River. On the one hand, it boasted splendid buildings, fine shops, theatres and museums (*see chapter* **Architecture**); on the other, it was a city of squalor, poverty, disease and prostitution. The residential areas were becoming polarised into districts with fine terraces, maintained by squads of servants 'below stairs', and slums of unimaginable poverty.

The growth of the metropolis in the century before Victoria came to the throne had been spectacular enough but, during her reign, thousands more acres of land were covered with housing, roads and railway lines. London had not seen the like of it before and has not since. Today, pick any street at random within five miles (8 km) of central London, and chances are its houses will be mostly Victorian. By the end of the century, the population had swelled to over six million.

Despite the social problems, by the end of the century great steps had been taken to improve the conditions of life for the great majority of people. The worst slums had been replaced by low-cost building schemes, funded by philanthropists, such as the American George Peabody, or by the new London County Council.

PUBLIC TRANSPORT

One of the greatest influences of the Industrial Revolution on Victorian London was the introduction of the railway and eventually the underground network. By the 1860s, traffic congestion in the capital had reached a point where people were prepared to accept any schemes that relieved the situation. The railway companies spent enormous sums of money designing ostentatious train stations to impress the cynical public. Euston Station's classical portico (destroyed by British Rail in 1963 in order to expand the station) cost nearly £40,000, though it fronted some very unspectacular railway sheds and platforms.

In 1863, the first underground line, between Paddington and Farringdon Road, proved an instant success, attracting over 30,000 travellers

on the first day. The Metropolitan and Circle lines at Baker Street and Great Portland Street are examples of mid-Victorian stations. The world's first electric track in a deep tunnel (the 'tube'), opened in 1890 between the City and Stockwell (later part of the Northern Line), followed by the Central Line. It was an American, Charles Tyson Yerkes, who laid the foundations for the modern tube, with his plans for the Bakerloo, Piccadilly and Northern Lines, which were completed by 1907. Examples of the early trains are on view at the **Science Museum**. For a comprehensive view of Victorian travel, from horse-drawn buses and hackney carriages to the underground system, visit the **London Transport Museum**.

THE GREAT EXHIBITION

The Great Exhibition in **Hyde Park** in 1851 captured the spirit of the age: discovery and invention. Prince Albert, the Queen's Consort, was personally involved in the organisation of this triumphant event, for which the Crystal Palace, a giant building in iron and glass (designed not by a professional architect but by the Duke of Devonshire's talented gardener Joseph Paxton), was erected in **Hyde Park**. During the five months that it was open, the Exhibition drew an estimated six million visitors from all parts of Great Britain and abroad, and the profits made inspired the Prince Consort to establish a permanent centre for the study of the applied arts and sciences: the result is the South Kensington Museums (*see chapter* **Museums**) and Imperial College. After the Exhibition, the Crystal Palace was moved to Sydenham and used as exhibition centre until destroyed by fire in 1936.

Metropolitan *extension to Aldgate (1877).*

Bedlam

In the seventeenth and eighteenth centuries you took your entertainment where you found it, and many took it touring Bethlehem Royal Hospital (also known as Bethlem Royal Hospital and Bedlam). The experience was not unlike visiting a zoo, except that the creatures chained up in squalid cages were humans suffering from mental illness, at whom it was considered great sport for visitors to jeer and shout abuse. It wasn't until 1770 that patients' feelings were taken into consideration and whips were no longer used.

Bedlam first cared for 'distracted' patients in 1377. Methods of care included being chained to walls and ducking, and among the inmates were young women whose reason for committal was simply that they were unmarried mothers. In 1675-76 the asylum was moved from its site outside Bishopsgate to Robert Hooke's building in Moorfields. A new building in Lambeth became its home in 1815 and to this building a year later were added blocks for the criminally insane, whose numbers, 30 years later, were to include the artist Richard Dadd. (The Lambeth building now houses the **Imperial War Museum**.)

Dadd (1819-87) was a promising young artist who, in 1843, had a mental breakdown and murdered his father. During his 20 years' incarceration in Bedlam he painted some of his most striking work, characterised by an obsessive attention to detail. *Portait of a Young Man* (1853), *Bacchanalian Scene* (1862) and *The Fairy Feller's Master Stroke* (1855-64, pictured) date from this period and can be seen in the **Tate**. A number of Dadd's watercolours, along with extraordinary works by the Russian dancer Nijinsky and Jonathan Martin, the failed arson-

Dadd's **The Fairy Feller's Master Stroke.**

ist of York Minster, can be seen in the hospital's museum (*0181 777 6611 ext 4307*) at its new site in Monk Orchard Road, Beckenham, Kent.

In 1993 a patient on a day-pass rehabilitation scheme wandered out of the hospital grounds and into a bank where he attempted to carry out an armed robbery – with a banana. Earl Lewis told police he couldn't see what the problem was, since he had no money and the bank had plenty. It makes you wonder why Lewis, like so many before him, was ever sent to Bethlem in the first place.

When the Victorians were not colonising the world by brute strength, they had the foresight to combine their conquests with scientific developments. The Royal Geographical Society (RGS) sent navigators to chart unknown waters, botanists to bring back new species, and geologists to study the earth. Many of these specimens ended up in the **Royal Botanic Gardens** at Kew; others found a home in the South Kensington museums. The most influential RGS expedition was Charles Darwin's voyage to the Galapagos Islands on HMS *Beagle*. The very foundations of science and religion were rocked when the naturalist published his theory of evolution in *The Origin of Species*. Darwin's home (Downe House) can be visited at Orpington, Kent.

The Victorian age had more than its fair share of intellectuals and artists. Uppermost among the

writers and thinkers of the period was Charles Dickens, much of whose work was concerned with social injustice (*see chapter* **Further Reading**). The designer, socialist and poet William Morris was also moved to write about the terrible conditions suffered by the working class. His house in Walthamstow now holds a collection of his wallpaper and textile designs (see **William Morris Gallery**).

At the same time, Karl Marx used the British Museum Reading Room to write *Das Kapital*, the seminal work of left-wing economics and politics. The artist Richard Dadd, who was born in Chatham, Kent, close to London, spent much of Queen Victoria's reign detained at her pleasure, first in Bethlehem Royal Hospital or Bedlam (*see above*) and later in Broadmoor.

Two World Wars

The capital suffered massive losses in terms of human life and property in World Wars I and II. The world was changing – it, and London, would never be the same again.

The old world order broke up in the early part of the twentieth century. New thinking, new inventions, faster communications and modernist buildings all began to transform ways of living, but the biggest upheavals in the first half of the century were from the two World Wars. Britain fought in both. London did not suffer great damage in WWI (1914-18) but the conflict was far more costly in terms of British lives lost abroad. The impact of WWII (1939-45) is more obvious: Hitler's bombs did more to change the city than anything since the Great Fire. Londoners were in the front line and thousands died in their homes, at factories, in offices or in defence of the city.

The course of the wars is charted at the **Imperial War Museum**. The British Army's role is explained at the **National Army Museum**; the **Royal Air Force Museum** charts the history of the Royal Air Force (RAF), while the **Museum of London** and the Britain at War Experience show how wartime affected the lives of Londoners.

THE EDWARDIAN DECADE

During the brief reign of Edward VII (in his sixtieth year when he came to the throne, with a reputation for high life, amours and gambling), London regained some of the gaiety and glamour lacking in the last years of Victoria's reign. Fashion was more flamboyant; women pinned enormous hats to their hair and wore off-the-shoulder dresses. A touch of Paris came to London with the opening of the **Ritz Hotel** in Piccadilly. The **Café Royal** was favoured by the more Bohemian artists and writers; the first Lyons Teashops opened providing what they called 'luxury catering for the little man', and the first American-style department store, **Selfridges**, opened in Oxford Street in 1909.

Road transport was revolutionised. Motor cars put-putted around London's streets. The first motor bus was introduced in 1904, and by 1911 the use of horse-drawn buses had been abandoned. Electric trams (double-deckers) started running in 1901 (though not through the West End or the City) and continued until 1952. The **London Transport Museum** has models and genuine examples of all the public transport of the period.

To the Edwardians, mass entertainment meant a night out at the music hall, now known as 'variety theatres'. Audiences cheered and jeered at the songs and jokes of Max Miller and Marie Lloyd right into the 1930s when the variety shows fell victim to cinema, radio and eventually television.

WORLD WAR I (1914-18)

London suffered its first air-raids in WWI. The first bomb over the City was dropped from a Zeppelin near **Guildhall**, in September 1915, to be followed by many nightly raids. Bombing raids from planes began in July 1917. **Cleopatra's Needle**, on the Victoria Embankment, was one of the minor casualties, with damage to the plinth and one of its sphinxes, which can still be seen. In all, several hundred people lost their lives. The most devastating casualties of WWI were in northern France and Belgium, where the opposing armies dug themselves in and fought from trenches. Millions of men on both sides were killed in the conflict, or died of disease in the terrible conditions. The Trench Experience at the **Imperial War Museum** tries to recreate some of the horrors of trench warfare in Flanders (Belgium).

Following the carnage, people in virtually every British town and village erected war memorials, mourning the loss of a generation of young men such as the ordinary 'Tommy' (slang for a British soldier) at **Paddington Station**, unarmed and reading a letter from home. Perhaps the most poignant is the Tomb of the Unknown Warrior at **Westminster Abbey** commemorating the hundreds of thousands of WWI dead whose bodies could not be identified. The remains of an unidentified soldier were covered with French soil, and Belgian marble was used for the memorial stone. The national monument is the **Cenotaph** (by Edwin Lutyens) in Whitehall, which is where the annual Remembrance Day Service for the dead of both World Wars takes place every November.

THE 1920S AND 1930S

London's population increased dramatically in the years between the wars, reaching its peak at nearly 8.7 million in 1939. To accommodate the influx, the suburbs expanded outwards in all directions at an alarming rate, particularly to the north-west with the extension of the Metropolitan Line (an area known as Metroland).

The London County Council (based at County Hall on the South Bank) began to make a greater

Suffragette City

Until the nineteenth century, the right to vote was restricted to the land-owning gentry, but pressure for political change grew as the industrial revolution shifted economic power towards the new capitalist class of merchants and industrialists. In 1832, the first Reform Act (vehemently opposed in some quarters) had extended the franchise to all middle-class men (in business and the professions). The second Act, in 1867, allowed 'settled tenants' (workers in towns) to vote. Working-class men and women were excluded altogether.

The working-class men began to form movements, such as the Chartists, who demanded a charter of rights, including the right to vote. Towards the end of the nineteenth century, a brave group of women set out to fight for equal rights for women, against much opposition (from women as well as men).

The leading light in the women's cause was Emmeline Pankhurst (1858-1928), wife of a barrister and radical reformer, who founded the Women's Social and Political Union (WSPU) in

Emily Davison (left) on Derby Day 1913.

1903, supported by her daughters Christabel and Sylvia, and women from all over the country. Dubbed 'the Suffragettes' by the *Daily Mail*, they launched a paper *Votes for Women* and organised mass meetings, first in Manchester and later in London, at Caxton Hall and the **Royal Albert Hall**. In 1908, realising that constitutional methods were getting them nowhere, they began to resort to militant tactics, chaining themselves to the railings in Downing Street and smashing windows at Parliament and West End stores, which made headline news. At first they were treated reasonably chivalrously, but as time went on, the police attacks became more violent, rousing sympathy for the cause and embarrassing the government.

One of the most militant members of the WSPU was Emily Davison, an Oxford graduate. She was arrested several times and sent to Holloway prison, where she went on hunger strike and was forcibly fed. On Derby Day 1913, she became the first martyr for the cause when she tried to catch the reins of the King's horse, and was fatally injured. Thousands of women, dressed in white, formed a silent procession at her funeral.

In the following year, a Velazquez painting, *The Rokeby Venus*, was slashed in the **National Gallery** (the skilful repair can still just be seen), but with the onset of war, the Suffragettes stopped their militant activities and threw themselves into war work. In 1918, their efforts were partially rewarded when women over 30 (and all adult men) were given the vote. Ten years later, in 1928 (the year that Emmeline Pankhurst died), the vote was extended to all adult women.

impact on London life, undertaking programmes of slum clearance and new housing schemes, creating more parks and open spaces, and taking under its wing education, transport, hospitals and clinics, libraries and the fire service.

FASHIONS BETWEEN THE WARS

After the trauma of WWI, a 'live for today' attitude prevailed among the young upper classes in the 'roaring '20s'. The new fashion for women was the 'flapper', with her bobbed hair, skin-tight boyish shimmy dress and cloche hat. Flappers would gather in cocktail bars to swap comments about sex, Freud and jazz. For men, plus-fours and diamond-patterned sweaters were casual-chic and a tuxedo *de rigueur*. Evening and tea

dances were popular at the **Ritz** and the **Savoy**.

The new medium of film became immensely popular, and a night at the flicks was soon regular entertainment for all social classes. Cinema-going was turned into an event with the advent of the 1930s art deco picture palace. The **Odeon Leicester Square** retains its dramatic geometric black frontage and tower.

Radio also took off in a big way in the 1920s and '30s. Families gathered round enormous Bakelite wireless sets, decorated with stylised sunbursts, to hear the latest sounds from the British Broadcasting Company (BBC, from 1927 becoming the British Broadcasting Corporation). TV broadcasts started on 26 August 1936, when the first BBC telecast went out live from the Alexandra Palace studios in Alexandra Park. The **Museum of the**

Moving Image (MOMI) has a fund of material from the early days of film and television.

The styles of the period are well represented at the **Victoria & Albert Museum**, with an array of fashion in the Dress Collection, and furniture, sculpture and art deco frippery in the Twentieth Century Primary Galleries. At the **Geffrye Museum** a 1930s living room has been recreated, complete with three-piece suite, Bakelite wireless, tiled fireplace and other modest art deco features.

Oswald Mosley *and the BUF, October 1936.*

POLITICS BETWEEN THE WARS

Political change happened quickly after WWI. Lloyd George's government averted revolution in 1918-19 by promising (but not delivering) 'homes for heroes' for the embittered returning soldiers. But the Liberal Party's days in power were numbered. The Labour Party, which had gained its first seats in Parliament at the turn of the century, enjoyed rapid growth. By 1924, the party had enough MPs to form its first government, with Ramsay MacDonald as Prime Minister.

Civil disturbances, caused by rising unemployment and an increased cost of living, resulted in the 1926 General Strike, when the working classes downed tools in support of the miners. Prime minister Baldwin encouraged volunteers to take over the public services, and the streets were teeming with army-escorted food convoys, aristocrats running soup kitchens and students driving buses. After nine days of chaos, the strike was called off by the Trades Union Congress.

Unlike much of Europe, Britain never had a strong nationalist movement in the 1930s. Though Oswald Mosley's British Union of Fascists (BUF) had some powerful friends among industrialists and the ruling classes, his party never gained mass support. When, in 1936, Mosley tried to organise an anti-Jewish march through the East End, a crowd of 500,000 locals packed Cable Street, in Stepney, to prevent it. But as Hitler's Nazi party in Germany grew in strength during the 1930s, another world conflict looked increasingly likely. During the Munich Crisis of 1938 there was a mass evacuation of London's children to the countryside. On Prime Minister Neville Chamberlain's proclamation of 'Peace in Our Time', these preparations for war temporarily ceased. But the appeasement stopped with Hitler's invasion of Poland; Britain declared war on 3 September 1939.

WORLD WAR II (1939-45)

When war was declared, the government implemented precautionary measures against the threat of enemy air raids. Night-time blackout was enforced (causing an increase in serious road accidents), trench shelters were dug in London parks, and some 600,000 children and pregnant mothers were rapidly evacuated from the capital to country districts. German and Italian males (many of them shopkeepers, who had lived here for years) were interned in camps in remote areas. The capital's treasures were sent to secret shelters (paintings from the **National Gallery** were stored in the slate mines of north Wales), sandbags prepared and millions of gas-masks made ready. The Home Guard was prepared to fight an invasion.

To everyone's surprise, the expected bombing raids did not happen during the autumn and winter of 1939-40, and many of the evacuees drifted back to the capital. As the months drew on, this period became known as the 'Phoney War'. In the spring of 1940, as Britain still waited for a German attack, the 66-year-old Winston Churchill replaced Neville Chamberlain as Prime Minister of the wartime coalition government. By June 1940, the Germans had advanced through northern Europe. France had been overcome and the beleaguered British forces had had to be rescued from Dunkirk. The German army was 100 miles (160 km) from London. The threat of invasion was very real and London's defences sorely stretched.

BATTLE OF BRITAIN

In July 1940, the Germans began preparations for an invasion of Britain. For the next three months, battle was waged in the air over southern and eastern England. Luftwaffe bombers set out to destroy airfields, while smaller fighter planes took on the RAF. Although the RAF's fighter pilots were outnumbered, it was the Luftwaffe that suffered the heaviest casualties. On 31 October 1940, the Germans stopped this line of attack, and the Battle of Britain was officially over, prompting Churchill's famous remark: 'Never in the field of human conflict was so much owed by so many to so few'. Many of the planes which took part on both sides are on display in the **Royal Air Force Museum** and occasionally still fly at the **Imperial War Museum**'s Duxford Airfield near Cambridge.

The Blitz

The Phoney War came to an abrupt end at tea-time on 7 September 1940, a hot Saturday afternoon which brought the first wave of German bombers. Hundreds of aircraft dumped their load of high explosives on east London and the docks, and a second wave followed with another raid on the same night. Whole streets were left burning and the dead and injured numbered over 2,000. The Blitz had begun.

The raids on London continued for 57 consecutive nights, then intermittently for a further six months. As the air-raid sirens sounded and giant searchlights scoured the skies above the blackened city, thousands of Londoners poured underground into home-made or specially built communal shelters, or underground stations; thousands more simply stayed in their homes.

The emergency services were stretched to breaking point during the first few weeks, but with hastily organised teams of civilian volunteers they managed to save thousands of people who were buried in the wreckage of their homes. Londoners reacted with tremendous bravery and stoicism and the period is still nostalgically referred to as 'Britain's finest hour'. The firemen became the heroes of the Blitz.

The worst night for London was 29 December 1940, the Sunday after Christmas. Thousands of fire bombs rained down on the City and threatened another Great Fire of London. To make matters worse, a low tide meant that water could not be pumped from the Thames. A famous photograph shows **St Paul's** riding the flames like a great ship in a sea of fire, but in spite of the destruction all around, **St Paul's** survived because of a heroic band of volunteers (including the poet Louis MacNeice) known as 'Paul's

Watch', who spent their nights in the dome of the Cathedral ready to deal with fire-bombs.

Churchill's War Cabinet and Defence Committee planned the Allies' moves from an underground warren near Whitehall, known as the **Cabinet War Rooms**. Churchill's room was so spartan that he preferred to kip at the **Savoy**, which often suffered from bomb damage – but then nowhere in central London was safe. **Buckingham Palace, Westminster Abbey** and **St Paul's Cathedral** were all hit (though not seriously damaged). BBC Radio's **Broadcasting House** – a prime target because of its propaganda role – was painted grey to elude the bombers' sight. It was eventually hit on 15 October 1940; newscaster Bruce Belfrage continued to read the headlines.

After a final massive raid on 10 May 1941, the Germans focused their action elsewhere, but by the end of the War about a third of the City and the East End was in ruins.

Two Apprehensive Shelterers, Henry Moore.

D-DAY

From 1942 the tide of the war began to turn. De Gaulle and other members of the French government-in-exile were based in London, and met at the **French House** pub to coordinate the resistance. By 1944, the British-based Allies were preparing for the D-Day invasion of Normandy, which began on 6 June. The main support ship for the landings was the battle-scarred cruiser **HMS Belfast**, now moored on the Thames near **Tower Bridge**.

DOODLEBUGS

In 1944, the V1s, or Doodlebugs, began to strike London. Pilotless planes, their engines would shut down over the city: when the buzzing stopped, the bomb would fall. Dozens were sent over every day

through the summer, causing widespread destruction. In September 1944, the V2 rocket was launched. These ground-to-ground missiles flew silently, giving no warning of approach, and could destroy whole rows of houses. Over the winter, 500 V2s fell on London, mostly in the East End; the last one fell on 27 March 1945 in Orpington, Kent.

PEACE AT LAST

Victory in Europe (VE Day) was declared on 8 May 1945. Thousands of people took to the streets. At **Piccadilly Circus**, a sailor climbed on to **Eros**'s pedestal and draped himself in a Union Jack.

Every year, in the week before Remembrance Sunday, many people don red poppies. A national ceremony is held at the **Cenotaph** in Whitehall.

Post-War London

A Labour government introduced the National Health Service, London hosted the Olympics and the Festival of Britain, and a new monarch was crowned – we'd never had it so good.

World War II left Britain almost as shattered as Germany. Soon after VE Day, a general election was held and Churchill was heavily defeated by the Labour Party under Clement Attlee. People wanted a change. A better Britain, the politicians promised, would be built from the rubble.

In London, the most immediate problem was a critical shortage of housing. Pre-fabricated bungalows provided a temporary solution (though many were still occupied 40 years later), but the huge new high-rise housing estates which the planners began to build did not subsequently prove a success (*see chapter* **Architecture**).

The Labour government established the National Health Service (in 1948), and began a massive nationalisation programme (including public transport services, electricity, gas, postal and telephone services). But for all the planned changes, life was drab, regimented and austere.

In the midst of this austerity, London hosted the Olympic Games in 1948. Three years later, the Festival of Britain (exactly one hundred years after the Great Exhibition in **Hyde Park**), was an attempt to inject colour and life into the city. The fairs and exhibitions that took over derelict land on the South Bank for the Festival provided the incentive to build the **South Bank Centre**, now the largest arts centre in western Europe.

THE 1950S

'Let's be frank about it; most of our people have never had it so good,' proclaimed Prime Minister Harold Macmillan in 1957. And perhaps he was right: the Welfare State was in operation, unemployment was low, prosperity was growing. The coronation of Queen Elizabeth II in 1953 had been the biggest television broadcast in history and there was the feeling of a new age dawning.

The craze for consumer durables and labour-saving devices came via the US. Many were British-made, such as Belling fridges and New World cookers. The annual Ideal Home Exhibition displayed what people had to buy to 'keep up with the Joneses'. Many of these 1950s household goods can be seen at the **Design Museum**; the **Geffrye Museum** has an exhibition on life in the 1950s, with mock-ups of pre-fabs and council houses.

Fashion-conscious, youthful rebellion arrived in the 1950s with rock 'n' roll. Elvis Presley replaced

England's World Cup win at Wembley, 1966.

sentimental crooners, and working-class lads adopted gravity-defying quiffs and fashionable neo-Edwardian clothes to become Teddy Boys. Teenage girls copied the American high-school look: skimpy polka-dot dresses, pony-tails and bizarrely framed sunglasses. The Saturday night 'hop' became a teen institution. London's hippest district, Soho, was a centre for Bohemians, beatniks and jazz. By the mid-'50s, international attention focused on Soho's jazz clubs; world-renowned **Ronnie Scott's** dates from 1959.

THE 1960S

Liberation was the buzzword of the 'swinging '60s'. The decade started with the censorship trial of DH Lawrence's *Lady Chatterley's Lover*. Banned for 32 years as too erotic 'for your wife or servants to read', it sold two million copies in six weeks after Penguin was allowed to publish it. Feminism made some advances, though the contraceptive pill (1961) turned out to be a mixed blessing in the fight for women's rights. Another overdue easing of restrictions occurred when homosexuality was decriminalised in 1967.

Fashion achieved great importance in London, and innovative styles by Mary Quant and others broke the stranglehold of Paris on couture. Skinny models such as Jean Shrimpton ('the Shrimp') and Twiggy dominated the fashion magazines. Boutiques blossomed along the King's Road, and Biba set the pace in Kensington. Soho's Carnaby Street became the focus of 'Swinging London', the fashion and music capital of the world.

Pillorying the Establishment became one of the great occupations of the 1960s. The TV show *That Was The Week That Was* led the way in highlighting hypocrisy and cant in the British ruling classes. Even so, when Winston Churchill died on 24 January 1965, thousands queued for hours to file past his coffin lying in state in Westminster Hall, to pay their last respects.

From 1964, off-shore 'pirate radio' stations revolutionised the music scene. The most famous was Radio Caroline, which played hits considered too racy for the BBC's mainstream radio stations and *Top of the Pops* TV programme. Meanwhile, as the Beatles rocketed to fame, London's music scene exploded with bands such as The Who, Manfred Mann and the Rolling Stones playing at the Marquee (*see chapter* **Music: Rock, Folk & Jazz**) and other venues.

The year of student unrest throughout Europe, 1968, saw the first issue of *Time Out* (a fold-up sheet for 5p) appear on the streets in August. The decade ended with the Beatles naming their final album *Abbey Road* after their recording studios in London NW8, and the Rolling Stones playing a free gig in **Hyde Park** (July 1969) which drew half a million people.

THE 1970S

Many Londoners remember the 1970s as a decade of economic strife. Inflation, the oil crisis and international debt caused chaos in the British economy. During 1974, Britain was put on a three-day working week, and a miners' strike brought down the Conservative government. This was also the period when the IRA started its bombing campaign on mainland Britain.

Against this background of strife and disunity, several important social and economic changes took place: Britain's idiosyncratic currency was replaced on 15 February 1971 with a decimal system (replacing the old pounds, shillings and pence); the UK joined the European Community in 1973; and racial discrimination was outlawed, as were practices that discriminated against women in the workplace. However, after almost two decades, society still has a long way to go before these last two laws prove effective.

For years, people sneered at the 1970s, decade of the Bee Gees, flared trousers and soul singers with a lurv thang. Excess was the by-word of '70s fashion. Music veered between over-produced pap-pop and the anarchy of punk. The corridors of Kensington Market still cater for punk purists, and Vivienne Westwood, who started selling outlandish garments in a tiny boutique on the King's Road, continues to sell her uncompromising collection of clothing design (*see chapter* **Shopping**).

THE 1980S

History will regard the 1980s as the Thatcher era. When the Conservatives won the general election in 1979, Britain's first woman Prime Minister – the propagandist for 'market forces' and Little Englander morality – set out to expunge socialism and the influence of the 1960s and '70s. A monetarist policy and cuts in public services savagely exacerbated the divide between rich and poor. While the professionals and 'yuppies' (young urban professionals) profited from tax cuts and easy credit, unemployment soared. In London, riots erupted in Brixton in 1981 and Tottenham in 1985; mass unemployment and policing methods were seen as contributing factors.

The Greater London Council (GLC) mounted spirited opposition to the Thatcher government. This included lowering the price of tickets on the tube and buses. However, Thatcher responded by abolishing the GLC and, since 1986, London has been without an elected governing body. County Hall (opposite the **Houses of Parliament**) lies empty, bought by a Japanese property developer.

The eyes of Caligula and the lips of Monroe, according to President François Mitterrand.

Trafalgar Square was the focus for 1990's **Poll Tax riot** *– Thatcher's days were numbered.*

The deregulation of the stock exchange (the Big Bang) in 1986 opened the market to overseas members through international computerised trading. It was followed a year later by a resounding crash on London's money market, though the consumer boom continued unabated as the Porsche-driving yuppies made serious money and took their pick of the smart new properties in Docklands. However, the spectacular rise in house prices at the end of the 1980s (reaching a peak in August 1988) was followed soon after by an equally alarming slump and the onset of a severe recession in the economy.

One of the biggest success stories of the decade was the growth of **Camden Market**, which continues to draw thousands of visitors at weekends. On the other hand, the Docklands development (one of the Thatcher enterprise schemes, set up in 1981, for creating a new business centre in the partly derelict docklands east of the City) has been hampered by the Government's over-reliance on market forces, and refusal to fund much-needed transport links.

THE 1990S

At the beginning of the 1990s, there was an upsurge of hope in London. The Berlin Wall had crumbled and (of more immediate relief to most Londoners) so too had Thatcher's leadership. A riot in **Trafalgar Square** had helped to see off both Margaret and her inequitable Poll Tax; in October 1990, she was replaced as leader of the Conservative Party by John Major.

Yet just as the 1990s got underway, Britain's economy slumped into its worst recession since the 1930s. In London, the yuppy accessory businesses of the 1980s have been among the worst hit: designer boutiques and restaurants have closed by the score. Much of the office space in Docklands remains empty; the owners of the **Canary Wharf** development went into receivership; it was bought and is now struggling to become viable. To cap it all, the British people, in an extraordinary act of masochism, voted in yet another Conservative government (the fourth in succession) in 1992. Shortly after the election, a massive IRA bomb in the City killed three people and obliterated the Baltic Exchange; after a second bomb, a year later, which shattered buildings around Bishopsgate, the City closed many of its streets to incoming traffic and manned the entrances with armed police.

But all is not gloom. The recession has meant that bargain shops and traditional street markets are thriving. And after overdosing on style in the 1980s, London's myriad restaurants are now concentrating on giving good value.

London Today

It may be a noisy, dirty, mess crying out for its own elected government, but London is still a major player on the world stage.

It used to be disasters like large fires and the Blitz which set off great waves of redevelopment and alteration in London. But now, during one of the most politically stable and disaster-free periods in its two millennia of history, the city is changing faster than ever before.

This is not unique to London; as the flow of information and new technology accelerates around the world, change is becoming the universal constant. But spend some time in London, or visit the city at two-year intervals, and you will see change on a bewildering and sometimes breathtaking scale. It ranges from the trivial (telephone booths seem to be redesigned every few months) to the colossal (enormous new office complexes where once there were docks and cargo ships).

Yet London does offer some powerful constants. It entered this century as Europe's largest and most important city and it will exit it with the same

*The **BT Tower** – enduring symbol of London.*

status – not the loveliest, not the most cultured, but indisputably the continent's biggest and most crucial. It is a capital of superlatives, with the world's busiest international airport, Europe's busiest stretch of motorway (the westernmost section of the M25), the greatest centre of international bank lending.

Its dominance of British national life – provincials might call it a stranglehold – remains unshaken; in fact, it's growing. Of course, London is top dog in politics and finance, but it also shows no sign of relinquishing pole position in the arts, heritage, the media and advertising, publishing, football, cuisine, fashion, shopping. With 12 per cent of the nation's population, it accounts for 20 per cent of UK Gross Domestic Product.

So there are things to hold on to in the seething sea of change that is London. But beware of one false conviction, firmly held by many Londoners and passed on to visitors – that theirs is a shrinking and increasingly inferior capital.

True, London's population did fall sharply in the decades after World War II and now stands at just under seven million. But it is now growing again, and the Government's population experts are forecasting a rise of nearly 10 per cent over the next 30 years. This increase will be partly homegrown, but immigration, mainly from Europe, will be the other key component. London will become a still more cosmopolitan city.

As for the inferiority complex… that's understandable. Britain has seen its international importance and relative wealth decline since ending World War II as the globe's third most powerful nation. The capital feels caught up in this shrinkage. The monarchy, very much a London-based outfit, has abruptly shed all its mystery and symbolism as the Queen ages and her children behave all too humanly. Londoners are always being told about or travelling to cities that seem superior because they have sunny beaches nearby, or more modern public transport, or more exciting new museums, public spaces and buildings.

There are plenty of things for Londoners to be ashamed of. Chief of these must be the widening gap between rich and poor and the appearance of beggars on streets and in the Underground. The tourists don't see the worst of it; the many bleak inner city and suburban estates where unemployment and fragmented families are rife and the

*The **Broadgate** development by Liverpool Street Station – modern architecture at its best.*

main sources of income are crime, drug-dealing and state benefits. We've still a long way to fall before we reach the depths of alienation and deprivation found in Washington and Detroit but, all the same, it's clear that prosperous London has turned its back on a dangerously high proportion of its poorer, less able citizens.

Then there is the lack of governance, planning and coherence. London, Europe's greatest capital, is the only one without an elected authority in overall charge of the city's strategic planning. Public sector services are run by central Government and 33 locally elected and highly disparate borough councils. Quarrels are frequent and debilitating. The overwhelming power of central government and the relatively low status of the boroughs has allowed corruption to raise its ugly head in a few councils run by both left- and right-wing administrations.

Postwar development has left London in a discordant mess. Skyscraper construction has been discouraged apart from in a few areas, most noticeably the City of London, and where it has happened it is unimpressive. Seen from a middle distance vantage point such as Tower Bridge, the City looks like the downtown of a second division US city.

While there relatively few skyscrapers, there are plenty of modern buildings which are bulky and high enough to oppress and diminish the many, tall, beautiful and elegant creations of earlier centuries – the Wren and Hawksmoor churches, St Paul's Cathedral, the Monument to the Great Fire.

London has some superb modern architecture and development; the great, concrete arts complex along the South Bank of the Thames, Broadgate next to Liverpool Street Station, even Canary Wharf on the Isle of Dogs has its own vulgar, yuppie magnificence. But so many handsome and historic buildings are spoilt by being surrounded by polluted air, indifferent or ugly new buildings and roads packed with snarling, deafening traffic.

Which brings us to another of London's great shames – its transport arrangement. Half of all journeys made inside the capital involve private cars, with unpleasant and dangerous levels of noise, pollution and congestion the result. Average driving speeds throughout the capital are 15 miles per hour (24 kmph), 2 mph slower than they were 25 years ago.

It's almost certainly going to get worse. For while the volume of traffic continues to rise, the Government has scaled back its road-building ambitions. It now talks about discouraging driving by using measures such as reducing the amount of car parking space in the centre. The hope is that drivers will transfer to a public transport system which has the highest fares in Europe. But public transport, in the shape of elderly or undermaintained diesel-powered taxis and buses, is part of the problem – they are to blame for much of the environmental damage in the heart of London.

Obvious ills such as these feed the widespread conviction that London is a capital in decline, and make one wonder why ten million overseas visitors bother to come each year. But it isn't in decline – not at all. In fact, developments in public transport are among several reasons for optimism. The system may be grubby and expensive, but it works. The rolling stock of the Underground and overground trains is being gradually renewed, while the biggest boom in track laying for decades is underway. The Jubilee Line is being extended for miles eastward; in the west, Heathrow Airport is at last getting a high-speed rail link to central London; and down south, a tramway is being planned for Croydon. More exciting, romantic and significant than any of these is the new express rail service to Paris and Brussels through the Channel Tunnel. It's worth going to Waterloo Station just to see the gleaming, sinuous giant train shed and the sleek blue and yellow Eurostar beasts which whisk you into Europe. There you see the beginning of a new travelling era.

Another great London strength is its greenery. One sixth of its area consists of parks, woods, farms, playing fields and vegetable plots – considerably more than most other major western cities. Add to that Londoners' beloved private gardens and the broad green belt which surrounds the city and prevents its further sprawl, and you have a remarkably verdant metropolis.

The city is also starting to deal with its huge quantity of waste within its borders rather than exporting it. Millions of tonnes of sewage sludge will soon be burnt in new incinerators instead of being dumped in the North Sea. Ever larger quantities of household garbage are also being incinerated instead of being carried to landfill dumps miles outside of London. The heat from burning both of these copious waste streams is used to generate electricity.

With the ceasefires in Northern Ireland the terrorist threat seems to be retreating in London while it advances in cities overseas. The capital's social and cultural places, its museums, theatres, bars and restaurants, are manifestly thriving despite economic uncertainty.

For London doesn't make much any more and it worries about how it will pay its way in the world and whether it can find work for its citizens. A dozen years ago one fifth of London jobs were in manufacturing; now the proportion is just over one tenth. Today and in the future its most important wealth-creating activities will be to trade in insurance and finance, to generate business ideas and to provide services to multinationals. London is a good place for these things; it has been doing them for centuries, it speaks English, the international business language, and it is conveniently positioned halfway between the time zones of North America and the eastern Pacific. Foreign companies have purchased many of the key British players in these areas.

Until quite recently, London's identity used to lie in being the capital of one of the world's most important countries. Today Britain matters less, but London has kept its place and its identity as one of the top five world cities – confused, messy, rich, colourful and ever changing.

London by Area

Central London

Cartographers identify the centre point as Trafalgar Square, the London Psychogeographical Association locates the omphalos in the Isle of Dogs, but the metropolitan heart beats wherever you can feel it.

London doesn't possess a main street. If you cross Oxford Street or Piccadilly, you can't really say that you've traversed the busiest thoroughfare with the most attractions, commercial or otherwise, in the capital. Instead, London has many different 'centres' around which significant buildings and streets revolve. That this hub of metropolis contains a number of centres is one of the reasons why central London is such a major tourist attraction and entertainment hotspot. Come rush hour though, the appeal fades quickly: the day can't be too far off when all of us have to carry around our own personal oxygen tank to combat the fumes. But if you're here in the evening, enjoy it – there is an awful lot to see and do.

Covent Garden

In Covent Garden, streets King and Henrietta face each other, separated by the Market building. Built around 1630, the roads are named after Charles I and his queen: this romantic air blankets Covent Garden; you are likely to see many couples holding hands around the various stalls and street shows that give the area its vitality. All through the week, jugglers, escape artists and mimics parade the pedestrianised area in front of **St Paul's Church**, often pulling large audiences, though the markets are open throughout the week. There are plenty of cafés to sample and the stalls are original and varied, offering unusual jewellery, toys and prints.

It has not always been an attractive little retreat from the combined horrors of Shaftesbury Avenue, Long Acre and the Strand. As long ago as the 1530s, medieval monks used the area to grow vegetables (it was known as Convent Gardens back then, belonging to **Westminster Abbey**) and enjoyed a lively market ambience from the late 1600s until, by the eighteenth century, the area took a bit of a nosedive and was soon populated by a nefarious breed of pimps and prostitutes. As recently as 1974, Covent Garden was in a mess, the market having moved to Nine Elms, south of the River. The now defunct Greater London Council wanted to tear the place down and replace it with office blocks. Protests mounted by local residents saved old Covent Garden. It has since managed to grab a little Continental charm for itself.

Despite the glut of markets, the best shopping is to be found in the smaller surrounding streets. Check out Neal Street, Shorts Gardens, Floral Street and the quaint Seven Dials which acts as a centre point to a number of small avenues (*see chapter* **Shopping & Services**). Beware the traffic; ludicrously, this tiny roundabout is open to drivers. All of these roads contain attractive shops and your capacity for window-shopping or mooching through goods on shelves will doubtless expand. Neal's Yard courtyard, in Shorts Gardens, especially, is a pleasure to visit as here you will find a health food shop, various vegetarian cafés, the superb Neal's Yard Dairy, which stocks dozens of cheeses, and the herbalist shop, famed for its natural medicines and massage oils.

Covent Garden also has a reputation for its theatre (it is no coincidence that **St Paul's Church** is known as 'the actors' church') and it is well served by the **Royal Opera House**, an internationally acclaimed centre for the art despite rising seat prices and accusations that its programme is elitist and obscure. One of its major aims is to put on a mammoth series of Verdi's works, leading up to the centenary of his death in 2001.

Covent Garden is one of those places that is busy morning, noon and night, serving a working public as well as the usual tourist influx.

Soho

Soho was called by its exotic name as early as 1636 and became an area of rapid development after 1685, when the Edict of Nantes was revoked and droves of French Protestant refugees peopled the houses springing up on Soho's streets. Growth was so acute that a royal proclamation condemned the buildings as eyesores which 'do choak up the air of His Majesty's palaces and parks'. Conditions are still hectic today and Buck House has remained conspicuously quiet. Soho is one of the busiest areas of central London, yet it has no tube station. It is served by the four underground stops which define its shape: Tottenham Court Road, Leicester Square, Piccadilly Circus, and Oxford Circus.

Though Soho Square sounds like the natural epicentre of Soho life, it is in fact popular only on sunny lunchtimes when office workers sit out to eat their sandwiches or doze on its turf. Not so back in the late seventeenth century, when it was known as King Square and contained a statue of the sovereign (which is still there) along with a fountain representing the Thames, Severn, Humber and Trent – seen as the four main rivers in England.

Over the years, many different ethnic types have settled in the area and introduced a diverse cuisine: much of London eats here as a precursor to a night out or as an alternative to going home after work. Chinatown is the most famous manifestation of gastronomic invasion, covering the area between Leicester Square and Shaftesbury Avenue (its heart is found, roughly, in Gerrard Street). Scores of Chinese restaurants line the backstreets, popular at all times of the day, especially lunchtime when dim sum dishes are on offer (*see* chapter **Restaurants**), or in the evenings either side of a visit to the major cinemas in Leicester Square (*see* chapter **Film**). These aren't the only cinemas to be found but the others are more in keeping with the seamier side of Soho, the Soho associated with prostitution and pornography which found a home here in the 1970s and stayed.

Westminster

A tour of London would not be complete without a stop at Westminster. In the summer months, the crowds around **Westminster Abbey** and the **Houses of Parliament** stand testament to this.

Perhaps the most remarkable of London's buildings, a genuine feat of architectural achievement, the **Houses of Parliament** are the centre of political thought in this country. It's a pity such beauty is wasted on a bunch of boorish, incompetent louts. The Palace of Westminster, as it is also known, is an imposing feature nestling against the bank of the Thames where it has stood, in one manifestation or another, since medieval times.

It is interesting to conceive of Westminster as a city in its own right. It was granted that status by royal charter on 29 October 1900, yet its standing in the years leading up to that date was less than befitting a municipality. The area around **Westminster Abbey** was shabby and thief-ridden,

Java Jive

Christopher Hemblade on Soho's 24-hour coffee culture.

It's become a truism that the cultural engine of the metropolis is Soho and coffee is its fuel. Where and how you drink your beverage defines who you are as much as the clothes you wear, the way you walk, who you are with, or what you say. The brand of mocha you consume can make the difference between being a labelled a player or a tourist.

And in Soho, you can drink it from one dawn to the next.

Nonchalantly sip a cup of strong ristretto from Aroma in Dean Street at 11-ish and fellow gazers will know you're rushing from one production meeting to an editing session; make that a fast food chain instead and they'll know you'll be back in Bournemouth before sunset. Huddle conspiratorially over an espresso at lunchtime in the Living Room, Bateman Street, or take a caffè latte from Caffe Nero in Frith Street and everyone will know you're a stylist sorting out the logistics of a Soho Square fashion shoot. During the afternoon, intellectuals devour Camus while draining cups in Patisserie Valerie, Old Compton Street, or Maison Bertaux in Frith Street. If you're caught grabbing a filter coffee (studded with coffee beans) in Freedom, Wardour Street, in the early evening, passers-by will foist the 'gay beau monde and their friends' tag upon you. Ditto with the Old Compton Café in Old Compton Street. As the night moves on, Bar Italia (open 24 hours) on Frith Street becomes host to the well-dressed club fraternity.

In Soho a coffee, more than bottled beer or even a Bill Amberg clutch bag, is treated as a fashion accessory. In reality, you don't have to *drink* your coffee to be a Soho habitué – being *seen* with it is what counts.

Manette Street

'We passed into Greek Street under the archway that was to become our favourite entrance to the area because it was like a border-post, the crossing-point where obligations could be left behind. We turned left. Robinson talked about how hard it was to find any remains of the shivering, naked heart of the city that Soho had once been: the countless creaking, winding stairs, leading to poky rooms, the ascendant lured up by whatever clumsy enticement was offered by the crudely hand-lettered card stuck next to the downstairs bell. On that first evening we collided with a man ducking out after his swift transaction upstairs, already moving at street speed as he came through the door.'

From *Robinson* (Jonathan Cape 1993, Vintage 1994) by Christopher Petit.

probably because of the Abbey's reputation as a sanctuary for criminals. The Abbey itself has not escaped the ravages of time, having undergone external repairs and renovations so frequently that its age can only be gauged by inspecting the ornate interior in which a sense of ceremony pervades: this is where British monarchs have been both invested and buried. Many visitors come for a view of Poets' Corner, which contains few bones but plenty of memorials: to William Shakespeare, Jane Austen and Charles Dickens, to name but three. Oscar Wilde has recently been taken into the Westminster hall of fame after years of prevarication over his gross indecency committal.

Among the many governmental offices scattered around Westminster, Downing Street can be found close to the **Cenotaph** on Whitehall, although large black gates (introduced by Margaret Thatcher) protect the Premier at Number 10 (prime ministers have used this residence since 1735) and his Chancellor at Number 11 from the lumpen proletariat, although they didn't prevent a mortar bomb attack by IRA terrorists in 1991 which caused plenty of damage but no injuries.

Whitehall itself is worthy of a look, a broad avenue lined with statues, including General Montgomery and Francis Drake, which connects Parliament Square to **Trafalgar Square**.

St James's

Shirts from **Turnbull & Asser**, cashmere from Lord's, luxury food from **Fortnum & Mason**. You're in St James's – gentlemen's London – where modish business types and aristocrats sip pre- and post-prandial drinks in sophisticated (some would say anachronistic) clubs.

The **Ritz** is a benchmark by which opulence can be measured. Treat yourself to tea here but make sure you've saved up and booked in advance. Such extravagance seems a long way from the hospital that once existed on the site of **St James's Palace** 'for fourteen maidens that were leprous' which Henry VIII saw fit to shift when he took a liking to the vicinity and claimed it for himself. Nowadays, the ambience is much more seductive and reaches to **St James's Park**, surely one of the best-kept and most elegant stretches of greensward in the capital. **Buckingham Palace** can be viewed from here by a stretch of water buoying swans and ducks in abundance. Squirrels inhabit the park too and have lost any of their timidity but beware their sharp claws and teeth if you fancy sharing a bag of nuts with them – a tetanus jab would be advisable if you get attacked.

If you suffer from hay fever or have had your fill of London's parks, try the hushed web of streets around Pall Mall, where gentlemen's clubs, such as the Atheneum and the Reform Club, try to stay the passage of time. Or the **ICA**, on The Mall (for another luxuriant view of **Buckingham Palace**), which stages many controversial performances in the arts of dance, film and theatre.

Mayfair – *separates Soho from Hyde Park.*

Bloomsbury

Bloomsbury evolved in the West End during the reign of Charles II. At the time, it was deemed too far away from Whitehall to be fashionable but its houses were coveted for their splendid views of Hampstead. This, of course, was long before the current phalanx of buildings blotted out the greenery beyond London's hub, yet now the area is renowned as one of the most peaceful districts of the capital – despite its panoramic paucity. Bloomsbury Square, with its Georgian terraces, is still a delight, as are squares Queen and Russell which are open to the public and provide a leafy retreat from fuming Tottenham Court Road.

Although most famous for its Bloomsbury Group, that rarefied clique with a monopoly on blue plaques throughout the area, including Virginia Woolf, EM Forster and TS Eliot, it should not be forgotten that the **British Museum, University College Hospital** and **University of London** and are based here. The University's headquarters occupies the stunning Senate House (1933, *see chapter* **Architecture**) on Malet Street.

The **British Museum** is well worth investing a day of your time for a decent exploration of its

The Brain of London

Jonathan Coe dissects the enduring appeal of Bloomsbury.

I can still remember the rush of excitement when I first penetrated the inner sanctum of the British Museum Reading Room: that vast, airy, resonant dome, lined with unthinkable numbers of books, their spines bronzed and glittering, and at its centre, coiled spirals of shelving containing the immense catalogues bound in hundreds of hardback folios. In Smithfield Market I had found London's stomach; travelling on the tube, I had explored its veins and criss-crossed arteries; but upon entering the Reading Room, I knew at once that I had found the nerve centre of the whole operation. This was the brain of London.

In a few years' time, the place will have been cleared, and its shifting population of students, international scholars and malodorous drop-outs re-located to the new building at King's Cross. So see it while you can: visitors are admitted daily. Getting a reader's ticket is a different matter. I arrived in London about nine years ago armed with a sheaf of what I took to be impeccable academic references, but it took weeks of persistent wheedling and persuasion before I got one of those treasured laminated passes in my hand. As soon as that happened, Bloomsbury became my unofficial second home.

At the time I was living in Bermondsey, claiming the dole and paying a princely £9 a week rent on my shared council flat. To cross the river by Waterloo Bridge every morning on the Number 1 bus, get off outside Foyle's and walk up Great Russell Street to the gates

of the British Museum was to be granted entry into a different world. And all for the price of a weekly Travelcard.

Like most provincial boys coming to live in London for the first time, I didn't exactly have the feeling of being smothered by a welcoming embrace. I remember one of my first visits to Bloomsbury, when it was bitterly cold and I was huddled up in a scruffy old overcoat recently bequeathed to me by my great uncle. A red-faced businessman in a camel hair coat passed me in the street and, seeing that I was about to ask him a question, he shook his head and shoved a self-protecting hand in my face. He thought I'd been about to ask him for money. In fact I'd been going to ask him the way to Dillons in Gower Street. I resolved to smarten myself up.

It was Russell Square that helped me settle into London. Sitting in its central circle, on one of the west-facing benches (all the east-facing ones have, bizarrely, been removed), you can see the BT Tower, the dome of the British Museum Reading Room and the tower of the University Library, and get a strong and exhilarating sense of the all-encompassing capital city.

But what I really like about Russell Square is the tacky little café in the corner, serving hot dogs and thin-crust pizza and big cups of brown soupy tea. Ever since I found it, it has felt like a little bit of the provinces, put there expressly to reassure all those, like me, for whom London can never be more than an adopted home.

labyrinthine walkways. Just shy of a hundred galleries, its floor space is crammed with ancient treasures and artefacts from all over the globe, many nabbed 'in the name of the Crown' by explorers in the eighteenth century. Highlights include the Elgin Marbles, the Rosetta Stone, the Magna Carta and Lindow Man, the remarkably well-preserved corpse of a first-century male, preserved in a Cheshire peat marsh until his discovery in 1984.

The farce of the British Library and its new St Pancras site has been an embarrassment to the Government since its budget went ballistic and the deadline for completion was missed (it is now four years late). Eighteen million volumes have yet to be transported to their new destination and, every year, copies of all publications, from books to newspapers to maps, are added to this figure.

Clerkenwell

A monk by the name of Fitz-Stephen was much taken by Clerkenwell's freshwater springs (it was probable that the area's name arose from the use of what was known as the clerk's fountain or well) back in medieval times. Perhaps it was this natural charity that affected him – a gift from the Earth. It was a gift that was to replicate itself during the Great Fire, when evacuees took to the lush meadows of Clerkenwell.

Now, Clerkenwell is a hotch-potch of intimate lanes and thundering carriageways. At the time of writing, it appears in a state of flux. For every building in fine fettle, there seem to be two or three shrouded in construction netting or framed by scaffolds. The fresh water springs are no longer in evidence; traffic is the only free-flowing form. That and the demolition ball. The junction of roads Farringdon and Clerkenwell is abuzz with JCBs.

Clerkenwell is an odd borderland between central and east London. It has the centre's congested mazes and east's sense of sprawl. The Barbican's residential towers, crenellated basilisks, watch over you as you meander through streets broad and narrow. Like this one, say: Leather Lane, noted for its market, which is a denuded affair and worth visiting only to hear vendors speaking in tongues. The clothes are cheap but they look cheap. At the end of the lane, you hit Clerkenwell Road and a pub called the Duke Of York. You can't miss it: fire-engine red, it shows up the rest of the thoroughfare like an ember in a bed of ashes.

Turn left on to Farringdon Road and you soon reach the home of the *Guardian* (No 119), perhaps this country's finest newspaper – certainly since the *Independent* was gobbled up by the Mirror Group and production standards faltered. Further along, the **Eagle** provides a palatable stop-off for lunch and a glass of wine but more basic fare can be found at Al's Café Bar at Exmouth Market. Breakfasts as well as the usual bap-snacks are

recommended. The long haul back to King's Cross via Gray's Inn Road is leavened somewhat by the sheer, glittering mass at number 200 where, among others, ITN and Reuters are based. There are many sandwich bars and café-cum-bars for the immediate working populace during lunchtimes; these gradually peter out as you shade into the shabby tributaries which become the Euston Road.

Scarlet Tracings

'Gull took Hinton by the elbow and drove him, the shortest course, down the central aisle of the great meat cathedral of Smithfield, under the sign of Absalom & Tribe Ltd, under the hooks and lanterns, through the beach of blooded sawdust.

'This night place; herds arriving, muffled in darkness, dressed for the table by morning; thick scent of fat clings to the clothes, buckets of dark ornaments, black and purple, glistening pebbles of skin. The animal inside-out. They walk into the stomach of an upended cow; they are lost in its iron ribs, milk turned by terror into acid.'

From *White Chappell, Scarlet Tracings* (Goldmark 1987, Paladin 1988, Vintage 1995) by Iain Sinclair.

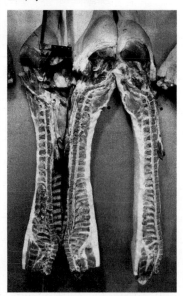

The City

The City, London's oldest quarter and lynchpin of the British economy, dies at the weekend. At such times, you should avoid it like the plague. Shops close, the streets are deserted; the entire effect is not unlike being stranded in a scene from *Batman*: Gothic buildings lurch out at you in among the cool, pristine architecture of the modern age (10 Fleet Lane looks like the nightmare mutation of a Rolodex and a filing cabinet) and the hush is utterly unexpected when you consider that, during the week, this famous square mile channels over a quarter of million people every day through its streets. Finding a lunch spot is a Herculean task.

As well as being the country's financial sector, the City contains some of the most arresting buildings London has to offer, including **St Paul's Cathedral** – one of around 50 churches dotting the area. This is just a third of the original number; the Reformation, the Great Fire of London in 1666 and the Blitz (1940) destroyed many places of worship.

You'll notice, as you trawl the City streets, how narrow and enclosed the main thoroughfares seem. It is one of London's best kept districts: the streets are comparatively litter free and there are a number of green zones which blend in nicely with the ancient arches and courtyards.

At the time of the Great Fire, the City was famous for its principal market on Cheapside (so called not for its bargains but because 'cheap' is a modernisation of the Old English word 'ceap' meaning 'barter'). Many of the attendant avenues were named after the goods located there: Pudding Lane (where the fire was started), Milk Street and Bread Street among others. Now, that sense of trade has survived writ large: the City is one of the most powerful players on the global market, highlighted by the enormity of 1992's sterling collapse, for ever consigned to the record books as 'Black Monday'. Places to spot are the **Bank of England** (the Old Lady of Threadneedle Street), the splendid **Lloyd's** building on Lime Street and the **Royal Exchange** on Cornhill. Smell the wealth.

The fire began in Farriner's Bakery, Pudding Lane at 1am on Sunday 2 September 1666. The **Monument** (the world's tallest free-standing column of stone) commemorates this disaster but a more visceral record can be found in Pepys' diaries: '... and all over the Thames, with one's face in the wind, you were almost burned by a shower of fire drops...' The fire raged until Wednesday. Five-sixths of the city was wiped out and eventually 13,000 destroyed houses were replaced by 9,000 new buildings, shaping the more spacious capital we know today (*see chapters* **Architecture** *and* **Tudors & Stuarts**).

Finsbury Circus – *on the edge of the City.*

Until recently, the nation's newspapers were to be found in the City's Fleet Street, world-famous HQ for hacks until the exodus to **Canary Wharf**. The *Daily Telegraph* still has a ghost to signify its place in Fleet Street: its name can be made out in its former building, evoking an earlier, romantic age of hot metal. Legal Britain has its base here too, the imposing structure of the **Royal Courts of Justice** a constant on television news.

Primarily though, the City is known for its business. If the 1980s were about pockets being lined with silver, the 1990s were their antithesis, the recession hitting as hard as the IRA bomb that destroyed the Baltic Exchange and the thirteenth-century St Ethelburga's church.

You could spend hours wandering these knotted avenues and, without a guide, it proves a daunting task. But you can't go wrong because there are many fascinating buildings to visit, from **Dr Johnson's House** (tucked away in a maze of backstreets at 17 Gough Square) to **St Paul's** itself or any of the churches which pop up with the frequency of London buses. Take time to visit one of London's finest pubs, **Ye Olde Cheshire Cheese**. Dr Johnson drank here, as did Pepys and Charles Dickens; it has retained much of the snug, jovial atmosphere that they must have enjoyed. (For further information on the City's churches *see chapters* **Sightseeing** *and* **Architecture**.)

West London

Its riches do not belong to the Duke of Westminster and the Belgravia squares, but to anyone who has ever walked across Albert Bridge, wandered through Holland Park or leaned into the Westway's curves.

Like a stately old grandmother looking down fondly upon her wayward offspring, west London is maturity and grace in equal measure. From the pale, likable terraces of Maida Vale to the attenuated atmosphere of Knightsbridge and Chelsea, you can't help feeling as though you've discovered a different place altogether – fewer postcard views but dozens of strange avenues and galleries in surroundings that could come from foreign lands.

Knightsbridge & Belgravia

Knightsbridge is synonymous with classy shopping and sumptuous residential pockets. Gaining its fashionable position was largely due to the pull of museums in South Kensington during the middle stages of the last century which gave the area a reputation for elegance and sobriety. If you're in this neck of the woods, chances are it's because of **Harrods**, a store that has matched the pace of our changing times without losing its grandeur. You'll find assistants, coaches and horses, even nannies, decked out in old-fashioned uniforms. Watch out for nearby shops that have cottoned on to Harrods' successful monopoly and produced their own subtle variations on that famous green and gold livery. This kind of thing has prompted action from the mother and father of all department stores in the past. Witness the débâcle when the Harrodian school in Barnes was jumped by the store in an attempt to stop it using the name. The case was thrown out of court and Harrods ordered to pay £130,000 costs. The embarrassment factor was doubled when bailiffs came to seize goods after the store dragged its feet over settling the bill.

Many of the smaller shops along Brompton Road and its attendant avenues are no less exclusive. If you're on the look out for an item of understated jewellery for your loved one, don't bother checking for prices – you won't find any, probably because the tags can't fit that many noughts on. Come to that, you won't find any understated jewellery either. A number of arcades vie with the boutiques: close to Knightsbridge tube are Knights Arcade and Brompton Arcade. Bargains are few, but for those deeply into the religion of shopping, Knightsbridge is as a Mecca for fat wallets.

If you're unlucky, you might bump into Princess Diana having a mooch down Beauchamp Place, her favourite haunt when she's got some pocket money. Packed with bijou boutiques, antique shops, signs and awnings, it recalls a more uncomplicated time; indeed, carry on into Walton Street and it's as though you've left the country altogether, stepping instead into a quiet, pretty lane where the walls are bright with colour, flowers and plants – the experience is almost Mediterranean. Check out the galleries along this street, chief among them the Durini Gallery which specialises in Latin American art and, at the time of writing, featured a stunning exhibition by Miguel A D'Arienzo. Many of the backstreets provide similar opportunities to escape the bustle. Discover bucolic squares and gardens – Cadogan Square,

Albert Bridge – *joins Battersea to Chelsea.*

Montparnasse, SW10

Alan Ross on the Fulham Road and environs.

I first came to South Kensington in 1949 and have never left it. Next to us in South Terrace was the actor Robert Newton who, often drunk, threw furniture out of the window and sometimes his wife. Opposite was Admiral Ingleby-Mackenzie who, on returning home from the Admiralty, exercised naked, my small step-daughter mistaking him for a polar bear. A few yards away the painter Matthew Smith, unassuming and quiet as a mouse, filled his studio with paintings of the most voluptuous models, landscapes and still lifes, transforming his part of Thurloe Square into something resembling Tahiti or the South of France.

I acquired an office for my magazine and publishing firm in Thurloe Place, opposite where the architects Casson and Conder practised, at work then on the handsome Ismaili Centre which now adorns the triangular site opposite the V&A. I used to eat at Jamshid, where Howard Marks the Oxford-educated drug smuggler and I were often the only customers. Now there is the excellent Kwality Tandoori, run by the Assam-born Mashud Khan, and next door Piccola Venezia, scene of congenial office lunchings attended by both famous and obscure writers. The area used to be a Polish enclave, inhabited by Polish emigrés, all reputed to be ex-generals or cabinet ministers. The owner of the tiny Polish restaurant where we ate succumbed to the demon drink, but Daquise, where the vodka and the strawberry tarts were more appetising than the food, survives.

Between the 1950s and the early 1980s the Fulham Road was a fairly featureless stretch notable mostly for the Queen Elms pub, the ABC cinema, the Chelsea football ground, and on the horizon Craven Cottage, home of Fulham FC, the only team with a river frontage, the sails of boats visible from the stands. Some great players performed in modest company.

In the last ten years or so the atmosphere has become more Montparnasse than old Fulham, with pavement cafés, brasseries, boutiques cheek by jowl as far as Putney and the River. Restaurants of every nationality – Italian, Chinese, Thai, Indian, Greek – exude national aromas within a hundred yards of each other. There are several art galleries in Park Walk and a famous painter, RB Kitaj, resident in Elm Park Road. Bookshops, with local stars Anita Brookner and Laurie Lee in nearby Elm Park Gardens, are open until late. You can see 11 different films within a five-minute walk if you are so minded.

There is still an agreeable, slightly knockabout feel to the Fulham Road, an occasional wino swaying about, a few frail patients from the Marsden taking the air, Chelsea supporters on Saturdays putting a brave face on the inevitable.

There is no shortage of garden squares and trees, of churches of every denomination, their elegant spires pointing inquisitively as dogs' noses into the sky. There are fewer Poles about, but in their place more Italians, French, Japanese, Indians. Sometimes you hardly hear a word of English, a relief on occasion. What is curious in an area so rich in high-class eating places and clothes shops is that you can no longer buy a fish or a button. But you can learn judo, tai-chi, play squash, swim, or go quietly to hell in your own sweet way. There is always the River, never far away, to take your pleasure by or jump into.

Egerton Gardens and Lennox Gardens – lush with vegetation and reeking with wealth; even the pigeons are of a better class.

At the junction with Sloane Avenue you'll see the splendid **Conran Shop** and, alongside it, the **Bibendum** oyster bar on Fulham Road housed in the attractive and spacious Michelin building.

Back towards Knightsbridge tube, you'll find **Harvey Nichols** (six floors of fashion and fine food), the jazzy Hyde Park Hotel and, next door,

Marco Pierre White's **The Restaurant** (get that definitive article). But don't fret, there are other, more modest eateries around: try Richoux opposite **Harrods**. Established in 1909, this attractive café offers all kinds of snacks and meals. Further along Brompton Road is a more modest tea room, **Patisserie Valerie**, offering a range of pastries and sandwiches with brisk, no-nonsense service.

Sloane Street offers more high-class couture, which peters out as you pass the Cadogan Hotel (the site of Oscar Wilde's arrest for gross indecency) and approach its bottom end, where Sloane Square offers you passage south-west to Chelsea via the King's Road, or north-east to Belgravia.

'Aristocratic' describes Belgravia, the clutch of land enclosed by Sloane Street, Knightsbridge, Grosvenor Place and Victoria. Property is stunning, both in terms of its stuccoed presence and asking price. Belgrave Square sits slap bang in the centre, an august place filled with embassies and fair quivering with importance. Yet in 1800, the area was nothing but fields; its development has been fast and recent, to rival equally flash Mayfair.

Kensington & Holland Park

If King William hadn't been asthmatic, chances are **Kensington Palace** wouldn't have been built and royals from the 1600s to the present (Princess Margaret is a current incumbent) wouldn't call this (another) home. Kensington High Street is another of London's primary shopping routes, full of the usual chainstore suspects but saved from dull homogeneity by Barkers, the department store, and fashion shops trying to be a little bit different.

Away from the mêlée, Kensington has pleasant, soporific avenues with eighteenth-century houses and lazy pubs. William Thackeray died at No 2 Palace Green (otherwise known as Millionaires' Row) which is now headquarters for the Israeli Embassy. Kensington Church Street, which takes you to Notting Hill Gate, is filled with interesting antique shops; off it lie a number of curious, quiet lanes which will reward exploration.

Kensington Gardens are a major enticement. Separated from **Hyde Park** by the Serpentine, they possess a more ordered, august character than their neighbour, though there's a statue of Peter Pan which proves popular with children and helps keep the Gardens just this side of stuffy.

Holland Walk would appear to be the man-made border between Kensington and equally desirable Holland Park, though many would agree that the latter falls under the aegis of the former, a small area with a glut of quite beautiful houses. **Holland Park** itself flaunts an open-air theatre which can seat up to 600 for plays and dance performances during the summer. There's a café, a Japanese garden and the odd peacock or two; the Park has a reputation as a gay trysting place. The **Belvedere** restaurant affords a delightful view of the Dutch Garden in which rhododendrons, azaleas and roses and dahlias riot during the hotter months.

Notting Hill

The Lonely Londoners, Sam Sevlon's pathos-ridden account of West Indians immigrating to London in the 1950s, is a brilliant introduction to one of the most colourful and interesting areas of west London. When the Western Islands folk turned up at Waterloo in a cold, alien country where ill-feeling was rife (due to the belief that they were here to steal jobs destined for the English) they brought with them their irrepressible love of music and dance. Bouts of insecurity and homesickness would be kept away by the introduction of a carnival, which has grown to become the largest street party in Europe, taking place over the August Bank Holiday weekend.

These days, although it has become an institution not beyond the threat of prohibition, the carnival sucks frightening numbers of people through the streets and avenues amid a clamour of steel bands, reggae and jungle. Excellent food is on offer and a dazzling array of floats peopled by extravagantly dressed, outrageously made-up exhibitionists. Part of the route includes Portobello Road, a world-famous glut of market stalls and antique shops stretching from Pembridge Road to north of the Westway (*see chapter* **Shopping: Markets**).

To those who love it, Notting Hill boasts many of the city's most fashionable restaurants and drop-dead trendy bars (**Beach Blanket Babylon** springs to mind on both counts), and some of the grandest architecture, often restored to its original, pristine white splendour. The detractors of W11 see the area as overpriced, self-consciously stylish and full of 'beautiful people' who like to

Holland Park roundabout – *the barometer.*

Way-out Westway

Will Self goes 'chnk-chnk-chnk'.

I come over all emotional when I think about the Westway. Really, I do. I can remember its completion in 1970 and my first 'grown-up' ride on it a few years later. High, on the pillion of a moped, caroming across all four lanes in the heat of a summer night. It was so shockingly Futuristic, an embodiment of all the science fictions I had ever read. A road sweeping across the city's Cubist scape; clean, shiny, slicing by block after block in elegantly plotted curve after curve. Then tantalising with a final rollercoaster plunge over the Marylebone flyover, before depositing you, dazed by the hubbub after the cool heights, in the bebop beat of central London.

Perhaps such eulogising seems excessive. I think not. The fundamental experience of driving the Westway remains the same today. On each occasion it never fails to work its magic. Especially when I come on at the White City junction and am driving on automatic, registering nothing but the subconscious 'chnk-chnk-chnk' of tyres over the deck sections of the flyover, only to come to when the road narrows at Paddington Green, and appreciate yet again the perfect movie-poster image that the windscreen provides as I swoop by the British Rail maintenance depot and commence my descent.

The flyover tends to have had a bad cultural press. Films of recent years, such as *Breaking Glass* and *Sammy and Rosie Get Laid*, have set scenes of riot and urban alienation under the grim lips of its jutting deck. One of the few entries the flyover makes into popular song is, predictably enough, in the Clash's 'London Calling'.

If you head west towards Latimer Road you enter an area where, despite the presence of workshops and a large children's daycare centre, the monumental presence of the flyover seems to have leached the life out of the adjacent streets, leaving behind boarded-up buildings, burnt matresses, zigzag graffiti, the detritus of urban decay.

Carrying on towards White City, the decks above divide to form the massive dilator of the elevated roundabout. It is here that, from below, the Westway is at its most visually spectacular. The sky is sliced into a series of curving wedges by the aerial carriageways. They form a basketry in the air that is at one and the same time free-floating and unbearably heavy.

think of themselves as bohemian (**Beach Blanket Babylon** again). But the area's reputation as a drug heaven and gathering point for drop-outs, as portrayed in Hanif Kureishi's *London Kills Me*, is largely inaccurate.

Chelsea

When you think of Chelsea, you think of its nonconformist past, coloured with iconoclasts; the cutting edge of artistic endeavour in the beatnik boom of the 1960s and '70s. But there is another side to it, possessing a quieter, more understated air, of Chelsea pensioners (conspicuous in red uniforms) and the ghosts of fictional spies (James Bond and George Smiley had apartments here). West of Sloane Square, the area is reached by the King's Road, a thoroughfare that became prominent for

its fashion two decades ago, thanks to the explosion of punk, but was established back in Stuart times when it was one of three private roads out of the capital used by royalty. Today, there are a number of antique shops, restaurants and cafés dotted around, as well as a farmer's market and trendy clothes stores including World's End which exhibits, amongst others, garments by arch-maverick Vivienne Westwood. This is the area infamous for its Sloane Rangers who cropped up in the money-mad 1980s, recognisable by their Range Rovers and Barbour jackets, partners of the braces and stripy shirts brigade who made a killing in the City before the slump.

Chelsea has a history of accommodating writers and painters, and Cheyne Walk, parallel to the Thames, is probably its most famous street in this respect. Dante Gabriel Rosetti the pre-Raphaelite painter lived at No 16 with a number of peacocks that were reputed to nettle the neighbours with early-morning cries. George Eliot lived at No 4 until her death in 1880; sea enthusiast JMW Turner worked on canvases at No 119 and Ian Fleming spent a while at Carlyle Mansions, which also sheltered Henry James and TS Eliot. Each of these houses has a view of the splendid **Albert Bridge** and you can look across to **Battersea Park** and the disused Battersea Power Station.

Other ports of call include the **Chelsea Physic Garden** on Royal Hospital Road where rock and herb gardens were designed and nurtured in an attempt to measure their restorative properties in medicine. Further along the same road lies the Royal Hospital itself, famous for being home to the Chelsea Pensioners, but also for providing a roof for any number of war veterans since the days of Charles II. A good view of the hospital can be had from **Ranelagh Gardens**, where the Chelsea Flower Show turns the air to perfume every summer. Next door, the **National Army Museum** gives an overview of the last 500 years, leading up to a grisly exhibition of Gulf War trophies.

South Kensington & Earl's Court

London's museum quarter begins here (*see chapter* **Museums**). The **Victoria & Albert** is at the western end of Brompton Road where it branches into Cromwell Road. A grand, imposing building, it was Prince Albert's attempt to crystallise the ethos of research and achievement in Arts and Sciences inspired by the Great Exhibition of 1851, which generated enough money to finance his project (and went towards constructing other major London museums). Since its erection at the turn of the century, it has proved to be a valuable asset to designers, artists and academics, boasting as it does an eclectic range of collections from many different eras, culminating recently in the securing of Antonio Canova's *The Three Graces*.

Down Cromwell Road, the **Natural History Museum** has escaped its dinosaur image of the past by introducing, amongst other things, dinosaurs. Except that these are life-size robotic replicas with moving parts, not the fusty old mountains of bone that usually typify such places of scholarly interest. The old Diplodocus, however, is still around to greet you upon entry. You can trawl galleries with evocative names such as the Blue Whale gallery, Creepy-Crawlies gallery or Ecology gallery to explore the various quirks of geology and biology.

Behind the neo-Gothic bulk of the **Natural History Museum**, the **Science Museum** on Exhibition Road is a must for any frustrated inventor. Packed with gadgets and interactive displays, the museum is a favourite with children of all ages and provides an extensive smorgasbord of scientific disciplines to choose from.

Famed for its museums, South Kensington is also a desirable residential area. Past tenants have included Winston Churchill (28 Hyde Park Gate) and John F Kennedy, when his father was US Ambassador to Britain in the late 1930s (14 Princes Gate). Also worth a visit are the darkly fascinating **Brompton Oratory** in Thurloe Place and, north of the museums, the **Royal Albert Hall** on Kensington Gore, a memorial to Victoria's consort and home of the Proms. Duck into any of the avenues that criss-cross this area and you'll be rewarded with a number of cafés, restaurants and shops.

By 1851, as London's development was gathering pace, Earl's Court – just down the Brompton Road from South Ken – was little more than a few linked farms. Recently, of course, Earl's Court has garnered a reputation for its busy, cosmopolitan atmosphere and is famous for its two immense exhibition halls, Earl's Court and Olympia, which house various major events such as the Ideal Home Exhibition and various motor shows. Bizarrely, Australians are a feature here more than most: you'll find them back-packing through the area or taking advantage of the reasonably priced hotels.

Mother London

'Kensal Green Cemetery came again into view, this time on the far side of the canal, looking like a magical forest. On his left the great gasholders towered, a vast abandoned fortress, and in their shadow was a high yew hedge hiding what he supposed must be some municipal construction, perhaps a relay station. He strode over an elaborately baroque cast-iron footbridge above a narrow basin in which was moored a single old-fashioned wooden rowing-boat, heavily varnished. Having crossed the bridge he stopped to salute from his side of the water a love that never was, the departed vessel which had carried all his dreams.'

From *Mother London* (Secker & Warburg 1988, Penguin 1989) by Michael Moorcock.

South London

Not even Korea has a north-south divide quite like London's, but when you get under the surface south of the River, you wonder why the north's had the upper hand for so long.

In a sense, there's no such thing as 'London'. The metropolis as we know it only came about in the last century, as scores of previously unrelated settlements, miles from the City of London, swelled and met to form a vaguely homogeneous whole – the 'twenty thousand streets under the sky' of Patrick Hamilton's 1930s London trilogy.

South London – that is, London south-of-the-River – betrays its hybrid origins at every turn. Watery pasture at Richmond and Barnes; rough common land with still recognisable villages at Clapham and Wimbledon; brooding warehouses at Bermondsey and Rotherhithe; breezy open spaces at Blackheath and Greenwich.

It would take the proverbial month of Sundays to visit the whole of south London, but the areas described below contain most of the highlights. If you're pressed for time, the 53 bus provides an excellent, no-frills tour, starting in central London (Oxford Street, Regent Street, Trafalgar Square), crossing the river at **Westminster Bridge** and trundling its way via the Old Kent Road, Shooters Hill and Blackheath to Woolwich. Unlike on tourist buses, you'll be surrounded by real Londoners; since they're English, you'll be under no obligation to speak to them.

Wimbledon

The soft 'puck' of tennis balls… Dan Maskell murmuring 'A superb backhand volley'… distant applause… there's something intrinsically English and permanently late-summer-afternoon about Wimbledon – for two weeks of the year anyway.

The rest of the time, the place is left to its own devices. Wimbledon Broadway is dominated by the Centre Court shopping centre, which has spread to adjoining municipal buildings such as the fire station and town hall. Wimbledon Theatre is an entertaining example of Edwardian architecture at its most feverish (the designer clearly didn't know when to stop when he reached the dome). It specialises in musicals and comedies; the adjoining Wimbledon Studio is a shade more literary. This end of the Broadway is well supplied with restaurants, as is Wimbledon Village, at the top of the formidably steep Wimbledon Hill Road. Beyond is Wimbledon Common – bigger, more woody

and certainly more horsey than, say, Clapham Common, and with a working windmill (built 1817) as a focal point. On the east side of the Common, a disused gravel pit now forms an idyllic lake and reed-beds, whose peace and quiet is barely disturbed by the murmur of traffic on Wimbledon Parkside. Crossing Parkside, a walk through south London suburbia (all pre-war villas and new Rovers at rest) brings you to the gates of the **All England Lawn Tennis Club** and the **Wimbledon Lawn Tennis Museum**. Wimbledon Park has public tennis courts and a large boating lake.

Kew & Richmond

Kew is, of course, best known for its **Royal Botanic Gardens** (also known as Kew Gardens), opened in the eighteenth century and still the world's principal botanical research centre. The quiet cul de sac outside Kew Station contains two good hostelries: the Flower and Firkin pub, whose conservatory backs on to the railway platform, offers free newspapers and has music at weekends. The Hothouse Café/Bar (9 Station Parade; open daily) has an airy, arty atmosphere (pictures for sale on the walls) and offers a wide-ranging selection of teas, coffees and beers – and a formidable all-day breakfast. The **Maids of Honour** teashop has a fabulous variety of home-made cakes and pastries. The World Tree (Station Parade) is a treasure trove of fossils, crystals and carved mammoth ivory, with friendly, knowledgeable staff. If you're heading for Kew Gardens, go via Kew Green, with its cricket ground surrounded by pubs and, in a corner, long, low, elegant St Anne's Church, built for Queen Anne in 1714. Its interior, with fine stained glass, is superbly clear and bright.

Richmond still looks much like what it once was: a busy, cramped English country town. Until the early sixteenth century the whole area was called Sheen, receiving its new name when Henry VII acquired the local manor house and called it after his earldom in Yorkshire (the surrounding area is still called North and East Sheen). Elizabeth I spent her last few summers at Richmond and died there in 1603, but Richmond Palace was allowed to fall into neglect. All that remains of it today is a gateway on Richmond Green, bearing the arms of Henry VII, and Old Palace Yard beyond. Richmond Green is less appealing than Kew Green, though it's enlivened at one end by the twin-cupola'd Richmond Theatre. The church of St Mary Magdalene in (where else but) Paradise Road is worth a look, if only for its hectic combination of architectural styles, dating from 1507-1904.

But Richmond is a place for enjoying the great outdoors. **Richmond Park** is, with the exception of Epping Forest, the last vestige of the great oak forests that surrounded London until medieval times. In 1727, the poet James Thomson exclaimed of Richmond Hill: 'Heavens! What a goodly prospect spreads around, of hills and dales, and woods, and lawns and spires and glittering towns and gilded streams'. The view has changed little, except that the glittering towns have merged to form a glittering city. Near the top of Richmond Hill, the Terrace Gardens descend steeply towards the river (there's a café halfway down). If the river isn't flooding, you can follow its meandering course towards Petersham and Ham and hail a ferry to row you across near Eel Pie Island. Alternatively you can hire a rowing boat or take a pleasure craft from Richmond Bridge. Flooding apart, the Thames is at its most tranquil here and, in the early morning and evening, Petersham Meadows are almost impossibly pastoral – brown cattle grazing on water meadows beside the misty river.

Battersea Power Station – *standing empty.*

In Saxon times Battersea was a small settlement known as Batrices Ege (Badric's Island), bounded by the Thames to the north and marshes to the south. Known for centuries as an area of market gardening (part of it is still called Lavender Hill), the character of Battersea changed dramatically with the Industrial Revolution. In the nineteenth century scores of factories sprang up, and the area was covered by a dense network of railway lines.

Battersea is still best approached by rail. The journey from Victoria gives the finest view of its best-known landmark, the gargantuan Battersea Power Station (1929-33). Closed in 1983, the building faces an uncertain future after a developer who had hoped to turn it into a theme park ran out of cash, leaving the central section partly demolished.

Battersea Park has a bloody history: in 1671 Colonel Blood hid in reeds near what is now the boating lake, waiting to shoot King Charles II as he bathed (his nerve failed him), and in 1829 the Duke of Wellington fought a pistol duel with Lord Winchilsea, who had accused him of treason for introducing the Catholic Emancipation Bill. Since 1985, the riverside front of the park has been dominated by a Peace Pagoda, complete with four huge golden Buddhas, built to commemorate Hiroshima Day. From here you get a good view of the River and of Chelsea on the opposite bank.

Battersea has long been a favourite spot of artists and writers: the old **Battersea Bridge** was the subject of Whistler's moody *Nocturnes*; Turner used to paint the River and its sunsets from **St Mary's Battersea**; more recently, Shane MacGowan and the Pogues celebrated **Battersea Bridge**'s next door neighbour in 'Misty Morning, Albert Bridge'. A raised walkway, overlooking river beaches and moored barges, takes you from **Albert Bridge** to **Battersea Bridge**, and from there it's a bus ride or longish walk to the thoroughfares of Lavender Hill, Battersea Rise and Northcote Road. Battersea Rise is a slightly arty stretch of road, with a good selection of restaurants. Northcote Road is dotted with a mix of local shops and Italian restaurants, as well as a lively fruit-and-vegetable market. At the bottom (beyond the junction with Bramfield Road), there's a section of antique shops. At 155a what appears to be one small shop turns out to be an enclosed market with around 30 traders, and a café to boot.

Clapham has two centres: Clapham Junction (technically part of Battersea) and Clapham Common. Clapham Junction was, until the coming of the railways, a country crossroads, with the **Falcon** inn providing refreshment for travellers. Nowadays, the **Falcon** provides respite for shoppers: the

Horniman Gardens – *balm for fevered souls.*

Grace Brothers-like department store Arding & Hobbs opposite has been serving the area since 1885. (The original store was burnt down in 1909, the flames burning so fiercely that meat in a nearby butcher's was cooked; the store was rebuilt the following year.) Clapham Junction Station was until recently the busiest in the world, with some 2,500 trains passing through every day.

A flat, grassy expanse held inside a triangle of roads, Clapham Common is somewhere between a park and a wild place; its bleak atmosphere has never been more vividly evoked than in Graham Greene's *The End of the Affair*. In the eighteenth century the Common was a haunt of highwaymen, and in 1722 a raid on vermin yielded 'nine hedgehogs and seven polecats'. The streets around Clapham Common tube fall into two sections: picturesque Old Town and the more routine Clapham High Street. There's more than a whiff of snobbery about Old Town, but it's worth a visit, if only to take in the villagey atmosphere – especially at its central point, where eighteenth-century pubs face on to an approximate square (complete with a small, country-ish bus terminus). The 88 bus, recently and rather self-consciously styled 'The Clapham Omnibus', starts its pleasantly circuitous route from here, to points north of the River.

Famous for its lush setting on the edge of the Common, Holy Trinity Church was well known in the nineteenth century as the headquarters of the Clapham Sect, a group of wealthy Anglicans who advocated muscular Christianity; one of them was William Wilberforce, the anti-slavery campaigner. The church was rebuilt after being hit by a V2 in 1945, and services are still held daily. North Street Potters (24 North Street) make and sell a variety of pottery and tableware, glazed blue and white swirling designs a speciality. The Tim Bobbin in Lillieshall Road is one of the more comfortable local pubs, popular at weekends with the local cricket-sweaters-and-velvet-headbands brigade. **Tea-time**, at 21 The Pavement, is determinedly camp and highly recommended.

Brixton, Stockwell & Oval

Brixton has existed, in various guises, for about a thousand years, of which the first 985 or so were relatively uneventful. Until the early nineteenth century, what we now know as the centre of Brixton was moorland, with the main settlement further north at Stockwell. Later, houses were built along the country roads, such as Coldharbour Lane and Brixton Road, that led to the City, forming a rudimentary suburbia; as the nineteenth century progressed, side roads were built between these long strands of development, filling in the paddocks and market gardens. Between the 1860s-'90s, development was intense as railways and trams linked Brixton with the heart of London. Around the turn of the century the social character began to alter, as the large houses that had been built along the trunk roads a century before were turned into flats and boarding houses. The latter were popular with theatre people working in the West End – hence the decision by John Major's father, a circus and music-hall artiste, to move to Coldharbour Lane in the late 1940s. Meanwhile, Brixton's ethnic identity was changing too, with the arrival of immigrants from the West Indies. A generation later, simmering hostility between the black community and the police, combined with continuing economic decline, culminated in serious rioting in 1981 and again in 1985.

Ten years on, Brixton is a calmer place, though still a visibly poor one. Brixton Market shows the area at its colourful, raucous best: it has the best selection of African and Caribbean food in Europe, as well as selling everything under the sun from wigs to ironing boards. The market sprawls, partly under cover, between Electric Avenue and Brixton Station Road. The former was so named in the 1880s, when it was the first street in the area to be lit by electricity; a century later it was recorded in song by Eddy Grant and, later, in Lenny Henry's treasurable parody ('I am in debt to the/Electric Company/And it's getting higher…').

Brixton is also a good entertainment spot. The Brixton Shaw Theatre ('The Brix') occupies part of St Mark's Church on Brixton Hill; the **Fridge** and the **Academy Brixton** are music venues; the **Ritzy**, formerly one of the best repertory cinemas in London, has undergone redevelopment and is due to have reopened in September 1995 as a five-screen cinema complex with bars and a restaurant.

Stockwell and Oval offer comparatively few rewards to the the visitor, without being entirely devoid of interest. A large pub, the Swan (corner of Stockwell and Clapham Road) offers high-quality music seven nights a week (mainly but not exclusively Irish) and an unpretentious disco at weekends. It's long been a favourite with London's Irish community. At Oval, there's a selection of above-average Indian restaurants along Brixton Road between Crewdson Road and Offley Road, together with an African restaurant, Taste of Africa (corner of Handforth Road).

Oval is best known for its cricket connections (*see chapter* **Sport & Fitness**). Oval Cricket Ground, home of Surrey Cricket Club, was opened in 1845 and has hosted not only the Test matches but most of the FA Cup Finals between 1870 and 1890. In World War II it served as a PoW camp. The large gasometer on the north side of Kennington Oval is a much loved sporting landmark.

South Bank & Waterloo

The arts complex on the South Bank represents London at its most self-consciously modern. The **Royal Festival Hall**, was built by the old London County Council (LCC) to mark the 1951 Festival of Britain, the nation's celebration of its emergence from post-war austerity, and displayed state-of-the-art architectural and building skills. In the mid-1960s the LCC stepped in again to give the building an entire new front and rear; meanwhile, work continued on the **National Theatre**, whose grey boxy appearance has been attracting mixed reviews since the day it opened in March 1976 (its first production featured Albert Finney in *Hamlet*).

Other buildings have proved less controversial. The **Queen Elizabeth Hall** and **Purcell Room** (both opened in 1967) specialise in small orchestral and chamber music concerts. The **Hayward Gallery** hosts a variety of international exhibitions; the wind-powered neon sculpture on the roof is a colourful landmark. Sheltering under a corner of Waterloo Bridge, the **National Film Theatre** **(NFT)** has been catering for serious cineastes since 1953. It also houses the **Museum of the Moving Image (MOMI)**, and a café and bar that are open to all (here's a tip: buy a drink from the NFT bar and take it outside to enjoy by the River).

The **South Bank Centre** is bounded at each end by bridges: Waterloo to the east, Hungerford to the west. The glorious view from **Waterloo Bridge**, especially during its distinctively bluey dusks, inspired The Kinks' 1967 hit 'Waterloo Sunset'. The little-used balcony on level 5A of the **Royal Festival Hall** is also recommended, especially if you want to photograph the river. At ground level the Riverside Walk has a good open-air book market at the **NFT** end and continues below the massive piles of **Hungerford Bridge** and past the bulk of the Shell Building (completed in 1963 but with a pre-war Manhattan look to it). A pathway (currently wheelchair-unfriendly but about to be improved) links the **Royal Festival Hall** to **Waterloo Station**, where the fleet of new Eurostar trains, at rest under their glass dome, are worth a look if you're train-minded.

The South Bank is currently in line for a facelift, though to what extent and when is uncertain. Oxo Tower Wharf, beyond the **National Theatre** and the black and white **London Weekend Television** building, is due to open as a shops-and-restaurants complex by the end of 1995; the art deco tower, built in 1930, was designed to circumvent London County Council rules on advertising. Richard Rogers has submitted plans for a massive Crystal Palace-style dome to cover the entire area between the **Queen Elizabeth Hall** and the **Royal Festival Hall**, and there have been proposals to build a giant Ferris wheel near **Westminster Bridge**. Neither project is likely to see the light of day before the year 2000, if at all.

Behind and below **Waterloo Station**, Lower Marsh (built on the ancient Lambeth Marsh) has a lively market on weekdays and, in **Marie's**, an eclectic mix of traditional caff fare and Thai cooking. Nearby Waterloo Road has the restored 1910 **Waterloo Fire Station,** reminiscent of Trumpton's, now a Modern British restaurant and bar.

Borough & Bankside

If you like literature, you'll love Borough. The **George Inn** is London's sole surviving galleried inn. In the days before purpose-built theatres, Shakespeare's predecessors would perform plays in the courtyard while spectators watched from the galleries. The White Hart Inn, where Mr Pickwick first meets Sam Weller in *The Pickwick Papers* (1837), stood in White Hart Yard until it was pulled down in 1889; on the other side of the **George**, Talbot Yard marks the scene of the Tabard Inn, where Chaucer's pilgrims meet at the beginning of the *Canterbury Tales* (c1390).

The church of St George the Martyr, on the corner of Borough High Street and Long Lane, is mentioned in Dickens' *Little Dorrit* (1855) – the heroine is born in the Marshalsea Prison which used to stand a few doors down. Dickens' own father had been imprisoned there for debt in 1824.

Borough has always been a congested place. Until 1750 **London Bridge** was the only crossing point into the City, and Borough High Street became an unofficial stagecoach terminus. The seventeenth-century poet Thomas Dekker described it as 'a continued ale house with not a shop to be seen between'. **Southwark Cathedral** provides, at the very least, welcome respite from the traffic, though not from the constant sound of trains rumbling into London Bridge Station. (Covered Borough Market, dating from the thirteenth century and probably London's oldest fruit and vegetable market, is also rather cathedral-like in its own way.) The war memorial at the top of Borough High Street (near Southwark Street), with its bronze reliefs of naval guns and World War I dogfights, is rather good, if you like that sort of thing. During the Great Plague, Londoners fled to the leather markets around Weston Street in the belief that the stench from the tanneries would keep the disease at bay. (It didn't.) The tanneries have gone, but the London Glassblowing Workshop can be found in their place (*7 The Leather Market, Weston Street*; open Monday-Friday and by appointment at weekends). The demonstrations of traditional techniques, and colourful, delicate designs, make it well worth a visit.

Bankside, which runs along the Thames to the north-east of Borough, once enjoyed a reputation as London's premier dissipation spot. For centuries, Londoners flocked to its taverns, brothels and bear- and bull-baiting pits. (Part of Bankside consisted of an unconsecrated graveyard for prostitutes.) Presiding over this sea of iniquity were the Bishops of Winchester, who owned the land and drew up rules and opening hours for the brothels – arguably an enlightened policy, which some local authorities are now beginning to emulate nearly 500 years later. Henry VIII ordered the brothels to be closed in 1546, but they soon reappeared and continued to flourish until the Puritans cleaned up the area in the seventeenth century. (The animal-baiting pits, however, continued until the 1830s.)

Today, a little of Bankside's past is re-emerging in the form of the replica **Globe Theatre**, gradually taking shape in Bear Gardens (a visitors' centre is already open). A little further on, you suddenly find yourself in the lee of the vast, oddly doom-laden Bankside Power Station (opened in 1963 and closed less than 20 years later but due to be redeveloped to house the new Tate Gallery of Modern Art by 2000). At low tide you can descend some (rather slippery) steps to the foreshore: from here, on summer evenings, the power station's single, massive brick chimney, and the three bridges across the river ahead, each packed with rush-hour traffic, are highly photogenic.

Bermondsey

It's hard to imagine it now, but at one stage there was probably more Christianity being practised in Bermondsey than anywhere else in London. The land here was first cultivated by medieval monks

Bankside Power Station – *future art gallery.*

and was later owned by the Knights Templar. One of its main thoroughfares, Tooley Street, was once home to no fewer than three abbots, a prior and its own church, St Olave's.

Until the advent of steam, the only industry in Bermondsey was a row of flour mills by the River, but by the early nineteenth century it was a busy, noisy place, especially after London Bridge Station opened in 1836. The area still has a Dickensian feel to it – check out St Saviour's Dock, a muddy creek between towering warehouses, visible over a low parapet on Jamaica Road. In Dickens' day the streets around here formed a notorious slum called Jacob's Island, where Bill Sikes gets his come-uppance in *Oliver Twist* (Jacob Street still exists, near Bermondsey Wall), and the abandoned warehouse on the left of Shad Thames, parallel to St Saviour's Dock, holds something of the oppressive quality of Dickens' darkest works (as you walk by, you can also catch a whiff of the spices it once contained).

Further down, Shad Thames is being redeveloped and slowly tamed, and the process is continuing at Hay's Wharf, beyond **Tower Bridge**. Hay's Galleria is an arresting development: a honey-coloured arcade topped by a soaring glass vaulted roof, with the Thames and **HMS Belfast** just outside. David Kemp's mechanical sculpture *The Navigators* (1987) makes a splendidly silly

The Course of the Heart

M John Harrison finds signs of life in south-east London.

RUSSIA DOCK WOODLAND AND STAVE HILL ECOLOGICAL PARK

Enter through Greenland Dock, via Norway Gate and South Sea Street. Though the docks vanished long ago they have been replaced by structures equally exotic. Walk round to the line of the vanished Grand Surrey Canal, passing beneath the human warehouses on Finland Quay, and you are surfing the eerie interface between money and sense.

The sides of the Redriff Road underpass are slotted for immense lock gates. Entering here in 1908 you would have been 20 or 30 feet under water. Now only the graffiti'd letters ANL give a clue to some of the new uses of the territory. Or is all this *still* somehow under water, a new dream of the drowned as they pass into Russia Dock Woodland?

The dock itself is a sip of standing water on soft earth colonised by pussy willow and gorse, bounded on one side by the great granite capstones and rusty iron bollards of the original quay: a brink no longer, nothing to teeter on the edge of, unless it's the smell of hawthorn in May. You might topple into that.

The traffic noise has receded very suddenly, and you could be anywhere. The success of this little park is its *density*, its sudden remoteness. Between here and the weird conical blister of Stave Hill, stretched across an area less than a mile long and half a mile wide, is a web of pathways and weedy ponds, waterworn boulders, tiny marshes and meadows, blackthorn hedges and shallow fords. The gorse smells like drugged sweets. A heron stands on one leg, stuffed, in the early morning light. Where Stave Dock was once a centre of softwood imports, there are cut-and-laid hedges. Rhetoric which promises – and nearly delivers – Warwickshire in Southwark.

Is this park an attempt to erase an embarrassing historical site? Or only to breathe? Are we under the water or over it? The signposts that might answer these questions are defaced. *Nelson Walk*, announces a mosaic in the Salter Road underpass, *near which existed–*. The rest is gone, along with all the little blue and white tiles. Retrace your steps, and, tired of the effort of imagining a vanished context, have a drink at the Wibbley Wobbley Floating Freehouse on the south side of Greenland Dock.

LEWISHAM REGISTER OFFICE

The dull exterior of 368 Lewisham High Street hides a quiet collision of the secular and the ceremonial, with paint peeling off the radiators and low armchairs tightly upholstered in dappled powder-blue leather – an altar set up in someone's office.

Before each ceremony the rings are placed in what looks like a tinfoil ashtray, next to a bowl of dried flowers. The Registrar is in her thirties with a light but surprisingly matronly voice. Her clerk wears a pink and black outfit in houndstooth check, with matching 1960s spectacles. But here comes the bride! – in her brief white skirt, with what looks like mistletoe in her hat. And Bol, or Bof, the bridegroom, with his patent-leather tango hair-do. All four of them look at one another nervously. The video camerawoman runs about. Someone's three-year-old runs about.

Finally the register, which resembles the visitors' book of a shabby bed and breakfast hotel in south Wales, is filled in. The Registrar, concerned about Bol or Bof's signature, quizzes him patiently. 'Yes, but what do you *sign*?' Meanwhile, the still camerawoman, forbidden to work in case her flash disturbs, looks anxiously on. The moment is escaping! But she mustn't worry. Every moment is escaping, after all: and, anyway, at the end of the ceremony, the whole process will be restaged for the cameras by the Registrar herself. Outside in the car park the next wedding is gathering itself together, like a bag-lady in a doorway picking up her bags.

focal point. Bermondsey Street itself is home to a superb antiques market (Fridays only, 5 am-noon), frequented by dealers and collectors.

Rotherhithe

Pepys knew Rotherhithe as Redriffe, though both names may derive from the Anglo-Saxon words 'redhra' and 'hyth' – 'mariner's haven'. The old name still holds good: Rotherhithe is relatively undisturbed by visitors, with superb views across the Thames to Wapping and two of the best riverside pubs in London, the Angel (101 Bermondsey Wall East) and the **Mayflower** – the *Mayflower* docked near here in 1620 before beginning her voyage to America. Both pubs are partly supported on piles directly over the river. The infamous Judge Jeffreys is said to have used the Angel as a vantage point from which to watch pirates being drowned on the opposite bank.

St Mary's, in St Mary Church Street, is a gem of a church, built by local seamen and watermen in the eighteenth century. Nowadays, thanks to acts of burglary and vandalism, the interior can only be viewed through reinforced glass. The communion table in the Lady Chapel and two bishop's chairs were made from timber from the warship *Fighting Temeraire*, the subject of Turner's painting now hanging in the **National Gallery**. The old school opposite the church, with its carved figures of eighteenth-century schoolchildren over the porch, is also rather charming. Walk from here down Elephant Lane and you get a sudden, magnificent view of the River, with **Tower Bridge** and the tangle of the City beyond.

Peckham & Dulwich

Narrowly beaten by the **Tower of London** for the coveted position of 'London's top tourist destination', Peckham has recently enjoyed a fresh wave of popularity – especially since the opening of a Holiday Inn on Peckham Rye. Joke. Nobody visits Peckham. Even people who live in Peckham don't go there any more than they can help it.

Seriously, Peckham's not half as bad as Londoners like to make out, and you can do a lot worse than use it as a starting point for some of the, let's say, more *mainstream* parts of south London. For a start, Peckham enjoys a surprisingly rich and colourful heritage. It's recorded in the Domesday Book as Pecheha, or 'village among the hills', the hills being those of nearby Honor Oak, Nunhead and Plow Garlick. Henry I thought sufficiently highly of the place to award it as a gift to his illegitimate son, the Earl of Gloucester.

Like many districts of south London, Peckham was a quiet, rural area until the Industrial Revolution. It was a favourite stopping place for cattle drovers on their way to markets in the City;

Dulwich Picture Gallery – *England's oldest.*

they would leave their herds grazing on the common, Peckham Rye, while they refreshed themselves in the inns along Peckham High Street. As a child, the poet William Blake saw a vision of angels on the Rye, and in her novel *The Ballad of Peckham Rye* (1960) Muriel Spark refers, without apparent irony, to 'the dusky scope of the Rye's broad lyrical acres'. (Drinkers: she also maps out a useful pub crawl on page 1.) The Victorian terraced houses that feature in the novel have now mostly gone, to be replaced by monolithic council estates and tower blocks (the stamping ground of Del and Rodney in *Only Fools And Horses*). But there's still a glint of former architectural glory in the carefully restored, pale-coloured almshouses in Choumert Road (you can walk down the tiny, floral mews behind the iron gate at the back). Further down Choumert Road, there are examples of the small, exotic African and Asian grocers' shops that have sprung up since the 1960s.

Peckham suffers from not having a tube station, but it's well served by buses. Lordship Lane, in neighbouring Dulwich, has an excellent selection of restaurants, and snakes down towards some of the best 'green lungs' south London has to offer. Dulwich Village is close to Dulwich Park (once a regular venue for duels) and **Dulwich Picture Gallery**, England's oldest gallery (founded in 1626) and a favourite of Mr Pickwick, who retires

*The **Royal Naval College** and **Queen's House**, seen from Island Gardens on the Isle of Dogs.*

to Dulwich in *The Pickwick Papers*. For a taste of the Gothic, try **Nunhead Cemetery**, one of the biggest Victorian burial grounds in London.

Honor Oak Park is said to be where Queen Boudicca was defeated by the Roman army in 61 AD. Dick Turpin used the oak on One-Tree Hill as a look-out, and the hill served as a beacon during the Napoleonic Wars.

The **Horniman Museum** was opened in 1890 to exhibit the objects accumulated by tea magnate Frederick Horniman during his travels around the world; the chunky art nouveau building is alone worth seeing. With its soft, lush flanks and fine views across London, Horniman Gardens offers balm to the fevered south London soul.

Greenwich

Greenwich is the playground of kings and queens. Henry VIII and his daughters Mary I and Elizabeth I were all born here, and Greenwich Palace (then called Placentia) was Henry's favourite residence. He could hunt in **Greenwich Park** and visit his beloved home fleet ('the wood wall of England') at anchor along the river. It was at Greenwich that Sir Walter Ralegh put his cloak over a puddle so that Elizabeth I wouldn't have to get her feet wet; here too Elizabeth signed the execution warrant of Mary Queen of Scots.

After the Tudors, the palace fell on hard times. Under Oliver Cromwell it became first a biscuit factory, then a prison. In 1660 the newly restored Charles II embarked on an ambitious scheme to

return Greenwich to its former glory. Work began on a new palace, though in the event only one river-side wing was actually built. William and Mary, who succeeded Charles, preferred the royal palaces at Kensington and Hampton Court and ordered Sir Christopher Wren to design another wing for the unfinished building, to create the Royal Naval Hospital. This is the great façade you see from the River today (since 1873 it's been the **Royal Naval College**), with a gap in the middle to allow an unobscured view of the **Queen's House** behind (now the main section of the **National Maritime Museum**).

The best way to arrive at Greenwich is still by river at Greenwich Pier (pleasure boats go to and from the **Thames Barrier**, Westminster, Charing Cross and the **Tower of London**). Alternatively, you can start from Island Gardens on the Isle of Dogs and take the Greenwich Foot Tunnel. Either way, you'll find yourself in the shadow of the **Cutty Sark**, built in 1869 and in dry dock here since 1954, after an adventurous life as one of the fastest tea clippers in the world. Dwarfed in comparison is the yacht **Gipsy Moth IV**, in which Sir Francis Chichester made the first solo round-the-world voyage in 1966-67 (on his return he was knighted with the same sword that Elizabeth I had used to knight Sir Francis Drake).

The town of Greenwich is a busy, traffic-laden place with a plethora of markets. The Trafalgar Tavern in Park Row was a favourite haunt of literary chums Dickens, Thackeray and Wilkie Collins, who came regularly for seafood dinners

(Dickens set a wedding feast here in *Our Mutual Friend*). **Goddard's Ye Old Pie House** has been serving home-made pies since 1890 (the queue can look daunting but moves remarkably fast). **St Alfege Greenwich** (1712-18) takes its name from the Archbishop of Canterbury who was martyred on this site by invading Vikings in 1012, after courageously refusing to sanction a demand for ransom which would have secured his release.

Hilly **Greenwich Park** is topped by the **Old Royal Observatory**, built during the reign of Charles II. The first astronomer royal, John Flamsteed, made some 30,000 observations of the heavens from here, for his star catalogue, *Historia Coelestis Britannica*. Greenwich Mean Time was introduced in 1880, the Greenwich Pips in 1924 and the Speaking Clock in 1936. Every day since 1833 the red time-ball on the north-eastern turret of the Observatory has dropped at precisely 1pm as a signal to shipmasters on the river to adjust their chronometers. You can also straddle the Greenwich Meridian Line and stand simultaneously in the Eastern and Western Hemispheres. The view from the Park, down to the **Queen's House** and the **Royal Naval College**, with the Thames, Docklands and the City beyond, is magnificent.

Charlton & Woolwich

In centuries gone by, few travellers relished the prospect of a journey along the Old Dover Road. At Shooters Hill in particular, the road was steep and the countryside wild; this was a favourite spot for footpads and highwaymen to lie in wait for easy prey. Robbers who were caught were themselves shown no mercy: they were hanged at a gallows at the bottom of Shooters Hill and their bodies displayed on a gibbet at the summit. In 1661 Samuel Pepys recorded that he 'rode under a man that hangs at Shooters Hill, and a filthy sight it was to see how the flesh is shrunk from his bones'.

Charlton was a nearby village, built around the Jacobean manor Charlton House (now a community centre and public library). Nearby Hornfair Park takes its name from the Charlton Horn Fair, which was held every year until 1872. According to local tradition, the fair was started after King John seduced the wife of a local miller and, in recompense, gave her wronged husband all the land visible from Charlton to Rotherhithe. The miller's neighbours named the riverside boundary of his new land 'Cuckold's Point' and established the annual Horn Fair (horns being the symbol of a cuckoldry). At its peak in the eighteenth and nineteenth century, the fair was attended by thousands of people, many arriving by boat wearing horns and dressed as kings, queens and millers. Hornfair Park is now tucked away at the corner of a housing estate; Maryon Park, used in Antonioni's *Blow Up* and closer to the River, is more pleasant.

One of the most spectacular sights on the River, the **Thames Barrier** stretches between Silvertown on the north bank and Woolwich on the south. Since its completion in 1982, at a cost of £500 million, the barrier has been raised more than 20 times to protect London from flooding. When raised, the four main gates are each the height of a five-storey building (normally they lie on the riverbed, allowing ships to pass over them). There's a visitors' centre and cafeteria on the Woolwich side (open daily) and the barrier is raised once a month (phone to check dates and times). Since July 1994, a retired Russian U-475 submarine has been moored near the Barrier (tours of the vessel daily).

Woolwich itself attracts fewer visitors than its more glamorous neighbour Greenwich, though it has plenty to offer above-average shopping centre. The long pedestrianised thoroughfare Powis Street also boasts two spectacular buildings at the river end: the ruddy Edwardian Central Stores building and, opposite, the creamy-tiled, art deco Co-op. Another fine art deco building, the Woolwich Coronet cinema, overlooks the river at the foot of John Wilson Street.

The character of Woolwich has been shaped by strong military and naval associations. The Woolwich Arsenal was established in Tudor times as the country's main source of munitions; the Royal Artillery later moved into Woolwich Garrison, built between 1776-1802 and boasting the longest Georgian façade in the country. It's best seen from Woolwich Common or from Grand Depôt Road, where the remains of the Royal Garrison Church of St George have been left as consecrated ground after being hit by a flying bomb in 1944 (the end walls and altar are still standing). For military aficionados, there is a **Museum of Artillery**.

Henry VIII established the Royal Dockyard at Woolwich in 1512, initially so that his new flagship, the *Great Harry*, could be built there (then the largest ship in the world, she was destroyed by fire in 1553, on a return visit to the yard). The Dockyard closed in 1869 and moved to Chatham. Just downstream from the Woolwich Ferry terminal, the stretch of river known as Gallions Reach was the scene of the Thames' worst-ever shipping accident. In 1878 a crowded pleasure steamer, the *Princess Alice*, was struck broadside by a collier, the *Bywell Castle*, with the loss of some 700 lives, including a dozen who managed to cling to the collier's side, only to be swept away when she dropped anchor. Four years later, the *Bywell Castle* herself disappeared without trace in the Atlantic.

The Woolwich Ferry has existed since the fourteenth century; the old paddle steamers were replaced by diesels as late as 1963. (There's also a foot tunnel.) Today the seating area outside the Waterfront Leisure Centre, next to the terminal, is a fine spot to watch a great river at work.

East London

As Canary Wharf finally begins to take off and the Jubilee Line edges closer, there are real signs of eastern promise.

This is what the tourists do. They get on the 15 bus at **Piccadilly Circus**, **Trafalgar Square** and the Aldwych, and make a bee-line for the coveted front seats upstairs. At the **Tower of London** the conductor will shout 'Tower!' three times, with decibel increments of approximately 30 per cent. After they've been disgorged and the conductor has carefully pointed out the stop opposite for the return journey, the bus moves off and the conductor can have a surreptitious sit-down, secure in the knowledge that anyone still on board is a local and can look after himself.

It needn't be this way. Stay on the bus as it sweeps round the corner and into Aldgate, where the City officially ends and real London begins. The East End starts here.

Whitechapel & Spitalfields

Whitechapel has always been the City's poor, rather embarrassing next-door neighbour. It first developed as a home for bell-founders and other metal-workers who were expelled from the City for being too noisy; the Whitechapel Bell Foundry (founded in 1520) and Gunmakers' Company Proof House still survive in Fieldgate Street and Commercial Road respectively. By Victorian times, the area was wretchedly poor, a contemporary social historian describing it as 'a shocking place... an evil plexus of slums that hide human creeping things'. Only crime – and especially prostitution – thrived (*see page 112* **Ripping Yarns**).

Whitechapel was enriched by successive waves of immigrants: Irish and Germans in the early nineteenth century; Jewish refugees from Eastern Europe from 1880-1914; and, as the Jews prospered and moved north, Indians and Bangladeshis, who between the 1950s-'70s took over textile businesses along Commercial Street and Commercial Road.

If you do travel in on the 15 bus, it's best to get off at Aldgate East (look out for Tubby Isaacs' jellied eel stall on the left), at the stop between Goulston Street and Old Castle Street. Commercial Street, which sweeps off to the left towards the

*The East End is riddled with cobbled alleys such as this one off **Whitechapel High Street**.*

City, is, frankly, pretty horrid but, for all that, worth a look.

For most of its length it's a wide swathe of forlorn-looking Victorian warehouses, with grim but fascinating side streets, some, such as Fleur de Lis Street, changing within a few paces, from the semi-gentrified to the irredeemably desolate. The enclosed **Spitalfields Market** provides a welcome oasis of warmth and life. The famous fruit and vegetable market, established in 1682, moved north-east to Leyton some years ago, but a small organic market continues on the old site, surrounded by a variety of eateries and small businesses such as the **Magpie Bookshop**.

By contrast, Hawksmoor's magnificent **Christchurch Spitalfields**, opposite, is now virtually closed, pending long-term renovation. After dark, this stretch of Commercial Street has a distinctly Hell's Kitchen look to it, with prostitutes standing at intervals along the kerb and anonymous figures clustering around the all-night mobile café that parks outside the church railings.

Fournier Street, which runs alongside **Christchurch** to link Commercial Street with Brick Lane, is a reminder of the Huguenots, eighteenth-century refugees from France, whose skill at silk-weaving brought them prosperity in the East End. The street's lined with their tall houses with distinctive shutters and ornate, jutting porches.

There are two excellent reasons to visit Brick Lane and the immediate area: **Brick Lane Market** and the plethora of cheap, authentic curry restaurants. Among the best are Nazrul (130 Brick Lane; unlicensed but you can bring your own booze); the barnlike Clifton (126 Brick Lane; open till 5 am); the Standard (48 Hanbury Street) where the service is especially charming; and the Sonar Bangla (46 Hanbury Street), specialising in baltis – curries eaten with nan bread, straight out of a hot iron pot.

Brick Lane's Jewish heritage survives in the **Brick Lane Beigel Bake** (No 159; open 24 hours). Playwright Arnold Wesker was brought up in nearby Fashion Street, while *Oliver!* composer Lionel Bart lived above the shoe shop at the corner of Brick Lane and Princelet Street (27 Brick Lane): when the atmosphere in the house grew too claustrophobic the young Bart would climb out on to the flat roof which is visible from the street. There's a dearth of good pubs in the Lane, but an exception is the Pride of Spitalfields in Heneage Street, which attracts a friendly local crowd.

Most visitors to Whitechapel come only for the Sunday markets at Brick Lane and nearby **Petticoat Lane**, but the whole area is worth exploring. **Bloom's** at 90 Whitechapel High Street is a local landmark: it has been serving good kosher fare for over half a century. Hidden at the end of an alley next to the Kentucky Fried Chicken, the Freedom Press publishes a wide variety of political and

Wapping High Street – *'filthy' no longer.*

anarchist literature. Further down, the art nouveau **Whitechapel Gallery** specialises in contemporary art. Whitechapel Public Library has a pleasantly well-thumbed atmosphere. A tile mural outside commemorates the hay market which was held in the High Street for 300 years until its abolition in 1928. A more modest clothing market continues to flourish along Whitechapel Road.

Whitechapel has special rewards for those prepared to put in the extra legwork. Fieldgate Street, off Plumbers Row, is worth a detour for a look at the Victorian bulk of Tower House, built as a hostel for the homeless, and only closed in the late 1980s. Stalin and Lenin stayed here while they were attending the Fifth Congress of the Russian Social Democratic Labour Party in nearby Fulbourne Street. The Blind Beggar pub on the corner of Whitechapel Road and Cambridge Heath Road is best known for its 1960s criminal connections (*see page 112* **Ripping Yarns**). Today it's a comfortable, if slightly anonymous place, popular with traders and visitors to the market outside.

For east London completists, the alley at Wood's Buildings is especially recommended. Turn left at the end and you'll find yourself in a wide, almost forgotten tract of land, dominated by a huge, ruined Victorian school (the rusty railings on top belonged to the roof playground). It's arguably the most desolate spot in the whole of the East End (it

Ripping Yarns

Ian Cunningham examines the East End's record for violent crime.

For centuries, the East End has been associated with crime. Traditionally this was due largely to widespread poverty and – while London Docks were thriving – a huge shifting population which conferred anonymity on perpetrators and victims of crime alike. By the late nineteenth century, Spitalfields and Whitechapel were virtually no-go areas in which prostitution thrived and rape, mugging and murder were commonplace.

Given this environment, it's rather surprising that Jack the Ripper remains the best-known criminal ever to have operated in the East End. Between August and October 1888 he stabbed and mutilated five prostitutes, mainly in the Whitechapel area: Mary Anne Nichols in Bucks Row (now Durward Street); Annie Chapman in Hanbury Street; Elizabeth Stride in Berner Street (now Henriques Street) off the Commercial Road, and – on the same night – Catherine Eddowes in Mitre Square; and Mary Kelly, in Miller's Court, between what are

now White's Row and Brushfield Street. After the murder of Mary Kelly, the killings abruptly stopped. Speculation over the Ripper's identity has kept criminologists entertained ever since, though post mortem photographs of the victims (not released by Scotland Yard until as late as 1972) are a sobering reminder of just how squalid and cruel the murders actually were.

Other East End murderers whose identities are known have tended to fade into obscurity. Among them is John Williams, the Ratcliff Highway Murderer, who in December 1811 hacked to death two entire families at 29 Ratcliff Highway

(now The Highway) and at the King's Arms in New Gravel Lane (now Garnet Street). Williams hanged himself in prison while awaiting trial and his body was driven in a cart through large crowds to the crossroads of Cannon Street Road and Cable Street, where he was buried in quicklime with a stake through his heart.

Britain's first railway murder was carried out by Franz Müller on a train between Bow and Hackney Wick in July 1864. Müller attacked and robbed a fellow passenger, Thomas Briggs, stealing his gold watch and throwing his body on to the line. However, in his hurry to escape he took Briggs's hat by mistake, leaving his own on the train. Scotland Yard detective Dick Tanner traced the hat to Müller, but by the time police arrived at his house Müller was on his way to New York on the SS *Victoria*. Undaunted, Tanner booked passage on the faster SS *City of Manchester* and was waiting at the harbour when Müller disembarked – still wearing the wrong hat and with Briggs's watch in his luggage. Reporting on his public execution later that year, the *Times* noted that 'robbery and violence, loud laughing, oaths, fighting, obscene conduct and still more filthy language reigned round the gallows far and near'. Partly as a result, public hangings were banned by Parliament in 1868 and were conducted inside prisons until the abolition of the death penalty in 1964.

In 1875 Henry Wainwright murdered and dismembered his (bigamous) wife in the brushmaker's shop he owned in the Whitechapel Road,

comes as no surprise to learn that Jack the Ripper's first victim died here) but one prays that the developers will continue to leave it exactly as it is.

Docklands

The history of London's Docklands is the history of Britain in microcosm. As the British Empire expanded in the eighteenth and nineteenth centuries, so too did the traffic along the River Thames, as ships arrived laden with booty from all corners of the globe. Different docks were built to specialise in various types of cargo: rum and hardwood at West India Docks on the Isle of

Dogs; wool, sugar and rubber at **St Katharine's Dock** by **Tower Bridge**; ivory, coffee and cocoa at London Docks in Wapping. During World War II the Docks suffered heavy bombing (including 57 consecutive nights of firebombing from 7 September 1940) but by the 1950s they had again reached full capacity.

When it came, the end came suddenly. As late as 1964, 61 million tons of cargo were handled. But the collapse of Empire, a series of crippling strikes and, above all, the introduction of deepwater container ships led to the closure, one by one, of all of London's docks from **Tower Bridge** to Barking Creek between 1967-84.

Jack the Ripper *territory (above and left).*

next to what is now the Andrew Sketchley Theatre. Wainwright's big mistake was to ask a passer-by, a man named Stokes, to keep an eye on the parcelled-up remains while he went to find a cab. While he was away, Stokes examined one of the parcels and a human hand fell out. At this point Wainwright reappeared, loaded the parcels into his cab and drove off; when Stokes ran up to two policemen to tell them what had happened they laughed at him. Meanwhile, Wainwright ordered the cab driver to pull up at an ironmonger's shop, presumably to buy a spade. By this time, Stokes had managed to find another policeman who would believe him, and Wainwright was found, arrested and subsequently hanged.

January 1911 saw the Siege of Sidney Street. In December a gang of Russian anarchists had been surprised by a passing constable while digging through the wall of a jeweller's shop in Houndsditch. In the shootout that followed, three policemen were killed and the anarchists escaped. On 3 January, two of the anarchists were cornered at their lodgings on the second floor of 100 Sidney Street by a contingent of Scots Guards. In the ensuing carnage, which was witnessed by the then Home Secretary Winston Churchill, the building was burned down and the two anarchists and a fireman were killed. The

anarchists' bodies were too badly burned to be identified, and their surviving comrades were acquitted of the three earlier murders through lack of evidence.

At St George's Town Hall in nearby Cable Street a mural commemorates the battle between local people and marching blackshirts led by the Fascist leader Sir Oswald Mosley, on 4 October 1936. The march, intended to intimidate the local Jewish population, was abandoned and the blackshirts were never seen in such numbers in the East End again.

On 8 March 1966, the jukebox in the Blind Beggar pub, Whitechapel Road, was playing the new number one, 'The Sun Ain't Gonna Shine Anymore', when Ronnie Kray entered and shot George Cornell. For ten years Ronnie and his twin brother Reggie had dominated organised crime from Woolwich to the City; Cornell was a member of the rival Richardson gang which operated south of the River. When the police arrived it appeared that no one in the pub had seen the shooting. In 1969, the Krays were each jailed for a minimum of 30 years, the judge commenting that 'society has earned a long rest from your activities'.

Between 1974-78 a trio of contract killers – Henry MacKenny, Terence Pinfold and John Childs – murdered six people. The bodies were cut into log-sized pieces and burned on an open gas fire in Childs' ground-floor flat at Dolphin House, Poplar High Street; Childs presided over the 'cremations' dressed in an undertaker's top hat. The bones were crushed to powder and scattered along roads, rivers and canals. The case made history in 1980 as the first mass murder trial to take place without a single body.

Rumours have long circulated that when parts of London Docks were drained in the 1980s, several sets of concrete-booted remains were found among the tyres and prams. As for the 1990s, if history is anything to go by, the East End criminals are still out there… somewhere.

In 1981 the Conservative government set up the London Docklands Development Corporation (LDDC). Its brief was to regenerate the eight and a half square miles of derelict land by building new offices and homes, and attracting new businesses. The LDDC's 14-year history has been far from smooth. From the outset it has been accused of favouring wealthy outsiders over the needs of local people. As the property market slumped from the late 1980s onwards, developers found themselves with empty buildings and no one to buy them.

For all this, Docklands remains one of the most spectacular areas of London, and it's becoming more accessible: the Docklands Light Railway

(DLR) now operates seven days a week, and the long-awaited extension to the Jubilee Line (due for completion in 1998) will add a much-needed tube link (*see chapter* **Getting Around**).

St Katharine's Dock to Shadwell

St Katharine's once housed over a thousand cottages, a brewery and the twelfth-century church of St Katharine, all of which were demolished without compensation to make way for a grandiose new docklands development scheme. This was in 1828. **St Katharine's Dock**, which was built over the old settlement, remained open until 1968;

in 1973 it re-emerged as the first, and perhaps the best, of the Docklands redevelopments. The Dock is now a yacht marina and home to a light-ship, the *Nore*, which was once moored in the Thames Estuary, and to a squadron of russet-sailed turn-of-the-century barges. A trio of Dock-lands riverbuses, introduced to the River in the 1980s but withdrawn when their operator went into receivership, has also found what appears to be a final resting place in one corner. There are numerous restaurants and cafés on the edge of the Dock, which attract legions of coach parties on summer nights.

In 1598, London historian John Stowe described Wapping High Street as a 'filthy strait passage, with alleys of small tenements or cottages... built and inhabited by sailors' victuallers'. Today, any-one expecting a *Mary, Mungo and Midge*-style High Street is in for a surprise: Wapping's is a quiet, rather sunless thoroughfare, hemmed in on either side by warehouses (those in Wapping Wall are the most spectacular) and new flats.

The River at Wapping is brimming with his-tory. Until well into the nineteenth century, con-victed pirates were taken at low tide to Execution Dock (near the River police station at Wapping New Stairs) and left there in chains until three tides had washed over them. The Captain Kidd pub (108 Wapping High Street) commemorates one of the most famous recipients of this brand of rough justice – Kidd had been despatched by the gov-ernment to capture pirates in the Indian Ocean but instead became one himself. Another pub, the Town of Ramsgate (62 Wapping High Street), is where the bloodthirsty Judge Jeffreys, who had sent scores of pirates to nearby Execution Dock, was himself captured as he tried to escape to Ham-burg disguised as a sailor (he died in the **Tower of London**). Captain Blood was also caught here after stealing the Crown Jewels. Dating from 1520, the Prospect of Whitby (57 Wapping Wall) is the oldest and most famous of the Wapping riverside pubs. Pepys, Dickens, Whistler, Turner – and Judge Jeffreys – were all regulars. In the early eighteenth century, the first fuchsia ever seen in Britain was sold here, by a sailor to a local market gardener. The White Swan and Cuckoo (corner of Wapping Lane and Prusom Street) has no river-side view and a beer garden that's best described as functional, but it serves award-winning food and is one of the friendliest pubs in east London.

Once part of the London Docks, Shadwell Basin is now surrounded by new flats designed by Richard Rogers. In summer, the 30-foot-deep Basin is alive with local children swimming. Stand at the western end of the Basin and you get an excellent view of **Canary Wharf**, nearly three miles away. It's best seen at sunset, when the rocket-like tower turns to seemingly impossible shades of pink, silver and gold. The Highway, beyond (*see page*

View of Canary Wharf from the **Barley Mow**.

112 **Ripping Yarns**), was described by a local magistrate in the 1860s as 'a scene of riots, de-baucheries, robberies and all conceivable deeds of darkness. From the public houses there constant-ly issued the sounds of loud laughter, mingled with shouting and fearful imprecations... If the sailors were not entirely fleeced inside the saloons, the process was completed by bullies and fighting men when they staggered out into the street.'

Today the Highway is a changed place, but not necessarily for the better. Rupert Murdoch's prison-like News International building ('Fortress Wapping') sprawls between St Katharine's Dock and **Tobacco Dock**, a much-heralded shopping centre which has yet to recover from the recession. Opposite, Hawksmoor's **St George-in-the-East** has fared better: although the interior was burnt out by a World War II incendiary bomb, the core of the church was rebuilt in the 1960s and contin-ues to flourish as a place of worship. Further down the Highway, beyond Shadwell, the river walkway at Free Trade Wharf gives you a good view of the River and, from this angle, the mountainous structure of Canary Wharf.

Limehouse

The name comes from the lime kilns that were built here in medieval times, but Limehouse's prosperity came from the sea. In 1610, a census revealed that half the working population were mariners, and Limehouse later became a centre for ship-building (one yard built most of the country's lifeboats between 1850-90). The importance of Limehouse is reflected in the immense size of **St Anne's, Limehouse** (corner of Commercial Road and Newell Street), built between 1712-24, in what were then open fields, and one of Nicholas Hawksmoor's most dramatic creations (the clock is the second highest in Britain after Big Ben's and was built by the same makers). Look out for the unusual stone pyramid in the churchyard: the carving on one side has been weathered almost completely away, but it's believed to have some Masonic significance known only to Hawksmoor himself.

Britain's first wave of Chinese immigrants (mainly seamen) settled in Limehouse in the nineteenth century. Their influence survives in some of the local street names (Ming Street, Canton Street) and in the scattering of Chinese restaurants around West India Dock Road. At that time, Limehouse was well known for its gambling and drug dens (Oscar Wilde's Dorian Gray comes here to buy opium) and features in stories by Sax Rohmer (creator of Fu Manchu) and Sir Arthur Conan Doyle. Charles Dickens knew Limehouse well: he regularly visited his godfather in Newell Street and he used the tiny, dark and still superb Grapes inn (76 Narrow Street) as the model for the Six Jolly Fellowship Porters in *Our Mutual Friend* (1865). The larger **Barley Mow**, also in Narrow Street, is useful if you want to sit outside– it's built on an open dock, overlooking the river.

Isle of Dogs

For many people, Docklands *is* the Isle of Dogs. Redevelopment has been at its most intense here, culminating in **Canary Wharf**, whose 800-foot tower makes it the tallest building in Britain.

There's little about the Isle that isn't subject to dispute. Some insist that it isn't an island at all but a peninsula (although the main section of West India Docks effectively splits it in two), and no one can agree on whether 'Dogs' refers to the royal kennels that were once kept here or to the dykes ('dijks') that were built by Flemish engineers in the seventeenth century. Above all, argument rages on whether the Isle of Dogs is, as the LDDC would claim, a crucible of economic progress, or a monstrous adventure playground for the very rich.

If the redevelopment around West India Docks has a toytown look from the Docklands Light Railway (DLR), at ground level it looks more like the set of a James Bond film. However, the Visitor Centre (3 Limeharbour; open daily) is a refreshingly user-friendly source of maps and other information. If epic buildings aren't for you, try Mudchute City Farm (open Monday-Saturday). Island Gardens offers an unparalleled view across

the Thames towards Greenwich (a foot tunnel takes you under the river to emerge next to the **Cutty Sark**). This was Sir Christopher Wren's favourite spot from which to admire his creation the **Royal Naval College** (Hawksmoor was his assistant); the building was split in the middle so as not to block the view of the **Queen's House** and **Royal Observatory** on the hill beyond.

In the eighteenth century, a subterranean forest, destroyed in a prehistoric earthquake, was discovered underneath Island Gardens. Follow the river walkway on the far side and you'll find yourself looking out towards Deptford, with a ship or two tied up. At low tide it's a pleasantly mournful scene of grey foreshores and wheeling gulls.

Bethnal Green & Hackney

In Victorian times Bethnal Green was the poorest district in London. In 1889 nearly half the population lived below subsistence level, with the Jago area around Old Nichol Street containing the worst ravages of poverty and squalor. New flats and the opening of what is now the **Bethnal Green Museum of Childhood** in the late nineteenth century, followed eventually by wholesale slum clearance in the twentieth, went some way towards improving the quality of life, but the area has remained impoverished. Bethnal Green suffered especially badly during World War II: on 3 March 1943, 173 people were killed in a stampede at the entrance to the tube station, then being used as an air raid shelter; towards the end of the war, many of Hitler's flying bombs were deliberately aimed at the area because of its large Jewish population.

Hackney, to the north, was originally an extended village, popular in the fifteenth and sixteenth centuries with merchants who wanted to live near, but not too near, the City. Hackney's oldest house, **Sutton House**, dates from this period. In his diary entry for 11 June 1664, Pepys records that he went 'with my wyfe only to take ayre, it being very warm and pleasant, to Bowe and Old Ford; and thence to Hackney. There… played at shuffle board, ate cream and good cherries; and so with good refreshment home'. The rural idyll continued until the nineteenth century, when Hackney's market gardens were gradually buried under terraced houses and workshops, themselves to be replaced by housing estates after World War II.

Hackney is best approached selectively and with caution. **Columbia Road** and **Ridley Road** have excellent markets; the former also offers a number of pottery shops specialising in terracotta, while the latter is home to the **Ridley Bagel Bakery** (open 24 hours). Other traditional East End food can be sampled close by: pies and eels at **F Cooke**; fish and chips at Faulkners (424/426 Kingsland Road). There are also several good Turkish restaurants, thanks to the local Kurdish community.

North London

How can an area that includes Hampstead Heath, Highgate Cemetery and Regent's Park – in addition to the world-renowned Camden Market – not be the most desirable in London?

North Londoners consider their area to be the best in the capital in terms of politics (a lazy, liberal, left-wing mood pervades here), places to live (not as ostentatious as South Ken or Belgravia, Hampstead and Islington still manage a louche classiness) and places to be seen (Camden Town – still the hottest and coolest draw). If the extent of this urban mix is too much, there is enough parkland to satisfy the most fervent country bumpkin, all of it within easy reach of most north London smogspots. Well served by public transport, teeming with bizarre hideaways in which to eat and shop, north London is the first choice of many looking for a place to live in the capital.

Camden Town

Camden boasts a rich heritage, developing around the canal at the time the Industrial Revolution found its feet in the 1830s. Thriving rapidly, it became a popular place to settle, a feature it has retained in the years since, thanks to its balance of bohemia and calm (**Regent's Park** is close by).

West Indian trade manifests itself in the multiform foodstuffs prepared and sold from small trolleys on Camden High Street. Many shops do a roaring trade in footwear, trinkets and jewellery; the various markets and cubby-hole shops are second to none. This place could find you that elusive gift for a difficult relative within minutes.

At the weekend, Camden becomes a people magnet, drawing around 100,000 visitors into the arterial road that includes Camden High Street and Chalk Farm Road. It's the best time to visit, because the markets don't open through the week. Good thing too really, for the roads would otherwise become impassable. There's a good case for pedestrianising some of this stretch, perhaps the area which includes the bridge over the Grand Union Canal (also known as the Regent's Canal, which offers you passage to **London Zoo** or Little Venice via towpath or waterbus) – it proves something of a death trap if you aren't wary. There's a real sense of community among the traders here, a salt-of-the-earth apprenticeship which means that while some of the gear you'll be considering might not be 100 per cent quality, the banter and friendliness are pukka. The buildings too get in on the act, many sporting giant models of the goods on offer: DMs, leather jackets, jeans. Though many buildings look the worse for wear, Camden has long held a reputation as a desirable place of residency, not least because it is one of the trendiest spots in town. You can track down any hedonistic pursuit in these parts.

Your senses will be assailed by all manner of extravagances, including incessant bass lines as passing vehicles and hand-held ghetto blasters pump out hip hop and reggae. Don't be surprised to see representatives of our burgeoning 'yoof' culture dancing in the road. The emphasis is on street cool and being tolerant to any eccentricity you might encounter. It's also incredibly relaxing if you can channel yourself away from the mainstream and find a seat outside one of the many excellent cafés along the thoroughfare; people-watching is a fine way to pass the time over a coffee if you've spent a hard day shopping or just hanging out.

Major crowd-pullers include, on Kentish Town Road, perhaps the oldest and best of London's secondhand vinyl stockists, **Rock On**, where obsolete artists grin down at you from record sleeves pinned to walls and ceiling. The **WKD** café, further along, is a modish location in which to be seen; smart dress is preferable while you tuck into a light snack or enjoy a drink. An other-world experience greets you when you see the Sainsbury's sign (17 Camden Road), odd among the fashionable shops despite the futuristic shell in which it nestles. Across the way from Camden Town tube lies the World's End – a monstrous pub which figures as a meeting place for weekend clubbers.

Regent's Park

This is one of London's main lungs, oxygenating the thin air above our polluted streets and rooftops. It beggars the imagination to consider what state the capital would be in without these punctuative green acreages, but while they exist, it would be folly not to enjoy them. For a while you are transported away from the manic world of bumper-to-bumper and angry horn-hitting to an oasis of calm where civility doesn't seem like too great an effort.

Surrounded by achingly beautiful white stucco terraces (Cumberland Terrace, Chester Terrace),

Hi-tech flats in Camden Town sandwiched between Sainsbury's and the **Regent's Canal**.

the park is a triumph of taste and grandeur constructed in 1812 by John Nash for the Prince Regent (later King George IV). Prior to that, it was a hunting ground and farmland but it has survived in its current state for almost 200 years.

London Zoo, which struggled through some lean years when the threat of closure seemed a certainty, has enjoyed a return to popularity thanks to sponsorship, though major changes in the treatment of animals have also helped its cause. Other attractions, beyond the green expanses, include Queen Mary's Gardens, with its beautiful rose garden; the domes and minarets of London Central Mosque; and the open-air theatre which puts on performances during the summer months.

Separated from **Regent's Park** by Prince Albert Road, **Primrose Hill** is a gentle slope with stunning views. Kites and Frisbees are de rigueur in the summer months, though some of the sleepy streets off Primrose Hill Road and Regent's Park Road offer quaint shops and cafés if your needs are less energetic. Don't miss the **Lansdowne** pub on Gloucester Avenue. Come 5 November, **Primrose Hill** is probably your best bet for a spectacular bonfire and firework display.

Hampstead

Perhaps more than any other place in London, Hampstead has retained a village atmosphere which lends it a restful air. This relaxed ambience might also be due to its position on a hill where, if the air is not exactly rarefied, it is a lot cleaner than

the chewable fare on offer down in the choked bowl of the city centre. A classy area, Hampstead is renowned for sheltering members of the well-heeled, but traditionally left-wing, middle class. Its housing is predominantly Georgian and highly desirable, its parkland (**Hampstead Heath** is another fine lung in the urban spread) is a big draw in the summer. Despite its pastoral charm, Hampstead boasts a great deal of what can be found in the metropolis proper. There are three major cinemas: the **Everyman**, the MGM and the **Screen on the Hill**. There are chic designer shops, delicatessens, countless cafés and restaurants. It is also the home of the **Royal Free Hospital**, distinguished for being the first hospital to train women doctors early this century.

Hampstead has enjoyed this superiority ever since the plague years of the mid-seventeenth century when Londoners with any nous decided to escape the diseased ginnels of the city for the healthier slopes at the city's outskirts and soon founded a trade in water – specifically, selling it to the riff-raff who didn't need much persuasion that Hampstead was synonymous with cleanliness. A couple of hundred years later, Hampstead became popular with the cutting edge of arts and letters. At various times, Keats, Constable and Lawrence lived here, as well as Freud (for **Keats' House** and **Freud's House** *see chapter* **Museums**).

The volume of traffic in Hampstead has become so heavy that its roads, never designed for the kind of hammering they receive these days, are constantly under strain. But there are plenty of side streets and mysterious enclaves to explore, and a quirky charity market in Hampstead Community Centre on Hampstead High Street where eccentric women sell you chunks of amber and the local colour nip in for cups of tea.

If the idea of shopping is too ghastly, the Heath is five minutes away, accessible via any of the avenues off the main thoroughfare on the tube side. Parliament Hill will afford you perhaps one of the two best views of the capital (the other is from Archway Bridge) if you can dodge the flapping kites, but the rest of the Heath is just as inviting. Of interest are the separate-sex bathing ponds and **Kenwood House**, a spectacular mansion which serves as a backdrop to open-air waterside concerts on weekend evenings during the summer.

The south-west section, roughly beginning at Jack Straw's Castle – a grand old pub which has been on West Heath Road in one form or another since the late fourteenth century – is a popular trysting place for gay men, but the area is policed during the evenings and arrests have been made in the past. Another pub, which has escaped the kind of facelift suffered by Jack Straw's, is the Spaniard's Inn on Spaniard's Road. Keats, Byron and Shelley quaffed liquid inspiration here. Nearby, you can sneer at the wealth on Bishop's Avenue, where scores of overblown houses prove that taste is not necessarily concomitant with opulence.

High on Parliament Hill, **Hampstead Heath***.*

Highgate

Hand in hand with Hampstead (as demonstrated by the free weekly tabloid for residents, the *Ham & High*) goes Highgate, another quaint village-like area which, while not sharing Hampstead's relaxed bustle, is nevertheless equally charming. Located on the opposite side of **Hampstead Heath**, Highgate has managed to keep some of that olde worlde magic, manifest in its tea shops, antique and secondhand book haunts on Highgate High Street. One of these shops, notable for its purple exterior, is the Great Expectations gallery, filled with piles of unusual antiques and art pieces. The proprietor will follow you around and give you a potted history of each item you scrutinise, the name of the artist for any of the brilliantly coloured pieces, no matter how obscure. Prices vary but some of the smaller works are pleasingly cheap. Other places of note are Pond Square, a little sanctuary nestled between Highgate High Street, South Grove and West Hill. Branching off the intersection south of this is The Grove, an arrestingly grand but quiet lane which was once home to Samuel Coleridge and JB Priestley.

Highgate is famous for its cemetery (*see chapter* **Parks & Gardens: Cemeteries**) which is bisected by Swains Lane. The western side is the older section, rescued from neglect by the Friends of Highgate Cemetery and now accessible only by guided tour (£3). The eastern side, still in use, is less atmospheric but dotted with famous graves, including those of Karl Marx, George Eliot and Sir Ralph Richardson. Admission is £1. A good hour or so can be spent trawling the gravelled paths and taking in the manifold headstones. Photographers must obtain a camera pass at the gate.

If you want more tranquillity, **Waterlow Park** shares land with **Highgate Cemetery**. The park is a small chunk of sloped green with ponds and trees (some of which would look better placed in a dark fairy tale), tennis courts and a play area for toddlers. As well as sharing a border with the cemetery, it also nudges up against the **Whittington Hospital** on Swains Lane. Towards Highgate High Street, the sixteenth-century **Lauderdale House**, once home to Charles II's mistress Nell Gwyn, is now a community arts centre and café.

Stoke Newington

There's something about Stoke Newington which is different to most places in London. Maybe it's the fact that it isn't served by a tube (try the 73 bus), or that it really has only one interesting street, if you ignore the long, dull shopping slog that is Stoke Newington High Street. Maybe it's the enduring rumour of bent bobbies within the local force. Whatever, Stoke Newington exudes an appeal beyond that which the metropolitan can

The Books of Blood

Kim Newman on Crouch End and the horrors that emanate from N8.

In the middle of 1994, I moved from Crouch End and now I'm worried.

To most people, Crouch End means Andy Kershaw going on about café society on radio documentaries and the story about Bob Dylan mixing up Crouch Hall Road and Crouch Hill Road while trying to find Dave Stewart and spending an hour in someone's front room waiting for 'Dave' to get home from work. But to a horror writer, Crouch End is a touchstone.

There is a Stephen King short story *called* 'Crouch End'. Though certainly not one of his better pieces, it's an odd circumstance that the Maine Man of Horror should write about the impossibility of reaching Crouch End by public transport and a sinisterly supernatural reason for this. The cold-souled realist might protest that King's protagonist could have avoided horrors if he took the tube to Finsbury Park and changed to the overground, getting off at Hornsey, but that's beside the point.

The reason King wrote the story is that he once got lost trying to visit his friend Peter Straub, who used to live in Crouch End. Strangely, several key genre works of the last 20 years were written within the confines of Crouch End. In one street, heavyweights Straub and Clive Barker, who didn't know each other, were near neighbours. Straub wrote his best-selling *Ghost Story* in Hillfield Avenue, but was long gone when Barker, just down the road, wrote *The Books of Blood*.

Skirting the area are the current or sometime residences of horror pros Brian Lumley (*Necroscope*) and Peter Tremayne (*Dracula Unborn*), gothic fringe master Scott Bradfield (*The Dream*

of the Wolf) and encyclopaedist Phil Hardy (*The Aurum Film Encyclopaedia: Horror*). Robert Holdstock reshaped modern fantasy with *Mythago Wood*, which was written just over the railway bridge in the Harringay Ladder, a peculiar rack of streets named after Elizabethan seafarers, which was also the place where Harry Adam Knight, split between two houses, came up with the greatest paperback gross-out of the 1980s, *The Fungus*.

It's hard to see why Crouch End should be such a magnet for the horrors. There is a bombed-out church at the bottom of Church Lane, a standing but shuttered spire with a stretch of graveyard, but it's park-like rather than doom-haunted. Martin Fido's *Murder Guide to London* mentions Crouch Hill, but only because a bar next to Scott Bradfield's flat used to be a chemist's shop where the 1911 Tollington Park poisoner Frederick Seddon bought his arsenic.

Otherwise it's a cheery, likable area with plenty of decent restaurants – my favourite is Florian's, which put up with my lengthy lunches – and entirely too many estate agents (like the rest of the planet). But obviously the Guardian Spirit of Horror hovers above, ensuring inspiration and prosperity for all.

I lived in Crouch End from late 1986 to mid-1994. During that period I sold my first novel and wrote a batch more, most of which were generously kissed by the muse of N8. Now I live somewhere else and I'll have to make do without that Guardian Spirit.

I wonder if it feels deserted.

---

offer. Perhaps, simply, it is one of those places that has a Sunday afternoon feel to it all week round.

Stoke Newington Church Street is a narrow row of exceptional shops (some of the bookshops rank alongside the best that Charing Cross Road has to offer) and attractive cafés, among them the **Blue Legume**, the trendy draw, and the Teapot, a more modest affair but perfect if you want to spend an hour or two dawdling over breakfast with a newspaper. They also sell an excellent variety of cakes.

A high proportion of the community is Turkish; on Green Lanes their shops sell typical fare, and a number of churches have been 'mosqued'.

Jazz lovers, not just in this area but all over London, find that the **Vortex** is one of the best spots for gigs, a trait that pulls Stoke Newington out of the nice-but-boring category. Clissold Park has the same quality, a comely spread perfect for relaxing strolls or the odd set on the tennis courts. **Abney Park Cemetery**, which has an entrance on Stoke Newington Church Street, is in the process of being restored but still enjoys the unkempt look that true graveyards deserve.

While you're in the area, pop up the road to Stamford Hill (the 253 is the most common bus), which has one of the largest concentrations of Hasidic Jews outside Jerusalem. Many attractive synagogues and orthodox Jewish schools grace the area and there is a preponderance of Volvo estates too. There is nothing of significant attraction in the noisy collision of roads Stamford Hill, Amhurst Park and Clapton Common unless you're hunting small food shops, a supermarket or pubs, but away from the main drag there are tranquil walks to enjoy – in Springfield Park (where there is a playing area, a marina and bowling greens) or alongside the canal opposite Walthamstow Marshes where there are several decent pubs to refresh you.

Islington

Islington's genesis was as an isolated settlement on a gravel ridge many years before the Norman Conquest. It was the checkpoint for all trade (usually farm-related) coming down from the wastelands of the north and locus of target practice for keen archer King Henry VIII (when he wasn't decapitating wives). Nowadays, Islington is a fashionable and attractive enclave (its avenues have been referred to in Dickens' work and an N1 postcode is a highly coveted status symbol), a position it has enjoyed since the seventeenth century. This popularity is in no small way apportioned to the existence of a spa which was said to cure all manner of ailments. It flaunts a trendy, left-wing bias and was conspicuous for its Champagne socialists in the 1980s. Artists and politicians have peopled the streets here over the years, including George Orwell, Evelyn Waugh and playwright Joe Orton, who was murdered by his lover Kenneth Halliwell in their Noel Street home in August 1967. Labour leader Tony Blair has a home in Islington and vanguards of the socialist movement Lenin and Trotsky did much of their work in the area.

If you find you're hungry during a visit, there are many good restaurants and ethnic eateries to explore, especially along Upper Street. **Rabieng Thai** (No 143) and Le Mercury (No 140A, on the corner with Almeida Street, home of the excellent **Almeida** theatre) can be highly recommended. Many of the pubs (such as the **King's Head** at No 115) put on entertainments throughout the week; comedy, music and theatre are well represented. One place that guarantees a good performance is the Tower Theatre on Canonbury Place which has been staging plays for 40 years.

Because of the lack of tourists the streets are pleasantly free of pedestrian jams, allowing you to peruse a few places that have been unable to make the grade as major attractions, such as Chapel

Market, which is open most days and provides Islington's population with its weekly groceries. Other goods can be purchased here or you might prefer the more stately wares on offer at **Camden Passage**, which specialises in antiques; though the merchandise may be of high quality, the stallholders are not averse to a spot of haggling. The **Business Design Centre** on the west side of Upper Street is also worth a look. Now used as an exhibition centre, it has been home to Cruft's dog show, cattle shows and even a bull fight.

Muswell Hill

Just because Muswell Hill isn't served by the tube doesn't mean you shouldn't pay a visit. Although on paper there doesn't appear to be much on offer here, there's enough to keep you amused for an evening – especially if you're on the look out for an evening of dinner and drink.

Go to East Finchley tube, jump on a 102 outside the station and alight at Muswell Hill Broadway. From the hub at its north-eastern end are spread a number of roads, all of them packed with shops, fast food pits and restaurants. Gastronomically, there's a lot to choose from but no real stand-outs. In fact, you might like to skip dinner altogether and buy some ready-made dishes from Mauro's at 229 Muswell Hill Broadway; the fresh pasta and home-made sauces are especially enticing.

The pubs are at the top of the steep Muswell Hill which sweeps down to Hornsey. The Swiss Village and the Tap and Barrel are next door to each other, the Green Man opposite. On summer evenings, the view down to London from here is breathtaking. For an even better panorama, nip into Alexandra Park and take a stroll round Alexandra Palace (broadly known as Ally Pally) – where the BBC were initially based. Now though, the Palace is an entertainment centre containing, among other enticements, an ice-rink.

From these grounds, the whole of London is cupped most conveniently and this world capital looks suddenly tame and ineffective. Exploration of the grounds here could bring dividends. A few deer are kept in enclosures and are quite happy to come and nose at human visitors.

Muswell Hill has some good and unusual shops in among the usual high street suspects. On the Broadway again, try Crocodile Antiques (No 122) for a number of original Victorian and art nouveau fireplaces and an intriguing shop (with café) filled with scatter cushions, wooden sculptures and scores of greetings cards that are a cut above the usual – the excellent Michael Sowa's understated and surreal cards are a fine example.

A poignant sight, tucked beneath another shop window, is a memorial to PC Keith Blakelock who worked in the area until his horrific murder at Broadwater Farm during the 1981 riots.

Eating & Drinking

Restaurants

Every taste and pocket are catered for as London's restaurant scene comes of age.

London is unmatched for diversity of cuisines. Here's our pick of the bunch; if you want to investigate further, the *Time Out* Eating & Drinking Guide (£7.50, updated annually) lists almost 1,500 of the city's restaurants, cafés and bars.

The average prices quoted below are based on the cost of a three-course meal (or the ethnic equivalent) for one person. They do not include alcohol.

Celebrated Chefs

Alastair Little

49 Frith Street, W1 (0171 734 5183). Leicester Square or Tottenham Court Road tube. **Lunch served** noon-3pm Mon-Fri. **Dinner served** 6-11.30pm Mon-Sat. **Average** £40. **Set lunches** £10 two courses (basement); £20 three courses. **Credit** A, AmEx, £TC, V.
Spartan, some would say shabby, surroundings and high prices are offset by Little's cooking. The menu constantly evolves, but the current source of inspiration is Italy. Service and atmosphere are relaxed.

Bistrot Bruno

63 Frith Street, W1 (0171 734 4545). Leicester Square or Tottenham Court Road tube. **Lunch served** 12.15-2.30pm Mon-Fri. **Dinner served** 6.15-11.30pm Mon-Sat. **Average** £25. **Credit** A, AmEx, DC, TC, V.
The menu at Bruno Loubet's critically acclaimed restaurant makes unsettling reading, but persevere as the combinations work. The décor is austere. Next door is Café Bruno, where the dishes are cheaper but fail to enthral. More exciting are Loubet's plans to open a huge brasserie, L'Odéon, on Regent Street in autumn 1995.
Branch: Café Bruno 64 Frith Street, W1 (0171 439 0606).

The Capital

22-24 Basil Street, SW3 (0171 589 5171). Knightsbridge tube. **Lunch served** noon-2.30pm, **dinner served** 7-11.15pm, daily. **Average** £25. **Set lunches** £21.50, £25, three courses incl coffee, service. **Set dinner** £25 three courses incl coffee, service. **Service** 12½%. **Credit** A, AmEx, DC, TC, V.
A recently refurbished townhouse hotel, best known for its restaurant. Philip Britten cooks an essentially French repertoire, integral to which are constant reminders of the English seasons. The wine list is one for oenophiles, but has a helpful selection at the front. Dress: smart.

Chez Nico at Ninety Park Lane

90 Park Lane, W1 (0171 409 1290). Hyde Park Corner or Marble Arch tube. **Lunch served** noon-2pm Mon-Fri. **Dinner served** 7-11pm Mon-Sat. **Average** £60. **Set lunch** £25 three courses incl service. **Service** 12½%. **Credit** A, AmEx, DC, £TC, V.
Nico Ladenis operates here under the wing of Forte, cooking very serious, very good food – the set lunch is a bargain. The long wine list includes a selection of just-about affordable bottles. Chefs trained the Nico way cook at the branches listed below (where the average is £25 a head and the atmosphere less grand). Dress: jacket and tie.
Branches: Nico Central 35 Great Portland Street, W1 (0171 436 8846); **Simply Nico** 48A Rochester Row, SW1 (0171 630 8061).

Clarke's

124 Kensington Church Street, W8 (0171 221 9225). Notting Hill Gate tube/12, 27, 28, 31, 52 bus. **Lunch served** 12.30-2pm, **dinner served** 7-10pm, Mon-Fri. **Set lunch** £22 two courses, £26 three courses, incl coffee, service. **Set dinner** £37 four courses incl coffee, service. **Credit** A, £TC, V.
Any criticisms of the no-choice policy in the evenings are quickly dispelled once Sally Clarke's distinctive, Californian-inspired food has been tasted. The ingredients are the best and the freshest and are skilfully combined in an open-plan kitchen. The wine list has lots of choice by the glass.

Fulham Road

257-259 Fulham Road, SW3 (0171 351 7823). South Kensington tube/14 bus. **Lunch served** noon-2.15pm Mon-Fri, Sun. **Dinner served** 7-11pm Mon-Sat; 7-10pm Sun. **Average** £35. **Set lunches** £14.50 two courses, £17.50 three courses. **Credit** A, AmEx, £TC, V.
Glorious food, delightful décor and unintimidating service made Stephen Bull's third venture winner of the 1995 *Time Out* Best New Restaurant Award. The beguiling combinations (beetroot bavarois with cured sea bass) are cooked by Richard Corrigan. The clientèle are wealthy but dull. The Bistro & Bar is the livliest and cheapest of the three.
Branches: Stephen Bull's Bistro & Bar 71 St John Street, EC1 (0171 490 1750); **Stephen Bull** 5-7 Blandford Street, W1 (0171 486 9696).

The Restaurant

Hyde Park Hotel, 66 Knightsbridge, SW1 (0171 259 5380). Knightsbridge tube. **Lunch served** noon-2.45pm Mon-Fri. **Dinner served** 6.30-11.15pm Mon-Sat. **Set lunch** £25 three courses incl coffee. **Set dinner** £65 three courses. **Credit** A, AmEx, DC, £TC, V.
Yorkshireman Marco Pierre White has left Wandsworth for the shelter of Forte's redbrick hotel. Tales of the not-quite-tamed punk of the kitchen's temperament are legion, yet these days the only shock you get is when the bill arrives. The three Michelin stars attained this year partly explain the prices, but Marco's cooking consistently draws high praise. Less challenging and more grown up than his reputation.

La Tante Claire

68 Royal Hospital Road, SW3 (0171 352 6045/0171 351 0227). Sloane Square tube. **Lunch served** 12.30-2pm, **dinner served** 7-11pm, Mon-Fri. **Average** £70 dinner. **Minimum** £45 dinner. **Set lunch** £25 three courses incl coffee, service. **Credit** A, AmEx, DC, TC, V.
Pierre Koffman rarely leaves his kitchen, which ensures a rare consistency which few restaurants in this league can match. Expect daring combinations and sensational flavours with an underlying gutsiness. Further bonuses are a pleasant atmosphere and a pretty, unfussy dining room. The wine list is massive but does contain some French country wines. Dress: jacket and tie.

*Mussels, frites and over 100 types of Belgian beer – get into the habit at **Belgo Centraal**.*

African

Calabash
The Africa Centre, 38 King Street, WC2 (0171 836 1976). Covent Garden tube. **Lunch served** 12.30-3pm Mon-Fri. **Dinner served** 6-11pm Mon-Sat. **Average** £15 incl 25p cover. **Service** 10%. **Credit** A, AmEx, DC, £TC, V.
A good starting point for a culinary tour of Africa.The menu carries clear explanations. Wines are from Algeria and Zimbabwe, beers from all over Africa. Service can be slow.

The Americas

Café Pacifico
5 Langley Street, WC2 (0171 379 7728). Covent Garden tube. **Meals served** noon-11.45pm Mon-Sat; noon-10.45pm Sun. **Average** £14. **Service** 12½%. **Credit** A, AmEx, £TC, V.
The chicest Mexican in town, sporting huge windows and a wooden interior. The bar is much to the fore, with a choice of bourbons and tequilas; the food (fajitas, tacos, chimighangas, guacamole) is less fine, but serves its purpose.

Christopher's
18 Wellington Street, WC2 (0171 240 4222). Covent Garden tube. **Brunch served** 11.30am-3pm Sun. **Lunch served** noon-2.30pm Mon-Fri. **Dinner served** 6-11.30pm Mon-Sat. **Average** £30. **Service** 12½% for parties of seven or more. **Credit** A, AmEx, DC, £TC, V.
One of the few places to do an American brunch with any conviction. The rest of the menu is worth having too: smoked tomato soup, New York strip steak with fries and oysters on the half shell. The prices are high, the dress smart casual.

Ed's Easy Diner
12 Moor Street, W1 (0171 439 1955). Leicester Square or Tottenham Court Road tube. **Meals served** 11.30am-midnight Mon-Thur, Sun; 11.30am-1am Fri, Sat. **Average** £7. **Minimum** £3.95 when busy. **Credit** LV, TC.
The 1950s diner ambience – neon, chrome, Formica and old

tunes – is not matched by the menu, which has a small selection of burgers, melts, chips and desserts. Food is cooked to order behind the diner counter – not bad for fast food.
Branches: 362 King's Road, SW3 (0171 352 1956); 16 Hampstead High Street, NW3 (0171 431 1958).

Hard Rock Café
150 Old Park Lane, W1 (0171 629 0382). Hyde Park Corner tube. **Meals served** 11.30am-12.30am daily. **Average** £14. **Minimum** main course when busy. **Service** 12½%. **Credit** A, AmEx, £$TC, V.
The hype surrounding the Hard Rock has obscured the fact that it's still the best theme diner in the city. The burgers are fine specimens and the thing to order, plus there are malts, shakes and floats, desserts and the odd veggie dish. Bookings not accepted.

Joe Allen
13 Exeter Street, WC2 (0171 836 0651). Covent Garden tube. **Lunch served** noon-4pm, **dinner served** 6pm-midnight, daily. **Average** £20. **No credit cards**.
A brass plaque identifies the route down to this darkened basement – once inside you find slack service, red-checked tablecloths and a menu of modern American dishes.

Planet Hollywood
Trocadero, Piccadilly, W1 (0171 287 1000). Piccadilly Circus tube. **Meals served** 11.30am-1am Mon-Fri; 11am-1am Sat; 11am-12.30am Sun. **Average** £20. **Service** 12½%. **Credit** A, AmEx, DC, £TC, V.
The movie ephemera is more interesting than the menu at the over-publicised Planet Hollywood. The food comes in sizable amounts, but at hefty prices. The door policy has improved; bookings are not accepted.

Belgian

Belgo Centraal
50 Earlham Street, WC2 (0171 813 2233). Covent Garden tube. **Meals served** noon-midnight Mon-Sat; noon-11pm Sun. **Average** £20. **Credit** A, AmEx, DC, £TC, V.

Bigger than the hip Camden branch, the same formula applies – mussels, frites and Belgian beer (over 100 types) served in a bustling environment by men in monks' garb. The jury is still out on the Ron Arad-designed interior.
Branch: Belgo Noord 72 Chalk Farm Road, NW1 (0171 267 0718).

British

See also below Fish & Chips.

Alfred

245 Shaftesbury Avenue, WC2 (0171 240 2566). Tottenham Court Road tube. Bar **Open** 5-11pm Mon-Sat. *Restaurant* **Lunch served** noon-3.45pm, 6-11.45pm, Mon-Sat. **Average** £20. **Credit** A, AmEx, DC, £TC, V.
Walls of shiny blue above dark brown paintwork, bare tables and Bakelite ashtrays – it's a designer caff, frill-free and utilitarian. Food is neo-yeoman, pulled off with panache. Starters are light and smart, main courses their antithesis: great platefuls of rabbit in beer and sage sauce, duck in cider with apple chutney, or toad in the hole. The commitment to traditional victuals extends to the drink; good British beers and some lethal native liqueurs.

F Cooke & Sons

41 Kingsland High Street, E8 (0171 254 2878). Dalston Kingsland BR/22A, 22B, 38, 67, 149, 243 bus. **Open** 10am-7pm Mon-Wed; 10am-8pm Thur; 10am-1pm Fri, Sat. **Average** £4. **Unlicensed. No credit cards**.
One of the prettiest of London's traditional pie and mash shops, fitted out with wooden benches and Victorian tiles. Minced beef pie, jellied eels, liquor (parsley sauce) and a wedge of mashed potato, plus cherry pie and custard pretty much sums up the menu. A bargain.

The People's Palace

Royal Festival Hall, South Bank, SE1 (0171 928 9999). Waterloo tube/BR. **Open** noon-3pm daily. **Dinner served** 5.30-11pm daily. **Average** £15. **Credit** A, AmEx, DC, JCB, LV, TC, V.
The initial reception to this glass-fronted restaurant was mixed, but the views are so wonderful and the menu so reasonably priced that it's worth a whirl. Chef Gary Rhodes' other joint, The Greenhouse, earns nothing but plaudits for its rejuvenation of British cuisine.
Branch: The Greenhouse 27A Hay's Mews, W1 (0171 499 3331).

Quality Chop House

94 Farringdon Road, EC1 (0171 837 5093). Farringdon tube/BR/19, 38 bus. **Lunch served** noon-3pm Mon-Fri; noon-4pm Sun. **Dinner served** 6.30-11.30pm daily. **Average** £16. **Credit** £TC.
Updated British food, served in cramped but splendid surroundings. The high-backed bench seating and tiled floor make an ideal space in which to sample bangers, mash and onion gravy or salmon fishcakes with sorrel sauce. Service is young and friendly.

St John

26 St John Street, EC1 (0171 251 0848). Farringdon tube/BR. Bar **Open** 11am-11pm Mon-Sat; noon-3pm Sun. *Restaurant* **Lunch served** noon-3pm daily. **Dinner served** 6-11.30pm Mon-Sat. **Average** £20. **Credit** A, AmEx, £TC, V.
An austere bar and restaurant replete with dining architects and the culinarily curious. Dishes are a mixture of earthy ingredients and diverting combinations, crusading a revival in British ingredients. The menu at the sister restaurant is equally robust, but with more of a Modern British spin.
Branch: French House Dining Room above the French House, 49 Dean Street, W1 (0171 437 2477).

Simpson's-in-the-Strand
Grand Divan Tavern

100 Strand, WC2 (0171 836 9112). Charing Cross tube/BR. **Lunch served** noon-2.30pm Mon-Sat; noon-2pm Sun. **Dinner served** 6-11pm Mon-Sat; 6-9pm Sun. **Average** £25. **Credit** A, AmEx, DC, JCB, £$TC, V.
Breakfasts fit for a king have been introduced at Simpson's. Now the best roast beef in town has been joined by the likes of quails' eggs with haddock, black pudding, kedgeree and bubble and squeak. The atmosphere is masculine, the décor stately. Dress: jacket and tie.

Sweetings

39 Queen Victoria Street, EC4 (0171 248 3062). Cannon Street tube/BR. **Lunch served** 11.30am-3pm Mon-Fri. **Average** £20. **No credit cards**.
An incredibly busy City fish restaurant where space is tight and puddings are of the old school. The canteen atmosphere (and paradoxically calm waiters) lend an informal air to proceedings. There's a bar at the front and a marginally more comfortable restaurant behind it – both are scenically old-fashioned but the seating leaves a lot to be desired.

Modern British

The boundaries between Modern British menus and those from other cuisines (eclectic, international, Cal-Ital and so on) are increasingly hard to define. The cuisine was an innovation of the 1980s, when talented chefs began experimenting with ingredients from around the world to create a new cuisine. The result is often exciting and

*Gary Rhodes' **People's Palace** at the RFH.*

unfailingly fashionable, but remains rooted in European culinary tradition. We list the star players below and in **Celebrated Chefs** (*above*).

The Belvedere

Holland House, Holland Park, off Abbotsbury Road, W8 (0171 602 1238). Holland Park or Kensington High Street tube. **Lunch served** noon-3pm daily. **Dinner served** *summer* 6-11pm, *winter* 7-11pm, Mon-Sat. **Average** £25. **Credit** A, AmEx, DC, £TC, V.
Housed in what was the ballroom of the former Holland House – a beautiful wisteria-clad building – is this attractive restaurant. The food necessarily takes second place, but at these prices it shouldn't disappoint as often as it does. Custom does keep rolling in though, as settings don't come much sweeter.

Bibendum

Michelin House, 81 Fulham Road, SW3 (0171 581 5817). South Kensington tube. **Lunch served** 12.30-2.30pm Mon-Fri; 12.30-3pm Sat, Sun. **Dinner served** 7-11.30pm Mon-Sat; 7-10.30pm Sun. **Average** £45. **Credit** A, AmEx, £TC, V.
Matthew Harris has taken over from Simon Hopkinson as head chef, but the formula remains the same: gorgeous surroundings, correct service and a menu which is frill-free but provides marvellous flavours. Dress: smart, not overly formal.

Blue Print Café

Design Museum, Butlers Wharf, SE1 (0171 378 7031). Tower Hill tube/Tower Gateway DLR/London Bridge tube/BR/47, 78 bus. **Lunch served** noon-3pm Mon-Sat; noon-3.30pm Sun. **Dinner served** 7-11pm Mon-Sat. **Average** £20. **Service** 15%. **Credit** A, AmEx, DC, £TC, V.
One of the many Sir Terence Conran ventures at Butlers Wharf, the Blue Print offers reliable Cal-Ital food. The setting alone is reason to visit the place – a bright, white room on top of the **Design Museum** with glorious river views.

The Chiswick

131 Chiswick High Road, W4 (0181 994 6887). Turnham Green tube. **Lunch served** 12.30-2.45pm Mon-Fri; noon-2.45 Sun. **Dinner served** 7-11.30pm Mon-Sat. **Average** £25. **Credit** A, AmEx, JCB, LV, TC, V.
A modern, no-frills establishment which serves up sublime grub (lamb with aubergine pesto, Szechuan pork salad, fab rhubarb trifle) at reasonable prices. Service is consistently friendly. Winner of the 1995 *Time Out* Award for Best Modern British Restaurant.

The Ivy

1 West Street, WC2 (0171 836 4751). Leicester Square tube. **Lunch served** noon-3pm, **dinner served** 5.30pm-midnight, daily. **Average** £30 incl £1.50 cover. **Credit** A, AmEx, DC, £TC, V.
An attractive, well-run restaurant that has remained a celebrity haunt while nurturing the public. The convivial, clubby setting is enlivened by stained glass and murals. The menu is a mix of fashionable, luxury and comfort food.
Branch: Le Caprice Arlington House, Arlington Street, SW1 (0171 629 2239).

Kensington Place

201 Kensington Church Street, W8 (0171 727 3184). Notting Hill Gate tube. **Lunch served** noon-3pm Mon-Fri; noon-3.30pm Sat, Sun. **Dinner served** 6.30-11.45pm Mon-Sat; 6.30-10.15pm Sun. **Average** £20. **Credit** A, TC, V.
A great glass hangar that is enduringly popular, despite the noise and the crush. The unfaltering kitchen and polished service bring in much of the trade, while the possibilities for people-watching ensure it's always packed.

For when the shopping gets on top of you.

Nicole's

158 New Bond Street, W1 (0171 499 8408). Bond Street or Green Park tube. **Breakfast served** 10-11am Mon-Fri; 10-11.30am Sat. **Lunch served** noon-3.30pm Mon-Fri; noon-4pm Sat. **Dinner served** 6.30-11pm Mon-Fri. **Average** £25. **Credit** A, AmEx, DC, LV, £TC, V.
Smart new restaurant for ladies-who-lunch beneath the Nicole Farhi clothes store. Well turned-out modish dishes – grilled chicken with sweet potatoes, Mediterranean vegetables with pesto – are served in sleek surroundings.

Museum Street Café

47 Museum Street, WC1 (0171 405 3211). Holborn or Tottenham Court Road tube. **Lunch served** 12.30-2.30pm, **dinner served** 6.30-9.30pm, Mon-Fri. **Average** £15. **Credit** A, AmEx, JCB, LV, £TC, V.
Refurbished, expanded and now licensed – much has changed at Museum Street. The good bits – a short menu of simple, often char-grilled dishes, unpretentious attitude and pleasant service – stay the same.

Le Pont de la Tour

Butlers Wharf Building, 36D Shad Thames, SE1 (restaurant 0171 403 8403/bar and grill 0171 403 9403). Tower Hill tube/Tower Gateway DLR/London Bridge tube/BR/47, 78 bus. **Brunch served** noon-3pm Sat. **Lunch served** noon-3pm Mon-Fri, Sun. **Dinner served** 6-11.30pm Mon-Sat; 6-11pm Sun. **Average** £45. **Service** 15%. **Credit** A, AmEx, DC, £TC, V.
The most formal of the Conran restaurants, with a sleek interior and a menu of French-biased dishes. The bar area is more relaxed and majors in shellfish. In the same complex are two more Conran ventures, **Cantina del Ponte** (0171 403 5403/Mediterranean, where prices are a little cheaper) and **Butlers Wharf Chop House** (0171 403 3403/British, and pretty expensive).

Quaglino's

16 Bury Street, SW1 (0171 930 6767). Green Park or Piccadilly Circus tube.
Restaurant **Lunch served** noon-3pm daily. **Dinner served** 5.30-11.30pm Mon-Thur, Sun; 5.30pm-12.30am Fri, Sat. **Average** £30.
Bar **Open** 11am-midnight Mon-Sat; 11am-11pm Sun. **Average** £10.
Both **Service** 15%. **Credit** A, AmEx, DC, £TC, V.
A couple of years after it first opened to enormous media fanfare, this restaurant is still delivering the goods. A meal here always feels like an occasion, and the food is much, much better than it has to be (fish and seafood in particular).

The Square

32 King Street, SW1 (0171 839 8787). Green Park or Piccadilly Circus tube. **Lunch served** noon-3pm Mon-Fri. **Dinner served** 6-11.45pm Mon-Sat; 7-10pm Sun. **Average** £38. **Credit** A, AmEx, DC, £TC, V.
The food is superlative, the décor glamorous, the prices high. There's an atmosphere of monied calm, despite the efforts of the young, welcoming staff. The wine list is a serious document, but there's a short choice of affordable bottles.

Caribbean

Brixtonian

11 Dorrell Place, off Nursery Road, SW9 (0171 978 8870). Brixton tube/BR. **Bar open** 5.30pm-midnight Mon; noon-midnight Tue, Wed; noon-1am Thur-Sat; 6.30pm-midnight Sun (women only). **Dinner served** 7-11.30pm Tue-Thur; 7-11.30pm Fri, Sat. **Set dinners** £14.95 two courses, £18.95 three courses. **Service** 12½%. **Credit** A, £TC, V.
Every six weeks the menu hops to another Caribbean island, but the quality of the cooking keeps to the same high standards. The Colonial-style room makes a pleasant setting. The bar downstairs is livelier. *See chapter* **Pubs & Bars**.
Branch: Brixtonian Backayard 4 Neal's Yard, WC2 (0171 240 2769).

Chinese

Fung Shing

15 Lisle Street, WC2 (0171 437 1539). Leicester Square tube. **Meals served** noon-11.30pm daily. **Average** £18. **Minimum** £8.50 (after 6.30pm). **Credit** A, AmEx, DC, £TC, V.
A reputable restaurant serving innovative and traditional dishes – hotpots and sizzling dishes being stand-out items. The cool green décor and attentive service add to the allure.

Imperial City

Royal Exchange, Cornhill, EC3 (0171 626 3437). Bank tube. **Meals served** 11.30am-8.30pm Mon-Fri. **Average** £20. **Service** 12½%. **Credit** A, AmEx, DC, £TC, V.
Strikingly stylish City Chinese in the cellars of the Royal Exchange. The menu, devised by Ken Hom, is MSG-free and fulfils expectations. The service is less sure.

Dim Sum

London has some of the world's finest Cantonese culinary talent, thanks to the exodus of top chefs from Hong Kong (before the colony reverts to Chinese rule in 1997). Perhaps the most distinctive manifestation of Cantonese cuisine is dim sum: snacks and dumplings, deep-fried or steamed, that are served every lunchtime and afternoon (never

after 6pm). Chinatown has numerous restaurants that serve these snacks; we list the best below.

China Court

Swiss Centre, 10 Wardour Street, W1 (0171 434 0108/0109). Piccadilly Circus tube. **Meals served** noon-11.30pm daily. **Dim sum** noon-5pm Mon-Sat; 11am-4.45pm Sun. **Average** £8 dim sum, £15 full menu. **Credit** A, AmEx, £TC, V.
A highly rated dim sum establishment. The best dishes are on the Chinese menu, and some members of staff aren't that helpful about divulging its contents, but if you're a dumpling fan, persevere. The spick and span interior is short on space.

Chuen Cheng Ku

17 Wardour Street, W1 (0171 437 1398). Piccadilly Circus tube. **Meals served** 11am-11.45pm daily. **Dim sum** 11am-5.30pm daily. **Average** £7 dim sum, £13 full menu. **Credit** A, AmEx, DC, £TC, V.
A vast, regal dining room, hung with chandeliers, where trolleys laden with dim sum go round and round over the red carpet. Just flag down a trolley and point at what you want.

Harbour City

46 Gerrard Street, W1 (0171 439 7859/0171 287 1526). Leicester Square or Piccadilly Circus tube. **Meals served** noon-11.30pm Mon-Thur; noon-midnight Fri-Sun. **Dim sum** noon-5pm daily. **Average** £7 dim sum, £15 full menu. **Service** 10%. **Credit** A, AmEx, DC, £TC, V.
Although many of Harbour City's diners are Chinese, the whole dim sum menu has been translated into English – a rare treat. The 'exotic' list contains the delicacies. All three floors have light, modern décor, and service is notably polite.

Hong Kong

6-7 Lisle Street, WC2 (0171 287 0324/0352). Leicester Square or Piccadilly Circus tube. **Meals served** 11am-11.30pm daily. **Dim sum** noon-5pm daily. **Average** £8 dim sum, £15 full menu. **Credit** A, AmEx, TC, V.
The dim sum at this large restaurant is among the best in Chinatown, although the evening menu is less promising.

Tai Wing Wah

7-9 Newport Place, WC2 (0171 287 2702). Leicester Square tube. **Meals served** noon-11.30pm Mon-Thur; noon-midnight Fri, Sat; 11am-10.30pm Sun. **Dim sum** noon-5pm Mon-Sat; 11am-5pm Sun. **Average** £8 dim sum, £15 full menu. **Credit** A, AmEx, DC, £TC, V.
Only part of the dim sum menu is in English, but the waiters here are usually happy to provide translations. Whatever you opt for, the results should be satisfying.

Fish & Chips

Brady's

696 Fulham Road, SW6 (0171 736 3938). Parsons Green tube. **Dinner served** 7-10.45pm Mon-Sat. **Average** £6. **No credit cards**.
Brady's offers prettily piscine décor and unadorned, well-cooked fish and chips in both branches. Starters (potted shrimps, cod's roe pâté) and puds (apple crumble, treacle tart) are above average.
Branch: 513 Old York Road, SW18 (0181 877 9599).

Geales

2 Farmer Street, W8 (0171 727 7969). Notting Hill Gate tube. **Meals served** noon-3pm, 6-11pm, Tue-Sat. **Average** £9.50 incl 15p cover. **Credit** A, LV, £TC, V.
The fish is fried in beef dripping here, producing a dark, crunchy and grease-free coating. The portions are ample. The restaurant gets very busy, so service can suffer.

Rock & Sole Plaice

47 Endell Street, WC2 (0171 836 3785). Covent Garden tube. **Meals served** 11.30am-10.30pm daily. **Average** £7. **Minimum** £1 (12.30-2.45pm). **Unlicensed. Corkage** no charge. **Credit** LV, £TC.

Ignore the unglamorous caff setting and focus on the quality of the limited range of fish. The mushy peas are good too. A bargain in the centre of town.

Sea Shell

49-51 Lisson Grove, NW1 (0171 723 8703/0171 724 1063). Marylebone tube/BR. **Lunch served** noon-2.15pm, **dinner served** 5.15-10.30pm, Mon-Fri. **Meals served** noon-10.30pm Sat. **Average** £10. **Minimum** £3.50. **Credit** A, AmEx, DC, LV, £TC, V.

This famous chippy has a dark wood and chintz interior and excellent fish. The menu is long and prices are higher than the norm.

Branch: Gutter Lane, Gresham Street, EC2 (0171 606 6961).

Upper Street Fish Shop

324 Upper Street, N1 (0171 359 1401). Angel tube. **Lunch served** noon-2pm Tue-Fri; noon-3pm Sat. **Dinner served** 5.30-10pm Mon-Sat. **Average** £12. **Minimum** £5. **Unlicensed. Corkage** no charge. **No credit cards.**

The mirrors, wood panelling and red-checked tablecloths suggest a bistro, but the menu is resolutely patriotic. Fried, grilled or poached fish is followed by the likes of bread and butter pudding with custard.

French

See also above **Celebrated Chefs.**

Canteen

Unit 4G, Harbour Yard, Chelsea Harbour, SW10 (0171 351 7330). Fulham Broadway tube then C3 bus. **Lunch served** noon-3pm Mon-Sat; noon-3.30pm Sun. **Dinner served** 6.30pm-midnight Mon-Sat; 6.30-11pm Sun. **Average** £22 incl £1 cover. **Credit** V.

Marco Pierre White and Michael Caine own this rather flashy outfit, which is decorated with a playing card motif. The cooking isn't fail-safe, but the prices aren't greedy for the overall quality: ink risotto and cod viennoise earned high marks; puddings are intricate.

Chez Bruce

2 Bellevue Road, SW17 (0181 672 0114). Wandsworth Common BR. **Lunch served** noon-2pm Tue-Fri; 12.30-3pm Sun. **Dinner served** 7-10pm Mon-Sat. **Set lunch** £15, three courses. **Set dinner** £18.50 two courses, £22 three courses. **Credit** A, AmEx, DC, TC, V.

An uneasy mix of decorative styles is about the only complaint we can make of Chez Bruce. It's comfortable and the food is excellent: lamb with tomato and aubergine gratin, and char-grilled brill with a buttery chive sauce were two of the dishes that thrilled.

Chez Gérard

8 Charlotte Street, W1 (0171 636 4975). Goodge Street or Tottenham Court Road tube. **Lunch served** noon-3pm Mon-Fri, Sun. **Dinner served** 6-11.30pm daily. **Average** £20 incl £1 cover. **Service** 12½%. **Credit** A, AmEx, DC, JCB, £TC, V.

French classics, some of them with a twist, keep Chez Gérard

Chez Bruce – brill brill and lovely lamb, uncommonly good for Wandsworth Common.

---

packed for lunch and dinner. Steak frites is a constant favourite. The décor is light and sunny, the service pleasant.

Branches: 31 Dover Street, W1 (0171 499 8171); 119 Chancery Lane, WC2 (0171 405 0290).

Chez Max

168 Ifield Road, SW10 (0171 835 0874). Earl's Court tube. **Lunch served** 12.30-2.30pm Tue-Fri. **Dinner served** 7-11pm Mon-Sat. **Set lunches** £13.50 one course, £15.50 two courses, £17.50 three courses. **Set dinner** £25.50 three courses. **Credit** A, £TC, V.

The Renzland twins, Max and Marc, come from Essex but have a perfect grasp of French cooking. Service is cheeky, the surroundings are cramped but the food is hard to fault. Go by public transport, as parking's impossible, and book.

Branch: Le Petit Max 97A High Street, Kingston-on-Thames, Surrey (0181 977 0236).

L'Escargot

48 Greek Street, W1 (0171 437 2679). Leicester Square or Tottenham Court Road tube. **Brasserie Lunch served** noon-2.15pm Mon-Fri. **Dinner served** 6-11pm Mon-Sat. **Average** £22. *Restaurant* **Lunch served** 12.15-2.30pm Mon-Fri. **Dinner served** 7-11pm Mon-Sat. **Average** £35. **Credit** A, AmEx, DC, TC, V.

A Soho stalwart, relaunched a couple of years ago with chefs Garry Hollihead and David Cavalier. The service, art-oriented décor and assured cooking make an urbane mix.

Mon Plaisir

21 Monmouth Street, WC2 (0171 836 7243/0171 240 3757). Covent Garden or Leicester Square tube. **Lunch served** noon-2.15pm Mon-Fri. **Dinner served** 6-11.15pm Mon-Sat. **Average** £25. **Service** 12½%. **Credit** A, AmEx, DC, £TC, V.

A useful, very Gallic bistro consisting of three rooms, all decorated differently. Classic dishes are competently executed and served at a good price for the centre of town. Book.

Branch: Mon Petit Plaisir 33 Holland Street, W8 (0171 937 3224).

Spread Eagle

1-2 Stockwell Street, SE10 (0181 853 2333). Greenwich BR. **Lunch served** noon-3pm daily. **Dinner served** 6.30-10.30pm Mon-Sat. **Average** £25. **Credit** A, AmEx, DC, £TC, V.

One of the few decent places to eat in Greenwich. A warren of parlour-like rooms decorated in different, old-fashioned styles. The straightforward food is somewhat secondary; eating à la carte pushes the price up considerably.

Villandry Dining Room

89 Marylebone High Street, W1 (0171 224 3799). Baker Street tube. **Open** 8.30am-5.30pm, **lunch served** 12.30-2.30pm, Mon-Sat. **Dinner served** once a month, or for parties of 15 or more. **Average** £15. **Minimum** £6.90. **Credit** A, AmEx, LV, £TC, V.

Cramped and more expensive than it first seems, but we wouldn't be without this tiny French restaurant. Each day a few simple dishes, expertly produced, are served to all-round satisfaction. Out front is an *épicerie*.

Greek

Greek Valley

130 Boundary Road, NW8 (0171 624 3217). St John's Wood tube/16, 98, 139 bus. **Dinner served** 6pm-midnight Mon-Sat. **Average** £10. **Meze** £8.50, £10.95. **Credit** A, £TC, V.

A standard Greek Cypriot menu with the odd surprise, and among the best baklava we've ever tasted. There's a good selection for vegetarians too. Run by a husband and wife team who offer a genuine welcome.

Lemonia

89 Regent's Park Road, NW1 (0171 586 7454). Chalk Farm tube/31, 168 bus. **Lunch served** noon-3pm Mon-Fri, Sun. **Dinner served** 6-11.30pm Mon-Sat. **Average** £10. **Meze** £9.50 per person (minimum two). **Credit** A, £TC, V.

Greek restaurant as brasserie – it works well and there's always a nice atmosphere, although things can get a little cramped. The Greek-Cypriot cooking is a cut above most.
Branch: Limani 154 Regent's Park Road, NW1 (0171 483 4492).

Mega-Kalamaras

76-78 Inverness Mews, W2 (0171 727 9122/2564). Bayswater or Queensway tube. **Dinner served** 6.30pm-midnight Mon-Sat. **Average** £22. **Service** 10%. **Credit** A, AmEx, DC, £TC, V.

The menu here makes compelling reading, as it concentrates on dishes from the Greek mainland and islands. Out go Greek-Cypriot grills, and in come unusual dishes, many of them vegetarian. From combinations of okra and tomato to lamb casseroled in wine, the food is commendable.
Branch: Micro-Kalamaras 66 Inverness Mews, W2 (0171 727 5082).

Hungarian

The Gay Hussar

2 Greek Street, W1 (0171 437 0973). Tottenham Court Road tube. **Lunch served** 12.30-2.30pm, **dinner served** 5.30-10.45pm, Mon-Sat. **Average** £22. **Set lunch** £15.50 three courses. **Service** 12½%. **Credit** A, AmEx, DC, £TC, V.

The clubby atmosphere and décor, and menu laden with meaty dishes from the old Hapsburg Empire, make the Gay Hussar a memorable experience. The wine list is tempting.

Indian

See also page 137 **The Curry Trail**.

Bombay Brasserie

Courtfield Close, Courtfield Road, SW7 (0171 370 4040). Gloucester Road tube. **Lunch served** 12.30-3pm, **dinner served** 7.30pm-midnight, daily. **Average** £30. **Minimum** £20 dinner. **Set buffet lunch** £13.95 incl coffee. **Credit** A, DC, TC, V.

Swirling ceiling fans, potted palms and a large conservatory provide the setting for elevated Indian food. Prices are high, and there's more competition than there used to be, but the menu contains some intriguing nuggets.

Chutney Mary

535 King's Road, SW10 (0171 351 3113). Fulham Broadway tube. **Lunch served** 12.30-2.30pm Mon-Sat; 12.30-3pm Sun. **Dinner served** 7-11.30pm Mon-Sat; 7-10pm Sun. **Average** £28 incl £1.50 cover. **Set buffet lunch** (Sun) £12.95. **Service** 12½%. **Credit** A, AmEx, DC, JCB, £TC, V.

An exciting menu based on the hybrid cooking of the British Raj. Dishes, such as scallop kedgeree with lentils or masala roast lamb, are usually good. Décor is expensive but bland.

Viceroy of India

3-5 Glentworth Street, NW1 (0171 486 3515). Baker Street tube. **Lunch served** noon-3pm, **dinner served** 6-11.30pm, daily. **Average** £18. **Credit** A, AmEx, DC, £$TC, V.

Good for a business lunch: huge, seating about 150 diners on two levels, with bare brick walls, a dash of marble, and ter-racotta statues. Most of the menu consists of expensive versions of workaday dishes, although the breads are good.

Irish

Mulligans

13-14 Cork Street, W1 (0171 409 1370). Oxford Circus or Piccadilly Circus tube.
Bar **Open** noon-11pm Mon-Sat. **Average** £6.
Restaurant **Lunch served** 12.30-2.15pm Mon-Fri. **Dinner served** 6.15-11.15pm Mon-Sat. **Average** £28. **Service** 12½%. **Credit** A, AmEx, DC, £TC, V.

Comfort food – oxtail, Irish stew and treacle tart – served in a smart basement reminiscent of a very smart pub. There's an oyster bar on the ground floor.

Italian

Al San Vincenzo

30 Connaught Street, W2 (0171 262 9623). Marble Arch tube. **Lunch served** 12.30-1.45pm Mon-Fri. **Dinner served** 7-10.15pm Mon-Sat. **Average** £30. **Credit** A, £TC, V.

A small, intimate restaurant where the service occasionally falters but the food rarely does. The rustic dishes – Italian sausages with white beans, or grey mullet with olive oil and mint – are matched by the staunchly Italian wine list.

Bertorelli's

44A Floral Street, WC2 (0171 836 3969). Covent Garden tube.
Café **Lunch served** noon-3pm, **dinner served** 5.30-11.30pm, Mon-Sat. **Average** £15.
Restaurant **Lunch served** noon-3pm Mon-Fri. **Dinner served** 5.30-11.30pm Mon-Sat. **Average** £20 incl £1.50 cover.
Both **Service** 12½%. **Credit** A, AmEx, DC, £TC, V.
Friendly service, a nice, light room and chef Maddalena at the helm make this one of the best bets in Covent Garden. Booking essential.

Del Buongustaio

283 Putney Bridge Road, SW15 (0181 780 9361). East Putney or Putney Bridge BR/14, 22, 220 bus. **Lunch served** noon-3pm Mon-Fri; 12.30-3.30pm Sun. **Dinner served** 6.30-11.30pm Mon-Sat. **Average** £20. **Credit** A, AmEx, V.

The interior is plain and parlour like, the service friendly but discreet, leaving all the flamboyance to the food. A daily changing menu of regional specialities delivers satisfying flavours and sizable portions. The wine list is, like the management, a mix of Australian and Italian. The sister restaurant is less expensive, more casual and can be slapdash.
Branch: Osteria Antica Bologna 23 Northcote Road, SW11 (0171 978 4771).

Orso

27 Wellington Street, WC2 (0171 240 5269). Covent Garden tube. **Meals served** noon-midnight daily. **Average** £25. **Credit** £TC.

An easygoing atmosphere, user-friendly menu and a star-studded clientèle mean that this noisy basement restaurant is invariably busy. The bill soon mounts up, but dishes such as rabbit with spinach, balsamic vinegar and new potatoes are generally worthwhile.
Branch: Orsino 119 Portland Road, W11 (0171 221 3299).

The River Café

Thames Wharf, Rainville Road, W6 (0171 381 8824). Hammersmith tube/11 bus. **Lunch served** 12.30-3pm Mon-Sat; 1-3pm Sun. **Dinner served** 7.30-9.30pm Mon-Sat. **Average** £28. **Service** 12½%. **Credit** A, £TC, V.

The refurbished River Café is now better than ever. The superlative food now has a suitable setting: white walls, blue

carpet and a 50-foot stainless steel bar. The ingredients are
the freshest, the techniques simple but effective, with char-
grilling to the fore. The all-Italian wine list is a talking point.

Japanese

Hamine
*84 Brewer Street, W1 (0171 439 0785/0171 287 1318).
Piccadilly Circus tube.* **Meals served** noon-2.30am Mon-
Fri; noon-1.30am Sat; noon-11.30pm Sun. **Average** £9.
No credit cards.
The first Japanese noodle bar in Britain continues the good
work, serving huge bowls of ramen (noodle soup), plus a few
rice dishes. Order from the counter, pay, sit down and gawp
at Japanese satellite TV.

Noto
*2-3 Bassishaw High Walk, London Wall, EC2 (0171 256
9433). Liverpool Street or Moorgate tube.* **Lunch**
served 11.30am-3pm Mon-Fri. **Dinner served** 5-10pm
Mon-Fri. **Meals served** 11.30am-9pm Sat. **Average** £8.
Credit £TC.
A ramen bar where diners perch on high stools round a
horseshoe bar to enjoy good-sized noodle dishes and gyoza
(dumplings). Portions are generous.
Branch: Bow Bells House, 7 Bread Street, EC4 (0171 329
8056)

Tokyo Diner
*2 Newport Place, WC2 (0171 287 8777). Leicester
Square tube.* **Meals served** noon-midnight daily.
Average £7. **No credit cards.**
The menu covers a wide range of the most popular Japanese
dishes: bento boxes, katsu curry, noodles, sashimi (raw fish)
and sushi. Décor is functional, but the location couldn't be
more central and the prices are reasonable (tips not accepted), making this a good starting point for novices.

Wagamama
*4 Streatham Street, WC1 (0171 323 9223). Tottenham
Court Road tube.* **Lunch served** noon-2.30pm Mon-Fri;
1.30-3pm Sat; 12.30-3pm Sun. **Dinner served** 6-11pm
Mon-Sat. **Average** £6. **Credit** LV, £$TC.
Still ridiculously successful, but deservedly so. This west-
ernised version of a noodle bar is big, stunningly designed
and has a fast turnover. Sit at long tables on bench seating
and try the interesting noodle and rice dishes. The ramen are
highly recommended. No smoking. A hectic, friendly atmosphere prevails, helping to make it a good place to strike up
conversations with total strangers.

Miyama
*38 Clarges Street, W1 (0171 499 2443). Green Park
tube.* **Lunch served** noon-2.30pm Mon-Fri. **Dinner
served** 6-10.30pm daily. **Service** 15%. **Credit** A, AmEx, DC, JCB, £TC,
V.
Very approachable for an upmarket Japanese. The atmosphere is relaxed, the clientèle are mixed and the set lunches
a steal. There's a teppan grill downstairs, along with the
sushi bar and private rooms. The City branch is a slightly
flashier place and has a sushi bar.
Branch: City Miyama 17 Godliman Street, EC4 (0171
489 1937).

Suntory
*72-73 St James's Street, SW1 (0171 409 0201). Green
Park tube.* **Lunch served** noon-2pm, **dinner served** 6-
10pm, Mon-Sat. **Average** £30 lunch, £60 dinner. **Credit**
A, AmEx, DC, JCB, £$YTC, V.
A famous, expensive, smart outfit. The food and service are
unbeatable, with only the very best ingredients used. The
set lunches offer an affordable way of experiencing them.

Jewish

Bloom's
*90 Whitechapel High Street, E1 (0171 247 6001/6835).
Aldgate East tube.* **Meals served** 11am-9.30pm Mon-
Thur, Sun; 11am-2pm Fri. **Average** £14. **Credit** A,
AmEx, DC, £TC, V.
Bloom's has been accused of resting on its laurels, and cer-
tainly the service and the food have their ups and downs.
Still, if it's borscht, latkes, carrot tzimmes and dumplings
you want, you may as well eat them at what has become an
institution. Kosher supervised (Beth Din).
Branch: 130 Golders Green Road, NW11 (0181 455
1338/3033).

Korean

Jin
*16 Bateman Street, W1 (0171 734 0908/0856). Leicester
Square or Tottenham Court Road tube.* **Lunch served**
noon-2.30pm, **dinner served** 6-11pm, Mon-Sat.
Average £16. **Service** 12½%. **Credit** A, AmEx, DC,
£TC, V.
An accessible menu (with clear instructions on how to order),
friendly service and a reliable kitchen all account for Jin's
popularity. Classic dishes include a meltingly tender yuk
hwe (fresh pear and raw beef) and barbecued beef strips.

Malaysian & Indonesian

Lam's
*100 High Street, N8 (0181 341 4754). Hornsey BR/W7
bus.* **Dinner served** 6.30-11pm Mon-Thur, Sun; 6.30pm-
midnight Fri, Sat. **Average** £12. **Minimum** £8. **No
credit cards.**
An exotic hideaway in the heart of Hornsey. Standards such
as sambal prawns and chicken with lemon dip are consistently good. Add a few chilled Tiger beers and you have
a very fine evening. Tables are big and round, the service
friendly and efficient.

Melati
*21 Great Windmill Street, W1 (0171 437 2745).
Piccadilly Circus tube.* **Meals served** noon-11.30pm
Mon-Thur, Sun; noon-12.30am Fri, Sat. **Average** £15.
Service 10%. **Credit** A, AmEx, DC, LV, £TC, V.
One of the best Malaysian restaurants in the centre of town,
Melati offers very good, reasonably priced food in congenial
surroundings. The seafood is particularly good and the menu
has many seldom-seen Indonesian dishes.
Branch: Minang 11 Greek Street, W1 (0171 287 1408).

Satay Malaysia
*10 Crouch End Hill, N8 (0181 340 3286). Bus 41, W2,
W7.* **Dinner served** 6-10.45pm Mon-Thur, Sun; 6-
11.45pm Fri, Sat. **Average** £12. **No credit cards.**
Malaysian standards served with charm, and at low prices,
guarantee this small restaurant continued local support.

Singapore Garden
*154-156 Gloucester Place, NW1 (0171 723 8233). Baker
Street tube/Marylebone tube/BR.* **Lunch served** noon-
2.45pm daily. **Dinner served** 6-10.45pm Mon-Thur,
Sun; 6-11.15pm Fri, Sat. **Average** £20. **Minimum** £9
dinner. **Service** 12½%. **Credit** A, AmEx, DC, £TC, V.
The best Singaporean food in London is served at these two
branches (although the menu also lists many standard
Chinese dishes). The plush setting and charming service add
to the appeal.
Branch: 83-83A Fairfax Road, NW6 (0171 328 5314/0171
624 8233).

Mediterranean

Daphne's

112 Draycott Avenue, SW3 (0171 589 4257). South Kensington tube. **Lunch served** noon-3pm Mon-Sat; noon-4pm Sun. **Dinner served** 7-11.30pm daily. **Average** £15 lunch, £25 dinner. **Service** 15%. **Credit** A, AmEx, DC, £TC, V.

Many gossip column inches have been written about this haunt of the rich and famous, but this swanky restaurant has more to it than that. The menu has salads, pastas, fish or grills, not too exorbitantly priced, and the cooking is skilful. Dress to be noticed.

est

54 Frith Street, W1 (0171 437 0666/0777). Leicester Square tube. **Lunch served** noon-3pm Mon-Fri. **Dinner served** 6-11pm Mon-Thur; 6-11.30pm Fri, Sat. **Average** £16. **Service** 12½%. **Credit** A, AmEx, DC, £TC, V.

Booking is essential at this small restaurant/bar. Boasting a glass bar, blond wood fitting and an enticing Italianate menu, it attracts a young, loud crowd.

Union Café & Restaurant

96 Marylebone Lane, W1 (0171 486 4860). Bond Street tube. **Meals served** 10am-10pm Mon-Fri. **Average** £18. **Credit** A, TC, V.

Fabulous cooking in no-frills, modern surroundings. Dishes use Mediterranean ingredients (only the best) to modish effect. Book lunch – though the room is large, it fills up fast.

Middle Eastern

Al Basha

222 Kensington High Street, W8 (0171 937 1030/0171 938 1794). High Street Kensington tube. **Meals served** noon-midnight Mon-Thur, Sun; noon-1am Fri, Sat. **Average** £25 incl £1.50 cover. **Service** 15%. **Credit** A, AmEx, DC, JCB, £$TC, V.

High standards are maintained at this classy Lebanese restaurant. The décor is pristine, the service correct and the food (grills and meze dishes in the main) top-notch.

Scandinavian

Anna's Place

90 Mildmay Park, N1 (0171 249 9379). Canonbury BR/38, 73, 141, 171A, 236, 277 bus. **Lunch served** 12.15-2.15pm, **dinner served** 7.15-10.45pm, Tue-Sat. **Average** £22. **Service** 10%. **No credit cards**.

Anna is on hand to ensure that diners in her woody, homely restaurant are happy. Fish, particularly cured herring, makes many appearances but all dishes have a modern slant.

Spanish

Albero & Grana

Chelsea Cloisters, 89 Sloane Avenue, SW3 (0171 225 1048/1049). Sloane Square or South Kensington tube. **Restaurant Lunch served** noon-2.30pm Mon-Sat. **Dinner served** 7.30-11pm Mon-Sat; 7-10.30pm Sun. **Average** £25.

Bar **Open** noon-4pm, 6pm-midnight, daily. **Average** £11. *Both* **Service** 12½% for parties of seven or more. **Credit** A, AmEx, DC, £PtaTC, V.

Contemporary variations on traditional dishes include lasañe de morcilla (lasagne of black pudding with green pepper sauce). The cooking is good but lapses do occur. The wine list disappoints. Superb tapas are available from the bar.

Thai

Bahn Thai

21A Frith Street, W1 (0171 437 8504). Leicester Square or Tottenham Court Road tube. **Lunch served** noon-2.45pm Mon-Sat; 12.30-2.30pm Sun. **Dinner served** 6-

*Delicious meze, tender meats and bright décor are the highlights at Covent Garden's **Sofra**.*

11.15pm Mon-Sat; 6.30-10.30pm Sun. **Average** £20 incl 75p cover. **Credit** A, AmEx, DC, £TC, V.
The long menu holds some wild and wonderful dishes, as well as many Thai standards. Authentic tastes are usually forthcoming, but the service can falter.

Khun Akorn
136 Brompton Road, SW3 (0171 225 2688).
Knightsbridge tube. **Lunch served** noon-3pm Mon-Sat, 12.30-2.30pm Sun. **Dinner served** 6.30-11pm Mon-Thur; 6.30-11.30pm Fri, Sat; 7-10.30pm Sun. **Average** £22.
Credit A, AmEx, DC, TC, V.
A classy joint with appropriate prices. Thai standards, plus more imaginative dishes, are wonderfully presented and taste twice as good.

Rabieng Thai
143 Upper Street, N1 (0171 226 2014). Angel or
Highbury and Islington tube. **Lunch served** noon-2.30pm Tue-Sun. **Dinner served** 6-11pm. **Average** £15. **Service** 10%. **Credit** A, AmEx, £$TC, V.
Service can be on the slow side but some fine dishes – the seafood is good – are prepared with great attention to detail and the atmosphere is very pleasant. The best Thai locally.

Sri Siam
14 Old Compton Street, W1 (0171 434 3544). Leicester
Square tube. **Lunch served** noon-3pm Mon-Sat. **Dinner served** 6-11.15pm Mon-Sat; 6-10.30pm Sun. **Average** £15. **Service** 12½%. **Credit** A, AmEx, DC, £TC, V.
The dining room is atmospheric and encourages lingering, while the menu has many tempting dishes, including a number of vegetarian ones.
Branch: Sri Siam City 85 London Wall, EC2 (0171 628 5772).

Turkish

Istanbul Iskembecisi
9 Stoke Newington Road, N16 (0171 254 7291). Dalston
Kingsland BR/22A, 22B, 38, 67, 149, 243 bus. **Meals served** 5pm-5am Mon-Sat; 2pm-5am Sun. **Average** £7.
Credit A, AmEx, DC, V.

Highly rated by the local Turkish community and notable for its tripe dishes and late opening times. A long menu includes meze dishes, grills and kebabs, and there's lots of choice for vegetarians too. Service is welcoming.

Mangal
10 Arcola Street, E8 (0171 249 0400). Dalston
Kingsland BR/67, 149 bus. **Meals served** noon-midnight daily. **Average** £8. **Unlicensed. Corkage** no charge. **No credit cards.**
Mangal is the nearest you'll get to a genuine Turkish restaurant without visiting Turkey. An uninviting exterior hides a neat caff interior with an ocakbasi (charcoal grill) from which emerge delights such as mixed kebab for two (chicken, quail, döner, köfte, Adana kebab and lamb chops, served with unlimited fresh bread and a crisp mixed salad). A real bargain.
Branch: Mangal II 4 Stoke Newington Road, N16 (0171 275 7745).

Sofra
36 Tavistock Street, WC2 (0171 240 3773).
Covent Garden tube. **Meals served** noon-midnight daily. **Average** £15. **Service** 12½%. **Credit** A, AmEx, DC, £TC, V.
Bright, airy and converting the masses in Covent Garden to Turkish food. Delicious meze, tender meats and excellent bread are the highlights, erratic service the low point.
Branch: 18 Shepherd Street, W1 (0171 493 3320).

Vietnamese

Golden Triangle
15 Great Newport Street, WC2 (0171 379 6330).
Leicester Square tube. **Lunch served** noon-3pm, **dinner served** 5-11pm, Mon-Thur. **Meals served** noon-11.30pm Fri-Sun. **Average** £13. **Service** 10%. **Credit** A, AmEx, DC, £TC, V.
A pleasantly unfussy space with an easygoing atmosphere. The northern Vietnamese owners offer a menu that takes in all the national variations, so classics such as chicken with lemongrass sit alongside interesting variations such as beef in coffee sauce. Pot dishes are recommended.

Not all dim sum menus in Chinatown are translated into English – **Harbour City***'s is though.*

Vegetarian

Mildred's

58 Greek Street, W1 (0171 494 1634). Tottenham Court Road tube. **Open** noon-11pm Mon-Sat. **Average** £10. **Credit** LV.

A short menu of interesting dishes (some of which contain fish) is served in a café setting just a few steps from the lunchtime bustle of Soho Square. Sharing tables is *de rigueur* at busy times, seating is cramped and tables are Formica-topped. No smoking.

Neal's Yard Dining Room

First floor, 14 Neal's Yard, WC2 (0171 379 0298). Covent Garden tube. **Meals served** noon-5pm Mon, Tues, Sat; noon-8pm Wed-Fri. **Average** £10. **Unlicensed. Corkage** no charge. **Credit** £TC.

A bare room dominated by huge windows and a horseshoe-shaped bar behind which is the kitchen. Quality ingredients go into the likes of Turkish meze, Indian thali (both are set meals) and Egyptian falafel, and results speak for themselves. There are fab puddings, such as lemon tart and baked cheesecake to follow. No smoking.

The Curry Trail ✓

Each of the restaurants listed is worth a special trip; the best needn't mean the most expensive.

Diwana Bhel Poori House

121 Drummond Street, NW1 (0171 387 5556). Euston Square tube/Euston tube/BR. **Meals served** noon-11.30pm daily. **Average** £8. **Set buffet lunch** (noon-2.30pm) £3.95. **Unlicensed. Corkage** no charge. **Credit** A, AmEx, DC, LV, £TC, V.

The Diwana offers a tried and tested formula of dosas, thalis and bhel poori, at bargain prices. Furnished in early 1970s stripped pine. Standards are more erratic at the Westbourne Grove branch.
Branch: 50 Westbourne Grove, W2 (0171 221 0721).

Jai Krishna

161 Stroud Green Road, N4 (0171 272 1680). Finsbury Park tube/BR. **Lunch served** noon-2pm, **dinner served** 5.30-10.30pm, Mon-Sat. **Average** £6. **Unlicensed. Corkage** 75p wine, 20p beer. **Credit** LV.

The low prices, friendly welcome and consistently good vegetarian dishes – the rasam (black pepper soup) and jeera aloo are especially recommended – make this cash-only caff very popular. Order from the counter.

Kastoori

188 Upper Tooting Road, SW17 (0181 767 7027). Tooting Bec or Tooting Broadway tube/131 bus. **Lunch served** 12.30-2.30pm Wed-Sun. **Dinner served** 6-10.30pm daily. **Average** £14. **Minimum** £4. **Thalis** £7.25, £11.25. **Credit** A, LV, £TC, V.

Kastoori is Gujarati-run, and has a growing list of Gujarati specials rarely found elsewhere. The Gujarati thali is a small feast which includes a couple of 'shaks' (curries) of aubergine and potato, a yellow dahl, and a choice of chapatis or mouthwateringly light pooris. Main courses come with superb home-made Gujarati chutneys. The best 'specials' are found on Sundays, market day for local Asians. The décor is bland but clean; service comes with a smile.

Karahi King

213 East Lane, North Wembley, Middx (0181 904 2760). North Wembley tube. **Meals served** noon-midnight daily. **Average** £10. **Unlicensed. Corkage** no charge. **No credit cards.**

A balti house par excellence in all but name; spicy meat dishes are served sizzling hot in karahis at very competitive prices. Stick to karahi dishes; birianis are less successful, but the tandoori paratha is wonderful. Karahi King is unlicensed, but you can bring in drink from the off-licence next door; many of the Gujarati men bring in bottles of Johnnie Walker, just as they might in India.

Madhu's Brilliant

39 South Road, Southall, Middx (0181 574 1897/0181 571 6380). Southall BR. **Lunch served** 12.30-3pm Mon, Wed-Fri. **Dinner served** 6-11.30pm Mon, Wed-Sun. **Average** £13. **Service** 10%. **Credit** A, AmEx, DC, £TC, V.

The most accessible (to westerners) of Southall's 'Indian' restaurants, with its drinks licence, comfortable folksy interior and racial mix of diners. But the food is indeed of a high calibre. Large dishes to be eaten communally are a speciality. The juicy butter chicken (£10 for four) is memorable. Breads are also good – don't miss the crisp, light bhatura. If you're after authentic Southall flavours in a near-curry-house ambience, this is it.

Rasa

55 Stoke Newington Church Street, N16 (0171 249 0344). Stoke Newington BR/73, 106, 149 bus. **Lunch served** noon-2.30pm, **dinner served** 6pm-midnight, daily. **Average** £11. **Credit** A, AmEx, DC, LV, £TC, V.

The best south Indian (and coincidentally vegetarian) food in London. The small room is pleasant enough, but it's the brilliant and rare Keralan dishes that are the talking point. Moru kachiathu (£3.10) is a sweet, mild curry from south India, and features plantain and mango flavoured with ginger and mustard seeds. Avial is a yoghurt and coconut curry mildly spiced with limbdi ('curry leaves') and containing colourful vegetables such as carrot and dudhi (Indian marrow). The attention to detail is impressive.

Sakoni

119-121 Ealing Road, Wembley, Middx (0181 903 9601). North Wembley tube/183 bus. **Meals served** 11am-10pm daily. **Average** £5. **Unlicensed. Credit** A, V.

This smart Gujarati vegetarian snack bar was extended last year, but the essence remains the same: monochrome décor, cheap prices and a predominantly East African Asian clientèle. Among the snacks are khichi, double-cooked rice flour dumplings eaten with oil and chilli powder. Don't miss the excellent fruit juices and shakes.

Tamarind

20 Queen Street W1 (0171 629 3561). Green Park tube. **Lunch served** noon-3pm Mon-Fri, Sun. **Dinner served** 6-11pm Mon-Fri; 7-11pm Sun. **Average** £22. **Credit** A, AmEx, DC, £TC, V.

A new, smart (interior designed by Emily Todhunter) restaurant with soignée staff and a very un-Indian atmosphere. The menu lists predictable north Indian fare, brilliantly cooked. The biriani (£10.50) is a splendid example, with large chunks of lamb in good rice, dum-cooked to seal in the flavours of cardamom, cloves and other spices. Expensive but impressive.

Cafés & Brasseries

Café culture comes to town – and not before time.

London has come a long way in just a few years. What used to be rather a formal city, with strict breakfast, lunch and dinner times, has been transformed into a city with a café culture. Londoners expect to be able to order a coffee at any time of the day (and not just any coffee either – a choice of flavours and styles is becoming the norm) and visitors, too, benefit from this revolution.

A number of chains have sprung up to cater to this new-found freedom in eating and drinking. Branches of the Dôme, Café Rouge and Café Flo brasseries are scattered throughout London, and all offer drinks and simple meals in undemanding surroundings at reasonable prices.

Central

Aroma
36A St Martin's Lane, WC2 (0171 836 5110). Leicester Square tube/BR. **Open** 8am-11pm Mon-Fri; 9am-11pm Sat; noon-8pm Sun. **Unlicensed. Credit** A, AmEx, DC, V.
A rapidly growing coffee chain, providing a choice of caffeine fixes, cakes and sandwiches amid brightly painted surroundings. There's even an outlet in the Charing Cross Road branch of **Books Etc** – yet more proof that where America leads, we follow.
Branches are too numerous to list here. Check the telephone directory for your nearest.

Bar Italia
22 Frith Street, W1 (0171 437 4520). Leicester Square tube. **Open** 24 hours daily. **Unlicensed. No credit cards.**
A touchstone of trendiness and coffee within Soho. The limited number of seats and generally cramped setting can't put a dent in its popularity. Italian football is constantly on at the back, and there are a few snacks, but the atmosphere is what counts.

Boulevard
40 Wellington Street, WC2 (0171 240 2992). Covent Garden tube. **Meals served** noon-midnight daily. **Credit** A, AmEx, DC, LV, £TC, V.
A cut above the brasserie chains and redecorated to boot. A light, sunny interior and a more interesting menu than its competitors compensate for occasional lapses in food.

The Box
32-34 Monmouth Street, WC2 (0171 240 5828). Leicester Square tube. **Open** 11am-11pm Mon-Sat; noon-10.30pm Sun. **Credit** A, AmEx, DC, LV, £TC, V.
During the day your sexual orientation is irrelevant, and the sandwiches, salads and cakes are worth dropping in for. In the evening the Box becomes a gay bar (Sunday is designated women's night). Small but stylish, with cheery décor.

Caffè Nero
43 Frith Street, W1 (0171 434 3887). Leicester Square tube. **Open** 8am-2am daily. **Unlicensed. No credit cards.**
Damn fine coffee and Italian cakes are the attractions at this rival to **Bar Italia**. The designer interior of beaten metal and chrome makes for uncomfortable seating, but people-watching opportunities along this stretch are first class.
Branch: 66 Old Brompton Road, SW7 (0171 589 1760).

Caffè Piazza
16-17 Russell Street, WC2 (0171 379 7543). Covent Garden tube. **Open** noon-11.30pm daily. **Credit** A, AmEx, £TC, V.
Prices are friendly at this large Italian brasserie, although the food blows hot and cold. The pale peach walls, checked tablecloths and long bar complete with TV make for an appealing atmosphere.

Carnevale
135 Whitecross Street, EC1 (0171 250 3452). Barbican tube/Old Street tube/BR. **Food served** noon-3pm, 5.30-10.30pm, Mon-Fri. **No credit cards.**
A dead mod sandwich bar and café where you can eat high-quality, original vegetarian food, or just have good coffee or freshly made lemonade.

Coffee Gallery
23 Museum Street, WC1 (0171 436 0455). Holborn or Russell Square tube. **Open** 8am-5.30pm Mon-Fri; 10am-5.30pm Sat. **Unlicensed. No credit cards.**
Good coffee and fabulous Italian savouries, salads and desserts – at slightly higher than average prices – served on pretty pottery. It's small and close to the British Museum, so

*Admirable attention to detail at **Carnevale**.*

A rare quiet moment at Waterloo's **Bar Central**, which has a branch on the King's Road.

finding a seat can be tricky. Owned by the people who run the King's Road Café and Table Café.

Cyberia
39 Whitfield Street, W1 (0171 209 0982). Goodge Street tube. **Open** 11am-9pm Mon, Sat; 11am-10pm Tue-Fri. **Unlicensed. No credit cards.**
Cakes and coffee take a backseat to playing on the Internet (£2.50 per half hour/£1.50 concessions). Cyberdudes rule, but for novices on-line tuition is available (phone for details). The *Time Out* Internet site is at *http://www.timeout.co.uk.* e-mail: *cyberia@easynet.co.uk.*

dell 'Ugo
56 Frith Street, W1 (0171 734 8300). Leicester Square tube. **Open** *café* 11am-midnight Mon-Sat. **Credit** A, AmEx, DC, LV, £TC, V.
Three storeys of chatter and noise. A Mediterranean-esque menu is served throughout, but prices are cheapest (and seating most cramped) in the ground-floor café.

Jerusalem Coffee House
55 Britton Street, EC1 (0171 253 3490). Farringdon tube/BR. **Open** 8am-6pm Mon-Fri. **No credit cards.**
The exterior looks intriguingly ancient, the interior is newly panelled and painted. Cakes, rolls and a few hot dishes provide the fuel, otherwise there's fine coffee served by the mug.

Leith's at the Institute
Chartered Accountants' Hall, Moorgate Place, Moorgate, EC2 (0171 920 8626). Moorgate tube/BR. **Open** noon-2.30pm Mon-Fri. **Credit** A, AmEx, MC, V.
A cavernous, split-level basement, that's both restaurant and wine bar. Prue Leith's involvement ensures innovative food and a diverse, if expensive, wine list.

The Living Room
3 Bateman Street, W1 (0171 437 4827). Tottenham Court Road tube. **Open** 10am-midnight Mon-Fri; 11am-midnight Sat; noon-11pm Sun. **Unlicensed. No credit cards.**
A mellow venue, kitted out with old sofas, rickety chairs and tables and a no-rush policy (that includes the staff). A long list of mix 'n' match sandwich fillings is chalked on a board; there's a choice of cereals, cakes, soft drinks and coffees. Young film biz types seem to be treating this place like, well, their living room.

Maison Bertaux
28 Greek Street, W1 (0171 437 6007). Leicester Square tube. **Open** 9am-8pm Mon-Sat; 9am-1pm, 3-7.30pm, Sun. **Unlicensed. No credit cards.**
Bertaux wins no prizes for décor, but the cakes, pâtisserie and pastry savouries – broccoli, leek or mushroom tarts – keep the customers rolling in to this Soho stalwart. The coffee – café au lait – disappoints some.

Patisserie Valerie
44 Old Compton Street, W1 (0171 437 3466). Piccadilly Circus or Tottenham Court Road tube. **Open** 8am-8pm Mon-Fri; 8am-7pm Sat; 10am-6pm Sun. **Credit** LV, £TC.
The Valerie empire continues to expand, but this is the original. The window display is a treat; inside pâtisserie and cappuccino are the order of the day, although other branches have longer menus featuring more savoury items. Expect to share a table at busy times.
Branches: 215 Brompton Road, SW3 (0171 823 9971); **Patisserie Valerie at Maison Sagne** 105 Marylebone High Street, W1 (0171 935 6240); 8 Russell Street, WC2 (0171 240 0064); 66 Portland Place, W1 (0171 580 5533).

Pelican

45 St Martin's Lane, WC2 (0171 379 0309). Charing Cross tube/BR. **Open** 11am-midnight Mon-Sat; 11am-10.30pm Sun. **Credit** A, AmEx, DC, LV, £TC, V.
One of the few brasseries in London with an authentic French feel (right down to the rather superior waiters). The menu runs from breakfast to dinner; the wine list is heavily biased towards France. One for grown-ups.

The Place Below

St Mary-le-Bow, Cheapside, EC2 (0171 329 0789). St Paul's tube. **Open** 7.30am-2.30pm Mon-Fri. **Average** £10 lunch. **Unlicensed. No credit cards.**
A self-service café. Dishes are inventive and light, this being one of the best vegetarian places in town. They no longer serve evening meals. No smoking.

Pret à Manger

77/78 St Martin's Lane, WC2 (0171 379 5335). Leicester Square tube. **Open** 8am-11pm Mon-Thur; 8am-midnight Thur-Sat; 9am-8pm Sun. **Unlicensed. No credit cards.**
Like Topsy, this chain just keeps on growing. And Londoners are very grateful, as the designer sandwiches here are well-filled (if sometimes a little sweet) and very fresh. Sushi, baguettes, cakes, puddings, inventive soft drinks and good coffee complete the picture. Not all branches have seats. **Branches** are too numerous to list here. Check the telephone directory for your nearest.

Ranoush Juice Bar

43 Edgware Road, W2 (0171 723 5929). Marble Arch tube. **Open** 8.30am-3am daily. **Unlicensed. No credit cards.**
Middle Eastern snacks and drinks, in a bland international airport setting. Juices include melon, orange and tamarind at around £1.50 a go.

Soho Soho

11-13 Frith Street, W1 (0171 494 3491). Tottenham Court Road tube. **Open** *bar* 11am-11pm Mon-Fri; noon-11pm Sat. *Rôtisserie* noon-12.45pm Mon-Sat. *Restaurant* noon-2.45pm, 6pm-midnight, Mon-Fri; 6pm-midnight Sat. **Credit** A, AmEx, DC, LV, £TC, V.
The noise in the open-plan ground floor bar and brasserie can exceed acceptable levels, but Soho Soho remains a popular meeting and greeting venue. Food is South of France-inspired, the décor bleached with splashes of colour. The first-floor restaurant is much more formal.

Star Café

22 Great Chapel Street, W1 (0171 437 8778). Tottenham Court Road tube. **Open** 7am-5pm Mon-Fri. **No credit cards.**
An upmarket version of the corner caff, where the likes of a mixed grill, pasta bake or crumble and custard are served amid a rash of vintage metal advertising signs.

West

La Brasserie

272 Brompton Road, SW3 (0171 584 1668). South Kensington tube. **Meals served** 8am-midnight Mon-Sat; 10am-11.30pm Sun. **Credit** A, AmEx, DC, LV, £TC, V.
A very French brasserie – efficient service, menu written in French (with vegetarians grudgingly catered for) and a French wine list. So popular that at busy times only meals are served.

Brasserie du Marché aux Puces

349 Portobello Road, W10 (0181 968 5828). Ladbroke Grove tube/15, 52, 295 bus. **Open** 10am-11pm Mon-Sat; 11am-4pm Sun. **Meals served** noon-11pm Mon-Sat. **Credit** A, AmEx, DC, LV, £TC, V.
A welcome sight after a hard day's shopping in **Portobello Road Market**. Dishes are brasserie-style with a twist, and worth having, although it's possible to order just a coffee; the atmosphere is laid-back.

Café Laville

453 Edgware Road, W9 (0171 706 2620). Edgware Road or Warwick Avenue tube. **Open** 10am-11pm Mon-Sat; 10am-8pm Sun. **No credit cards.**
A designer café overlooking Regent's Canal. Food runs from croissants to more substantial fare, but the view's the thing.

Café Minema

43 Knightsbridge, SW1 (0171 823 1269). Hyde Park Corner or Knightsbridge tube. **Open** 9am-9.30pm Mon-Sat; noon-7pm Sun. **Credit** A, AmEx, DC, LV, V.
A chic, glass-fronted café next to the **Minema** cinema. High prices are charged for small portions and a drinks list which includes coffee and Champagne.

Daquise

20 Thurloe Street, SW7 (0171 589 6117). South Kensington tube. **Open** 10am-11pm daily. **Credit** £TC.
One of the few un-gentrified hang-outs in South Ken. You

Ice Creams

The Fountain

Fortnum & Mason, 181 Piccadilly, W1 (0171 734 8040 ext 492). Green Park or Piccadilly Circus tube. **Open** 9.30am-6pm Mon-Sat. **Credit** A, AmEx, DC, £$TC, V.
Ice creams with a bit of class. Sit amid chandeliers, *trompe-l'oeil* panels and starched white napery and let one of the uniformed waitresses bring you one of the super sundaes.

Häagen-Dazs on the Square

14 Leicester Square, WC2 (0171 287 9577). Leicester Square tube. **Open** 10am-midnight Mon-Thur, Sun; 10am-1am Fri, Sat. **Licensed. Credit** £TC.
Excellent ices in bland surroundings. The choice of flavours, toppings and sauces is bewildering, but with the likes of dark chocolate chip available, you don't begrudge the effort.
Branches: 75 Hampstead High Street, NW3 (0171 794 0646); Unit 6, The Piazza, WC2 (0171 240 0436); 83 Gloucester Road, SW7 (0171 373 9988).

Marine Ices

8 Haverstock Hill, NW3 (0171 485 3132). Chalk Farm tube. **Open** 10.30am-11pm Mon-Sat; 11.30am-10pm Sun. **Credit** A, MC, V.
A family-run gelateria that supplies many London restaurants. The ice cream is good but the sorbets are unbeatable. Just the tonic after a hard afternoon at **Camden Market.**

Neal's Yard Beach Café

13 Neal's Yard, WC2 (0171 240 1168). Covent Garden tube. **Open** 9.30am-8pm daily. **Unlicensed. No credit cards.**
A newcomer, decked out in tutti frutti colours, serving ice creams, sorbets and soya milk ices. There are lots of fruit juice combos too.

won't see ladies-who-lunch tucking in to the Polish cakes, coffee and flavoured vodkas served here. It's handy for Exhibition Road and the museums.

Fifth Floor Café
Harvey Nichols, Knightsbridge, SW1 (0171 235 5000). Knightsbridge tube. **Open** 10am-10.30pm Mon-Sat; noon-5pm Sun. **Credit** A, AmEx, DC, LV, £TC, V.
The Julyan Wickham-designed fifth floor contains a food hall (*see chapter* **Shopping**), a restaurant (*see chapter* **Restaurants**), a café (serving modish dishes and teas) and a bar. Prices aren't bad, but at busy times it's all go.

Lisboa Patisserie
57 Golborne Road, W10 (0181 968 5242). Ladbroke Grove tube. **Open** 8am-8pm daily. **No credit cards**.
A Portuguese pastelaria with a beautiful tile painting and a hissing Gaggia. Cakes, such as the pasteis de nata (custard tarts), are baked on the premises.

Maison Pechon
127 Queensway, W2 (0171 229 0746). Bayswater tube. **Open** 7am-7pm Mon-Wed; 7am-8pm Thur-Sat; 7.30am-7pm Sun. **No credit cards**.
A narrow room with a pâtisserie counter running the length of one side. The assorted gâteaux steal the show, but there are a few hot dishes too.

Le Metro
28 Basil Street, SW3 (0171 589 6286). Knightsbridge tube. **Open** 7.30am-10.30pm Mon-Sat. **Credit** A, AmEx, DC, LV, V.
A sleek refurbishment, knockout food and many great wines available by the glass make this basement brasserie a must. Ideally placed for Knightsbridge shoppers.

South

Annabel's Patisserie
33 High Street, SW19 (0181 947 4326). Wimbledon tube/BR. **Open** 9am-7pm Mon-Thur, Sun; 9am-10.30pm Fri, Sat. **Credit** A, AmEx, DC, LV, £TC, V.
A tea-room and brasserie, serving patisserie and French-accented meals. The cream cakes are good if a bit pricey, but there's little competition nearby.

Bar Central
131 Waterloo Road, SE1 (0171 928 5086). Waterloo tube/BR. **Meals served** noon-midnight Mon-Sat; noon-11pm Sun. **Credit** A, MC, V.
So successful is this bar/brasserie that several more branches are planned. The menu is more interesting to read than most, the food more competent, but popping in for a few drinks is not discouraged.
Branch: 316 King's Road, SW3 (0171 352 0025).

Café Portugal
5A & 6A Victoria House, South Lambeth Road, SW8 (0171 587 1962). Vauxhall tube/BR. **Open** 9am-11pm Mon, Tue, Thur-Sun. **Credit** A, MC, V.
A little piece of Portugal. The possibilities at this Portuguese café include tapas, cake and ice cream, plus beers and Portuguese liqueurs from the bar.

The Depot
Tideway Yard, Mortlake High Street, SW14 (0181 878 9462). Barnes Bridge or Mortlake BR. **Open** 11am-11pm Mon-Sat; 11am-10.30pm Sun. **Meals served** 11am-3pm, 6-11pm, Mon-Sat; 11am-3.30pm, 7-10.30pm, Sun. **Credit** A, AmEx, DC, LV, £TC, V.
The river views account for some of the Depot's popularity, the user-friendly menu and relaxed atmosphere do the rest.

Magazines and beans at **Crowbar Coffee**.

The laid-back atmosphere and brasserie-style menu make it a relaxing place. A favourite with families.

Maids of Honour
288 Kew Road, Kew, Surrey (0181 940 2752). Kew Gardens tube/BR. **Open** 9.30am-1pm Mon; 9am-6pm Tue-Sat. **Licensed**. **No credit cards**.
A slice of olde worlde England, so it's popular with tourists. Standards are not what they were, and don't attempt to order cakes during lunch (12.30-2.30pm), but the cream teas and pastries remain worth mentioning. Last orders 30 minutes before closing.

Marie's
90 Lower Marsh, SE1 (0171 928 1050). Waterloo tube/BR. **Meals served** 7am-5pm Mon-Fri; 7am-1pm Sat. **Unlicensed**. **No credit cards or cheques**.
Tucked away in the middle of a bustling street market, this tiny caff is run by Thais, who serve up a range of greasy spoon grills and Thai dishes to a mix of traders, office workers and, always a good sign, Thais. At £2.80 the pad pakkad-dong – that's pork or chicken stir-fried with mustard, green chilli, onions, carrots, ginger and rice – was further proof that Marie's is worth more than one visit. A cherry pie, however, was merely routine. The décor is rudimentary: helicopter fan, shiny pews and well-used Formica-topped tables.

Off the Rails
Greenwich Station, 187 Greenwich High Road, SE10 (0181 293 4513). Greenwich BR. **Open** 7am-7pm Mon-Fri; 10am-6pm Sat, Sun. **Unlicensed**. **No credit cards**.
A tiny, red-painted room in Greenwich Station where coffee reigns supreme. To soak it up there are well-made sandwiches, cakes and soups.

Pierre
11 Petersham Road, Richmond, Surrey (0181 332 2778). Richmond BR. **Open** 11am-11pm Mon-Sat; 11am-10pm Sun. **No credit cards**.
A smart, pastel-coloured café serving a mix of pastries (European and eastern), baguettes and Middle Eastern snacks and grills.

Tea-time
21 The Pavement, SW4 (0171 622 4944). Clapham Common tube/35, 37, 45, 88, 137, 155 bus. **Open** 11am-6pm daily. **Unlicensed**. **No credit cards**.
An exercise in nostalgia, with Lloyd Loom chairs, patterned china and an enticing choice of sweet and savoury dishes.

Waterloo Fire Station
150 Waterloo Road, SE1 (0171 620 2226). Waterloo tube/BR. **Open** noon-11pm Mon-Sat. **Meals served** 12.30-2.30pm, 6.30-11pm, Mon-Sat. **Credit** A, AmEx, DC, LV, £TC, V.

Large premises (a former fire station) housing a sprawling, crowded bar and a marginally more formal restaurant area. Dishes are robust Modern British at very nice prices.

East

The Cherry Orchard
241-245 Globe Road, E2 (0181 980 6678). Bethnal Green tube. **Open** 11am-4pm Mon, Thur, Fri; 11am-7pm Tue, Wed. **Unlicensed. Credit** A, V.
A vibrantly painted, spacious self-service vegetarian café. The usual range of salads, stews, bakes and soups is done with flair, and the atmosphere encourages lingering.

North

Bar Gansa
2 Inverness Street, NW1 (0171 267 8909). Camden Town tube. **Open** 10.30am-midnight Mon-Thur; 10.30am-1amFri, Sat; 10.30am-11.30pm Sun. **Credit** A, V.
A tapas bar with a buzz. The food is more varied than you'd find in Spain, so there's lots of choice for vegetarians. Round the corner the **Crown & Goose** is run by the same people.

Blue Legume
101 Stoke Newington Church Street, N16 (0171 923 1303). Bus 73. **Open** 9.30am-6.30pm Tue-Fri; 10.30am-6.30pm Sat, Sun. **Licensed. No credit cards.**
Blue Legume has fast become a local favourite. The bric-à-brac and bare-boards interior is a relaxed setting, and the menu is user-friendly, running from organic mushrooms on toast to sticky cakes.

The Coffee Cup
74 Hampstead High Street, NW3 (0171 435 7565). Hampstead tube. **Open** 8am-11.30pm Mon-Sat; 9am-11.30pm Sun. **Unlicensed. No credit cards.**
The long, varied menu is the draw at this snug, wood-panelled café. Tea and toast, mixed grills or ice cream, served with a smile. There are tables outdoors in clement weather.

Cosmo
4-6 Northways Parade, Finchley Road, NW3 (0171 722 1398). Finchley Road or Swiss Cottage tube. **Open** 8.30am-10.30pm daily. **Meals served** noon-10.30pm daily. **Credit** A, AmEx, DC, LV, £TC, V.
Step into *mittel* Europe at Cosmo, where no one is in a rush. Lemon tea, omelettes and substantial cakes make for a better menu than the one in the next-door restaurant.

Crowbar Coffee
406 St John Street, EC1 (0171 713 1463). Angel tube. **Open** 8am-midnight Mon-Sat; 9am-8pm Sun. **Unlicensed. No credit cards.**
A strikingly modern design, an unusually short menu and an appealingly large number of magazines are the ingredients at Crowbar. The coffee is good, the few rolls and pastries excellent.

Gill Wing Café
302-304 St Paul's Road, N1 (0171 226 2885). Highbury & Islington tube/BR. **Open** 9.30am-10.30pm daily. **Credit** £TC.
The service can be dippy and the food over-ambitious at this neighbourhood brasserie, but the atmosphere is mellow and newspapers are provided.

Lauderdale House
Waterlow Park, Highgate Hill, N6 (0181 341 4807). Archway tube. **Open** 9am-6pm Tue-Sun. **Licensed. No credit cards.**
On a sunny day, jostle with the middle-class families of NW3 as they fight for tables on the terrace of this magnificent house. The range of hot dishes includes several tempting vegetarian choices, among them stuffed baked avocado and spinach quiche with salad or chips; otherwise there are the usual snacks. Waterlow Park itself is beautiful, and near the café there's a tiny aromatic herb garden, with name badges written in Braille. Alternatively you can sit inside, then have a wander round the craft stalls.

Patisserie Bliss
428 St John Street, EC1 (0171 837 3720). Angel tube. **Open** 8am-7pm Mon-Fri; 9am-6pm Sat, Sun. **Unlicensed. No credit cards.**
Much-admired pastries (notably the almond croissants) are baked at this tiny pâtisserie in premises formerly occupied by the cosy Italian Marinella's. A range of teas are served alongside the usual coffees.

Primrose Patisserie
136 Regent's Park Road, NW1 (0171 722 7848). Chalk Farm tube. **Open** 8am-10pm daily. **Unlicensed. No credit cards.**
A popular Polish-run hangout. The menu features dishes such as goulash and rice alongside a selection of cakes.

Wisteria
14 Middle Lane, N8 (0181 348 2669). Bus 14A, W2, W3, W7. **Open** 11.30am-5.45pm Tue-Fri; 10am-5.45pm Sat; 11am-5.45pm Sun. **Unlicensed. No credit cards.**
The delight of the Wisteria is that it's so unexpected in London. The cluttered tea-room offers cakes, trifle, sandwiches and unusual tea-time savouries. No smoking, not even in the walled patio.

Top Teas

The Capital
22 Basil Street, SW3 (0171 589 5171). Knightsbridge tube. **Tea served** 3.30-5pm daily. **Set tea** £10.
Go for the silver samovar, the freshest cream tea and the lovely loos.

Claridge's
Brook Street, W1 (0171 629 8860). Bond Street tube. **Tea served** 3-5pm daily. **Set tea** £15.50.
Take tea as it used to be taken, amid glorious décor and with liveried flunkeys.

Lanesborough
Hyde Park Corner, SW1 (0171 259 5599). Hyde Park Corner tube. **Tea served** 3.30-6pm daily. **Set teas** £14.50-£21.50.
Try conspicuous consumption in over-the-top surroundings at this brash newcomer.

The Ritz
Piccadilly, W1 (0171 493 8181). Green Park tube. **Tea served** 2-6pm daily. **Set tea** £16.50.
The most famous tea in town in now strictly production line, but it remains a glamorous setting.

Savoy
The Strand, WC2 (0171 836 4343). Charing Cross tube/BR. **Tea served** 3-5.30pm daily. **Set tea** £15.95.
A more casual affair than you might expect, but the supply of tea, sandwiches and cakes seems endless.

Pubs & Bars

From real ale to really silly cocktails, we line them up.

Central

The American Bar
Savoy Hotel, Strand, WC2 (0171 836 4343). Charing Cross tube/BR. **Open** 11am-3pm, 5.30-11pm, Mon-Sat; noon-3pm, 7.30-10.30pm, Sun. **Credit** A, AmEx, DC, £$TC, V.
Prices are high (this *is* the **Savoy**) but the bartenders are first class. Champagne cocktails cost about £9, other mixes about £7, all with nibbles. Men must wear a jacket and tie.

Atlantic Bar and Grill
20 Glasshouse Street, W1 (0171 734 4888). Piccadilly Circus tube. **Drinks served** noon-3am Mon-Sat; noon-10.30pm Sun. **Credit** A, AmEx, £TC, V.
The over-hyped basement bar and restaurant complex is popular enough to warrant a door policy by mid-evening. At its best the Atlantic is colourful, diverse and louche; at worst it's little better than a pretentious provincial hotel bar.

Bleeding Heart
Bleeding Heart Yard, off Greville Street, EC1 (0171 242 8238). Chancery Lane tube/ Farringdon tube/BR. **Open** noon-10.30pm Mon-Fri. **Credit** A, AmEx, DC, V.
All the wines (19 at last count) on the list at this ancient wine bar are served by the bottle and by the glass, useful if you want to experiment. The menu has a French emphasis.

Bradley's Spanish Bar
48 Hanway Street, W1 (0171 636 0359). Tottenham Court Road tube. **Drinks served** 11am-11pm Mon-Sat. **Credit** A, AmEx, DC, LV, £TC, V.
A tiny bar with orange Formica tables, red velvet stools, juke box, faded posters and mock-flocked walls. A faithful band of aficionados squash in to drink draught and bottled beer.

Coach & Horses
29 Greek Street, W1 (0171 437 5920). Leicester Square tube. **Open** 11am-11pm Mon-Sat; noon-3pm, 7-10.30pm, Sun. **No credit cards.**
Norman, self-styled 'rudest publican in Britain', presides over the quintessential Soho pub, second home to the staff of *Private Eye* and other louche characters.

Cork & Bottle
44-46 Cranbourne Street, WC2 (0171 734 7807). Leicester Square tube. **Open** 11am-midnight Mon-Sat; noon-10.30pm Sun. **Credit** A, V.
Incredibly, a pleasant, rambling wine bar just off Leicester Square, with a wondrous wine list and excellent food. It's even open late enough so you can pop in after the cinema.

The Dog House
187 Wardour Street, W1 (0171 434 2116). Tottenham Court Road tube. **Open** noon-11pm Mon-Sat. **Credit** A, AmEx, £TC, V.
A basement bar where space is at a premium and bar snacks are better than they need to be. A haunt of young groovers.

The Eagle
159 Farringdon Road, EC1 (0171 837 1353). Farringdon tube/BR. **Open** noon-11pm Mon-Fri. **Credit** £TC.

This revamped pub was the first of the new breed. The combination of skilful, unfussy cooking and stripped down décor showed the way to a score of pretenders. One of the best updates of the traditional British boozer. It's a large, bright interior that still looks like a pub, but the food is a delight, and there are half a dozen wines by the glass, plus a range of beers. Very crowded.

Flamingo Bar
9 Hanover Street, W1 (0171 491 1558). Oxford Circus tube. **Open** 5.30pm-3am Mon-Fri; 8pm-3am Sat. **Credit** A, AmEx, £TC, V.
Dick Bradsell's cocktails are the star attraction at this quietly hip, discreet basement bar, although there are beers too. Early in the evening the place is quiet, later the pace hots up.

Fox & Anchor
115 Charterhouse Street, EC1 (0171 253 4838). Farringdon tube/BR. **Open** 7am-9.30pm Mon-Fri; 8am-11am Sat. **Breakfast served** 7-10.30am Mon-Fri; 8-10.30am Sat. **Lunch served** noon-2.15pm Mon-Fri. **Credit** A, AmEx, LV, V.
Strictly off-bounds for the squeamish (**Smithfield Market** is not a pleasant site), this Smithfield market pub offers gut-busting breakfasts (including, strangely, one for vegetarians) and the best steaks in town.

Freedom
60-66 Wardour Street, W1 (0171 734 0071). Piccadilly Circus tube. **Drinks served** 9am-11pm Mon-Sat. **Credit** V.
A cosmopolitan, busy but relaxed blend of bar and café. It's mainly gay, but during the day anyone can feel at home. The drinks list runs to 250 items, from Black Sheep Ale to 16 types of iced tea. Snacks come in generous portions.

Freuds
198 Shaftesbury Avenue, WC2 (0171 240 9933). Covent Garden or Tottenham Court Road tube. **Open** 11am-11pm Mon-Sat; noon-10.30pm Sun. **Credit** £TC.
The interior – bare concrete walls, distressed metal doors and slate tables – disguises the fact that this is actually a friendly centre-of-town bar. Beers, cocktails and sizable bar snacks fuel the chatter.

The Hope
15 Tottenham Street, W1 (0171 637 0896). Goodge Street tube. **Open** 11am-11pm Mon-Sat; noon-3pm, 7-10.30pm, Sun. **Meals served** noon-2.30pm Mon-Fri. **Credit** A, LV, V.
A genuine local in the West End. Upstairs, during the day, sausages (including a veggie one) from Simply Sausages are served with either fresh mash or chips and beans, plus a range of superior mustards.

Lamb & Flag
33 Rose Street, WC2 (0171 497 9504). Covent Garden tube. **Open** 11am-11pm Mon-Thur; 11am-10.45 Fri, Sat; noon-3pm, 7-10.30pm, Sun. **No credit cards.**
A small, rickety pub tucked up a side alley. In the seventeenth century, Dryden was beaten up here – now it's a popular meeting place and one of the only decent pubs in Covent Garden. Upstairs is quieter.

The Hope, *also known as the Sausage Pub.*

A restaurant within the shell of a pub. Italianate food, wheat beers and a great wine list make this worth the trek.

Princess Louise
208 High Holborn, WC1 (0171 405 8816). Holborn tube. **Open** 11am-11pm Mon-Fri; noon-3pm, 6-11pm Sat; noon-2pm, 7-10.30pm Sun. **No credit cards**.
A Grade II listed pub that excels on Desperate Dan-sized sandwiches and a wide range of cask-conditioned ales. Thai food is served upstairs.

Riki Tik
23-24 Bateman Street, W1 (0171 437 1977). Tottenham Court Road tube. **Open** 11am-1am Mon-Sat.
Late in the evenings there's a door policy (admission £3 after 11pm), but at other times this trendy Soho bar is laidback enough for all comers.

Three Greyhounds
25 Greek Street, W1 (0171 734 8799). Leicester Square tube. **Open** noon-11pm Mon-Sat; 7-10.30pm Sun. **Credit** A, V.
Recently overhauled, but mercifully unruined, this remains one of Soho's best pubs. It's run by the inimitable Roxy Beaujolais, who doles up fine food, beer and banter from behind the mock-medieval bar.

Trader Vic's
Basement, London Hilton, Park Lane, W1 (0171 493 7586). Hyde Park Corner tube. **Drinks served** 5.30pm-1am Mon-Sat; 7-11.30pm Sun. **Service** 15%. **Credit** A, AmEx, DC, TC, V.
The preposterously kitsch cocktail bar of the Hilton is decked out like a B-movie South Sea Island bar. The cocktails are great and the choice includes many rum-based numbers.

Ye Olde Cheshire Cheese
Wine Office Court (off Fleet Street), EC4 (0171 353 6170). Chancery Lane tube/City Thameslink BR.
Bar **Open** 11.30am-11pm Mon-Sat; noon-3pm Sun. **Lunch served** noon-2.30pm daily. **Dinner served** 6-9pm Mon-Thur.
Restaurant **Lunch served** noon-2.30pm, **dinner served** 6-9pm Mon-Sat.
Both **Average** £17. **Credit** A, AmEx, DC, LV, £TC, V.
The venerable Cheese has been a pub since the Great Fire. It's a wooden, creaky place with hard bench seating (which you'll usually have to share), sawdust on the floor, and old-fashioned waiters. Food is well-cooked British nosh.

Ye Olde Mitre
1 Ely Court, Ely Place, EC1 (0171 405 4751). Chancery Lane tube. **Open** 11am-11pm, **meals served** 11am-10.30pm, Mon-Fri. **No credit cards**.
An atmospheric little pub, dating back to 1514, tucked down an alley. Food is limited to sandwiches.

West

Beach Blanket Babylon
45 Ledbury Road, W11 (0171 229 2907). Notting Hill Gate tube. **Open** 11am-11pm Mon-Sat; 11am-10.30pm Sun.
A Gaudi-esque design and a reputation as a fashionable hangout have made BBB very busy indeed. The dungeon-like restaurant serves Mediterranean food.

La Copita
63 Askew Road, W12 (0181 743 1289). Shepherd's Bush tube. **Open** 12.30-2pm Wed, Thur, Fri; 6-midnight Mon-Sat. **Credit** A, V.
Excellent neighbourhood tapas bar offering mouthwatering snacks, cold Portuguese beer and charming service.

Lamb Tavern
10-12 Leadenhall Market, EC3 (0171 626 2454). Liverpool Street tube/BR. **Open** 11am-9pm Mon-Fri. **Credit** A, V.
A restored Victorian pub, packed with suits at lunch on account of the hot roast beef sandwiches. The upstairs bar is no-smoking.

Moon & Sixpence
181-185 Wardour Street, W1 (0171 734 0037). Oxford Circus or Tottenham Court Road tube. **Open** 11am-11pm Mon-Sat; noon-3pm, 7-10.30pm, Sun. **Meals served** 11am-10pm Mon-Sat. **Lunch served** noon-2.30pm, **dinner served** 7-9.30pm, Sun. **Credit** A, LV, V.
The JD Wetherspoon chain sticks to a formula: no music, a range of good, well-kept beers, and a menu that includes baked potatoes and pasta.

O'Hanlons
8 Tyson Street, EC1 (0171 837 4112). Farringdon tube/BR. **Open** 11am-11pm Mon-Fri. **No credit cards**.
The home-made soda bread, stew and guinness are the genuine articles. Probably the most Irish of Irish pubs in London.

Old Crown
33 New Oxford Street, WC1 (0171 836 9121). Holborn or Tottenham Court Road tube. **Open** 11.30am-11pm Mon-Sat. **Credit** A, AmEx, DC, V.
A pub/bar hybrid, serving an international choice of dishes and drinks, plus beers by the pint. The pace hots up at night.

Peasant
240 St John Street, EC1 (0171 336 7726). Angel tube/Farringdon tube/BR. **Open** 12.30-3pm Mon-Fri; 5.30-11pm Mon-Sat. **Lunch served** 12.30-2.30pm Mon-Fri. **Dinner served** 6.30-10.30pm Mon-Sat. **Credit** A, DC, V.

The Cow

89 Westbourne Park Road, W11 (0171 221 0021).
Westbourne Park tube. **Open** noon-3pm, 5.30-11pm,
daily. **Credit** A, £TC, V.
Sir Terence's son Tom has converted an old pub into a place
where Notting Hill's gilded and grungey can chew the cud.
Excellent seafood.

The Dove

19 Upper Mall, W6 (0181 748 5405). Ravenscourt Park
tube. **Open** 11am-11pm Mon-Sat; noon-3pm, 7-10.30pm,
Sun. **Credit** £TC.
The Dove occupies a small, seventeenth-century building
overlooking the Thames. Graham Greene and Ernest
Hemingway drank here (but presumably not together).

Ebury Wine Bar

139 Ebury Street, SW1 (0171 730 5447). Sloane Square
tube/Victoria tube/BR. **Open** 11am-11pm Mon-Sat; noon-
2pm, 7-10pm, Sun. **Credit** A, AmEx, DC, £TC, V.
A jolly place which fills up quickly after office hours. The
food is worth having, and there's a decent wine list.
Branches: Carriages 43 Buckingham Palace Road,
SW1 (0171 834 0119); **Draycotts** 114 Draycott Avenue,
SW3 (0171 584 5359).

Ferret & Firkin

114 Lots Road, SW10 (0171 352 6645). Fulham
Broadway tube. **Open** 11am-11pm Mon-Sat; noon-3pm, 7-
10.30pm, Sun. **No credit cards**.
The ... & Firkin chain has a number of fine boozers in town:
all of them brew their own beers in the basement and serve
decent pub nosh. This one attracts a hearty, Chelsea crowd.

Julie's Bar

137 Portland Road, W11 (0171 727 7985). Holland
Park tube. **Open** 11am-midnight daily. **Credit** A, AmEx,
£TC, V.
Overpriced food and drink in a delightful setting. The rooms
have 1970s/Gothic fittings and a mellow atmosphere.

Nag's Head

53 Kinnerton Street, SW1 (0171 235 1135).
Knightsbridge tube. **Open** 11am-11pm Mon-Sat; noon-
3pm, 7-10.30pm, Sun. **No credit cards**.
Like walking into a country pub. Bar-wedged locals, friendly staff and a beautiful mews location make this a soporific
refuge from central London chaos.

Orange Brewery

37 Pimlico Road, SW1 (0171 824 8002). Sloane Square
tube. **Open** 11am-11pm Mon-Sat; noon-3pm, 7-10.30pm,
Sun. **Credit** A, AmEx, V.
A recent face-lift hasn't altered the top three reasons for visiting: SW1, SW2 and Pimlico Porter. Brewery tours can be
arranged and take-away kegs for the really desperate.

Paradise by Way of Kensal Green

19 Kilburn Lane, W10 (0181 969 0098). Kensal Green
tube/BR/Kensal Rise BR. **Drinks served** 5-11pm Mon-
Thur; 5-11pm Fri, Sat; 11am-3pm, 7-11pm, Sun. **Credit**
A, £TC, V.
Funky, unaffected staff; subtle imaginative décor; decent
modern European food and a poseur-free bunch of regulars
make this the most charismatic and bohemian bar in town
albeit on the wrong side of the Harrow Road. Beers on tap
include Beamish, Guinness and John Smith's, or there are
vodka shots, Normandy cider and Champagne.

Sporting Page

Camera Place, SW10 (0171 352 6465). Sloane Square
tube. **Open** 11am-11pm Mon-Sat. **Credit** A, £TC, V.
Sells more Bollinger than any other outlet in London. Ignore
the mobile phones and rugby shirts and enjoy the great food.

Westbourne Tavern

101 Westbourne Park Villas, W2 (0171 221 1332).
Royal Oak tube. **Open** 11am-11pm Mon-Sat; noon-3pm, 7-
10.30pm, Sun. **Credit** A, AmEx, V.
The latest local to fall into the hands of well-connected foodies. Closely following the **Eagle**'s flightpath, it offers Modern

You've 250 drinks to choose from at the cosmopolitan **Freedom** *bar/café, Wardour Street.*

British pub grub in a media-filled scrum, with the obligatory 'pine and leather' look interior. Go on a weekday lunchtime and enjoy one of the best pints of Guinness in London.

White Horse
1 Parson's Green, SW6 (0171 736 2115). Parson's Green tube. **Open** 11.30am-11pm Mon-Fri; noon-11pm Sat; 11am-3pm, 7-10.30pm, Sun. **Lunch served** noon-2.45pm Mon-Fri; 11am-2.45pm Sat, Sun. **Dinner served** 5.30-10.30pm Mon-Fri; 7-10.30pm Sat; 7-10pm Sun. **Credit** A, AmEx, LV, V.
A refined interior – leather sofas and half-panelled walls – is matched by a great range of beers. There are always two guest bitters, you might find Bavarian beers on draught, plus unusual English brews. Every so often, the landlord holds a beer festival.

Windsor Castle
114 Campden Hill Road, W8 (0171 727 8491). Notting Hill Gate tube. **Open** 11am-11pm Mon-Sat; noon-3pm, 7-10.30pm, Sun. **Credit** A, AmEx, £TC, V.
A warren of rooms in old wood and a pretty, walled garden are enough of an attraction in themselves. The clincher is the splendid British pub food. Obviously it gets crowded.

South

The Alma
499 Old York Road, SW18 (0181 870 2537). Wandsworth Town BR. **Open** noon-11pm Mon-Sat; noon-3pm, 7-10.30pm, Sun. **Credit** A, AmEx, TC, V.
A pub with a much-lauded Frenchish restaurant, that occasionally suffers the effects of its popularity. The interior is dark wood, the beer Young's. The Ship (*below*) is a sister pub.

Anchor Bankside
34 Park Street, SE1 (0171 407 1577). Monument tube/Cannon Street or London Bridge tube/BR. **Open** 11.30am-11pm Mon-Sat; noon-3pm, 7-10.30pm, Sun. **Credit** A, AmEx, DC, LV, £TC, V.
This Forte-run pub serves adequate food and a reasonable choice of beers, but the views over the Thames provide the reason for being here. There are lots of tables outdoors.

Belle Vue
1 Clapham Common Southside, SW4 (0171 498 9473). Clapham Common tube. **Open** 11am-11pm Mon-Sat; 11am-3pm, 7-10.30pm, Sun. **No credit cards.**
A renovated pub within popcorn-throwing distance of the **Clapham Picture House**, but with food good enough to make movie munching redundant. Beers on tap.

Brixtonian
11 Dorrell Place, SW9 (0171 978 8870). Brixton tube/BR. **Drinks served** 4.30pm-midnight Mon; noon-midnight Tue, Wed; noon-1am Thur-Sat; 7pm-midnight Sun. **Happy hour** 5.30-7pm Mon-Fri. **Credit** A, AmEx, £TC, V.
Mellow, relaxed and serving moreish rum-based cocktails. An unpretentious mix of locals sit inside on rattan sofas or pastel Formica chairs or, thanks to braziers and canopies, outside in any weather. There's a restaurant on the first floor (*see chapter* **Restaurants**).

The Dog House
293 Kennington Road, SE11 (0171 820 9310). Kennington tube/3, 109, 159 bus. **Open** noon-11pm Mon-Fri; 6-11pm Sat; noon-3pm, 7-10.30pm, Sun. **Meals served** noon-9pm Mon-Sat; noon-3pm Sun. **Credit** A, LV, £TC, V.
A refurbished pub where the décor's studiedly bohemian. Dishes are standard but change every day. An extensive New World wine list is joined by an array of imported beers.

Garden House
Castlenau, Barnes (0181 563 9003). Hammersmith tube. **Open** 11am-11pm Mon-Sat; 11am-3pm, 7-10.30pm, Sun. **Credit** A, AmEx, V.
The emphasis here is on size (large). Huge pub, garden, wine list and food portions make this a welcome new addition to Barnes.

George Inn
77 Borough High Street, SE1 (0171 407 2056). Borough tube/London Bridge tube/BR. **Open** 11am-11pm Mon-Sat; noon-3pm, 7-10.30pm, Sun. **Lunch served** *pub* noon-2.30pm daily; *restaurant* noon-2pm Mon-Fri. **Dinner served** *restaurant* 6.30-9pm Mon-Fri by advance booking only. **Credit** A, AmEx, DC, V.
London's only surviving coaching inn, which makes it a must-see for tourists, and if you're looking for a quiet drink in the summer, go elsewhere. Food is disappointing, but the beers include Boddingtons and Flowers.

Masons Arms
169 Battersea Park Road, SW8 (0171 622 2007). Battersea Park BR. **Open** 11am-11pm Mon-Sat; noon-3pm, 7.30-10.30pm, Sun. **Credit** A, V.
This revamped boozer has a pleasing dark green and wood interior, sturdy furniture and loud music. The blackboard menu changes regularly and is slightly wine bar-ish in tone. Drinks include beers on draught, wines and Champagne.

Mayflower
117 Rotherhithe Street, SE16 (0171 237 4088). Rotherhithe tube. **Open** 11.30am-11pm Mon-Sat; noon-3pm, 7-10.30pm, Sun. **Credit** A, AmEx, £TC, V.
A historic pub with a jetty sticking out over the Thames and a snug interior. The food is run-of-the-mill.

The Ship
41 Jews Row, SW18 (0181 870 9667). Wandsworth Town BR/28, 95, 291 bus. **Open** 11am-11pm Mon-Sat; noon-3pm, 7-10.30pm, Sun. **Credit** *food* A, AmEx, £TC, V.
Hopelessly busy, especially on Sundays and for summer barbecues, but worth it if you go midweek. The riverside location and splendid food are what pack them in.

Slug & Lettuce
Riverside House, Water Lane, Richmond, Surrey (0181 948 7733). Richmond tube/BR. **Open** 11am-11pm Mon-Sat; noon-3pm, 7-10.30pm, Sun. **Lunch served** noon-3pm Mon-Thur; noon-2.45pm Sun. **Dinner served** 6-9pm Mon-Thur. **Meals served** noon-6pm Fri, Sat. **Credit** A, LV, £TC, V.
The large interior has good-sized tables, staff are friendly and the menu lists the likes of pan-fried lambs' kidneys on granary muffin. More expensive than the average pub, but the riverside location makes it a fine place to spend a sunny Sunday afternoon – get there early if you want a seat.

Sun
The Pavement, Clapham Common, SW4 (0171 622 4980). Clapham Common tube. **Open** 11am-11pm Mon-Sat; 10.30am-3pm, 7-10.30pm, Sun. **Credit** A, V.
One of a constellation of pubs in the old part of Clapham which has broken away from the rest with a splurge of Technicolor paint. Food is pub grub Italian-style and there are more than a dozen wines, three lagers and two real ales on draught and the usual range of bottled beers.

Tearoom des Artistes
697 Wandsworth Road, SW8 (0171 652 6526). Wandsworth Town BR/77, 77A, 156 bus. **Drinks served** 5-11pm Wed-Sat; noon-1am Sun. **Credit** A, AmEx, DC, £TC, V.
A well-established hang-out for south London bohemians

and thirtysomethings, the Tearoom is a mixture of bar, restaurant and music venue. The atmosphere is more Amsterdam than Battersea. Drinks are pretty cheap, the menu is vegetarian.

White Cross Hotel
Water Lane Riverside, Richmond (0181 940 6844).
Richmond tube/BR. **Open** 11am-11pm Mon-Sat; noon-3pm, 7-10.30pm, Sun. **Credit** A, LV, £TC, V.
A popular Richmond riverside haunt, with excellent views and Victorian front parlour decoration. Above average fare is served alongside fine ales and a decent choice of wines.

East

Barley Mow
44 Narrow Street, E14 (0171 265 8931). Limehouse DLR. **Open** 11am-11pm Mon-Sat; 11am-3pm, 7-10.30pm, Sun. **Credit** A, AmEx, LV, £TC, V.
The views from what was the dockmaster's house are spectacular both up- and downstream and across to the south bank, but the food is uninspired and the beer prices cheeky. Sit outside to watch the sun set upstream and you may find your drinks last longer.

Corney & Barrow
10 Cabot Square, E14 (0171 512 0397). Canary Wharf DLR. **Drinks served** 11am-11pm Mon-Fri. **Credit** A, AmEx, DC, JCB, V.
Wine merchants Corney & Barrow operate good-humoured bars where business people can wind down from (or continue) working. The design here is hi-tech, service is efficient, the beers are unusually intriguing and the wines, as might be expected, are superb. The food ain't bad either.
Branches are too numerous to list here. Check the telephone directory for your nearest.

The Dove
24-26 Broadway Market, E8 (0171 275 7617). Bus 6, 55, 106, 253. **Open** 11am-11pm Mon-Sat; noon-3pm, 7-10.30pm, Sun. **No credit cards.**
An imaginative and thoughtful pub. Nice food, much of it vegetarian, is served (not Sunday evening). There's TV for football matches, and drinks include stouts, lagers and real ales. Another bar area serves Belgian beers.

North

The Albion
10 Thornhill Road, N1 (0171 607 7450). Angel or Caledonian Road tube. **Open** 11am-11pm Mon-Sat; noon-3pm, 7-10.30pm, Sun.
There are several pubs called The Albion in the area – or at least that's what it feels like after you've visited them all – but this is the best, by virtue of its charming garden.

Cottons Rhum Shop, Bar & Restaurant
55 Chalk Farm Road, NW1 (0171 482 1096). Chalk Farm tube/31, 168 bus. **Open** 5pm-midnight Mon; 11am-midnight Tue-Sun. **Credit** A, £TC, V.
The Caribbean food takes third place here, after the atmosphere and the drinks (potent cocktails included). Distressed décor and loud reggae and soul complete the picture.

Crown & Goose
100 Arlington Road, NW1 (0171 485 2342). Camden Town tube. **Open** 11am-11pm Mon-Sat; 10.30am-3pm, 7-10.30pm, Sun. **Credit** LV.
A favourite locally, and so invariably busy, but the staff remain welcoming. A plainly converted pub is the setting for a short menu of no-nonsense dishes and a pleasing choice of drinks (draught and bottled beer, wine by the glass).

NW1's finest, the award-winning **Engineer.**

The Flask
77 Highgate West Hill, N6 (0181 340 7260). Highgate tube. **Open** 11am-11pm Mon-Sat; noon-3pm, 7-10.30pm, Sun. **Credit** LV.
A venerable pub, north of Highgate Cemetery, which in its time has offered succour to Hogarth and Coleridge. There's a smallish beer garden.

Holly Bush
22 Holly Mount, NW3 (0171 435 2892). Hampstead tube. **Open** 11am-3pm, 5.30-11pm, Mon-Fri; 11am-4pm, 6-11pm, Sat; noon-3pm, 7-10.30pm, Sun. **Credit** LV.
A maze of a pub, with lots of dark, low-ceilinged rooms arranged around an ancient wooden bar. The splendid collection of beers helps you to ignore the paltry pub grub.

The Engineer
65 Gloucester Avenue, NW1 (0171 722 0950). Chalk Farm tube. **Open** 11.30am-11pm Mon-Sat; noon-3pm, 7-10.30pm, Sun. **Credit** A, £TC, V.
A spruced-up pub with a restaurant to one side, serving an array of modern dishes, such as squid with black olives and coriander. There's Beamish and Adnam's on draught, and a list of wines from Bibendum wine cellars. Winner of the 1995 *Time Out* Eating & Drinking Award for Best Bar.

Lansdowne
90 Gloucester Avenue, NW1 (0171 483 0409). Chalk Farm tube/31, 168 bus. **Open** 6-11pm Mon; 11am-11pm Tue-Sat; noon-3pm, 7-10.30pm, Sun. **Credit** £TC.
Sparse decoration and an inventive menu are what you get at this new wave pub. Prices are high for a pub, but then so is the quality. Wine is also a strong point.

Magpie & Stump
132 Stoke Newington Church Street, N16 (0171 275 9407). Bus 73. **Open** 11am-11pm Mon-Sat; noon-3pm, 7-10.30pm, Sun. **No credit cards.**
A charming local, much loved by the thirtysomethings of Stoke Newington. It's another bare-boards boozer, with a small garden at the back and a relaxed atmosphere. Food is served but they're just as happy if you order a pint and a bag of crisps.

WKD
18 Kentish Town Road, NW1 (0171 267 1869). Camden Town tube. **Drinks served** noon-2am Wed-Sat; noon-midnight Sun. **Happy hour** noon-10pm Wed-Sun. **Admission** £2-£3 after 9.30pm. **Credit** A, AmEx, £TC, V.
A funky Camden venue that's a mix of café, bar, club and exhibition space. Despite the minimalist décor – bare breeze-block walls, concrete floor and bar – the atmosphere is warm. Soul and gospel bands often play, and there are regular jamming and DJ nights. Drinks run from hot chocolate through fashionable beer to cocktails.

Shopping & Services

Shopping & Services

When it comes to buying and selling, London shrinks to manageable proportions – like attracts like as types of stores congregate.

Bookshops cluster around Charing Cross Road. Denmark Street wouldn't be Denmark Street without its music shops. Look up Tottenham Court Road in the dictionary and it says something about 'street with lots and lots of hi-fi outlets'. Clothes shops gather according to type of fashion and price range. Head for Knightsbridge for top department stores; Covent Garden for street style; Islington for secondhand gear. Go to Savile Row for your bespoke needs, and get all shirty in Jermyn Street.

Sales run just after Christmas and in June/July. Bargains can be found in the department stores.

You're entitled to a refund or replacement if a purchase is faulty. Always keep your receipt.

Department Stores

London's big department stores sell everything from apples to zucchini, after-shave to zoom lenses. Below we take a look at fashion and food halls.

Dickins & Jones

224-244 Regent Street, W1 (0171 734 7070). Oxford Circus tube. **Open** 9.30am-6pm Mon-Wed, Fri, Sat; 9.30am-8pm Thur. **Credit** A, AmEx, DC, SC, £TC, V.
The House of Fraser fashion leader, devoted to fashion and beauty. Ranges fall into four categories: classics, updated classics, contemporary and directional. Designers currently available include Ghost, Nicole Farhi, Joseph, Amanda Wakeley, MaxMara and Mugler pour Mugler.
Baby-changing facilities. Bureau de change. Beauty salon. Cafés and restaurants. Delivery service. Disabled: access, toilet. Hair salon. Mail order.

Fortnum & Mason

181 Piccadilly, W1 (0171 734 8040). Piccadilly Circus tube. **Open** 9.30am-6pm Mon-Sat. **Credit** A, AmEx, DC, JCB, £TC, V.
Fortnum's has been a tourist attraction since the Great Exhibition in 1851. The food hall was redesigned in 1981 to make way for modern contraptions such as the semi-circular cold cabinet from which raised pies, deluxe canapés, portions of beef wellington and lobster thermidor are dispensed, but there are still fancy dressed assistants with cut-glass accents on hand to proffer help. But there's more to Fortnum's than teas and pongy pot pourri – it also sells top designer clothes. The menswear includes the Fortnum & Mason Collections and definitive soft suits by Ermengildo Zegna; the womenswear Missoni, Jean Muir, MaxMara and Georges Rech.
Catalogue. Delivery service (international). Disabled: access; toilet. Export scheme. Mail order. Baby-changing facilities. Cafés and restaurant.

Harrods

87 Brompton Road, SW1 (0171 730 1234). Knightsbridge tube. **Open** 10am-6pm Mon, Tue, Sat; 10am-7pm Wed-Fri. **Credit** A, AmEx, DC, JCB, SC, £$TC, V.
The 18 departments in the food hall fill seven elaborately decorated rooms, encompassing 35,000sq ft. There's a pâtisserie hall for tea, coffee, luxury chocs and more flans, pastries and tarts than you can shake a stick at. The fruit and vegetable hall has strawberries all year round, as well as tamarillos, starfruit, cactus fruit and mangosteens. The meat, fish, poultry and bacon hall is perhaps the highlight. There are 60 fashion departments at Harrods, including a good swimwear section and the infamous Way In. The menswear department is well stocked with modish names. No seriously ripped jeans, cut-offs or cycling shorts can be worn.
Baby-changing facilities. Bureau de change. Cafés and restaurant. Car park. Cakes made to order. Delivery service (within M25, free on orders over £50). Disabled: access; toilet. Hair salon. Mail order.

Harvey Nichols

109-125 Knightsbridge, SW1 (0171 235 5000). Knightsbridge tube.
General **Open** 10am-7pm Mon, Tue, Thur, Fri; 10am-8pm Wed; 10am-6pm Sat; noon-5pm Sun.
Fifth Floor **Open** 10am-8pm Mon-Fri; 10am-6pm Sat.
Both **Credit** A, AmEx, DC, £$TC, V.
Always boasting the finest window displays in London, this is the fashion addict's first stop. It incorporates one of the lunching ladies' favourite havens, the Fifth Floor café, as well as a perfumery. Calvin Klein, Ozbek and Dolce & Gabbana continue to be the best sellers but MaxMara, Mani, Margaret Howell, Nicole Farhi and John Rocha are also popular. On the lower ground floor you'll find menswear. The roof-top foodies' paradise – food hall, café, bar and restaurant – was opened in 1993. Fruit and flowers separate the groceries from the café; the restaurant and bar are hidden behind a glass wall. The emphasis is on food fashion: the pasta shelves are packed with every shape, size and flavour imaginable.
Baby-changing facilities. Bureau de change. Car park. Delivery service (within London area). Disabled: access; toilet. Mail order.

John Lewis

278-306 Oxford Street, W1 (0171 629 7711). Oxford Circus tube. **Open** 9.30am-6pm Mon, Tue, Wed, Fri; 9am-6pm Sat; 10am-8pm Thur. **Credit** SC.
Famed for its 'never knowingly undersold' policy and its fabrics selection, John Lewis devotes the first floor to women's separates, including Liz Claiborne, Episode, Betty Berkley, Jaeger and Jacques Vert. Menswear includes Levi's, Pepe, Wrangler, own brand, Jaeger, Bernhard and Aquascutum. *Alterations to own goods. Baby-changing facilities. Delivery service. Disabled: access, toilets. Export bureau. Mail order. Restaurants.*

Liberty

*Regent Street, W1 (0171 734 1234). Oxford Circus
tube.* **Open** 9.30am-6pm Mon, Tue, Fri, Sat; 10am-6pm
Wed; 9.30am-7.30pm Thur. **Credit** A, AmEx, DC, JCB,
SC, £$TC, V.

Think of Liberty and scarves and endless leather accessories
spring to mind. While it is true that Liberty's Arts and
Crafts heritage suffuses every inch of the store, there is much
more besides. It is well stocked with textile designers
and top designer fashion – a new own label joins menswear
and womenswear from Miyake, Galliano, Liza Bruce and
Vivienne Westwood.

*Café. Delivery service. Disabled: access, lifts, toilets.
Export bureau. Mail order. Restaurant.*

Branch: Unit RU20, Terminal 3 Departures, Heathrow
Airport, Hounslow, Middx TW6 1JH (0181 754 8488).

Marks & Spencer

*458 Oxford Street, W1 (0171 935 7954). Marble Arch
tube.* **Open** 9am-7pm Mon-Wed, Fri, Sat; 9am-8pm Thur.
Credit SC.

The company that revolutionised the TV dinner and regularly persuades its customers to part with £1.09 for half a
dozen eggs has turned its hand to the deli counter. Called
'speciality delicatessens', these have assistants ready to dispense salads, pastries, barbecue specials or fish. Some stores
have new 'butcher's shops', with osso bucco, lime and coriander chicken kebabs, prime Aberdeen Angus beef and lamb
saddle steaks with apricot and almond stuffing. M&S, with
Paul Smith as design consultant, is to be thanked for revo-
lutionising high-street fashion in the 1980s. Its menswear
and womenswear go from strength to strength. New lines
and more avant garde designs are test-marketed at the
Marble Arch branch.

*Bureau de change. Delivery service. Disabled: access, lifts.
Export bureau. Mail order.*

Branches are too numerous to list here. Check the
telephone directory for your nearest.

Selfridges

*400 Oxford Street, W1 (0171 629 1234). Bond Street
tube.* **Open** 9.30am-7pm Mon-Wed, Fri, Sat; 9.30am-8pm
Thur. **Credit** A, AmEx, DC, EC, JCB, SC, £$TC, V.

The food hall was remodelled and expanded in 1989 and
though it might lack the architectural splendour of Harrods
or Fortnum's, this is probably the most user-friendly of the
food halls. It provides an international range of food, with
counters devoted to India, Japan, China, Mexico and Jamaica.
The meat and fish counters are small but still manage to
stock venison, pheasant, partridge and pigeon in season
and exotic fish. There's a separate wine shop, a branch of
Prêt à Manger tucked into one corner and an oyster bar.
New developments in fashion include the launch in autumn
1995 of a Selfridges women's coordinates collection comprising nine pieces. The best sellers are currently MaxMara,
Mani, CK, Cerrutti, Betty Jackson, Caroline Charles and
Jasper Conran.

*Baby-changing facilities. Café. Delivery service. Disabled:
access, lifts, toilets. Export scheme. Free catalogue. Mail
order. Restaurant. Services arcade (in basement).*

Simpson

*203 Piccadilly, W1 (0171 734 2002). Piccadilly Circus
tube.* **Open** 9am-6pm Mon, Wed, Fri, Sat; 9.30am-6pm
Tue; 9am-7pm Thur. **Credit** A, AmEx, DC, JCB, SC,
£$TC, V.

Classic British fashion for men and women with everything
erring on the expensive side. Laroche, Synonyme by George
Rech, Mulberry, Dax, Genny Way and Joseph do well here.
Of the two floors of fashion the fourth floor is younger top
end and casual and the fifth floor classic.

*Catalogue. Delivery service. Export scheme. Gift wrapping.
Mail and telephone credit order. Restaurant/sushi bar.
Wine bar/café.*

Food

For food halls *see above* **Department Stores.**

Bakeries & Pâtisseries

& Clarke's

*122 Kensington Church Street, W8 (0171 229 2190).
Notting Hill Gate tube.* **Open** 8am-8pm Mon-Fri; 9am-
4pm Sat. **Credit** A, V.

Set up by Sally Clarke next door to her restaurant, this small,
attractive shop sells Clarke's famous Mediterranean-style
breads, with bestsellers including walnut, hazelnut and
raisin, and green olive and herb.

Cheese Shops

Neal's Yard Dairy

*17 Shorts Gardens, WC2 (0171 379 7646). Covent
Garden tube.* **Open** 9am-7pm Mon-Sat; 11am-5pm Sun.
Credit A, V.

Shelves are stacked with truckles, wedges and pyramids,
rinds glowing golden, blue-green or flossy white. Staff are
enthusiastic and you are encouraged to sample the bewildering array of varieties sold.

Paxton & Whitfield

*93 Jermyn Street, SW1 (0171 930 0259). Green Park or
Piccadilly Circus tube.* **Open** 9am-5.30pm Mon-Sat.
Credit A, AmEx, DC, £TC, V.

Inside these premises, sandwiched between the bootmakers
and suitmakers of Jermyn Street, the narrow room is stacked
on one side with cheeses, plus a few sides of ham and bacon,
pots of pâté and hand-raised pork pies, and on the other with
jars of preserves, chutneys and pickles.

Confectioners

Charbonnel et Walker

*1 The Royal Arcade, 28 Old Bond Street, W1 (0171 491
0939). Green Park or Piccadilly Circus tube.* **Open** 9am-
6pm Mon-Fri; 10am-5pm Sat. **Credit** A, AmEx, DC, JCB,
V.

This dapper shop for chocaholics continues to sell beautifully packaged chocolates made with cocoa-rich chocolate
and fresh cream.

Rococo Chocolates

*321 King's Road, SW3 (0171 352 5857). Sloane Square
tube.* **Open** 10am-6.30pm Mon-Sat. **Credit** A, AmEx, V.

The place for those who take their cocoa content seriously.

Delicatessens

Butlers Wharf Gastrodome

*Butlers Wharf Building, Shad Thames, SE1 (0171 403
3403). London Bridge tube/BR.* **Open** times vary. **Credit**
A, AmEx, DC, V.

Conran's temple to food contains four smart shops – **Chop
Shop, Oils & Spice Shop, Le Pont de la Tour Food
Store** and **Smoked Fish & Crustacea** – intended to com-
plement both each other and the restaurants housed in the
Butlers Wharf complex.

Randall & Aubin

*16 Brewer Street, W1 (0171 437 3507). Piccadilly Circus
tube.* **Open** 8am-6.30pm Mon-Fri; 8am-6pm Sat. **Credit**
A, V.

Despite its central location, this beautiful old Anglo-French
grocer's is very much a neighbourhood store supported by
loyal regulars.

Delivery

Room Service

(City and central London deliveries 0171 586 5800/north-west London deliveries 0171 586 6000). **Credit** A, AmEx, DC, V.
Room Service has an arrangement with restaurants which provide it with meals to order that are then delivered.

Health Food

Neal's Yard Wholefood Warehouse

21-23 Shorts Gardens, WC2 (0171 836 5151). Covent Garden tube. **Open** 9am-7pm Mon-Wed, Fri; 9am-7.30pm Thur; 9am-6.30pm Sat; 10am-5.30pm Sun. **Credit** A, V.
All your wholefood and health food needs catered for.
Disabled: access.

Wild Oats

210 Westbourne Grove, W11 (0171 229 1063). Bayswater or Royal Oak tube. **Open** 9am-7pm Mon-Fri, Sun; 9am-6pm Sat. **No credit cards**.
Stock is extensive, from the organic greengrocery to the bread section, which offers over 30 varieties.
Disabled: access.

International

Carluccio's

28A Neal Street, WC2 (0171 240 1487). Covent Garden tube. **Open** 11am-7pm Mon-Thur; 10am-7pm Fri; 10am-6pm Sat. **Credit** A, AmEx, V.
There are so many pre-prepared dishes at this high-class, high-fashion Italian deli, your senses reel.
Catering. Delivery service (local).

Reza Patisserie, Meats & Greengrocery

347 Kensington High Street, W8 (0171 603 0924). High Street Kensington tube. **Open** 9am-9pm daily. **No credit cards**.
Delicious variants of zolbia (Middle Eastern pastry dipped in syrup and honey, flavoured with rosewater), as well as baklava and raisin cookies. There are round, sweet lemons and white salmon (actually smoked grass carp); unroasted pistachios; and saffron-flavoured ice-cream.

See Woo

18-20 Lisle Street, WC2 (0171 439 8325). Leicester Square tube. **Open** 10am-7.45pm daily. **No credit cards**.
This Chinese store's frozen section is good: wun-tun pastry, whole milkfish, nilefish, water catfish, tilapia, snakehead-fish, silver and black pomfrets, ducks' tongues and quails. The basement is packed with crockery and chopsticks.

Southall

Southall BR.
Once known for its northern Indian specialities as retailed by Sikhs, Southall has experienced a noticeable influx of Moslems from Birmingham in its Asian community of late. The result is a proliferation of halal butcher's shops. The tastiest street snacks are the kebabs, served Punjabi-style, straight from the charcoal grill. Indian and Pakistani grocery shops remain plentiful.

Traiteur Pagnol

170 Regent's Park Road, NW1 (0171 586 6988). Chalk Farm tube. **Open** 9.30am-4pm Mon; 9.30am-8pm Tue-Fri; 9.30am-6pm Sat. **No credit cards**.
Soups, tartes, terrines, roasted meats, cassoulet, fish en papillote, seafood tagliatelle, wild duck, blue lentils with pancetta and roasted vegetables are prepared on the premises.
Delivery service.

Yaohan Plaza

399 Edgware Road, NW9 (0181 200 0009). Colindale tube. **Open** 10am-7pm Mon-Thur; 10am-8pm Fri, Sat; noon-6pm Sun. **Credit** A, JCB, V.
The huge food department with Japanese retailers including the sweet makers Minamoto Kichoan *(0181 205 0988)* and sushi makers Dalkichi *(0181 200 0009)*.

Drink

Wines & Spirits

Berry Bros & Rudd

3 St James's Street, SW1 (0171 396 9600). Green Park tube. **Open** 9am-5.30pm Mon-Fri. **Credit** A, AmEx, DC, V.
Classic regions, plus a selection of New World wines.
Case discount. Delivery service. Mail order. Storage. Wine tasting.

Corney & Barrow

194 Kensington Park Road, W11 (0171 221 5122). Ladbroke Grove or Notting Hill Gate tube. **Open** 10am-8pm Mon-Sat. **Credit** A, AmEx, V.
Classic lines with good ranges from down under and Italy.
Case discount. Delivery service. Mail order. Storage. Wine tasting.

Beer

The Beer Shop

8 Pitfield Street, N1 (0171 739 3701). Old Street tube/BR. **Open** 11am-7pm Mon-Fri; 10am-4pm Sat. **Credit** A, £TC, V.

Regional breweries supply **The Beer Shop**.

Draught beer from regional breweries is sold in polypins and upwards, and there's a wide selection of bottled beers from around the world.
Delivery service (local). Discounts negotiable on large orders. Glass hire. Sale or return party service.

Coffee & Tea

Algerian Coffee Stores
52 Old Compton Street, W1 (0171 437 2480). Leicester Square tube. **Open** 9am-7pm Mon-Sat. **Credit** A, AmEx, DC, JCB, V.
Over 35 coffees, with a further 20 flavoured varieties. There's even a section called 'coffee additives', which turns out to be rather healthier than it sounds: it includes ground roasted figs, orange peel and cardamom for flavouring your favourite brew. Teas are sold also, including Gunpowder Green and Darjeeling first flush.
Mail order.

The Costume Studio
6 Penton Grove, off White Lion Street, N1 (0171 388 4481/837 6576). Angel tube. **Open** 9.30am-6pm Mon-Fri; 10am-5pm Sat. **Credit** A, AmEx, V.
More than 5,000 outfits with which to knock 'em dead at that most terrifying of ordeals, the fancy dress party.

Party Party
11 Southampton Road, NW5 (0171 267 9084). Belsize Park tube/Hampstead Heath BR. **Open** 9.30am-5.30pm Mon-Sat. **Credit** A, AmEx, V.
Party Party will inspire you to throw one, and invest in one of the spectacular custom-made cakes for which this jolly-looking shop is famous.

Health & Beauty

Culpeper Herbalists
8 The Market, Covent Garden Piazza, WC2 (0171 379 6698). Covent Garden tube. **Open** 10am-8pm Mon-Thur; 9am-8pm Fri, Sat; 10am-6pm Sun. **Credit** A, AmEx, EC, JCB, V.
Drawers containing 50 medicinal herbs attract the punters to this delightful corner shop.
Mail order.
Branch: 21 Bruton Street, W1 (0171 629 4559).

Crabtree & Evelyn
6 Kensington Church Street, W8 (0171 937 9335). High Street Kensington tube. **Open** 9.30am-6pm Mon-Wed, Fri, Sat; 9.30am-7pm Thur. **Credit** A, AmEx, V.
Fanciful toiletries and gift foods, all beautifully packaged in a Victorian-esque style. The chain only dates back to the 1970s but with wafting classical music and traditional wooden features, you'd pitch it much earlier.
Disabled: access.
Branches: 30 James Street, WC2 (0171 379 0964); 239 Regent Street, W1 (0171 409 1603); 134 King's Road, SW3 (0171 589 6263).

Floris
89 Jermyn Street, SW1 (0171 704 0299). Piccadilly Circus tube. **Open** 9.30am-5.30pm Mon-Fri; 10am-5pm Sat. **Credit** A, AmEx, DC, JCB, V.
Mahogany showcases filled with bottle upon bottle of perfumes and soaps. Upper crust clientèle are greeted by the aromas of three ranges for men. Women can choose from the gamut of traditional smellies, such as Lily of the Valley.
Mail order.

The Green Room
165 Kensington High Street, W8 (0171 937 6595). High Street Kensington tube. **Open** 9am-9pm Mon, Tue, Thur, Fri; 10am-9pm Wed; 9am-7pm Sat. **Credit** A, AmEx, V.
Body Shop products are used alongside the Green Room's own aromatherapy oils and the most PC wax in town: made from naturally seeping Cyprus tree resin rather than beeswax, it's suitable for vegans. Natural tanning is popular.
Branches are too numerous to list here. Check the telephone directory for your nearest.

Neal's Yard Remedies
15 Neal's Yard, WC2 (0171 379 7222). Covent Garden tube. **Open** 10am-6pm Mon-Fri; 10am-5.30pm Sat; 11am-4pm Sun. **Credit** A, V.
Over 200 medicinal herbs; herbal capsules and nutritional supplements; herbal and Chinese herbal tinctures. Skincare products and toiletries based on herbal/essential oil recipes.
Mail order (01865 245 436)
Branches: Chelsea Farmers' Market, Sydney Street, SW3 (0171 351 6380); 9 Elgin Crescent, W11 (0171 727 3998); 68 Chalk Farm Road, NW1 (0171 284 2039).

Nelsons Pharmacy
73 Duke Street, W1 (0171 629 3118). Bond Street tube. **Open** 9am-5.30pm Mon-Fri; 9am-4pm Sat. **Credit** A, V.
Over 3,000 remedies, including Bach Flower remedies. There are aromatherapy oils, books and nutritional supplements.
Mail order.

Penhaligon's
41 Wellington Street, WC2 (0171 836 2150). Covent Garden tube. **Open** 10am-6pm Mon-Sat. **Credit** A, AmEx, DC, EC, JCB, £TC, V.
Purveyors of English luxury gifts including traditional perfumes for men and women.
Branches: 16-17 Burlington Arcade, W1 (0171 629 1416); 20A Brook Street, W1 (0171 493 0002); 8 Cornhill, The Royal Exchange, EC3 (0171 283 0711).

The Porchester Spa
Queensway, W2 (0171 792 3980). Bayswater, Queensway or Royal Oak tube. **Open** women 10am-10pm Tue, Thur, Fri; 10am-4pm Sun. Men 10am-4pm Mon, Wed, Sat. Mixed 4-10pm Sun. **Admission** £15.40. **No credit cards.**
A Westminster Council-run spa with original 1920s features, now past their former glory. Some find the Porchester tatty, others characterful. A central kidney-shaped plunge pool is surrounded by marble walls, pillars and golden ceilings. Sweating is an essential part of the Porchester experience and there is no shortage of places to cook: three interconnected Turkish hot rooms of variable heat; a Russian steam room and a traditional sauna. Also a full-size swimming pool.

The Sanctuary
12 Floral Street, WC2 (0171 240 9635). Covent Garden tube. **Open** 10am-6pm Mon, Tue; 10am-10pm Wed, Thur, Fri; 10am-6pm Sun. **Credit** A, AmEx, £$TC, V.
Luxurious spa facilities for women only, with everything your heart could desire for a day of self-indulgence.

Hairdressers

Antenna
27A Kensington Church Street, W8 (0171 938 1866). High Street Kensington tube. **Open** 10am-7pm Mon-Fri; 10am-6pm Sat. **Credit** A, DC, £TC, V.
Nothing is too outrageous for high-tech Antenna, which specialises in monofibre hair extensions, as invented by the owner, Simon Forbes. These are attached to the natural hair by means of a tiny plastic seal at the root.

Bladerunners

158 Notting Hill Gate, W11 (0171 229 2255). Notting Hill Gate tube. **Open** 10am-7pm Mon-Fri; 10am-6pm Sat. **Credit** A, AmEx, V.

A new arrival on the scene specialising in Afro and European hair. It's got a relaxing feel to it, with maple floors, a waterfall and fresh coffee smells.

Fish

30 D'Arblay Street, W1 (0171 494 2398). Tottenham Court Road tube. **Open** 10am-7pm Mon-Wed, Fri; 10am-8pm Thur; 10am-5pm Sat. **Credit** A, EC, V.

Located in a former fishmonger's, Fish retains some of the original 1950s fittings. It caters for a stylish Soho crowd, who are expertly coiffed in big dentist's chairs.

Molton Brown

58 South Molton Street, W1 (0171 629 1872). Bond Street tube. **Open** 10am-5.30pm Mon, Fri; 10am-7pm Tue, Thur; 10am-6pm Wed; 9am-4.30pm Sat. **Credit** A, £TC, V.

Molton Brown pioneered the 1980s craze for long bendy hair rollers. A relaxed atmosphere prevails. **Branch:** 54 Rosslyn Hill, NW3 (0171 794 2022).

Vidal Sassoon

60 South Molton Street, W1 (0171 491 8848). Bond Street tube. **Open** 9am-6pm Mon, Tue, Fri; 9am-6.45pm Wed, Thur; 9am-4.30pm Sat. **Credit** A, £TC, V.

Thirty years on from Sassoon's heyday and it hasn't lost its edge, with the emphasis on precision cutting and innovation. **Branches:** 130 Sloane Street, W1 (0171 730 7288); 45A Monmouth Street, WC2 (0171 240 6635); Whiteleys of Bayswater, 151 Queensway, W2 (0171 792 2741).

Trevor Sorbie

10 Russell Street, WC2 (0171 379 6901). Covent Garden tube. **Open** 9am-6pm Mon, Tue; 9am-8pm Wed-Sat. **Credit** A, AmEx, JCB, £TC, V.

Revered as style leaders, the Sorbie team reckon to be one step ahead of fashion. Trevor was the man who invented the wedge in 1974 and scrunch drying in the 1980s.

GF Trumper

9 Curzon Street, W1 (0171 499 1850). Green Park tube. **Open** 9am-5.30pm Mon-Fri; 9am-1pm Sat. **Credit** A, AmEx, JCB, £TC, V.

This flagship shop of the grandiose Trumper chain boasts

Double vision? **Arthur Morrice** *is your man.*

a line of Victorian mahogany cubicles, green marble sink-tops and ten stylists smartly clad in traditional waistcoats. **Branches:** 20 Jermyn Street, SW1 (0171 734 1370); **Simpson's of Piccadilly** W1 (0171 734 2002).

Opticians

Cutler & Gross

16 Knightsbridge Green, SW1 (0171 581 2250). Knightsbridge tube. **Open** 9.30am-6pm Mon-Sat. **Credit** A, AmEx, DC, V.

Handmade on the premises, the frames come in hundreds of chic styles, many based on 1940s designs. A popular range at the time of writing is in a super-light stainless steel. *Eye test £25. Repair service.*

Arthur Morrice

13 Beauchamp Place, SW3 (0171 584 4661). Knightsbridge tube. **Open** 9.30am-6pm Mon, Tue, Thur-Sat; 9.30am-7pm Wed. **Credit** A, AmEX, DC, JCB, V.

In addition to the usual suspects (Oliver Peoples, Paul Smith, LA Eyeworks), Morrice stocks unworn antique frames, including a solid gold item (1926) made for Morrice's grandfather, also an optician. Priced at £2,000, it could have found a permanent home in the shop. Go on, prove us wrong. Morrice and his colleagues provide the friendliest, most attentive service you'll receive, eye-wise, in London. *Eye test £15. Repair service. Same-day service.*

Fashion

Designer

Agnès B

34-36 Floral Street, WC2 (0171 379 1992). Covent Garden tube. **Open** 10.30am-6.30pm Mon-Sat; 10.30am-7pm Thur. **Credit** A, AmEx, £TC, V;

'There is no place for fashion today; it is an anachronism,' says Agnes B, who has been selling the same trimmed T-shirts since she set up in business in 1973. Ranges for men, women and children. *Alterations (larger branches only). Mail order.* **Branches:** 111 Fulham Road, SW3 (0171 225 3477); 235 Westbourne Grove, W11 (0171 792 1947).

À La Mode

36 Hans Crescent, SW1 (0171 584 2133). Knightsbridge tube. **Open** 10am-6pm Mon, Tue, Thur-Sat; 10am-7pm Wed. **Credit** A, AmEx, DC, £$TC, V.

À La Mode is a rare stockist of US designers Richard Tyler and Mizrahi, as well as Belgian designer Demeulemeester. *Alterations. Delivery service. Export scheme. Mail order.*

Betty Jackson

311 Brompton Road, SW3 (0171 589 7884). South Kensington tube. **Open** 10am-6pm Mon, Tue, Thur-Sat; 10am-7pm Wed. **Credit** A, AmEx, £TC, V.

Betty Jackson makes reliable clothes for loyal customers. Jackie O dresses in washed satin, A-line knitted skirts, and jackets come lined in bright floral prints. *Alterations. Delivery service. Export scheme. Mail order.*

Browns

23-27 South Molton Street, W1 (0171 491 7833). Bond Street tube. **Open** 9.30am-6pm Mon-Wed, Fri, Sat; 10am-7pm Thur. **Credit** A, AmEx, DC, JCB, £$TC, V.

Owner Joan Burstein can be relied upon to supply the best in womenswear, while menswear buyer Inno Aquib always keeps up with new names. Designer wear includes Jil Sander, Donna Karan and Rifat Ozbek in the main shop, and more names in the growing fashion empire that trails down South Molton Street. *Alterations. Delivery service. Export scheme.*

Branches: 6C Sloane Street, SW1 (0171 493 4232);
G Gigli 38 South Molton Street, W1 (0171 495 1509);
Romeo Gigli 62 South Molton Street, W1 (0171 495
6730); **Browns Own Label** 50 South Molton Street, W1
(0171 491 7833); **Genny** 18 South Molton Street, W1
(0171 629 1080); **Labels for Less** First Floor, 38 South
Molton Street (0171 491 7833).

Comme des Garçons

59 Brook Street, W1 (0171 493 1258). Bond Street tube.
Open 10am-6pm Mon-Wed, Fri, Sat; 10am-7pm Thur.
Credit A, AmEx, DC, EC, JCB, £$TC, V.
CdG designer Rei Kawakubo was one of the Japanese who
changed the fashion canvas in the early 1980s by challenging all our ideas about shape, fabric and tailoring. Her experiments with synergy (the mixing of unexpected fabrics such
as silk and boiled wool) have been equally breathtaking.
Alterations. Export scheme.

DKNY – Donna Karan

27 Old Bond Street (0171 499 8089). Bond Street tube.
Open 10am-6pm Mon-Wed, Fri, Sat; 10am-7pm Thur.
Credit A, AmEx, DC, EC, JCB, £$TC, V.
Famous for working magic with cashmere and reviving the
bodysuit, this quintessential Manhattan designer was the
first to tackle the problem of what women wear to work.
Alterations. Delivery service. Export scheme.

Dolce & Gabbana

*175 Sloane Street, SW1 (0171 235 0335). Sloane Square
tube.* **Open** 10am-6pm Mon-Fri; 10am-6pm Sat.
Credit A, AmEx, DC, EC, JCB, £$TC, V.
Opened in March 1995, the Dolce shop is the first freestand-
ing store for the infamous Italian design duo.
Alterations. Delivery service. Export scheme.

Egg

*36 Kinnerton Street, SW1 (0171 235 9315).
Knightsbridge tube.* **Open** 11am-7pm Tue-Sat. **Credit** A,
AmEx, £TC, V.
Elegant clothing and beautiful accessories for rich women.
A strange but seductive shop.
Export scheme.

Emporio Armani

*187-191 Brompton Road, SW3 (0171 823 8818).
Knightsbridge tube.* **Open** 10am-6pm Mon, Tue, Thur-
Sat; 10am-7pm Wed. **Credit** A, AmEx, £TC, V.
Off-the-peg perfection for men and women. This branch is
housed in an old Victorian bank.
Alterations. Delivery service. Export scheme. Mail order.
Branches: 57 Long Acre, WC2 (0171 917 6882); 111-112
New Bond Street, W1 (0171 491 8080).

Issey Miyake

*270 Brompton Road, SW1 (0171 581 3760). South
Kensington tube.* **Open** 10am-6pm Mon-Sat. **Credit** A,
DC, JCB, £TC, V.
As the millennium approaches, it is widely accepted that the
future of fashion lies in the laboratory; fabrics, not hemlines,
are the key. Japanese designer Miyake, like Westwood, isn't
tied to current trends, but forges out in his own direction.
Alterations. Delivery service. Export scheme.

Jean Paul Gaultier

*Galerie Gaultier, 171-175 Draycott Avenue, SW3
(0171 584 4648). South Kensington tube.* **Open**
10am-6pm Mon, Tue, Thur-Sat; 10am-7pm Wed.
Credit A, AmEx, V.
In recent seasons Jean Paul Gaultier has catapulted Mongo-
lians, Buddhas and other cultural sushi onto the catwalks.
This is a well-designed shop, carrying a decent amount of
Gaultier's more wearable stuff.
Alterations. Delivery service. Export scheme.

Off-the-shoulder look at **Vivienne Westwood.**

John Richmond

*62 Neal Street, WC2 (0171 379 6020). Covent Garden
tube.* **Open** 10am-7pm Mon-Sat; 1-6pm Sun. **Credit** A,
AmEx, DC, £TC, V.
'Destroy' clothes should be avoided at all costs, but John
Richmond's menswear is justly popular.
Export scheme.
Branches: 2 Newburgh Street, W1 (0171 734 5782);
Boutique Destroy 57-59 Neal Street, WC2 (0171 379
1896).

Jones

Men's: *13 Floral Street, WC2 (0171 240 8312)*
Women's: *15 Floral Street, WC2 (0171 379 4299).*
Both: *Covent Garden tube.* **Open** 10am-6.30pm Mon-Sat;
1-6pm Sun. **Credit** A, AmEx, DC, JCB, £$TC, V.
The store supplies the best of fashion's latest flights of
fancy – be they Dries van Noten, Corinne Cobson, Martin
Margiela, Hussein Chalayan or Lawler Duffy shoes. It's rare
among designer shops in that it's as well stocked for men
as it is for women.
Alterations. Delivery service. Export scheme. Mail order.

Joseph

*23 Old Bond Street, W1 (0171 629 3713). Bond
Street tube.* **Open** 10am-6.30pm Mon-Wed; 9.30am-6pm
Sat; 10am-7pm Thur; noon-5pm Sun. **Credit** A, AmEx,
DC, £$TC, V.
Joseph Ettedgui began selling clothes from the basement of
his hairdressing salon in the 1970s. He is world renowned
for his keen fashion sense and almost magical ability to read
the future. This new store in Bond Street focuses on his own
lines: knitwear, suits, jackets and jeans for men and women.
Alterations. Delivery service. Export scheme. Mail order.
Branches are too numerous to list here. Check the
telephone directory for your nearest.

Katharine Hamnett

20 Sloane Street, SW1 (0171 823 1002). Knightsbridge tube. **Open** 10am-6.30pm Mon, Tue, Thur, Fri; 10am-7pm Wed, Sat. **Credit** A, AmEx, DC, £TC, V.
Well known for her work to protect the environment – notably with a project called Eco Cotton 2000 – Katharine Hamnett is a fearless campaigner, most recently against the use of environment-damaging PVC. Her manner is astringent, her designs clever.
Alterations. Delivery service. Export scheme. Mail order.

The Library

268 Brompton Road, SW3 2AS (0171 589 6569). Knightsbridge tube. **Open** 10am-6.30pm Mon, Tue, Thur, Fri; 10am-7pm Wed; 12.30-5pm Sun. **Credit** A, AmEx, V.
This is the place to head for if you like stylish menswear and photography books. Also in stock are knitwear by Martin Kidman and suits by former Comme des Garçons designer Nigel Curtiss.
Alterations. Export scheme. Mail order.

MaxMara

32 Sloane Street, SW1 (0171 235 7941). Knightsbridge tube. **Open** 10am-6pm Mon, Tue, Thur-Sat; 10am-7pm Wed. **Credit** A, AmEx, DC, EC, JCB, £TC, V.
Upmarket continental womenswear including the perfect work suit. Designer wear, but without all the fuss.
Branch: 153 New Bond Street, W1 (0171 491 4748).

Nicole Farhi

158 New Bond Street, W1 (0171 499 8368). Bond Street tube. **Open** 10am-6pm Mon-Wed, Fri, Sat; 10am-7pm Thur. **Credit** A, AmEx, DC, £TC, V.
Farhi has recently opened a restaurant in the basement of the shop; both are flourishing. She appeals to creative/media types who want one part fashion, two parts comfort.
Alterations. Delivery service. Export scheme. Mail order.
Branches: 11 Floral Street, WC2 (0171 497 8713); 25-26 St Christopher's Place, W1 (0171 486 3416); 27 Hampstead High Street, NW3 (0171 435 0866); 193 Sloane Street, SW1 (0171 235 0877).

Paul Smith

40-44 Floral Street, WC2 (0171 379 7133). Covent Garden tube. **Open** 10.30am-6.30pm Mon-Wed, Fri; 10.30am-7pm Thur; 10am-6.30pm Sat. **Credit** A, AmEx, DC, JCB, £TC, V.
Smith has recently made a successful transition into womenswear, mostly classics with a twist. Charismatic and down to earth, Smith has fought long and hard for the British fashion industry and is currently a design consultant for M&S.
Alterations. Delivery service. Export scheme. Mail order.

Pellicano

63 South Molton Street, W1 (0171 629 2205). Bond Street tube. **Open** 10am-6pm Mon-Wed, Fri, Sat; 10am-7pm Thur. **Credit** A, AmEx, DC, £TC, V.
A jewel of a shop, Pellicano is to be applauded for giving new designers exposure to the fashion radar.
Alterations. Delivery service. Export scheme.

Prada

44-45 Sloane Street, SW1 (0171 235 0008). Sloane Square tube. **Open** 10am-6pm Mon, Tue, Wed-Sat; 10am-7pm Wed. **Credit** A, AmEx, DC, JCB, £TC, V.
The unobtrusive label makes this Italian brand gold dust for fashion freaks.
Alterations. Export scheme. Mail order.

Red Or Dead

1 & 23 Thomas Neal's Centre, Earlham Street, WC2 (0171 240 5576). Covent Garden tube. **Open** 10am-7pm Mon-Sat; noon-6pm Sun. **Credit** A, AmEx, DC, JCB, £TC, V.

Secondhand club chic at Oxfam's **No Logo.**

Wayne Hemmingway's shoe empire, born ten years ago on a stall in Camden Market, has now expanded to sell clothes.
Export scheme. Mail order (0181 908 3602).
Branches: 36 Kensington High Street, W8 (0171 937 3137); 33 Neal Street, WC2 (0171 379 7571); 186 Camden High Street, NW1 (0171 482 4423).

Space NK

Thomas Neal's Centre, Earlham Street, WC2 (0171 379 7030). Covent Garden tube. **Open** 11am-7pm Mon-Sat; 1-6pm Sun. **Credit** A, AmEx, DC, £$TC, V.
Medicine-cabinet whiteness and space-age modernity predominate in the décor here, setting off the products of British design talents such as Abe Hamilton.
Export scheme. Mail order.

Vivienne Westwood

6 Davies Street, W1 (0171 629 3757). Bond Street tube. **Open** 10.30am-6pm Mon-Wed, Fri, Sat; 10.30am-7pm Thur. **Credit** A, AmEx, DC, JCB, £$TC, V.
Ms Westwood invented punk and revived the crinoline, the bustle and the bust-thrusting corset. Head to Davies Street for couture, or to World's End for cheaper, street-style items.
Alterations. Export scheme. Mail order.
Branches: World's End 430 King's Road, SW3 (0171 352 6551); **Vivienne Westwood Sale Shop** 40-41 Conduit Street, W1 (0171 439 1109).

Whistles

12-14 St Christopher's Place, W1 (0171 487 4484). Bond Street tube. **Open** 10am-6pm Mon-Wed, Fri, Sat; 10am-7pm Thur. **Credit** A, AmEx, DC, £$TC, V.
Lucille Lewin ushered in a revolution in designer shopping when she opened Whistles ten years ago. Always à la mode.
Branches are too numerous to list here. Check the telephone directory for your nearest.

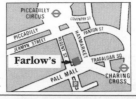

Yvonne Damont

2 The Square, Richmond, Surrey (0181 940 0514).
Richmond tube/BR. **Open** 10am-5.30pm Mon-Sat. **Credit**
A, AmEx, £$TC, V.
Along with Rita Britton of Pollyanna in Barnsley, Yvonne
Damont is rated as one of the best independent retailers
around. She loves fashion, as the décor and clothes testify.
Head for Demeulemeester; Damont is a rare stockist.
Export scheme. Mail order.

Designer Discount

70

70 Lamb's Conduit Street, WC1 (0171 430 1533).
Holborn or Russell Square tube. **Open** 10am-6pm Mon-
Fri; 10am-5pm Sat. **Credit** A, AmEx, JCB, £TC, V.
Mainly menswear, changing rapidly. In the past we've found
incredible reductions on Paul Smith jeans, shirts and T-shirts
(£55-£80), Stone Island, Versace, Armani and Valentino.

Paul Smith

23 Avery Row, W1 (0171 493 1287). Bond Street tube.
Open 10.30am-6.30pm Mon-Wed, Fri, Sat; 10.30am-7pm
Thur. **Credit** A, AmEx, £$TC, V.
The end of the line for Paul Smith's classic menswear and
womenswear, children's clothes and toiletries. The majority
are a half off and some a third off.

Street

Ad Hoc

38A Kensington High Street, W8 (0171 938 1664). High
Street Kensington tube. **Open** 10am-6.30pm Mon-Sat;
10am-7pm Thur. **Credit** A, AmEx, EC, £TC, V.
Obscene and supreme, these cramped premises hold garments made from every kinky fabric under the sun. Rubber-
ised catsuits, PVC shirts and the widest selection of hosiery
for miles make this essential for clubwear.
Branch: 153 King's Road, SW3 (0171 376 8829).

Boxfresh

2 Shorts Gardens, WC2 (0171 240 4742). Covent
Garden tube. **Open** 11am-6.30pm Mon-Sat. **Credit** A, EC,
£TC, V.
Friendly menswear shop stocking own-label sweatshirts,
plus Ben Sherman shirts and John Smedley knitwear.

Duffer of St George

27 D'Arblay Street, W1 (0171 439 0996). Oxford Circus
tube. **Open** 10.30am-6.30pm Mon-Wed, Fri, Sat; 10.30am-
7pm Thur. **Credit** A, AmEx, EC, £TC, V.
If you don't want to be sniffed at superciliously when you
venture out to your favourite club, you'd better get kitted out
in Duffer, pioneering menswear designers extraordinaire.
Branch: 29 Shorts Gardens, WC2 (0171 379 4660).

Hyper Hyper

26-40 Kensington High Street, W8 (0171 938 4343).
High Street Kensington tube. **Open** 10am-6pm Mon-Wed,
Fri, Sat; 10am-7pm Thur. **Credit** varies.
The neo-classical statues which front this indoor market
never fail to bestow a frisson of excitement within the
bosoms of all those who enter its portals. Hyper Hyper
provides a good home for 52 young designers.

Kensington Market

49-53 Kensington High Street, W8 (0171 938 4343).
High Street Kensington tube. **Open** 10am-6pm Mon-Sat.
Credit varies.
The most claustrophobic indoor market in London. Tattoo
parlours and tarot reading stalls add character, and there's
something to cater for every sartorial need. Fetish stalls sit
comfortably next to 1970s retro units.

Shop

4 Brewer Street, W1 (0171 437 1259). Leicester Square
tube. **Open** 10am-6pm Mon-Sat. **No credit cards**.
Expect to find imaginative, well-constructed garments from
styling supremo Judy Blame and T-shirts from clubwear
fanatics Gorgeous.

Sign of the Times

15 Shorts Gardens, WC2 (0171 240 6694). Covent
Garden tube. **Open** 10.30am-6.30pm Mon-Sat. **Credit** A,
AmEx, DC, EC, £TC, V.
Sign of the Times has been selling sexy, tight Ts for years;
it still stocks the best from Jimmy Jumble, Karen Savage and
Suburban Genius. Many items are one-offs, nothing is under-
stated and practicality has been firmly damned.

Mid-range

American Retro

35 Old Compton Street, W1 (0171 734 3477). Piccadilly
Circus tube. **Open** 10.15am-7pm Mon-Sat. **Credit** A,
AmEx, £TC, V.
Smedley knitwear, Dolce & Gabbana underwear, some club
wear and lots of accessories.

Ted Baker

1-2 Langley Court, WC2 (0171 497 8862). Covent
Garden tube. **Open** 10am-7pm Mon-Wed, Fri, Sat;
10am-7.30pm Thur; noon-5pm Sun. **Credit** A, AmEx,
DC, £TC, V.
Impressive selection of men's shirts and T-shirts.
Branches: phone 0171 436 4104 for information.

Episode

172 Regent Street, W1 (0171 439 3561). Oxford
Circus tube. **Open** 10am-6.30pm Mon, Tue; 10am-7pm
Wed, Fri; 10am-8pm Thur; 9.30am-7pm Sat. **Credit** A,
AmEx, £TC, V.
With Isabella Rossellini modelling what she describes as
intelligent clothes, this Hong Kong-based company is becom-
ing firmly imprinted on the fashion map.
Branches: 53 Brompton Road Knightsbridge, SW3 (0171
589 5724); Bishopsgate Arcade, Liverpool Street Station,
EC2 (0171 628 8691).

French Connection

Men's: *56 Long Acre, WC2 (0171 379 6560).*
Women's: *11 James Street, WC2 (0171 836 0522).*
Both: *Covent Garden tube.* **Open** 10.30am-6.30pm Mon-
Wed, Fri, Sat; 10.30am-8pm Thur; noon-6pm Sun. **Credit**
A, AmEx, £TC, V.
At the time of writing FC's men's fashion is a bit off the boil
– Breton tops look passé, while the Double Axed brand is
unremarkable. Womenswear is more of the moment – linen
jackets and short skirts in cream, aqua and lavender pastels.
Branches are too numerous to list here. Check the
telephone directory for your nearest.

The Gap

31 Long Acre, WC2 (0171 379 0779). Covent Garden
tube. **Open** 10am-8pm Mon-Sat; 12.30-6.30pm Sun.
Credit A, AmEx, EC, £TC, V.
The American chain provides an eager public with basic mix
and match clothes, such as knitted twinsets and skirts, T-
shirts and chinos. Certain branches stock Baby Gap.
Branches are too numerous to list here. Check the
telephone directory for your nearest.

Jigsaw

31 Brompton Road, SW3 (0171 584 6226).
Knightsbridge tube. **Open** 10am-7pm Mon, Tue,
Sat; 10am-8pm Wed; 10am-7.30pm Thur, Fri.
Credit A, AmEx, £TC, V.

Practical clothes for women – styles are classic, with a nod to current fashion. A large outlet at 9-10 Floral Street, WC2 (0171 240 5651) now stocks menswear exclusively.
Branches are too numerous to list here. Check the telephone directory for your nearest.

Karen Millen
Unit 4, Barker's Arcade, High Street Kensington, W8 (0171 938 3758). High Street Kensington tube. **Open** 10am-6.30pm Mon-Wed, Fri, Sat; 10am-8pm Thur. **Credit** A, AmEx, DC, EC, JCB, £TC, V.
Kent-based Millen keeps her prices down and yet her clothes are as desirable as many designer items.
Branch: 46 South Molton Street, W1 (0171 495 5297); 59 King's Road, SW3 (0171 823 4071); 34 Great Marlborough Street, W1 (0171 287 1350); 7-9 Church Street, Kingston-Upon-Thames, Surrey (0181 547 0135); The Glades, Bromley, Kent (0181 466 5262).

Oasis
13 James Street, WC2 (0171 240 7445). Covent Garden tube. **Open** 10am-7pm Mon-Wed, Fri, Sat; 10am-8pm Thur; noon-7pm Sun. **Credit** A, AmEX, DC, EC, JCB, £$TC, V.
With its Modigliani-inspired mannequins, Oasis stands out from the rest of the high street. The beauty of these clothes is that they're trendy but non-alienating.
Branches are too numerous to list here. Check the telephone directory for your nearest.

Warehouse
96 King's Road, SW3 (0171 584 0069). Sloane Square tube. **Open** 10am-6.30pm Mon, Tue, Fri; 10am-7pm Wed, Thur; 12.30pm-6.30pm Sun. **Credit** A, AmEx, EC, JCB, £TC, V.
Since fashion director Yasmin Yusuf joined the company 18 months ago, this chain has gone from strength to strength.
Branches are too numerous to list here. Check the telephone directory for your nearest.

Budget

Hennes
261-271 Regent Street, W1 (0171 493 4004). Oxford Circus tube. **Open** 10am-6.30pm Mon-Wed, Fri; 10am-8pm Thur; 9.30am-6pm Sat. **Credit** A, AmEx, EC, £TC, V.
The Swedish chain's range of competitively priced womens-wear seems invested with more glamour than its rivals.
Branches: 481 Oxford Street, W1 (0171 493 8557); 123B Kensington High Street, W8 (0171 937 3329).

Miss Selfridge
40 Duke Street, W1 (0171 318 3833). Bond Street tube. **Open** 9.30am-7pm Mon-Wed, Fri; 9.30am-8pm Thur; 9.30am-7pm Sat. **Credit** A, AmEx, EC, £TC, V.
This flagship store seems to be aiming for a street market feel, with concessions from Sue Rowe, Sub Couture, Ann Baynham and North.
Branches are too numerous to list here. Check the telephone directory for your nearest.

Top Shop/Top Man
214 Oxford Street, W1 (0171 636 7700). Oxford Circus tube. **Open** 10am-7pm Mon-Wed, Fri, Sat; 10am-8pm Thur. **Credit** A, AmEx, DC, EC, £TC, V.
Giant TV screens playing chart hits lure customers down to budget heaven. The Souled Out range lends a 'market' feel to proceedings and always attracts the crowds. As well as Top Shop's own label, there's the Lipsy range of clubwear, plus Pink Soda, Paul Tunstall, Zack and Ego. Designer Joe Casely-Hayford also has an exclusive Top Shop line.
Branches are too numerous to list here. Check the telephone directory for your nearest.

Unusual Sizes

1647
69 Gloucester Avenue, NW1 (0171 722 1647). Camden Town tube. **Open** 10am-6pm Mon-Sat. **Credit** A, AmEx, £TC, V.
Forty-seven per cent of British women are size 16 or over. 1647, set up in 1991 by Dawn French and designer Helen Teague, aims to offer them something a bit different. Designs are all unstructured, comfortable and fashionable.

Base
55 Monmouth Street, WC2 (0171 240 8914). Leicester Square tube. **Open** 10am-6pm Mon-Sat. **Credit** A, AmEx, DC, £TC, V.
Sizes 16-28 are sold here. Women's clothes are sourced from Scandinavia, the US, Germany and Israel. Designers stocked include Ville, August Silk and Joyce Ridings.

High & Mighty
83 Knightsbridge, SW1 (0171 589 7454). Knightsbridge tube. **Open** 9am-5.30pm Mon-Tue, Thur-Fri; 9am-6pm Sat; 9am-6.30pm Wed. **Credit** A, AmEx, DC, V.
For men over 6ft 3in, with waistlines measuring more than 34-60in. There are polo tops, suits and linen jackets by designer Louis Feraud.
Branches: 145-147 Edgware Road, W2 (0171 723 8754); The Plaza, 120 Oxford Street, W1 (0171 436 4861).

Fetish

Detainer
2 Hoxton Street, N1 (0171 739 2199). Old Street tube/BR. **Open** 10.30am-6pm Mon-Sat. **Credit** A, EC, MC, JCB, £TC, V.
If your idea of dressing up is getting tied up then Detainer is essential. No videos, poppers or mags – just some of the best bespoke leather and latex gear this side of Amsterdam. *Mail order.*

SH!
22 Coronet Street, N1 (0171 613 5458). Old Street tube/BR. **Open** 11.30am-6.30pm Mon, Wed-Sat. **Credit** A, EC, £TC, V.
This mainly womenswear fetish shop has re-opened as a 'women's erotic emporium' after Hackney Council tried to take them to court for being a sex shop (the case was thrown out). Rubber, leather and PVC at reasonable prices. *Catalogue. Mail order.*

Leather

Blakes
4 Langley Court, WC2 (0171 240 3878). Covent Garden tube. **Open** 10.30am-6.30pm Mon-Sat; 12.30-5.30pm Sun. **Credit** A, AmEx, DC, £TC, V.
Prices are kept fairly low here and items are stylish.

Natural Leather
33 Monmouth Street, WC2 (0171 240 7748). Covent Garden tube. **Open** 11am-7pm Mon-Sat. **Credit** A, £$TC, V.
Leather jackets, jeans, bags, wallets and belts. *Alterations, cleaning and repair.*

Secondhand

Blackout II
51 Endell Street, WC2 (0171 240 5006). Covent Garden tube. **Open** 11am-7pm Mon-Fri; 11am-6pm Sat. **Credit** A, AmEx, DC, EC, V.
One-off gems that could easily turn into wardrobe essentials.

Chenil Galleries
181-183 King's Road, SW3 (0171 351 0795). Sloane Square tube. **Open** 10am-5.30pm Mon-Sat. **Credit** A, AmEx, V.
This indoor antiques market houses three antique clothing stalls: Persiflage, Enigma and Fothergill Crowley.

Cornucopia
12 Upper Tachbrook Street, SW1 (0171 828 5752). Victoria tube/BR. **Open** 11am-6pm Mon-Sat. **Credit** A, V.
Womenswear from 1910-60. Most come in small sizes.

Laurence Corner
126-130 Drummond Street, NW1 (0171 388 6811). Warren Street tube. **Open** 9am-5.30pm Mon-Sat. **Credit** A, AmEx, DC, V.
Astounding selection of militaria.

No Logo
26 Ganton Street, W1 (0171 437 7338). Oxford Circus tube. **Open** 11am-6pm Mon-Sat. **No credit cards.**
If Oxfam have a flagship store, this is it. Clothes designed to appeal mainly to hippy students and spangly clubbers.

Pandora
16-22 Cheval Place, SW7 (0171 589 5289). Knightsbridge tube. **Open** 10am-6pm Mon-Sat. **Credit** A, V.
Whole sections devoted to Chanel, Armani, Alaia and other major designers: all garments are in excellent condition.

Rokit
225 Camden High Street, NW1 (0171 267 3046). Camden Town tube. **Open** 10am-6pm Mon-Fri; 4.30-6.30pm Sat, Sun. **Credit** A, AmEx, V.
Rokit runs a wholesale company and imports clothes from the US, the best of which it snaps up for its shop.

Souled Out
Unit 25, Portobello Green Arcade, 281 Portobello Road, W11 (0181 964 1121). Ladbroke Grove tube. **Open** 10am-6pm Mon-Thur; 9am-6pm Fri, Sat. **Credit** A, V.
On a 'green' scale of one to ten, owner Frank Akinsele gives himself an eight for his recycled clothing shop, which caters to the Portobello beau monde by deconstructing salvaged garments and reinventing them as club classics.

Underwear

Agent Provocateur
6 Broadwick Street, W1 (0171 439 0229). Leicester Square tube. **Open** 10.30am-6.30pm Mon-Sat. **Credit** A, AmEx, V.
The brainchild of Serene Rees and Joseph Corre, Agent Provocateur sells mainly women's lingerie with 1950s glamour appeal, most of it from France and the US. *Mail order.*

Janet Reger
2 Beauchamp Place, SW3 (0171 584 9360). Knightsbridge tube. **Open** 10am-6pm Mon-Sat. **Credit** A, AmEx, JCB, V.
For wildly glamorous women's lingerie, a tough one to beat.

Weddings

Anello and Davide
49 Dorset Street, W1 (0171 486 2930). Baker Street tube. **Open** 10am-5.30pm Mon-Fri; 10am-4.30pm Sat. **Credit** A, AmEx, V.
A range of contemporary wedding shoes. It has won the British Bridal Award for shoe design two years running.

Moss Bros
88 Regent Street, W1 (0171 494 0666). Oxford Circus or Piccadilly Circus tube. **Open** 9am-6pm Mon-Wed; 9am-7pm Thur; 9am-6pm Fri, Sat. **Credit** A, AmEx, DC, JCB, SC, £$TC, V.
This and the Covent Garden branch have the widest selection, but all Moss Bros stores offer a hire service.
Branches are too numerous to list here. Check the telephone directory for your nearest.

Tomasz Starzewski
4 Pont Street, SW1 (0171 235 4526). Knightsbridge tube. **Open** by appointment only. **Credit** A, AmEx, V.
Tomasz Starzewski is best known for the classic but witty suits that have attracted society ladies to this boutique but his wedding dress designs are equally beautiful. Knightsbridge address or not, the atmosphere is unintimidating and the service attentive.

Fashion Accessories
General Accessories

Octopus
King's Walk Mall, 122 King's Road, SW3 (0171 589 7715). Sloane Square tube. **Open** 10am-6pm Mon-Sat. **Credit** A, AmEx, V.
Nobody who enters Octopus can fail to be enchanted: the accessories are almost unbearably cute, without ever descending into kitsch. All are specially commissioned from individual makers, and everything is beautifully finished.

Robot
37 Floral Street, WC2 (0171 836 6156). Covent Garden tube. **Open** 10am-6.30pm Mon-Wed, Fri, Sat; 10am-7pm Thur; noon-5.30pm Sun. **Credit** A, AmEx, DC, V.
Great accessories at this menswear emporium include Redskins bridle leather belts, Achile socks from France and original 1950s winkies. The emphasis is on quality. *Export scheme. Mail order. Repairs to own goods.*

James Smith & Sons
53 New Oxford Street, WC1 (0171 836 4731). Tottenham Court Road tube. **Open** 9.30am-5.30pm Mon-Fri; 10am-5.30pm Sat. **Credit** A, V.
A dazzling array of umbrellas and walking sticks. Most sticks and umbrellas come in a choice of lengths and walking umbrellas can be cut to size while you wait. *Export scheme. Mail order. Repairs to own goods.*

Hats

Fred Bare
118 Columbia Road, E2 (0171 729 6962). Old Street tube/BR. **Open** 10am-2pm Sun. **Credit** A, V.
Young and funky hats also available at department stores.

The Hat Shop
58 Neal Street, WC2 (0171 836 6718). Covent Garden tube. **Open** 10am-7pm Mon-Sat. **Credit** A, AmEx, V.
From Kangol and Fred Bare to way-out numbers by trendy milliner Stephen Jones, and dressy hats by Peter Bottley. *Export scheme.*

Herbert Johnson
30 New Bond Street, W1 (0171 408 1174). Bond Street tube. **Open** 10am-6pm Mon-Fri; 10am-5pm Sat. **Credit** A, AmEx, DC, JCB, V.
Herbert Johnson makes all kinds of hats for men and women. There is a bespoke service available, for equestrian and military headwear as well as for less specialised models. *Export scheme. Mail order. Repairs.*

Leather Goods

Anya Hindmarch
*91 Walton Street, SW3 (0171 584 7644). South
Kensington tube.* **Open** 9.30am-6pm Mon-Fri; 10am-4pm
Sat. **Credit** A, AmEx, V.
The very fashionable Anya Hindmarch brings out a new
collection of beautiful, desirable bags every season.
Export scheme. Mail order. Repairs to own goods.

Mulberry Company
*11-12 Gees Court, W1Y (0171 493 2546). Bond Street
tube.* **Open** 10am-6pm Mon-Wed, Fri, Sat; 10am-7pm
Thur. **Credit** A, AmEx, DC, V.
Definitive shoulder bags, weekend bags, 'small leathers' and
other items of luggage in Mulberry's two-colour designs.
*Brochure. Export scheme. Mail order. Repairs to own
goods.*

VB Morrison
*50 Neal Street, WC2 (0171 836 0928). Covent Garden
tube.* **Open** 1-6pm most days. **No credit cards.**
The eccentric Morrison opens when he feels like it. There are
no refunds, no exchanges and no repairs, but it's all done in
a bid to keep prices down.

Osprey
*11 St Christopher's Place, W1 (0171 935 2824). Bond
Street tube.* **Open** 11am-6pm Mon-Sat; 11am-7pm Thur.
Credit A, AmEx, EC, JCB, £TC, V.
Browse through the range of beautifully proportioned, clean-
lined, handmade bags and everything else will seem garish.
Export scheme. Mail order.

Jewellery

Beau Gems
*418 Strand, WC2 (0171 836 7356). Charing Cross
tube/BR.* **Open** 9.30am-5.30pm Mon-Sat. **Credit** A,
AmEx, DC, JCB, V.
Specialists in buying and selling antique and modern jewellery, who will also repair fine examples of both.
Disabled: access. Valuations.

Butler & Wilson
*189 Fulham Road, SW3 (0171 352 8255). South
Kensington tube.* **Open** 10am-6pm Mon, Tue, Thur-Sat;
10am-7pm Wed. **Credit** A, AmEx, JCB, V.
B&W is among London's most glamorous jewellers and is
the place to go for jewel-encrusted diamante creations.
Disabled: access. Repair service (on own jewellery).
Branch: 20 South Molton Street, W1 (0171 409 2955).

Janet Fitch
*37A Neal Street, W1 (0171 240 6332). Covent Garden
tube.* **Open** 11am-7pm Mon-Sat; 1-6pm Sun. **Credit** A, V.
The 30 or so young designers whose work is temptingly
arranged at Janet Fitch are among the best.
Branches: 25A Old Compton Street, WC2 (0171 287
3789); 188A King's Road, SW3 (0171 352 4401).

Frontiers
*39 Pembridge Road, W11 (0171 727 6132). Notting Hill
Gate tube.* **Open** 11am-6.30pm Mon-Sat. **Credit** A,
AmEx, DC, JCB, V.
Proprietress Alby Nall-Cain collects antique and tribal jewellery on her travels around the world and then sells it from
this small shop.

Garrard & Co
*112 Regent Street, W1 (0171 734 7020). Oxford Circus
or Piccadilly Circus tube.* **Open** 9am-5.30pm Mon-Sat.
Credit A, AmEx, DC, JCB, V.
Well-heeled tourists flock to Garrard & Co to see fine English
jewellery displayed in museum-like surroundings.
Disabled: access. Repair and resizing service. Valuations.

Into You
*144 St John Street, EC1 (0171 253 5085). Angel
tube.* **Open** noon-7pm Tue-Fri; noon-6pm Sat. **No
credit cards.**
At London's pioneering piercing shop, proprietress Teena
Marie will pierce everything from your abdomen to your
penis. She uses sterilised equipment and advises extensively on aftercare. There's a wide selection of body jewellery,
including classic designs and more ornamental pieces.
Disabled: access.

Jess James
*3 Newburgh Street, W1 (0171 437 0199). Oxford Circus
tube.* **Open** 11am-6.30pm Mon-Fri; 11am-7pm Thur;
11am-6pm Sat. **Credit** A, AmEx, DC, JCB, V.
Jess Canty and James Knight's showcase for many of the
world's best and most innovative designers continues to go
from strength to strength.
Repair and resizing service.

Tiffany & Co
*25 Old Bond Street, W1 (0171 409 2790). Green Park or
Piccadilly Circus tube.* **Open** 10am-5.30pm Mon-Sat.
Credit A, AmEx, DC, JCB, V.
Tiffany has one of the best selections of fine jewellery in the
world. Classics include the silver screwball keyring, the sil-
ver T-clip ballpoint pen and the 18 carat gold diamond ring.
Disabled: access. Repair and resizing service. Valuations.

Watches & Clocks

City Clocks
*31 Amwell Street, EC1 (0171 278 1154). Angel
tube/King's Cross tube/BR.* **Open** 9.30am-5.30pm Mon-
Fri; 9.30am-4pm Sat. **Credit** A, AmEx, DC, V.
Staff are trained to repair Rolex, Longines, Cartier and Patek
watches and can restore antique timepieces.

The Swatch Store
*313 Oxford Street, W1 (0171 493 0237). Bond Street or
Oxford Circus tube.* **Open** 10am-7pm Mon-Wed, Fri;
10am-8pm Thur; 9am-7pm Sat. **Credit** A, V.
This official outpost of the Swatch empire stocks the entire
cheap and cheerful range of over 100 models.
Disabled: access.

Shoes

Manolo Blahnik
*49-51 Old Church Street, SW3 (0171 352 3863). Sloane
Square tube then 11, 19, 22 bus.* **Open** 10am-6pm Mon-
Fri; 10.30am-5.30pm Sat. **Credit** A, AmEx, V.
Simply the most beautiful, to-die-for shoes in the business.
Export scheme. Repairs to own shoes.

Patrick Cox
*8 Symons Street, SW1 2TJ (0171 730 6504). Sloane
Square tube.* **Open** 10am-6pm Mon, Tue, Thur-Sat;
10am-7pm Wed. **Credit** A, AmEx, V.
It's not unusual to find Cox-hungry wannabes salivating outside while a bouncer ensures no riot breaks out.
Export scheme. Mail order. Repairs to own shoes.

Dr Martens
*1-4 King Street, WC2 (0171 497 1460). Covent Garden
tube.* **Open** 10am-7pm Mon-Wed, Sat; 10am-8pm Thur,
Fri; noon-6pm Sun. **Credit** A, AmEx, EC, JCB, £TC, V.
Six floors offer a selection of stationery, clothing, footwear,
workwear and a customising service.

Emma Hope

33 Amwell Street, EC1 (0171 833 2367). Angel tube.
Open 10am-6pm Mon-Wed, Fri, Sat; 10am-7pm Thur.
Credit A, V.
Designer Emma Hope is known for making long, lean shoes in beautiful materials, such as a soft linen/viscose knit, but she's not averse to using leather and suede.
Export scheme. Mail order on bridal shoes only. Repairs to own shoes.

Natural Shoe Store

21 Neal Street, WC2 (0171 836 5254). Covent Garden tube. **Open** 10am-6pm Mon, Tue; 10am-7pm Wed-Fri; 10am-6.30pm Sat; noon-5.30pm Sun. **Credit** A, AmEx, DC, V.
Where possible, shoes have been produced without cruelty or environmental damage.
Export scheme. Mail order. Repairs to own shoes.

Office

60 Neal Street, WC2 (0171 497 2463). Covent Garden tube. **Open** 10am-7pm Mon-Sat; noon-6pm Sun. **Credit** A, AmEx, V.
As well as the foot-friendly Caterpillar and Converse labels, Office also sells its own very funky range of footwear.
Export scheme. Mail order (0181 838 4447). Repairs to own goods.

Pied à Terre

31 Old Bond Street, W1 (0171 491 3857). Green Park tube. **Open** 10am-6.30pm Mon-Wed, Fri, Sat; 10am-7pm Thur. **Credit** A, AmEx, DC, EC, V.
Three ranges are available here: Rouge, handmade ladies' shoes, Original and Basics.
Export scheme. Repair service.
Branches are too numerous to list here. Check the telephone directory for your nearest.

Red Or Dead

61 Neal Street, WC2 (0171 379 7571). Covent Garden tube. **Open** 10.30am-7.30pm Mon-Fri; 10am-7pm Sat; noon-6pm Sun. **Credit** A, AmEx, DC, EC, JCB, V.
Wacky, gimmicky footwear season after season.
Export scheme. Mail order. Repairs to own shoes.
Branches are too numerous to list here. Check the telephone directory for your nearest.

Shellys

266-270 Regent Street, W1 (0171 287 0939). Oxford Circus tube. **Open** 9.15am-6.15pm Mon-Wed, Fri, Sat; 9.15am-7.15pm Thur. **Credit** A, AmEx, DC, V.
Street-smart boots and shoes for men and women.
Export scheme. Mail order. Repairs to own shoes.
Branches are too numerous to list here. Check the telephone directory for your nearest.

Shoemakers

John Lobb

9 St James's Street, SW1 (0171 930 3664). Green Park tube. **Open** 9am-5.30pm Mon-Fri; 9am-4pm Sat. **Credit** A, AmEx, JCB, V.
Generally considered to make the best shoes in the world.
Export scheme. Mail order. Repair service.

Shoe Repair

Michael's Shoe Care

10-12 Procter Street, WC1 (0171 405 7436). Holborn tube. **Open** 8am-6.30pm Mon-Fri. **Credit** A, V.
A range of shoecare, including every colour of polish under the sun; plus scarves, belts, umbrellas and briefcases.
Handbag repair.

Branches: 66 Ludgate Hill, EC4 (0171 248 4640); 9 Camomile Street, EC3 (0171 929 3887); 11A New London Street, EC3 (0171 265 1991).

Dry-Cleaning & Repairs

Danish Express Laundry

16 Hinde Street, W1 (0171 935 6306). Baker Street or Bond Street tube. **Open** 8.30am-5.30pm Mon-Fri; 9.30am-12.30pm Sat. **Credit** A, AmEx, DC, V.
Branch: Janet's Laundry 281A Finchley Road, NW3 (0171 435 6131).

Deluxe Cleaners

30 Brewer Street, W1 (0171 437 8541). Piccadilly Circus tube. **Open** 8.30am-6pm Mon-Fri. **No credit cards**.
Staff use ozone-friendly perchloroethylene solvent in their machines. Most garments can be cleaned.

Duds'n'Suds

49-51 Brunswick Shopping Centre, Russell Square, WC1 (0171 837 1122). Russell Square tube. **Open** 8am-9pm Mon-Sat; 8am-6pm Sun. **No credit cards**.
Fifty-two washing machines and tumble dryers, plus comfy chairs, a pool table, Sky television and a smart-looking snack bar dispensing cappuccino, Danish pastries and the like.

Invisible Menders of Knightsbridge

161 Gloucester Road, SW7 (0171 373 0514). Gloucester Road tube. **Open** 8.30am-6pm Mon-Fri; 9am-4pm Sat. **No credit cards**.
David Frost and Kylie Minogue are regular customers.
Delivery service (local).

Jeeves of Belgravia

10 Pont Street, SW1 (0171 235 1101). Knightsbridge tube. **Open** 8.30am-5.30pm Mon-Fri; 8.30am-5pm Sat. **Credit** A, AmEx, V.
There is no major conversion work that Jeeves feels unable to complete. Bespoke fitting service and dry-cleaning.
Collection and delivery service (free).

Dressmakers

Lisa Galea

4A Delancey Passage, NW1 (0171 387 1907). Camden Town tube. **Open** by appointment only. **No credit cards**.
Galea says the designs she is being asked to do (by the likes of Dannii Minogue and Alison Moyet) are less flouncy than in recent years. She can work with most fabrics.

Tanseem Haberec

98 St Paul's Churchyard, EC4 (0171 248 1022). St Paul's tube. **Open** 10am-8pm Mon-Fri. **Credit** A, EC, £$TC, V.
Since Tanseem Haberec left the Royal College of Art in 1979 she has been custom-making clothes for prominent businesswomen. She plans to start doing men's tailoring.

Tailors

47/47A Carnaby Street

Carnaby Street, W1. Oxford Circus tube.
Westminster Council has made sure that the traditional Soho trade of tailoring will not die out by making it impossible for anyone to use these buildings for any other purpose. Businesses include Keith Watson (47A Carnaby Street; 0171 437 2327), Franco Santoro (47 Carnaby Street; 0171 437 8440) and Brian Staples (47 Carnaby Street; 0171 734 5069).

Oswald Boateng
274 Portobello Road, W11 (0181 964 1465). Notting Hill tube. **Open** by appointment only. **No credit cards.**
Last July Oswald Boateng became the first tailor to show a couture collection for men in Paris. With a client list that includes Lenny Henry and Tori Amos, it's no suprise he's in demand. He's also almost entirely self-taught.

Timothy Everest
32 Elder Street, E1 (0171 377 5770). Liverpool Street tube/BR. **Open** 9.30am-6pm Mon-Fri; 10am-4pm Sat; also by appointment. **Credit** A, AmEx, V.
Everest tailors for people in government, media, banking and entertainment. It's no surprise: he's the bee's knees.

Gieves & Hawkes
1 Savile Row, W1 (0171 434 2001). Piccadilly Circus tube. **Open** 9am-6pm Mon-Wed, Fri, Sat; 9am-7pm Thur. **Credit** A, AmEx, DC, JCB, £TC, V.
G&H seems to have moved from its bespoke roots with a shop offering off-the-peg pieces and an 'At Ease' collection. The name is pronounced Geeves rather than Jeeves.
Branches: 18 Lime Street, EC3 (0171 283 4914); **Harrods** 87-135 Brompton Road, SW1 (0171 730 1234); **Selfridges** 400 Oxford Street, W1 (0171 629 1234).

Richard James
31 Savile Row, W1 (0171 434 0605). Piccadilly Circus tube. **Open** 10am-6pm Mon-Fri; 11am-5pm Sat. **Credit** A, AmEx, £$TC, V.
One of the newest, trendiest and friendliest tailors around.

John Pearse
6 Meard Street, W1 (0171 434 0738). Leicester Square tube. **Open** 10am-7pm Mon-Sat. **Credit** A, V.
John Pearse is ranked alongside Timothy Everest, but takes a grander approach, believing that if people are prepared to buy bespoke, they'll be happy to spend a substantial amount.

Shirtmakers

Hilditch & Key
73 Jermyn Street, SW1 (0171 930 5336). Green Park or Piccadilly Circus tube. **Open** 9.30am-6pm Mon-Fri; 9.30am-5.30pm Sat. **Credit** A, AmEx, DC, EC, JCB, £$TC, V.
Utterly approachable shirtmakers who offer off-the-peg shirts as well as bespoke poplin numbers.

Turnbull & Asser
23 Berry Street, SW1 (0171 930 0502). Green Park or Piccadilly Circus tube. **Open** 9.30am-5.30pm Mon-Sat. **Credit** A, AmEx, DC, EC, £$TC, V.
With Prince Charles, Michael Caine and Zsa Zsa Gabor as fellow customers, you'll be in good company.
Branches: 71-72 Jermyn Street, SW1 (0171 930 0502).

Bookshops
Departmental Bookshops

Books Etc
120 Charing Cross Road, WC2 (0171 379 6838). Tottenham Court Road tube. **Open** 9.30am-8pm Mon-Sat; noon-6pm Sun. **Credit** A, AmEx, DC, £TC, V.
Endowed with a small café, this bright, modern, well-stocked store looks inviting to anyone stumbling confused out of Foyle's across the road. The free *Fiction Etc* anthology of extracts from new novels has been a popular innovation. *Company accounts. Gift wrap. Gift vouchers. Mail order.* **Branches** are too numerous to list here. Check the telephone directory for your nearest.

Dillons the Bookstore
82 Gower Street, WC1 (0171 636 1577). Goodge Street tube. **Open** 9am-7pm Mon, Wed-Fri; 9.30am-7pm Tue; 9.30am-6pm Sat; noon-6pm Sun. **Credit** A, AmEx, £TC, V.
Dillons has everything you'd expect of a major bookstore – a massive amount of stock, clear departmental layout, helpful staff – and this branch stocks a wide range of magazines. *Catalogues of new medical, nursing, business, education and ELT titles. Company and individual accounts. Disabled: access, lifts, toilets. Mail order.*
Branches are too numerous to list here. Check the telephone directory for your nearest.

Foyles
119 Charing Cross Road, WC2 (0171 437 5660). Tottenham Court Road tube. **Open** 9am-6pm Mon-Wed, Fri, Sat; 9am-7pm Thur. **Credit** A, AmEx, £$TC, V.
The sheer range of titles makes Foyles well worth spending time in. Gone to earth in musty corners on the upper floors are out-of-print rarities and even the occasional ex-library book. The range of hardback fiction outshines that of any other shop we have visited, and the staff know their stuff. *Export scheme for records/tapes/CDs. Magazine (monthly). Mail order.*

Waterstone's
121-125 Charing Cross Road, WC2 (0171 434 4291). Tottenham Court Road tube. **Open** 9.30am-8pm Mon-Sat; noon-6pm Sun. **Credit** A, AmEx, £TC, V.
The model bookstore. Waterstone's staff appear uniquely well informed and enthusiastic about books. Stores are clearly laid out and have a huge stock including lots of backlist titles and independent presses well represented, so that shopping or browsing in any branch is a delight. Watch out for programmes of author talks and readings. *Book search. Catalogue of new titles. Mail order from Milsom Street, Bath, Avon BA1 1DA.*
Branches are too numerous to list here. Check the telephone directory for your nearest.

Miscellaneous

Books For Cooks
4 Blenheim Crescent, W11 (0171 221 1992). Ladbroke Grove tube. **Open** 9.30am-6pm Mon-Sat. **Credit** A, AmEx, DC, £TC, V.
Take 8,000 books about food, blend with actual cooking smells from test kitchen, then squeeze both into agreeable Notting Hill premises. Add a dash of style, then season with signings and celebrity customers. *Cookery demonstrations (Sat, phone for details).*

Cinema Bookshop
13-14 Great Russell Street, WC1 (0171 637 0206). Tottenham Court Road tube. **Open** 10.30am-5.30pm Mon-Sat. **Credit** A, £TC, V.
Charming service and a huge collection of books (new and secondhand) and magazines on the seventh art. *Mail order.*

Compendium
234 Camden High Street, NW1 (0171 485 8944/0171 267 1525). Camden Town or Chalk Farm tube. **Open** 10am-6pm Mon-Sat; noon-6pm Sun. **Credit** A, £TC, V.
Probably London's best selection of fringe political, hardline feminist, Third World, environmentalist and generally weird stuff in addition to new fiction, home-grown and imported, an excellent selection of poetry, reference books, body art mags and anarchist newspapers. Proprietor Mike Hart and his staff know their business and are friendly and helpful. *Book lists. Disabled: access to ground floor only. Mail order.*

Daunt Books

83 Marylebone High Street, W1 (0171 224 2295). Baker Street or Bond Street tube. **Open** 9am-7.30pm Mon-Sat. **Credit** A, £TC, V.

Skylights, galleries and green lampshades makes this one of the most attractive bookshops in the UK. There's a good general section and three floors of travel books. Fiction and non-fiction titles are racked alongside guides and maps. *Mail order.*

Dillons Arts Bookshop

8 Long Acre, WC2 (0171 836 1359). Covent Garden tube. **Open** 9.30am-10pm Mon-Sat; noon-7pm Sun. **Credit** A, AmEx, DC, EC, £TC, V.

Bright, airy, refined and well stocked. It also functions as a rare retail outlet for literary magazines. *Catalogue. Mail order.*

Forbidden Planet

71 New Oxford Street, WC1 (0171 836 4179). Tottenham Court Road tube. **Open** 10am-6pm Mon-Wed, Sat; 10am-7pm Thur, Fri. **Credit** A, AmEx, £TC, V.

Comics, magazines and merchandise have taken over the ground floor while sf, fantasy and horror books occupy the basement. Author signings are well advertised. *Gift tokens. Telephone order service (0171 497 2150).*

French's Theatre Bookshop

52 Fitzroy Street, W1 (0171 387 9373). Warren Street tube. **Open** 9.30am-5.30pm Mon-Fri. **Credit** A, AmEx, DC, EC, £TC, V.

French's aims to carry all play scripts written in the English language currently in print. *Catalogue. Mail order. Mailing list.*

Gay's The Word

66 Marchmont Street, WC1 (0171 278 7654). Russell Square tube. **Open** 10am-6pm Mon-Wed, Fri, Sat; 10am-7pm Thur; 2-6pm Sun. **Credit** A, AmEx, £TC, V.

Gay's The Word is the only gay and lesbian bookshop in London, although more bookshops now have gay/lesbian sections. The premises are small but the selection wide. *Mail order.*

Grant & Cutler

55-57 Great Marlborough Street, W1 (0171 734 2012). Oxford Circus tube. **Open** 9am-5.30pm Mon-Wed, Fri, Sat; 9am-7pm Thur. **Credit** A, £TC, V.

The foreign-language bookshop for students and others with a yen for literature in its *version originale.* *Catalogue. Mail order.*

Housmans

5 Caledonian Road, N1 (0171 837 4473). King's Cross tube/BR. **Open** 10am-6.30pm Mon-Sat; noon-4pm Sun. **Credit** A, £TC, V.

An eclectic mix of fiction and non-fiction. The big anarchist section is suspiciously well-organised.

Magpie Bookshop

53 Brushfield Street, E1 (0171 247 4263). Liverpool Street tube/BR. **Open** noon-3pm Mon-Wed; 11am-5pm Thur, Fri; 11am-4pm Sat; 10am-5pm Sun. **Credit** A, V.

A section devoted to first editions of capital chronicler Iain Sinclair's poetry and novels. Also occult and secondhand.

Murder One

71-73 Charing Cross Road, WC2 (0171 734 3485). Leicester Square tube. **Open** 10am-7pm Mon-Wed; 10am-8pm Thur-Sat. **Credit** A, AmEx, £TC, V.

The ground floor has crime and romance, with stacks of sf, fantasy and horror downstairs. Owner/writer/editor/publisher Maxim Jakubowski organises signings. *Catalogue. Mail order.*

Neal Street Books

37 Neal Street, WC2 (0171 240 3319). Covent Garden tube. **Open** 10am-7.30pm Mon-Fri; 11am-7pm Sat; noon-5pm Sun. **Credit** A, AmEx, £TC, V.

Lots of author-signed books and a fine range of titles share the limited space in this pleasant Covent Garden bookstore, which also has a range of cards.

Branches: Books on Sport Lillywhites, Piccadilly Circus, SW1 (0171 930 3181); **Dulwich Books** 6 Croxted Road, SE21 (0181 670 1920); **The Highgate Bookshop** 9 Highgate High Street, N6 (0181 348 8202).

Silver Moon Women's Bookshop

68 Charing Cross Road, WC2 (0171 836 7906). Leicester Square tube. **Open** 10am-6.30pm Mon-Wed, Fri, Sat; 10am-8pm Thur. **Credit** A, AmEx, EC, £TC, V.

The country's only women's bookshop stocks a reasonable selection of fiction by women writers, plus biographies and books on various subjects. Men are not encouraged to linger in the lesbian section in the basement, but the atmosphere is friendly to all. *Catalogue (four times a year, subscription £2). Disabled: access to ground floor only. Mail order.*

Sportspages

Caxton Walk, 94-96 Charing Cross Road, WC2 (0171 240 9604). Leicester Square tube. **Open** 9.30am-7pm Mon-Sat. **Credit** A, AmEx, DC, £TC, V.

Surely the best shop anywhere for books on sport, Sportspages also stocks footy fanzines, magazines and videos. *Mail order (specialist sports' lists available).*

Edward Stanford

12-14 Long Acre, WC2 (0171 836 1915). Leicester Square tube. **Open** 10am-6pm Mon, Sat; 9am-7pm Tue-Fri. **Credit** A, AmEx, DC, £TC, V.

Stanford's is stuffed with international maps, gazetteers, illuminated globes and Lonely Planets. The basement contains more Ordnance Survey maps than you'll ever need, plus town plans for more or less the whole country. *Mail order (0171 836 1321).*

Zwemmer Media Arts

80 Charing Cross Road, WC2 (0171 240 4157). Leicester Square tube. **Open** 9.30am-6pm Mon; 10am-6pm Sat. **Credit** A, AmEx, DC, £TC, V.

Photography and cinema are the specialisations at this charming link in the Zwemmer chain of specialist shops. **Branches**: are too numerous to list here. Check the telephone directory for your nearest.

Secondhand/Antiquarian

Bell, Book & Radmall

4 Cecil Court, WC2 (0171 240 2161). Leicester Square tube. **Open** 10am-5.30pm Mon-Fri; 11am-4pm Sat. **Credit** A, AmEx, £TC, V.

It specialises in first editions of nineteenth- and twentieth-century English and American literature.

Maggs Brothers

50 Berkeley Square, W1 (0171 493 7160). Green Park tube. **Open** 9.30am-5pm Mon-Fri. **Credit** A, V.

Pre-twentieth-century books on travel, literature, natural history, early printing and bibliography are the specialities.

Skoob

15 Sicilian Avenue, WC1 (0171 404 3063). Holborn tube. **Open** 10.30am-6.30pm Mon-Sat. **Credit** A, AmEx, DC, EC, JCB, V.

Excellent stock of fiction: Penguin, Vintage and Picador get their own shelves. A genuine students' favourite. *Discount (10%) for students and unwaged.*

Henry Sotheran

2-5 Sackville Street, W1 (0171 439 6151). Piccadilly Circus tube. **Open** 9.30am-6pm Mon-Fri; 10am-4pm Sat. **Credit** A, AmEx, DC, JCB, £TC, V.

The Folio Society shares the lower ground floor with Sotheran's collection of architecture books. The ground floor has glass cases of children's first editions, travel books, military, and natural history sections.
Branch: 80 Pimlico Road, SW1 (0171 730 8756).

Unsworth, Rice & Coe

12 Bloomsbury Street, WC1 (0171 436 9836). Tottenham Court Road tube. **Open** 10am-8pm Mon-Fri; 10am-7pm Sat; noon-7pm Sun. **Credit** A, AmEx, DC, JCB, £TC, V.

The stock includes remainders and out-of-print books as well as an antiquarian section and lots of secondhand fiction.

Newsagents

A Moroni & Son

68 Old Compton Street, W1 (0171 437 2847). Piccadilly Circus tube. **Open** 7.30am-7pm Mon-Sat; 8am-2.30pm Sun. **No credit cards.**

Many titles arrive at this bulging international newsagent the same day they are published in their home countries.
Branches: 308 Regent Street, W1 (0171 580 3835); 75 Marylebone High Street (0171 935 3275)

Electronics

Audio Visual

Radio Rentals

87-89 Baker Street, W1 (0171 486 8338). Baker Street tube. **Open** 9am-5.30pm Mon-Sat. **Credit** A, V.

Basic TV/VCR packages are available here.
Branches are too numerous to list here. Call 01734 304 000 for your nearest.

Hi-Fi

The Cornflake Shop

37 Windmill Street, W1 (0171 631 0472). Goodge Street tube. **Open** 10am-6pm Tue-Sat; 10am-7pm Thur. **Credit** A, AmEx, £TC, V.

Cornflake Shoppers don't browse; they've already read the reviews of the system they're after and now they've come to hear it in one of the purpose-designed demonstration rooms.

Hi-Fi Experience

227 Tottenham Court Road, W1 (0171 580 3535). Tottenham Court Road tube. **Open** 10am-6pm Mon-Fri; 9am-6pm Sat. **Credit** A, AmEx, DC, £TC, V.

A wide range of stock includes quality British products from Mission, Cyrus, Musical Fidelity, Arcam, Audiolab, Tannoy, KEF, TDL, Quad, Monitor Audio and Rogers.

Richer Sounds

2 London Bridge Walk, SE1 (0171 403 4710). London Bridge tube/BR. **Open** 10am-6pm Mon-Wed, Fri; 10am-7pm Thur; 10am-5pm Sat. **Credit** A, V.

Julian Richer's shops specialise mostly in last year's models, at lower-than-last-year's prices. It's mainly mid-market stuff.

Computers

Computer Exchange

143 Whitfield Street, W1 (0171 916 3110). Goodge Street or Tottenham Court Road tube. **Open** 10am-7pm Mon-Sat; noon-5pm Sun. **Credit** A, £TC, V.

The leading secondhand computer dealer in the West End for both Apple Macintoshes and PCs. Reasonably current secondhand software is also stocked. There is an extensive range of hard drives and accessories on offer, all at huge discounts. Staff are well-informed computer fanatics.

Gultronics

15 & 223 Tottenham Court Road, W1 (0171 436 3131). Goodge Street tube. **Open** 9am-6pm Mon-Wed, Fri, Sat; 9am-7pm Thur. **Credit** A, V.

From electric typewriters to fax machines and PCs, Gultronics stocks the lot, although laptops are a speciality. The showroom at No 223 is piled high with heavily discounted goods. Special offers change weekly.
Branch: 43 Church Street, Croydon, Surrey (0181 666 0303).

Hobbies, Arts & Crafts

Atlantis

146 Brick Lane, E1 (0171 377 8855). Aldgate East tube. **Open** 9am-5.30pm Mon-Fri; 10am-5.30pm Sat, Sun. **Credit** A, V.

Britain's largest art materials store.

The Bead Shop

43 Neal Street, WC2 (0171 240 0931). Covent Garden tube. **Open** 1-6pm Mon; 10.30am-6pm Tue-Fri; 11.30am-5pm Sat. **Credit** A, V.

Heaven for amateur jewellery junkies and an essential stop for professionals, this is the original self-service bead shop. Books on jewellery making are also stocked.
Catalogue (£3.75). Mail order from JRM Beads, 16 Redbridge Enterprise Centre, Ilford IG1 1TY (0181 553 3240).

Beatties

202 High Holborn, WC1 (0171 405 6285/8592). Holborn tube. **Open** 10am-6pm Mon; 9am-6pm Tue-Fri; 9am-5.30 Sat. **Credit** A, AmEx, DC, V.

This branch of the excellent toy and model chain has the most to offer model railway enthusiasts. The floor space is currently being expanded to accommodate a growing Virtual Reality stock. There are also kits for boats, planes and cars.
Mail order from 70 The Parade, High Street, Watford, Herts, WD1 2AW).
Branches: are too numerous to list here. Check the telephone directory for your nearest.

Borovik Fabrics

16 Berwick Street, W1 (0171 437 2180/0520). Oxford Circus or Tottenham Court Road tube. **Open** 8.30am-6pm Mon-Fri; 8.15am-5pm Sat. **No credit cards.**

The huge stock of fabrics runs from showy brocades, lamés, taffetas, velvets and bridal laces to tweeds and wool mixes.
Postal delivery.

The Cloth Shop

290 Portobello Road, W10 (0181 968 6001). Notting Hill Gate or Ladbroke Grove tube. **Open** 10.30am-6pm Mon-Sat. **No credit cards.**

This textile Mecca stocks over 400 types of cloth – calico, muslin, viscose, Lycra, English wools, French cottons.

Contemporary Applied Arts

43 Earlham Street, WC2 (0171 836 6993). Covent Garden tube. **Open** 10am-6pm Mon-Sat. **Credit** A, AmEx, DC, V.

This showcase shop and gallery, for a charity founded in 1948 as the Crafts Centre, presents and markets the work of its members, who include most of the leading figures in all areas of crafts in Britain as well as a steady stream of new names creating hip, stylish designs.

L Cornelissen & Son

*105 Great Russell Street, WC1 (0171 636 1045).
Tottenham Court Road tube.* **Open** 9.30am-5.30pm Mon-
Fri; 9.30am-5pm Sat. **Credit** A, JCB, V.
Rare pigments, oil paints, pastels, canvases and gouache.
Export scheme. Mail order. Price lists.

Crafts Council Gallery Shop

44A Pentonville Road, N1 (0171 278 7700). Angel tube.
Open 11am-6pm Tue-Sat; 2pm-6pm Sun. **Credit** A, V.
The Crafts Council's headquarters house a small, attractive
shop with a frequently changing stock of high-quality work.

Creative Quilting

*3 Bridge Road, Hampton Court, East Molesey, Surrey
(0181 941 7075). Hampton Court BR.* **Open** 9.30am-
5.30pm Mon-Sat; noon-4pm Sun. **Credit** A, V.
London's only quilting and patchwork shop, CQ has American cottons by Concord, VIP, Hoffman and other designers.
Catalogue (£3). Classes. Mail order.

Creativity

*45 New Oxford Street, WC1 (0171 240 2945). Holborn
or Tottenham Court Road tube.* **Open** 9.30am-6pm Mon-
Wed, Fri, Sat; 9.30am-7pm Thur. **Credit** A, V.
Creativity's reputation is built on its wide range of stock for
knitting, tapestry, needlepoint and embroidery.
Mail order.

Electrum Gallery

*21 South Molton Street, W1 (0171 629 6325). Bond
Street tube.* **Open** 10am-6pm Mon-Fri; 10am-1pm Sat.
Credit A, AmEx, DC, JCB, V.
This jewellery gallery offers one of the widest selections
of modern craft jewellery in Britain, with any number of
stylish and surprising but very wearable designs.

Falkiner Fine Papers

*76 Southampton Row, WC1 (0171 831 1151). Holborn
tube.* **Open** 9.30am-6pm Mon-Sat. **Credit** (accepted for
purchases over £10) A, AmEx, £TC, V.
Beautiful rare papers, including hand-marbled, parchment
and sheets with pressed flowers.
Catalogue. Export scheme. Mail order.

Fitch's Ark

*6 Clifton Road, W9 (0171 266 0202). Paddington
BR.* **Open** 11am-7pm Mon-Sat; 11am-3pm Sun. **Credit**
A, EC, V.
The Ark stocks craft items of all sizes and kinds – so long
as they're based on animal imagery.

Iron Age

*25 North End Parade (top of North End Road), W14
(0171 603 1282). West Kensington tube.* **Open** 9am-
5.30pm Mon-Fri; 9am-2pm Sat. **No credit cards.**
London's only remaining blacksmith and ornamental ironmonger has in stock a sizable range of free-standing pieces.

MacCulloch & Wallis

*25-26 Dering Street, W1A (0171 409 0725). Bond Street
tube.* **Open** 9am-6pm Mon-Fri; 10.30am-4.30pm Sat.
Credit A, V.
M&W is everything a haberdasher should be, stocking the
lot, from interlinings, silks and accessories to needles and
pins and tailor's dummies.
Catalogue (0171 409 0725). Mail order.

Russell & Chapple

*23 Monmouth Street, WC2 (0171 836 7521). Leicester
Square tube.* **Open** 8.30am-5pm Mon-Fri. **Credit** A, V.
Rolls of canvases, cottons, linens and hessians line the walls
on the ground floor of London's biggest canvas supplier.
Export scheme. Mail order. Price list.

Spink and Son

5 King Street, SW1 (0171 930 7888). Green Park tube.
Open 9.30am-5.30pm Mon-Fri. **Credit** A, V.
Britain's leading authority on numismatory matters is also
a fascinating and beautiful shop. The collector can inspect
coins, medals, bullion and bank notes of outstanding rarity.

Stanley Gibbons International

*399 Strand, WC2 (0171 836 8444). Covent Garden
tube/Charing Cross tube/BR.* **Open** 8.30am-6pm Mon-Fri;
9.30am-5.30pm Sat. **Credit** A, AmEx, DC, V.
SG estimates it has about 3 million stamps, the majority of
which cost between 30p and 50p.
Catalogues. Mail order.

Music Shops

African Music Agency

*120 Kentish Town Road, NW1 (0171 267 1928).
Camden Town tube/Camden Road BR.* **Open** 11am-8pm
Mon-Sat. **No credit cards.**
You won't find a wider range of African instruments in
London – drums, mbiras, African xylophones and jembes.
Export scheme. Mail order. Repair service.

Andy's Guitar Centre & Workshop

*27 Denmark Street, WC2 (0171 916 5080). Tottenham
Court Road tube.* **Open** 10am-8pm Mon-Sat; 12.30-
6.30pm Sun. **Credit** A, AmEx, DC, £TC, V.
Long-established guitar shop aiming for the quality end of
the market. Prices are fair. Repairs undertaken.
*Delivery service (free). Export scheme. Finder service.
Mail order. Repair service. Tuition.*

Boosey & Hawkes

*295 Regent Street, W1 (0171 580 2060). Oxford Circus
tube.* **Open** 9am-6pm Mon-Fri; 10am-4pm Sat. **Credit** A,
AmEx, DC, £TC, V.
A wide selection of mainly classical scores.
Catalogues (free). Mail order. Postal delivery.

The Folk Shop

*Cecil Sharp House, 2 Regent's Park Road, NW1 (0171
284 0534). Camden Town tube.* **Open** 10am-6pm Mon-
Sat. **Credit** A, AmEx, EC, V.
The Early Music Shop's ready-to-make kits for harpsichords,
crumhorns, citterns, lutes and the like join Hobgoblin's range
of guitars, fiddles, bells and accordions and so on in this spacious and well laid-out basement. A full range of strings and
reeds and the widest range of folk publications in London.
*Catalogue. Export scheme. Mail order. Repair and
renovation service.*
Branch: Hobgoblin Music 17 The Parade, Northgate,
Crawley, Sussex (01293 515858).

Music & Video Exchange

*56 Notting Hill Gate, W11 (0171 229 4805). Notting
Hill Gate tube.* **Open** 10am-8pm daily. **Credit** A, AmEx,
DC, £TC, V.
The buyer need not beware at this busy and well-stocked
secondhand store – there are plenty of bargains. It's the sellers who usually get much less than they expected. The music
and electrical stock changes all the time, but you can usually pick up everything needed to start a band or orchestra.

World of Music

*8, 20, 21-24 Denmark Street WC2 (0171 379 3384).
Tottenham Court Road tube.* **Open** 10am-6pm Mon-Sat.
Credit A, AmEx, DC, Musicard, £TC, V.
Several previously individual shops are now lumped under
the WoM banner. Argent's (named after 1960s keyboard man
Rod) now eschews the ivories in favour of brass, woodwind
and a wide range of classical and pop/rock sheet music;

Sutekina handles keyboards and hard-disk recording equipment; TPA, guitars and PA equipment; World of Pianos, digital and acoustic pianos; Rhodes covers the top end of the guitar range; and Hank's handles acoustic and semi-acoustic guitars. The Drum & Bass Cellar is also on these premises. *Export scheme. Mail order.*

Photographic

Keith Johnson & Pelling
93-103 Drummond Street, NW1 (0171 380 1144).
Euston Square tube. **Open** 9am-5.30pm Mon-Fri. **Credit** A, AmEx, DC, V.
KJP is one of the biggest, most popular and professional photographic shops, covering the whole pro-am spectrum. Staff are hugely experienced.
Camera hire. Delivery service. Mail order. Repair service.
Branches: Ramilles House, 1-2 Ramilles Street, W1 (0171 439 8811); Perseverance Works, 38 Kingsland Road, E2 (0171 729 0019); Eagle Wharf Studios, 49 Eagle Wharf Road, N1 (0171 253 5174).

Leeds Camera Centre
20-22 & 24-26 Brunswick Centre, WC1 (0171 833 1661). Russell Square tube. **Open** 9am-5pm Mon-Fri. **Credit** A, V.
A main stockist for Hasselblad and Mamiya and also carries Nikon, Metz and Sinar plus all Polaroid formats, lighting, studio accessories, light boxes and a range of film.
Catalogue. Delivery service. Export scheme. Mail order. Rental and repair service.

Sendean
105 Oxford Street, W1 (0171 439 8418/9). Oxford Circus or Tottenham Court Road tube. **Open** 9am-5.30pm Mon-Fri. **Credit** A, EC, V.
Sendean provides a reliable repair service for all cameras. *Export scheme. Mail order.*

Sky Photographic Services
Ramilles House, 2 Ramilles Street, W1 (0171 434 2266). Tottenham Court Road tube. **Open** 9am-6.30pm Mon-Fri. **Credit** A, V.
Both the price and the turnaround time (six hours) for printing and mounting slide film make Sky's service competitive.
Branches: 64A/B Cannon Street, EC4 (0171 236 1019); 17-23 Southampton Row, WC1 (0171 242 2504); 16 Andrews Road, E8 (0171 254 4313).

Records, Tapes & CDs
Megastores

HMV
150 Oxford Street, W1 (0171 631 3423). Oxford Circus tube. **Open** 9.30am-7pm Mon-Wed, Fri, Sat; 9.30am-8pm Thur. **Credit** A, AmEx, DC, £TC, V.
Clearly laid-out rock, pop and soul sections. The specialist departments in the basement are equally impressive. *Mail order.*
Branches: 363 Oxford Street, W1 (0171 629 1240); 4 Trocadero, Coventry Street, W1 (0171 439 0447).

Tower Records
1 Piccadilly Circus, W1 (0171 439 2500). Piccadilly Circus tube. **Open** 9am-midnight Mon-Sat; noon-6pm Sun. **Credit** A, AmEx, £TC, V.
It's hard work just walking from one section of this vast store to another. Always plenty of imports from Japan and the US. *Disabled: access. Export scheme. Mail order.*
Branches: 62-64 Kensington High Street, W8 (0171 938 3511); 151B Queensway, W2 (0171 229 4550).

Virgin Megastore
14-30 Oxford Street, W1 (0171 631 1234). Tottenham Court Road tube. **Open** 9.30am-8pm Mon, Wed-Sat; 10am-8pm Tue; noon-6pm Sun. **Credit** A, AmEx, £TC, V.
Virgin's revamp has done away with the cluttered feel of the place, making it easier to locate things.
Disabled: access. Export scheme. Listening facilities. Mail order.
Branch: 527-531 Oxford Street, W1 (0171 491 8582).

Miscellaneous

58 Dean Street Records
58 Dean Street, W1 (0171 734 8777/0171 437 4500). Piccadilly Circus tube. **Open** 10am-6.30pm Mon-Sat. **Credit** A, DC, £TC, V.
An exemplary selection of film soundtracks, mainly on vinyl. There are rare titles in abundance.
Listening facilities. Mail order.

Black Market
25 D'Arblay Street, W1 (0171 437 0478). Oxford Circus tube. **Open** 10am-7pm Mon-Sat. **Credit** A, AmEx, £TC, V.
Black Market stocks all the hippest 12in imports. *Listening facilities.*

Black Music Centre
12 Berwick Street, W1 (0171 494 1081/0171 437 3535/fax 0171 287 0022). Piccadilly Circus tube. **Open** 10am-7pm Mon-Sat. **Credit** A, £TC, V.
Daddy Kool, central London's premier reggae stockists, has recently moved two doors up the road to share premises with Rockin' Sarah's Jazz and Soul Shop – and this is the result. *Catalogue (send SAE). Listening facilities. Mail order.*

Dub Vendor
274 Lavender Hill, SW11 (0171 223 3757). Clapham Junction BR. **Open** 9am-7pm Mon-Wed, Sat; 9.30am-8pm Thur, Fri. **Credit** A, V.
Reggae specialists stocking the latest releases from Jamaica. There's a fine back-catalogue selection too.
Catalogue and monthly lists (£2 per year). Listening facilities.
Branch: Dub Vendor Record Shack 155A Ladbroke Grove, W10 (0181 969 3375).

Fat Cat Records
19 Earlham Street, WC2 (0171 209 1071). Covent Garden tube. **Open** 10.30am-6.30pm Mon-Sat. **No credit cards.**
A unparalleled selection of trance, techno and dub. *Listening facilities. Mail order.*

Honest Jon's
278 Portobello Road, W10 (0181 969 9822). Notting Hill Gate tube. **Open** 10am-6pm Mon-Sat; 11am-5pm Sun. **Credit** A, AmEx, £TC, V.
London's finest shop for black music offers a selection of new releases on CD and secondhand LPs. In the basement there's the modern jazz section including a fine selection of highly coveted Blue Note records.
Listening facilities. Mail order.

Intoxica!
231 Portobello Road, W11 (0171 229 8010). Ladbroke Grove tube. **Open** 10.30am-6.30pm Mon-Sat. **Credit** A, £TC, V.
Secondhand jazz, soundtracks, exotica, soul and 1960s, plus new US independents and dance in the basement.
Catalogue (for new records, send SAE). Listening facilities. Mail order.

Mole Jazz
311 Gray's Inn Road, WC1 (0171 278 0703). King's Cross tube/BR. **Open** 10am-6pm Mon-Thur, Sat; 10am-8pm Fri. **Credit** A, AmEx, DC, £TC, V.
Upstairs is devoted to secondhand LPs, with a great many collector's items. Downstairs it's CD heaven.
Export scheme. Mail order. Postal auctions.

Mr Bongo
47 Lexington Street, W1 (0171 287 1887).
Oxford Circus tube. **Open** 11.30am-6.30pm Mon-Sat.
Credit A, V.
The latest Latin and Brazilian releases, plus jazz and soul.
Listening facilities. Mail order.

Ray's Jazz Shop
180 Shaftesbury Avenue, WC2 (0171 240 3969).
Leicester Square or Tottenham Court Road tube. **Open** 10am-6.30pm Mon-Sat. **Credit** A, £TC, V.
While the rest of the world has deserted to the delights of CD, Ray's still stocks as much as possible on vinyl.
Listening facilities. Wheelchair access (Monmouth Street entrance).

Reckless Records
30 Berwick Street, W1 (0171 437 4271). Oxford Circus tube. **Open** 10am-7pm daily. **Credit** A, £TC, V.
Top secondhand outlet; main lines are rock, soul and jazz.
Mail order from Upper Street branch (below).
Branch: 79 Upper Street, N1 0NU (0171 359 2222).

Rhythm Records
281 Camden High Street, NW1 (0171 267 0123).
Camden Town tube. **Open** 10.30am-6.30pm daily. **Credit** A, £TC, V.
Hardcore punk, 1960s psychedelia, electronic and country.
Listening facilities.

Rock On
3 Kentish Town Road, NW1 (no phone). Camden Town tube. **Open** 10.30am-6pm Mon-Sat; 11am-6pm Sun. **No credit cards.**
A long-standing collectors' favourite for rockabilly and soul.

Rough Trade
130 Talbot Road, W11 (0171 229 8541). Notting Hill Gate tube. **Open** 10am-6.30pm Mon-Sat. **Credit** A, AmEx, V.
A great selection of independent releases from across the world and plenty of other stuff besides.
Listening facilities. Mail order.
Branch: 16 Neal's Yard, WC2 (0171 240 0105).

Selectadisc
34 Berwick Street, W1 (0171 734 3297). Oxford Circus tube. **Open** 9.30am-7pm Mon-Sat. **Credit** A, AmEx, V.
Although indie music in all its aspects is the main theme here, other genres, notably dance and jazz, are well covered.

Stern's African Record Centre
116 Whitfield Street, W1 (0171 387 5550/0171 388 5533). Warren Street tube. **Open** 10.30am-6.30pm Mon-Sat. **Credit** A, AmEx, £TC, V.
Stern's boasts a glorious selection of African music from every country in the continent, on all formats.
Listening facilities. Mail order.

Vinyl Experience
18 Hanway Street, W1 (0171 636 1281/0171 637 1771). Tottenham Court Road tube. **Open** 10am-6.30pm Mon-Sat. **Credit** A, AmEx, £TC, V.
Vinyl Experience specialises in records and memorabilia for the serious collector.
Listening facilities. Mail order.

Sport

The Kite Store
48 Neal Street, WC2 (0171 836 1666). Covent Garden tube. **Open** 10am-6pm Mon-Wed, Fri; 10am-7pm Thur; 10.30am-6pm Sat. **Credit** A, AmEx, £TC, V.
Kites, kites and more kites, from a basic Peter Powell stunt-kite to a 12ft/4m-wide Flexifoil.

Lillywhite's
24-36 Lower Regent Street, SW1 (0171 930 3181). Piccadilly Circus tube. **Open** 9.30am-7pm Mon-Fri; 9.45am-7pm Sat; 9.30am-6pm Sun. **Credit** A, AmEx, JCB, V.
Six floors filled with equipment for just about any sport imaginable. The range of skiing and skating gear is as comprehensive, if not better, than any of the specialist outlets around town.

Olympus Sports
301-309 Oxford Street, W1 (0171 409 2619). Oxford Circus tube. **Open** 9.30am-7pm Mon-Wed, Fri; 9.30am-8pm Thur; 11am-5pm Sun. **Credit** A, AmEx, V.
Olympus aims at the mainstream sports and general fitness market. Footwear is a major part of the business.
Branches are too numerous to list here. Check the telephone directory for your nearest.

Antiques
Arcades

Alfie's Antique Market
13-25 Church Street, NW8 (0171 723 6066). Edgware Road tube/Marylebone tube/BR. **Open** 10am-6pm Tue-Sat. **Credit** varies.
A scruffy, sprawling place, largely aimed at dealers, with more than its share of tat.
Delivery service. Shipping. Valuations.

Antiquarius
131-141 King's Road, SW3 (0171 351 5353). Sloane Square tube/11, 19, 22 bus. **Open** 10am-6pm Mon-Sat. **Credit** varies.
The strong areas are buttons, textiles and art deco but there's also silverware, jewellery, ceramics, and collectibles.

Camden Passage
Camden Passage, off Upper Street, N1 (0171 359 9969). Angel tube. **Open** 10am-5pm Tue-Sat. **Credit** varies.
Numerous arcades, plus an outdoor market on Wednesday and Saturday mornings (see page 172 **Markets**). There's silverware, porcelain, jewellery, brass, prints, dolls and lighting and, in the Angel Arcade, a dealer specialising in globes.
Restoration. Shipping.

Chelsea Antiques Market
245A-253 King's Road, SW3 (0171 352 5689). Sloane Square tube/11, 19, 22 bus. **Open** 10am-6pm Mon-Sat. **Credit** varies.
Highlights are the Optical Department, with a range of microscopes, telescopes, sextants, compasses and surgeons' implements, and antiquarian booksellers Harrington Bros.

Grays Antique Market
58 Davies Street, W1 & 1-7 Davies Mews, W1 (0171 629 7034). Bond Street tube. **Open** 10am-6pm Mon-Fri. **Credit** varies.
An excellent first stop for anyone wanting a good browse among an eclectic range of stalls run by unpretentious and enthusiastic dealers.
Bureaux de change. Engraving. Jewellery repairs & restoration. Shipping. Valuations.

*You never know what you'll find at **LASSCo**.*

any other textile you care to imagine. There's a dreamy range of 1920s-'40s evening wear, along with the Gallery's own reproduction clothes, soon to be stocked by Liberty. *Shipping.*

Furniture & Decorative

Whiteway & Waldron
305 Munster Road, SW6 (0171 381 3195). Fulham Broadway or Hammersmith tube/74, 211 bus. **Open** 10am-6pm Mon-Fri; 11am-4pm Sat. **No credit cards**.
A dusty treasure trove of ecclesiastica, where you can expect to find anything from chapel chairs, brass candlesticks and pews to plaster Madonna statues and stained glass windows. *Delivery service. Shipping. Valuations.*

Glass & Ceramics

Cobb Antiques
39B High Street, SW19 (0181 946 2811). Wimbledon tube/BR. **Open** 10am-5.30pm Mon-Sat. **Credit** A, AmEx, DC, EC, JCB, V.
One of the few shops in London to specialise in antique glass. *Shipping. Valuations.*

Metalwork

The House of Steel
400 Caledonian Road, N1 (0171 607 5889). Caledonian Road tube/Caledonian Road & Barnsbury BR. **Open** 11.30am-5pm Mon-Fri; by appointment Sat. **No credit cards**.
A shrine to antique ironwork and reproduction steel, this company restores, designs and makes everything from chairs and tables to curtain poles, sundials, garden furniture and spiral staircases. *Delivery service. Casting replacements. Invisible mending. Mail order. Restoration. Shipping. Valuations.*

Architectural

LASSCo
St Michael's Church, Mark Street (off Paul Street), EC2 (0171 739 0448). Old Street tube/BR. **Open** 10am-5pm daily. **Credit** A, AmEx, EC, V.
Housed in a flamboyant Victorian church, LASSCo is a paradise for anyone who loves architectural salvage. The owner has the breadth of imagination to take in anything from part of Westminster Bridge to Dudley Moore's glittery red bathroom suite. Other eye-catchers have included a William Kent-style neoclassical doorway, a pair of mosque doors and a sixteenth-century gryphon carved out of Cotswold limestone. *Delivery service. Shipping.*

Mirrors & Frames

House of Mirrors
597 King's Road, SW6 (0171 736 5885). Fulham Broadway tube/11, 22 bus. **Open** 9am-6pm Mon-Fri; 10am-6pm Sat. **No credit cards**.
A varied selection of mostly gilded nineteenth-century mirrors, ranging in style from extravagant rococo to refined neo-classical and in price from £1,000 to £2,500. *Delivery service. Restoration. Shipping.*

Silverware

London Silver Vaults
Chancery House, 53-63 Chancery Lane, WC2 (0171 242 3844). Chancery Lane tube. **Open** 9am-5.30pm Mon-Fri; 9am-1pm Sat. **Credit** varies.
There are now 40 shops offering everything from 1920s napkin rings to an extraordinary 1860 centrepiece featuring a palm tree, a giraffe, an ostrich and a deer. Bargains are to be had at David S Shure's: everything on one shelf costs £5. *Shipping. Valuations.*

Carpets & Textiles

David Black Oriental Carpets
96 Portland Road, W11 (0171 727 2566). Holland Park tube. **Open** 10am-6pm Mon-Fri; 11am-5.30pm Sat. **Credit** A, AmEx, DC, £TC, V.
The carpets here are not only oriental: at last visit there were Arts and Crafts carpets, an Icelandic rug and African textiles. Black and his assistant are approachable and aim to always have some relatively affordable pieces in stock. *Delivery service (free locally). Cleaning and repairs. Shipping. Valuations.*

Gallery of Antique Costume and Textiles
2 Church Street, NW8 (0171 723 9981). Marylebone tube/BR. **Open** 10am-5.30pm Mon-Sat. **Credit** A, AmEx, £TC, V.
The Gallery is a glory hole of sumptuous antique brocades, appliqués, paisleys, silks, chenilles, needlepoints, velvets and

Twentieth-century

Art Furniture
158 Camden Street, NW1 (0171 267 4324). Camden Town tube/Camden Road BR. **Open** noon-5pm daily. **No credit cards**.
A large warehouse shared by several dealers specialising in Arts and Crafts, art deco and the odd 1950s or '60s piece. *Delivery service. Shipping.*

Markets

You can look but you can't touch – fruit and veg buying, **Brick Lane**-style, on a Sunday.

Antiques

Bermondsey (New Caledonian) Market

Bermondsey Square, SE1. Borough tube/London Bridge tube/BR. **Open** 5am-2pm Fri; starts closing noon.

For many, this is London's best antiques market, attracting dealers (both buyers and sellers) from all over. Most dealers have disappeared by 9am, to be replaced by tourists and collectors. Around the market are several antiques-packed warehouses, cubby holes and shops.

Camden Passage Market

Camden Passage, off Upper Street, N1 (0171 359 9969). Angel tube. **Open** 7am-2pm Wed; 9am-3.30pm Sat.

A quaint walkway with bookshops, restaurants and antiques shops. Come market days, traders take up every available space along the passage and under awnings opposite Islington Green. Silverware, jewellery and toys, and nineteenth-century magazines and prints form the bulk of their stock.

Crafts

Jubilee and Apple Markets

Jubilee Market *Jubilee Hall, off Southampton Street, WC2;* **Apple Market** *The Piazza, Covent Garden WC2. Covent Garden tube.* **Open** 9am-5pm daily.

Given their position, these two markets could scarcely be anything other than tourist traps. However, both manage to attract interesting work from craftworkers and designers. The Apple Market, inside the Piazza, has jewellery in leather and metal, expensive chunky knitwear, toys, hats and a regularly changing parade of novelty goods. Jubilee Hall has antiques on Monday, crafts at the weekend, and clothes, cosmetics, snacks, bags and tourist tosh the rest of the week.

General

Berwick Street Market

Berwick Street, Rupert Street, W1. Leicester Square or Piccadilly Circus tube. **Open** 9am-6pm Mon-Sat.

Shop around and some beautifully fresh fruit and vegetables can be had. Several of Soho's restaurateurs buy here. Berwick Street also has household goods and fabrics. The market continues, after a seedy passage, into Rupert Street. Secondhand records, leather handbags and clothes reside here.

Brixton Market

Electric Avenue, Pope's Road, Brixton Station Road, SW9. Brixton tube. **Open** 8.30am-5.30pm Mon, Tue, Thur-Sat; 8.30am-1pm Wed.

A startling assortment of Afro-Caribbean foodstuffs is up for grabs at Brixton: everything from calves' heads, goat's meat and pigs' tails to yams, plantain and breadfruit. Head for Electric Avenue or the slightly frayed charm of the Granville and Market Row arcades for the best of the provisions. But there's much more than food at this scintillating market. Reggae throbs out from the record stalls; Rastafarian priests light incense and proffer religious tracts; herbs and potions are sold under a bridge as trains thunder overhead.

Ridley Road Market
Ridley Road, E8. Dalston Kingsland BR/38, 149, 243 bus. **Open** 9am-3pm Mon-Wed; 9am-noon Thur; 9am-5pm Fri, Sat.
Ridley Road provides a vibrant mix of cultures. First there are the cockney fruit and veg sellers; then the bagel bakery and, further up, Milly's tiny smoked salmon stall. Asia is represented by the Turkish lock-ups, with their tins of pulses and olive oils, and the south Asian halal meat traders selling dozens of garotted chickens. Interspersed with all this are various household goods, jeans, womenswear and fabric stalls.

Lunchtime

Leadenhall Market
Whittington Avenue, off Gracechurch Street, EC3. Bank or Monument tube. **Open** 7am-4pm Mon-Fri.
Though it is open all morning, Leadenhall comes into its own at lunchtime. Mallard, teal, partridge and woodcock are all sold in season. Ashdown the fishmonger's puts on an unparalleled display of seafood and sells superb oysters, while other stalls specialise in high-class delicatessen, cheeses and chocolates. Expensive but delectable.

Organic

Spitalfields Market
Commercial Street (between Lamb Street and Brushfield Street), E1 (0171 247 6590). Liverpool Street tube/BR. **Open** *organic market* 11am-3pm Fri; 9am-3pm Sun. *General market* 11am-3pm Mon-Fri; 9am-3pm Sun.
Only part of the vast structure is used by the stalls; a sports centre, a party venue and farm take up the rest of the space. Crafts and antiques stalls are set up through the week, but it's on Friday and especially Sunday that the market comes alive. A dozen or so organic producers appear. The craft section has a stall with handloom bedspreads made by the Bengal Women's Union; handmade jewellery and pottery; wooden toys; and underwear made from unbleached cotton.

Weekend

Brick Lane Market
Brick Lane (north of railway bridge), Cygnet Street, Sclater Street, E1; Bacon Street, Cheshire Street, Chilton Street, E2. Aldgate East or Shoreditch tube/Liverpool Street tube/BR. **Open** 6am-1pm Sun.
From 6am the down-at-heel traders from Bethnal Green Road offer various old tat. At 7.30am things get under way on Sclater Street, given over to pet foods, provisions, electrical goods and tools. Off Cygnet Street, new bicycles, meat, fruit and vegetables and frozen food are up for grabs. Brick Lane itself is where to find leather jackets, cheap jewellery, a fruit and veg stall and a jellied eel stand.

Around Cheshire Street are stalls selling cheap cassettes and household goods, lock-ups full of junk, and, further up, an indoor warehouse packed with secondhand goods, collectibles and a discount book stall.

Camden Market
Camden Lock, Buck Street, Electric Ballroom, Chalk Farm Road, Commercial Place, NW1. Camden Town tube. **Open** *Camden Lock* 9.30am-5.30pm daily; *the rest* 10am-6pm Sat, Sun.
At weekends Camden Market now has outposts in every bit of space on and off Chalk Farm Road between Camden Town tube and Hawley Street. First stop out of the tube is the Electric Ballroom with its laundered secondhand fashions. There are more clothes, new and secondhand, around Buck Street. The Lock, a cobbled courtyard leading to the canal, is where the market started and it still attracts the most impenetrable crowds. Handmade crafts, hippyish clothes and vegetarian fast food stalls are the highlights. Antiques, pine furniture, secondhand books, records and more clothes occupy the area off Chalk Farm Road. Generally, secondhand goods are a few notches above the junk of Brick Lane, but below the manicured objets of Portobello.

Greenwich Market
College Approach, Stockwell Street and corner of High Road and Royal Hill, SE10. Greenwich BR. **Open** 9am-5pm Sat, Sun.
In the mish-mash of stallzs off Greenwich High Road, there's a wealth of tacky secondhand clothes. West of the Hotel Ibis are trestle tables piled with coins, medals and banknotes, secondhand books and art deco furniture. Stockwell Street has new T-shirts and jewellery, as well as army surplus stalls, secondhand records and an indoor book market.

Petticoat Lane Market
Middlesex Street, Goulston Street, New Goulston Street, Toynbee Street, Wentworth Street, Bell Lane, Cobb Street, Leyden Street, Strype Street, Old Castle Street, Cutler Street, E1. Liverpool Street tube/BR. **Open** 9am-2pm Sun (Wentworth Street also open 10am-2.30pm Mon-Fri).
Hundreds of stalls swamp the area around Middlesex Street, attracting thousands of customers, but the range of goods isn't correspondingly large: leather jackets, watches, jewellery, novelty goods, underwear, socks, shirts, shoes. Yet there are plenty of pitches worth perusing: window-shop at the old gold stalls on Cutler Street, or flick through the CDs and tapes on Goulston Street and Bell Lane.

Portobello Road Market
Portobello Road, W10 and W11. Ladbroke Grove or Notting Hill Gate tube. **Open** *antiques and junk* 7am-5.30pm Sat; *general market* 9am-5pm Mon-Wed, Fri, Sat; 9am-1pm Thur.
The top end is of most interest to antiques buffs, with over 2,000 stalls containing objets d'art, jewellery, old medals, paintings, silverware and disparate collectibles. Further down the hill is a fruit and veg market, also open Monday to Saturday. Prices are generally low. The next transformation comes under the Westway – food gives way to clothes, jewellery and records. From here up to Golborne Road, it becomes increasingly run-down.

D & A Binder
34 Church Street, NW8 (0171 723 0542). Edgware Road tube/Marylebone tube/BR. **Open** 10am-5pm Mon-Sat. **Credit** A, AmEx, V.
Binder's specialises in pre-war shop fittings, which it renovates, refurbishes and French polishes itself.
Delivery service. French polishing. Restoration. Shipping. Valuations.

Risky Business
44 Church Street, NW8 (0171 724 2194). Edgware Road tube/Marylebone tube/BR. **Open** 10am-5.30pm Mon-Sat. **Credit** A, AmEx, EC, £TC, V.
Devoted to early-twentieth-century sports and travel goods. *Restoration. Shipping.*

Auctions

Bonhams
Montpelier Street, SW7 (0171 584 9161). Knightsbridge tube. **Open** 9am-6pm Mon; 9am-4.30pm Tue-Fri; 11am-4pm Fri. **Sales** phone for a schedule/catalogue. **Viewing** usually 3-4 days before sale; phone to check.
The charged atmosphere, the drama of big-money sales and the variety of goods make Bonhams an excellent introduction to the heady world of buying at auction.
Branch: Bonhams New Chelsea Galleries 65-69 Lots Road, SW10 (0171 393 3900).

Christie's
8 King Street, SW1 (0171 839 9060). Green Park tube. **Open** 9.30am-4.30pm Mon, Wed-Fri; 9.30am-8pm Tue; 2.30-5pm Sun (viewing only Sun). **Sales** weekly; phone for a schedule. **Viewing** phone to check.
London's oldest fine art auctioneer's is hardly a bargain-hunter's paradise, although prices in the South Kensington branch tend to be more in the hundreds than the thousands.
Branch: Christies South Kensington 85 Old Brompton Road, SW7 (0171 581 7611).

Phillips
101 New Bond Street, W1 (0171 629 6602). Bond Street tube. **Open** 8.30am-5pm Mon-Fri; 2-5pm Sun (viewing only Sun). **Sales** see catalogue for details. **Viewing** see catalogue for details.
When Phillips auctioned the entire contents of Elizabeth David's kitchen in 1994, cookery books with gravy stains, wooden spoons and old storage jars were snapped up by enthusiasts for a few pounds each. A rare piece of delftware from Southwark, however, sold for £276,000.
Branch: Phillips West 10 Salem Road, W2 (0171 229 9090).

Sotheby's
34-35 New Bond Street, W1 (0171 493 8080). Green Park tube. **Open** 9am-4.30pm Mon-Fri for buying and viewing; noon-4pm Sun for occasional viewing (phone to check). **Sales** see catalogue for dates and times.
London's oldest auctioneer's is now has branches all over the world. Expect to find anything from a Manet painting to Jimi Hendrix's guitar going under the hammer.

Furniture Retailers
Designer

Furniture Union
46 Beak Street, W1 (0171 287 3424). Piccadilly Circus tube. **Open** 11am-6pm Mon-Sat. **Credit** A, EC, V.
Mandy Taylor-Jones set up the Furniture Union in 1993 to promoting the work of British furniture designers. *Catalogue. Delivery service (from £20). Mail order.*

Mid-range

The Conran Shop
Michelin House, 81 Fulham Road, SW3 (0171 589 7401). South Kensington tube. **Open** 9.30am-6pm Mon, Wed-Sat; 10am-6pm Tue; noon-5pm Sun. **Credit** A, AmEx, EC, £TC, V.
The light and airy interior of the Michelin House is a perfect setting for Conran's design showcase. The work of top international designers vies with exclusive pieces by the Conran Design Group. The basement houses swish kitchenware, china, books, stationery, toys and food.
Delivery service (free in London for goods over £200). Export scheme. Interior design.

Heal's
196 Tottenham Court Road, W1 (0171 636 1666). Goodge Street tube. **Open** 10am-6pm Mon-Wed; 10am-8pm Thur; 10am-6.30pm Fri; 9.30am-6.30pm Sat. **Credit** A, AmEx, SC, V, DC, £TC.
The best known of London's furniture stores, Heal's continues to maintain the standards of quality and style that it set over a century ago. The range of furniture includes pieces from the top names in international design.
Delivery service (£25, free on orders over £200). Export scheme. Mail order.

Designers Guild
267-271 & 277 King's Road, SW3 5EN (0171 351 5775). Sloane Square tube. **Open** 9.30am-5.30pm Mon, Tue, Thur, Fri; 10am-5.30pm Wed, Sat. **Credit** A, EC, £TC, V.
Tricia Guild now employs 165 people in the company she founded in 1970. At first, she concentrated on designing quality furnishing fabrics, wall-coverings and accessories, but furniture is becoming an increasingly important part of the business. There are seven upholstered ranges, all designed and made in house.
Delivery service (£25 within M25). Interior design. Mail order.

Purves & Purves
80-81 & 83 Tottenham Court Road, W1 (0171 580 8223). Goodge Street or Warren Street tube. **Open** 9.30am-6pm Mon-Wed, Fri, Sat; 9.30am-7.30pm Thur. **Credit** A, AmEx, EC, £TC, V.
Andrew and Pauline Purves mix the best of British design with a sprinkling of top Europeans. The furniture is sleek and witty, but comfort is rarely sacrificed for style. *Catalogue. Delivery service (free on orders over £1,000). Mail order.*

Budget

IKEA
Brent Park, 255 North Circular Road, NW10 (0181 208 5600). Neasden tube. **Open** 10am-8pm Mon-Fri; 9am-6pm Sat; 11am-5pm Sun. **Credit** A, AmEx, SC, V.
Never before has such a huge range of well-designed, good-quality household goods been available in the UK at such low prices. Get there early and be prepared for long waits. *Baby changing facilities; supervised playroom for children aged 3-7; video room for children under 11; pushchairs. Catalogue. Delivery service (£5 within 5 miles, £15 within M25). Free parking. Roof racks for rent or sale.*
Branch: Valley Park, Purley Way, Croydon, Surrey (0181 208 5600).

Secondhand

After Noah
121 Upper Street, N1 (0171 359 4281). Angel tube. **Open** 10am-6pm Mon-Sat, noon- 5pm Sun. **Credit** V, A.

A cannily chosen mix of new and secondhand household accessories and furniture dating from the 1940s.
Delivery service (free on goods over £500).

Art Furniture
158 Camden Street (loading bay and parking at 3B Prowse Place), NW1 (0171 267 4324). Camden Town tube/Camden Road BR. **Open** noon-5pm daily. **No credit cards.**
Housed in the railway arches by Camden Road BR station, this warehouse is like the Tardis – small from the outside but spacious within. Most stock is good-quality Edwardian, art deco and Arts and Crafts furniture in tip-top condition.
Delivery service (negotiable).

Grove Green Antiques
108 Grove Green Road, E11 (0181 558 7885). Leyton tube. **Open** 9am-5.30pm Mon-Sat; 10am-4pm Sun. **No credit cards.**
If you like to see your antiques in situ, then come to this off-beat, almost sinister shop – it's set up in adjoining houses, the stock squeezed into ramshackle, draughty rooms.
Delivery service (negotiable).

The Old Cinema
160 Chiswick High Road, W4 (0181 995 4166). Turnham Green tube. **Open** 9.30am-6pm Mon-Wed, Fri, Sat; 9.30am-8pm Thur, noon-5pm Sun. **Credit** A, EC, V.
For serious furniture-buying you should visit these 10,000 sq ft of sales space spread over three rambling floors. There's a vast selection of antique and secondhand furniture.
Delivery service (negotiable).

Home Accessories

Barclay & Bodie
7-9 Blenheim Terrace, NW8 (0171 328 7879). Maida Vale or St John's Wood tube. **Open** 9.30am-5.30pm Mon-Sat. **Credit** A, AmEx, V.
Inspiring gift and home accessories shop run by two former interior designers.
Catalogue (£2). Mail order.

The Candles Shop
30 The Market, Covent Garden, WC2 (0171 836 9815). Covent Garden tube. **Open** 10am-8pm Mon-Sat; 10am-7pm Sun. **Credit** A, AmEx, V.
Many brightly coloured candles, plus touristy souvenirs.
Branch: 50 New King's Road, SW6 (0171 736 0740).

The Kasbah
8 Southampton Street, WC2 (0171 379 5230). Covent Garden tube. **Open** 10am-7pm Mon-Wed, Fri, Sat; 10am-8pm Thur. **Credit** A, AmEx, £TC, V.
Atmospheric Moroccan store, with an in-house travel agent and tented area for the ad hoc imbibing of mint tea.
Catalogue. Mail order.

Muji
26 Great Marlborough Street, W1 (0171 494 1197). Oxford Circus tube. **Open** 10am-9pm Mon-Sat; 10am-7.30pm Thur, Fri. **Credit** A, AmEx, DC, V.
Japanese homewares: brown stationery, aluminium storage boxes, grey cotton underwear and sleek kitchen accessories.
Branch: 39 Shelton Street, WC1 (0171 379 1331); 157 Kensington High Street, W8 (0171 376 2484).

Nice Irma's
46 Goodge Street, W1 (0171 580 6921). Goodge Street tube. **Open** 10am-6pm Mon-Wed, Fri; 10am-7pm Thur; 10am-5pm Sat. **Credit** A, AmEx, £TC, V.
Well-known purveyor of ethnic housewares, and worth a visit for the Indian bedspreads, china, glass and candelabra.

Vintage Magazine Store
39-43 Brewer Street, W1 (0171 439 8525). Piccadilly Circus tube. **Open** 10am-7pm Mon-Fri; 10am-8pm Sat; noon-8pm Sun. **Credit** A, AmEx, V.
Large choice of film and rock memorabilia.
Branches: 247 Camden High Street, NW1 (0171 482 0587); 7-8 Greenland Place, NW1 (0171 482 5083).

Gardens & Flowers

The Chelsea Gardener
125 Sydney Street, SW3 (0171 352 5656). Sloane Square or South Kensington tube/11, 19, 22, 49 bus. **Open** 10.30am-6pm Mon-Sat; 11am-5pm Sun. **Credit** A, AmEx, £TC, V.
Seasonal and temperature-related sections.
Delivery service. Export scheme. Gift tokens. Interflora. Landscaping.
Branch: Crews Hill, Enfield, Middx (0181 367 9323).

Columbia Road Market
Columbia Road, between Gosset Street and the Royal Oak pub, E2. Old Street tube/BR/26, 48, 55 bus. **Open** 8am-1pm Sun.
A must for lovers of gardens, flowers and street markets. Come early to avoid crushing the flowers and plants.

Fulham Palace Garden Centre
Bishops Avenue (off Fulham Palace Road), SW6 (0171 736 2640). Putney Bridge tube. **Open** 9.30am-5.30pm Thur; 9.30am-6pm Mon-Fri, Sat; 10am-5pm Sun. **Credit** A, AmEx, V.
Bedding and window-box plants available through the year.
Delivery service (Tue, Wed, from £5). Garden consultancy.

Value Added Tax

Visitors who live outside the European Community (EC), and who stay no longer than three months, can claim back the Value Added Tax (VAT, currently 17.5 per cent) charged on most goods in Britain: the catch is that you'll probably have to spend over £50 or £75 first, depending on the shop. The procedure is simple: take along your passport, then fill in a form at the shop which the assistant will stamp (there may be a service charge), and hand the completed document to the customs office at the airport or port (officials may want to see the goods). There's normally a six-week wait before you get the money back, and payment will be by cheque or by accreditation to your credit card. Not all shops offer this scheme, so it's best to check first before spending any money. If you are having your goods shipped directly by the shop, you can usually persuade them to deduct the VAT prior to payment. But not all shop assistants are as well-informed about this system as they should be.

Harper & Tom's

13 Elgin Crescent, W11 (0171 792 8510). Ladbroke Grove tube. **Open** 9am-7pm Mon-Sat. **Credit** A, V.
Specialists in floral fashions, including Japanese Ikebana.
Delivery service.

The Wild Bunch

22 Earlham Street, WC2 (0171 497 1200). Covent Garden tube. **Open** 10am-8pm Mon-Sat. **No credit cards**.
The blooms are banked up, from fragile violet posies and grape hyacinths, to branches of May blossom and willow.

Gifts & Stationery

Anything Left-handed

57 Brewer Street, W1 (0171 437 3910). Piccadilly Circus tube. **Open** 9.30am-5pm Mon-Sat. **Credit** A, V.
Utilitarian and novelty items for this maligned minority.

BladeRubber Stamps

2 Neal's Yard, WC2 (0171 379 7391). Covent Garden tube. **Open** 10am-6pm Mon-Sat. **Credit** A, AmEx, DC, V.
Rubber stamps and ink pads in a variety of colours.
Catalogue. Mail order.

Jack Duncan Cartoons & Books

44 Museum Street, WC1 (0171 242 5335). Holborn or Tottenham Court Road tube. **Open** 10am-6pm Mon-Fri; 10am-5pm Sat. **Credit** A, £TC, V.
Signed cartoons and caricatures, books and playing cards.

Get Stuffed

105 Essex Road, N1 (0171 226 1364). Highbury & Islington tube/BR/38, 56, 73, 171A, 277 bus. **Open** 10.30am-4.30pm Mon-Wed, Fri; 10.30am-1pm Thur; 11am-4pm Sat. **No credit cards**.
Eye-catching taxidermist's stuffed with various animals.
Delivery service. Export scheme. Hire service.

Graham & Green

7 Elgin Crescent, W11 (0171 727 4594). Ladbroke Grove tube. **Open** 10am-6pm Mon-Fri; 9.30am-6pm Sat; 11am-5pm Sun. **Credit** A, AmEx, DC, £TC, V.
Pens, jewellery, frames, bags, clocks, vases and candlesticks.
Branches: 4 & 10 Elgin Crescent, W11 (0171 727 4594); 164 Regent's Park Road, NW1 (0171 586 2960).

The Museum Store

37 The Market, The Piazza, WC2 (0171 240 5760). Covent Garden tube. **Open** 10.30am-6.30pm Mon-Sat; 11am-5pm Sun. **Credit** A, AmEx, DC, £TC, V.
Amusing items from museum shops around the world.
Branches: 50 Beauchamp Place, SW3 (0171 581 9255); 4A-5A Perrins Court, NW3 (0171 431 7156).

Oggetti

135 Fulham Road, SW3 (0171 581 8088). South Kensington tube. **Open** 9.30am-6pm Mon-Sat. **Credit** A, AmEx, DC, V.
Smart gifts and expensive playthings for grown-ups.
Branch: 143 Fulham Road, SW3 (0171 584 9808).

Theatre Tokenline

(0171 240 8800). **Open** 24 hours daily. **Credit** A, AmEx, DC, V.
Theatre tokens are redeemable at all West End box offices.

The Tintin Shop

34 Floral Street, WC2 (0171 836 1131). Covent Garden tube. **Open** 10am-6pm Mon-Wed, Fri, Sat; 10am-7pm Thur; noon-5pm Sun. **Credit** A, AmEx, DC, JCB, £TC, V.
Home to all things Tintin-related.

Mysteries

11 Monmouth Street, WC2 (0171 240 3688). Tottenham Court Road tube. **Open** 10am-6pm Mon-Sat. **Credit** A, EC, V.
Stacks and stacks of New Age literature and equipment. Accessories include music, posters, jewellery, candles and a phrenology head. You can do a six-week course in qabalah.
Catalogue. Delivery service. Export scheme. Mail order.

Paperchase

213 Tottenham Court Road, W1 (0171 580 8496). Goodge Street tube. **Open** 9am-6pm Mon, Wed; 10am-6pm Tue; 9am-7pm Thur, Fri; 9.30am-6.30pm Sat. **Credit** A, V.
This flagship branch of the stationery chain is an excellent source not only of cards and wrapping paper, but also of art materials, papers, pens and desk accessories. One room alternates between Christmas essentials (September to January) and a décor collection.
Branches are too numerous to list here. Check the telephone directory for your nearest.

The Pen Shop

199 Regent Street, W1 (0171 734 4088). Oxford Circus tube. **Open** 9.30am-6pm Mon, Tue, Fri, Sat; 10am-6pm Wed; 9.30am-7pm Thur. **Credit** A, AmEx, DC, V.
A selection of over 1,000 pens, including Mont Blanc, Waterman, Lamy, Rotring and Tombow.
Export scheme. Mail order.
Branch: Debenhams 344 Oxford Street, W1 (0171 493 0215).

Smythsons

44 New Bond Street, W1 (0171 629 8558). Bond Street tube. **Open** 9.15am-5.30pm Mon-Fri; 10am-1.30pm Sat. **Credit** A, AmEx, DC, JCB, V.
Pukka stationery.
Mail order.
Branch: 135 Sloane Street, SW1 (0171 730 5520).

Games & Magic

See chapter **Children: Shopping**.

Office & Studio

Business Matters

203 Lewisham High Street, SE13 (0181 318 1235). Lewisham BR. **Open** 8.30am-6.30pm Mon-Fri; 9am-10pm Sat. **Credit** A, AmEx, DC, EC, V.
Staff will answer the telephone for you on a general line. Messages will then be posted or faxed to you.
Brochure.

London Graphic Centre

107-115 Long Acre, WC2 (0171 240 0095). Covent Garden tube. **Open** 9am-5pm Mon-Fri; 10.30am-6pm Sat. **Credit** A, AmEx,£TC, V.
LGC has moved into Apple Macintoshes to supplement its existing range of art materials and stationery.
Catalogue. Delivery service. Export scheme. Mail order.
Branches: 12 Tottenham Street, W1 (0171 637 2199); 254 Upper Richmond Road, SW15 (0181 785 9797).

Neal's Yard Desktop Publishing Studio

14 Neal's Yard, WC2 (0171 379 5113/fax 0171 379 0135). Covent Garden tube. **Open** 9am-10pm Mon-Fri; noon-5pm Sat, Sun. **Credit** A, V.
There are 14 Apple Macintoshes for hire and a free introductory lesson. Other services offered include image setting, scanning and disk translation.
Catalogue.

Galleries & Museums

Royal Academy of Arts

Piccadilly, London W1

⊖ Green Park or Piccadilly Circus

Situated in the heart of London's West End, the Royal Academy of Arts is one of the country's leading galleries holding major exhibitions of old masters as well as shows of contemporary art.

Highlights for 1995/6 include **Africa: The Art of A Continent, Gustave Caillebotte** and **The Twentieth Century: The Age of Modern Art.**

The Royal Academy also has a shop and restaurant.

For further details and opening times, telephone the Royal Academy's recorded information line on **0171-439 4996/7**.

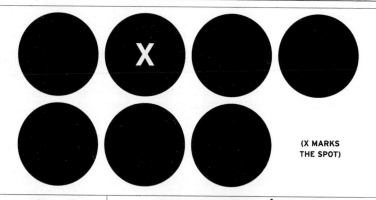

Art Galleries

A new flock of young British artists is being shepherded by wily gallerists who know how to separate the sheep from the goatees – but is the public having the wool pulled over its eyes?

London has reinvented itself as a City of Art. The capital of philistinism now boasts the most exciting community of artists in the world, and it's been created not by the money-minded gallery owners (although adman Charles Saatchi has been a key player in fostering new talent), but by the artists themselves.

Although the public remains traditionally deeply sceptical of all modern art, the raw talent evinced by a series of provocative exhibitions across town is finally attracting attention. Much of their new work can be seen for nothing at the commercial galleries in Cork Street, Dering Street and at the mainstream public galleries. The same names keep cropping up but they are only part of a swarming hive of artistic activity. Keep your eyes peeled for Damien Hirst, Fiona Rae, Mat Collishaw, John Frankland, Marc Quinn and Anya Gallacio, to mention but a few of the not-so-secret agents of change on the contemporary art scene.

Although the work of young artists is particularly vibrant at the moment, the historic public collections at the **National Gallery**, the **Courtauld Institute**, and the **Dulwich Picture Gallery** remain veritable eye-openers. Major and minor oils on canvas down the ages can be found here in suitably lavish period settings as well as at various other lesser known but equally rewarding locations (*see* **Collections**). Under the directorship of Nicholas Serota, the **Tate Gallery**, the city's much-loved collection of modern and British art, has just opened a gallery for new art, Art Now, and has plans for expansion.

The **Royal Academy of Arts** on Piccadilly hosts prestigious but pricey exhibitions with international reputations. One such is the London-wide exhibition in September 1996 being masterminded by the Academy. A major critical historical appreciation of modernism, The Twentieth Century: The Age Of Modern Art looks set to be the exhibition of the epoch. As well as Picassos in Piccadilly, three other important London galleries will participate. The **Whitechapel Gallery** will exhibit modern masters on the theme of 'Dream',

*New developments at the **Tate Gallery** include the Art Now gallery, for contemporary work.*

from De Chirico and Chagal to Hopper. The **Hayward Gallery** will cover 'Abstraction' from Mondrian to Richard Long, and the **National Portrait Gallery** will explore the portrait as a means of psychological enquiry.

The **Serpentine Gallery** in Hyde Park is probably the most beautiful space in London in which to view mainly contemporary international art. The **Saatchi Gallery** in St John's Wood should not be missed: it's a superb space in which to see the best of Young British Art. Combine a visit to **Interim Art** and **Flowers East** in east London with a look at the latest installation at **Matt's Gallery**. Late June and early July is the time to catch the fine art degree shows at the London colleges: you'll find details in the press.

ART PUBLICATIONS

The London art scene inspires reams of articles, critiques and commentary. All the daily and Sunday papers have their art critics, but some of them have been around a little too long. The most authoritative of the younger generation, Andrew Graham-Dixon is currently on sabbatical leave from the *Independent*, and you'll find Tim Hilton in its sister paper, the *Independent on Sunday*, espousing gestural painting. At the other end of the scale, Brian Sewell expounds his vehemently anti-avant garde views in the daily *Evening Standard*. For a solid, respected and decidedly didactic stance, check out Richard Cork in the *Times*. He was conceptualism's greatest supporter in the 1970s, and now puts his energies into patiently explaining the avant garde to his readers. Read one of the very few women to be given a voice in the art world, Sarah Kent, in *Time Out* magazine, which also carries reviews of current exhibitions and up-to-date listings of what's on.

Other notable magazines include *Frieze* (£3.50, monthly) – hip and utterly wonderful to hold and behold. Its expansive brief means it happily embraces areas such as fashion, photography and film, alongside painting and sculpture. But it can be wilfully dense and self-conscious. *Tate* (£3), which was launched by the gallery in September 1993 and appears three times yearly, aims to be equally trendy, but with more nods to the mainstream and a greater emphasis on accessibility.

If you fancy something more middle-brow look for *Modern Painters* (£4.50, quarterly), the glossy magazine made infamous by the contentiously reactionary views of its founder Peter Fuller, who died in 1990. And for the best of the earnest brigade, buy *Art Monthly* (£2.25, monthly), for a safe and scholarly look at the art world. Magazines are for sale in most gallery shops, but even better is **Dillons Art Bookshop** in Covent Garden. It sells a quantity of art, photography, fashion and culture journals you may have found hard to believe actually existed.

Collections

Courtauld Institute Gallery

Somerset House, Strand, WC2 (0171 873 2526). Covent Garden tube. **Open** 10am-6pm Mon-Sat; 2-6pm Sun. **Admission** £3; £1.50 under-15s, OAPs, UB40s. **Credit** A, £TC, V.
The Courtauld Collection is housed in the Strand block of George III's Somerset House, allowing 80 per cent of its hoard to be hung. A recent re-hang promises to improve further the presentation of the largest collection of post-Impressionist works in London. To get round the 32 Rubens paintings, Bellinis, Veroneses and the Impressionists, it's worth buying a guide, or booking a guided tour.

Dulwich Picture Gallery

College Road, SE21 (0181 693 5254). North or West Dulwich BR; P4, 12, 37, 78, 176 bus. **Open** 10am-5pm Tue-Fri; 11am-5pm Sat; 2-5pm Sun. Closed Bank Holidays. **Admission** £2; £1 OAPs UB40s; free Fri (under-16s at all times). **No credit cards**.
This was the first national gallery to be built, designed by Sir John Soane in 1817, and is as famous for its architecture as for its paintings. The Gallery offers a flavour of Regency taste, when collecting was moving into the public domain after centuries as a purely private activity. The interesting collection consists mainly of seventeenth- and eighteenth-century Continental masters: Rubens abounds along with Poussin romanesques and a few Van Dyks. The compact hanging, also in Regency style, includes some impressive Gainsboroughs as well. Rembrandt's *Girl at a Window* is one of the Gallery's most celebrated possessions.

Iveagh Bequest, Kenwood

Hampstead Lane, NW3 (0181 348 1286). Hampstead tube/Golders Green tube then 210 bus. **Open** *1 April-30 Sept* 10am-6pm daily; *1 Oct-31 Mar* 10am-4pm daily. **Admission** free, donations gratefully received.
Set in the leafy environs of Hampstead, the first Earl of Mansfield's home was brilliantly remodelled by Robert Adam. Beneath his neo-classical façade, exciting attempts are being made to restore the original exotic colouring to the hallway. The ornate ceiling's moulded vines with clusters of grapes and grinning animal skulls testify to the room's dual purpose as porch and dining room. Beyond, the house is full of interesting paintings and furniture: look out for one of Rembrandt's self-portraits (guaranteed original unlike so many of the others), several rare Vermeers in the dining room, and Reynolds' portrait of Nelson's mistress, Lady Hamilton, dressed up as a nun. The charming ambience of the handsome Library draws in many admirers at weekends. The English Heritage staff are knowledgeable, friendly and quite willing to answer enquiries.
Audio cassettes £1. Disabled: access to ground floor and car parking. Facilities for the hard of hearing. Foreign-language guides. Group tours. Open-air summer concerts, indoor recitals (0171 973 3427). Restaurants: Coach House, open noon-2.30pm daily; Old Kitchen, open 9am-6pm daily April-Sept, Sunday lunchtimes throughout the year. School visits.

Leighton House Museum

12 Holland Park, W14 (0171 602 3316). High Street Kensington tube/9, 93 bus. **Open** 11am-5.30pm Mon-Sat. **Admission** free but donations appreciated.
The painter Lord Leighton fulfilled his vision of a palace of art when he had this house built in 1864. It now houses his collection of pre-Raphaelite and High Victorian work as well as bearing witness to his fascination with the East. In 1996, the centenary of Lord Leighton's death, the place will be transformed for an exhibition demonstrating the

Marc Quinn's 'Self' in the **Saatchi Collection**.

eminent Victorian's life and times. In what must be one of London's most interesting interiors, a highlight is the Arab Hall: an Islamic tiled, wooden-latticed room, based on a Moorish palace in Palermo.

National Gallery

Trafalgar Square, WC2 (0171 839 3321). Leicester Square or Piccadilly Circus tube/Charing Cross tube/BR. **Open** 10am-6pm Mon-Sat; 2-6pm Sun. **Admission** free. **Credit** A, AmEx, £$TC, V.

Founded in 1824 with just 38 pictures, the National Collection of Paintings now contains over 2,000 western European paintings from the thirteenth to the twentieth century, including works from all the major schools of art. The leather Chesterfield-style sofas, marble, and creaking wooden floors add to the olde-worlde atmosphere. There is a guided tour for the daunted, which concentrates on the major paintings on the ground floor. Robert Venturi and Denise Scott Brown's Sainsbury Wing, opened in 1991, provides breathtaking exhibition space for the fine collection of early Renaissance works. And don't miss the Micro Gallery, where at the touch of a screen you can see any painting in the collection, print out a reproduction or construct a customised tour around your own favourites, which may include some of the following: Van Gogh's *Sunflowers*, Van Eyck's *The Arnolfini Portrait*, Titian's *Bacchus and Ariadne*, Constable's *The Hay Wain* or Turner's *The Fighting Temeraire*.
Bookshop. Brasserie: lunch 11.45am-2.45pm Mon-Sat; tea 2-5pm daily. Café. Disabled: access Orange Street/Sainsbury Wing. Films. Lectures. Guided tours. Micro Gallery open 10am-5.30pm Mon-Sat; 2-5.30pm Sun. Parent/baby room.

National Portrait Gallery

2 St Martin's Place, WC2 (0171 306 0055). Leicester Square tube or Charing Cross tube/BR. **Open** 10am-6pm Mon-Sat; noon-6pm Sun. **Admission** free. **Credit** A, AmEx, DC, £TC, V.

You can trace the history of the nation in the faces of its key players down the ages at the National Portrait Gallery. Founded in 1856 to collect pictures of royal and political figures, it now also houses the only known portrait of William Shakespeare, neither royal nor a politician. Start on level 4 – the Medieval landing – and work downwards. The present generation of the royal family is on Level 2, with Brian Organ's well-known portrait of the Princess of Wales. A new gallery of twentieth-century portraiture opened in November 1993, including a photography gallery. The gallery will be hanging the portraits from the city-wide The Twentieth Century: The Age Of Modern Art from September 1996.
Bookshop. Group visits by prior appointment. Lunchtime lectures. Talks. Videos.

Queen's Gallery

Buckingham Palace, Buckingham Palace Road, SW1 (0171 930 4832/recorded information 0171 799 2331). St James's Park tube. **Open** 9.30am-4pm daily. **Admission** £3.50; £2.50 OAPs; £2 under-17s.

The Queen heads a committee that decides which paintings to show here from her vast collection. Each season an artist is selected for special attention, often one of the great British masters such as Reynolds, Gainsborough or Stubbs.

Saatchi Collection

98A Boundary Road, NW8 (0171 624 8299). St John's Wood tube/139 bus. **Open** noon-6pm Thur-Sat. **Admission** £2.50; Fri, Sat; free Thur.

Charles Saatchi's advertising fortune enabled him to become an influential mover of modern art. Seven years ago he visited the Freeze exhibition in Docklands and fell in love with contemporary British art. Whoever he buys now, everyone else will be watching. Richard Wilson's *20:50*, an installation in sump-pump-oil and galvanised steel is now a fixture at his gallery. Not surprisingly, the large purpose-built space

has also seen some extraordinary temporary exhibitions. Of the three shows a year, one usually concentrates on young British artists. Names to look out for in 1996 include Brad Lochore, Jenny Saville, Gary Hulme, John Frankland and Marcus Harvey.

Tate Gallery

Millbank, SW1 (0171 887 8000). Pimlico tube/C10, 77A, 88 bus. **Open** 10am-5.50pm Mon-Sat; 2-5.50pm Sun. **Admission** free; *special exhibitions* prices vary.

Many people's favourite London gallery, the Tate perhaps owes its popularity to the satisfying combination of its collection of international modern art with the national collection of British paintings housed under one splendid neo-classical roof. However, the Clore Gallery extension, designed by James Stirling to grace the marvellous collection of Turner's paintings, has also proved a great success and further improvements are in the offing. In 1995 a new gallery space opened dedicated to Art Now, which in its first year exhibited work by contemporary artists Marc Quinn, Miroslaw Balka and Genevieve Cadieux. The development heralds the role contemporary art is expected to play here and at the proposed Tate Gallery of Modern Art, projected to open in 2000 at Bankside Power Station. The conversion by Swiss architects Herzog and de Meuron will provide the nation's first museum of modern art, leaving the Millbank building to become the Tate Gallery of British Art. Meanwhile, the gallery will be mounting an eagerly awaited full-scale retrospective of Cézanne's work in 1996.

Wallace Collection

Hertford House, Manchester Square, W1 (0171 935 0687). Bond Street tube. **Open** 10am-5pm Mon-Sat; 2-5pm Sun. **Admission** free. **Credit** A, £TC, V.

The hallway and state drawing room of Sir Richard Wallace's late eighteenth-century house have been meticulously restored to the splendour of his original design, right down to the crimson silk hangings and damask curtains. The illegitimate heir of the Marquis of Hertford, he nonetheless inherited the ardent Francophile's extraordinary collection of furniture (including one of Marie Antoinette's writing desks), paintings and porcelain purchased for safe-keeping in London after the revolution. An impressive clutch of Old Masters, including Franz Hals' *The Laughing Cavalier*, vies for space with arms and armour and a display of Catherine the Great's crockery. Just off Oxford Street, this engrossing house seems to have been left over from the last century.
Library (by appointment only). Public lectures. Tours and study days (contact education officer).

Public Galleries

Barbican Art Gallery

Level 3, Barbican Centre, Silk Street, EC2 (0171 638 4141 ext 306/recorded information 0171 588 9023). Barbican tube or Moorgate tube/BR. **Open** 10am-6.45pm Mon, Wed-Sat; 10am-5.45pm Tue; noon-6.45pm Sun. **Admission** £4.50; £2.50 OAPs, under-15s. **Credit** A, AmEx, £TC, V.

The Barbican lives up to its name in terms of inaccessibility. That said, the main gallery regularly mounts interesting exhibitions of modern and historical works. There will be a retrospective of American photojournalist Eve Arnold's work in the summer of 1996, and the Belgian expressionist James Ensor's hallucinatory turn-of-the-century meditations on death and society will be on show in 1997.

Camden Arts Centre

Arkwright Road, corner of Finchley Road, NW3 (0171 435 2643). Finchley Road tube. **Open** noon-8pm Tue-Thur; noon-6pm Fri-Sun. **Admission** free. **Credit** A, V.

The borough of Camden's community arts centre includes three gallery spaces, which host contemporary exhibitions and

*The **Hayward Gallery** stages a retrospective of Claes Oldenburg's work in summer 1996.*

one historical show a year. Barnett Newman's work will be exhibited into 1996. A recent development is the chance to see the exhibition artists at work through the rolling artists-in-residence scheme. School groups come in the morning and there are educational tours. Talks are given on Sundays at 3pm by artists, usually responding to the current exhibition.

Chisenhale Gallery
64 Chisenhale Road, E3 (0181 981 4518). Bethnal Green or Mile End tube/D6, 8, 277 bus. **Open** 1-6pm Wed-Sun. **Admission** free.
In a vast late-Victorian warehouse backing on to a canal, contemporary, innovative work can be found here in an exciting variety of forms. Sculptor Simon Patterson and painter Juan Davila are two artists whose strange pieces have recently occupied the echoing empty space.

Crafts Council
44A Pentonville Road, N1 (0171 278 7700). Angel tube. **Open** 11am-6pm Tue-Sat; 2-6pm Sun. **Admission** free. **Credit** *shop* A, AmEx, V.
Housed in an elegantly converted Georgian house in Islington, the Crafts Council's gallery showcases the nation's crafts output. Exhibitions often take a theme and demonstrate craftspeople's contribution in that area. Codes And Messages in early 1996 looks at craft and communications with a display of calligraphy and ceramic telephones.

Hayward Gallery
Belvedere Road, South Bank Centre, SE1 (0171 928 3144/recorded information 0171 261 0127). Waterloo tube/BR. **Open** 10am-6pm Mon, Thur-Sun; 10am-8pm Tue, Wed. **Admission** £5; £3.50 OAPs, under-18s. **Credit** A, V.
Part of the South Bank Centre, the Hayward is one of London's finest venues for temporary exhibitions of both contemporary and historical art. The relatively high admission charges are usually justified by the quality of the work curated. Until 5 May 1996, Spellbound: Art And Film In Britain promises to be an interesting exploration of our contemporary artists' relationship with the moving image. It looks set to be another example of the Hayward's trail-blazing appeal. Also in 1996, as well as the Age of Modern Art, Claes Oldenburg: An Anthology will be a major summer retrospective of the American sculptor's lurid monumental everyday objects.

ICA Gallery

The Mall, SW1 (0171 930 3647/membership enquiries 0171 930 0493/recorded information 0171 930 6393). Piccadilly Circus tube or Charing Cross tube/BR. **Open** noon-7.30pm Mon-Thur, Sat, Sun; noon-9pm Fri. **Admission** free with membership. **Membership** £22 per year; £12 per year OAPs; £1.50 per day (£1 concs). **Credit** A, AmEx, DC, £TC, V.

At its opening in 1948, the great art historian and anarchist Herbert Read declared that the Institute of Contemporary Arts would be different from all the others. Much to its credit, it has maintained its reputation for being a challenging place to witness all forms of artistic expression. The Upper Gallery is an elegant suite of rooms which host exhibitions of every type of work produced by the avant garde. The Concourse Gallery attracts more attention because of its position by the café. Many leading artists had their first London exhibitions at the ICA, including Moore, Picasso, Max Ernst and Helen Chadwick.

Bar. Bookshop. Café. Cinema. Group discount. Lectures. Workshops.

Independent Art Space

23A Smith Street, SW3 (0171 259 9232). Sloane Square tube. **Open** 11am-6pm Thur-Sat. **Admission** free.

Founded in 1994 as a project space for contemporary artists, the IAS invites in four independent curators a year. The exhibitions of neo-conceptual British and Continental artists have proved popular. Finely bound limited edition programmes of the shows are produced, which are given signed to subscribing members, or are available unsigned at the door for £10. **NB** The IAS is not open all year round.

Matt's Gallery

42 Copperfield Road, E3 (0181 983 1771). Mile End tube. **Open** noon-6pm Wed-Sun. **Admission** free.

The latest installations can be seen at Matt's Gallery. Artists are invited by owner Robin Klassnik to do with this East End space what they will, and the results range from the epistemic to the plain incomprehensible.

RIBA

66 Portland Place, W1 (0171 580 5533). Oxford Circus tube. **Open** 8am-7pm Mon, Wed, Fri; 8am-9pm Tue, Thur; 9am-5pm Sat. **Credit** A, V.

The Royal Institute of British Architects is housed in a monumental edifice built by Grey Wornham in 1934. The gallery exhibits the great and the good: Nicholas Grimshaw, Tadao Ando and Santiago Calatrava, to name but a few.

Riverside Studios

Crisp Road, W6 (0181 741 2251). Hammersmith tube. **Open** 10am-11pm Tue-Sun. **Admission** free.

Ten shows a year in the gallery and foyer space contribute to the fine art commitment of this independent west London theatre and cinema. Sculpture, paintings, drawings and installations by young British unknowns as well as high-profile international artists are shown.

Royal Academy of Arts

Burlington House, Piccadilly, W1 (0171 439 7438). Green Park or Piccadilly tube. **Open** 10am-6pm daily. **Admission** £3-£6. **Credit** A, AmEx, £TC, V.

Britain's first art school (it opened in 1768), the Royal Academy of Arts also held the country's first annual open exhibitions of living artists. This persists as the Summer Exhibition (*see chapter* **London by Season**) where thousands of paintings, sculptures and architectural works are on view, and visitors number around 150,000 each year. Whatever the exhibition, the RA's reputation and history ensure huge crowds of weekend gallery wanderers, and long queues to get in. Early on Sunday morning is the quietest time at the weekend. Exhibitions scheduled for 1996 include The Twentieth Century: The Age Of Modern Art , and a centennial exhibition of Frederic, Lord Leighton's work (*see above* **Leighton House**). The RA's postgraduate school stages its Premium Show every January.

Simon Schofield's 'Sizewell B in Ruins' (1994) features in April/May 1996 at **Camerawork**.

Serpentine Gallery
Kensington Gardens, Hyde Park, W2 (0171 402 6075).
Lancaster Gate or South Kensington tube. **Open** 10am-
6pm daily. **Admission** free.
The Serpentine pursues an independent and lively curatorial policy which has won it many regular visitors. It's housed
in a tranquil former tea pavilion, and the french windows
look out on to Hyde Park, imbuing the exhibitions with varying qualities of natural light (depending on the weather)
and enhancing the peaceful atmosphere in which to con-
template the works. Informal talks given by invited artists
on Sunday afternoons can also be very lively and there's a
well-stocked bookshop.

Whitechapel Gallery
80-82 Whitechapel High Street, E1 (0171 522 7878
recorded/0171 522 7888 other enquiries). Aldgate East
tube. **Open** 11am-5pm Tue, Thur-Sun; 11am-8pm Wed.
Admission free.
The Whitechapel remains one of the most interesting galleries in London – it is independent and puts on a variety of
exciting temporary shows. In 1996, apart from the Age Of
Modern Art, there will be exhibitions of the work of German
Expressionist Emil Nolde, and 15 of Canadian artist Jeff
Wall's monumental photographic tableaux in lightboxes.
The gallery has a number of artists-in-residence who give
lectures and run workshops. The annual Whitechapel Open
is the only major show of east London artists.

Commercial Galleries

Central: Cork Street

Cork Street has been at the hub of the art world
since the end of World War II. So long as you are
prepared to brave the snooty demeanour of the
assistants, the galleries will provide an insight into
the shape of the market for both historical and
contemporary artworks, and they're all free to
enter. Many close in August, while their customary
clientèle are in the Bahamas.

Bernard Jacobson Gallery
14A Clifford Street, W1 (0171 495 8575). Green Park or
Piccadilly Circus tube. **Open** 10am-6pm Mon-Fri; 10am-
1pm Sat. **No credit cards.**
Jacobson's space, formerly an old gaming club, now hosts
the work of British painters such as Bomberg and Nicholson,
as well as the more recent abstract black and white compositions of Ian McKeever.

Entwistle
37 Old Bond Street, W1 (0171 409 3484). Green Park
tube. **Open** 10am-5.30pm Mon-Fri, 11am-4pm Sat.
Entwistle specialises in showing young British, Japanese
and American artists. Exhibitions have ranged from Sarah
Staton and Andrew James' sculptures to Bridget Smith's
huge photographs. Proud to be the first gallery in Bond
Street to give room to work in film and video, its summer
'fashion' show played off the proximity of their famous
neighbour Versace.

Marlborough Fine Art
6 Albermarle Street, W1 (0171 629 5161). Green Park
tube. **Open** 10am-5.30pm Mon-Fri; 10am-12.30pm Sat
(closed Bank Holiday weekends). **No credit cards.**
This gallery concentrates on exhibiting modern British masters such as Moore, Kitaj and Hepworth. Its famous mixed
summer show is considered an important date for the diary.
The print room shows the Marlborough's own artists, including Frank Auerbach and Paula Rego's figurative paintings.

Check **Waddington's** *for Peter Blake's work.*

Raab Boukamel Gallery
9 Cork Street, W1 (0171 734 6444). Green Park tube.
Open 10am-6pm Mon-Fri; 10am-2pm Sat. **Credit** A,
AmEx, V.
Contemporary international figurative works on a large scale
are the Raab's speciality. They represent an impressive variety of European artists including Luciano Castelli, Gerard
Garouste and Daniel Spoerri. Ken Currie's figurative paintings represent part of the British contingent.

Mayor
22A Cork Street, W1 (0171 734 3558). Green Park tube.
Open 10am-5.30pm Mon-Fri; 10am-1pm Sat.
One of the first galleries to open in Cork Street in 1933, Mayor
now specialises in twentieth-century masters such as Klee,
Ernst and Sir Roland Penrose. It also claims to be the largest
single exhibition space in the area, and there's the peculiar
old squash court to peer into from the balcony.

Victoria Miro
5-6 Cork Street, W1 (0171 734 5082). **Open** 10am-
5.30pm Mon-Fri; 11am-1pm Sat. **No credit cards.**
Victoria Miro's gallery, designed by Claudio Silvestrin, well
suits the mixed clutch of contemporary artists she represents: Andrew Gursky, Stephen Pippin, and the sculptors
Jake and Dinos Chapman.

Waddington's
11, 12 & 34 Cork Street, W1 (0171 437 8611). Green
Park or Piccadilly Circus tube. **Open** 10am-5.30pm Mon-
Fri; 10am-1pm Sat (34 Cork Street closed in August). **No**
credit cards.
The Waddington Galleries are one of the major forces to be
reckoned with by modern and contemporary art dealers.
They exhibit modern masters such as Picasso, Matisse
and Dubuffet, as well as Peter Blake, Patrick Caulfield,
Barry Flanagan and William Turnbull. Contemporary artists

represented include Ian Davenport, Fiona Rae and Alison Jakes. In collaboration with Karsten Schubert their recent compilation of the latest work by young British artists, From Here, drew a confused response.

Central: Dering Street

Annely Juda Fine Art
23 Dering Street, W1 (0171 629 7578). Bond Street tube. **Open** 10am-6pm Mon-Fri; 10am-1pm Sat. **No credit cards.**
Annely Juda tends to concentrate on modern British masters such as Anthony Caro, David Nash and Alan Green. The fact that Cristo, Miro and Eduardo Chillida have also been exhibited here conveys an impression of the gallery's stature: the summer show is always worth a visit.

Anthony d'Offay
9, 21, 23 & 24 Dering Street, W1 (0171 499 4100). Bond Street tube. **Open** 10am-6pm Mon-Sat. **Credit** *books and catalogues only* A, AmEx, V.
Since opening in 1980 with Joseph Beuys and Gilbert & George, d'Offay has become renowned for his exhibitions of significant modern art. Work by big names can often be seen here, including Warhol, Lichtenstein and Pollock.

Anthony Reynolds Gallery
5 Dering Street, W1 (0171 491 0621). Bond Street tube. **Open** 10am-5.30pm Mon-Fri; 10am-1pm Sat. **Credit** A, AmEx, V.
Anthony Reynolds moved to this space in 1987. Here he has focused mainly on contemporary British art in every type of medium. Artists recently represented include David Austen, Geogina Start and Mark Wallinger.

Fine Art Society
148 New Bond Street, W1 (0171 629 5116). Bond Street tube. **Open** 9am-5.30pm Mon-Fri; 10am-1pm Sat. **Credit** A, V.
The Fine Art Society has an olde-worlde atmosphere that complements the portfolio of artists on show. If you are a devotee of the cult being made of mid-twentieth-century painter Eric Ravilious's work, this is the place to seek it out.

Gimpel Fils
30 Davies Street, W1 (0171 493 2488). Bond Street tube. **Open** 10am-5.30pm Mon-Fri; 10am-1pm Sat (closed Sat in Aug). **No credit cards.**
Gimpel Fils is known for its twentieth-century French painting and sculpture. It has also shown the work of British painter Terry Atkinson, and abstracts by the Scot Alan Davie. The gallery space has room for works on a large scale, such as Niki de Saint Phalle's sculptures.

Central: Other Galleries

Austin/Desmond Fine Art
Pied Bull Yard, 15A Bloomsbury Square, WC1 (0171 242 4443). Holborn tube. **Open** 10am-5.30pm Mon-Fri. **No credit cards.**
John Austin specialises in modern British painting and carries a wide selection of contemporary prints by artists such as Ivan Hitchens and William Scott.

Frith Street
60 Frith Street, W1 (0171 494 1550). Tottenham Court tube. **Open** 10am-6pm Tue-Fri; 11am-4pm Sat. **No credit cards.**
Opened in 1989, Frith Street's four interlinked rooms provide an intimate space for exhibitions of contemporary artists from home and abroad, including Juan Munoz and newer arrivals such as painter Marlene Dumas and the multi-media artist Tacita Dean.

Karsten Schubert
41, 42 Foley Street, W1 (0171 631 0031). Goodge Street tube. **Open** 10am-6pm Tue-Fri; 11am-3pm Sat. **No credit cards.**
A visit here is essential if you want to keep up with the very latest developments in contemporary art. The gallery focuses on British and American work. Artists represented include Matt Collishaw, Keith Coventry, Bridget Riley and Lynne Cohen.

Laure Genillard Gallery
38A Foley Street, W1 (0171 436 2300). Goodge Street tube. **Open** 11am-6pm Tue-Fri; 11am-3pm Sat. **No credit cards.**
Laure Genillard's is a small space which manages to maintain an emphasis on installations and minimalism. Tania Kovats' light sculptures and drillings by Craig Wood have been the subject of recent shows.

Rebecca Hossack
35 Windmill Street, W1 (0171 436 4899). Tottenham Court Road tube. **Open** 10am-6pm Mon-Sat. **No credit cards.**
Responsible for the city's only central sculpture garden next to St James's, Piccadilly, Rebecca Hossack also specialises in Aboriginal art at her recently refurbished space: look out for her yearly 'songlines' exhibition in July and August. Last year a mixed range of artists was shown, including David Page's *Fifteen Bitches And A Pig*.

White Cube
44 Duke Street, St James's, SW1 (0171 930 5373). Green Park tube. **Open** noon-6pm Fri, Sat.
Jay Jopling's space, designed by Claudio Silvestrin, has witnessed some of the most promising exhibitions of recent years. Jopling has a sure eye for the artists of the future and his relentless self-promotion has put the White Cube at the forefront of the contemporary art scene. If evidence is needed, witness his stable of artists, which includes young turks Gavin Turk (he of the Sid Vicious self-sculpture and blown egg with *oeuvre* written on it), Itai Doron and Marc Quinn (who froze nine pints of his own blood to create the bust *Self*).

West

Jibby Beane
Flat 6, 143-145 Gloucester Terrace, W2 (0171 723 5531). Paddington tube/BR. **Open** noon-6pm Wed, Thur (or by appointment). **No credit cards.**
One of the colourful newcomers on the gallery scene, ex-Vivienne Westwood model Jibby Beane has opened her own living room as a gallery to show young artists, who, in 1995, have included Marcus Coates, Emma Smith and Jonathan Goslan.

England & Co
14 Needham Road, W11 (0171 221 0417). Bayswater or Notting Hill Gate tube. **Open** 11am-6pm Tue-Sat. **Credit** A, AmEx, V.
Jane England is well known for her annual international Art In Boxes show. She also stages regular successful re-appraisals of contemporary and modern British and international work which are enhanced by the intensity of this small space.

Francis Graham-Dixon
17 Great Sutton Street, EC1 (0171 250 1962). Barbican tube. **Open** 11am-6pm Mon-Sat.
Opened in 1987 in a Victorian glovemaker's workshop, the gallery specialises in contemporary British, European and North American abstracts in a variety of media. In 1995 there were exhibitions of Geoffrey Rigden's and Julia Farrer's paintings, and some 'autocollages' by Jiri Kolar.

'Game Boys II' by Bosnian war artist Peter Howson, exhibited at **Flowers East**, *E8.*

London Print Workshop

421 Harrow Road (opposite Bravington Road), W10 (0181 969 3247). Westbourne Park tube/18, 31, 36 bus. **Open** 2-6pm Mon; 10.30am-9pm Tue; 10.30am-6pm Wed-Fri; 1-5pm Sat. **No credit cards.**
The workshop has six exhibitions a year, and offers open access to artists. The shows are wide and varied, and often affiliated to other galleries such as Flowers East. Recent shows have included Ken Kiss and Harvey Daniels.

Todd Gallery

1-5 Needham Road, W11 (0171 792 1404). Bayswater or Notting Hill Gate tube. **Open** 11am-6pm Tue-Fri; 11am-4pm Sat. **No credit cards.**
A large, sparse, purpose-built space provides ample room for Jenny Todd's eclectic variety of artists. She has shown work by young British, American and European painters such as Simon Lewis, Joanna Kirk and Maria Lalic.

North

Lisson Gallery

67 Lisson Street, NW1 (0171 724 2739). Edgware Road tube. **Open** 10am-6pm Mon-Fri; 10am-5pm Sat. **Credit** A, AmEx, V.
Although slightly out of the way, this modernist gallery, with its recent, seriously minimalist extension, is well worth a visit. The Lisson offers space to the young and established, and represents a number of sculptors of international repute including Sol Lewitte, Tony Cragg, Anish Kapoor and Granville Davie.

East

Flowers East

199-205 Richmond Road, E8 (0181 985 3333). Bethnal Green tube/6, 35, 55, 106, 253 bus. **Open** 10am-6pm Tue-Sun. **Credit** A, V.

With two spaces – Flowers East, London Fields – Flowers has plenty of room to show its 30-strong stable. The art is mostly British and ranges from the abstract to the figurative. Those represented here include Bosnian war artist Peter Howson, John Keane and Patrick Hughes.
Branches: London Fields 282 Richmond Road, E8 (0181 533 5554).

Interim Art

21 Beck Road, E8 (0171 254 6907). Bethnal Green tube. **Open** 11am-6pm Fri, Sat.
This important gallery in two rooms of a converted Victorian terrace has made a broad move in policy from innovative, international work towards young British artists. There are those who might consider that tautologous, but Interim Art's reputation remains secure with recent exhibitions by painters Julie Roberts and Mark Francis, and Gillian Wearing's video installations.

Paton Gallery

London Fields, 282 Richmond Road, E8 (0181 986 3409). Bethnal Green tube/106, 253 bus. **Open** 11am-6pm Tue-Sat; noon-6pm Sun. **No credit cards.**
The dynamic Graham Paton moved his gallery to larger premises in London Fields in 1993. With double the space, he hopes to expand beyond his core artists and show some more experimental works.

Reed's Wharf Gallery

Mill Street, SE1 (0171 252 1802). Tower Hill tube/BR. **Open** 10am-6pm Tue-Fri; 11am-3pm Sat. **No credit cards.**
Seven shows a year are put on at this gallery overlooking the Thames. The owner claims to be 'looking for artists with a unique voice' and is refreshingly passionate about the work he shows. The gallery is blessed with good natural light and high ceilings, perfect for displaying the Chinese dissident artist Qu Lei Lei's huge, deep-toned visual diaries, which are scheduled for late 1995.

South

Cabinet
8 Clifton Mansions, 429 Coldharbour Lane, SW9 (0171 274 4252). Brixton Tube. **Open** noon-6pm Fri, Sat.
Occupying two rooms in the strangely Italianate Clifton Mansions, Cabinet has established itself recently as the place to look for interesting new developments. Youngish contemporary artists shown include Rod Dickinson, Simon Bill and, from the States, Jason Fox.

Alternative

Alternative Art Galleries
c/o 47A Brushfield Street, E1 (0171 375 0441).
Telephone enquiries 10am-6pm Mon-Fri. **Shops open** 11am-5pm Tue-Sat.
One of the most rewarding ways to buy art is direct from the artist. With this in mind, and the desire to make art accessible, Alternative Arts has struck upon a brilliant scheme – it borrows empty shops, selects artists who haven't had the mainstream attention they deserve and invites them to hang and invigilate their own shows. The spaces are scattered along Chiltern Street and Marylebone High Street, both in W1. The work is in all media – from exquisitely sculpted paper wall hangings to vibrant semi-abstract oils and Mondrian-inspired sculpture – and the quality is high. Expect to pay anything from £50 to £2,000. Trading laws forbid making purchases on site, which may mean writing a cheque on the pavement or making a trip to the artist's studio. Alternative Arts also runs an art market at Spitalfields once a month from May to December; phone for details.

Photography Galleries

The Association Gallery
The Association of Photographers, 9-10 Domingo Street, EC1 (0171 608 1441). Barbican or Old Street tube.
Open 9.30am-6pm Mon-Fri. **Admission** free. **Credit** A, AmEx, V.
The two-floored Association Gallery opened in 1986 to showcase work commissioned for advertising and editorial purposes and it puts on an annual show of Association of Photographers' award-winners each February. It also puts on 20 contemporary photographic exhibitions a year.

Camerawork
121 Roman Road, E2 (0181 980 6256). Bethnal Green tube. **Open** 1-6pm Mon-Sat. **Admission** free.
Camerawork's brief is a worthy one: to show adventurous, challenging, issue-based work. The 1996 programme includes a group show examining the effects of the Chernobyl disaster (April-May), a series of exhibitions from or about eastern Europe (June-Aug), and interactive work from Japan and Europe in collaboration with galleries in Newcastle and Glasgow (Nov-Dec).

Hamilton's
13 Carlos Place, W1 (0171 499 9493). Bond Street or Green Park tube. **Open** 10am-6pm Tue-Sat. **Admission** free. **Credit** A, AmEx, £$TC, V.
Rubbing shoulders with Mayfair's fine-art galleries, Hamilton's has always had an exclusive international clientèle and exhibited high-profile photographers. It shows photography as fine art; prints start at about £250 and go on upwards. Choose from over 3,000 prints by names such as Bailey, Penn, Avedon and Newton. It's a great space and has excellent exhibitions, concentrating on more fashionable contemporary names, from Linda McCartney's 1960s pop stars to the controversial Joel-Peter Witkin.
Disabled: access. Print room.

Photofusion
17A Electric Lane, SW9 (0171 738 5774). Brixton tube/BR. **Open** 1.30-5.30pm Tue-Fri; noon-4pm Sat.
Admission free. **No credit cards.**
Aided by council and commercial grants, this co-operative has kept to its community roots and concentrates on social documentary photography, showing some unsettling images of London's communities. It will also be contributing to the current vogue for all things east European with an exhibition of work by Slovak photographers Rudo Prekop, Camil Varga and Peter Zupnik. Expanding into the premises next door will consolidate Photofusion's real work of staging the debates, talks and educational events which have created a south London photography forum.
Children's workshops. Courses, events, talks. Darkroom and studio facilities by prior appointment. Disabled: access; chair-lift entrance; toilets. Monthly membership available. Picture library 9.30am-5.30pm Mon-Fri.

Photographers' Gallery
5 Great Newport Street, WC2 (0171 831 1772). Covent Garden or Leicester Square tube. **Open** 11am-6pm Tue-Sat. **Admission** free. **Credit** A, AmEx, DC, V.
In 1971 the Photographers' Gallery, devoted to photography, was the first of its kind to open in England. It has been promoting contemporary photography ever since, especially social documentary and reportage, and has been instrumental in encouraging national galleries to hold photographic shows. It has 24 shows a year.
Café. Disabled: access. Facilities for the deaf. Membership available. Print room. Reference library. Shop. Workshops, talks, discussions, teachers' evenings.

Special Photographers' Company
21 Kensington Park Road, W11 (0171 221 3489). Ladbroke Grove or Notting Hill Gate tube. **Open** 10am-6pm Mon-Fri; 11am-5pm Sat. **Admission** free. **Credit** A, V.
Opened in the 1980s in the heart of trendy Notting Hill, the Special Photographers' Company gallery aimed to represent the work of serious photographers, while taking advantage of the growing market of wealthy thirtysomethings looking for entertaining and beautiful images to hang on their walls. It seems to have achieved this, by exhibiting a wide range of work from Joyce Tenneson to Clare Park and Herman Leonard's classic jazz images. Not limited by a specifically fine-art or documentary tradition, the gallery holds a large collection of prints from landscape to abstract, which start at £60, and a number of Spanish images, including startling work by the fashion photographer Javier Vallhonrat. The gallery is on two levels: the ground floor and a spacious basement area.
Disabled: access (ground floor only). Print room, no appointment necessary.

Zelda Cheatle Gallery
8 Cecil Court, WC2 (0171 836 0506). Leicester Square or Charing Cross tube/BR. **Open** 11am-6pm Tue-Fri; 11am-4pm Sat. **Admission** free. **Credit** A, AmEx, V.
When Zelda Cheatle broke away from the Photographers' Gallery in 1989, she took with her a background in documentary work and a following of serious, especially US, collectors. Her small gallery shows some excellent British, American and European photography. Predominantly exhibiting portrait, documentary, landscape and abstract work, the gallery has featured work by David Hiscock, Eve Arnold, Steve Pyke and Manuel Bravo. In 1996 she will be mounting an exhibition that compares and contrasts contemporary Anglo-Japanese work. Cheatle's own publications include John Blakemore's *This Stilled Gaze* and Steve Pyke's striking *Philosophers*. The print collection contains work by Calum Colvin, Annie Liebowitz, Robert Doisneau, as well as vintage Czechoslovak and modern Mexican works.
Disabled: access (ground floor only).

Museums

London's museums are where to go if you don't like museums – nowhere in the history of glass cases has so much been put on display so enticingly for so many.

There's no doubt that visiting museums is not what it used to be. Even the most venerable repositories of the past are now falling over themselves in the bid to entice more visitors. No more gazing blankly at some inexplicably shapen antiquity resting snugly beneath plate glass. You're more likely to find it rotating slowly in many-angled light with explanatory audio-visual back-up. London's museums are reaching for their Manuals of User-Friendliness in the drive to keep their turnstiles spinning and their collections appealing.

Abandoning the traditional curatorial policy of static displays accompanied by a learned guidebook has inevitably provoked reaction. Objections tend to be lodged on the grounds that attention-grabbing gimmicks diminish the opportunity for individual voyages of discovery.

Nowadays interesting relics have much sterner competition. TV satisfies much of the curiosity that museums aroused in the Victorians. Some modern attractions even avoid using the word 'museum', which is ironic considering the root of the word's connection with inspiration rather than conservation.

There are still museums that buck the trend. Most obviously the large museums, such as the **Victoria & Albert Museum**, which remains aloof in its attitude to all but the cognoscenti of art and design, and the **British Museum**. Their collections are simply too large to admit more than superficial alterations to their presentation. On the other hand, there seems little justification for the resolutely recondite approach of some of the military museums (with the notable exception of the **Imperial War Musuem**) and other specialist museums.

The **Science Museum**, appropriately enough, was the pioneer of the interactive exhibit and 'hands-on' activity. Its neighbour, the **Natural History Museum**, has now stolen its thunder, bringing nature to life with the latest technological wizardry. Equally up-to-the-minute in its organisation and consequently usually very busy is the **Museum of the Moving Image (MOMI)** attached to the **National Film Theatre (NFT)**.

Other museums have perfected a combination of the two approaches. The **Museum of London** uses atmospheric sound and light to complement its largely object-oriented collection; but this in no way detracts from individuals' ability to imagine their own versions of London's past. The **National Maritime Museum** also saves the hi-tech explication for the Twentieth Century Seapower gallery, leaving the history of seafaring to be told by old paintings and scale models.

The remarkable variety of museums guarantees that the most arcane enthusiasm will find inspiration somewhere. The difficulty will be deciding where to begin to enjoy the endless treasures of the past that seem to have fetched up in London.

Major Museums

See also page 190 **Exhibition Road** *and page 195* **British Museum**.

Museum of London
150 London Wall, EC2 (0171 600 3699). Barbican tube/St Paul's tube/Moorgate tube/BR. **Open** 10am-5.50pm Tue-Sat, Bank Holidays; noon-5.50pm Sun. **Admission** £3.50; £1.75 OAPs, under-15s; free after 4.30pm.
The concrete 'drawbridge' across a 'moat' of traffic makes an appropriate approach to this exploration of London's history, purpose-built in the middle of a busy City roundabout. Inside you'll find one of the most imaginatively designed museums in the capital. It traces the growth of London from prehistoric times to the last war with an absorbing combination of models, period artefacts and reconstructions. The Roman interior, with its original mosaic pavement, is particularly impressive. Look out also for the Cheapside hoard: a staggering cache of fine jewels, dating from 1560-1640, which were found in a box under a shop. The Great Fire Experience, an illuminated model with sound effects and commentary is only partially successful in depicting the fire that destroyed four-fifths of the City of London in 1666. On the ground floor, the Lord Mayor's ceremonial coach , as well as shop and restaurant interiors from Victorian and Edwardian London (including Selfridge's art deco elevator), provide a good impression of the extreme conditions of wealth and poverty still glaringly obvious today.
Disabled: access; toilets. Films. Lectures (induction loop for the hard of hearing). Restaurant (10am-5pm Tue-Sat; noon-5pm Sun). Shop. Workshops.

National Maritime Museum
Romney Road, SE10 (0181 858 4422). GreenwichBR/Maze Hill BR/Island Gardens DLR then Greenwich foot tunnel/1, 177, 188 bus/boat to Greenwich Pier. **Open** *Mar-Oct* 10am-5pm daily. *Nov-Feb* noon-5pm Sun. **Admission** *passport to all sections £6.95; £4.95 disabled, OAPs, students, UB40s, under-16s; £13.95 family; free under-7s. Any one of National Maritime Museum, Queen's House, East Wing Exhibition or Old*

Exhibition Road

From beneath his mock-medieval memorial, Prince Albert broods over his brainchild: 87 acres of London developed with the profit from the massively popular Great Exhibition of 1851 into a permanent centre for industrial education. Down Exhibition Road today, you will find the **Victoria & Albert Museum**, the **Science Museum**, the **Natural History Museum**, as well as **Imperial College of Science and Technology**, the **Royal College of Art** and **Royal College of Music**. Sir Henry Cole was appointed to draw up the plans for the area and The **V&A** (first called the Museum of Manufactures, and later the Museum of Ornamental Art) was his first major achievment. The original, highly functional building was moved in 1872 and became the Bethnal Green Museum which is still a branch of the V&A dedicated to childhood. The more artistic Edwardian building designed by Aston Webb in 1890 now more appropriately houses the largest and finest collection of decorative art in the world.

The museum is also home to the national sculpture collection. In 1996, its most famous works of fine art, the *Raphael Cartoons*, which arrived from Hampton Court in 1865, will be on show again after a two-year restoration programme. The vast space available to the Museum means that nearly all of the staggering four-million-piece collection is on view to the public. It's divided over four levels into galleries of Art and Design, where the exhibits are arranged thematically by place and date, and galleries of Materials and Techniques, arranged by type or material.

Although the scale of the museum can be confusing, the arrangement allows even the casual browser an insight into the development of either style or textile through the ages. Not to be missed are the TT Tsui Gallery of Chinese Art, a fascinating display illuminating all facets of Chinese daily life and worship; the adjacent Toshiba Gallery of Japanese Art and the Frank Lloyd Wright Gallery, which houses the actual office that the American architect designed for Edgar J Kaufmann in the 1930s. One of the latest additions is the Glass Gallery which opened in January 1994. The café is spacious and serves good, but expensive, food.

The **Natural History Museum**, built on the site of another less popular Great Exhibition in 1862, opened in 1881 to exhibit the **British Museum**'s burgeoning variety of natural history specimens. Alfred Waterhouse's fine neo-gothic building still stands in all its pink and gold terracotta glory, gleaming from its 1970s cleaning as if built last year. One of London's most innovative museums, its collection is arranged in a series of Life Galleries ranging in theme from prehistory to global warming. The dinosaurs exhibition has guaranteed the museum's survival but the robotic models and colossal skeletons are only the beginning of the museum's wonders. Equally impressive are the Creepy-Crawlies (lots of animated arthropods), Human Biology, Ecology, and the Story of the Earth, which features a simulated earthquake and a piece of moon rock. The upstairs rooms are more traditional and the preserve of geological enthusiasts. Discovering Mammals, showing some of the biggest and rarest mammals in the world, is also a popular display.

Opened in its present building in 1913, the **Science Museum** capitalises on its reputation as the happening museum of the moment. Taking full advantage of Britain's heritage as the pioneer of industrialisation, many of the original machines that powered civilisation towards the millennium are lovingly preserved here. Filling five floors, the applications of technology are demonstrated, explained and celebrated. On the ground floor, the Apollo 10 command module and Stephenson's first steam train, the *Rocket*, illustrate how far our expertise in transportation has taken us.

On the first floor, The Launch Pad, a great favourite with kids, shows how technology works: you can push bubbles through silicone oil or whizz round on a turntable. There's also one of the first electric telegraph machines from 1846, a far cry

The Edgar J Kaufmann Office at the **V&A**.

The **Natural History Museum** – *last cleaned in the 1970s, but looking as good as new.*

from the mobile phone. The second-floor galleries reveal the secrets of nuclear physics and computing. Higher up, Flight Lab allows children to test the principles of flight for themselves by climbing into a cockpit to take the controls. Staff are 'Explainers'. Talks on flight, space and power are enthusiastic and lively. Buy the recently updated guide and avoid the less interesting galleries. Miss the school parties by visiting early in the morning.

The Victoria & Albert Museum

Cromwell Road, SW7 (0171 938 8500/recorded information 0171 938 8441). South Kensington tube. **Open** *noon-5.50pm Mon; 10am-5.50pm Tue-Sun. Print Room 10am-4.30pm Tue-Fri; 10am-1pm, 2-4.30pm, Sat.* **Admission** *free, donation requested: £2; 50p OAPs, students, UB40s, under-16s.* **Credit** *shop A, AmEx, £TC, V.*
Children's tours. Craft workshops. Disabled: access. Education department. Language tours: book in advance. Library facilities. Opinion days 2.30-4.30pm Tue. Short courses. Specialised gallery talks 2.30pm Mon-Sat. Study days. Restaurant (noon-5pm Mon; 10am-5pm Tue-Sun). Sunday jazz brunch.

Natural History Museum

Cromwell Road, SW7 (0171 938 9123/recorded information same number out of hours). South Kensington tube. **Open** *10am-5.50pm Mon-Sat; 11am-5.50pm Sun.* **Admission** *£5.50; £3 OAPs, UB40s; £2.80 under-17s; £15 family (2 adults, 4 children); membership scheme.* **Free** *after 4.30pm weekdays; after 5pm weekends, Bank Holidays.* **Credit** *shop A, AmEx, £TC, V.*
Bookshop. Café and restaurant (10am-5pm Mon-Sat; 11am-5pm Sun). Disabled: access. Discovery centre. Gallery shops. Group visits by prior appointment. Library facilities. Multilingual souvenir guides. School parties (free if pre-booked).

Science Museum

Exhibition Road, SW7 (0171 938 8008/8080/recorded information 0171 938 8123). South Kensington tube. **Open** *10am-6pm Mon-Sat; 11am-8pm Sun.* **Admission** *£4; £2.10 OAPs; £17 family (2 adults, 4 children); season tickets available.* **Free** *after 4.30pm.* **Credit** *shop A, AmEx, £TC, V.*
Bookshop. Café (10am-5pm, lunch noon-2.30pm, daily). Disabled: access by prior arrangement. Facilities for the visually impaired. Foreign-language guides. Group discounts. Library. Tours, free for schools.

*An American P15D Mustang at the **Imperial War Museum**, housed in what was Bedlam.*

Royal Observatory £5.50; £4.50 disabled, OAPs, students, UB40s; £3.50 under-16s; free under-5s. All prices include a free repeat visit in the next 12 months. **Credit** A, AmEx, £TC, V.

The logic of combining a visit to the National Maritime Museum with the **Old Royal Observatory** is more than purely economic. The Museum provides the background to the importance of the Meridian line to British and world trade. Popular special exhibitions aside, the permanent displays include delicate contemporary scale models of eighteenth-century ships of the line, a portrait gallery of the famous explorers, navigators and their monarchs (look out for John Bettes' famous portrait of Queen Elizabeth I) and a new hi-tech Nelson Gallery, opening in 1995. On the ground floor, the twentieth-century Seapower Gallery lets you take command in the Operations Room of a Type 22 Frigate and grasp the significance of the secret Zone Z to the D-Day landings. Surprisingly, despite developments in road, air and rail freight, world sea trade has increased eightfold since 1945. *Educational department. Disabled: access (ground floor only). Group discount. Library. Restaurant. Shop.*

Armed Services

Cabinet War Rooms

Clive Steps, King Charles Street, SW1 (0171 930 6961). Westminster or St James's Park tube/24, 29, 53, 88 bus. **Open** 9.30am-5.15pm daily. **Admission** £4; £3.10 OAPs; £3 students; £2 under-16s, UB40s; £6 family ticket (1 adult, 2 children).

The austere underground headquarters for Churchill's War Cabinet during World War II. All the rooms have been left exactly as they were – the all-important Map Room (manned night and day throughout the war to pinpoint the movement of troops and enemy), Churchill's bedroom (complete with nightshirt), and the telephone hotline to the White House. From time to time the (recorded) air raid sirens wail to complete the time warp. The guided tape tour fills in the details. *Disabled: access; toilet. Free audio guides. Group discount. Shop.*

Imperial War Museum

Lambeth Road, SE1 (0171 416 5000). Lambeth North tube/Elephant & Castle tube/Waterloo tube/BR. **Open** 10am-6pm daily. **Admission** £3.70; £2.75 OAPs, students, UB40s; £1.85 under-16s; free under-5s; £9.50 family (2 adults, 2 children). **Credit** *shop* A, V.

The early nineteenth century's most famous lunatic asylum, known as **Bedlam**, now houses this century's memorial to its two World Wars. A rotating clock-hand in the basement symbolises the cost of war in terms of human lives, a bodycount that it estimates will exceed 100 million by 1999. Most of the Museum's many visitors are there to remember or learn about the conflicts, but they must also be entertained. Operation Jericho, a fairground ride that supposedly simulates flying on a World War II bombing mission, is the most disturbingly bungled example of this phenomenon. The Museum's other two 'Experiences', of the Trenches and the Blitz, are far more genuinely educational and avoid vicarious thrills without being boring. In the vast atrium, you can see pristine restored and cut-away examples of a selection of the combatants' hardware: tanks, planes and mini-subs. Avoid the crowds by visiting either early or late in the day. *Disabled: access; toilets. Films. Group discounts. Lectures. Library. Research facilities. Restaurant. Shop.*

Guards' Museum

Wellington Barracks, Birdcage Walk, SW1 (0171 414 3271). St James's Park tube. **Open** 10am-4pm daily. **Admission** £2; £1 ex-guardsmen, OAPs, students; under-16s; £4 family (2 adults, 3 children). **No credit cards.**

This small museum in honour of the history of the five Guards regiments which were founded in the seventeenth century under Charles II occupies a basement beneath the impressive William IV barracks in Birdcage Walk. The oldest medal (awarded by Oliver Cromwell to Officers of his New Model Army at the Battle of Dunbar in 1651) and a bottle of Iraqi whisky captured in the Gulf War notwithstanding, this is predominantly an exhibition of uniforms and oil paintings accompanied by stirring martial music. See the Guards in ceremonial action every day at 11.30am when they form up to march to **St James's Palace** and **Buckingham Palace** to relieve their comrades on guard duty. The toy soldier shop claims to be the most important of its kind in London.

Disabled: access; no toilets. Group discount. Tour by prior arrangement. Toy soldier shop.

Museum of Artillery

The Rotunda, Repository Road, SE18 (0181 316 5402). Woolwich Dockyard BR. **Open** *1-4pm Mon-Fri.* **Admission** free.

The Museum of Artillery is worth visiting if only for the fine eighteenth-century architecture of the building by John Nash, but you'll also find artillery pieces here ranging from a 1346 Bombard, a kind of stubby mortar, to a four-barrelled 14.5mm anti-aircraft gun used in the Gulf. Model weapons, guidance systems and guns are dotted across the three acres of grounds. Swords, photographs and regimental regalia are kept on the other side of Woolwich Common in the old military academy.

Disabled: access. Shop.

National Army Museum

Royal Hospital Road, SW3, next to Royal Hospital (0171 730 0717). Sloane Square tube/11, 19 or 239 bus. **Open** *10am-5.30pm daily.* **Admission** free.

Yet to catch up with many of London's museums, the NAM does not go out of its way to make its collection accessible. Apart from the temporary exhibitions, which often focus on intriguing aspects of military history, even the Road to Waterloo exhibition, which includes a vast illuminated model of the battlefield, now seems dated. The skeleton of Napoleon's horse, Marengo, is the most bizarre exhibit. A new gallery devoted to the role of women in the armed forces seems to be a concession to political correctness.

Disabled: access. Reception and conference facilities. School talks arranged. Shop.

Royal Air Force Museum

Grahame Park Way, NW9 (0181 205 2266/recorded information 0181 205 9191). Colindale tube/Mill Hill Broadway BR/32, 226, 292 bus. **Open** *10am-6pm daily.* **Admission** £5.20; £2.60 OAPs, students, UB40s, under-15s; free registered disabled; £12 family (2 adults, 2 children; £1.10 per additional child). **Credit** *shop A, £TC, V.*

Hendon Aerodrome bills itself as the birthplace of aviation in Britain and here you can see how baby has grown. The awesomely hi-tech Phantom jet is the most recent acquisition, dwarfing the Spitfire and Hurricane fighters that won the Battle of Britain. You can have a close look at these on a guided tour. The main hangar houses planes plucked from aviation's history. Opposite you'll find the harbingers of the terrible rain from Bomber Command.

Car park (free). Classroom. Disabled: access. Educational films. Restaurant (10am-5pm daily). Shop. Tour by prior arrangement.

The Royal Armouries

HM Tower of London, EC3 (0171 480 6358). Tower Hill tube. **Open** *Mar-Oct 9am-5.45pm Mon-Sat; 10am-5.45pm Sun.* **Admission** £6.70; £4.50 disabled, OAPs, students, UB40s; £3.35 children. **Credit** *shop A, V.*

London's oldest museum contains exhibits from the Dark Ages to the present day. Major attractions include a Tudor and Stuart gallery with the armours of Henry VIII and Charles I. There's an oriental armoury with the world's largest suit of armour, designed for an Indian elephant.

Disabled: access. Group discount.

Art & Design

Design Museum

Butlers Wharf, Shad Thames, SE1 (0171 403 6933). Tower Hill tube or London Bridge tube/BR/15, 78 bus. **Open** *10.30am-5.30pm daily.* **Admission** £3.50; £2.50 children, OAPs, students, UB40s. **Credit** *shop A, V.*

The sights and smells of the **Chelsea Physic Garden** *– one of London's hidden pleasures.*

The British Museum

More people visit the British Museum than any other single place of interest in Britain and it's not hard to see why. It's one of only two institutions in the world (the other being the Smithsonian in Washington DC) that fulfil the Enlightenment concept of gathering all branches of human knowledge under one roof: a real-life encyclopaedia. Although its vast size can prove bewildering, it guarantees that curious crowds will find something here of more than passing interest.

The Museum's small beginnings can be traced to royal physician Dr Hans Sloane's 'cabinet of curiosities', bequeathed to the nation in 1753, a substantial miscellany of books, paintings, classical antiquities and stuffed animals. Over the next century the plunder of Empire, including the Elgin Marbles from Greece and various massive Egyptian monuments, overwhelmed the storage space available. In 1847 Robert Smirke designed the present impressive neo-classical edifice, with its grand colonnaded façade and ample interior. It was the the British Library, in fact, originally part of the museum, which was to make further expansion necessary. The Copyright Act of 1851 required that a copy of every book published in the land be deposited here. The repercussions are still being felt today, with the Library making fraught attempts to move to a much larger site at St Pancras. At the time the answer was provided by Antonio Panizzi, whose remarkable domed reading room opened in 1857. It's hardly changed since Marx penned *Das Kapital* in row G.

Highlights

As you walk in at the door, the British Library is to your right, with the reading room straight ahead. On your immediate left, past the bookshop, is the entrance to the Museum's displays on the ground floor. The larger part of the Museum's antiquities are collected together by area of origin. The Greek and Roman antiquities can be found on the extreme left of the building on the ground floor, upstairs and in the basement (rooms 1-15, 68-73 and 77-89 respectively). In room 7 the three graceful 'sea breezes' carved in clinging wet-look folds of marble are the Nereid Monument (400 BC). Next door in room 8 are the extraordinarily moving sculptures from the Parthenon brought to London by Lord Elgin in 1806. Upstairs with other exhibits from the Roman Empire, you'll find the Portland Vase (room 70), carved with mythological scenes in blue and white glass. Egyptian antiquities are on the right-hand side of the left wing of the building. Look out for the Rosetta Stone, inscribed with a decree in three languages which enabled Egyptian hieroglyphics to be deciphered for the first time. Western Asian antiquities (from ancient Assyria, Syria, Palestine and Iran) are in the middle, with long galleries containing the superb Assyrian reliefs of King Ashurbanipal's lion hunting. Upstairs in the medieval galleries, you'll find the Sutton Hoo ship burial's extraordinary hoard of Dark Age treasures and the Lindow Man, sliced in half by a bog-cutter centuries after his ritual sacrifice by mutilation and asphyxiation.

It's worth going on a guided tour if you want to get the most out of the musuem's displays. Although the exhibits are carefully labelled, the information panels in each room only provide the background in a drily informative fashion. The souvenir guide by John Julius Norwich is more entertaining, but hardly does justice to the less popular or downright strange objects dotted about the rooms. If you want to go it alone, you should allow time to make one rapid tour of the collection, and then go back to the rooms that you found particularly interesting. The museum is quietest early in the morning during the week. At any other time, expect company.

The British Museum

Great Russell Street, WC1 (0171 636 1555/recorded information 0171 580 1788). Holborn, Russell Square or Tottenham Court Road tube. **Open** 10am-5pm Mon-Sat; 2.30-6pm Sun. **Admission** free but donations welcome. **Exhibitions** £3.50; £2 children, OAPs, students, UB40s. **Credit** *shop* A, AmEx, DC, £TC, US, V.
Bookshop. Buffet/restaurant (10.15am-4.30pm; lunch served 11.45am-2.45pm). Café (10.15am-4.30pm Mon-Sat; 2.30-5.30pm Sun). Disabled: access (information 0171 637 7384). Parent and baby room. Reading room access only with educational pass. Schools and groups book in advance (0171 323 8511/8854). Shop. Sketching: contact information desk (0171 636 1555). Touch tours for the partially sighted. Tours, lectures, gallery talks, including free tours.

The British Museum*'s Japanese Gallery.*

The white and glass modernist building on Butlers Wharf is the ideal venue for a collection of innovative design. Sir Terence Conran, the man who introduced design to the high street, was the driving force behind the museum. Inside are spacious, airy galleries. Until April 1996, True Brit, an exhibiton devoted to fashion designer Paul Smith, will be in the Review Gallery on the first floor. The rather small section at the back is for other temporary exhibitions. Upstairs, the Conran Collection Gallery takes a historical look at cultural and technological influences on design and the development of mass-produced consumer objects. It won't take you long to get round, but it's worth coming here for the great river views and a quick overview of 1980s architecture in the surrounding streets. The **Blueprint Café** which shares the building, with its balcony overlooking the Thames, is an appropriately stylish establishment.

Bar/café. Disabled: access. Education programme for schools. Guided tours by prior arrangement. Research library (10.30am-1.30pm, 2.30-5.30pm, daily). Shop and mail order (to check availability phone 0171 403 4933).

Fan Museum

12 Crooms Hill, SE10 (0181 305 1441/0181 858 7879). Greenwich BR/boat to Greenwich Pier/1, 177, 180, 185, 188, 286 bus. **Open** *workshop* by appointment; *museum* 11am-4.30pm Tue-Sat; noon-4.30pm Sun. **Admission** £2.50; £1.50 OAPs, students, under-16s; free OAPs 2-4pm Tue. **Credit** A, V.

Mr and Mrs Alexander's independent museum in two converted Georgian town houses hosts the world's only permanent display of hand-held, folding fans. True to their coy usage, only part of the enormous collection is ever on view at once: their elasticity necessitates periodic rest. The exhibitions collect them according to themes varying from their design to their social history. In 1996 the doyen of English Victorian fan-makers, Monsieur Duvelleroy, will receive attention, while fans from the Hermitage Museum in St Petersburg are promised for 1997.

Disabled: access; toilets. Shop. Tour by prior arrangement.

Geffrye Museum

Kingsland Road, E2 (0171 739 9893). Old Street tube/BR, then 243 bus/Liverpool Street tube/BR, then 22A, 22B or 149 bus. **Open** 10am-5pm Tue-Sat; 2-5pm Sun, Bank Holidays. **Admission** free, under-8s must be accompanied by an adult.

These beautiful almshouses, built in 1715, were turned into a museum of furniture and interior design in 1914. A dedicated team have staved off the aura of purely specialist interest that title might suggest. A series of rooms facing the front lawns, reconstructed in period style, amount to an atmospheric voyage through the ages from the Elizabethan era to the 1950s. Some are accompanied by contemporary music (listen out for the 1930s Bakelite radio tuned into jolly morale-boosting tunes). All are interestingly explained and contain fascinating details: in the Stuart parlour a turtle's skull, stuffed baby crocodile and stuffed armadillo reflect the period's nascent interest in natural history. For December the rooms are resplendent with their appropriate Christmas decorations. Outside there's a new walled herb garden which makes a pleasant extra 'outdoor room' in fine weather.

Coffee bar. Facilities for people with disabilities. Herb garden. School and group tours by prior appointment. Shop.

Percival David
Foundation of Chinese Art

53 Gordon Square, WC1 (0171 387 3909). Euston Square tube/Goodge Street tube/Russell Square tube/Euston tube/BR. **Open** 10.30am-5pm Mon-Fri; closed Bank Holidays. **Admission** free, but donations welcome. Children under 14 must be accompanied by an adult.

Next to Lytton Strachey's house in Gordon Square, the heart of London's academia, three floors are given over to Sir Percival David's extensive collection of Chinese ceramics. At ground level you'll find the popular Ming (circa seventeenth-century) vases and some fascinating contemporary woodcuts on their production. Upstairs, older pieces from the tenth century include some extraordinarily beautiful china plates. The top floor is home to probably the most famous items, two large blue vases from the Yuan dynasty. The Foundation's peaceful, scholarly atmosphere suits the serenity of the antiques on display.

Catalogues, slides, postcards sold at the entrance. Group visits by prior arrangement. Library facilities available (£25 per week/£35 per year).

Botanical

Chelsea Physic Garden

66 Royal Hospital Road, SW3 (0171 352 5646). Sloane Square tube/11, 19, 22, 239 bus. **Open** Apr-Oct 2-5pm Wed; 2-6pm Sun. **Admission** £3.50; £1.80 students, UB40s, under-16s. **No credit cards.**

A refuge from the traffic thundering along the Chelsea Embankment, this walled garden was the first London botanical garden. Developed by Dr Hans Sloane (also founder of the **British Museum**) in 1712, it retains an atmosphere redolent of its roots in medieval monastery gardens. Formally divided into beds of plants with different uses, there are intriguing discoveries to be made, considerably facilitated by the informative labelling. Amongst the dye plants you'll find woad, fermented in stale urine by the pre-Roman Britons to paint their faces a disturbing blue. In the greenhouses are the types of yams from which modern contraceptives and steroids were synthesised and there's meadowsweet, which contained the active ingredient of aspirin, discovered in 1899. Although the sights and sweet smells are intoxicating (you can squeeze and sniff a variety of aromatherapeutic plants), the garden's main purpose is academic. With the knowledge that 50 per cent of the world's flora (89 per cent of which is unscreened for medical purposes) exists in only 7 per cent of its land area (in the rain forests), the greenhouse displays and the alternative disciplines explained in the Garden of World Medicine take on new significance.

Disabled: access. Guided tours by appointment (£10 inclusive price, up to 25 people). Shop. Tea (3.15-4.45pm).

Museum of Garden History

St Mary-at-Lambeth, Lambeth Palace Road, SE1 (0171 261 1891). Waterloo tube/BR/507, C10 bus. **Open** mid Mar-mid Dec 10.30am-4pm Mon-Fri; 10.30am-5pm Sun. **Admission** free; donations requested.

Inside St Mary-at-Lambeth church, antique horticultural tools and photographic panels on famous garden designers and plant-hunters illustrate the development of the English passion for gardening. A replica of a seventeenth-century garden has been created in the tiny church courtyard. Apart from its intrinsic curiosity value, it offers visitors an oppportunity to take tea in classic English style.

Café. Disabled: access. Lectures. Shop. Tour by prior arrangement.

Childhood

Bethnal Green Museum of Childhood

Cambridge Heath Road, E2 (recorded information 0181 980 2415). Bethnal Green tube/BR. **Open** 10am-5.50pm Mon-Thur, Sat; 2.30-5.50pm Sun. **Admission** free.

Itself a child of the **V&A**, this museum is housed in a nineteenth-century building in the East End and contains a mammoth number of dolls, doll's houses, trains, cars, children's clothes, books and puppets. According to the staff, everything is worth seeing, but the sheer tedium of looking at endless glass cases means that it's easier to stick to the doll's houses on the ground floor and the international doll collection on the first floor. The doll's houses in cabinets, originating in seventeenth-century Holland, and the new Japanese ceremonial dolls, must be seen.

Café. Disabled: access (by prior arrangement). School sessions. Shop (10am-5.20pm Mon-Thur; 10.15am-1pm, 2-5.20pm, Sat; 2.30-5.20pm Sun). Workshops (11am, 2pm Sat, phone for details).

London Toy and Model Museum

21 Craven Hill, W2 (recorded information 0171 262 7905/9450). Queensway tube/Paddington tube/BR/12, 15, 94 bus. **Open** 10am-4.30pm daily. **Admission** £3.50; £2.50 OAPs, students, UB40s; £2 under-16s; £6 family (2 adults, 2 children); free under-5s. **Credit** £TC.
Completely refurbished by its new owners (the Japanese Fujita Corporation), the museum has expanded to fill 20 galleries on five floors, packed with historic toys and working models, including ships, trains, aeroplanes and even a coal mine. All ages will enjoy gawping at the extraordinary Baywest City and wondering at the latest in toy technology.
Activity room. Café. Garden. Group discount. Shop. Tour by prior arrangement. Videos. Worksheets. Workshop.

Pollock's Toy Museum

1 Scala Street, W1 (0171 636 3452). Goodge Street tube. **Open** 10am-5pm Mon-Sat. **Admission** £2; 75p under-18s; under-3s free. **Credit** *shop* A, AmEx, V.
Hidden away behind Goodge Street, the museum looks like the Gingerbread House, and you half expect a wizened white-haired toymaker to descend the steep stairs. Instead, there's Mrs Fawdy who collects Pollock's old toy theatres and puts on live model theatre shows. One of the world's oldest bears, born in 1906, lives here, along with some colourful Mexican and Indian dolls. The excited voices of seven- to 12-year-olds show what a fine place this is. Take your own children and you're unlikely to leave the shop downstairs with a full purse.
Shop. Toy theatre (during school holidays).

Ragged School Museum

46-48 Copperfield Road, E3 (0181 980 6405). Mile End tube. **Open** 10am-5pm Wed, Thur; 2-5pm first Sun of month. **Admission** free.
The ragged schools were founded by Dr Barnado to educate and feed poor children. This canal-side warehouse was once one of the largest ragged schools and has changed little. The museum contains a reconstructed Victorian classroom complete with role-playing pupils.
Café. Guided tours. Shop. Temporary exhibitions.

Ethnography

Commonwealth Institute

Kensington High Street, W8 (0171 603 4535). Earl's Court, High Street Kensington or Holland Park tube. **Open** 10am-5pm Mon-Sat; 2-5pm Sun. **Admission** £1 adults; 50p under-14s. **No credit cards.**
This imposing building with its Zambian copper roof was opened in 1962 to replace the old Imperial Institute. Each of the 50 member nations of the Commonwealth (spot their flags fluttering outside) are represented by displays around the wide circular galleries on their customs, costumes and culture. The Institute plays a vital educational role and during the day the place is often being busily explored by school parties. The national festivals of the member nations are celebrated throughout the year, and the two art galleries mount interesting exhibitions of indigenous art.
Art gallery. Disabled: access. Educational resource centre. Group visits/coach bookings by prior arrangement. Restaurant. Schools reception and dining room. Shop.

Egyptian pot burial at the **Petrie Museum**.

Horniman Museum

London Road, SE23 (0181 699 1872; education dept ext 124/recorded information 0181 699 2339). Forest Hill BR/176 bus. **Open** 10.30am-5.30pm Mon-Sat; 2-5.30pm Sun. **Admission** free.
The major ethnographic hall of this idiosyncratic musuem is closed for redevelopment. It's a testament to its charm that it's still worth travelling from central London to find; children enjoy it enormously. The essence of nineteenth-century tea merchant Frederick Horniman's peculiar ethnic collection has been put on view in the natural history hall. Here a stuffed walrus presides gruffly over an eclectic display of other specimens. The surprising Apostle's Clock enacts a famous episode from the Gospels daily at 4pm. In the Music Room you can play and listen to all kinds of instruments from around the world. The Living Waters Aquarium demonstrates the life in a river on its way to the sea, a source of endless curiosity to children. In the summer, the formal and sunken gardens with fine views over London are an added attraction, as is the small zoo with farmyard animals.
Café. Disabled: access; toilets. Shop.

Museum of Mankind

6 Burlington Gardens, W1 (0171 437 2224/recorded information 0171 580 1788). Green Park, Oxford Circus or Piccadilly Circus tube. **Open** 10am-5pm Mon-Sat; 2.30-6pm Sun. **Admission** free. **Credit** *shop* A, AmEx, DC, £TC, US, V.
Artefacts from societies with no sources of power except the human body and domestic animals comprise the British Museum's vast ethnographic collection. The Museum's impressive classical exterior belies an unfortunately small but intriguing selection: two permanent exhibitions include shrunken heads from Ecuador, a cunningly carved big bass Yoruba drum, and Hoah Hakanan'ia, an Easter Island statue. Dodge the baleful grimace of the Hawaiian war god

The Bakelite radio, the art deco picture frame – it's the **Geffrye Museum***'s 1930s room.*

Ku Kukailimoku half-way up the stairs and make your way up to the treasures of the collection. Other rooms are given over to special exhibitions. If nothing else, the Museum provides a peaceful haven a stone's throw from Piccadilly.
Activity room. Bookshop. Café (10am-4.30pm Mon-Sat; 2.30-5pm Sun). Disabled: access. No tours/guides. Sketching permits might be required.

Petrie Museum of Egyptian Archaeology

DMS Watson Library, University College London, Malet Street, WC1 (0171 387 7050 ext 2884). Russell Square tube. **Open** 10am-12noon, 1.15-5pm, Mon-Fri (Closed Christmas and Easter and for four weeks in the summer). **Admission** free (donations requested).

The father of Egyptian archaeology, Sir Flinders Petrie, bequeathed the result of his desert digs, a collection of the minutiae of ancient Egyptian life, to **University College London** in 1933. It's hard to find, but even Indiana Jones would have considered the effort worthwhile. On display among traditional ranks of glass cabinets full of pots, carvings and ornaments, you'll discover the oldest garment in the world (from 3000BC), and the Qua bead-net erotic undergarment (2400BC). More disturbing exhibits include the exhumed pot-burial in the corner with its skeletal occupant squatting inside, and the coiffured head of a mummy with eyebrows and lashes still intact.

Film

Museum of the Moving Image (MOMI)

South Bank, SE1 (box office 0171 928 3232/recorded information 0171 401 2636/administration 0171 928 3535). Embankment tube/Waterloo tube/BR. **Open** 10am-6pm daily; last entry 5pm. **Admission** £5.50;

£4.70 students; £4 children, OAPs, UB40s; £16 family (2 adults, 4 children). **Credit** A, V.

Opened in 1988 in a purpose-built space squeezed beneath **Waterloo Bridge**, MOMI has become one of London's most popular museums. Its success relies not only on the innate appeal of its subject but also on the museum's encouragement of participation. The first part describes the birth of cinema with static displays of early attempts at animation, optical toys and the first cine cameras. Things really get moving with the dawn of the silent era, followed by a multitude of clips covering cinema's many genres: cartoons, Russian classics (shown in an agitprop train), newsreels and Hollywood favourites. Along with these, numerous working models allow you to explore the technical aspects of film and TV: fly with Superman, be interviewed by Barry Norman or direct your own animated feature. The actor guides tend to have their work cut out entertaining the hordes of children. You could happily spend many entertaining hours here, but unfortunately there's no re-admission.

Audio cassettes for the visually impaired. Bookshop. Disabled: access; help points. Films shown in evenings. Foreign-language guides. Regular exhibitions and events. Shop. Sign-interpreted tours (contact Education Dept).

Historical Figures

Baden-Powell Museum

Queen's Gate, SW7 (0171 584 7030). Gloucester Road tube/South Kensington tube/C1, 74, bus. **Open** 8am-8.30pm daily; closed for two weeks over Christmas. **Admission** free. **Credit** A, V.

This small exhibition located in London's major museum area pays tribute to Lord Robert Baden-Powell, founder of the Scout and Guide movement. It gives a good idea of the energy and vision of the man whose adventure club for boys now has 16 million members in 150 countries around the world. Much anecdotal detail of his life as secret agent, commander, writer, horseman and actor informs the display of Scouting memorabilia. A handset commentary at the commemorative bust of Big-Hat, as he was known to the Ashanti tribe, exhorts modern-day Scouts to 'keep yourself healthy and help others'. Although chiefly of interest to parties of Scouts doing homage, the exhibition will move anyone susceptible to the evident sincerity of this icon of Empire. A brief visit gives a fascinating insight into the attitudes and values of one individual who contributed to the culture that threw up the vast **V&A** over the road.

Accommodation bookable in the hostel for any scout or guide worldwide (single £24.60; double £19). Disabled: access. Restaurant. Shop.

Carlyle's House

24 Cheyne Row, SW3 (0171 352 7087). Sloane Square tube. **Open** 11am-5pm Wed-Sun. **Admission** £2.90; £1.10 under-16s. **No credit cards.**

The 'awesome sage of Chelsea', Thomas Carlyle, lived in this tall, roomy terraced house from 1834 until his death in 1881. His epic historical works are now much neglected, but his home remains lovingly preserved almost exactly as he left it. Above the piano in the front room, a contemporary painting depicts the famous Scotsman and his wife Jenny in their characteristically frugal accommodation, and you can judge for yourself how little it has changed. Today you will find the live-in custodian, his wife and their labrador dog William Cobbett most welcoming. All credit to them for managing to convey the impression that they are only house-sitting while the Carlyles are away on holiday, dispelling the atmosphere that sometimes pervades the mothballed abodes of the great and the dead. *Disabled: limited access. Souvenirs.*

Florence Nightingale Museum

St Thomas' Hospital, 2 Lambeth Palace Road, SE1 (0171 620 0374). Westminster tube/Waterloo tube/BR. **Open** 10am-5pm Tue-Sun. **Admission** £2.50; £1.50 OAPs, students, UB40s, under-16s; £5 family (2 adults, 2 under-16s). **Credit** A, AmEx, V.

This museum celebrates Florence Nightingale, the nurse heroine of the Crimean War (1854-56), who became known as the 'Lady of the Lamp' because of her nightly ward rounds. The story of her campaign to improve the conditions for the wounded is told with photographs, her personal effects and a reconstruction of a hospital scene from the time. *Film. Group discount. Shop. Study and resource centre on application to curator.*

Freud's House

20 Maresfield Gardens, NW3 (0171 435 2002/5167). Finchley Road tube/Finchley Road & Frognal BR. **Open** noon-5pm Wed-Sun. **Admission** £2.50; £1.50 OAPs, students, UB40s; free under-12s. **Credit** A, AmEx, V.

In this attractive symmetrical redbrick house Sigmund Freud lived for the last year of his life in forced exile from Vienna under the Nazis. His wife Anna remained here with her death in 1982. On the first floor you'll find her library and the loom she used in her work on child psychology. Also on the first floor, Freud In His Time provides an insight into his personality through an exhibition of his diary, the 'Shortest Chronicle'. Spread around the house is his collection of antiquities from Egypt, Japan, India and Greece. It's reassuring to discover that the man who made such a profound impact on the West was so fascinated by artefacts from other cultures. On the ground floor, if you're really interested in Freud's work, you'll need binoculars to read the titles of the books on his library shelves, but the couch is here and also the small green armchair at its head where the great psychoanalyst sat and listened. *Guided tours by prior arrangement. Lectures. Shop. Videos.*

Keats' House

Wentworth Place, Keats Grove, NW3 (0171 435 2062). Hampstead tube. **Open** *Apr-Oct* 10am-1pm, 2-6pm, Mon-Fri; 10am-1pm, 2-5pm, Sat; 2-5pm Sun. *Nov-Mar* 1-5pm Mon-Fri; 10am-1pm, 2-5pm, Sat; 2-5pm Sun. **Admission** free.

In 1925 an American bequest allowed this house to be opened in commemoration of the romantic poet John Keats. In fact he lived here only briefly, after his brother Tom's death. Even so, his most famous poem 'Ode to a Nightingale', was written beneath a tree in the front garden, the spot now marked with a commemorative sapling. Not much of the original furniture remains but the house has been extensively restored. In Keats' day, Hampstead was a small village some distance outside London. Today you could almost believe it had not been absorbed into the metropolis. *Audio cassettes. Disabled: limited access.*

Leighton House Museum

12 Holland Park, W14 (0171 602 3316). High Street Kensington tube. **Open** 11am-5.30pm Mon-Sat. **Admission** free but donations appreciated.

Leighton House, designed by Lord Leighton in 1866 in collaboration with George Aitchison, derives its inspiration directly from the East. Its most striking feature is the exotic Arab Hall added in 1879. This domed structure, with its elaborate Persian tiles, mosaic floor and square fountain, has a startling cupola of stained glass. Leighton, himself an artist of no mean repute, collected a variety of works that are now on permanent display.

William Morris Gallery

Lloyd Park, Forest Road, E17 (0181 527 3782). Blackhorse Road tube/Walthamstow Central tube/BR then 34, 97, 215, 257 or 275. **Open** 10am-1pm, 2-5pm, Tue-Sat, first Sun every month. **Admission** free.

Freud's House – *Sigmund lived here in exile.*

Opened in 1950, this house was the childhood home of William Morris, the influential late-Victorian designer, craftsman and socialist. Externally the house is little altered. Probably as he would have wished, the gardens, including the moated island where he used to play, are now a public park. In four rooms on the ground floor, Morris's biography is expounded through his work and political writings. Upstairs there are galleries devoted to the work of his associates, Burne-Jones, Philip Webb and Ernest Gimson, who assisted in contributing to the considerable popularity Morris's style retains today. The centenary of Morris's death will be marked in 1996 with a major exhibition of his company's tile work, including fireplaces and lintels.
Disabled: access (ground floor only). Guided tours by arrangement. Lectures. Mail-order service. Reference library, by prior arrangement. Shop.

Sir John Soane's Museum
13 Lincoln's Inn Fields, WC2 (0171 405 2107). Holborn tube. **Open** 10am-5pm Tue-Sat; 6-9pm first Tue of month. **Admission** free.
Britain's smallest national museum is also its most unusual. Sir John (1753-1837) was not only a superb architect and rival of John Nash but also a collector of beautiful objects, from Hogarth's *The Rake's Progress* to the sarcophagus of Seti I, pharaoh of Egypt 1303-1290 BC. Happily for us, Soane left his house and contents for later generations to explore.
Disabled: access.

Livery Companies

Clockmakers' Company Museum
The Clockroom, Guildhall Library, Aldermanbury, EC2 (0171 332 1865). Bank, Mansion House, Moorgate or St Paul's tube. **Open** *museum* 9.30am-4.45pm Mon-Fri; *library* 9.30am-5pm Mon-Sat. **Admission** free.
The oldest collection of clocks in the world includes John Harrison's prize-winning marine timekeeper. This remarkable invention first made it possible for ships at sea to find their longitude, giving the edge to Britain's Empire-builders. Sir George White, the keeper of the museum, gives fascinating

tours of the timepieces, usually on Mondays. It's worth booking on to one because the labelling is not particularly informative. Nowhere is it mentioned, for example, that one silver watch kept George Vancouver (of western Canadian seaboard fame) on time aboard HMS *Discovery*. Luckily for visitors' sanity, not all one thousand clocks and watches are kept ticking.
Disabled: access; toilets. Library.

Freemasons' Hall
Great Queen Street, WC2 (0171 831 9811). Covent Garden or Holborn tube. **Open** 10am-5pm Mon-Fri; 10.30am-1pm Sat. **Admission** free.
You need to book a tour to see the Grand Temple inside this massive and disturbing art deco edifice, the Grand Lodge of the Freemasons. The massive doors swing open to reveal acres of white marble and green jade right up to the ornate ceiling. The traditions of the sixteenth-century cathedral-building Stone Masons still play a part in the modern Masonic ritual. The Hall is the central meeting place for the 8,500 Masonic lodges (local centres) throughout the UK. Next door at Letchworth's you can buy souvenirs.
Disabled: access. Guided tours.

Merchant Taylors Hall
30 Threadneedle Street, EC2 (0171 588 7606). Bank or Monument tube. **Open** tours arranged by appointment only (contact three weeks in advance). **Admission** free.
The Merchant Taylors can trace its roots to 1327 when it began life as a religious and social guild for the Taylors and Linen Armourers (linen was worn under armour), controlling the measurement of cloth in the City of London. Now the guild concentrates on maintaining alms houses for the elderly and educational grants and scholarships. It has been in 'Thread needle' Street since 1347, and most of the library, court room and great kitchen has survived the Great Fire and the Blitz. The central point is the Cloisters Hall, rebuilt in the late 1940s, and used for livery dinners and conferences. Part of the organ housed here dates back to 1722. But all rooms have been beautifully restored; another highlight is the kitchen – three floors high and in use since 1425, with the original stone wall still visible.
Disabled: access.

*Nathan Meyer Rothschild's Book of Esther from the collections of the **Jewish Museum**.*

*The **Theatre Museum** – in the heart of Covent Garden and always a big hit with children.*

Religions & Societies

The Jewish Museum
129 Albert Street, NW1 (0171 284 1997). Camden Town tube. **Open** 10am-5pm Mon-Thur, Sun. **Admission** £3; £1.50 OAPs, students, UB40s; free children.

Recently relocated to this smart new building in Camden, the Museum is now much more commodious and accessible. The ground floor is dedicated to the history of Jewish life in Britain. A map panel lights up to show the distribution of Jewish communities across the land down the ages, and there are portraits of some of their eminent members, presided over by Jacob Epstein's striking bronze bust of Chaim Weizmann, the first president of Israel. If you're not that familiar with Judaic ceremonial, it's worth watching the 15-minute video on the significance of their ritual objects (hanucah lamps, mezuzahs and tephillins) before going upstairs to see the very fine collection of examples. There are social history displays also at the Finchley site of the Jewish Museum (80 East End Road, N3, 0181 349 1143).
Disabled: access. Group visits by appointment. School workshops with audio-visuals. Shop.

Museum of Methodism and John Wesley's House
Wesley Chapel, 49 City Road, EC1 (0171 253 2262). Old Street tube/BR. **Open** 10am-4pm Mon-Sat; noon-2pm Sun. **Admission** *museum and house* £3; £1.50 OAPs, students, UB40s; £8 family; 10 per cent reduction for groups over 20. Second visit free with ticket (same month).

In 1778 John Wesley, the founder of Methodism, converted the foundry of the Honourable Artillery Company (the turreted castle opposite) into his main chapel. In 1984 it was opened as a museum of the man's work. Appropriately enough, **Bunhill Fields**, just across the City Road, is the burial ground of many of London's dissenters. Wesley's unorthodox assemblies got him slung out of the Anglican Church but resulted in the establishment of a Church that now has a following of over 50 million around the world. Despite voting for reunion with the Church of England, it has recently twice been rejected. In the crypt of the neo-classical church, the exhibition provides a well-illustrated testament to the rise of the Church. Highlights include the pulpit and a large oil portrait of the scene at his death bed, Wesley in radiant white surrounded by sundry sombre admirers. In his house next door you can see his night cap, preaching gown and personal experimental electric-shock machine.
Disabled: access (museum only). Films. Groups must book in advance. Shop. Tours.

Museum of the Order of St John
St John's Gate, St John's Lane, EC1 (0171 253 6644). Barbican or Farringdon tube. **Open** 10am-5pm Mon-Fri; 10am-4pm Sat. Grand Priory Church and other Gate House rooms open only on guided tours (11am, 2.30pm Tue, Fri, Sat). **Admission** free, donations appreciated.

The old Gatehouse of the sixteenth-century Priory of Clerkenwell, for 400 years the London base of the Knights Hopitaller, is now isolated in the middle of the City. In 1874 it was given to the Order of the Hospital of St John of Jerusalem, a nineteenth-century organisation established to continue the tradition of the medieval knights, defenders of Christendom during the Crusades. Two years later the St John Ambulance was founded, the uniformed voluntary first-aid service now a reassuringly familiar presence at almost every major public event in Britain. The Museum holds a wonderful illuminated manuscript of the Mass from 1504, the Rhodes Missal, and two fifteenth-century panels from a Flemish triptych.
Disabled: access (ground floor only). Groups must book in advance. Reference library open by appointment. Shop.

Science

Kew Bridge Steam Museum
Green Dragon Lane, Brentford, Middlesex (0181 568 4757). Gunnersbury tube/Kew Bridge BR/27, 65, 237,

267 bus. **Open** 11am-5pm daily. **Admission**
Mon-Fri £2; £1 OAPs, students, under-16s; £5
family (2 adults, 3 children); *Sat, Sun, Bank Holidays*
£3.25; £1.80 OAPs, students, under-16s; £8.50 family.
No credit cards.
A Victorian riverside Pumping Station is now home to this
museum of water supply. At 3pm on weekends one of the
two largest steam engines in the world, the 90-inch Cornish
Beam engine (built in 1845 for use in the tin mines), stirs pon-
derously into motion. Like the working waterwheel and five
steam engines, it has been restored by enthusiastic volunteers to its former working order. Apart from the constant
clicking of the triple-expansion engine, once all the engines
are pumping away the museum remains strangely quiet.
*Disabled: limited access. Group discount. Guided tour by
prior arrangement. Shop. Tour tapes included in
admission fee.*

Vintage Wireless Museum

*(Private residence, for appointment telephone 0181 670
3667). West Dulwich BR/2, 322 bus.* **Open** *by
appointment only* 11am-7.30pm Mon-Sat. **Admission**
free (donation requested).
Gerry Wells has turned his home into an exhibition of his
abiding enthusiasm for everything radiophonic. His two-and-
a-half-hour tour lovingly details some of his favourite things
about a selection from his 1,000-piece collection of radios,
1950s TVs, telephones and news footage. He also offers a
repair service to help pay for the museum, which is run on
visitors' donations.
*Disabled: access. Lectures. Restoration and repair service.
Tea and biscuits on the hour.*

Sport

MCC Museum

*Marylebone Cricket Club, Lord's Ground, NW8 (0171
289 1611). St John's Wood tube.* **Open** *tours* (phone
0171 266 3825 for availability) noon, 2pm daily; *match
days* 10am, noon, 2pm. **Admission** *guided tours* £4.50;
£3 OAPs, students, UB40s, under-16s. **Credit** *shop* A, V.
Cricket fans will be delighted by this anecdotal exhibition
of the game's memorabilia. Among the paintings, photos
and significantly battered bats, there's a reconstruction
of the shot that killed a passing sparrow in 1936, complete
with stuffed bird and its nemesis, the ball. The Ashes reside
here: not much bigger than an egg cup, the sport's most
hard-won trophy (recently in England's case more easily
lost) contains the charred remains of one of the bails from
the 1882 Test series between England and Australia. On
match days, non-members (who include all women) are not
allowed into the Long Room, cricket's sacred shrine to its
finest sons.
*Disabled: access (ground floor only). Guided tour. Shop
(10am-5pm Mon-Fri, match day weekends).*

Rugby Football Union Museum

*Gate 7, Rugby Football Union Stadium, Rugby Road,
Twickenham (0181 892 8161 ext 246/tours 0181 892
5161). Twickenham BR or Hounslow East tube, then 281
bus.* **Open** 9.30am-1pm, 2.15-5pm, Mon-Fri. **Admission**
free; *tours* £1; 50p students, children, OAPs, UB40s.
Credit *shop* A, V.
Rugby's increasing popularity might mean that more fans
make the journey down to the Mecca of the sport at Twickenham. The museum has responded with a major overhaul
of its collection and relocation to an improved site in the stadium. The tour, from the dressing rooms to the hallowed
ground itself, is excellent. Combined tours with **Wimbledon
Lawn Tennis Museum** are also run; book two to three
weeks in advance.
*Tours (normally 10.30am-2.15pm Mon-Fri; book in
advance). Shop (9am-5pm Mon-Fri).*

Wimbledon Lawn Tennis Museum

*Church Road, SW19 (0181 946 6131). Southfields
tube/39, 93, 200 bus.* **Open** 10.30am-5pm Tue-Sat; 2-
5pm Sun. *During championships (spectators only)*
10.30am-7pm daily. **Admission** £2.50; £1 OAPs, under-
16s. **Credit** *shop* A, V.
More than 150 years of social and sporting history, dating
from the invention of the lawn mower in the 1830s, is
encapsulated in this newly redesigned, well-lit museum.
More interesting than the rows of cases filled with rackets
and balls is a mock-up of an Edwardian tennis party, touch-
button commentaries on past and present Wimbledon
stars, and videos of past championships. It's packed with
unusual information: yellow balls were first used in 1986;
they are kept at 20°C and can reach a speed of 140 mph
(220 kmph). For groupies, the collection includes personal
memorabilia such as Pat Cash's headbands and Boris
Becker's autograph.
*Café (10am-5pm Tue-Sat). Disabled: access. Library open
by prior arrangement. Shop.*

Theatre

Shakespeare Globe Exhibition

*New Globe Walk, Bankside, London SE1 (0171 928
6406). Mansion House tube or London Bridge tube/BR.*
Open 10am-5pm daily. **Admission** £3; £2 OAPs,
students, UB40s, under-16s. **No credit cards**.
Sadly Sam Wanamaker, the American actor and director, did
not live to see his visionary campaign to reconstruct the
Elizabethan Globe Theatre fully realised. Now almost complete, as we go to press, the theatre has indeed been painstakingly recreated, right down to the hand-turned oak balusters
around the balconies and the ring of thatched roof, Shakespeare's 'wooden O'. Regular daytime plays are due to take
place on the open-air stage from June 1996. By 1998 it is
hoped that the indoor Inigo Jones Theatre, a permanent exhibition of Elizabethan theatre, and a restaurant will be open.
The old Bear Gardens site of the museum now houses the
Globe Education Centre.
*Disabled: limited access. Education programme:
conferences, workshops, courses, lectures. Group visits
(phone Globe Education Centre, 0171 602 0202). Shop.*

Theatre Museum

*IE Tavistock Street, WC2, entrance off Russell Street,
(0171 836 7891/2330/First Call credit card bookings
0171 497 9977). Covent Garden tube.* **Open** 11am-7pm
Tue-Sun. **Admission** £3; £1.50 OAPs, students, UB40s.
Credit A, £TC, V.
Appropriately sited near the oldest West End theatre, the
Theatre Royal Drury Lane, the basement galleries here feel
like an aquarium of theatre history. Instead of water and fish,
the rows of tanks contain diverting illustrations and artefacts from the Elizabethan theatre to the present day. The
theatrical effect is enhanced by low light in the long corridors and flickering neon advertisements. In another gallery
you can explore the creative development of the Royal
National Theatre's production of *The Wind in the Willows*:
try on Toad's webbed gloves, play at being stage manager,
or watch videos of rehearsals in progress and first-night
nerves. The museum also holds the National Video Archive
of the Performing Arts, with continuous showings of performances that would otherwise be lost in time. A recent
addition is Painting The Players, the Somerset Maugham
collection of 100 portraits of legendary thespians and theatres: look out for Elizabeth I's striking resemblance to Bette
Davis in the first painting. The ground floor hosts Don't Clap
Too Hard, a fund-raising exhibition for the modernisation
of the **Royal Opera House**.
*Celebrity interviews, phone box office for details. Disabled:
access. Play readings in the Painters' Gallery. Shop. Study
days. Study room by appointment only. Workshops.*

Transport

London Transport Museum

39 Wellington Street, WC2 (0171 379 6344). Covent Garden tube. **Open** 10am-6pm daily. **Admission** £4.25; £2.50 children, OAPs, students, UB40s; free under-5s and registered disabled; £10.50 family (2 adults and 2 children). **Credit** *shop* A, V.

The £4 million pound facelift of London Transport's Covent Garden museum puts an optimistic front on the future of the world's most ancient metropolitan public transport system. Gathered behind the glass façade are the road and rail vehicles that have struggled to serve the city's increasing population since 1870. Beside the first electric trams, an audio-visual display prophesies their return – Sheffield and Manchester have introduced successful tram systems in recent years and plans are being drawn up for a scheme in Croydon – while another extolls the virtues of the apparently timeless red double-decker. (Traditional Routemasters have been replaced on many routes and those that remain are being refurbished.) Reasonably enough, it berates the continuing boom in car ownership. The most exciting part of the exhibition, especially for children, is the story of the development of the Underground. There is usually a queue to go in the simulator of a tube driver's perspective, featuring the 'dead man's handle' emergency cut-off device. You can also practise bus-driving or watch the video wall celebrating the 1940s development of leafy 'Metroland' for commuters made homeless by the Blitz.

Café. Disabled: access; lifts; toilets. Foreign-language guides. Guided tours weekends and school holidays. Information centre. School room. Shop.

North Woolwich Old Station Museum

Pier Road, E16 (0171 474 7244). North Woolwich BR/pedestrian tunnel/ferry from Woolwich BR. **Open** 10am-5pm Mon-Thur, Sat; 2-5pm Sun, Bank Holidays. **Admission** free.

The North Woolwich Old Station Museum is dedicated to the London and North Eastern Railway, which ran from the East End of London to Suffolk and Norfolk and back into Liverpool Street. On the first Sunday of every month the *Coffee Pot* and *Pickett* steam engines chug up and down outside. Inside, trains, tickets, station signs and a 1920s ticket office are on display and plans are afoot to include more aspects of local history. For railway enthusiasts it's worth a special trip to this otherwise rather charmless outpost of east London.

Disabled: access. Lectures by prior arrangement. Shop.

Other Specialist Museums

Bank of England Museum

Bartholomew Lane, EC2 (0171 601 5545). Bank tube. **Open** 10am-5pm Mon-Fri. **Admission** free.

Sir John Soane's design for the Bank of England was mostly demolished in an enlargement carried out between the wars, but this well thought out museum contains a restoration of the Bank Stock Office designed by Soane in 1793. Original artwork for banknotes is displayed inside closely monitored cabinets that check humidity and thieving hands.

Disabled: access by prior arrangement. Educational films. Lectures by prior arrangement. Tour and touch sessions for the visually impaired by prior arrangement.

Crystal Palace Museum

Anerley Hill, SE19 (0181 676 0700). Crystal Palace BR/2B, 3, 63, 108B, 122, 137, 157, 227, 249 bus. **Open** 11am-5pm Sun, Bank Holidays. **Admission** free (donation requested).

Crystal Palace aimed to educate the public about architecture, history and science. The original 1851 Great Exhibition building moved from Hyde Park to this site in Sydenham,

later to be named Crystal Palace. The museum is housed in one of the few original buildings left on site, the old engineering school, where Baird invented the television. It tells the history of the original Crystal Palace (burnt down in 1936) with a display of archive photographs. Its devoted staff don't manage to liven up the dull exhibits, but the 1850s models of prehistoric animals dotted around the gardens do, and are a reminder of just how quirky Crystal Palace was.

Tours and school parties by prior arrangement (£1; 50p children, OAPs, students, UB40s). Shop.

Museum of Richmond

Old Town Hall, Whittaker Avenue, Richmond (0181 332 1141). Richmond tube. **Open** *all year* 11am-5pm Tue-Sat; *May-Oct* 2-5pm Sun. **Admission** £1; 50p under 16s, OAPs, students, UB40s. **No credit cards**.

The Victorian Old Town Hall, close to the River, houses one of London's best local museums, naturally dwelling on Richmond's popularity as a royal resort, though it doesn't ignore its newer commuterland role.

Café (10am-5pm Mon-Sat; 2-5pm Sun). Disabled: access. Shop.

Musical Museum

368 High Street, Brentford, Middlesex (0181 560 8108). Gunnersbury tube/Kew Bridge or Brentford Central BR/65, 237, 267 bus. **Open** *Apr-June, Sept, Oct* 2-5pm Sat, Sun; *July, Aug* 2-5pm Wed-Sun. **Admission** £2; £1.50 OAPs, under-16s. **No credit cards**.

Occupying a converted church, the museum concerns itself with musical devices of all types, shapes and sounds. On the 90-minute tour by dedicated guides, you can hear some of the most celebrated instruments, such as the Steinway Duo-Art grand piano or the Wurlitzer cinema organ. There's also a series of popular summer concerts.

Disabled: access. Education service. Group discount. Guided tour/demonstration (2pm, 3.30pm; free). Sat evening concerts, phone for details. Shop.

National Postal Museum

King Edward Building, King Edward Street, EC1 (0171 239 5420). Barbican or St Paul's tube. **Open** 9.30am-4.30pm Mon-Fri. **Admission** free.

The three floors of this Edward VII building cover everything from the history of uniforms and telegraph services, to stamps, seals and delivery. The museum is a philatelists' paradise, with various rare sheets of penny reds and blacks. There's also a display of model post vans and two genuine BSA Bantam motorcycles once used by telegram boys.

Disabled: access by prior arrangement. Shop. Tour by prior arrangement.

✓ Public Records Office Museum

Chancery Lane, WC2 (0181 876 3444). Chancery Lane tube. **Open** 9.30am-5pm Mon-Fri. **Admission** free.

This very small museum provides a tiny glimpse of the national archives, notably photographs of the *Titanic* and the *Lusitania*, and the Domesday Book (literally the Day of Judgement book), a record of the lands of England made in 1086, painstakingly written by one scribe.

Shop.

St Thomas' Old Operating Theatre

9A St Thomas' Street, SE1 (0181 806 4325). London Bridge tube/BR. **Open** 10am-4pm Tue-Sun. **Admission** £2; £1.50 under-15s. **No credit cards**.

Visitors climb a narrow flight of 37 stairs to the belfry of an old church. In a well-lit adjoining room, ancient banks of viewing stands rise in semi-circles round a crude wooden bed. Close your eyes and you can almost hear the screams from an unanaesthetised, blindfolded patient as the blood-stained surgeon carefully saws through his leg.

Shop.

Arts & Entertainment

Media

With global mergers and takeovers, Britain's media industry is big business – but is it any different from anywhere else in the world?

The peculiarly British practice of displaying naked women in our best-selling national newspaper says a lot about the nation's psyche. Behind our Victorian values we're clearly obsessed with sex. Or at least the media think we're obsessed with sex. Or is it that the media are obsessed with sex? Whatever – there's no doubt that sex sells in Britain. It's the premise behind top TV shows (such as *Blind Date*) and the country's most popular papers (the *Sun* and the *News of the World*). Don't be alarmed – it's not mandatory. And beyond the populist pap produced by the publishing and broadcasting industries, there's some quality. The world-famous BBC continues to produce the occasional TV or radio gem, and newspapers such as the *Guardian* and the *Independent* have continued to retain a degree of editorial integrity. The media are in a healthier state than in many other countries at present, but the growth of international media moguls and restrictions imposed by our own Government could threaten that. For now, enjoy what you can.

Newspapers

There's no doubt that Britain's newspapers have a worldwide reputation for quality. Sadly, the reality fails to live up to it. Why? The reasons are simple – cash, cash and cash. Current newspaper practice seems to be twofold: sack senior experienced journalists and replace them with junior journos who cost a quarter of the salary; and buy a TV and radio station so that the same 'news' can be palmed on to different audiences. The result is that your hard-bitten hack seeking out the truth has all but disappeared, as bright young multi-media experts take over. These are the trendy darlings who regurgitate facts on to pages, screens and over the airwaves – often all at the same time. True, technology is moving on so quickly that we'll soon be able to source our own individually targeted news through the Internet, but for now Grub Street is looking grubbier than ever.

Tabloids

There's a huge demand for, to put it politely, 'bit 'n' tum' papers, led by the *Sun*, which for 25 years has successfully dragged the nation's morals into the slime. Typical headline – 'Lesbian Vicar Stabbed My Dog, Says Soap Star – full story in pictures pages 1, 2, 3, 4, 8-12, 17-34'. The *Daily Mirror* and the *Daily Star* tread a similar path although the *Mirror* has a reputed slight left-of-centre leaning in its editorial policy. Nevertheless, the front pages of all are likely to be dominated by actors and actresses, pop stars, footballers, snooker players and hamsters. The three papers have a combined circulation of more than seven million – that's more than half of the 14 million newspapers sold in Britain every day. News content – indiscernible.

Middle Range

Tabloid-sized papers such as the *Daily Mail* are the defenders of British middle-class moralities but are as interesting as dead sheep. Typical headline – 'Government promises enquiry'. The *Daily Express* is very similar to the *Mail* while *Today* is a less popular rival. Also within this arena is London's only daily paper, the *Evening Standard*. Despite its name, it can be found on newsstands by mid-morning but has several other editions throughout the day. The last edition, and therefore the most up-to-date news, is the West End Final. In practice, most of the editions carry the same articles, with just changes to front and back pages and two or three inside news pages. News content – about half, the rest is magazine-type features.

Qualities

Broadsheet papers may be difficult to handle but they offer the best news coverage, particularly of international events. Typical headline – 'Millions injured in earthquake but no British casualties reported'. These days, most broadsheets are in two sections, with City and sport generally making up the second section. The *Guardian* uniquely offers a tabloid-sized second section with a different theme, such as education or media, each day. The *Daily Telegraph* offers a comprehensive sport section on Mondays while on Fridays the *Independent* includes *Metro*, a third section devoted to 'the week ahead in London'. The *Times* has long been the least interesting of the broadsheets but is notable for leading a price war among the quality papers. It's probably no surprise that the paper is owned by Rupert Murdoch, whose plans for world media domination have often resorted to sleazier tactics. News content – good, with strong pictures.

Weekend Papers

At the weekend the papers go through a transition, becoming more departmentalised and much heavier (and more expensive). The champion heavyweight is the *Sunday Times* with 12 sections, from Style to Personal Finance. It's only to be taken with full English breakfast and extra coffee, and to be avoided if you have the remotest hangover. Far more fun on Sundays are the tatty tabloids with their tales of vicars, tarts and politicians' mistresses. The *News of the World* is the people's favourite but look out for the *People*, which normally wins the nipple count, and the *Sunday Mirror*. If you crave news, try the *Observer*, the *Independent on Sunday* or the *Sunday Telegraph* which have fewer sections but provide entertaining moments. Middle-brow tabloids the *Mail on Sunday* and the *Sunday Express* are best left to the kind of people who want to read these papers.

Saturday has also become a heavyweight paper day but don't think you'll be getting extra value for money. The Saturday editions generally cost more than their weekday counterparts and the extra 'padding' is mainly advertising-driven.

Magazines

You'll find magazines for virtually every taste in Britain – there are more than 6,500 titles available. And while many have closed in the 1990s, there have been many new periodicals. There are around 2,500 consumer publications – the rest are business or trade magazines – and the bulk of them are owned by a few major publishers. The biggest is Reed Elsevier, which owns IPC, followed by EMAP, and both these companies are on their way to becoming international concerns. Reed Elsevier is, in fact, half Dutch-owned. Many of the magazines published by the leading companies reflect their international ambitions and are available, in different formats, all over the world. Names such as *She, Elle, Reader's Digest* and *Hello!* (or *Ola*) will be seen in bookstalls across the globe.

Women's

The most crowded area of magazine publishing has always been the women's market. There are weeklies, monthlies and all kinds of specialist magazines. General issues are dealt with by everything from *Woman* to *Cosmopolitan*. Market research has allowed these magazines to become highly targeted at selective age or class groups – so, in theory, it should be easy to spot which magazine is aimed at you. There are specialist publications such as *Slimmer* or *Wedding & Home*, whose titles are self-explanatory. And as market research becomes more sophisticated, there's set to be even more tightly targeted launches to come to meet potential gaps.

Men's

It's only recently that men's magazines have become successful in the UK. *Maxim* is the latest launch, following on from success stories such as *GQ, Esquire* and *Loaded*. It's traditionally been a hard market for publishers to crack, and they've relied on specialist titles such as *The Gardener* or *Angling Times* to meet men's needs. That has changed in recent years, although there's a long way to go before the men's magazine market becomes as saturated as the women's.

Lifestyle

Magazines such as *The Face* and *Arena* have successfully lifted the following of fashion almost to an art form. The magazines border on manic pretentiousness but never fail to entertain, albeit unwittingly. The *Time Out*-owned *i-D* offers a more palatable mixture of hard fashion and self-deprecating humour.

News & Issues

If you're looking for something a bit more hard-hitting there's a real lack in the UK. The *Spectator* and *New Statesman & Society* are the closest you'll get, but can prove to be a little high-minded. *Private Eye* offers a twice-monthly satirical look at politics and news events and is well-worth seeking out, as is *The Big Issue*, which is sold on the street by homeless people. It deals mainly with issues affecting the homeless, but also offers news and reviews. The *Economist* covers business issues, and you'll also find the international editions of *Time* and *Newsweek* at most newsagents.

Sport

There are plenty of sport magazines in Britain – even London's own football monthly, *Kick it City*, which gives comprehensive coverage of London's 13 professional soccer clubs. You'll also find UK magazines devoted to those peculiarly American sports – basketball and Gridiron football.

Specialist

There's a magazine for virtually every need. Computer freaks are well-served, but then so are railway enthusiasts. And if you can't see what you want, ask. The vendor will know if there's a magazine for your particular taste and will be able to order it for you.

Radio

The proliferation of radio stations in London has been quite remarkable in recent years. All broadcasting in the UK is governed by the state, and the Radio Authority grants licences to broadcast. Its recent policy has seen the setting up of more-

Channel 4 – HQ of ground-breaking TV.

specialised stations, aimed at jazz or country audiences, while the state-owned BBC, with its five nationwide stations, has seen its total radio market-share fall below 50 per cent for the first time. As well as those listed here, there's still a thriving pirate network, which you may come across in your trawl up the dial.

Station Information

BBC Radio 1
97.6-99.8 FM.
The current controller of this station has stated his aim to play more 'new' music, but the fun-loving Radio 1 Jocks continue to blast out chart hits and 'cracker' jokes to their 12 million audience. However, John Peel and Andy Kershaw are worth a listen.

BBC Radio 2
88.0-90.2 FM.
It was recently voted radio station of the year, but it's hard to understand why. A selection of avuncular presenters play a selection of soporific MOR hits. Your auntie will love it.

BBC Radio 3
90.2-92.4 FM.
The BBC's own classical music station. Definitely not easy-listening.

BBC Radio 4
92.4-94.6 FM, 198 LW, 720 MW.
A speech-only station offering everything from chat to hot debates. Contains many 'much loved' programmes such as *The Archers* and *Desert Island Discs*. A slightly cosy world which can be a joy, or a pain.

BBC Radio 5 Live
693, 909 MW.
All the news and sport you need, 24 hours a day. Live coverage of major sporting events is restrained and informative.

GLR (BBC Greater London Radio)
94.9 FM.
The BBC's local London station offers plenty of regional news interspersed with adult rock.

BBC World Service
648 MW, 6.195, 9.410 SW.
Transmitted worldwide but available in the UK for a distillation of the best of all the other BBC stations.

Capital FM
95.8 FM.
London's liveliest commercial station offers a non-stop madcap mix of music, quizzes and commercials.

Capital Gold
1548 MW.
Plays 1960s, '70s and '80s pop but also features fantastically exuberant football commentaries.

Choice FM
96.9 FM.
South London soul station.

Classic FM
100-102 FM.
The accessible classical music offered makes for a pleasant listening experience.

Country 1035
1035 MW.
If you like country music then tune in.

Freedom FM
104.9 FM.
Twenty-four-hour lesbian and gay radio station.

JFM
102.2 FM.
Formerly known as Jazz FM but there's precious little jazz left on this station which had to go mainstream in order to be a success.

Kiss FM
100.0 FM.
Kiss offers a wide selection of dance music.

London Greek
103.3 FM.
Only available in the Haringey area of north London.

London News
97.3 FM.
This station offers 24-hour news, weather, motoring and business information.

London Newstalk
1152 MW.
Phone-ins and more chat.

Melody FM
105.4 FM.
London cabbies' favourite station offering non-stop instrumental versions of old Carpenters hits.

Spectrum Radio
558 MW.
Station researched, produced and presented by ethnic communities, including Asian, Arabic, Chinese, Hispanic, Jewish, Persian and Italian.

Sunrise
1458 MW.
Asian-orientated programming.

Talk UK
1053, 1089 MW.
So-called shock jocks such as Caesar the Geezer offer 24-hour gibberish and insults.

Virgin
105.8 FM, 1197, 1215 MW.
Album rock from Richard Branson's station.

Viva!
963 MW.
Women's radio station promising politics, sex and environmental issues all from a woman's perspective.

Television

Cable and satellite have helped increase the number of channels available, although many viewers still only receive the four main UK stations, two run by the BBC and two commercial stations. Even if limited to these four, there's still plenty to see (*Time Out* magazine lists full programme details every week) but for the latest films or for a lot of live sport, you'll either need to get access to a satellite dish, or just go and watch in a pub. A new nationwide station, Channel Five, is due to go on air by 1997 at the latest. As we go to press, the franchisees were due to be announced. The highest bid came from a consortium put together by the Canadian broadcaster CanWest Global Communications.

BBC 1
BBC1 represents all that is 'Auntie BBC' – the Corporation's mass-market station. It has no commercials, which considerably reduces the length of US imports. There's a fair smattering of soaps and game shows but also the odd quality programme. Daytime programming, however, stinks. Typical programmes – *EastEnders, Antiques Roadshow.*

BBC 2
Also a commercial-free station but, in general, BBC2 is free of crass programmes. That doesn't mean that the programmes are riveting, just not insulting. It offers a cultural cross-section – the station is happy to feature modern dance or traditional jazz, for instance. Typical programmes – *The Natural World, Newsnight.*

ITV – Carlton
Mass-appeal programmes are punctuated by commercial breaks every 15 minutes or so. It's not quite the lowest-common denominator, more the highest-possible audience. Its biggest problem is that any successful formula is then repeated ad infinitum. The station broadcasts from Monday to Friday only. Typical programmes – *Coronation Street, This Morning.*

ITV – London Weekend
LWT takes over from Carlton at the weekend to offer much of the same, if not more downmarket. A redeeming feature is the action movies it tends to broadcast, which can help liven up a dull Saturday night. Typical programmes – *Blind Date, Beadle's About.*

Channel 4
C4 offers a lot of minority viewing but is responsible for some of the best programmes produced in Britain in the last decade. Ground-breaking is, for a change, an apt adjective to describe this station. Typical programmes – *Brookside, The Big Breakfast.*

Satellite & Cable

There are new stations being launched all the time which are only available with a satellite receiver or cable. Greater choice doesn't mean better programmes, however. But if you're looking for rubbish, you'll find it. The listing of typical programmes will give you an idea of the kind of thing to expect.

Bravo
Generally a retro channel offering TV classics from the 1960s and '70s. Typical programmes – *The Avengers, Hogan's Heroes.*

CNN
Offers news and background. Typical programme – news.

Eurosport
One of three sport-only channels, offering marginal-interest events. Typical programmes – truck racing, weightlifting.

Family
Safe programming policy. Typical programmes – *Trivial Pursuit, Dangermouse.*

MTV
Rock and pop channel which borrows heavily from its American counterpart. Typical programmes – *Music Non-Stop, Beavis and Butt-Head.*

Sky Movies
Various blockbusters. Typical programmes – *Sliver, Surf Ninjas.*

Sky Movies Gold
Classic movie channel. Typical programmes – *Alfie, Rio Bravo.*

Movie Channel
More films. Typical programmes – *Buffy the Vampire Slayer, Much Ado About Nothing.*

Sky News
Twenty-four-hour news and features. Typical programmes – news.

Sky One
Channel with general appeal. Typical programmes – *The Simpsons, Letterman.*

Sky Sports
Buying up more and more of the major sporting events. There's also a Sky Sports 2 channel which broadcasts at weekends. Typical programmes – live rugby league, Premiership football.

TNT
Offers cartoons all day then classic TV programmes in the evening. Typical programmes – cartoons.

UK Gold
Buys wholesale from BBC and ITV, repeating yesterday's successful formulae. Typical programmes – *EastEnders, Neighbours.*

UK Living
Aimed at people spending all day at home. Typical programmes – *Agony Hour, Crosswits.*

VH-1
Rock station featuring extensive album coverage. Typical programmes – *Old Grey Whistle Test.*

Comedy

Funny, isn't it, how London has become the world capital of comedy?

London contains more comedy clubs than any other city in the world. There are several in the central area (including the **Comedy Store**, just off Piccadilly Circus), but the majority are found in outer London districts where local audiences provide the main support.

Comedy traditionally happens in pubs, though there are exceptions to this rule (*see* **Comedy Café**, **Comedy Empire**, **Cosmic Comedy Club**, **Hackney Empire**, **Jongleurs Camden Lock**, **Riverside Studios** and **Up the Creek**). The seating and décor can range from the plush to the functional. But all the clubs listed below are run by promoters who create a situation where comics can give their best and audiences can be guaranteed a good night out.

Stand-up comedy is the staple ingredient almost everywhere. Anyone in search of more varied bills with speciality acts (excluding stand-ups) should try **Circus Space**. Otherwise, it's a matter of scanning the weekly listings in *Time Out* magazine (always advisable, since the selection below is only a small number of the clubs currently operating), and deciding which show seems most suitable. You'll discover that the atmosphere can be very different from club to club.

None of the clubs listed take credit cards.

Central

Chuckle Club
Underground Bar, London School of Economics, Houghton Street (off Aldwych), WC2 (0171 476 1672). Holborn tube. **Open** 7.45pm Sat. **Performances** 9pm. **Admission** £6; £4 concs.
Host Eugene Cheese brings many of the strongest acts in the country to this student venue. Non-students are welcome too.

Comedy at Soho Ho
The Crown & Two Chairmen, Dean Street, W1 (0181 348 2085). Leicester Square or Tottenham Court Road tube. **Open** 8pm Sat. **Performances** 8.30pm. **Admission** £5; £4 concs.
A small and lively pub venue where the bills bring a good cross-section of the hundreds of comics performing on the London circuit.

Comedy Spot
The Spot, Maiden Lane, WC2 (0171 379 5900). Covent Garden tube. **Open** 8pm Mon. **Performances** 9pm. **Admission** £8 (incl free meal if you book before 8pm); £6; £3 concessions after 8pm.
One of few comedy clubs in London open on a Monday night and with its mix of experienced performers and newer acts the Comedy Spot is always good value .

Comedy Store
Haymarket House, Oxendon Street, SW1 (information 01426 914433; bookings 0171 344 4444). Piccadilly Circus tube. **Open** 6.30pm Tue-Sun. **Performances** 8pm Tue-Thur, Sun; also midnight Fri, Sat. **Admission** £8-£10.
The most famous club in the country and the place where the new movement in comedy was launched 15 years ago. All the best stand-ups appear here. On Wednesdays and Sundays the Comedy Store Players serve up high-class improvisation.

Guilty Pea
The Wheatsheaf, 25 Rathbone Place, W1 (0171 986 6861). Tottenham Court Road tube. **Open** 8.15pm Sat. **Performances** 8.45pm. **Admission** £5; £4 concs.
With comedy, just as with jazz, intimate surroundings often create the most memorable nights. The Guilty Pea has been running for many years. Its capacity is around 60.

Hurricane Club
The Black Horse, 6 Rathbone Place, W1 (0171 580 0666). Tottenham Court Road tube. **Open** 8.30pm Sat. **Performances** 9pm. **Admission** £5.50; £4.50 concs.
A long-established resident team performs highly enjoyable comedy impro games with a special guest each week drawn from the top rank of stand-up comics.

West

Acton Banana
The King's Head, Acton High Street, W3 (0181 992 0282). Acton Town tube/Acton Central BR. **Open** 8.30pm Fri. **Performances** 9pm. **Admission** £6; £4 concs.
The west London offshoot of Banana Cabaret (*see* **South**) and consequently a guarantee of good entertainment.

Cosmic Comedy Club
177 Fulham Palace Road, W6 (0171 381 2006). Hammersmith tube. **Open** 7.30pm Tue, Wed, Fri, Sat. **Performances** 8.30pm. **Admission** £2-£8; £1-£5 concs.
A relatively new club run by knowledgeable promoters where Tuesday and Wednesday nights are devoted to untried acts and the more impressive bills are reserved for the weekends.

Ha Bloody Ha
The Viaduct Inn, Uxbridge Road, W7 (0181 566 4067). Boston Manor tube/Hanwell BR. **Open** 8.30pm Fri, Sat. **Performances** 9pm. **Admission** £5-£6; £4 concs.
Way out west (it's not that far from Heathrow Airport), but well worth a visit if you're anywhere nearby for its good-humoured atmosphere and the chance to see performers who could be very big names in the near future.

Riverside Studios
Crisp Road, W6 (0181 741 2255). Hammersmith tube. **Performances** times vary. **Admission** £6-£8.50.

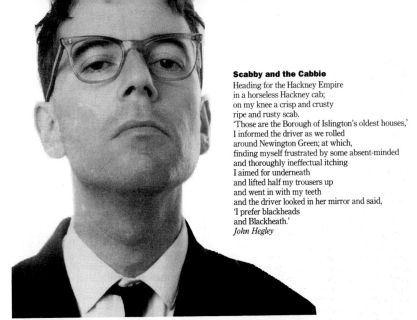

Scabby and the Cabbie

Heading for the Hackney Empire
in a horseless Hackney cab;
on my knee a crisp and crusty
ripe and rusty scab.
'Those are the Borough of Islington's oldest houses,'
I informed the driver as we rolled
around Newington Green; at which,
finding myself frustrated by some absent-minded
and thoroughly ineffectual itching
I aimed for underneath
and lifted half my trousers up
and went in with my teeth
and the driver looked in her mirror and said,
'I prefer blackheads
and Blackheath.'
John Hegley

Poet laureate of dogs, glasses and Luton Town, John Hegley pops up at the **Hackney Empire**.

A recently refurbished centre for the performing arts where top comics from Britain and other countries bring their solo shows. It mounted the first London Comedy Festival in 1994 – the next one will be in the last month or so of 1995. There are also seasons of late-night stand-up comedy (mainly on Saturdays).

South

Aztec Comedy Club
The Borderland, 47-49 Westow Street, SE19 (0181 771 0885). Crystal Palace or Gypsy Hill BR. **Open** 8pm Fri, Sun. **Performances** 9.30pm Fri, 9pm Sun. **Admission** £4-£4.50; £3.50-£4 concs.
A pleasant room above a Tex-Mex restaurant.

Banana Cabaret
The Bedford, 77 Bedford Hill, SW12 (0181 673 8904). Balham tube/BR. **Performances** 9pm. **Admission** £6; £4 concs.
One of the most enterprising and enjoyable clubs in London with two separate spaces running simultaneously in the same building on Saturday nights.

Cartoon at Clapham
The Plough, 196-198 Clapham High Street, SW4 (0171 738 8763). Clapham Common tube. **Open** 8.15pm Sat. **Performances** 9pm. **Admission** £6; £4 concs.
A large pub venue with good bills representative of what's fashionable in comedy.

East Dulwich Cabaret
East Dulwich Tavern, 1 Lordship Lane, SE22 (0181 299 4138). East Dulwich BR. **Open** 8.30pm Sat. **Performances** 9.15pm. **Admission** £5; £4 concs.
Well run with a reliable line-up and relaxed atmosphere.

Jongleurs Battersea
The Cornet, 49 Lavender Gardens, SW11 (0171 924 2766). Clapham Junction BR. **Open** 7.30pm Fri; 6pm, 10.30pm, Sat. **Performances** 8.45pm Fri; 7.15pm, 11.15pm, Sat. **Admission** £8-£10; £6-£7 concs.
Along with the Comedy Store, this is one of the the leading London comedy clubs, though with more varied line-ups not just confined to stand-up comedy. *See also* **Jongleurs Camden Lock**.

Up the Creek
302 Creek Road, SE10 (0181 858 4581). Greenwich BR. **Open** 8pm Fri, Sun; 7.30pm Sat. **Performances** 9.30pm Fri, Sun; 9pm Sat. **Admission** £6-£10; £4-£7 concs.
A fine, noisy bearpit of a club which tests even the best comics. Not for the faint-hearted.

East

Circus Space
Coronet Street, N1 (0171 613 4141). Old Street tube. **Open** 8pm Sat. **Performances** 8.30pm. **Admission** £7; £5 concs.
Acrobats, trapeze artists, physical comics and many other kinds of circus acts and street performers are the mainstay of the fortnightly shows in this splendid building situated in what was once Shoreditch Power Station.

Comedy Café
66 Rivington Street, EC2 (0171 739 5706). Old Street tube. **Open** 7.30pm Wed-Sat. **Performances** 8.30pm. **Admission** free Wed, Thur; £5-£7 Fri, Sat.
One of the few clubs in London customised for comedy. The Wednesday shows are for new acts; the Thursdays are great value, since they're free.

Hackney Empire
291 Mare Street, E8 (0181 985 2424). Hackney Central/Hackney Downs BR. **Performances** times vary. **Admission** £3-£8.
Comedy of every kind, from star-studded and occasionally riotous shows to special solo performances, in a large and lovely Edwardian variety theatre.

Downstairs at the King's Head – *well worth a trip to Crouch End, Saturdays and Sundays.*

North

Bound & Gagged Palmers Green

The Fox, 413 Green Lanes, N13 (0181 830 5233).
Palmers Green BR. **Open** 8.30pm Sat. **Performances**
9.15pm. **Admission** £6.50; £4.50 concs.
Good mixed bills in an ideal comedy space (capacity 200)
with more speciality acts than you'll find in most places.

Comedy Empire

Church Road, NW10 (0181 459 2917). Neasden tube.
Open 8pm Sat. **Performances** 9pm. **Admission** £8;
£5 concs.
Like the Hackney Empire, this impressive building used to
be an old variety theatre. It's run by the same team as Up
the Creek.

Downstairs at the King's Head

2 Crouch End Hill, corner of The Broadway, N8 (0181
340 1028). Finsbury Park tube/BR then W7 bus. **Open**
8pm Sat; 7.45pm Sun. **Performances** 8.30pm.
Admission £3.50-£5; £2.50-£4 concs.
One of the oldest clubs in the capital and deservedly popular, since the emphasis is on providing the best possible situation for the performers and giving audiences a good time.

Hampstead Comedy Club

The Washington, Englands Lane, NW3 (0171 483
3647). Belsize Park or Chalk Farm tube. **Open** 8pm Sat.
Performances 9pm. **Admission** £5; £4 concs.

A newcomer to the club scene set up by Ivor Dembina, a
comic with a huge amount of experience. It looks set to run
for years.

Jongleurs Camden Lock

Dingwalls Building, Middle Yard, Camden Lock, NW1
(0171 924 2766). Camden Town tube. **Open** 7pm Fri;
6pm, 10.30pm, Sat. **Performances** 8.15pm Fri; 7.15pm,
11.15pm, Sat. **Admission** £8-£10; £6-£7 concs.
A comfortable, purpose-built comedy venue on the American
model with excellent bills.

Meccano Club

Market Tavern, 2 Essex Road (opposite Islington Green),
N1. Angel tube. **Open** 8.30pm Fri, Sat. **Performances**
9pm. **Admission** £5; £4 concs.
A splendid, unpretentious basement venue that consistently brings out the best in comics. The Market Tavern also
houses Monday night shows (though not under the Meccano
banner) where well-known comics try out new ideas.

Red Rose Cabaret

Plimsoll Arms, 52 St Thomas's Road, N4
(0181 675 3819). Finsbury Park tube. **Open**
8pm Fri, Sat. **Performances** 9pm. **Admission** £6;
£3.50-£5 concs.
Old club, new place. Red Rose Cabaret has an impeccable
pedigree – few people who ever saw Andrew Davies clam-
ber on stage in his deep-sea diving suit will disagree. Here,
as elsewhere in the past, satisfaction is a virtual certainty.

Clubs

If there's one aspect of London life that moves faster than Ben Johnson on speed, it's the club scene. Here's a freeze-frame.

You can't move for bright young things and beautiful people – The Next Big Thing at **Iceni**.

Variety is the spice of nightlife in London. At first sight, it may look as if every dance floor shakes to the same Housey soundtrack but don't be fooled. New one-nighter clubs are constantly opening up. Most are inspired by the latest dance trends, with the DJ as the main attraction. You can hustle at 1970s party nights; jazz-dance to the latest trip-hop tracks; learn to lambada like a Brazilian; sweat on down to phat rap; or practise lindyhopping to big band swing. Not that dancing is the only essential activity. Kitschy throwbacks are definitely *in* this year. There are board-game clubs, easy-listening clubs and retro-supper clubs all competing for their 15 minutes of fame.

Clubbers are so used to venues staying open as late as 10am, that many don't bother going out until well after midnight. Unfortunately, the new timetable only applies to the dance floor. At the bar, for the time being, we're stuck with antiquated licensing laws, so after 3am alcohol gives way to fruit juices and 'psycho-active' drinks. Unfortunately, weekend clubbing is more expensive than ever. Admission often tops £10 on Fridays and Saturdays, at least until 3am, when the price drops to encourage club crawling.

If it all seems a bit hectic, there are plenty of intimate (and sober) venues where it's possible to communicate without shouting. Mature groovers should try some of the smarter, more expensive clubs in the West End, Mayfair, Kensington or Chelsea. Every week you'll find listings of about 200 different clubs and one-nighters in the Clubs section of *Time Out* magazine. Meanwhile, bear in mind a number of suggestions to ensure that your night on the town lives up to expectations.

MEMBERSHIP

Venues are prohibited from selling alcohol after 11pm unless they have either a music-and-dance licence or a club licence. Most opt for the latter, since it gives them the freedom to select members. However, most clubs' membership regulations are quite flexible. Many venues include a membership fee as part of the admission price, while most one-nighters only claim to be 'Members Only' if they don't think you would 'fit in'.

DRESS CODE

Most nightspots have a vague 'smart but casual' dress code. Jeans, T-shirts and trainers (sneakers) are frowned upon at the smarter venues, but are

*All smiles at the **Velvet Underground** on a Wednesday – well, almost all smiles anyway.*

the 'uniform' elsewhere. Although fashion isn't as important as it used to be, bear in mind that if a club has a reputation for a particular kind of music there's usually a style to go with it. Turn up in a suit to a club full of goths, and you might be glad if the bouncers refuse you entry.

TRANSPORT

Unless you can dance until breakfast time, you'll usually leave a club well after the Underground network has stopped running. Taxis can be hard to find early in the morning, so if at all possible it's worth arranging homeward transport in advance. You could take a minicab – although it may be unwise for a single woman to do so; reputable cab companies are listed in *chapter* **Getting Around**. Night buses are the cheapest means of transport, and they may offer an entertaining ride home. We've listed the night buses for clubs in districts outside central London, but if you're in the West End, head for Trafalgar Square, from where most night buses depart.

The Clubs

Bar Rumba

36 Shaftesbury Avenue, W1, next to Trocadero (0171 287 2715). Piccadilly Circus tube. **Open** 10pm-3.30am Mon-Fri; 7pm-6am Sat. **Admission** £3-£6 Mon-Fri; £10-£12 Sat.
This Latin bar and club has veered towards radical jazz fusion and phat funk on Mondays and Thursdays respectively. The rest of the week is usually given over to short-lived House nights.

The Blue Note

1 Hoxton Square, N1 (0171 729 8440). Old Street tube/BR. **Open** 8pm-2am Tue-Thur; 10pm-5am Fri, Sat; noon-6pm, 7pm-midnight Sun. **Admission** £5-£8 Tue-Thur; £6 Fri; £8-£10 Sat; £3-£5 Sun.
Formerly called the Bass Clef. The Acid Jazz Record label recently took over this small, atmospheric Hoxton Square club, thereby saving it from demolition and providing a platform for their weekly programme of midweek live shows and weekend jazz retreats. *See chapter* **Music: Rock, Folk & Jazz**.

The Borderline

Orange Yard, Manette Street, WC2 (0171 734 2095). Leicester Square or Tottenham Court Road tube. **Open** 11.30pm-3am Mon-Sat. **Admission** £6-£10.
Lively, unpretentious dance nights underneath a Tex-Mex restaurant; the music shifts from rock to funk to upfront dance. Thursdays is indie rock; bands play at weekends. *See chapter* **Music: Rock, Folk & Jazz**.

Camden Palace

1A Camden High Street, NW1 (0171 387 0428). Camden Town tube. **Open** 9pm-2.30am Tue-Thur, Sat; 9pm-4am Fri. **Admission** £4-£10.
Amid a great fanfare the Palace re-opened in the winter of 1994/95 to reveal its new interior – which looks as if a spaceship has crash-landed in the middle of the old dance floor. Still, it's always crowded, and best at Tuesday's indie-rock fest Feet First or the lively 1960s and '70s pop and R&B night on Wednesdays.

Cuba

11-13 Kensington High Street, W8 (0171 938 4137). High Street Kensington tube. **Open** 8pm-1am daily. **Admission** £1-£4.
Unassuming and friendly café/bar for local Latinophiles who gradually edge out the after-work drinkers as the tiny dance floor starts to shake to diverse worldbeat fusion.

Electric Ballroom

184 Camden High Street, NW1 (0171 485 9006).
Camden Town tube. **Open** 10.30pm-3am Fri; 10.30pm-
2.30am Sat. **Admission** £5-£6.
A large two-tiered venue which draws the weekend crowds
by playing everything from rock and glamour punk to funky
hip hop and House on the huge main floor, with jazz or hard
rock upstairs.
Disabled: access.

Emporium

62 Kingly Street, W1 (0171 734 3190). Oxford Circus
tube. **Open** 10pm-4am Wed-Sat. **Admission** £8-£12.
Emporium looks like an Ibizan dance club, transported brick-
by-brick to London. At weekends, the lavish open-plan
dance floor draws hordes of West End wannabes and the
occasional celeb.

Equinox

Leicester Square, WC2 (0171 437 1446). Leicester
Square tube. **Open** 9pm-3.30am Mon-Sat. **Admission**
£5-£7 Mon-Thur; £8-£10 Fri, Sat.
A mainstream club capable of keeping up to 1,500 dancers
happy if they like chart/dance music. The club is feature-
packed with plenty of bars and seats, a spectacular laser
system and an appalling carpet.

The Garage

20-22 Highbury Corner, N5 (0171 607 1818). Highbury
& Islington tube/BR. **Open** 7.30pm-2am daily. **Music**
9pm. **Admission** £3-£9.
Straightforward local club right by the tube station. Presents
bands in the evening and carries on with a club into the night.
Indie rocking to guitar-driven stormers is a speciality.

The Gardening Club

4 The Piazza, WC2 (0171 497 3154). Covent Garden
tube. **Open** 10pm-3.30am Mon-Thur; 10pm-6am Fri-Sat.
Admission £4-£7 Mon-Thur; £10-£12 Fri-Sat.
This coolly styled Covent Garden hangout consistently hosts
packed and pumpin' one-nighters which reduce the place
to a sweatbox on weekends, so arrive early if you want to
be included.

Hanover Grand

6 Hanover Street, W1 (0171 499 7977). Oxford
Circus tube. **Open** 10.30pm-4.30am Thur-Sat.
Admission £10-£12.
The owners behind SW1 shrewdly redesigned this spacious
hotel ballroom with a booming system – and little else.
Saturdays look set to run and run at Malibu Stacey where
happy handbag heads come to play while the queues outside
stretch into the distance.

Heaven

Underneath the Arches, Villiers Street, WC2 (0171 839
3863). Embankment tube or Charing Cross tube/BR.
Open 10pm-3am Mon; 10.30pm-3am Tue-Sat.
Admission £6-£7.50.
London's major gay club (*see chapter* **Gay & Lesbian**) is
also one of the best dance venues in town; a maze of bars,
corridors and pumping dance floors with excellent lasers,
sound systems and light shows. London's very own mini-
Glastonbury, Megatripolis, touches down on Thursdays.

The Hippodrome

Cranbourn Street, WC2 (0171 437 4311). Leicester
Square tube. **Open** 9pm-3.30am Mon-Sat. **Admission**
£4-£8 Mon-Wed; £6-£9 Thur-Sat.
Superb lighting and sound systems, but a chrome-clad disco
dinosaur as far as interior decoration goes. The club usually offers a 'commercial' mix of dance music for a smartly
dressed crowd of out-of-towners and tourists, with trapeze
artists and fire-eaters among the entertainment.

HQs

West Yard, Camden Lock, NW1 (0171 485 6044).
Camden Town tube. **Open** 9pm-3am Wed-Fri; 8pm-2am
Sat; 9pm-2am Sun. **Admission** £4-£7.
Not a purpose-built club by any means, but what this
canal-side haunt lacks in dance floor technology it certainly
makes up for with an atmosphere that can sometimes reach
inspirational levels.

Iceni

11 White Horse Street, off Curzon Street, W1 (0171 495
5333). Green Park tube. **Open** 10pm-3am Wed-Sat.
Admission £5-£8.
Still one of the most popular venues in town, with five rooms
on three stylish floors, making it ideal for clubs which make
a virtue of musical diversity and fun-funky interactive entertainment. Wednesdays and Saturdays are excellent funky
affairs with jam sessions, films, board games and great
crowds; the beautiful people and the Chelsea club set take
over on Fridays.

Jazz Café

5 Parkway, NW1 (0171 344 0044). Camden
Town tube. **Open** *club nights* 11.30pm-2am
Fri, Sat. *Performances* 7pm-midnight Mon-Thur, Sun;
7pm-2am Fri, Sat. **Admission** *club nights* £5-£6;
performances £7-£15.
Jazz fans come from far and wide to hear some of the best
music in the capital (from Afro-Latin jazz to rap). There
are a couple of bumpy jazzy-funk nights at the weekend
to expand the experience. *See chapter* **Music: Rock, Folk
& Jazz**.

Legends

29 Old Burlington Street, W1 (0171 437 9933).
Green Park or Piccadilly Circus tube. **Open** 10pm-3am
Wed, Thur; 10pm-6am Fri; 10.30pm-4.30am Sat.
Admission £5-£15.
Sleek 'n' steel nightclub venue designed by Eva Jiricna which
plays host to busy Housey nights at weekends. Drinkers will
appreciate one of the best stocked bars in clubland.

The Leisure Lounge

121 Holborn, EC1 (0171 242 1345). Chancery
Lane tube. **Open** 11pm-5am Fri; 11pm-10am Sat.
Admission £10-£12.
A large open-plan space, with huge back-lit photos of London
luminaries and excellent slide visuals wherever you look. If
you're still going on Sunday morning join the Happy House
hedonists at Sunny Side Up.

Limelight

136 Shaftesbury Avenue, W1 (0171 434 0572). Leicester
Square tube. **Open** 10pm-3am Mon-Sat. **Admission** £5-
£8 Mon-Thur; £10 Fri; £12 Sat.
Once a church, now a temple to funk, Garage and House
music. Black-clad 1980s revivalists take the venue over on
Wednesdays for the ever-popular Planet Earth.

Madame Jo Jo

8-10 Brewer Street, W1 (0171 734 2473). Piccadilly
Circus tube. **Open** 8pm-2am Mon-Sat; 2pm-midnight Sun.
Admission £5-£7.
This plush, intimate, late-night cabaret (very *La Cage Aux
Folles*) hosts easy-listening Indigo on a Tuesday night;
at other times it's a hunting ground for six-foot glamour-
pusses and the odd Soho mac man.

Mars

12 Sutton Row (opposite The Astoria), W1
(0171 439 4655). Tottenham Court Road tube. **Open**
10pm-3am Mon-Thur; 10.30-5am Fri; 11pm-6am Sat.
Admission £3-£10.
Mars' stark interior is certainly in marked contrast to its

Blag Blag Blag

Ben Bellman gets in for free.

Clubbing is an expensive business these days. Big weekend nights often top 12 quid, but like everything else it's negotiable. (Well not like everything else actually. You wouldn't think of haggling over cinema entrance on the grounds that your mate knows someone who worked on the film, but there you go.) A copy of *Time Out* is a good way to start. Welcomed at the better venues about town, it can often save you a third of the admission price if you just flash the cover. Check the listings to see where the deals are. Otherwise look out for reduced-rate club flyers that litter most Soho record shops and don't forget your NUS or student ID card.

Of course the reason that the really busy nights are expensive is that so many people get in free. Economics dictates that if half the punters wangle in on the guest list then the other half have to pay through the nose to compensate, so you've got the added irritant of knowing that your hard-earned cash is contributing to somebody's free evening. The more fashionable the club, the more dependent it is on attracting the beautiful people – and the beautiful people do not pay. To their credit, club runners have tried everything to squeeze a few quid out of London's free-loading community. But even the rattle of a collection box habitually fails to induce more than a few shameful excuses. Sad but true to form. Still if you can't beat 'em….

Blagging has its down side. You've got to be prepared for endless queuing and the possibility of a knock-back that ruins your night, but, like shop-lifting, it does add a certain frisson to what can otherwise be a rather predictable activity. Here are a couple of tried and tested scams which should provide a starting point for the potential ligger. They work best with a healthy dollop of self confidence and/or artificially induced Dutch courage. Try to maintain a slightly superior air but never appear patronising. Remember most bouncers and door people are sad and inadequate and get their thrills from herding people, so tread carefully and avoid igniting any short fuses. Decisive timing and the ability to think on your feet are also essential.

Scam one. Patiently wait your turn in the guest list queue. When asked for your name, mumble incoherently about some important-sounding foreign record company. This should draw the door person in close enough to cop a split-second glance

down the names and pick one out. 'Oh it might be under…' Works every time. This was used to spectacular effect at a recent party for Kate Moss where the doorman was actually inviting punters to point out their names on the list. Within minutes the club was full of people who didn't have any right to be there, while the celeb invitees were kept out in the rain on the grounds that they had already been crossed off.The high-tech version of this scam involves renting the house opposite and using high-powered binoculars and one of those hearing aid-type things.

Scam two. Another sure-fire lig that relies on club runners' unending pandering to anyone who mixes two records together for a living. Hang about until the DJ turns up and tag along at the back of his entourage. This works particularly well with Big Name American DJs who are usually so bewildered/out of it that they genuinely don't know who's with their party. You should be able to carry it off well into the night.

So it's free drinks, VIP passes and trips to the mixing booth. Another cheeky variable is the notorious 'I am the DJ and here's my guest list' tactic. Most jocks are so anonymous these days, you should have no problem convincing the security. After all, no one would go to the lengths of carrying heavy record boxes around just to get into a club. To this end, the problem has always been what to do with the boxes once you get in. I find that flight cases loaded down with cans of Red Stripe offer the best option. Happy blagging!

sister club the Velvet Underground, and it tends to attract a more single-minded dance crowd who appreciate the small but perfectly formed layout.

Maximus

14 Leicester Square, WC2 (0171 734 4111). Leicester Square tube. **Open** 10.30pm-3.30am Wed; 10pm-3am Thur; 10.30pm-6am Fri; 11pm-6am Sat; 9.30pm-3am Sun. **Admission** £5-£12.

A long-serving former disco, currently playing host to ever-changing one-nighters, with Thursday's Soul Kitchen and a stream of Saturday one-offs among the many attractions.

Ministry of Sound

103 Gaunt Street, SE1 (0171 378 6528). Elephant & Castle tube. **Open** 11pm-7am Fri; 11pm-9am Sat. **Admission** £12 Fri; £15 Sat.

An essential pilgramage for House and Garage enthusiasts. Security at the door is tighter than a micro-skirt, it's only open weekends and it's expensive, but, on a good night, the sheer energy of the place will take your breath away.

The Office

3-5 Rathbone Place, W1 (0171 255 1098). Tottenham Court Road tube. **Open** 6pm-2am Wed, Fri-Sat; 8.30pm-3am. **Admission** £3-£6.

The 1970s throwback that was Shuffles has been funkily overhauled and now hosts a range of off-beat nights. On Wednesday there's a madcap board game experience, The Double Six Club, while Saturday night attracts loads of goateed beatniks.

Le Palais

242 Shepherd's Bush Road, W6 (0181 748 2812). Hammersmith tube. **Open** 9.30pm-2.30am Wed; 9.30pm-3am Thur; 9pm-3am Fri, Sat. **Admission** £3-£7.

Redecorated in art deco revival style, west London's major disco comes complete with the requisite light show, lasers, video walls and a restaurant, but it's still like a dance hall in an aircraft hangar.

Plastic People

37-39 Oxford Street, W1 (no phone). Tottenham Court Road tube. **Open** 11pm-4am Mon-Thur; 11pm-6am Fri, Sat. **Admission** £5-£8.

A friendly, unpretentious dance dive which was recently given another makeover and a pumping new sound system. A roster of Housey one-offs usually fills the dance floor, which is small enough to give the impression that you're dancing among friends.

RAW

112A Great Russell Street, WC1 (0171 637 3375). Tottenham Court Road tube. **Open** 10pm-4am Thur; 10.30pm-5am Fri, Sat. **Admission** £4-£10.

Packed and pumping, this dance bunker deep below the earth's crust boasts a three-room homage to funky clubland style which draws streetwise regulars of all major musical persuasions.

The Site

196 Piccadilly, W1 (0171 439 1245). Green Park or Piccadilly Circus tube. **Open** 10pm-6am Thur-Sat. **Admission** £5-£12.

Central but characterless, this revamped discotheque provides a home for nomadic monthly House nights and a long-running women-only session on the first Thursday of every month.

Stringfellow's

16 Upper St Martin's Lane, WC2 (0171 240 5534). Covent Garden or Leicester Square tube. **Open** 9pm-3.30am Mon-Sat. **Admission** £8-£10 Mon-Thur; £10-£15 Fri, Sat.

Once Stringfellow's was the Mecca for tabloid celebs, but these days you're more likely to meet a computer programmer from Basildon. The menu is a mite pricey, but it's also one of the only decent restaurants in a club that we know of.

Subterania

12 Acklam Road, W10 (0181 960 4590). Ladbroke Grove tube. **Open** 8pm-2am Mon-Thur; 10pm-3.30am Fri, Sat. **Admission** £7-£8.

Nestling under the flyover and well worth a visit. Bands dominate the action during the week, with plenty of diverse turntable action at weekends. Friday's Rotation funk night is massive.

Disabled: access; toilet.

SW1

191 Victoria Street, SW1 (0171 828 7455). Victoria tube/BR. **Open** 9pm-6am Wed; 10pm-3am Thur; 10pm-6am Fri; 10.30pm-5am Sat. **Admission** £10 (£5 after 3am).

There's a bizarre contrast between the setting and the sounds at SW1. The venue: an Edwardian dance hall with traditional oak panelling on two floors. The music: tuff House. The attractions: serious dancers and chunky sound.

Tokyo Joe

85 Piccadilly, W1 (0171 409 1832). Green Park tube. **Open** 8.30pm-3.30am Mon-Sat. **Admission** £10 (£5 if dining).

A plush nightclub with accompanying restaurant serving Italian food. Unsurprisingly, it tends to attract well-heeled adults. Phone in advance to check on sartorial requirements.

United Kingdom

Buckhold Road (beside the Arndale Complex), SW18 (0181 877 0110). East Putney tube. **Open** 10pm-6am Fri, Sat. **Admission** £6-£12.

UK shook up conventional nightlife wisdom by opening in untrendy Wandsworth a couple of years ago. It's worth the trip if you're devoted to European-style Techno and Housey dance music at Friday's Final Frontier, otherwise its three huge rooms, fairly kitsch décor and purple chill-out area are probably best left to the locals.

Velvet Underground

143 Charing Cross Road, WC2 (0171 439 4655). Tottenham Court Road tube. **Open** 10pm-3am Mon-Thur; 10.30pm-4am Fri, Sat; 7pm-midnight Sun. **Admission** £4-£10.

They didn't call this the Velvet Underground fer nuthin': this well-designed club is velvet-swagged in red, blue and yellow, with sleek seating areas and a neat dance floor where Nicky Holloway and friends spin happy, thumping House beats to a twentysomething crowd.

The Venue

2A Clifton Rise, SE14 (0171 326 0969). New Cross Gate tube/BR. **Open** 8pm-2am Fri-Sat. **Admission** £5-£6.

South-east London's most popular club if the queues are anything to go by. You're advised to arrive early for the bands and alternative/indie rock sessions that pack this spacious retro dancehall.

The Wag Club

35 Wardour Street, W1 (0171 437 5534). Leicester Square or Piccadilly Circus tube. **Open** 10.30pm-3.30am Mon-Thur; 10.30pm-6am Fri, Sat. **Admission** £4-£6 Mon-Thur; £7 Fri; £10 Sat.

The club to be seen in during the mid-1980s is still an attractive proposition, with two floors playing host to a range of dance music: Wednesdays is rockin' with bands, Saturdays is for fans of funk and hip hop, Thursdays draw a diverse crowd of jazz bohos, and on Tuesdays the club is packed for its Bhangra, Rap and Swingbeat session.

Dance

Whatever your preferred form, you'll find a dance company from somewhere in the world performing it somewhere in London – at a price to suit.

London offers every style of dance from classical ballet and contemporary to Brazilian capoeira and Indian dance. Venues vary widely as well, from lavish theatres to open-air stages. Ticket prices are generally not prohibitive: even theatres with companies performing on the grandest scale have standby tickets or restricted-view seats for a fiver.

All world-class dance companies visit London at some point in their touring lives. In 1995, the Kirov Ballet, the Royal Swedish Ballet, the Royal Danish Ballet and Angelin Preljocaj all visited. Working within London itself are a multitude of companies and individual dancers. Virtually every culture of the world is represented here and this is reflected in dance. The best regional companies also include London on their touring circuits.

From the least initiated to the most discerning, everyone can find an affordable and creative dance event to suit them in London.

Major Venues

ICA
The Mall, SW1 (0171 930 3647/membership enquiries 0171 930 0493). Piccadilly Circus tube or Charing Cross tube/BR. **Open** *box office noon-9.30pm daily; noon-6.30pm advance bookings.* **Tickets** *prices vary.* **Credit** A, AmEx, DC, £TC, V.
Since its opening in 1948, the Institute of Contemporary Arts (ICA) has maintained a reputation for provocative and challenging art. Dance tends to be of the performance art genre mixing movement, music, text, films and design. The theatre has seating for approximately 200, enhancing its sense of intimacy and contact with the performance. ICA day membership, included in the ticket price, entitles you not only to roam the superb, airy, avant garde art galleries, but also to use the late bar, ideal for relaxing over after-theatre drinks. (*See also chapters* **Art Galleries**, **Film** *and* **Theatre**.) *Bar. Bookshop. Café. Group discount. Lectures. Workshops.*

The London Coliseum
St Martin's Lane, WC2 (0171 836 3161/credit card bookings 0171 240 5258/recorded information 0171 836 7666). Leicester Square tube or Charing Cross tube/BR. **Open** *box office 10am-8pm Mon-Sat.* **Tickets** *£8-£43.* Day tickets on sale to personal callers after 10am Mon-Thur: 55 stalls seats at £18; 100 balcony seats at £6. Standby seats Mon-Sat. **Credit** A, AmEx, DC, £$TC, V.
The Coliseum was originally intended to provide entertainment for visitors arriving at Charing Cross and from 1909-31 the world's greatest artists performed here. There are two main seasons of dance a year, during the summer and the week before Christmas. As one of London's most spacious

and lavish theatres it is first choice for many foreign ballet companies. In 1995 the Royal Swedish Ballet presented *Romeo and Juliet*, and the Kirov performed *Swan Lake* and *Sleeping Beauty*. Plush Champagne and coffee bars are dotted around, offering sandwiches and desserts; seek out the Edwardian Dutch bar in the basement. Meals can be pre-ordered for pre-performance or to gulp down in the interval. *Disabled: access; toilets. Group & family discount (0171 836 0111 ext 318). Shop (10am-7.30pm Mon-Sat).*

The Place
17 Duke's Road, WC1 (0171 387 0031). Euston tube/BR. **Open** *box office noon-6pm Mon-Sat.* **Tickets** *£4-£12.50.* **Credit** A, £TC, V.
Excellent sightlines, a large stage, occasionally superlative performances and cheap tickets combine to give The Place an edge over the more remote stages of the West End. Contemporary dance here ranges from exuberant athleticism and comic dance through to minimalist Eurocentric choreography and oriental works. Formerly famous for the London Contemporary Dance Theatre, The Place is currently home to a number of leading contemporary dance companies including Richard Alston Dance Company, Cholmondleys and Featherstones. London Contemporary Dance School is still here and continues to provide a hallmark of contemporary dance training. An active evening school provides a wide range of classes. The added presence of resource centres Dataplace and Videoplace makes The Place a hotbed of dance-related activity. The Turning World season showcases the best contemporary work from Europe. Also over the last five years The Place has presented Indian dance in Indian Summer and Vivarta. A foyer bar and home-cooked food in the café are also recommended. *Disabled: access.*

Riverside Studios
Crisp Road, W6 (0181 741 2255). Hammersmith tube. **Open** *box office noon-8pm daily.* **Tickets** *£7-£9.* **Credit** A, V.
Sadly the large performance spaces and intimate theatres of Riverside Studios have not been in use for dance in the last couple of years. Of the two performance spaces one has one of the largest stage areas in the country, making it an ideal venue. There are plans to return contemporary dance to the Riverside in 1996. It also intends to share in dance festivals such as Dance Umbrella, held in conjunction with The Place, South Bank Centre and Sadler's Wells. There's also an art gallery, cinema and bar/café. *Bar/café. Bookshop. Disabled: access. Restaurant.*

Royal Opera House
Covent Garden, WC2 (0171 240 1066/0171 304 4000). Covent Garden tube. **Open** *box office 10am-8pm Mon-Sat.* **Tickets** *£2-£130.* **Credit** A, AmEx, DC, V.
Opera and ballet are presented here on the grandest scale in the traditional horse-shoe-shaped theatre seating 2,000. It is the home of the Royal Ballet and the touring Birmingham Royal Ballet, formerly Sadler's Wells Ballet. It also plays host to the world's top ballet and opera companies. A programme of extensive refurbishment aims to renew the grandeur of

the ROH. This will also enable it to bring a number of activities of the Royal Ballet on to one site. Ticket prices have rocketed in recent years. However, 65 rear amphitheatre seats are sold from 10am on the day of the performance. Fifty standing places in the stalls circle are also sold on the day 90 minutes before curtain up. Getting standby tickets means queuing at the Floral Street box office from daybreak and tickets are limited to one per person.
Disabled: access; toilets. Opera and ballet education officers. Shop.

Sadler's Wells Theatre

Rosebery Avenue, EC1 (0171 278 8916). Angel tube. **Open** *box office* 10am-8pm Mon-Sat (till 6.30pm when no performance). **Tickets** £5-£35. **Credit** A, AmEx, DC, £TC, V.

Situated close to trendy Upper Street, the theatre is a magnet for excellent British and international ballet and dance companies. It holds up to 1,600 seats on three tiers and is the only theatre in London that presents contemporary as well as classical work on such a lavish scale. In 1995 Sadler's Wells has been visited by, among others, Les Ballets de Monte Carlo making their UK début, Paco Pena, Chitrasena Dance Ensemble from Sri Lanka and the Nederlands Dans Theater. The Turning World season of contemporary dance

is hosted here and at The Place. There are three bars and a café serving snacks before and after performances.
Restaurant. Disabled: access to main theatre; toilets.

South Bank Centre

South Bank, Belvedere Road, SE1 (box office 0171 928 8800/general information 0171 928 3002). Embankment tube/Waterloo tube/BR. **Open** *box office* 10am-9pm daily. **Tickets** £2.50-£30, some free events and children's events. **Credit** A, AmEx, DC, V.

Open-air festivals on the South Bank's balconies and terraces during the summer allow you to combine performance-watching with soaking up sunshine – both for free (the Great Outdoors and Ballroom Blitz festivals, for example). Inside there are three theatres to choose from. The **Royal Festival Hall** (RFH), seating 3,000 people, is the largest. It offers excellent viewing no matter where you sit. The English National Ballet presents two seasons a year here, during the summer and just after Christmas. The **Queen Elizabeth Hall** (QEH) holds 1,000 people and is designed like a lecture hall but with good sightlines. The **Purcell Room**, sharing foyer and bar with the QEH, seats 375 people. There is an extensive range of other facilities at the South Bank – galleries, meeting rooms, bookshop, poetry library, a number of bars and restaurants. The ballroom floor in the RFH foyer

Indian Dance

In the last few years there has been an explosion of Indian dance in London. All the classical dance styles – Bharatanatyam, Kathakali, Odissi, Kathak, Manipuri, Kuchipudi and Mohiniattyam – can be seen performed by touring artists from India as well as by those resident in Britain. And as time moves on, there's a greater tendency towards experimentation, drawing on other contemporary dance styles and rhythmical shapes, forms, movements and postures. Complex footwork, intricate hand gestures, expressive faces, transforming shapes and movements can be seen in different contexts, themes and costumes as never before.

While classical is continuing to flourish, innovation is being pushed to the limit, while retaining dignity and integrity. Companies range from the established Shobana Jeyasingh Dance Company to the small but exhilarating Bannerjee Sisters Maya Dance. An intriguing and interesting style of Indian dance can be seen in young British Asians whose language and vocabulary are yet to be clearly defined and are evolving all the time. Now is an exciting time for anyone interested in Indian dance, with choreographers' imaginations running wild, reflecting the richness of socio-cultural development in Britain.

In London, venues are beginning to reflect this tryst – classical and modern, traditional and contemporary Indian dance flourishing side by side – while the folk element has its place in Bhangra and Garba nights at social gatherings,

community centres, clubs and discos. So there is even an opportunity to participate for fun.

You can catch up with Indian dance at the Bhavan Centre, The Place Theatre, South Bank Centre, Watermans Arts Centre, Jacksons Lane, Old Bull Arts Centre, Tara Arts Centre, Paul Robeson Theatre, Tom Allen Arts Centre, Chisenhale Dance Space and Ravi Shankar Hall.

Different communities also have their own particular, graceful dances, for example the Bengali Dance Dramas of Tagore. These are frequently performed in community centres and at specially organised community functions. To attend, keep your eyes peeled for posters at venues or phone the London Boroughs Arts and Entertainment Sections.

Bannerjee Sisters Maya Dance Company.

is the venue for daily free events, usually bands or dance during festivals. These can be viewed from the raised bar, with seating all round the ballroom floor.
Car Park. Disabled: access; toilets. Free exhibitions. Front seats for the partially sighted by prior arrangement. Guided tours. Infra-red audio for the hard of hearing. Poetry library. Restaurants & cafés. Shops for books, music, records and gifts.

Other Venues

Albany Theatre
Douglas Way, SE8 (0181 692 4446). Deptford BR or New Cross tube/BR.
The Albany is a large round theatre where the emphasis is on contemporary Afro-Caribbean dance.

The Bhavan Centre
Old Church Building, Castletown Road, W14 (0171 381 3086). Barons Court or West Kensington tube.
The Institute operates as a forum for Indian classical dance and music as well as education and training in the culture.

Bloomsbury Theatre
15 Gordon Street, WC1 (0171 833 8822). Euston tube/BR.
Contemporary regional companies visit this theatre which is operated by London University.

Broadgate Arena
Corner of Liverpool Street and Eldon Street, EC2 (0171 588 6565). Liverpool Street tube/BR. **Performances** *May-Sept* 12.30-2pm Mon-Fri. **Tickets** free.
This outdoor site in the middle of the Broadgate complex becomes an amphitheatre during the summer. Used mainly as a music venue, it also presents some dance companies. The format includes free lunch-time performances.

Centrespace
Paul Robeson Theatre, Treaty Centre, High Street, Hounslow. Hounslow Central tube.
Centrespace presents a range of fringe dance works, with particular emphasis on south Asian dance.

Chats Palace
42-44 Brooksby's Walk, E9 (0181 986 6714). Homerton BR.
Chats Palace presents a monthly performance of Egyptian dance, *Rock the Pyramids*, by the Benat el Medina dance group (normally last Wednesday of the month, only £1).

Chisenhale Dance Space
64-84 Chisenhale Road, E3 (0181 981 6617). Bethnal Green or Mile End tube. **Open** *box office* 10am-6pm daily; *café* 6.30-8.30pm on performance evenings.
Chisenhale supports experimental dance, with programmes including performances, workshops, adults' and children's classes, residencies and commissions. In 1995 the East Winds Festival was the first festival in the UK devoted to Butoh, a radical dance art pioneered in late 1950s Japan now commanding a worldwide following.

Cochrane Theatre
Southampton Row, WC1 (0171 242 7040). Holborn tube.
The Cochrane Theatre hosts occasional dance performances, usually contemporary dance.

Drill Hall Arts Centre
16 Chenies Street, WC1 (0171 637 8270). Goodge Street tube.
The Drill Hall is a surprisingly large venue tucked away off the busy Tottenham Court Road and presenting an array of work often with a gay and lesbian emphasis.

Greenwich Dance Agency
The Borough Hall, Royal Hill, SE10 (0181 293 9741). Greenwich BR or Island Gardens DLR.
The Dance Agency is a fairly active outer London venue.

Hackney Empire
291 Mare Street, E8 (0181 985 2424). Bethnal Green tube or Hackney Central BR.
The Hackney Empire presents traditional variety, new variety, comedy, music and dance as well as children's shows.

Holland Park Theatre
Holland Park, Kensington High Street, W8 (0171 602 7856). Holland Park or High Street Kensington tube.
The Royal Ballet School performs every summer in the 600-seat open-air theatre.

Jackson's Lane Community Centre
269A Archway Road, N6 (0181 341 4421). Highgate tube.
Jackson's Lane presents performances, classes, jazz bands in the bar, and regular festivals of dance and music. Programming has recently been transformed, tending to select the best innovative contemporary dance. Look out for a season of experimental dance and music in autumn 1995.

Lilian Baylis Theatre
Arlington Way, EC1 (0171 713 6000). Angel tube.
Although managed by Sadler's Wells, the Lilian Baylis has developed a strong separate identity, presenting a range of contemporary new work. Look out for its Mosaics season.

Old Bull Arts Centre
68 High Street, Barnet, Herts (0181 449 0048). High Barnet tube.
The Old Bull presents a wide range of work from the classical to the contemporary, representing different cultures.

Ravi Shankar Hall
21 Hanway Place, WC1 (0171 323 0660/0171 580 3470). Tottenham Court Road tube.
Occasional classical Indian dance events are held here.

Studio Theatre
North Westminster School, North Wharf Road, W2 (0171 224 8421). Edgware Road tube.
This small theatre presents a range of events, from a summer festival of traditional dance to jazz and contemporary.

Tara Arts Centre
356 Garratt Lane, SW18 (0181 874 1458). Earlsfield BR.
This Asian arts centre provides an intimate venue.

Turtle Key Arts Centre
74 Farm Lane, SW6 (0171 385 4905). Fulham Broadway tube.
The emphasis at Turtle Key is on contemporary dance.

Union Chapel
Compton Avenue, N1 (0171 226 1686). Highbury & Islington tube/BR.
Occasional dance performances grace the Union Chapel's Studio Theatre.

Watermans Arts Centre
40 High Street, Brentford, Middlesex (0181 568 1176). Kew Bridge/Brentford BR.
Watermans is strong on Asian performing arts.

Yaa Asantewa Arts Centre
1 Chippenham Mews, W9 (0171 286 1656). Royal Oak or Westbourne Park tube.
The Yaa Asantewa puts on African and Caribbean dance.

Film

Tracking shot of boy and girl approaching a cinema, checking times and prices, having a last look at the movie poster, then, decided, striding in to buy another two hours' worth of dreams.

The big West End cinemas should be the best places to see major mainstream movies – they're certainly the most expensive – and in their main auditoria you may well get your money's worth in the shape of 70mm prints, giant screens and Dolby or THX sound. But most of them have been sub-divided, and their smaller screens can be small and cramped, with poor technical facilities. It pays to choose your cinema carefully: check *Time Out*.

The mainstream cinema scene is dominated by MGM and Odeon. Opportunities to see less run-of-the-mill fare have been diminished by the closures of the Parkway and the Plaza in Camden. Even so, London's circuit of art-house, independent and repertory movie houses still offers a wide choice. Expect to pay from about £6-£9 for an evening show in the West End. Most big cinemas have a complicated tangle of reduced prices at strange times if you fulfil various criteria – phone cinemas or check *Time Out*. Independent and Repertory cinemas are cheaper. Where advertised, late shows take place on Fridays and Saturdays. Many cinemas now charge extra for credit card bookings, so you often have to pay to reserve a specific seat.

Classifications: U – suitable for all ages; PG – parental guidance advised; 12 – no one under age 12; 15 – no one under 15; 18 – no one under 18.

The Majors

Barbican
Silk Street, EC2 (0171 638 8891). Barbican tube or Moorgate tube/BR. **Tickets** £6; £4 concs; £3 Mon. **Credit** A, AmEx, V.
In addition to the theatre and concert spaces – and the library, coffee bars, conservatory and waterside terrace – there are two well-equipped cinemas presenting a mixture of mainstream releases and subtitled films.
Advance booking. Car park. Cafés. Disabled: access; toilets. Restaurant. Shops.

Empire
Leicester Square, WC2 (0171 437 1234/credit card booking 0990 888990). Leicester Square tube. **Tickets** £8, £6.50. **Credit** A, AmEx, V.
There are few experiences to match sitting in the front row in the 1,000-seater Empire 1. Empires 2 and 3 are small.
Advance booking. Coffee bar. Late shows. Video bar.

MGM Haymarket
Haymarket, W1 (recorded information 0171 839 1527/credit card bookings 0181 970 6016). Piccadilly Circus tube. **Tickets** £6.50; £3.50 concs. **Credit** A, V.

Of the three screens here, only number one is big enough to do justice to Hollywood blockbusters. All the MGM cinemas offer reduced prices Mondays and before 6pm daily.
Late shows.

MGM Panton Street
Panton Street, SW1 (recorded information 0171 930 0631/credit card bookings 0181 970 6021). Piccadilly Circus tube. **Tickets** £6; £3.50 concs. **Credit** A, V.
An uncomfortable little four-screen used by MGM to show unusual, less profitable films considered a bit risky for their main houses. You'd be better off renting a video.

MGM Piccadilly
Piccadilly, W1 (0171 437 3561). Piccadilly Circus tube. No advance booking. **Tickets** £6; £3.50 concs. **No credit cards**.
Two screens with 150 seats each. Its late shows and gay programmes attract a loyal following.
Weekend late shows.

MGM Shaftesbury Avenue
135 Shaftesbury Avenue, W1 (0171 836 6279/credit card booking 0181 970 6013). Leicester Square or Tottenham Court Road tube. **Tickets** £6.50; £3.25 Mon. **Credit** A, V.
One of the best and most comfortable of the major MGMs, with two big screens showing a mix of Hollywood and European films. Recommended.
Advance booking.

MGM Swiss Centre
Swiss Centre, Leicester Square, WC2 (0171 439 4470). Leicester Square or Piccadilly Circus tube. **Tickets** £6; £3.50 concs. **Credit** A, V.
Small screens showing European art house movies.

MGM Trocadero
Trocadero, WC2 (0171 434 0031/credit card booking 0181 970 6015). Piccadilly Circus tube. **Tickets** £7; £4 concs. **Credit** A, V.
MGM's seven-screen flagship. Screen 1 is the biggest with 548 seats. Screens 6 and 7 are tiny.

MGM Tottenham Court Road
30 Tottenham Court Road, W1 (0171 636 6148/credit card booking 0181 970 6032). Tottenham Court Road tube. **Tickets** £6; £3.50 concs. **Credit** A, V.
Small, three-screener showing European and independent US and British films. It – and you – could do better.
Late shows.

Odeon Haymarket
Haymarket, W1 (01426 915353/credit card bookings 0171 839 7697). Piccadilly Circus tube. **Tickets** £8, £7, £6.50. **Credit** A, V.
Exclusive presentations of critically acclaimed films, mostly Hollywood. Reduced prices are available before 5pm. The screen is big, the technical facilities good.
Advance booking.

On Location

Nicholas Royle on London through the lens.

The montage of sights – Buckingham Palace, Piccadilly Circus, Nelson's Column, Big Ben's clock tower – has been used many times to signify that the action is moving to London. In American films and British regional movies, this stream of library pictures and postcard images instills a degree of recognition, a sense of familiarity – you may not live there, but you feel as if you do. But for those of us who do live in the capital, our sense of being an insider is only enhanced when the location shots are taken off the beaten track – and we recognise them.

1. High Hopes

The lugubrious Mike Leigh's hilarious clash of cultures was played out against the instantly recognisable span of the St Pancras train shed and the black and red King's Cross gasholders. Leigh has his leading couple living in the doomed, scruffy splendour of the Battle Bridge Road/Stanley Buildings community. Much-loved London landmarks, the gasholders are due to be dismantled to allow the construction of the international terminal at King's Cross and then re-erected if their old iron can take the strain.

2. The Tall Guy

When Emma Thompson gets up a ladder with Jeff Goldblum to deface the posters for Ron Anderson's (Rowan Atkinson's) show, it's the walls of the Shaftesbury Theatre they're scaling. Thompson's nurse works at the Royal Free Hospital in Hampstead and it's outside that very establishment that they meet for their first date. Goldblum later turns silhouette cartwheels over the top of Primrose Hill. Who wouldn't?

3. Truly, Madly, Deeply

Another film that uses its London locations ingenuously and which, to the despair of mis-

anthropes, wears its heart on its sleeve. Juliet Stevenson's widow wanders distressed over the Archway Bridge, known locally as Suicide Bridge, from which the view of London is unmistakable to anyone who has ever taken the same route. (Some of the streets she walks are in fact Bristol's, not Highgate's, but thanks to a sensitive location scout there's no awareness of this until the credits roll.) Later, on the South Bank,

she meets Michael Moloney, whose chat-and-hop routine had some cinema viewers reaching for the mental remote control.

4. Performance

First port of call for Nicolas Roeg completists when they come to London is the big white house at 81 Powis Square – it was for me, anyway. I

longed to ring the doorbell and for it to be answered by Anita Pallenberg wearing a fur coat and a smile. Roeg and Donald Cammell's 1970 psychedelic masquerade will for ever imbue that corner of W11 with a tangy, mushroomy flavour.

5. Radio On

Christopher Petit's first feature – a grim, plot-free road movie that found in the Westway a stretch of macadam worthy of the genre – created a fusion of rock/electronic/new wave music and oneiric monochrome to enhance the ambiguous qualities of its locations. The cheerless protagonist parks his old Rover at Gillette Corner off the Great West Road, Hounslow; he heads west out of town on the M4 past the

Agfa building at Brentford listening to David Bowie's 'Always Crashing In The Same Car'.

6. Hellraiser

The antithesis of *Truly, Madly, Deeply*, Clive Barker's first movie as director – an ambitious and in parts brilliantly successful film that will never let you hear again the words 'Jesus wept' without picturing *that* scene – was filmed in an empty house high on a leafy Dollis Hill avenue. Yet when Andy Robinson and family move in, they're treated to removal men whose transatlantic overdubs are (a) crap and (b) a million miles from synchronisation. And come the climactic conflagration, we seem to be standing not on Dollis Hill, but on some desolate docklands plain ten miles away.

7. Edge of Darkness

This one's cheating because it was made for TV, but it's so good and it's been shown at the National Film Theatre. When Bob Peck's Ronnie Craven comes to London to investigate his daughter's death he's dropped off outside the Kensington Hilton and is later abandoned outside BBC Television Centre because his host has to escort the Prime Minister. At an early morning meeting Ronnie is filmed with a long shot through a group of Americans playing softball in Regent's Park.

8. Blow Up

If you see *Blow Up* shortly after you move to London, as I did, you long to know in which park David Hemmings takes his photographs of the supposed murder, so you can trek out there and assume the POV (or you do if you've nothing better to do – 'sad' is the fashionable word for this kind of behaviour). It's like when Michael Caine finally escapes from his 'Albanian' captors in *The Ipcress File* and finds he's not in Tirana but somewhere in London. Where though? South or north? It matters, it's important. Later you discover that for *Blow Up*, Antonioni shot Hemmings shooting someone shooting someone else (if there was a shooting at all) in Maryon Park, Woolwich. It's a long way to go to see some grass.

9. The Passenger

Antonioni again. An early scene has Maria Schneider sitting on a bench in the Brunswick Centre, WC1 while Jack Nicholson descends a flight of concrete steps. The steps have now been blocked off, but not before I press-ganged

a couple of friends into re-enacting the scene for my own scrap of ersatz movie history.

10. Mona Lisa

Someone on set went overboard on King's Cross. 'Make it like that scene in *The Year of Living Dangerously*,' they must have said. 'The one where all the prostitutes come pawing at the car window.' I'm sorry, but there just aren't that many tarts in King's Cross, nor were there in the mid-1980s when it was shot. I know, I lived there. That aside, the film takes its locations seriously, from Simone's (Cathy Tyson's) assignations in the Park Lane Hotel to her flat in Trinity Court, an art deco block on Gray's Inn Road. And she doesn't even have Bob Hoskins drop her off outside the real Trinity Court before walking on to a set in Pinewood – when he accompanies her into the building and is attacked, the fight takes place in and around the staircase and elevator shaft of Trinity Court. Even when you think an error has been made – when Bob turns left off Victoria Embankment and takes his beautiful 3.4 litre Jag south over Westminster Bridge following Simone's request to be taken home – you soon realise it really would be quicker to cross the River, nip up York Road, back over Waterloo Bridge and up Kingsway than go round Parliament Square, back up Whitehall and fight his way round Trafalgar Square. Good old Bob.

Every film in London, every week.

London has more cinemas than Hollywood. Every week there are over 200 films to choose from. How will you find your way through the celluloid maze?

Every film in London, every week.

London has more cinemas than Hollywood. Every week there are over 200 films to choose from. How will you find your way through the celluloid maze?

Odeon Kensington

*High Street Kensington, W8 (01426 915353/credit card
bookings 0171 371 3166). High Street Kensington
underground.* **Tickets** £6.60, £6. **Credit** A, V.
Hollywood hits are the order of the day.
*Advance booking. Disabled: access to Screens 2, 3 and 4.
Late shows.*

Odeon Leicester Square

*Leicester Square, WC2 (01426 915683/credit card
bookings 0171 930 3232). Leicester Square or Piccadilly
Circus tube.* **Tickets** £9, £8, £7. **Credit** A, AmEx, V.
The biggest cinema in London (but not the biggest screen,
which is at the Odeon Marble Arch), and still the prestige
venue for the British premières of major new Hollywood
productions. Technical presentation is excellent.
Advance booking. Disabled: access; toilets. Late shows.

Odeon Marble Arch

*10 Edgware Road, W2 (01426 914501/credit card
bookings 0171 723 2011). Marble Arch tube.* **Tickets**
£8, £7, £6. **Credit** A, V.
London's biggest screen. Definitely a front-row experience.
Advance booking. Late shows.

Plaza

*17-25 Lower Regent Street, SW1 (0171 437 1234/credit
card bookings 0800 888997). Piccadilly Circus tube.*
Tickets £6.50. **Credit** A, AmEx, DC, V.
Comfortable four-screener showing new mainstream movies.
Beware the fact that the so-called circle in screen 1 is not a
circle at all – it's basically the rear stalls with a bit of a rake.
Advance booking. Late shows.

UCI Whiteleys 8 Cinema

*Second Floor, Whiteleys of Bayswater, Queensway, W2
(box office 0171 792 3303/credit card bookings 0800
888907). Bayswater or Queensway tube.* **Tickets** £5.75.
Credit A, V.
London's first multiplex cinema, with eight screens, sticks
to a solid diet of new commercial releases with no surprises.
Only screens 1 and 2 are large. Reduced prices before 3pm.
Advance booking. Disabled: access; toilets.

Warner West End

*Leicester Square, WC2 (recorded information 0171 437
3484/credit card bookings 0171 437 4343). Leicester
Square tube.* **Tickets** £7.50; £4 concs. **Credit** A, EC,
£TC, V.
Sound and vision only impress in the 400-seater screen 5.
There are eight more screens, all showing new Hollywood
releases. Reduced prices are available before 6pm Monday
to Friday. Larger and in no way recommended is Warner's
ten-screen multiplex in Acton, west London.
Advance booking. Disabled: access.

Independents

Chelsea Cinema

*206 King's Road, SW3 (0171 351 3742). Sloane Square
tube.* **Tickets** £7, £6; £4 first show daily. **Credit** A, V.
Lots of foreign-language and art-house movies are shown in
this smart, classy cinema.
Advance booking.

Curzon Mayfair

*38 Curzon Street, W1 (0171 465 8865/advance booking
0171 369 1720). Green Park tube.* **Tickets** £7, £6.
Credit A, AmEx, V.
Curzon cinemas are the best places to find Merchant/Ivory
releases and prestige French and international movies. Their
flagship house is in a posh area, with prices to match, but
you're also paying for comfort.

Branches: Curzon Phoenix 110 Charing Cross Road,
WC2 (0171 369 1721); **Curzon West End** Shaftesbury
Avenue, W1 (0171 369 1722).
Advance booking.

Gate Cinema

*87 Notting Hill Gate, W11 (0171 727 4043). Notting Hill
Gate tube.* **Tickets** £6; £3.50 concs before 6pm Mon-Fri
& late shows. *Sun matinées £4; £3 concs.*
This likable cinema has a good mix of art-house, classic and
cultish programmes. If you arrive early you can always go
and browse in **Waterstone's** a few doors down, or **Music
& Video Exchange** across the road.
Advance booking. Disabled: access. Weekend late shows.

Lumière

*42 St Martin's Lane, WC2 (0171 836 0691). Leicester
Square tube.* **Tickets** £7.50, £6.50; £5 first show daily;
£3 concs first show daily. **Credit** A, AmEx, £TC, V.
One of the country's finest, best-equipped cinemas with a
beautiful auditorium. Major new art-house releases.
Advance booking. Late shows. Disabled: access.

Metro

*11 Rupert Street, W1 (recorded message 0171 437
0757/box office 0171 734 1506). Leicester Square or
Piccadilly Circus tube.* **Tickets** £6; £4 first show Mon-Fri
concs. **Credit** A, EC, V.
Two-screen (screen 2 only 86 seats) cinema, showing new
indie releases, with artworks on display around the bar. Far
too indulgent to Hal Hartley – they should install reclining
seats for his next release, so we can all get some proper sleep.
Advance booking.

Minema

*45 Knightsbridge, SW1 (0171 235 4225). Hyde Park
Corner tube.* **Tickets** £6.50. **Credit** A, V.
Tiny but gorgeous independent showing high-quality inter-
national films. Reduced prices for afternoon shows.
Advance booking.

Notting Hill Coronet

*Notting Hill Gate, W11 (0171 727 6705). Notting Hill
tube.* **Tickets** £5.75; £2.75 concs. **Credit** A, V.
This shabby, nicotine-stained old place is one of the last two
smoking cinemas in London (the other is the Turnpike Lane
Coronet, which we recommend – for demolition).

Renoir

*Brunswick Centre, Brunswick Square, WC1 (0171 837
8402). Russell Square tube.* **Tickets** £6. **Credit** A,
AmEx, V.
Mainly subtitled films at this excellent two-screener beneath
the Brunswick Centre.
Advance booking.

The Ritzy

Brixton Oval, SW2 (0171 737 2121). Brixton tube/BR.
Tickets tbc. **Credit** tbc.
Due to have re-opened, following redevelopment, in September 1995. The restoration, under the auspices of English
Heritage, was to have retained the main theatre while adding
four more screens, plus a bar and café. The programming
will feature art house, US, European and British independent
movies and should still incorporate a repertory element.
Late shows.

Screen on Baker Street

*96 Baker Street, NW1 (0171 935 2772). Baker Street
tube.* **Tickets** £5. **Credit** A, V.
The smallest of this three-cinema chain. A mix of quality
Hollywood and international cinema. Prices are reduced at
all Screens on Mondays and for the first show each day.
Advance booking. Late shows.

Screen on the Green
83 Upper Street, N1 (0171 226 3520). Angel tube.
Tickets £5. **Credit** A, V.
This single-screen cinema is great for a night out in Islington, often showing the best of the latest US releases. The Bookshop Islington Green is just up the road, the Slug & Lettuce pub just *across* the road and **Pizza Express** the other side of the Green itself.
Advance booking. Weekend late shows.

Screen on the Hill
203 Haverstock Hill, NW3 (0171 435 3366). Belsize Park tube. **Tickets** £5.50. **Credit** A, V.
Another in the excellent chain, showing a mix of commercial and art-house releases. Booking often advisable. The late shows here are worth staying up for.
Advance booking. Disabled: access. Late shows.

Repertory

Repertory programmes change frequently. Some of these cinemas are clubs, with cheap, instant membership available on the door.

Electric Cinema
191 Portobello Road, W11 (0171 792 2020). Notting Hill Gate tube. **Tickets** £6. **Credit** A, V.
The oldest purpose-built cinema in London. Programmes now often feature new releases plus revivals.

Everyman
Hollybush Vale, NW3 (0171 435 1525). Hampstead tube. **Tickets** £5, £4.50. **No credit cards.**
London's longest-established repertory cinema offers good food, friendly staff and two films every day. Art-house staples and Hollywood classics are offered. If anything could be improved, it's the seating, which is a little on the desperately uncomfortable side.
Café. Disabled: access; toilets.

French Institute
17 Queensberry Place, SW7 (0171 589 6211). South Kensington tube. **Tickets** £4, £3. **No credit cards.**
Classic and contemporary French cinema.

Goethe Institute
50 Princes Gate, Exhibition Road, SW7 (0171 411 3400). South Kensington tube. **Tickets** £2. **No credit cards.**
Milestones of German cinema (often without subtitles).
Personal & postal bookings only.

ICA Cinema
Nash House, The Mall, SW1 (0171 930 3647). Piccadilly Circus tube. **Tickets** £6.50 (incl day membership); £5 members, concs, Mon, first show Tue-Fri. **Membership** £25 per year; £15 per year concs; £1.50 per day; £1 per day concs. **Credit** A, AmEx, DC, £TC, V.
Films too obscure for other houses as well as more standard art house fare. Day membership also allows you to visit the exhibitions and café.
Advance booking. Bar. Bookshop. Café. Group discount. Lectures. Workshops.

ICA Cinémathèque
Nash House, The Mall, SW1 (0171 930 3647). Piccadilly Circus tube. **Membership** £25 per year; £1.50 per day; £1 per day concs. **Tickets** £4 (incl day membership). **Credit** A, AmEx, DC, £TC, V.
Seasons of directors' work, together with avant garde work, short films and animated features.
Advance booking. Bar. Bookshop. Café. Group discount. Lectures. Workshops.

NFT – *no better place to see a film in the UK.*

National Film Theatre (NFT)
South Bank, SE1 (0171 928 3232). Waterloo tube/BR.
Tickets £4.35 non-members; £3.95 members.
Membership £11.95 per year; £8 concs. **Credit** A, AmEx, £TC, V.
One of the few cinemas in London where you get the feeling people have made a conscious decision to see a particular film rather than whatever happens to be on. A thoroughly recommended cinema experience. We can't say the same for the bar since it was refurbished and the floor-level seating and tables removed. But you can't go wrong if you take your drinks and sit outside overlooking the River.
Advance booking. Bar, café and restaurant. Disabled: access; toilets.

Phoenix
52 High Road, N2 (0181 444 6789/recorded information 0181 883 2233). East Finchley tube. **Tickets** £5, £4.50.
No credit cards.
Lovely old local cinema with a mixed programme.
Advance booking. Disabled: access by prior arrangement.

Prince Charles
Leicester Place, WC2 (0171 437 8181). Piccadilly Circus or Leicester Square tube. **Tickets** £2. **No credit cards.**
Big screen, daily changing rep programme, cheap seats.
Late shows.

Rio
107 Kingsland High Street, E8 (0171 249 2722/recorded information 0171 254 6677). Dalston Kingsland BR/67, 76, 149, 243 bus. **Tickets** £4.50; £3.50 concs. *Children's cinema club* £1.50 (£2.50 adults). **No credit cards.**
Charming old theatre. Everything from acclaimed European films to cult American pictures is shown as double-bills here.
Disabled: access; toilets. Late shows.

Riverside Studios
Crisp Road, W6 (0181 741 2255). Hammersmith tube. **Tickets** £4.50; £4.50 concs. **Credit** A, V.
A great mix of British films, art house favourites and cinema classics in a very pleasant environment. Good screen.
Advance booking. Bar. Bookshop. Café. Disabled: access. Restaurant

Festivals

London Film Festival
(Information 0171 815 1323). **Dates** November.
Hundreds of new films both at the **NFT** and an increasing number of cinemas around the West End. The emphasis is on reflecting the full range of world cinema. Major productions are usually booked up weeks in advance. For other films it can be surprisingly easy to pick up tickets.

Music: Classical & Opera

Home to some of the world's greatest orchestras, London is also blessed with an abundance of the finest classical venues.

On almost any night of the year, more classical music is performed in London than in any other capital – in concert halls, recital venues, churches and music colleges – yet London barely has the audience to fill them all. It's quite embarrassing some nights how many great musicians and international soloists are prepared to come and entertain, compared to the numbers of people who are prepared to leave their homes and listen. London doesn't always deserve the music it gets.

At present there are four international symphony orchestras, one BBC orchestra, four chamber orchestras, two period instrument ensembles and an indeterminate number of ad hoc groups, all based in London and vying to keep themselves in work. The **Royal Philharmonic Orchestra** (founded by Sir Thomas Beecham in 1946) is the only one of the big four which generates most of its own income through ticket sales and recording contracts. This can work to its detriment as it means that more time is spent in the recording studio and less in rehearsal. Nonetheless, after trying times in the early 1990s when the reputation of the orchestra plummeted, the RPO has taken on a new management team and fought back to its old illustrious position. The young tyro conductor Daniele Gatti is replacing Vladimir Ashkenazy as music director.

The **London Symphony Orchestra** was the first London orchestra to have a permanent home when it moved into the **Barbican** in 1982. The LSO is also the oldest of the capital's orchestras (founded 1904) and currently revels in its reputation as the country's best. It is also reputedly the most recorded orchestra in the world; there's a steely quality and a bright edge to their playing. New principal conductor Colin Davis took up his position in September 1995.

The **London Philharmonic Orchestra**, resident at the **South Bank Centre**, is going through something of a rough patch at the moment. Its talented principal conductor Franz Welser Most has never really found his feet either with them or with London, and although he's due to leave in 1996 for an opera post in Zürich, no replacement for him has yet been named.

The **Philharmonia** is London's only orchestra without a home, although it maintains a successful annual summer residency at the Théâtre du Châtelet in Paris. Their attitude to life, like their playing, is soft, warm and modest. They have a tendency to creep up and surprise audiences. They are probably the busiest orchestra in the country, if not the world, with recording and concert commitments on every continent. The list of principal and guest conductors includes some of the greatest names of the century in Karajan, Klemperer and Muti.

The **BBC Symphony Orchestra**, under principal conductor Andrew Davis, has a huge and well-deserved international reputation but really comes to the fore during the Proms. The **BBC Concert Orchestra**, the **London Concert Orchestra** and the **London Festival Orchestra** tend to rely on Vivaldi for income but do frequently make forays into uncharted modernist exercises when necessary.

John Eliot Gardiner's **Orchestra of Enlightenment** and the **New Queen's Hall Orchestra** are the principal period instrument ensembles. The

Michael Nyman's film scores introduced a new generation to classical music.

English Chamber Orchestra, the **Academy of St Martin-in-the-Fields** and the **London Mozart Players** are the leading chamber groups, and Richard Hickox's delightful **City of London Sinfonia** is as committed an orchestra to the new and untried as any.

London's choirs rank among the best in the world. The boys' choirs at **St Paul's Cathedral**, **Westminster Abbey** and **Westminster Cathedral** astound everyone the first time they hear them. Such small individuals; such mature noises. The Monteverdi Choir, Gothic Voices and The Sixteen are the professional bodies where they end

up when they become adults who have stayed on in music. The splendid Bach Choir and the Royal Choral Society are the enthusiastic amateur ensembles where they end up if they haven't.

Major Venues

Barbican Centre

Silk Street, EC2 (0171 638 8891). Barbican tube or Moorgate tube/BR. **Open** *box office* 9am-8pm daily. **Tickets** £6-£30. **Credit** A, AmEx, V.

This grim cultural stalag was the City's gift to London's arts world. And London never stops grumbling about it. The Barbican concert hall is home to the London Symphony

*Part of the **South Bank Centre**, the Royal Festival Hall is perfect for symphony concerts.*

Orchestra and the English Chamber Orchestra – though both bodies hop across the river to the **South Bank** (*see below*), for large-scale choral and orchestral works that the Barbican's designers neglected to plan for. Despite the whining, the Barbican is well worth checking out, as it maintains an excellent standard of music festivals and theme cycles, and, better still, you can now find the entrance. The erection of the seven gold muses above the porch in 1995 and the hanging of tiny waving, glinting mirrors on the underside of the entrance canopy have at last given the Barbican Centre a front door that looks like one.
Car Park. Disabled: access; toilets. Restaurant & cafés. Shops.

The London Coliseum

St Martin's Lane, WC2 (box office 0171 632 8300/booking for disabled patrons 0171 836 7666). Leicester Square tube or Charing Cross tube/BR. **Open** *box office* 10am-8pm Mon-Sat. **Tickets** £5-£50; *day tickets* available from 10am each day to personal callers: 100 balcony seats, £5; 46 dress circle seats (weekdays only), £25. **Credit** A, AmEx, DC, £TC, V.
The largest auditorium in London (2,500 seats) has in its time been a cinema, variety house, theatre and freak show venue where the great 7ft 11in Fräulein Brunnhilde, the tallest pianist in the world, made her name. Since 1968 it has been an opera house and home of English National Opera (ENO), a company which hires home-grown talent and always sings in the vernacular. This practice was a way of making sense of foreign opera to people who, unlike the Covent Garden crowds, made no pretence at understanding other languages. However, now the Royal Opera has stolen a march on ENO by introducing sur-titles, and the current debate is whether ENO will do the same. ENO productions range through the repertoire, from Monteverdi to the moderns, but above all, they exist as theatre – sometimes controversial, sometimes outrageous, sometimes a brilliantly successful gamble. The nearby Coliseum shop has an excellent selection of records, videos, libretti, books and magazines.
Disabled: access; toilets. Group & family discount (0171 836 0111 ext 318). Shop (10am-7.30pm Mon-Sat).

Royal Albert Hall

Kensington Gore, SW7 (information 0171 589 3203/box office 0171 589 8212). High Street Kensington or Knightsbridge tube. **Open** *box office* 9am-9pm daily. **Tickets** £3.50-£30. **Credit** A, AmEx, V.
The Royal Albert Hall is the major host of the best music festival in the world, the BBC Henry Wood Promenade Concerts. The Proms run from mid-July to mid-September and include a variety of orchestras, ensembles and performers from all over the world; tickets are at subsidised prices. The hall is rich in atmosphere and has been a well-loved venue for over a century. It has had acoustical problems but there have been improvements in recent times. The old place comes into its own with massed choirs and big orchestral forces. The 'Kensington Bowl', as Proms audiences have fondly dubbed it, won a clutch of 'best venue' awards in 1994 and the refurbishment and general updating are not even finished yet. It is now the home to the Royal Philharmonic Orchestra under new music director Daniele Gatti in a move designed to encourage audiences away from the **Barbican** and **South Bank**. There's nearly always a queue for the 1,600 prom tickets on sale each evening.
Disabled: access by prior arrrangement; toilet. Guided tours (May-Oct). Induction loops for the hard of hearing.

Royal Opera House

Covent Garden, WC2 (0171 304 4000). Covent Garden tube. **Open** *box office* 10am-8pm Mon-Sat. **Tickets** £2-£130; *day tickets* 65 rear amphitheatre seats for sale on day of performance from 10am, £12.50-£29.50 (one per person). **Credit** A, AmEx, DC, £TC, V.
The Royal Opera House is London's answer to La Scala, the

Met, the Bastille and the Vienna Staatsoper. Government cuts have meant that seat prices have risen to levels previously unheard of, and the Royal Opera has painted itself into a Thatcherite corner by its emphasis on private funding, sponsorship and business support. There are signs that the Royal Opera House has taken criticisms to heart and is struggling to be more accessible, but prices are still out of reach for the average music lover. Audiences, including the block-booked businessmen who off-set the exorbitant prices against tax, pay as much as £134 a seat in the Grand Tier (only they know whether it is worth it or not); the impecunious queue patiently for a seat in the gods at £12.50 (definitely worth it).
Disabled: access; toilets. Opera and ballet education officers. Shop.

St James's Church

Piccadilly, W1 (0171 734 4511/booking 0171 437 5053). Piccadilly Circus tube. **Admission** lunchtime free, donation of £2 appreciated; festivals £5-£15; tickets available at the door one hour before performance starts. **Credit** A, V.
The shady Indian Bean tree in the courtyard advises visitors that to touch its bark is to contact Mother Earth. Sir Christopher Wren's Piccadilly masterpiece is a wholesome, beautiful, slightly cranky church with lunchtime recitals from Wednesday to Friday each week, and concerts are combined with such activities as talks, discussions and a health and healing centre. The Lufthansa Festival (a regular summer event) yields a feast of baroque music which attracts some of the best international performers of early music (information *0181 241 5513*/box office *0171 437 5053*). The RTZ Festival of Young Musicians takes place in St James's Church during October.
Craft market. Gardens. Restaurant (vegetarian).

St John's Smith Square

Smith Square, SW1 (0171 222 1061). Westminster tube. **Open** 10am-5pm Mon-Fri; till start of concert on concert nights. **Tickets** £5-£15. **Credit** A, £TC, V.
The new £800,000 Johannes Klais organ has made St John's an even more impressive venue, even if audiences do have to listen to it with their backs turned. Otherwise, chamber orchestras and choirs come across best in this converted church. Christmas and Easter programmes always tend to be strong here. BBC lunchtime concerts provide a frequent bargain (Mondays at 1pm).
Restaurant.

South Bank Centre

South Bank, Belvedere Road, SE1 (box office 0171 928 8800/recorded information 0171 633 0932). Waterloo tube/BR. **Open** *box office* 10am-9pm daily. **Tickets** £5-£50. **Credit** A, AmEx, DC, V.
The South Bank Centre consists of three concert halls: the daddy-sized **Royal Festival Hall** for symphony concerts and amplified events with large popular appeal; the mummy-sized **Queen Elizabeth Hall** for chamber orchestras and concerts which attract smaller audiences; and the baby-sized **Purcell Room** for solo recitals and debut concerts. The South Bank Arts Centre has come to emphasise the 'theme' series as a way of beating the jaded palates of the musically over-fed. The centre is also the home of Opera Factory, whose abrasive productions under director David Freeman frequently shock, jolt and even – as with their *dolce vita* beach-bum version of *Così fan tutte* – prove a revelation. The complex has a more friendly, welcoming atmosphere than most international venues with its restaurants and bars, its bookshops, record stalls and art galleries.
Car park. Disabled: front seats for the partially sighted by prior arrangement; infra-red audio for the hard of hearing; wheelchair access; toilets. Free exhibitions. Poetry Library. Restaurants & cafés. Shops for books, music and records.

World Series

Amsterdam Berlin Madrid New York Prague Rome

New editions in September 1995

London & Paris

New titles in February 1996

Budapest & San Francisco

Wigmore Hall

36 Wigmore Street, W1 (0171 935 2141). Bond Street tube. **Open** *box office* 10am-8.30pm Mon-Sat; *Dec-Mar* 10.30am-1pm, 3.15-5.30pm, Sun; *Apr-Oct* 10.30am-1pm, 6.15-8.30pm, Sun. **Performances** 7.30pm Mon-Sat; *Dec-Mar* 11.30am, 4pm, Sun; *Apr-Oct* 11.30am, 7pm, Sun. **Tickets** £6-£30. **Credit** A, AmEx, DC, JCB, £TC, V.

The perfect concert hall. Acoustically it is unbeatable, wherever you sit. Since its recent refurbishment, it is also one of the most comfortable and well-equipped. The hall is a favourite location for recitals and chamber music and offers the most civilised pastime for Sunday morning in its mid-morning concerts which include coffee or sherry. There is an old-fashioned, unhurried atmosphere that suggests management untainted by the late-twentieth-century need to sell, sell, sell. With just one concert a night, there is no danger that the staff will have to share their priorities and indeed there is every indication that the music is what is treasured above all. Prices are reasonable, but popular concerts sell out fast. *Café/bar (open 11.30am-one hour after performance, 5.30pm-one hour after performance, Sat). Disabled: access. Restaurant (open noon-3pm, 5.30-8pm, Mon-Fri; 5.30-8pm Sat; noon-4pm Sun).*

Open-air Venues

It is supposed to rain. Summer outdoor concerts in London just would not be the same without the communal blankets, courtesy plastic macs and curtailed performances by international stars. At all of the following places, you can take a picnic and spread out a blanket. Weatherline (*0839 500951*) warns of imminent storms.

City of London Festival

Venues in and around the City (festival box office 0171 638 8891/information 0171 377 0540).
An international line-up of soloists, string quartets, orchestras and choirs give concerts in City churches, **Livery Halls**, **Guildhall**, **St Paul's Cathedral**, the **Barbican** and other venues all over the Square Mile. Ring the box office for a free brochure listing the events.

Holland Park Theatre

Holland Park, Kensington High Street, W8 (box office 0171 602 7856/information 0171 603 1123). High Street Kensington tube. **Performances** 7.30pm or 8pm, June-Aug. **Tickets** £12-£18. **Credit** A, AmEx, £TC, V.
The Holland Park Theatre cheats as it has a canopy over both stage and audience. It's also a spectacular venue for regular opera concerts: the gardens are inhabited by peacocks and the Jacobean house is one of the finest in London. *Disabled: access; toilets.*

Kenwood Lakeside Concerts

Kenwood House, Hampstead Lane, NW3 (information 0171 973 3427/advance booking from Ticketmaster 0171 413 1443). Archway or Golders Green tube, then 210 bus/East Finchley tube, then courtesy bus on concert nights. **Tickets** £5.50-£13.50; *day tickets box office on site from 2pm on the day.* **Credit** A, AmEx, DC, V.
Every Saturday (7.30pm) throughout the summer (10 June to 9 September), different orchestras perform concerts of safe, popular classics while picnickers across the lake lie in the grass or dream in deckchairs and know they have never had a lovelier evening. Firework displays usually terminate the evening. Tickets are sold for the lakeside enclosure, but prices have rocketed in the past few years. However, you can have a pleasant evening, and still hear the music, if you sit on the grassy slopes just outside the barrier. *Disabled: access.*

Marble Hill Concerts

Marble Hill Park, Richmond Road, Twickenham. (information 0171 973 3427/bookings through Ticketmaster 0171 413 1443). Richmond tube/BR, then 33, 90, 290, H22, R70 bus. **Tickets** £8-£13; *day tickets available on the two hours before the concert begins.* **Credit** A, AmEx, DC, V.
On summer Sunday evenings at 7.30pm the public sit outside in the beautiful Marble Hill Park on the riverside near Richmond and attend concerts of favourite works by major orchestras in white tuxedos and summery evening gowns. The dates for the summer are normally in July-August; all the concerts end with fireworks (with the exception of the Glenn Miller evening).

BOC Covent Garden Festival

Venues in and around Covent Garden, WC2 (Box office 0171 312 1990/information 0181 944 9467). **Tickets** £7-£30. **Credit** A, AmEx, V.
The Covent Garden festival kicks off in mid-May, a musical extravaganza of opera and the arts with the accent on new performers. Venues are provided by the Freemasons' Hall and the majesty of **St Paul's Cathedral**. Previous highlights have included Gilbert and Sullivan's *Trial by Jury* in Bow Street Magistrates' Court, a fringe festival boasting Tibetan Monks and Poets from the Underground and a festival stage behind **St Pauls** giving free weekend concerts from opera to gospel choirs.

Hampton Court Palace Festival

Hampton Court, East Molesey, Surrey (festival box office 0171 344 4444). East Molesey BR. **Tickets** £25-£100. **Credit** A, AmEx, V.
The gravel crunches, stilettos spear the grass and security men apologise for having to search you. But this is a splendid open-air festival in the first courtyard of the Tudor Palace. Be warned: tickets are about £100 each.

Spitalfields Festival

Christchurch Spitalfields, Commercial Street, E1 (festival office 0171 377 0287/box office 0171 377 1362). Liverpool Street tube/BR, Aldgate or Aldgate East tube/67 bus. **Tickets** £5-£25.
Chamber music and early and contemporary music concerts are featured in this popular annual festival in Nicholas Hawksmoor's impressive East End church (*see also chapter* **Sightseeing: Cathedrals & Churches**). The pick of the concerts are relayed live to overflow audiences gathered in **Spitalfields Market** across the road. *Disabled: access.*

Lunchtime Concerts

Most of the City churches give up their premises to lunchtime concerts once or twice a week.

St Anne and St Agnes

Gresham Street, EC2 (0171 373 5566). St Paul's tube.
St Anne and St Agnes not only puts on lunchtime concerts (starting at 1.10pm Mon and occasional Fri) but has performances of liturgical music in the church services. As a Lutheran church it excels in the music of Bach, performed as part of the Sunday service as originally intended. *Disabled: access with assistance.*

St Bride's

Fleet Street, EC4 (0171 353 1301). Blackfriars tube/BR.
Lunchtime concerts are held in St Bride's, also known as the Journalists' church, on Tuesday, Wednesday and Friday, beginning at 1.15pm and lasting for 35 minutes. They feature either professional musicians or senior students. They stop during August, Advent and Lent. *Disabled: access to ground floor only.*

St Lawrence Jewry
Guildhall, EC2 (0171 600 9478). Bank or St Paul's tube.
A handsome Wren church (1678) which has a rather unusual Mander organ salvaged from the Blitz. Lunchtime piano recitals are held on Mondays, and organ recitals on Tuesdays, both starting at 1pm. During August, there's a lunchtime festival, with a concert every weekday.
Disabled: access with assistance.

St Margaret Lothbury
EC2 (0171 606 8330). Bank tube.
Adjacent to the Bank of England, the church functions as a lunchtime church for Christians of all persuasions working in the City (there must be a few at large in the temples of Mammon), and it contains a recently restored English pipe organ of 1801, one of the finest in London. The Lothbury Singers give concerts here, and elsewhere, and organ recitals (1.10pm Thur) feature guest organists from all over Europe.

St Martin-in-the-Fields
Trafalgar Square, WC2 (0171 930 0089). Leicester Square tube or Charing Cross tube/BR.
Young artists give lunchtime recitals on Mondays, Tuesdays, Wednesdays and Fridays (1.05-2pm, donations welcome), and there are evening concerts on Thursdays, Fridays and Saturdays (tickets £6-£15).
Bookshop. Café. Disabled: access; toilets.

St Martin-within-Ludgate
Ludgate Hill, EC4 (0171 248 6054). St Paul's tube or Blackfriars tube/BR.
A striking Wren church (1684) with a magnificent spire. Recitals are given on Wednesday lunchtimes at 1.15pm, and cover a wide spectrum, from classical to Palm Court.

St Mary-le-Bow Church
Cheapside, EC2 (0171 248 5139). St Paul's tube.
This beautiful church provides a sympathetic environment for early, medieval and Renaissance music. Recitals are on Thursdays, starting at 1.05pm. On Tuesday at 1.05pm the Bow Dialogue takes place: a discussion between the vicar and a prominent personality.

St Michael's Cornhill
Cornhill, EC3 (0171 626 8841). Bank tube.
The organ at St Michael's is old enough for Purcell and Handel to have played on, which they almost certainly did. An excellent organ recital tradition continues on Monday lunchtimes (1pm, except Bank Holidays) throughout the year.
Guided tours by arrangement.

St Olave's Hart Street
Hart Street EC3 (0171 488 4318). Tower Hill tube/Fenchurch Street BR.
St Olave's lunchtime chamber music recitals, every Wednesday and Thursday at 1.05pm, feature a selection of solo, duo and trio instrumentalists.
Disabled: access.

Around & About

Almeida Theatre
Almeida Street, N1 (0171 359 4404). Angel tube or Highbury & Islington tube/BR or Essex Road BR. **Open** box office 10am-6.30pm Mon-Sat. **Tickets** £5-£15.50. **Membership** £10 per year. **Credit** A, AmEx, DC, V.
This small theatre in Islington has gained a remarkable reputation for avant garde productions of international theatre

*The annual **Spitalfields Festival** brings chamber music to Nicholas Hawksmoor's towering Christchurch Spitalfields.*

and new music, as well as a heady mix of well-performed contemporary and classic plays. The Almeida Opera, the annual festival of new stage works interspersed with concerts, takes place in July. (*See also chapter* **Theatre**.)
Café. Disabled: access; toilet.

Blackheath Concert Halls
23 Lee Road, Blackheath, SE3 (box office 0181 318 9758/information 0181 463 0100). Blackheath BR/54, 75, 89, 108 bus. **Open** box office 8am-7pm Mon-Sat. **Tickets** £1-£50. **Credit** A, V.
A venue for high-powered series and cycles.
Educational projects. Café and bar. Disabled: access to ground floor only; toilets.

British Music Information Centre
10 Stratford Place, W1 (0171 499 8567). Bond Street tube. **Open** noon-5pm Mon-Fri. **Recitals** 7.30pm Tue, Thur. **Tickets** £3-£5.
A unique collection of scores, taped music, records, CDs and videos about composers are kept here. There's usually a recital (predominantly new British music) on Tuesday and Thursday evenings (except August).

Burgh House
New End Square, NW3 (0171 431 0144). Hampstead tube. **Tickets** £4-£6.
Regular concerts by local musicians are given in this museum venue. There's no set evening for music, so check *Time Out* magazine's listings for details.

Dulwich Picture Gallery
College Road, SE21 (0181 693 5254). West Dulwich BR/P4, 12, 37, 78, 176 bus. **Open** 10am-5pm Tue-Fri; 11am-5pm Sat; 2-5pm Sun. **Admission** gallery free Fri; £2 adults, £1 OAPs, students, UB40s, free under-15s Tue-Thur, Sat, Sun; closed Mon. **Concerts** £5-£10. **No credit cards.**
The oldest art gallery in England is also a venue for prom concerts on one Saturday a month at 11.30am. Recitals are held in the evenings (at 8pm), also about once a month.
Disabled: access. Guided tours. Lectures.

Fenton House
Hampstead Grove, NW3 (0171 435 3471). Hampstead tube. **Open** *Apr-Oct* 11am-5.30pm Sat, Sun & Bank Holidays; 2-5.30pm Mon-Wed. **Admission** £6; £12 for celebrity concerts.
Fenton House contains the treasured Benton Fletcher collection of early keyboard instruments. First-class musicians give recitals of baroque music on occasional Wednesday evenings between May and September.
Disabled: access to ground floor only.

Lauderdale House
Waterlow Park, Highgate Hill, N6 (0181 348 8716/0181 391 2032). Archway tube. **Open** 11am-4pm Tue-Fri. **Tickets** £3.50-£6. **No credit cards.**
You can treat children to a fair or a puppet show on Saturday morning, then enjoy a recital in the evening at this family venue. Performances might be by a local professional trying out a programme before appearing at the Wigmore Hall. Saturdays and Sundays tend to be the music days, but telephone for details.

National Sound Archive
29 Exhibition Road, SW7 (0171 412 7440). South Kensington tube. **Open** 10am-5pm Mon-Wed, Fri; 10am-9pm Thur.
A unique museum of recorded sound. It has several million exhibits, all free, though some must be booked in advance. World premières of obscure modernist compositions share spool space with Hitler's Nuremberg speeches and common or garden sound-effects from raspberries to volcanoes.

Your passport to London

TimeOut

At newsagents every Wednesday

Music: Rock, Folk & Jazz

From Pizza on the Park to Sparks, Andy Sheppard to the Shepherd's Bush Empire, London's music scene is pumpin'.

Shepherd's Bush Empire *and* **Forum** *hosted Sparks' first UK gigs for years in 1994 and '95.*

Rocksteady, bluebeat and ska and all kinds of hot music are performed nightly in rocking London. The only big star of the rock era never to perform in London, or indeed in the UK, was Elvis Presley. This was more to do with some strange stratagem developed by his manager, Colonel Tom Parker, than any avoidance of this great city. But he's probably the only star of the rock era who could afford not to visit London and still retain his vast following. The man made the myth, and the myth has subsequently fed off itself.

Everyone else knows that London is an important part of that world tour. Which, for Londoners, means we never have to travel to see anyone; we know that eventually they'll come to us. That does not mean that Cockneys are cocky – no, it means

they're wallowing in the richness and variety of London's music scene. From the smallest sweat-stained smoky bar to the largest aircraft-hangar-like venues, there's room beneath the capital's sky for music, music and more music. And you've got nothing to lose except your inhibitions.

One word of warning: touts. Another word: scalpers. In whatever language you understand, these leeches roam London's streets looking for unsuspecting punters to rip off. You buy tickets off someone selling in the street at your peril. Not only may they be forgeries, but it's also illegal and London's bobbies are cracking down. If you can't get tickets through the normal channels for your chosen gig, then choose something else, there's always plenty more happening.

*Tuesday night is Irish folk night at the **Amersham Arms**, SE14 – expect a lively evening.*

Major Venues

There are enough large venues in London to accommodate most of the world's stars, although there are always those whose egos would never fit on to the continent, let alone a 70-foot stage. The drawback with large venues is often a lack of atmosphere, but it can often be the only way to see your favourites.

Academy Brixton

211 Stockwell Road, SW9 (0171 924 9999). Brixton tube/BR tube. **Open** 7pm-late, depending on show. **Admission** £10-£20. **Credit** A, V.
Has a capacity of around 4,000 but still somehow manages to offer a degree of intimacy. Attracts a lot of top rock names, but also books many interesting acts, ranging from soul to jazz funk. Only a few yards' walk from the station and so easy to get to.

Apollo Hammersmith

Queen Caroline Street, W6 (0171 416 6080). Hammersmith tube. **Open** 7.30-10.30pm. **Admission** £11-£25. **Credit** A, AmEx, DC, £TC, V.
All-seated venue retains part of its previous cinema (it was the Hammersmith Odeon) atmosphere. Plenty of top names appear and it's generally packed. Don't go along expecting a wild night, though, dancing is strictly in the aisles.

Astoria

157 Charing Cross Road, W1 (0171 434 0403). Tottenham Court Road tube. **Open** 7-11pm Mon-Thur; 11pm-3.30am Fri; 10pm-6am Sat. **Admission** £4-£7. **No credit cards**.
Ever-popular venue equally happy showcasing indie, reggae or blues. Good views of the bands but can get very packed, and consequently sweaty.

Astoria 2

157 Charing Cross Road, W1 (0171 434 0403). Tottenham Court Road tube. **Open** 7.30pm-2am. **Admission** £6 average. **No credit cards**.
Favoured by indie bands and their fans. Smaller than the Astoria but just as popular.

Forum

9-17 Highgate Road, NW5 (0171 284 2200). Kentish Town tube/BR/N2 bus. **Open** 7-11pm Mon-Thur, Sun; 7pm-2am Fri-Sat. **Admission** £7.50-£17.50. **Credit** A, V.
Roomy venue offers a range of well-known rock and indie bands. If there's no room on the often-packed dancefloor, there's a sweeping staircase to sit on, or to use to go up to the theatre-style seats upstairs. Booking policy seems to involve mainly established acts.

The Grand

St John's Hill, Clapham Junction, SW11 (0171 738 9000). Clapham Junction BR. **Open** 7pm-2am (nights vary). **Admission** £12-£16. **Credit** A, V.
A refurbished theatre which has come to be one of the Capital's most popular venues, offering a selection of well-known rock and soul successes. Owned by the mighty Mean Fiddler group which also owns north London's larger Forum, among others. Literally across the road from Clapham Junction station, which is itself only five minutes from either Victoria or Waterloo rail stations.

Marquee

105 Charing Cross Road, WC2 (0171 437 6601). Leicester Square or Tottenham Court Road tube. **Open** 7-11pm Mon, Wed; 7-10.30pm Tue, Thur-Sun. **Admission** £3-£8. **Music** 8pm. **Credit** A, V.
Has a long history encompassing most music styles in the last four decades, from jazz and blues through to indie and goth. These days there are more hopefuls than heroes but this compact venue still retains a rock-style atmosphere.

Shepherd's Bush Empire

Shepherd's Bush Green, W12 (0181 740 7474).
Shepherd's Bush tube. **Open** 7.30pm-midnight.
Admission £8-£15. **Credit** A, V.
Formerly the BBC Television Theatre, the Empire has rapidly grown to be one of London's premier venues. Its three-tiered seating arrangement ensures good views of the top rock acts which appear. Expect to see well-known British and American groups nightly.

Wembley Arena

Empire Way, Wembley, Middlesex (0181 900 1234).
Wembley Park tube/Wembley Central tube/BR. **Open**
6.30-11pm. **Music** 7.30pm. **Admission** £15-£25. **Credit**
A, AmEx, DC, V.
This 12,000-seater indoor venue attracts only the bigger stars. It's a shame because the place is hard to get to, far too big to generate any kind of enjoyable atmosphere, and too expensive. Fans of bands appearing may not have another opportunity to see their idols, although the size of the place precludes any real chance of getting close to the stars. Strictly for the sterile.

Wembley Stadium

Empire Way, Wembley, Middlesex (0181 900 1234).
Wembley Park tube/Wembley Central tube/BR.
Open 7.30-11pm. **Admission** £14-£25. **Credit** A,
AmEx, DC, V.
Madonna and Michael Jackson touch down here when they tour the UK. It holds more than 70,000 which, after a week's residency, means the megastars can claim to have performed to around half a million. The fact is, only a handful actually get to see the stars, the rest have to gaze at their images on huge screens from a distance. An uncomfortable experience in every way, although being in the open air means there's a chance of a shower or storm to enliven the evening.

Pubs & Wine Bars

British beer is distinctive and it's developed its own music scene where drinking is intrinsically entwined with listening. But the pub rock scene encompasses far more than ageing never-quite-made-it rockers. Everything from reggae to blues is regularly featured, and the British music pub is a traditional stamping ground of tomorrow's stadium-bound stars.

Bull & Gate

389 Kentish Town Road, NW5 (0171 485 5358).
Kentish Town tube/BR. **Open** 11am-11pm Mon-Sat;
7.30-11.30pm Sun. **Music** 9-11pm. **Admission** £4.
No credit cards.
See them here before they become famous. Indie and alternative bands pay their dues at venues such as the Bull & Gate. Pub rock it ain't, but it's a great pub.

Camden Falcon

234 Royal College Street, NW1 (0171 485 3834).
Camden Town tube. **Open** 5.30-11pm Mon-Sat; 7-
10.30pm Sun. **Music** 9pm. **Admission** £3.50. **No
credit cards.**
Up to 150 punters are often crammed into the back bar of this Camden pub to see live alternative music. Dingy and uninviting, but that's rock 'n' roll. Isn't it?

Dublin Castle

*94 Parkway, NW1 (0171 485 1773). Camden Town
tube.* **Open** 11am-midnight Mon-Sat; 7-10pm Sun. **Music**
8.30pm. **Admission** £3.50-£5. **No credit cards.**
When bands such as Blur want to play secret gigs, they

choose the Dublin Castle. Compact, without being intimidating. Fun, without being over friendly. You'd normally expect to come across some up-and-coming hopeful at this basement venue.

Half Moon

93 Lower Richmond Road, SW15 (0181 780 9383).
Putney Bridge tube. **Open** 11am-11pm Mon-Sat; noon-
3pm, 7-9.30pm, Sun. **Music** 8.30pm. **Admission** £2-£6.
No credit cards.
Taking a trip down the District Line to Putney can lead to a pleasant evening drinking by the River, or a great evening's entertainment at the Half Moon. Fairly straight selection of music, but all of good quality. You won't be shaken, but you may be stirred.

King's Head

*115 Upper Street, N1 (0171 226 1916). Angel
tube/Highbury & Islington tube/BR/N92 bus.* **Open**
11am-midnight Mon-Sat; 9.30pm Sun. **Music** 9.30pm.
Admission free. **No credit cards.**
Packed Islington pub which pays homage to its past with a tongue-out-of-cheek reverence. Famous for its theatre, which retains the support of many grand knights and dames of the British stage. Less well-known are the music performers playing mainly acoustic sets. Very popular as it's a good place for a drink even if the music's no good.

The Robey

*240 Seven Sisters Road, N4 (0171 263 4581). Finsbury
Park tube/BR/N21, N29, N90 bus.* **Open** 11am-12.30am
Mon-Thur; 11am-6am Fri-Sat; 7-10.30pm Sun. **Music**
9pm. **Admission** £3-£5. **No credit cards.**
Standing in the shadow of the long-departed Rainbow, the Robey fits in up to 300 sweaty goths or punks. No guitar solos here, but plenty of loud guitar music to bleed to.

Station Tavern

*41 Bramley Road, W10 (0171 727 4053). Latimer
Road tube/295 bus.* **Open** 11am-11pm Mon-Sat; noon-
3pm, 7-10.30pm, Sun. **Music** 9pm. **Admission** free.
No credit cards.
It's a long, lonely journey, singing the blues, and the same applies if you want to and hear the blues. Making the trip can be a bit of a lottery as you never know how good the music is going to be. But the blues is the blues – especially if it's free.

Swan

*1 Fulham Broadway, SW6 (0171 385 1840). Fulham
Broadway tube/N11, N14 bus.* **Open** noon-midnight
Mon-Wed; noon-1am Thur; noon-2am Fri, Sat; noon-3pm,
7-10.30pm, Sun. **Music** 9pm Mon-Sat; 1pm, 9pm, Sun.
Admission £3-£6. **No credit cards.**
Loud rock music played by loud rock bands.

Torrington Arms

*4 Lodge Lane, High Road, North Finchley, N12 (0181
445 4710). Woodside Park tube.* **Open** 11am-11pm Mon-
Sat; 7-11pm Sun. **Music** 9pm. **Admission** £3-£5. **No
credit cards.**
Located in the heady reaches of north London, but this backroom pub venue can come alive with the right band. A mixed bag of blues, soul and rock.

World's End

21-23 Stroud Green Road, N4 (0171 281 8679).
Finsbury Park tube/BR. **Open** 11am-midnight Mon-Sat;
noon-3pm, 7-11pm, Sun. **Music** 9.30pm. **Admission** free.
No credit cards.
Large, lively Finsbury Park pub, moments from the tube and bus station, offering a variety of music. Generally fun and undemanding blues, rock, whatever. Rhythm 'n' booze, reasonably priced with a good range of beers.

Club Venues

Club culture is mainly geared around dancing but many clubs have an excellent live music policy as well. Be prepared to face up to whatever is the current fashionable door policy when trying to get in.

The Borderline
Orange Yard, Manette Street, Charing Cross Road, WC2 (0171 734 2095). Tottenham Court Road tube. **Open** 8pm-midnight Mon, Tue; 8.30pm-3am Wed-Sat. **Music** 9.30pm. **Admission** £6-£10. **Credit** A, V.
Bingo Hand Job (aka REM) chose this venue to play their only London gigs for more than five years, and there have been other secret gigs here over the years. Most nights, however, it's sweaty rock. For a complete evening, try Break for the Border, the Mexican restaurant next door.

Camden Palace
1A Camden Road, NW1 (0171 387 0428). Camden Town tube/N2, N93 bus. **Open** 9pm-2.30am Tue, Wed; 9pm-3.30am Thur; 9pm-4am Fri; 10pm-6am Sat. **Music** midnight. **Admission** £4-£10. **No credit cards.**
Very much a club, as well as a live venue; on Saturday nights expect to queue for an hour or more. Normally showcases indie bands on Tuesdays.

The Garage
20-24 Highbury Corner, N1 (0171 607 1818). Highbury & Islington tube/BR/N92 bus. **Open** 8pm-midnight Mon-Thur; 8pm-2am Fri-Sun. **Admission** £4-£9. **Credit** A, V.
Smallish (capacity 500) but popular. Features a mixture of name crowd-pullers and up-and-coming acts. Club nights at the weekend follow the gigs.

Mean Fiddler
28A High Street, NW10 (0181 961 5490). Willesden Junction tube/BR/N18 bus. **Open** 8pm-2am Mon-Thur; 8pm-3am Fri, Sat; 7.30pm-1am Sun. **Music** 9.30pm. **Admission** £4-£8. **Credit** A, V.
Rock, pop and country at the main Mean Fiddler venue, while the Acoustic Room offers folk and no electric guitars. Good music and reasonable beer helped the owner of the Mean Fiddler launch a career which now encompasses half of London's main music venues, from the **Forum** to the **Jazz Café**. But the monopoly is founded on sensible logic; the customers can drink and listen to music in good surroundings. Come to where it all started. A confusing one-way traffic systems means it's a good idea to come by tube, bus or cab.

Orange
3 North End Crescent, North End Road, W14 (0171 371 4317). West Kensington tube/N11, N31, N97 bus. **Open** 8.30pm-midnight. **Music** 9.30pm. **Admission** £4-£5. **No credit cards.**
Not the best of views, but the music is often good. This compact venue can pack in 300, but thankfully there remains room to breathe.

Rock Garden
The Piazza, Covent Garden, WC2 (0171 836 4052). Covent Garden tube. **Open** 8pm-3am Mon-Thur; 4-10pm Sat; noon-3pm, 8pm-midnight, Sun. **Admission** £5. **Credit** A, AmEx, DC, V.
Showcasing young bands with regular indie, blues, funk and pop nights. If you eat in the upstairs burger restaurant first you'll get free entry on non-club nights. Traditionally a tourist joint, the Rock Garden keeps threatening to improve.

Subterania
12 Acklam Road, W10 (0181 960 4590). Ladbroke Grove tube/N18, N50 bus. **Open** 8pm-2am Mon-Thur; 10pm-3.30am Fri-Sat. **Music** 9pm. **Admission** £7-£8. **Credit** A, V.
Sparse double-tiered west London club venue that mainly features dance music but also includes rap, soul, techno and funk. Door policy can be a little heavy, but, once you're inside, the venue is usually buzzing.

Music Festivals

May

USSU Festival
Stanmer Park, Brighton (info 01273 774890/tickets 0171 344 4444).
A two day outdoor event with an indie, dance and hip hop-influenced bill.

Hothouse Blues Festival
Corn Exchange, Market Square, Witney, Oxon (info 01608 810987/tickets 01993 774890).
One for old dudes and bluesy rocksters.

June

Fleadh
Finsbury Park, N4 (info 0181 963 0940/tickets 0171 344 0044).
A Celtic-orientated pop and folk festival.

Glastonbury Festival
Worthy Farm, Pilton, Somerset (info 01839 668899/tickets 01179 767686).
A three-day Greenpeace benefit with over 1,000 bands and 17 stages representing every kind of music.

July

Phoenix Festival
Long Marston Airfield, Stratford-Upon-Avon (info 0181 963 0940/tickets 0181 963 0940).
Not as established as Glastonbury or Reading; generally an impressive line-up with an indie bias.

Womad
Rivermead, Richfield Avenue, Reading, Berks (info & tickets 01734 591591).
A roots, dance and world music festival.

Cambridge Folk Festival
Cherry Hinton Hall Grounds, Cambridge (info & tickets 01223 463346).
A long-established festival of more rootsy acts.

August

Reading Festival
Little John's Farm, Reading, Berks (info 0181 963 0940/tickets 0171 344 0044).
A more rock-orientated affair. Stay in one of the nearby hotels if possible, as thefts from tents are rife.

The Underworld

174 Camden High Street, NW1 (0171 482 1932).
Camden Town tube/N2, N93 bus. **Open** 8pm-1am.
Music 9.30pm. **Admission** £5-£8. **No credit cards.**
Beneath the World's End pub directly opposite the tube, the
Underworld features a surprising number of well-known
bands. It's standing room only and so, unless you push to
the front, you'll see little. But there's nothing wrong with
drinking happily at the back, is there?

The Venue

2A Clifton Rise, SE14 (0181 692 4077). New Cross
tube/BR/New Cross Gate tube/BR/N77 bus. **Open** 8pm-
2am Fri; 8pm-3am Sat. **Admission** £5-£6. **Credit**
(advance bookings only) A, V.
It may seem a long way south but the Venue in New Cross
is one of the best indie places in London. It's also a popular
home for the fast-growing number of tribute bands current-·
ly doing the rounds.

Folk & Roots Venues

It's a long time since London's beatnik coffee
bars swung to the sounds of the latest long-haired
folk music, but there's still a thriving and lively
folk scene, offering some rewarding evenings.
These days, British folk is an integral part of
the bustling world music scene, so you're as likely to see a performer from Senegal as you are from
Potter's Bar.

Africa Centre

38 King Street, WC2 (0171 836 1973). Covent Garden
tube. **Open** 9.30pm-3am Fri-Sat. **Music** 10.30pm.
Admission £6-£7. **No credit cards.**
The Africa Centre plays host to a number of top African
bands. During the day the Africa Centre shop offers an excellent range of goods. There's also a specialist bookshop on
the first floor.

Amersham Arms

388 New Cross Road, SE14 (0181 692 2047). New Cross
tube/BR. **Open** 11am-11pm Mon-Sat; noon-3pm, 7-
10.30pm, Sun. **Music** 8pm. **Admission** free Tue; varies
other nights. **No credit cards.**
Tuesday is Irish folk night and sessions are usually lively.
Sunday nights also feature Irish bands, while other nights
are variously themed, including indie rock on Wednesdays
and C&W on Saturdays. A bit of a trek from the centre
of town but there are few experiences to rival seeing and
hearing a good traditional Irish group in full swing.

Cecil Sharpe House

2 Regent's Park Road, NW1 (0171 485 2206).
Camden Town tube/N2, N29, N93 bus. **Open**
7.30-11pm Thur-Sat. **Music** 7.30pm. **Admission**
£3-£5. **No credit cards.**
A folkie's dream, with all sorts of traditional English music
and dancing activity. But don't be put off – there's some great
fun to be had. File Gumbo, held on the first Friday of the
month, for instance, is cajun dancing at its best, and includes
a beginner's session to get you going.

Halfway House

142 The Broadway, W13 (0181 567 0236). Ealing
Broadway tube/207, N50, N89 bus. **Open** 11am-11pm
Mon-Thur; 11am-midnight Fri-Sat; noon-3pm, 7pm-
10.30pm, Sun. **Music** 9.30pm Fri-Sun. **Admission** free.
No credit cards.
Irish community feel, with good music and Guinness.
Features other lively music, such as cajun, as well as Irish.

Swan

215 Clapham Road, SW9 (0171 978 9778). Stockwell
tube/N87 bus. **Open** 11am-11pm Mon-Wed; 11am-2am
Thur-Sat; noon-3pm, 7pm-10.30pm, Sun. **Music** 9pm.
Admission £2-£6. **No credit cards.**
As Irish as they come with strictly traditional Irish sounds.

Weavers Arms

98 Newington Green Road, N1 (0171 226 6911).
Highbury & Islington tube/BR. **Open** 8.30pm-midnight
Mon-Sat; 8pm-10.30pm Sun. **Music** 9pm. **Admission**
£2-£6. **No credit cards.**
Attracts groups from Europe and the States, and fans from
all over London. Expect to see cajun, celtic, roots and blues,
and plenty of good dancing.

Jazz Venues

There's a very lively jazz scene in London and
there are countless small clubs and bars offering
perfectly good combos, often as free entertainment.
A walk around Soho will throw up a good selection of these, but even in far flung parts of the
capital, there are some jazz gems to be found.

100 Club

100 Oxford Street, W1 (0171 636 0933). Tottenham
Court Road tube. **Open** 7.30pm-midnight Mon-Wed;
8pm-1am Thur; 8.30pm-3am Fri; 7.30pm-1am Sat; 7.30-
11.30pm Sun. **Admission** £5-£8. **No credit cards.**
Famed venue which featured The Who and the Rolling
Stones in the 1960s, the Sex Pistols and The Clash in the
1970s, but since has concentrated on jazz and blues and a
smattering of swing and jive.

606 Club

90 Lots Road, SW10 (0171 352 5953). Fulham
Broadway tube/11, 22, N11 bus. **Open** 8.30pm-2am Mon-
Sat; 8.30-11.30 Sun. **Music** 9.30pm Mon-Wed, Sun; 10pm
Thur; 10.30pm Fri-Sat. **Admission** (non-members) £3.95
Mon-Thur, Sun; £4.50 Fri-Sat. **Credit** A, V.
Basement club featuring much of the best young British jazz
talent around. Membership brings slightly cheaper entrance
charges. Difficult to find, but it's worth the search.

The Blue Note

1 Hoxton Square, N1 (0171 729 8440). Old Street tube
and BR. **Open** 9pm-6pm daily; varies in evening, phone
for details. **Music** from 8.30pm. **Admission** £3-£7. **No**
credit cards.
Funk, jazz and Latin grooves at this friendly venue in an
unlikely location. Has its own café offering a selection of
reasonably priced meals from lunchtime onwards.

Bull's Head, Barnes

Barnes Bridge, SW13 (0181 876 5241). Hammermith
tube then bus 9/Barnes Bridge BR/N14, N65 bus. **Open**
11am-11pm Mon-Sat; 12.30-3pm, 7-10.30pm, Sun.
Admission £3-£7. **No credit cards.**
The Bull's Head's riverside location makes this ideal for
pleasant jazz. Well worth the trip, but don't expect anything
too hot or far out.

Jazz Café

5 Parkway, NW1 (0171 916 6060). Camden Town
tube/N93 bus. **Open** 7pm-midnight Mon-Thur; 7pm-2am
Fri-Sat; noon-4pm, 7pm-midnight, Sun. **Admission** £7-
£15. **Credit** A, V.
Great booking policy means you're as likely to see some of
the famous names of jazz as some rising hip hop star at this
excellent venue. Latin, fusion and ragga fans are all catered
for, but if you really want to see and hear the music, book a

table. As with other trendy locations, much of the audience comes to be seen and heard rather than watch and listen.

Pizza Express

10 Dean Street, W1 (0171 437 9595). Tottenham Court Road tube. **Open** 8pm-12.30am. **Music** 8.30pm-midnight Mon-Thur; 9pm-midnight Fri-Sat. **Admission** £1.50-£18. **Credit** A, AmEx, DC, V.

The difference in admission prices reflects the wide variety of artists on offer in the excellent Soho basement venue. Top US jazz stars can be followed the next night by some youthful local combo. Look out for residencies by big names and best nights. The pizzas upstairs are among the best offered in London from a consistently excellent chain.

Pizza on the Park

11 Knightsbridge, SW1 (0171 235 5550). Hyde Park Corner tube. **Open** 8pm-midnight. **Music** 9.15pm. **Admission** £8-£18. **Credit** A, AmEx, DC, V.

A Pizza Express franchise, so good food and mainly mainstream jazz from names you're likely to recognise. The offices above the restaurant were once consulting rooms at **St George's Hospital** (now relocated to Tooting, leaving its shell to be inhabited by the **Lanesborough** hotel). It's said that part of the restaurant housed the former morgue. Goodness knows what went on in what is now the basement Jazz Room.

Ronnie Scott's

47 Frith Street, W1 (0171 439 0747). Leicester Square, Picadilly Circus or Tottenham Court Road tube. **Open** 8.30pm-3am Mon-Sat. **Music** 9.30pm. **Admission** £12-£14. **Credit** A, AmEx, DC, V.

Club run by the British saxophonist which consequently attracts stars from over the pond. This is what Soho jazz is all about – the drinks are very expensive, the views are poor, unless you book a table early, but the music is the best. What can you do?

Union Chapel

Compton Terrace, N1 (0171 226 1686). Highbury & Islington tube/BR/N19, N65, N92 bus. **Open** 7-11pm. **Music** 8.30pm. **Admission** £5-£10. **No credit cards**.

A 50-foot ceiling helps make the acoustics at this venue among the best in London. It's a former congregational church, but it really come to life when it stages jazz concerts. Only the bigger names appear, it holds more than 1,000, but sells out quickly. It's a remarkable venue which deserves its high reputation, although concerts are held infrequently.

Vortex

Stoke Newington Church Street, N16 (0171 254 6516). Stoke Newington BR/67, 73, 76, 106, 243 bus. **Open** 11am-11pm Mon-Thur; 11am-midnight Fri, Sat; 11am-10.30pm Sun. **Music** 8.30pm. **Admission** £3-£6. **Credit** A, V.

Regular north London haunt, featuring many north London jazz musicians. Good venue for reasonably priced jazz.

Other Venues

New locations to stage rock and jazz concerts spring up all the time as promoters seek exciting and different venues. In the past there's been live music at such diverse places as **HMS Belfast**, the warship turned tourist attraction moored near **Tower Bridge**, and the **London Dungeon**, the scary waxworks near **London Bridge**. You'll need to keep an eye on *Time Out* for any of these special events. Many of London's theatres have in the past staged concerts, particularly when they're quiet on a Sunday. There are also several open-air

*Tip up to the **Jazz Café**'s Sunday lunchtime jam session and you could end up on stage.*

*Siouxsie and the Banshees have played everywhere from the **Grand** to the **Royal Albert Hall**.*

venues, with major festivals held annually (*see page 239*). Universities and colleges are another good source of live music.

Palladium

8 Argyle Street, W1 (0171 494 5038). Oxford Circus tube. **Open** 6.45pm-10.30pm. **Music** 7.30pm. **Admission** £8.50-£29. **Credit** A, AmEx, V.

This theatre holds more than 2,000 and is occasionally used by some of the larger acts as a central London venue. It offers excellent acoustics and good facilities, generally a lot more professional than most straight-ahead music venues.

Royal Albert Hall

Kensington Gore, W1 (0171 589 8212). Gloucester Road, Knightsbridge or South Kensington tube/9, 10, 52 bus. **Open** varies, box office opens 9am-9pm. **Admission** £15-£30. **Credit** A, AmEx, V.

It may seem incongruous that this paean to all things Victorian has become one of the most exciting rock venues around. From the Beatles to the Banshees – not forgetting God himself – they've all packed out this venue, despite the terrible acoustics. But don't turn up on spec, especially during the summer months, as the Albert Hall generally plays host to black-tie classical concerts. Oh and another thing, it's a myth about Hitler's other ball.

South Bank Centre

South Bank, SE1 (0171 928 8800). Waterloo tube/BR. **Open** varies, box office 10am-9pm daily. **Admission** £6-£25. **Credit** A, AmEx, DC, V.

Occasional contemporary music venue. Recent concerts have featured a spectacular performance by Laurie Anderson at the **Royal Festival Hall**, featuring music, lasers and split-screen video, and Andy Sheppard at the **Queen Elizabeth Hall**. Call for details of any upcoming events.

Sport & Fitness

London isn't just swinging, it's stepping, swimming, stretching and slam-dunking itself into shape.

Paul Merson, *Arsenal and England winger.*

If there was one thing which characterised yuppie London better than any other, better even than red-rimmed spectacles and the Filofax, it was the 1980s health craze. Stroll through Islington on a Sunday morning and you're still more likely to get knocked over by a gang of joggers than a Suzuki Jeep. In the 1990s, fitness is fast becoming everybody's business. The capital has evolved a weird and wonderful selection of public and private sporting facilities, ranging from the cheap and cheerful to the expensive and terribly serious.

Football and rugby are the main winter spectator sports, and London boasts numerous high-profile club sides for each. Summer belongs to cricket and the gentle sound of leather on willow.

Check out the Sport section of *Time Out* magazine for the pick of the action, as well as details of contacts and classes in virtually every kind of physical activity. Alternatively, phone Sportsline *(0171 222 8000)* or contact your local leisure centre (*see below* **Sport & Leisure Centres**).

Participation Sports

Archery

Mike Parry School of Archery
Fatima Community Centre, Commonwealth Avenue/India Way, W12 (0171 383 5022). White City tube.
Membership £50 per year.
Find out if your aim is true by signing up for one of Mike Parry's three-hour evening 'taster' sessions, where a qualified instructor will point you in the right direction for £15. Grades of achievement are awarded for excellence in the advanced lessons, which are available at £36.

Athletics

The following offer track and field training facilities, and their resident clubs host meetings in the National and Southern Leagues. For a less intense workout, check the Sportsboard in *Time Out*.
Barnet Copthall Stadium *Great North Way, NW4 (0181 203 4211). Mill Hill East tube.*
Croydon Sports Arena *Albert Road, SE25 (0181 654 3462). Norwood Junction BR.*
Crystal Palace National Sports Centre *Ledrington Road, SE19 (0181 778 0131). Crystal Palace BR.*
Mayesbrook Park *Lodge Avenue, Dagenham (0181 593 3539). Upney tube.*
New River Stadium *White Hart Lane, N22 (0181 881 2310). Wood Green tube.*
Paddington Recreation Ground *Randolph Avenue, W9 (0171 798 3642). Maida Vale tube.*
Parliament Hill *Highgate Road, NW5 (0171 435 8998). Gospel Oak BR.*
Queen Elizabeth Stadium *Donkey Lane, Enfield, Middx (0181 363 7398). Enfield Town BR.*
Terence McMillan Stadium *Maybury Road, E13 (0171 511 4477). Plaistow tube.*
Tooting Bec Track *Tooting Bec Road, SW17 (no phone). Tooting Bec tube.*
West London Stadium *Du Cane Road, W12 (0181 743 4030). White City tube.*

Baseball

British Baseball Federation
Wendy MacAdam, 66 Belvedere Road, Hessle, North Humberside HU13 9JJ (01482 643551).
The National Baseball League is run by the BBF, consisting of a premier division and three regional conferences. London is covered by the southern conference. Wendy MacAdam can help to put you in touch with your local team.

Bungee Jumping

UK Bungee Club
Chelsea Bridge Tower, Battersea Wharf, Queenstown Road, SW8 (0171 720 9496). Battersea Park BR.
If simply looking at London's famous monuments isn't enough, why not safely throw yourself off one with the UK Bungee Club? Battersea Observation Tower stands 325 feet above ground level and the impressive, if fleeting, view of the capital skyline should make all the nerves worthwhile. If you prefer, the Club will happily catapult you 250 feet upwards and over the Thames. Everyone from first-timers to seasoned addicts are welcomed. Phone for prices.

Croquet

Hurlingham Club
Ranelagh Gardens, SW6 (information 0171 736 3148). Putney Bridge tube.
If you were expecting a French version of cricket, forget it.

Croquet, or the process of hitting balls through hoops with big mallets, is as English as cucumber sandwiches. For most Britons, the game is at its finest fooling around in the back garden on a summer evening after a few beers. Hurlingham is the game's spiritual home and setting for the British Open Championships every July. Send a stamped addressed envelope for details of your nearest teams and clubs.

Cycling

Eastway Cycle Circuit
Temple Mills Lane, E15 (0181 534 6085). Leyton tube. **Open** 9am to dusk daily. **Admission** £2 for two hours with own bike.
Catering for BMX, road racing and cyclo-cross, with events taking place most weekends, Eastway offers a selection of purpose-built cycle tracks.

Herne Hill Velodrome
Burbage Road, SE24 (0171 737 4647). Herne Hill BR. **Open** daily. **Admission** free for coaching sessions; £2.50 for leagues Mon & Wed eves and special events. Contact Gerald Wallis.
Herne Hill velodrome is the oldest cycle stadium in the world. If the grounds themselves might be feeling the wear, the track is only three years old and officially *the* fast racing surface in the UK. It's now the only velodrome in London, and international events are staged over holiday periods. Track bike hire is available, but serious speed freaks should call 0171 635 9761 for details on renting a recumbent.

Dance

Dance Attic
368 North End Road, SW6 (0171 610 2055). Fulham Broadway tube. **Open** 9am-10pm Mon-Fri; 9am-5pm Sat; 10am-5pm Sun. **Membership** £25 for six months; £40 per year; £1.50 per day. **Classes** £2.50-£3.
Dance Attic boasts a gym to complement its highly popular dance and rehearsal studios.Tuition is offered in ballet, jazz, flamenco, historic dance, lambada and rock 'n' roll. A range of aerobics and step classes is also available. Phone or write with a stamped addressed envelope for full timetable.

Danceworks
16 Balderton Street, W1 (0171 629 6183). Bond Street tube. **Open** 8am-10.30pm Mon-Fri; 10am-6pm Sat, Sun. **Membership** £75 per year (£35 students, nurses, UB40s); £22 per three months. **Classes** £4.
Danceworks is a popular centre situated just off Oxford Street offering a comprehensive range of dance, fitness and movement classes to suit all abilities. Natureworks, an in-house medicine centre, houses more than 25 practitioners.

Pineapple Dance Centre
7 Langley Street, WC2 (0171 836 4004). Covent Garden tube. **Open** 9.30am-9pm Mon-Fri; 9.30am-6pm Sat; noon-3.30pm Sun. **Membership** £80 per year; £35 per year Equity, students, UB40s; £25 for three months; £4 per day. **Classes** £4.
Pineapple made its name during the 1980s fitness boom, and with over 150 classes per week to choose from, it's still noted for variety and high standards of tuition. Drop-in classes are available to the public. Phone for timetable details. **Branch**: 38 Harrington Road, SW7 3HL (0171 581 0466).

Golf

Courses
Airlinks *Southall Lane, Hounslow (0181 561 1418). Hayes & Harlington BR.* **Course** 18 holes. **Fee** £10.75 per round Mon-Fri; £13.50 Sat, Sun.

Beckenham Place *Beckenham Hill Road, SE6 (0181 650 2292). Beckenham Hill BR.* **Course** 18 holes. **Fee** *winter* £8 per round Mon-Fri; £13 per round Sat, Sun.
Brent Valley *Church Road, Cuckoo Lane, W5 (0181 567 1287). Hanwell BR.* **Course** 18 holes. **Fee** £7.95 per round Mon-Fri; £12 Sat, Sun.
Chingford *Bury Road, E4 (0181 529 5708). Chingford BR.* **Course** 18 holes. **Fee** £9 per round Mon-Fri; £12.50 Sat, Sun.
Lee Valley Leisure *Picketts Lock Lane, N9 (0181 803 3611). Ponders End BR.* **Course** 18 holes. **Fee** *members* £7.50 Mon-Fri, £10.50 Sat, Sun; *non-members* £9 Mon-Fri, £12 Sat, Sun.
Richmond Park *Roehampton Gate, Richmond Park, SW15 (0181 876 3205). Barnes BR.* **Course** two 18-hole courses. **Fee** £9.25 per round Mon-Fri; £13 per round Sat, Sun.
Stockley Park *Stockley Park Golf Course, Heathrow (0181 813 5700). Heathrow Terminal 1, 2, 3 tube, then U5 bus.* **Course** 18 holes. **Fee** £17.50 per round Hillingdon residents Mon-Fri, £22.50 Sat-Sun; £25 non-residents Mon-Fri, £30 Sat-Sun.

Regent's Park Golf School
Outer Circle, Regent's Park, NW1 (0171 724 0643). Baker Street tube. **Open** 8am-9pm daily.
For £5, day visitors can work off Londonitis by hammering 50 balls off the highly popular driving range. Every bucket thereafter is £2, and for the highly stressed an annual membership is only £60. As for proper lessons, 30 minutes with the club pro will cost you £16 (£14 members), or £70 buys a course of six. You can have your swing computer-analysed for £35, and the fee is waived if you buy a set of clubs.

Ice Skating

Broadgate Ice Rink
Eldon Street, EC2 (0171 588 6565). Liverpool Street tube. **Open** *late Oct-mid Apr* daily. **Admission** £5; £3 under-16s. **Skate hire** £2; £1 under 16s & OAPs.
The only outdoor ice rink in the UK this compact, friendly arena caters for skaters of all ages and abilities. The EXCO Broomball League is also staged here, a game in which teams attempt to 'sweep' a football into goals using, of all things, brooms. Phone for information on opening times, private hire facilities and how to set up your own Broomball team.

Queens Ice Skating Club
17 Queensway, W2 (0171 229 0172). Queensway or Bayswater tube. **Sessions** 10am-4.30pm, 7.30-11pm, Mon-Fri; 10am-12.30pm, 2.30-5pm, 7.30-11pm Sat, Sun. **Admission** £5 adults; £3.50 children. **Skate hire** £1.50.
This fashionable Bayswater rink attracts a mixture of serious skaters and trendy young things, all to the accompaniment of thumping dance music. Not a cool place to fall over.

Streatham Ice Rink
386 Streatham High Road, SW16 (0181 769 7771). Streatham BR. **Sessions** 10am-4pm, 7.30-10.30pm, Mon-Fri; 11am-4.45pm, 8-11pm, Sat, Sun; **Admission** £5 adults (£4 under-12s) incl skate hire; £3.70 Adults (£2.70 under-12s) with own skates.
This spacious and newly refurbished suburban rink offers good value for those who have their own skates, and stages ice hockey from time to time.

Karting

Whether you're a budding Damon Hill or just looking to burn some rubber after a hard day at the office, London's indoor tracks can provide the ideal setting for your thrills and spills.

An Ayrton Senna (tenner) buys you 15 minutes of madness at **Daytona & Indianapolis**.

National Karting Association *David Williams, Unit 4, Parish Wharf Trading Estate, Harbour Road, Portishead BS20 9DA (Freefone 0500 135145)*. Contact the Association for information about the sport and details of your nearest circuit.

Daytona & Indianapolis Raceways *54 Wood Lane, W12 (0181 749 2277). White City tube.* **Fee** £10-£40 per person. **Sessions** daily. Phone for availability.
This busy indoor track caters for all levels of racers – £10 will buy you a 15-minute practice session, whilst £40 is the standard private entry fee for a race.

Fast Lane Leisure *Knight Road, Strood, Rochester, Kent (01634 713383). Strood BR.* **Fee** £27.50 per person. **Sessions** daily. Phone for availability.

Playscape Pro Racing *Clapham Kart Raceway, Triangle Place, SW4 (0171 498 0916). Clapham Common tube.* **Fee** £37.50 per driver. **Sessions** daily. Phone for availability.

Spitfire Racing *26 Browells Lane, Feltham (0181 893 2104). Feltham BR.* **Fee** *racing* £25 per person; *15-minute trial* £10 per person. **Sessions** daily. Phone for availability.

Trak 1 Racing *Unit 2A, Wyvern Way, Barnsfield Place, Uxbridge (01895 258410/811303). Uxbridge tube.* **Fee** £34.50 per person. **Sessions** daily. Phone in advance.

Martial Arts

British Council of Chinese Martial Arts
14 Stevenson Way, Larkfield, Aylesford, Kent ME20 6UN (01732 848065).
Deals with queries about organisations and clubs.

British Karate Federation
Smalldrink, Parsonage Lane, Begelly, Kilgetty, Dyfed SA68 0YL.

Venues
Jujitsu Club of London *Westminster Cathederal Hall, Ambrosden Avenue, Victoria SW1 (0171 352 7716). Victoria tube.* Yes, it's located in Westminster Cathederal

Hall, but the club offers excellent tuition in all levels of Jujitsu, Karate, Aikido and Tai Chi. Phone for details.
London School of Capoeira Dance *Studio 8, The Place, 17 Dukes Road WC1 (0171 354 2084). Euston tube/BR.* Capoeira is a blend of dance and martial arts. Free demonstration sessions are held every Friday evening between 9-10pm. A beginners' monthly course of four lessons costs £75 (£65 concessions).

Riding

Belmont Riding Centre
Belmont Farm, The Ridgeway, NW7 (0181 906 1255). Mill Hill East tube. **Open** 9am-9pm Tue-Fri; 9am-5pm Sat, Sun. **Lessons** *group* £13.50 per hour; *private* £19 per hour.
Apart from the 150 acres and cross-country course, Belmont is very proud of its indoor school and two menages. Competition and hunt riders have a high reputation.

Hyde Park Stables
63 Bathurst Mews, W2 (0171 723 2813). Lancaster Gate tube. **Open** 7.15am-7pm Tue-Fri; 9am-5pm Sat, Sun. **Lessons** from £25 per hour.
Smart stables offering pleasant treks through Hyde Park.

Wimbledon Village Stables
24 High Street, SW19 (0181 946 8579). Wimbledon tube/BR. **Open** 8am-5pm daily. **Rides/lessons** from £19 per hour.
Approved by the BHS (British Horse Society, not the soft furnishings shop) and situated only five minutes from the tube, these friendly stables are known for having some of the best horses in London for nervous and experienced riders.

Rollerskating & Skateboarding

Skate Attack
95 Highgate Rd, NW5 (0171 485 0007). Kentish Town tube. **Open** 9.30am-6pm Mon-Fri; 9am-6pm Sat; 10am-2pm Sun. **Credit** A, AmEx, £TC, V.

Skate Attack is the largest shop of its kind in Europe, dedicated to everything skate-like and offering a service facility for wonky wheel disorders. There's a small teaching ring on site (an hour's training costs £7); longer sessions are conducted at the Sobell and Mornington Leisure Centres.

Softball

National Softball Federation – Greater London Region

Contact Bob Fromer, Birchwood Hall, Storridge, Malvern, Worcs WR13 5EZ (01886 884203).
Bob Fromer can provide on-the-spot information for beginners and seasoned players, ranging from contacts for your local London teams, leagues and coaching sessions, to advice on how to become an umpire. All enquiries are welcomed.

Swimming

To find your nearest pool (they're everywhere), try *Yellow Pages* or Sportsline (*0171 222 8000*). Here are a few of the better known ones (*see also below* **Sport & Leisure Centres**).
Gurnell Baths *Ruislip Road East, W13 (0181 998 3241). Ealing Broadway tube.* **Open** 8am-7pm Mon, Fri; 8am-9pm Tue-Thur; 8am-4.45pm Sat, Sun. **Admission** £2.10; £1.05 children.
Highbury Pool *Highbury Crescent, N5 (0171 226 4186). Highbury & Islington tube.* **Open** 7am-8.30pm Mon-Fri; 7.30am-5pm Sat, Sun. Adult swim only, 7am-

---

Getting Involved

Getting involved in your local sports scene can be one of the most rewarding decisions you'll ever make. It can seem intimidating – some advice might be useful.
1. Stop talking about it… **do it**. Actions speak louder than words, talk is cheap and at the end of the day when the ball's in the back of the net, it's a game of two halves, Brian. Probably.
2. Ask for **advice**. You won't be treated like a visitor from another planet. All sports and organisations thrive on new recruits and, unless otherwise stated, all the contact addresses and numbers listed in this section will happily offer help and advice to participants of all ages and abilities.
3. Organise a **group of friends** or colleagues. Hiring half a sports hall for a kickabout might cost £30-40 between you. A deposit or small fee is customary for the hire of a soft ball.
4. Visit a local **leisure centre**. They will offer details of all the classes and courses they run, and can often tell you where to find ones they don't.
5. Check *Time Out*'s **Sportsboard**, in the Sports section of the magazine each week.

9am every morning. Women only, 6.30pm Tuesday. **Admission** £2 adult; 90p children.
Ironmonger Row Baths *Ironmonger Row, EC1 (0171 253 4011). Old Street tube.* **Open** 7.30am-7.30pm Mon-Fri; 9am-4.30pm Sat. Pool closed Sun. **Admission** £2.20 adults; 1.10 children.
Latchmere Leisure Centre *Latchmere Road, SW11 (0181 871 7470). Clapham Junction BR.* **Open** 7.30am-9pm Mon-Thur, Sat, Sun; 7.30am-5.30pm Fri. **Admission** £1.90 (£1.65 off-peak: 9am-5pm Mon-Fri); £1.20 children.
Marshall Street Leisure Centre *14-16 Marshall Street, W1 (0171 287 1022). Oxford Circus tube.* **Open** 7.15am-7pm Mon-Fri; 8.30am-7pm Sat; 9am-noon Sun. **Admission** £2.40 adults; 90p children.
Newham Leisure Centre *Prince Regent Lane, E13 (0171 511 4477). Prince Regent DLR (Mon-Fri) or Custom House BR then bus.* **Admission** £1.80 adults; £1.05 children.
The Oasis *32 Endell Street, WC2 (0171 831 1804).* **Open** 7.30am-8pm Mon-Fri; 9.30am-5pm Sat, Sun. **Admission** £2.50 adults; 85p children.
The Oasis has an indoor as well as an outdoor pool.

Tennis

The Tarmac courts in most London parks usually cost nothing at quiet times (weekday mornings). Be prepared to pay around £3 per hour and wait your turn at the weekends. Private facilities and coaching cost more, but Sportsline (*0171 222 8000*) may be able to help you shop around.

The Lawn Tennis Association (LTA) Trust

Queen's Club, Pallister Rd, W14 (0171 385 4233). Baron's Court tube.
The LTA produces a highly useful guide, 'Where to Play Tennis in London', outlining facilities and coaching opportunities. Send a stamped addressed envelope for your copy.

Islington Tennis Centre

Market Road, N7 (0171 700 1370). Caledonian Road tube. **Open** 8am-10pm Mon-Fri; 9am-10pm Sat, Sun.
Courts outdoor £4-5 per hour; indoor £12-13.50 per hour.
Set up to nurture the sport in an area starved of facilities, the centre provides three outdoor, three indoor and three mini-courts for general use. Besides at the centre itself, coaching courses are held at Highbury Fields and Finsbury Leisure Centre, priced £30-£40. Ask for membership details.

Kensington & Chelsea Sports Development Team

(0171 352 2275).
LTA-qualified instructors offer six-hour, one-weekend intensive group coaching courses at venues throughout the borough for £45. Six-week, one-hour courses for intermediates cost £35, while individual tuition is available at £20 per hour.

Tennis Network

195 Battersea Church Road, SW11 3ND.
Tennis Network exists to match up local players of similar ability. Write enclosing a stamped addressed envelope.

Ten-Pin Bowling

Finding a bowling alley in London is a tortuous experience. Lord knows why, but there simply aren't that many of them. The ones that do exist are modern, safe and crammed with other distractions. Rowans has a limited number of lanes, but also houses a fitness centre, bar, pool tables and a

*Jet-ski with **Docklands Watersports Club**.*

vast amusement arcade. A similarly impressive
array of facilities can be found at GX Superbowl.
GX Superbowl *Units 1-2, 15-17 Alpine Way, E6 (0171
511 4440). Beckton DLR/East Ham tube then 101 bus.
Phone for prices.*
Rowans Leisure *10 Stroud Green Road, N4 (0181 800
1950). Finsbury Park tube/BR. Phone for prices.*

Watersports

Behind the office blocks and endless building sites,
the once still waters of the Docklands are rippling
again with all manner of watery pursuits. To
obtain the excellent guide, 'Watersports in London
Docklands', send a stamped addressed envelope to
Visitor Centre, 3 Limeharbour, London E14 9TJ.

Docklands Watersports Club
*Gate 15, King George V Dock, Woolwich Manor Way,
E16 (0171 511 7000). Gallions Reach DLR (Mon-Fri) or
North Woolwich BR.* **Open** 10am-dusk Mon, Tue, Thur-Sun.
Go jet-skiing in the heart of London! The club provides good
training facilities for riders of all levels. Charges start around
£20 for 30 minutes, which includes hire of vehicle, wetsuit
and use of club facilities.

Lea Valley Watersports Centre
*Greaves Pumping Station, North Circular Road, E4
(0181 531 1129). Angel Road BR.* **Open** 10am-dusk daily.
Windsurfing, sailing, water-skiing and canoeing are the
main pursuits on the 90-acre (36-hectare) Banbury Reservoir.
There are RYA-approved coaching courses in all activities.

London Sea School
*Royal Victoria Dock, E16 (0171 537 2626). Royal
Victoria DLR (Mon-Fri).*
The Sea School offers training in boat handling and off-shore
sailing, held in the comfort of the Royal Victoria Docks,
before going off to sea for the full heave-ho experience.

Royal Docks Waterski Club
*Gate 16, King George V Dock, Woolwich Manor Way,
E16 (0171 511 2000). North Woolwich BR.* **Open** 10am-
dusk daily.
The only Waterski club in central London offers courses for
all skill levels, and beginners are made to feel particularly
welcome. For more experienced skiers there are mono,
slalom, jump and tricks courses to select from. The water is
regularly tested and conforms to EC standards.

Women's Rowing Centre
The Promenade, Duke's Meadows, W4 (0181 840 4962).
The centre runs courses on the River for beginners. Leave a
message on the answerphone if there's no one in the office.

Sport & Leisure Centres

The best place to head for to get an appraisal of
your local sporting scene, leisure centres cater for
all sorts of activities (check the noticeboard) at
affordable prices, but tend to home in on the following: aerobics (and 'step'), badminton, basketball, martial arts, indoor cricket nets, indoor and
outdoor hockey, squash, indoor and outdoor soccer, swimming, volleyball, weight training and
yoga. Day fees are minimal where applicable, and
most are open seven days a week. Always phone
ahead if you're hoping to book a court or hall.

Look for their numbers in *Yellow Pages* under
Leisure Centres, or call Sportsline *(0171 222
8000)*. Below we list a geographical spread of the
better-known centres.

Elephant & Castle Leisure Centre
*22 Elephant & Castle, SE1 (0171 582 5505). Elephant &
Castle tube.* **Open** 7.15am-9.30pm Mon-Fri; 9am-5pm Sat,
Sun.
The E&C is no beauty spot, but this modern, compact centre opposite the pink shopping mall is a real gem and the
facilities are great value. There's squash, swimming, a sports
hall and loads of classes. Phone for prices.

Jubilee Hall Leisure Centre
*30 The Piazza, WC2 (0171 836 4835). Covent Garden
tube.* **Open** 6.30am-10pm Mon-Fri; 10am-5pm Sat, Sun.
Membership £50 per year; £5-9 day fee for non-
members. Phone for full details.
A busy, well-equipped centre is one of the highlights at this
centre, known also for its selection of martial arts classes.

Michael Sobell Leisure Centre
*Hornsey Road, N7 (0171 609 2166). Holloway Road or
Finsbury Park tube.* **Open** 9am-10.30pm Mon-Fri; 10am-
9.30pm Sat, Sun.
This huge north London centre has excellent facilities and
the sports hall is often used as a basketball venue.

London Central YMCA
*112 Great Russell Street, WC1 (0171 637 8131).
Tottenham Court Road tube.* **Open** 7am-10.30pm Mon-
Fri; 10am-9pm Sat, Sun. **Membership** £39.50 per week
peak times (7-10.30am; 4.30-10.30pm); £26 off-peak
(10.30am-4.30pm).
One of the most comprehensive ranges of facilities in town.
The centre is popular with the gay community.

Mornington Sports & Leisure Centre
*142-150 Arlington Road, NW1 (0171 267 3600).
Camden Town tube.* **Open** 12pm-2.30pm, 4.30pm-9.30pm
Mon-Fri; closed Sat-Sun.
The closure of Mornington Crescent tube until 1997 has hit
the trade at this backstreet centre, but skateboarding and
rollerskating sessions are still held here by the groovy guys
from **Skate Attack** (see **Skateboarding & Rollerskating**).

Queen Mother Sports Centre
*223 Vauxhall Bridge Road, SW1 (0171 798 2125).
Victoria tube/BR.* **Open** 6.30am-7.30pm Mon-Thur;
6.30am-8.30pm Fri; 7.30am-8pm Sat, Sun; 9am-8pm Sun.
A £1 million facelift means there's a new gym, dance studio
and crèche as well as squash, badminton and swimming.

Seymour Leisure Centre
*Seymour Place, W1 (0171 723 8019). Edgware Road or
Marble Arch tube.* **Open** 7am-10pm Mon-Fri; 7am-8pm
Sat; 8am-8pm Sun.

Besides the pool, the Seymour runs the highly rated Move It programme of exercise classes (£3.60), aerobic and 'step' classes (£3.70), and has a new cardio-vascular fitness room.

Yoga

YBT Yoga Therapy Centre
4th Floor, Royal London Homeopathic Hospital, 60 Great Ormond Street, WC1 (0171 833 7267). Russell Square tube.
Founded by the charitable Yoga Biomedical Trust, the centre provides treatment for stress-related illnesses, back pains, respiratory problems, MS and Parkinson's disease. In addition, 'drop-in' yoga classes are offered to the public at lunchtimes and early evenings throughout the week. Fees range from £10 for a small group class to £25 for personal tuition. A range of individual health assessments is also offered.

Spectator Sports
American Football

London Monarchs
White Hart Lane, High Road, N17 (0171 396 4525). White Hart Lane BR.
Given the relatively high levels of coverage and enthusiasm the sport is afforded over here, it's a bit sad to find that the imperiously-titled World League of American Football actually consists of only six teams. Joining London, teams from Amsterdam, Barcelona, Düsseldorf, Edinburgh and Frankfurt jostle for dubious 'world' domination. The Monarchs should again be contenders, with new QB Brad Johnson (on loan from Minnesota Vikings) expected to be a key figure.

Basketball

Recent visits here by Shaq 'Attack' O'Neal and Magic Johnson have triggered a surge in the popularity of UK basketball. The Leopards and the Towers are London's premier slam-dunking sides, both in the National Budweiser Basketball League. Barking & Dagenham Bobcats and London Heat play in the women's Division One.
London Leopards *London Arena, Limeharbour, E14 (0171 515 8515). Crossharbour DLR or D8/D9 weekend bus service.*
London Towers *'Wembley Court', Wembley Exhibition Centre, Empire Way, Wembley (0181 900 1234). Wembley Park tube.*
Brixton Topcats *Brixton Recreation Centre, Station Road, SW9 (0171 274 7774). Brixton tube/BR.*
Crystal Palace *Crystal Palace National Sports Centre, Ledrington Road, SE19 (0181 778 0131). Crystal Palace BR.*
Barking & Dagenham Bobcats *Gorebrook Leisure Centre, Ripple Road, Dagenham (0181 592 5555). Becontree tube.*
London Heat *Lee Valley Sports Centre, Quartermile Lane E10 (0181 519 0017). Leyton tube.*

Boxing

Details of big fights tend to be fly-posted throughout the capital: seats can cost anything between £20-£200, depending on the size of the draw. For boxing nostalgists, the Old Kent Road, SE1 provides the gritty backdrop for the famous Henry Cooper and Thomas A'Beckett pubs, both of which have ringside gyms upstairs. The following venues hold regular bouts: phone for details.

*All enquiries to the **UK Bungee Club**.*

York Hall *Roman Road, E2 (0181 980 2243). Bethnal Green Tube.*
Royal Albert Hall *Kensington Gore, SW7 (0171 589 3203). High Street Kensington or Knightsbridge tube.*
Lewisham Theatre *Catford, SE8 (0181 690 0002). Catford/Catford Bridge BR.*

Cricket

Wickets. Googlies. Leg Stumps. Silly Mid-Offs. It's not the rules of England's national summer game that cause all the confusion, but the baffling terminology used to describe the goings-on in the middle. Most league matches take four days to complete, if indeed they are completed at all, so it's generally advisable to take in one of the limited-overs matches on Sunday afternoons. Every summer, the England team gets roundly trounced by the touring visitors: in 1995 the mighty West Indies will once again be serving up the carnage. Book well in advance for international fixtures.

Lord's
St John's Wood Road, NW8 (Middlesex 0171 289 8979/Marylebone Cricket Club – national administrative body – 0171 289 1611). St John's Wood tube.
The marbled halls and immaculate playing surface of Lords are the spiritual and administrative home of the game. Middlesex County Cricket Club is also based here, playing league and cup matches from April until September. Tickets are easy to obtain and should cost less than £10.

Foster's Oval
Kennington Oval, SE11 (0171 582 6660). Oval tube.
The gasworks behind the main stand tells you you're not at Lord's any more, but, with one of the finest batting pitches in the country, the Oval has a reputation for producing thrilling cricket. Also the home of Surrey County Cricket Club, the Oval traditionally stages the final – and often the deciding – game in each summer's International Test Series.

Football
London takes pride in the strength and diversity of its clubs. Arsenal and Chelsea have featured prominently in the European Cup-Winners' Cup recently, and after Spurs' failure to hang on to Jürgen Klinsmann for more than one brief, brilliant season at White Hart Lane, Chelsea manager Glen Hoddle has shown himself to be just as sharp-minded off the field as on by bringing Dutchman Ruud Gullit to Stamford Bridge.

Club Sides
Arsenal *Arsenal Stadium, Avenell Road, N5 (0171 226 0304). Arsenal tube.* **Tickets** £11-£23. FA Carling Permiership.
Barnet *Underhill Stadium, Westcombe Drive, Barnet (0181 441 6932). High Barnet.* **Tickets** *standing* £6-8; *seats* £12.50-15. Endsleigh League Div 3.
Brentford *Griffin Park, Braemar Road, Brentford (0181 847 2511). Brentford BR.* **Tickets** *standing* £7.80; *seats* £13. Endsleigh League Div 2.
Charlton Athletic *The Valley, Floyd Road, SE7 (0181 293 4567). Charlton BR.* **Tickets** £10-£14. Endsleigh League Div 1.
Chelsea *Stamford Bridge, Fulham Road, SW6 (0171 385 5545). Fulham Broadway tube.* **Tickets** £10-£30. FA Carling Permiership.
Crystal Palace *Selhurst Park, Park Road, SE25 (0181 771 8841). Norwood Junction/Crystal Palace/Selhurst BR.* **Tickets** £16-£25. Endsleigh League Div 1.
Fulham *Craven Cottage, Stevenage Road, SW6 (0171 736 6561). Putney Bridge tube.* **Tickets** *standing* £7-7.50; *seats* £10.50. Endsleigh League Div 3.
Leyton Orient *Leyton Stadium, Brisbane Road, E10 (0181 539 2223). Leyton tube.* **Tickets** *standing* £7; *seats* £9-11. Endsleigh League Div 3.
Millwall *The New Den, Senegal Fields, Zampa Road, SE16 (0171 232 1222). South Bermondsey BR.* **Tickets** £10-£20. Endsleigh League Div 1.
Queens Park Rangers *Rangers Stadium, South Africa Road, W12 (0181 749 5744). White City tube.* **Tickets** £11-£25. FA Carling Permiership.
Tottenham Hotspur *White Hart Lane, High Road, N17 (0171 396 4567). White Hart Lane BR.* **Tickets** £13-£25. FA Carling Permiership.
Watford *Vicarage Rd, Watford (01923 230933). Watford High Street BR.* **Tickets** £9-£11.50. Endsleigh League Div 1.
West Ham United *Boleyn Ground, Green Street, E13 (0181 548 2748). Upton Park tube.* **Tickets** £11-£20. FA Carling Permiership.
Wimbledon *Selhurst Park, Park Road SE25 (0181 771 2233). Norwood Junction/Crystal Palace/Selhurst BR.* **Tickets** £10-£22. FA Carling Permiership.

UEFA Euro '96 England
Euro '96, PO Box 1996, Newcastle-Under-Lyme, Staffs ST5 1LE (helpline 0178 274 1996).
In June 1996, the European Football Championships will be held in England for the first time. Wembley stages England's opening round matches and the final, but is the only London venue to be selected and, not surprisingly, tickets are already selling very fast. Other matches will be played at all-seater stadia in Birmingham, Leeds, Manchester, Liverpool, Newcastle, Sheffield and Nottingham. To apply for tickets, write to the address above, or pick up an application form at any branch of Midland Bank.

Golf
Two of the UK's most famous courses lie within easy reach of London. Wentworth has become the regular venue for the European PGA tournament every May. Sunningdale no longer accommodates the European Open, but is still prominent on the Volvo European tour. Admission prices vary.
Sunningdale *Ridgemount Road, Sunningdale, Ascot (01344 21681). Sunningdale BR.*
Wentworth Golf Club *Wentworth Drive, Virginia Water, Surrey (01344 842201). Virginia Water BR.*

Greyhound Racing
Providing a cheaper and more down-to-earth alternative to horse racing, watching the dogs hurtle through the sand is a fun night out. All tracks have a bar and restaurant.
Catford Stadium *Ademore Road, SE26 (0181 690 2261). Catford Bridge BR.* **Admission** £2.50-3.50
Races 7.30pm Mon, Thur, Sat.
London Stadium Hackney *Waterden Road, E15 (0181 986 3511). Hackney Wick BR or W15 bus.* **Admission** £3.50 (£1 Tue, Sat). **Races** 7.30pm Mon, Wed, Fri, Sat; 11am Tue, Sat.
Walthamstow Stadium *Chingford Road, E4 (0181 531 4255). Walthamstow Central tube.* **Admission** £2-4 (£1-4 Sun). **Races** 7.30pm Tue, Thur, Sat; noon Sun.
Wembley Stadium *Stadium Way, Wembley (0181 902 8833). Wembley Park tube.* **Admission** £2.50-3.50 (free Sun). **Races** 7.30pm Mon, Fri; 12.25pm Sun.
Wimbledon Stadium *Plough Lane, SW19 (0181 946 5361). Wimbledon Park tube.* **Admission** £2.50-4 (£2 Thur). **Races** 7.30pm Tue, Wed, Fri, Sat.

Hockey
National League games are generally held on Saturdays and Sundays. We list the venues of London's top clubs. Phone for details of matches.
Hounslow Riverside Drive *Duke's Meadows, Great Chertsey Road, W4 (0181 994 9470). Chiswick BR.*
Indian Gymkhana Feltham School *Browells Lane, Feltham (0181 890 8882). Feltham BR.*
Old Loughtonians *Luxborough Lane, Chigwell (0181 504 7222). Chigwell tube.*
Southgate Broomfield School *Sunningdale, off Wilmer Way, N14 (0181 361 2932). Arnos Grove tube.*
Teddington School *Broom Road, Teddington (0181 977 0598). Teddington BR.*

Horse Racing
Whether it's Champagne and roast beef sandwiches at Ascot, or a chip butty in the Tattersalls at Kempton, a day at the races can provide you with a unique taste of British sporting pomp and occasion. Half the fun is sizing up the odds along with the teeming crowd that surrounds the trackside bookies, who usually accept a minimum stake of £5 on a win-only bet. Bets

can also be made with the Tote, which gives no odds until all the bets have been placed and divides the pool between the winners. Nearly all races are run on grass.

Ascot
High Street, Ascot (01344 22211). Ascot BR. **Admission** *Silver Ring £3; Grandstand £9; Club £15.*
The Royal Meeting in June is the highlight of the Racing society calendar, when the rest of the population watches on TV to marvel at the oddly sculpted hats. Ascot is commonly acknowledged to be Britain's premier flat course, and the racing is always highly competitive.

Epsom
Racecourse Paddock, Epsom (01372 726311). Epsom BR. **Admission** *Enclosure £4; Grandstand £9; Club £13.*
With its meandering slopes and lopsided home straight, Epsom is one of the world's oldest and most idiosyncratic courses. It's also one of the fastest, with numerous record-breaking times set here over the years. It's the home of the Derby and the Oaks, both run in June.

Kempton Park
Staines Road East, Sunbury-on-Thames (01932 782292). Kempton Park BR. **Admission** *Silver Ring £4; Tattersalls £9; Club £13.*
An unpretentious but cheerful course on the south-west boundary of London, Kempton has recently been given a somewhat overdue facelift. The annual highpoint is the Tripleprint George VI Stakes, run on Boxing Day (Dec 26), but if you'd rather not brave the cold, the summer meetings which stretch into the evenings are also very popular.

Sandown Park
The Racecourse, Esher Station Road, Esher (01372 463072). Esher BR. **Admission** *Silver Ring £5; Grandstand £12; Club £15.*
Generally deemed to be the best-equipped of the London tracks, Sandown's major occasions are the Whitbread Gold Cup (April) and the Coral Eclipse Stakes (July). Easy access from Waterloo via train and close proximity to the A307 make it popular with city day-trippers.

Windsor
Maidenhead Road, Windsor (01753 865234). Windsor & Eton Riverside BR. **Admission** *Silver Ring £4; Tattersalls £8; Club £12 .*
Best experienced on a hazy summer evening, Windsor takes full advantage of its Thames-side setting, with a shuttle boat service operating from Barry Avenue Promenade in the town before and after racing. The course is set in a figure eight with a head-on view of the last five furlongs, making it difficult to work out which horse is winning. You may not even care, such is the balmy ambience of this delightful course. There are good restaurants and bars in the Club Enclosure.

Motor Sport

Silverstone Circuit
Silverstone, near Towcester, Northants (01327 857271). Northampton BR.
The British Formula One Grand Prix is held here every July, indicating Silverstone's status as the UK's number-one circuit. Trouble is, you'll need a car of your own plus a good map reader and hours to spend in traffic jams just getting there. GP tickets are £60, or £120 for a Grandstand seat.

Major Sporting Events in London

American Football
August – American Bowl, Wembley Stadium.

Athletics
January – WICB Tournament, Crystal Palace.
April – London Marathon.
July – TSB Games, Crystal Palace.
August – Crystal Palace Invitation.

Badminton
March – England Championships, Wembley Arena.

Basketball
April – Budweiser Basketball Championships, London Arena.

Cricket
May – One-Day Internationals, Lord's and The Oval.
July – B&H Cup Final, Lord's.
September – Nat West Trophy Final, Lord's.

Equestrianism
May – Royal Windsor Horse Show, Windsor Great Park (01753 860633).
September – Horse of the Year Show, Wembley.
December – Showjumping Championships, Olympia.

Football
April – Coca Cola Cup Final, Wembley Stadium.
May – FA Cup Final, Wembley Stadium.
June 1996 – UEFA European Football Championships, Wembley Stadium and across the country (0178 274 1996).
August – FA Charity Shield, Wembley Stadium; League season starts.

Horse Racing
June – The Oaks, Epsom; The Derby, Epsom; Royal Ascot.
July – King George VI & Queen Elizabeth Diamond Stakes, Ascot; Glorious Goodwood.
September – Festival of British Racing, Ascot.
December – King George VI Tripleprint Chase, Kempton Park.

Ice Hockey
April – British Championships, Wembley Arena.

Rowing
March – Varsity Boat Race.
June – Henley Regatta.

Rugby League
April – Silk Cut Challenge Cup Final, Wembley.
October 1995 – World Cup, Great Britain (0178 274 1995).

Rugby Union
January-March – Five Nations Championship, Twickenham (0181 892 8161).
May – Pilkington Cup Final and Middlesex Sevens, Twickenham.
December – Varsity Match, Twickenham.

Snooker
February – B & H Masters, Wembley Arena.

Tennis
June – Stella Artois Championships, Queen's Club; Wimbledon Championships.

Wimbledon Stadium

Plough Lane, SW17 (0181 946 5361). Wimbledon Park tube. **Admission** £6.50 adults; £3 children.

If you've never taken in an evening of bangers, hot-rods or stock car racing before, then it's well worth the trek down to Wimbledon just to sample the chaos. Sunday evenings are the regular nights and the season takes a break in June.

Polo

The Guards Polo Club

Smiths Lawn, Windsor Great Park, Englefield Green, Egham (01784 437797). Windsor & Eton Central BR.

Nothing at all to do with circular mints, Polo is an undeniably glamorous sport with more than a dash of elitism. However much it might seem like hockey on horses, it provides a pleasant day out in the shadow of Windsor Castle.

Rugby League

London Broncos

Barnet Copthall Stadium, Great North Way, NW4 (0181 203 4211). Mill Hill East tube.

It was always going to take something exceptional to propel London's finest into the top flight after years of trawling the lower leagues, and sure enough, there'll be a place for the Broncos in Rupert Murdoch's tenuously-made-for-TV multi-million-buck Super League, due to kick off in summer 1996. The issue of who's 'in' and who's 'out' is a highly contentious (and, as we go to press, unresolved) one, but media and commercial forces mean that several famous old clubs will sadly have to merge or pack up. In contrast, the Super League is a gift-horse for the Broncos, who badly need the extra cash and exposure, but their place in the sun is still more likely to be in Murdoch's national newspaper than on Manly beach.

Rugby Union

England have got better at rugby over recent years, and the introduction of high-powered marketing and professional standards to this once staunchly amateur code definitely has something to do with it. Interest is resurgent, and several leading internationals play their club rugby in London, most notably with Harlequins, London Irish and Wasps. The rugby union season runs from September to May and games are played on Saturday afternoons.

Club Rugby

Blackheath *Rectory Field, Charlton Road, SE3 (0181 858 1578). Blackheath BR.*
Harlequins *Stoop Memorial Ground, Craneford Way, Twickenham (0181 892 0822). Twickenham BR.*
London Irish *The Avenue, Sunbury-on-Thames (01932 783034). Sunbury BR.*
London Scottish *Athletic Ground, Kew Foot Road, Richmond (0181 332 2473). Richmond tube/BR.*
Richmond *Athletic Ground, Kew Foot Road, Richmond (0181 940 0397). Richmond tube/BR.*
Rosslyn Park *Upper Richmond Road, Priory Lane, SW15 (0181 876 1879). Barnes BR.*
Saracens *Bramley Ground, Chase Side, N14 (0181 449 3770). Cockfosters tube.*
Wasps *Repton Avenue, Sudbury (0181 902 4220). Sudbury Town tube.*

Twickenham

Whitton Road, Twickenham (0181 892 8161). Twickenham BR.

Twickenham is the home of English rugby, hosting England internationals as well as representative league games and cup finals. The stadium itself has been magnificently rebuilt over recent years, raising capacity to 60,000 and making it probably *the* most impressive modern stadium in England. Tickets for matches in the Five Nations Championship, from January-March, are distributed through clubs and are almost impossible for casual spectators to obtain. Tickets for cup finals and other matches played here are less difficult to come by, and the box office will be able to provide details.

Tennis

All England Lawn Tennis Club

Church Road, SW19 (0181 944 1066/ticket information 0181 946 2244). Wimbledon Park or Southfields tube.

As you might expect, gaining admission to the-one-they-all-want-to-win remains one of life's less attainable quests. Tickets for the main court are allocated by ballot, and for an application form you should write (with stamped addressed envelope) to the club between 1 September-31 December. A few tickets are available on the day, but be prepared for a scrap. For most people, the outer courts are therefore a more realistic proposition. You'll need to be extremely good at queuing but once you're in, the freedom to wander from one court to another means you're never far from the best of the action. Take an umbrella and a sizeable dowry for the famously expensive strawberries.

Queen's Club

Palliser Road, W14 (0171 385 2366/ticket information 0171 497 0521). Barons Court tube.

Every June these west London grass courts host the Stella Artois tournament, featuring most of the stars from the men's circuit as they limber up for The Big One down the road. Plan ahead: it's increasingly popular with spectators.

Major Stadia

Crystal Palace National Sports Centre

Ledrington Road, SE19 (0181 778 0131). Crystal Palace BR. **Open** *box office* 9.30am-5pm Mon-Fri.

London's premier athletics stadium hosts a Grand Prix meeting every summer, and the sports centre itself is a venue for a host of events ranging from basketball to weightlifting.

London Arena

Limeharbour, London E14 (0171 515 8515). Crossharbour DLR or D8/D9 weekend bus.

Lurking incongruously in the shadow of Canary Wharf, the Arena was recently rescued from financial ruin incurred during the 1980s. It may resemble an aircraft hangar but it provides a modern, comfortable and atmospheric setting for major indoor sports. Londoners know it best as the home of the Leopards basketball team (*see above* **Basketball**).

Wembley Complex

Empire Way, Wembley, Middlesex (0181 900 1234). Wembley Park tube. **Open** *box office* 9.30am-9pm Mon-Sat; 10am-6pm Sun.

Comprising the cavernous 80,000 capacity stadium and the indoor arena, Wembley is the setting for many of the nation's greatest sporting occasions. Top soccer matches such as the Coca Cola and FA Cup Finals are played here (normally selling out months in advance). Wembley will host England's games in the European Football Championships, Euro '96, and the final, whether we get there or not. Exhibition rugby league and American football are staged here in the summer and, most strangely of all, local greyhound racing is held three nights a week. The Arena accommodates major snooker, gymnastics, equestrianism, tennis, ice hockey, boxing and basketball events. The box office number above provides ticket information for both venues.

Theatre

From Andrew Lloyd Webber to the Royal Shakespeare Company, London is caught in the limelight.

With up to 24 openings a week in the West End, Off-West End and sprawling Fringe, London is the undisputed capital of the theatre world. It has two of the greatest subsidised acting companies, in the **Royal Shakespeare Company (RSC)** and the **National Theatre**; two of the richest and most influential musical impresarios, in Andrew Lloyd Webber (*Sunset Boulvard, Cats*) and Cameron Macintosh (*Miss Saigon, Oliver!*); and at any one moment there are over 150 venues hosting some 200 shows.

Choice is a nice concept, but choice can also be a hindrance when you're trying to work out what to see and, more importantly, what to avoid. London heaves with an unhealthy number of actors and egos, many of whom – particularly on the Fringe – think nothing of inflicting their monumental lack of talent on an unsuspecting public. So even the hardest heart should have a modicum of sympathy for the devil… in this case the theatre critic whose job it is to sift through the layers of mediocrity for the odd rare gem. A simple rule of thumb is to consult the Critics' Choice selection in *Time Out* magazine.

The big musicals are traditionally the biggest draws. Many visitors collect them like souvenirs (*Grease* or *Les Miserables*); many collect them for individual performances (Jonathan Pryce in *Oliver!*). A tip to bear in mind when choosing from these is to avoid the long-distance hype. Musicals that have been running for years tend to get very jaded; and endless cast changes and half-empty houses turn shows very stale. By the time a production has reached its third change of cast it might no longer be recognisable as the show that the critics raved about.

Word of mouth and seat availability have always been better indications of a show's state of health than the quotes pinned in lights on the outside of the theatre. Do note also that for matinée performances the 'stars' are often replaced by their stand-ins, which is why matinée tickets tend to be cheaper.

Like any other big business which attracts visitors, the theatre also attracts the unscrupulous. There are plenty of ticket touts out there who are quite happy to charge you twice or even three times the face value of tickets. Unless you're really desperate, avoid buying tickets off the street outside the venues. Not only is this illegal but it's also cripplingly expensive if, for instance, it's a top-price seat for *Phantom of the Opera* (£30). Deal directly with the box office in person or by telephone; all big venues take credit cards. They may charge you a commission if booking by telephone, usually 10 to 12 per cent of the ticket price; if it's much more than that be suspicious and/or complain.

Although the West End is strongly delineated and fairly straightforward to get around, a visit to the Off-West End or the Fringe, where the work is frequently more exciting and where London has an avant garde edge over any other city in the world, can be a baffling affair. This is definitely territory for the more adventurous.

If the Fringe is the major scouting ground for raw new talent, the Off-West End is the most exciting mix of experience and inexperience. Vanessa Redgrave, Corin Regrave, Diana Rigg and Ralph Fiennes all graced an Off-West End stage in 1995. There are few certainties at any level of theatre, but outside the subsidised domain of the **National Theatre**, the **RSC** and the **Royal Court** (the West End theatre that's historically and most strongly identified with controversy and new writing), it is the Off-West End venues which are producing the most consistently challenging work. The Fringe, of course, will always continue to inspire – particularly the work done in venues such as the **Old Red Lion**, the **New End** and the **Greenwich Studio** – for without its roots theatre in London would wither and die.

See also chapter **London by Season** for information on the world's largest arts bonanza, the **Edinburgh Festival**. Every two years, London plays host to the London International Festival of Theatre (LIFT), an innovative and avant garde festival of performers from around the world. It's next due in town in June 1997.

From summer 1996 there is every chance that the rebuilt **Globe Theatre** will finally have risen from its 300-year-old ashes, so you'll be able to see Shakespeare's plays in the setting for which they were written. *See chapter* **Sightseeing** for further details.

Fiona Shaw as Richard II at the **National Theatre**. *'The most suitable Richard I could think of,' said director Deborah Warner.*

*Comprising the Olivier, the Lyttelton and the Cottesloe – the **National Theatre**, South Bank.*

Tickets for West End musicals can be the most difficult to obtain and are easily the most expensive (approximately £10-£36). In association with many theatre box offices, Ticketmaster (*0171 344 4444*) and First Call (*0171 497 9977*) provide tickets in advance for all West End shows. Expect to pay a telephone booking fee (roughly 10 per cent extra) for some productions if you buy tickets through an agency. To avoid booking fees buy direct from the box office.

Artsline
54 Chalton Street, NW1 (0171 388 2227). Camden Town tube. **Open** 9.30am-5.30pm Mon-Fri.
A free advice and information service on access for people with disabilities to arts and entertainment in London. Ask staff to send you the free monthly arts listings magazine *Disability Arts in London.*

Half-Price Ticket Booth
Ticket Booth Leicester Square, WC2 (no phone). Leicester Square or Piccadilly Circus tube. **Open** 2.30-6.30pm Mon-Sat; noon-6.30pm on matinée days. **Tickets** for some shows half price plus £2 service charge (£1.25 on tickets under £12.50). **No credit cards.**

The ticket booth in Leicester Square, run by the Society of London Theatre (SOLT), has a limited number of tickets for most West End shows on the day of performance at half price (cash only) on a first come first served basis. Tickets are restricted to four per person and you cannot return tickets to the booth, though the theatre might accept returns. Watch out for touts trying to sell you tickets while you queue. A list of theatres that use this standby scheme is available from SOLT, Bedford Chambers, The Piazza, Covent Garden, WC2 (0171 836 0971).

Major Theatre Companies

National Theatre
South Bank, SE1 (box office 0171 928 2252/information 0171 633 0880). Waterloo tube/BR. **Open** *box office* 10am-8pm Mon-Sat. **Performances** 7pm, 7.15pm or 7.30pm Mon-Sat; matinées 2pm, 2.15pm, 2.30pm Tue-Thur, Sat. **Tickets** *Olivier and Lyttelton £7-£22; Cottesloe* £14. **Credit** A, AmEx, V.
The National Theatre has established itself as Britain's leading theatrical hot-house. Under current director Richard Eyre, who retires in 1997, the building has mounted a huge spread of plays and acting styles. The building itself – an imposing concrete structure on the South Bank – comprises three theatres: the **Olivier** (large, open-platform stage), the **Lyttelton** (proscenium arch) and the **Cottesloe** (small, flexible studio space). From September 1995, Sean Mathias

directs Dame Judi Dench and Sir Ian McKellen in Stephen Sondheim's *A Little Night Music*. Diana Rigg stars in Brecht's *Mother Courage* from November 1995.
Disabled: access; toilets. Bookshop. Gallery. Restaurants and cafés.

Royal Court (English Stage Company)
Sloane Square, SW1 (0171 730 1745). Sloane Square tube. **Open** *box office* 10am-8pm Mon-Sat.
Performances phone for details. **Tickets** £5-£18.
Credit A, AmEx, £TC, V.
The Royal Court, situated in the chic heart of Chelsea, has always been the bad boy of West End theatre. And its young artistic director, Stephen Daldry, has upheld the controversial image with natural flair. Writers such as Caryl Churchill, Edward Bond and Timberlake Wertenbaker have made their names here. But more recently, a hard-hitting number of young turks, who have caused some minor sensations (most notably Sarah Kane's orgy of violence *Blasted* above the main house in the Royal Court Theatre Upstairs, are starting to get their breaks on the main stage.
Disabled: assistance (0171 730 5174); access. Group discount (0171 730 5174). Tour by prior arrangement (0171 328 7558). Induction loop.

The Royal Shakespeare Company
Barbican Centre, Silk Street, EC2 (0171 638 8891/information 0171 628 2295). Barbican tube/Moorgate tube/BR. **Performances** phone for times.
Tickets £6-£22. **Credit** A, AmEx, £TC, V.
The RSC, which employs and trains some of the greatest Shakespearean actors and directors in the world, has two homes: one in London at the **Barbican Centre** (incorporating the Barbican Theatre and The Pit) and the other in Shakespeare's birthplace, Stratford-upon-Avon (*see chapter* **Trips Out of Town**). Stratford's Royal Shakespeare Theatre is the only venue that stages nothing but Shakespeare; the others all have an equal commitment to new writing and the classics. What is seen in Stratford one season comes to London the next. London's **Barbican Centre** is hard to find and confusing inside, although the new layout and grand entrance arch have improved matters. Sightlines are good though.
Car park. Disabled: access; toilets. Restaurants and cafes. Shops.

Long Runners & Musicals

Arcadia
Haymarket Theatre Royal, Haymarket, SW1 (0171 930 8800). Piccadilly Circus tube. **Performances** 7.30pm Mon-Sat; *matinées* 2.30pm Wed, Sat. **Tickets** £9-£23.
Tom Stoppard's masterpiece is an enormously stimulating play about facts and fiction. Set in a Derbyshire country house, the action switches from a present day investigation by two historical sleuths into a scandal involving Lord Byron and the relationship between a tutor and his brilliant female pupil in 1809.

Blood Brothers
Phoenix Theatre, Charing Cross Road, WC2 (0171 369 1733). Leicester Square or Tottenham Court Road tube. **Performances** 7.45pm Mon-Sat; *matinées* 3pm Thur, 4pm Sat. **Tickets** £27-£50.
This ambitious melodrama, about Liverpudlian twins separated at birth and brought up in radically different environments, is now ten years old and feeling its age. Willy Russell and Bob Tomson's musical scrapes by on sentimentality and memorable songs.

Buddy
Victoria Palace Theatre, Victoria Street, SW1 (0171 834 1317). Victoria tube/BR. **Performances** 8pm Mon-Thur; 8.30pm Fri, Sat; *matinées* 5.30pm Fri, 5pm Sat. **Tickets** £6-£27.50.
Alan Janes' show tells the true and tragic story of the bespectacled rock 'n' roll star who was killed in a plane crash at the age of 21. It's a revue show of Buddy Holly's most famous songs and has been running for several years now. Only for the most dedicated fan.

Cats
New London Theatre, Drury Lane, WC2 (0171 405 0072). Holborn or Covent Garden tube. **Performances** 7.45pm Mon-Sat; *matinées* 3pm Tue, Sat. **Tickets** £10.50-£30.
The most successful Andrew Lloyd Webber musical of them all, based on TS Eliot's *Old Possum's Book of Practical Cats*, still generates enough fizz to keep packing audiences in despite being London's longest-running musical.
Disabled: access.

Ten Tips for Cheap Theatre-Going

1. The Half-Price Ticket Booth in Leicester Square (*see above* **Information & Tickets**) has a number of cheap tickets for most West End shows. These are sold on a first come, first served basis (cash only).
2. Matinée performances are much cheaper than evenings but in some instances understudies replace the stars. Seats for Monday-Thursday evening performances in the West End are uniformly cheaper than Friday or Saturday nights.
3. Pay for a restricted-view seat in the stalls (not all theatres have them), then move to a better seat when the lights go down. This is only possible when the show isn't sold out.
4. The cheapest seats are usually in the 'gods' at the top of the theatre, but you'll need a pair of binoculars to see the show.
5. Buy tickets direct from the box office to save on credit card charges, telephone booking fees (usually 10 per cent) and agency commissions.

6. Go to previews of West End and Off-West End shows. The tickets are considerably cheaper as the critics haven't had a chance to pan the show yet.
7. The National Theatre sells a number of tickets for shows on the day from 10am at the box office: 40 for the Olivier; 40 for the Lyttelton; 20 for the Cottesloe. Queues start at 8am for the popular shows.
8. Some theatres have reduced-price nights: at BAC you 'pay what you can' on Tuesdays; at the Royal Court all tickets are £5 on Monday nights; the Theatre Royal Stratford East has the lowest concessionary rates for students, OAPs and the unemployed. There's also a Student Standby Theatre Line (*0171 379 8900*), open after 2pm, which advises on ticket availability.
9. Many theatres, such as the Donmar and the National, sell standing-room tickets at vastly reduced prices. It's well worth enquiring about these if the show is either sold out or you're extremely broke.
10. Look out for special offers in *Time Out* magazine.

Copacabana

Prince of Wales Theatre, Coventry Street, W1 (0171 839 5987). Leicester Square tube. **Performances** 8pm Mon-Sat; *matinées* 3pm Wed, Sat. **Tickets** £20-£30.

Barry Manilow's musical, directed by Roger Redfarn and based almost entirely on Manilow's song 'Copacabana', is a wonderful over-the-top spectacular full of pirates in tights, chorus girls wearing teepees of ostrich feathers and go-go girls wearing fruit in all the wrong places. One of the slickest and most glamorous musicals in town.

Crazy For You

Prince Edward Theatre, Old Compton Street, W1 (0171 734 8951). Leicester Square or Tottenham Court Road tube. **Performances** 7.45pm Mon-Sat; *matinées* 3pm Thur, Sat. **Tickets** £11.50-£30.

A reworking of Gershwin's *Girl Crazy*, with showstopping numbers, great dancing and big portions of heart-stopping romance. Apart from the big ticket songs, the star of the evening is Susan Stroman's exhilarating choreography.

Grease

Dominion Theatre, Tottenham Court Road, W1 (0171 416 6060). Tottenham Court Road tube.
Performances 7.30pm Mon-Sat; *matinées* 3pm Wed, Sat. **Tickets** £10-£27.50.

The coach-party favourite based on the film with a heart as big as a Cadillac. All-round family entertainment and a triumph of energy over good taste.

Les Miserables

Palace Theatre, Shaftesbury Avenue, W1 (0171 434 0909). Leicester Square tube. **Performances** 7.30pm Mon-Sat; *matinées* 2.30pm Thur, Sat. **Tickets** £7-£30.

This RSC production of Alain Boublil's and Claude-Michel Schonberg's epic adaptation of Victor Hugo's novel is still going strong. Sit right up high in the cheapest seats to see how the slick scene changes work, and take a hankie for those tragic moments.

Miss Saigon

Drury Lane Theatre, Catherine Street, WC2 (0171 494 5000). Covent Garden tube. **Performances** 7.45pm Mon-Sat; *matinées* 3pm Wed, Sat. **Tickets** £8.50-£30 (telephone booking fee £1.50, £1).

Another outing by Boublil and Schonberg, directed by British theatre darling Nicholas Hytner, this sumptuous update of *Madame Butterfly* – complete with spectacular floor shows, dream sequences and a helicopter – takes place around the fall of Saigon in 1975. An American GI falls in love with a Vietnamese prostitute. Wearing its heart on its sleeve. Doomed love, indeed.
Disabled (0171 494 5470): access; toilets.

The Mousetrap

St Martin's Theatre, West Street, WC2 (0171 836 1443). Leicester Square tube. **Performances** 8pm Mon-Sat; *matinées* 2.45pm Tue, 5pm Sat. **Tickets** £8-£22.

Agatha Christie's charming institution of a play continues to stroll along at a sedate 1930s pace towards the 21st century, supported by some of the most innocently camp acting in the West End.

Oliver!

London Palladium, Argyll Street, W1 (0171 494 5020) Oxford Circus tube. **Performances** 7.30pm Mon-Sat; *matinées* 2.30pm Wed, Sat. **Tickets** £10-£30 (telephone booking fee £1).

Cameron Mackintosh's rousing revival of Lionel Bart's original musical restores those great anthems to demanding more gruel and picking pockets. Currently stars one of the finest British actors of stage and screen, Jonathan Pryce, as Fagin and Sally Dexter as Nancy. A visually busy show, but not a patch on the film. Directed by Sam Mendes.

Phantom of the Opera

Her Majesty's Theatre, Haymarket, SW1 (0171 494 5000/5400). Piccadilly Circus tube. **Performances** 7.45pm Mon-Sat; *matinées* 3pm Wed, Sat. **Tickets** £9-£30 (telephone booking fee 12½%).

Now in its ninth year, Andrew Lloyd Webber's lavish smash hit continues to attract long queues of hopeful tourists waiting for returns. You already know the story – hideous monster falls in love with beautiful opera singer – and most of the songs too, no doubt.
Disabled (0171 494 5470): access; toilets.

Starlight Express

Apollo Victoria Theatre, Wilton Road, SW1 (0171 416 6070). Victoria tube/BR. **Performances** 7.45pm Mon-Sat; *matinées* 3pm Tue, Sat. **Tickets** £12.50-£30.

The world's only roller-skating musical, performed at high speed on tracks before, around and above the nightly packed audience, has recently undergone a major overhaul involving new songs and direction. But the circus atmosphere is its greatest strength.

Sunset Boulevard

Adelphi Theatre, Strand, WC2 (0171 344 0055). Charing Cross tube/BR. **Performances** 7.45pm Mon-Sat; *matinées* 3pm Thur, Sat. **Tickets** £17.50-£35.

Andrew Lloyd Webber's latest extravaganza, based on the Billy Wilder film of the same name and directed by Trevor Nunn, had a successful revamp in 1994. It has more bite, more songs, and Betty Buckley in the lead role gives it a livelier feel. Worth seeing for the sets alone.

Woman in Black

Fortune Theatre, Russell Street, WC2 (0171 836 2238). Covent Garden tube. **Performances** 8pm Mon-Sat; *matinées* 3pm Tue, 4pm Sat. **Tickets** £8.50-£20.

Susan Hill's popular ghost story adapted by Stephen Mallatrat. Performed by just two actors, is still capable of sending tingling ripples of fear down the spine and producing an uncomfortable lurch in the stomach.

Open-air Theatre

See also chapter **Music: Classical & Opera** for outdoor opera at **Holland Park**.

Regent's Park

Open Air Theatre, Regent's Park, W1 (0171 486 2431/1933). Baker Street tube. **Tickets** phone for details. **Repertory** season May-Sept, phone for details.

This is a magical venue for outdoor theatre but it lives and dies according to the fickle English weather. It is well and truly open to the elements – starlings fly overhead, midges bite, trees rustle – and despite hot summer days, can get quite chilly in the evening after the sun sets. Plays here run in repertoire so it's worth checking the listings in *Time Out* magazine if you've set your heart on the annual favourite, *A Midsummer Night's Dream*.

Off-West End

Almeida

Almeida Street, N1 (0171 359 4404). Angel tube or Highbury & Islington tube/BR. **Open** box office 10am-6pm Mon-Sat.

Guided by the firm hands of artistic directors Ian McDiarmid and Jonathan Kent, the Almeida, a stone's throw from Islington's Upper Street, regularly turns out impressively selected, acted and directed productions, tending towards the modern and the seriously avant garde. (*See also chapter* **Music: Classical & Opera**).

BAC

176 Lavender Hill, SW11 (0171 223 2223).
Clapham Junction BR. **Open** box office 10am-6pm
Mon; 10am-10pm Tue-Sun. **Tickets** £4-£8.50; 'pay
what you can' Tue.
Dubbed 'the National Theatre of the Fringe' because of the
sheer number of visiting productions that sweep into the
venue every two or three weeks, BAC (formerly the Battersea
Arts Centre) is a theatre factory. After an adventurous tenure
under artistic director Paul Blackman, it will be interesting
to see how the venue does under new management. It also
has a very strong stand-up comedy tradition and boasts a
bookshop and a gallery space that features several major
photography exhibitions.

The Bush

Shepherd's Bush Green, W12 (0181 743 3388).
Goldhawk Road or Shepherd's Bush tube. **Open**
telephone booking 10am-7pm Mon-Sat.
This small theatre above The Bush pub has one of the
strongest commitments to new writing in Britain. It's reputation is such that the company have been able to shift many
of their impressive plays into the West End after opening
here. The best place to sit is right up at the back so you don't
have to sit with people's knees pressing into your back.
Scunthorpe-based Richard Cameron's hard-hitting comedy
dramas première here and are well worth watching out for.

Donmar Warehouse

Thomas Neal's, Earlham Street, WC2 (0171 369 1732).
Covent Garden tube. **Open** box office 10am-8pm Mon-Sat.
Tickets £10-£18.
This is one of the most exciting, but also one of the most
expensive, of the Off-West End venues with tickets for some
shows at West End prices. The stage is circular.

Drill Hall

*16 Chenies Street, WC1 (0171 637 8270). Goodge Street
tube.* **Open** box office 10am-8pm Mon-Fri; 12.30pm-8pm
Sat. **Tickets** £6-£10.
Gay, lesbian, feminist and politically aware theatre is the
speciality of the studio-style Drill Hall. It's backed up by a
vegetarian café in the basement, a women-only bar night on
Mondays, a no-smoking day on Thursdays and a crèche on
Friday evenings.

The Gate

*The Prince Albert, 11 Pembridge Road, W11 (0171 229
0706). Notting Hill Gate tube.* **Open** box office 10am-6pm
Mon-Fri.
A small pub theatre with a gigantic reputation, the Gate has
established a critical vogue with revivals of little-known
European classics. Under the new artistic direction of young
turk David Farr, it will be interesting to see if it will now
branch into the contemporary and experimental.

Hampstead Theatre

*Avenue Road, NW3 (0171 722 9301). Swiss Cottage
tube.* **Open** box office 10am-7pm Mon-Sat.
Tickets £8-£13.
It's not unusual for plays to transfer from this charming theatre to the West End, or to see big names on the stage.

King's Head

*115 Upper Street, N1 (0171 226 1916). Angel tube or
Highbury & Islington tube/BR.* **Open** box office 10am-
8pm Mon-Sat; 10am-4pm Sun. **Tickets** £9-£10.
London's oldest pub theatre is still lively after all these years
and is one of last bastions of lunchtime theatre – short
plays you can watch over your burger. In the evening it takes
on a bohemian cabaret atmosphere, serves inexpensive pre-
theatre suppers and has recently produced several notable
musical revivals. Bands play in the bar after shows, and the
late drinking licence (until midnight) makes it popular.

Orange Tree

1 Clarence Street, Richmond, Surrey (0181 940 3633).
Richmond tube/BR. **Open** box office 10am-7pm Mon-Sat.
Tickets £5.50-£11.50.
Under Sam Walters, this beautiful theatre in the round
has produced consistently sterling work. It attracts a loyal
local audience and is an ideal place to visit after a day trip
to the riverside town of Richmond (*see* **London By Area:
South London**).

Theatre Royal Stratford East

Gerry Raffles Square, E15 (0181 534 0310).
Stratford tube/BR. **Open** box office 10am-6pm Mon-Fri;
10am-3pm Sat.
This is a fascinating place – a crumbling Victorian theatre
(surrounded by a dismal shopping centre) that consistently
puts on high-quality drama which appeals to locals as well
as West End theatre-goers.

Tricycle

269 Kilburn High Road, NW6 (0171 328 1000).
Kilburn tube. **Open** box office 10am-8pm Mon-Sat.
Tickets £7.50-£13.
The Tricycle not only justifiably takes pride in running a
brave programme, but its comfortable premises and excel-
lent bar make it one of the livelier venues Off-West End.

Young Vic

66 The Cut, SE1 (0171 928 6363). Waterloo tube/BR.
Open box office 10am-6pm Mon-Sat. **Tickets** £6-£18.
The Royal Shakespeare Company took temporary residence
in this Waterloo venue in 1995, but its fortunes had already
been turned around through some exciting programming by
artistic director Tim Supple.

Fringe Venues

Check out the venues below to sample the best of
London's ever-active fringe.
Brick Lane Music Hall *152 Brick Lane, E1 (0171
377 8787). Aldgate East, Shoreditch or Liverpool Street
tube.* **Open** box office 10am-6pm Mon-Fri; dinner from
7.30pm; show 9pm.
Etcetera Theatre *Oxford Arms, 265 Camden High
Street, NW1 (0171 482 4857). Camden Town tube.*
Open box office 10am-8pm Mon-Sat.
The Finborough *Finborough Arms, Finborough Road,
SW10 (0171 373 3842). Earl's Court tube.* **Open** box
office 11am-8pm Mon-Sat.
Greenwich Studio *Prince of Orange Pub, 189 High
Road, SE10 (0181 858 2862). Greenwich BR.* **Open** box
office 11am-8pm Mon-Sat.
Hen & Chickens *Highbury Corner, N1 (0171 704
2001). Highbury & Islington tube/BR.* **Open** box office
noon-7pm Mon-Sat.
Man in the Moon *392 King's Road, SW3 (0171 351
2876/5701). Sloane Square tube then 11, 19, 22 bus.*
Open box office 10am-7pm Mon-Sat.
New End Theatre *27 New End, NW3 (0171 794
0022). Hampstead tube.* **Open** box office 10am-8pm
Mon-Sat.
Old Red Lion *St John Street, EC1 (0171 837 7816).
Angel tube.* **Open** box office 10am-11pm daily.
Southwark Playhouse *62 Southwark Bridge Road,
SE1 (0171 620 3494). Borough tube.* **Open** box office
11am-8pm Mon-Sat.
Turtle Key Arts Centre *74A Farm Lane, SW6 (0171
385 4905). Fulham Broadway tube.* **Open** box office
10am-8pm Mon-Sat.
White Bear *138 Kennington Park Road, SE11
(0171 793 9193). Kennington tube.* **Open** box office
10am-6pm Mon-Sat.

After Hours

***In the wee small hours of the morning, when the whole
wide world is fast asleep...***

If you're visiting London and you've just come
from Naples, say, or Amsterdam or Paris – or any
other major city in Europe – or if you've come over
from New York, New Orleans… wherever, you'll
notice that come midnight London pretty much
closes down. Tubes stop around 12.30am, after
which you join the mostly good-natured crowds
on a night bus or pay through the nose for a cab.

Having said which, there are encouraging signs
around Soho that the 24-hour lifestyle might slowly be creeping into the capital. More and more
shops of all kinds are staying open later. For more
information on what to do after hours, *see chapters*
**Shopping & Services, Comedy, Film, Gay
& Lesbian, Music: Rock, Folk & Jazz** *and*
Clubs. For emergencies *see chapter* **Survival**.

Transport

Last tubes from central London are between midnight and 12.30am. London Regional Transport
operates night buses until the tubes start again at
6am (8-9am on Sunday). The focal point is Trafalgar Square; most night buses run to and from
there. BR runs an irregular service of trains to com-
muter stations on the outskirts through the night
from Euston, King's Cross (main line and Thameslink stations), Victoria and Waterloo. For further
information on times for the tubes, night buses and
overland trains call the LRT enquiry service on
0171 222 1234 which is open round the clock.

You can catch a taxi or minicab any time, day
or night. You'd be advised to pick up the phone
rather than rely on being picked up off the street.
See chapter **Getting Around**.

Comedy

The **Comedy Store**, **Jongleurs Camden Lock**,
and **Up the Creek** will keep a smile on your face
into the early hours. *See chapter* **Comedy**.

Drinking

There are relatively few ways to drink after pub
hours, although the situation is gradually improving. The rule is: you can keep drinking if you have
paid to do something else. So, if you go to dance,
eat or watch comedy, keep drinking until thrown

out. Pubs throughout central London are employing DJs or musicians as entertainment and having
their licences extended to 2am or later. Look for a
pub or bar that charges an entry fee. Otherwise,
see chapters **Comedy, Music: Rock, Folk &
Jazz** *and* **Clubs** for late night bars disguised as
entertainment hotspots.

Atlantic
*20 Glasshouse Street, W1 (0171 734 4888). Piccadilly
Circus tube/night buses from Trafalgar Square.* **Open**
noon-3am Mon-Sat; 7-10.30pm Sun. **Credit** A, AmEx, V.
If you just want to drink, you have to queue until there's
room inside. If you want to eat late, book a table.

Café Bohème
*13-17 Old Compton Street, W1 (0171 734 0623).
Tottenham Court Road or Leicester Square tube/night
buses from Trafalgar Square.* **Open** 8am-3am Mon-Sat;
9am-10.30pm Sun. **Drinks served** 11am-3am Mon-Sat;
11am-3pm, 7-10.30pm, Sun. **Credit** A, AmEx, £TC, V.
Drinks are served without food until closing time, but there's
an admission charge for drinkers late in the evening.

Cuba Libre
*72 Upper Street, N1 (0171 354 9998). Angel tube/N19,
N73, N92 N96 night bus.* **Open** noon-2am Mon-Sat;
noon-10.30pm Sun. **Credit** A, AmEx, DC, £TC, V.
Ersatz Cuban restaurant, lively music and late drinking.

Eating

London does have plenty of decent and half-decent
restaurants that stay open late. It also has plenty
of restaurants best avoided whatever the time of
day or night. *See chapter* **Restaurants** or for a
more detailed look at the scene, buy the latest edition of the *Time Out Eating & Drinking Guide*.

Bar Italia
*22 Frith Street, W1 (0171 437 4520). Tottenham Court
Road tube/night buses from Trafalgar Square.* **Open** 24
hours daily. **Unlicensed**. **No credit cards**.
The coffee is what counts, although there are a few snacks.

Ed's Easy Diner
*12 Moor Street, W1 (0171 439 1955). Leicester Square
tube/night buses from Trafalgar Square.* **Open** 11.30am-
midnight Mon-Thur, Sun; 11.30am-1am Fri, Sat. **Credit**
LV, £TC.
Mock 1950s US diner style, mini-jukeboxes, meaty burgers.

Häagen Dazs
*14 Leicester Square, WC2 (0171 287 9577). Leicester
Square tube/night buses from Trafalgar Square.* **Open**
10am-midnight Mon-Thur, Sun; 10am-1am Fri, Sat. **No
credit cards**.
For if it's just *got* to be ice cream.

In the event of insomnia, it's either Brick Lane's **Beigel Bake** *or that Hal Hartley video.*

Yung's

23 Wardour Street, W1 (0171 437 4986). Leicester Square tube/night buses from Trafalgar Square. **Open** noon-4.30am daily. **Credit** A, AmEx, DC, £TC, V.
Even at 4am the food is well above average in this popular Chinatown eaterie.

WKD Cafe

18 Kentish Town Road, NW1 (0171 267 1869). Camden Town tube/N1, N2 night bus. **Open** noon-2am Wed-Sat; noon-midnight Sun. **Admission** £2-£3 after 9.30pm. **Credit** A, AmEx, £TC, V.
Mix of café, restaurant, club. What do you care, it's open late.

Film

For cinemas which run late shows on Fridays and Saturdays, *see chapter* **Film**. Cinemas do change programmes, so keep an eye on *Time Out*. Late shows usually start around 11pm.

Music

See also chapter **Music: Rock, Folk & Jazz**.

100 Club

100 Oxford Street, W1 (0171 636 0933). Tottenham Court Road tube/N1, N2, N5, N98 night bus. **Open** 7.30pm-midnight Mon-Wed; 8pm-1am Thur; 8.30pm-3am Fri; 7.30pm-1am Sat; 7.30-11.30pm Sun. **Admission** £5-£8. **No credit cards**.
Gone are the Sex Pistols, in are jazz, blues, swing and jive.

Ronnie Scott's

47 Frith Street, W1 (0171 439 0747). Leicester Square, Piccadilly Circus or Tottenham Court Road tube/night buses from Trafalgar Square. **Open** 8.30pm-3am Mon-Sat. **Admission** £12-£14. **Credit** A, AmEx, DC, V.
Expensive drinks but worth it for the standard of the jazz.

Mean Fiddler

28A High Street, NW10 (0181 961 5490). Willesden Junction tube/BR/N18 bus. **Open** 8pm-2am Mon-Thur; 8pm-3am Fri, Sat; 7.30pm-1am Sun. **Admission** £4-£8. **Credit** A, V.
Pop, rock and country, plus folk in the Acoustic Room.

Shopping

See also chapters **Shopping & Services** *and* **Survival**.

Pharmacists

Bliss

5 Marble Arch, W2 (0171 723 6116/6219). Marble Arch tube/N3, N56, N99 bus. **Open** 9am-midnight daily. **Credit** A, AmEx, DC, £TC, V.
Branches: 33 Sloane Square, SW1 (0171 730 1023); 149 Edgware Road (0171 723 2336).

Warman Freed

45 Golders Green Road, NW11 (0181 455 4351). Golders Green tube/N13 bus. **Open** 9am-midnight daily. **Credit** A, AmEx, DC, V.

Groceries

There are lots of 24-hour petrol stations dotted around the capital; many of them stock certain groceries, such as bread, milk and chocolate. The 7-Eleven chain has sprouted also. Open 24 hours, they do not take credit cards. They are expensive but stock a range of goods, from frozen food to hot snacks. Check the phone book for your nearest.

Beigel Bake

159 Brick Lane, E1 (0171 729 0616). Aldgate East tube/N76, N95, N98 night bus. **Open** 24 hours daily. **No credit cards**.
Unbeatable bagels for unsleepy people.

Ridley Bagel Bakery

13-15 Ridley Road (0171 923 0666). Dalston Kingsland BR/N83 night bus. **Open** 24 hours daily. **No credit cards**.
Terrific filled bagels round the clock.

Riteway

57 Edgware Road, W2 (0171 402 5491). Marble Arch tube/N18, N56, N59, N79 night bus. **Open** 24 hours daily. **No credit cards**.
Groceries, magazines, newspapers, cigarettes and sweets.

In Focus

Business

Whether you want to flog your new line in Hawaiian shirts or try your hand at corporate raiding, London is the biz.

A precious moment of tranquillity in the City.

Well over half of London's ten million foreign visitors each year are involved in business of some sort and many are drawn not only by the international financial centre in the City but also by the reputation of its supporting business services. This section gives you the full range of those services. If you want to import, export, patent a revolutionary toaster design, find your first secretary, or simply check out the competition, it's all here.

Banking

Arrange banking facilities with your own bank before leaving home: chances are, it'll have a reciprocal arrangement with a British bank, and you may need to obtain references. The head offices of the 'big four' commercial banks are listed below. *See chapter* **Essential Information** for opening hours and further information.

Barclays Bank
54 Lombard Street, EC3 (0171 626 1567). Bank tube.

Lloyds Bank
71 Lombard Street, EC3 (0171 626 1500). Bank tube.

Midland Bank
Poultry, EC2 (0171 260 8000). Bank tube.

National Westminster Bank
41 Lothbury, EC2 (0171 726 1000). Bank tube.

Business Information

The *Financial Times* is the best newspaper to consult for an update on facts and figures in the City

and all over the world. If you enjoy a little more analysis, however, try the *Economist*.

American Chamber of Commerce
75 Brook Street, W1 (0171 493 0381). Bond Street tube. **Open** 9am-5pm Mon-Fri; *library* 10.30am-2.30pm Mon-Thur.
Want to sell it in America? Got something they'll just love? The Chamber publishes a trade directory, but only member companies may use the library and research facilities. The commercial library of the American Embassy *(0171 499 9000)* is another good source of US business addresses.

Anglo-Japanese Economic Institute
Morley House, 314-322 Regent Street, W1 (0171 637 7872). Piccadilly Circus tube. **Open** 9.30am-5.30pm Mon-Fri by appointment.
A good source of reference material on all Japanese economic matters. Each year it publishes the invaluable *Japanese Addresses in the UK* (£7.50).

Business Design Centre
52 Upper Street, N1 (0171 359 3535/fax 0171 226 0590). Angel tube. **Open** 9am-5pm Mon-Fri.
A trade centre for commercial interior design, this impressive building contains showrooms, an exhibition centre and a conference centre. The exhibitions display products used in commercial design, and they usually change weekly.

Business Information Service
British Library, 25 Southampton Buildings, Chancery Lane, WC2 (0171 412 7454). Chancery Lane tube. **Open** *library* 9.30am-9pm Mon-Fri; 10am-1pm Sat. *Phone enquiries* 9.30am-5.30pm Mon-Fri.
The most comprehensive collection of business information in the UK is held here, including company reports, house journals and, for those inclined, CD-ROM services. There's a quick query service on the number above, or a Priced Research Service *(0171 412 7457/fax 0171 412 7453)* which will undertake on-line searches of the library records, and provide market overviews, company profiles, distributor details and mailing lists.

Chamber of Commerce and Industry
33 Queen Street, EC4 (0171 248 4444/fax 0171 489 0391). Mansion House tube. **Open** 9am-5.30pm Mon-Fri; *export documents dept* 9.30am-4.30pm Mon-Fri; *reference library (members only)* 9.15am-5.15pm Mon-Fri.
The largest Chamber of Commerce in the UK. No matter how shiny your suit, the chamber is only open to members and overseas visitors, who may avail themselves of the lounge and function rooms.

EC Information Unit
8 Storeys Gate, SW1 (0171 973 1992). St James's Park or Westminster tube. **Open** 10am-1pm (also 2-5pm by appointment) Mon-Fri; *information point* 10am-6pm Mon-Fri.
The small London office of the European Commission will provide information on Brussels' initiatives. There's also a

'Men and women... sucked up through an infinitely complicated respiratory apparatus of trains and termini into the mighty congested lungs...' – 'The Slaves of Solitude', Patrick Hamilton.

reference library open to all. The information point is packed with free literature on what the EC gets up to.

Extel Financial

Fitzroy House, 13-17 Epworth Street, EC2 (0171 825 8000/fax 0171 251 3525). Liverpool Street tube/BR or Moorgate tube/BR. **Open** *enquiries* 10am-5.30pm Mon-Fri; *help desk and computer desk* 24 hours daily.

Extel publishes financial data on easy-to-read sheets about more than 9,000 British and foreign businesses. It costs £29 to take one of these cards away. The firm also does British and overseas company searches and deals with all kinds of corporate financial queries and problems.

Financial Times Cityline

(recorded information 0891 123456/list of all lines 0898 123099/information 0171 873 4378). **Open** 24 hours daily.

There are 28 *FT* Cityline recorded information services, updated constantly with news from financial markets. Calls cost 48p a minute peak time, 36p a minute cheap rate.

Jordan & Sons Company Information

20-22 Bedford Road, WC1 (0171 400 3333/fax 0171 251 0825). Old Street tube/BR. **Open** 8.30am-5.30pm Mon-Fri.

Need the low down on a competitor before you go any further? Jordan's will find out everything short of the colour of their pants. A full company search costs £29.44 and takes up to 48 hours. Company formations are also organised (Britain and overseas); telephone for a quote.

London Law Agency

84 Temple Chambers, EC4 (0171 353 9471). Temple tube. **Open** 9am-5.30pm Mon-Fri.

If you want to form a company in the UK, this agency is one of many that can cut through the red tape, for a fee. It can also provide status reports on UK companies (£20 per company) so you can vet your potential trading partner.

London World Trade Centre

International House, 1 St Katherine's Way, E1 (0171 488 2400). Tower Hill tube. **Open** 9am-5.30pm Mon-Fri.

In common with the other 240 or so Trade Centres around the world, complete office and business support services are offered here. The Centre will also provide lists of prospective buyers or suppliers for your product in this country, trade leads and business information.

Reference Libraries

See also chapter **Survival**.

Chamber of Commerce & Industry Reference Library

33 Queen Street, EC4 (0171 248 4444/fax 0171 489 0391). Mansion House tube. **Open** 9.15am-5.15pm Mon-Fri.

The Chamber of Commerce and Industry's comprehensive library is open to members and overseas visitors. You'll find general commercial information and detailed information on export and international trade.

City Business Library

1 Brewers Hall Garden, EC2 (0171 638 8215/recorded information 0171 480 7638). Moorgate tube. **Open** 9.30am-5pm Mon-Fri.
The City Business Library keeps an excellent range of business reference works, including newspaper cuttings, Extel cards and world directories.

London Business School Library

Sussex Place, Regent's Park, NW1 (0171 262 5050). Baker Street tube or Marylebone tube/BR. **Open** 9am-11pm Mon-Fri; also during term-time 9am-5pm Sat, 1-9pm Sun **Admission** £20 a day.
The library has a collection of by-country and by-industry information files, plus a comprehensive stock of standard business reference works, including Extel and McCarthy press-cutting cards. The LBS Research Service *(0171 723 3404)* will do the work for you at a rate of £60 per hour.

Communications

British Monomarks

Monomarks House, 27 Old Gloucester Street, WC1 (0171 405 4442/404 5011/fax 0171 831 9489). Holborn tube. **Open** 9.30am-5.30pm Mon-Fri; *telex bureau* 8am-8pm Mon-Fri. **Credit** A, AmEx, £$TC, V.
At British Monomarks you may use a telex or fax machine, have mail forwarded, or arrange to use the 24-hour telephone answering service. Leave a deposit and phone in your telex messages, 24 hours a day.

Business Matters

203 High Street, SE13 (081 318 1235/fax 0181 318 1439). Lewisham BR. **Open** 8.30am-8.30pm Mon-Fri; 8.30am-noon Sat. **Credit** A, AmEx, DC, £TC, V.
Dictate a message over the telephone and Business Matters will fax or telex it for you anywhere in the world. Its telephone answering service costs £30 a month plus VAT, to be paid in advance.

Hanway Print Centre

102-106 Essex Road, N1 (0171 226 6868). Angel tube. **Open** 9am-5.30pm Mon-Fri. **Credit** A, £TC, V.
The Hanway Print Centre offers a comprehensive and reasonably priced photocopying (colour and black & white) and print service, including high speed Xeroxing. You can send a fax for £1 a page within the UK.

Company Legislation

Institute of Trading Standards Administration (ITSA)

3/4/5 Hadleigh Business Centre, 351 London Road, Hadleigh, Essex (0702 559922/fax 0702 559902). Hadleigh BR.
The Administration will provide details of your local Trading Standards Office, which is responsible for enforcing current legislation on fair and safe trading. It will also offer help and advice.

Patent Office

25 Southampton Buildings, WC2 (0171 438 4700). Chancery Lane tube. **Open** 10am-4pm Mon-Fri.
It costs £25 to file a patent here, although in all cases the office recommends employing a qualified agent for its precise wording. The patent examiners also offer a Search and Advisory Service (SAS). For £200 or more, they will also gather information from the world's largest single source of technical information. The Patent Office library (open 9.30am-9pm Mon-Fri; 10am-1pm Sat) contains the national collection of patent documentation.

Conferences

London Tourist Board

26 Grosvenor Gardens, SW1 (no phone/fax 0171 730 9367). Victoria tube/BR. **Open** 8am-7pm Mon-Sat; 8am-4pm Sun.
The London Tourist Board will assist with the organisation of conventions or exhibitions. By letter or fax, request its free guide *Convention and Exhibition London,* which lists hotels and centres that host events, together with their facilities.

Queen Elizabeth II Conference Centre

Broad Sanctuary, SW1 (0171 222 5000/enquiries 0171 798 4060/fax 0171 798 4200). St James's Park tube. **Open** 8am-6pm Mon-Fri; 24-hour conference facilities.
This purpose-built centre has some of the best conference facilities in London. There's a choice of rooms with capacities from 12-1,000; communication equipment is available and there's a TV studio equipped to broadcast-specifications.

Couriers

Harley Street Runners

65 Great Portland Street, W1 (0171 323 5595/fax 0171 323 5867). Oxford Circus tube. **Open** 8am-7pm Mon-Fri; 8am-3pm Sat. **Credit** A, AmEx, DC, JCB, V.
A van, cycle, motorbike and foot messenger service. The couriers will go anywhere in mainland Britain for a fixed amount. The company can also organise direct mailing, removals, Datapost and foreign deliveries.

Parcel Force Datapost

Datapost Service Centre, 4th floor, 20-23 Greville Street, EC1 (Freephone 0800 88 4422/fax 0171 250 2938). Farringdon tube/BR. **Open** 8.30am-5.30pm Mon-Fri. **Credit** A, AmEx, DC, V.
Parcel Force Datapost is a Post Office parcel service. Use it to send packages anywhere in Britain; next-morning delivery is guaranteed. There's also an international service. Parcels are accepted at any main post office and same-day delivery can often be arranged. ●

Equipment Hire

ABC Business Machines

59 Chiltern Street, W1 (0171 486 5634). Baker Street tube. **Open** 9am-5.30pm Mon-Fri; 9.30am-12.30pm Sat. **Credit** A, £TC, V.
Answerphones, calculators and audio equipment are among the equipment you can hire from ABC. Electronic typewriters cost £35 a month, fax machines £53 a month. Copiers and computers start at £90 a month.

Network Office Equipment

63 Lupus Street, SW1 (0171 821 8186/fax 0171 630 5160). Pimlico tube. **Open** 9am-5.30pm Mon-Fri. **Credit** A, AmEx, £$TC, V.
All types of office electrical equipment can be bought or hired from Network. Short-term rental charges (per month) start from £45 for electronic typewriters, £75 for a Cannon fax machine and £195 for IBM computers with laser printers.

Import & Export

Within EC countries, import licences are needed only for raw steel and restricted items (firearms, for example). Importers from outside the EC need licences for a wide variety of goods, including clothing and shoes, textiles, agricultural goods, foodstuffs and ceramics. An application, which must be made for each product to be imported, takes from three to five days to clear. Licences are valid from three months to a year. Commercial goods must be declared on arrival and an SAD (Single Administrative Document) completed. But for merchandise carried as baggage (valued under £600) a customs declaration may not be needed. There's a standard rate of 17.5 per cent Value Added Tax (VAT) on most imported goods, based on the value of the goods plus the duty payable.

The exporting of certain goods – arms, electronic and chemical equipment – requires licences issued by a Tory MP or, more seriously, the **Department of Trade & Industry** (*see below*).

British Overseas Trade Board
123 Victoria Street, SW1 (office hours 0171 215 5000/ 5.30pm-9am 0171 215 5000). **Open** 9am-5pm Mon-Fri.
The OTB was set up in 1972 to advise the government on overseas trade. Over 200 experts are available to give practical advice to anyone wishing to export goods to any destination in the world.

Companies House
55-71 City Road, EC1 (general information 0171 253 9393/company search 0222 380801). Old Street tube/BR. **Open** 8.30am-5.30pm Mon-Fri (last company search 3pm).
In order to export goods from Britain, you should register here as a UK company (for taxation purposes). You can also gain access to information on companies, British and foreign (if registered here).

Customs & Excise
New King's Beam House, 22 Upper Ground, SE1 (0171 620 1313 ext 3997/fax 0171 865 5625). Waterloo tube/BR. **Open** 9am-5pm Mon-Fri.
The New King's Beam House deals with telephone enquiries only. You can call in person at Dorset House, Stanford Street, SE1, during office hours. Phone for the addresses of local London centres giving advice on VAT and excise.

Department of Trade & Industry (DTI)
Queensway House, West Precinct, Billingham, Cleveland, TS23 2NF (01642 553671/fax 01642 533557). **Open** 9am-5pm Mon-Fri.
Export Licensing Unit *Kingsgate House, 66-74 Victoria Street, SW1 (0171 215 8070/fax 0171 215 8564). Victoria tube/BR.* **Open** 9am-5pm Mon-Fri.
Contact the Billingham DTI office with enquiries about, or applications for, import licences. The Export Licensing Unit deals with enquiries on export controls and licences.

Export Market Information Centre
DTI, Kingsgate Housee, 66-74 Victoria Street, SW1 (0171 215 5444/business statistics 0633 812973/fax 0171 215 4231). Victoria tube/BR. **Open** 9am-8pm Mon-Fri.
Everything you could possibly want to know about exporting is kept here. The database – the British Overseas Trade Information System – provides information on products, markets, overseas agents and export opportunities.

Institute of Export
64 Clifton Street, EC2 (0171 247 9812). Liverpool Street tube/BR. **Open** 9.15am-5pm Mon-Fri.
A professional body that aims to 'raise the standards of export management... through the exchange of information and ideas between exporters'. Enquiries about Institute membership are welcomed.

Institute of Freight Forwarders
Redfern House, Browells Lane, Feltham, Middx (0181 844 2266/fax 0181 890 5546). Hatton Cross tube or Feltham BR. **Open** 9am-5pm Mon-Fri.
The Institute gives information about sending freight and baggage, and puts callers in touch with reputable companies who handle air and sea freight. Ask either for the Air or Sea division, as appropriate.

Removals
Bishop's Move
102 Stewarts Road, SW8 (0171 498 0300). Vauxhall tube/BR. **Open** 9am-5.30pm Mon-Fri. **Credit** by arrangement.
This reliable family-owned company has been shipping, removing and distributing goods for 140 years. It will undertake almost any scale of work, but specialises in handling valuable furniture.

Evan Cook
134 Queen's Road, SE15 (0171 635 0224). Queen's Road Peckham BR. **Open** 9am-5pm Mon-Fri. **Credit** by arrangement.
A good London firm that has been specialising in office removals since 1893.

Secretarial
More typing services are advertised on bookshop noticeboards and in *Time Out*'s classified ads.

Reed Employment, Staff Agency
143 Victoria Street, SW1 (0171 821 5593/fax 0171 821 5598). Victoria tube/BR. **Open** 8.45am-5.30pm Mon-Fri.
Reed supplies secretarial, computing, accountancy and technical services to registered companies.

Typing Overload
67 Chancery Lane, WC2 (0171 404 5464/fax 0171 831 0878). Chancery Lane tube. **Open** 9.30am-5.30pm Mon-Fri. **Credit** A, AmEx, DC, £$TC, V.
Come here for a speedy and professional typing service for any job that can be done on a word-processor.
Branch: Knightsbridge Secretarial Services 170 Sloane Street, SW1 (0171 235 6855).

Translation
AA Technical & Export Translation
The London International Press Centre, 76 Shoe Lane, Fleet Street, EC4 (0171 583 8690/fax 0171 353 3133). Chancery Lane tube or Blackfriars tube/BR. **Open** 10am-6pm Mon-Fri. **No credit cards.**
AA provides native speakers of most languages; it has on its books 612 translators speaking 50 languages. Rates vary from £8 to £21 per 100 words depending on the language and complexity of the text. Interpreters cost between £220 and £500 per day. AA is a member of the Association of Translation Companies and a holder of the International Export Association Seal of Approval.

Central Translations
2-3 Woodstock Street, W1 (0171 493 5511). Bond Street tube. **Open** 9am-5pm Mon-Fri. **No credit cards.**
Conveniently situated in the West End, Central offers typesetting and proof-reading of pretty well every language under the sun, as well as translation and interpreters. Rates for translation into English range from about £8.50 to £25 per 100 words depending on how esoteric the copy is.

Children

*From ghosties and ghoulies to Sumatran tigers and teddy bears'
picnics, every day is Funday in London.*

London is a wonderful city for children. They love
the noise and confusion, the museums, cinemas,
parks, pomp and junk food, the heave and swelter
of its streets. After years of treating their children
with a sort of weary intolerance, of late the British
have thrown themselves into the rearing and entertainment of their offspring with a manic intensity.
It is now actually fun to be a child in London.

The one drawback to all this becomes apparent
the moment you take your first lungful of London's
reeking, pestilential air. British governments (incredibly, there's no such thing as a *London* government) have seemed hell-bent on turning their
capital into the world's most polluted city. Read
the papers for air quality reports (the *Guardian*
and *Evening Standard* carry them) and if WHO
safety levels are exceeded, as is common in the
summer, get your kiddies off the streets and into
a museum. Or *see chapter* **Trips Out of Town**...

Sightseeing & Attractions

See **Index** to locate more details for these ten suggestions and *chapter* **Sightseeing** for more.

Buckingham Palace
What could be more exciting to children than a real palace
where a real Queen lives? Okay, it's pretty boring once you're
inside (and the queues can be long), but the tramping of red-
coated guards in the square outside keeps everyone amused.
Nearby: **Green Park** and **St James's Park**, for
letting off steam; **Royal Mews** for horses and coaches.

Changing the Guard
To avoid the big crowds round the Palace railings (*see above*),
go early and wait near the Barracks in Birdcage Walk to see
the Guard march across to the Palace.
Nearby: The **Royal Mews** and **Westminster
Cathedral** tower (take the lift to the top).

Covent Garden Market
Full of shops, stalls and street entertainers. Don't miss the
Cabaret Mechanical Theatre and Eric Snook's Toyshop.
Nearby: **London Transport Museum**, **Theatre
Museum**, **St Paul's Church** garden for a picnic and
the **Oasis** outdoor and indoor pools.

Greenwich
Choose a fine day and take the riverboat to explore Greenwich and **Greenwich Park** (a 15-minute walk from the
pier), then walk under the River Thames (through the pedestrian tunnel from Greenwich Pier to the Isle of Dogs) to return
on the Docklands Light Railway from Island Gardens to
Tower Gateway or Bank.
Nearby: **Cutty Sark**, **Gipsy Moth IV**, **National
Maritime Museum** and **Greenwich Market**.

HMS Belfast
A great place for children, with seven huge decks to explore;
the best way to get there is by ferry boat from Tower Pier.
Nearby: **Tower Bridge**, **Tower Hill Pageant** and the
gruesome **London Dungeon**.

Kew Gardens
Climb up high in the giant glasshouses to look down on a
jungle of plants, swelter in the steamy Aroid House, or just
take a picnic in the most beautiful gardens in London.
Nearby: **Kew Bridge Steam Museum** and the
Musical Museum (both across Kew Bridge).

Piccadilly Circus
The big attractions are **Rock Circus**, Planet Hollywood and
the **Trocadero**. Evenings are the best time to visit.
Nearby: Chinatown, Leicester Square cinemas.

The South Bank
The River, its bridges and its traffic are an inspiration. Start
at the riverside terraces of the **Royal Festival Hall**, where
there are cafés, free foyer exhibitions and special events on
summer weekends. Then stroll along the South Bank to
Gabriel's Wharf, with its small shops, tea room, pizza restaurant, and open-air music and dance evenings in the summer.
Nearby: NFT, MOMI, National Theatre.

St Paul's Cathedral
Climb to the Dome for a breathtaking view over the City. You
need a head for heights and plenty of stamina.
Nearby: Postman's Park, the **Museum of London** and
the **Barbican Centre**.

Trafalgar Square
On a fine day, Trafalgar Square is a good place to spend a
credit card-free hour. Take a camera, and marvel at how long
the under-12s enjoy feeding the pigeons, climbing on the
lions, playing around the fountains and watching the world
go by. When they tire of this, round them up, cross the road
to the **National Gallery** (free admission), and head straight
for Room 18 to see the extraordinary van Hoogstraten
peepshow *Views of the Interior of a Dutch House*.
Nearby: **National Portrait Gallery**, The Mall (leading to
Buckingham Palace), Downing Street.

Meet the Animals

The British love their animals. London's parks
are teeming with wildlife, its streets and buildings
are mobbed by pigeons and its pavements are
encrusted with dog effluent. Your best bet is to
head for the city farms – 18 altogether – the
biggest of which is Mudchute Park & Farm, Pier
Street, Isle of Dogs, E14 (*0171 515 5901*). For a
full list contact the National Federation of City
Farms, AMF House, 93 Whitby Road, Brislington,
Bristol BS4 3QF (*0117 971 9109*). *See also below*
Theme & Safari Parks.

Battersea Park Children's Zoo

Battersea Park, SW11 (0181 871 7540). Sloane Square tube then 19 or 39 bus/Battersea Park BR. **Open** *Easter-Oct* 10am-5pm daily (last admission 4.30pm); *Oct-Easter* 11am-3pm (weekends only). **Admission** £1; 40p under-15s, OAPs.

There are meerkats and lots of animals to stroke, including pygmy goats, rabbits and a pot-bellied pig. The caged monkeys are rather sad, the snakes suitably menacing.

Bocketts Farm

Bocketts Farm Park, Young Street, Fetcham, Near Leatherhead, Surrey (01372 363 764). Fetcham or Leatherhead BR, then taxi/by car A24, then A246. **Open** 10am-6pm daily. **Admission** £2.50; £2 under-17s; £1.35 2 years; free under-2s.

A lovely farm that's close enough to London to make it accessible. There are farm animals (goats, shire horses, pigs, chickens) to stroke and nuzzle, some tame deer, a huge, hay-stuffed barn and playgrounds. It's very popular, particularly in spring (all those lambs), so try to visit on a weekday.

Kentish Town City Farm

1 Cressfield Close, Grafton Road, NW5 (0171 916 5421). Kentish Town tube/BR/Gospel Oak BR. **Open** 9am-5.30pm Tue-Sun. **Admission** free.

London's original city farm is set on five acres (two hectares) of land, and boasts a riding club for young Camden residents. There are horses, cows, goats and free-range chickens.

London Zoo

Regent's Park, NW1 (0171 722 3333). Camden Town tube/Baker Street tube then 74 bus. **Open** 10am-5.30pm daily. **Admission** £7; £6 OAPs; £4 under-15s; free under-4s; £20 family ticket (2 adults, 2 children). **Credit** A, AmEx, £$TC, V.

Coram's Fields – *no unaccompanied adults.*

The revamped Children's Zoo now has new buildings and landscaping, along with numerous interactive displays scattered among the interactive animals. It's here that your toddler, who's been straining to forge a meaningful relationship with the Sumatran tiger, can finally get her sticky paws on the wildlife: there are sheep and goats to fondle, pigs with hairy backs to scratch and downy-haired wallabies to clinch in a tight embrace. The emphasis is on British wildlife and farm animals, and there are some wonderful rare breeds, but you'll also meet reindeer, llamas and a lugubrious Bactrian camel. For a review of the main Zoo, *see chapter* **Sightseeing**. *Disabled: access to most areas. Restaurant.*

Parks & Playgrounds

Regent's Park has boating lakes, playgrounds and **London Zoo**; **Kensington Gardens** has two playgrounds and the Round Pond. Londoners' favourites are **Hampstead Heath** (especially Parliament Hill Fields for kite flying, children's playgrounds and a huge open-air lido); **Battersea Park** (with a boating lake and Children's Zoo); **Holland Park** in Kensington; and, in the north, Alexandra Park (with an indoor ice rink, mini-golf course, boating lake, animal enclosure and a great view over London). We list three of interest to children below; *see also chapter* **Parks & Gardens**.

Coram's Fields

93 Guilford Street, WC1 (0171 837 6138). Russell Square tube. **Open** *Easter-end Oct* 9am-8pm daily; *Nov-Mar* 9am-5pm daily. **Admission** free.

Right in the centre of London, this children's park has a café where visitors can enjoy their meals and teas. The pet animal area has sheep, goats, rabbits, guinea pigs, pigs, ducks, chickens and an aviary. They also have an under-fives play area, paddling pool and drop-in centre (open 2-4pm Mon-Fri), and a play area and sports ground for older children. No dogs, and **no adults admitted without a child.** *Disabled: access; toilets.*

Crystal Palace Park

Thicket Road, Penge, SE20 (0181 778 9496). Crystal Palace BR. **Open** 7.30am-dusk daily. **Admission** free.

A quirky park, home to the **Crystal Palace National Sports Centre.** Attractions include a farmyard, with pigs, goats and horses, a boating lake with bizarre Victorian dinosaurs prowling on the islands, a maze, a 'land train' (that's a dressed-up tractor to most of us) and a Children's Funfair.

Syon Park & London Butterfly House

Syon Park, Brentford, Middlesex (0181 560 0378/recorded information 0181 560 7272). Gunnersbury tube then 237, 267 bus. **Open** *Oct-Apr* 10am-3.30pm daily; *May-Sept* 10am-5.30pm daily. **Admission** £2.75; £1.75 under-16s, OAPs; family £6.95 (2 adults, 4 children). **Credit** A, V.

In the grounds of Syon Park is a huge tropical greenhouse full of foliage and thousands of butterflies, including the Atlas Moth (largest in the world) and a room full of insects and arachnids including scorpions, tarantulas and ants. *Café. Restaurant.*

One O'Clock Clubs

These are play clubs within parks where pre-school children can play in safety. Most have sandpits, Wendy houses, paints, slides and climbing frames. Children must be accompanied by an adult.

Proof, if it were needed, that you don't have to be a child to enjoy a day out at **Chessington**.

Barnard Park

Barnsbury Road, N1 (0171 278 9494). Angel tube/Caledonian Road & Barnsbury BR. **Open** *one o'clock club* noon-3.30pm Mon-Fri.

Battersea Park

Albert Bridge Road, SW11 (0181 871 6349). Battersea Park/Queenstown Road BR/19, 39, 44, 45, 49, 130, 137, 170 bus. **Open** 7am Mon-Fri (closing times vary throughout year); *adventure playground* 3.30-7pm Mon-Fri; 10.30am-6pm Sat, Sun (closed Mon during term-time).

Holland Park

Abbotsbury Road entrance, W8 (0171 603 2838). Holland Park tube. **Open** *one o'clock club* 12.30-5.30pm Mon-Fri; 10.30am-5.30pm Sat, Sun (10.30am-5.30pm daily during school holidays).

Paddington Recreation Ground

Randolph Avenue, W9 (0171 625 7024). Maida Vale tube. **Open** phone for details of under-5s club.

Theme & Safari Parks

See chapter **London by Season** for the dates of funfairs in London.

Chessington World of Adventures

Leatherhead Road, Chessington, Surrey (01372 729560/recorded information 01372 727227). Chessington South BR/bus Flightline 777 from Victoria Coach Station. **Open** *July-Oct* 9.30am-9.30pm, *Oct-July* 10am-5.45, daily (last admission 3pm). **Admission** £14.50; £11.50 4-14s; £6.25 OAP; £5.75 disabled; under-4s free. **Credit** A, AmEx, V.

A frenetic 65-acre/26-hectare theme park and zoo. If you take the train (35 minutes from Waterloo), hang on to your train tickets because there's usually reduced-price admission for BR passengers. Arrive as early as you can because it fills up rapidly, particularly during school holidays, with queues for the most popular rides. The latest is Rameses Revenge, a huge swinging chair swooping violently through the air. Mobster Magic, an attraction on a gangster theme, replaces the Circus Big Top, and there's a new ride, Sea Storm. Other favourites include the Runaway Mine Train, the breathtaking Vampire (a suspended rollercoaster) and the Safari Skyway Monorail for a panoramic view over the park and zoo. *Baby changing facilities. Cafés. Disabled: access. Restaurants. Shop.*

Thorpe Park

Staines Road, Chertsey, Surrey, KT16 8PN (01932 569393). Staines BR/Hatton Cross tube, then link bus to Thorpe Park/by car M25 junction 11 or 13. **Open** *Apr-Oct* 10am-5.30pm daily. **Admission** £13.25; £11.25 children; family £40 (2 adults, 4 children); free children under 1m tall.

A Disneyesque theme park in Surrey, massively revamped and now attracting one million frenzied visitors a year. The pleasantly landscaped site covers 500 acres close to London and rounds up all the usual suspects: terrifying rides, stunt shows, a working farm, 'fungle jungle' adventures, ghost rides, oversized cartoon characters and enough junk food to down Marlon Brando. Loads of fun for all the family.

Whipsnade Wild Animal Park

Dunstable, Bedfordshire, LU6 2LF (01582 872171). Luton or Hemel Hempstead BR, then bus/by car M1 junction 9 or 12; M25 junction 21. **Open** *Apr-Oct* 10am-6pm Mon-Sat, 10am-7pm Sun; *Nov-Mar* 10am-4pm daily. **Admission** £7.30; £5.50 3-13s; £6 OAPs, disabled.

London Zoo's out-of-town safari park makes for a much breezier and more cheering day out. About 600 acres of prime English countryside are stocked with rhinos, giraffes, tigers, bears, lions, herds of zebra, hippos, cheetahs, penguins, elephants and the unpronounceably rare Przewalski's horse. Favourites with children are the sea-lions, the chimps and the kids' farm. There's no driving: you take the Whipsnade railway, the free road-train or you walk.

Woburn Safari Park

Woburn Park, Bedfordshire, MK17 9QN (01525 290407/8). By car M1 junction 13. **Open** *Mar-Oct* 10am-5pm daily; *Nov-Feb* 11am-3pm Sat, Sun. **Admission** £7.90; £5.40 children; free under-3s.

The Duke of Bedford's vast grounds have been turned over to a rather grand safari park. There are lions, tigers and elephants, of course, but the place is becoming better for close interaction with animals, less alarming species. There's a tiny tot safari trail, badger valley, playgrounds, pet's corner and, new in 1995, 'rainbow landing', an idea borrowed from San Diego Zoo where visitors can be dive-bombed by lorikeets (they're birds). The main part of Woburn remains the drive-through safari and the unsettling experience of having your car mobbed by hungry baboons. Adults may want to see the lovely Woburn Abbey later, but they won't be allowed to.

Horrors & Spooks

Truth be told, and despite the earnest efforts of generations of teachers and parents, all that any self-respecting child craves is blood; preferably by the bucketful and ideally incorporating torture, severed heads and a lingering, sacrificial death. So if your offspring is whimpering with tedium in yet another dusty museum or grimly stroking the umpteenth ickle fluffy bunny, it's time to unleash the brute on one of the places below.

Chislehurst Caves

Old Hill, Chislehurst, Kent (0181 467 3264). Chislehurst BR from Charing Cross station (about 25 mins). **Open** *Easter-Sept* 11am-5pm daily; *Oct-Easter* 11am-4.30pm Wed-Sun. **Admission** *short tour* £3; £1.50 accompanied under-15s, OAPs; free under-5s. *Long tour* (2.30pm Sun, Bank Holidays) £5; £2.50 under-15s; no under-5s.

Take a spooky lamplight tour (45-50 minutes) through this maze of ancient man-made chalk tunnels and caves. Previous occupants include the Druids, the Romans and war-time Londoners sheltering from air-raids. The place is largely untouched and there are chilling stories of druid sacrifices and ghosts. The long tour takes 90 minutes, delving deeper. *Café (open school holidays and weekends).*

London Dungeon

28-34 Tooley Street, SE1 (0171 403 0606). London Bridge tube/BR. **Open** 10am-6.30pm daily (last admission one hour before closing). **Admission** £7.50; £4.50 under-14s; £6 students, OAPs; free entry for under-5s and disabled. **Credit** A, AmEx, £TC, V.

Grisly waxwork displays of torture, execution, murder, plague and other incidents of foul play make this one of the worst places to take a young child with a nervous disposition. Older children lap it up, even the grotesquely exploitative Jack The Ripper Experience. *Café. Disabled: access. Group discount.*

Madame Tussaud's

Marylebone Road, NW1 (0171 935 6861). Baker Street tube. **Open** *May-Sept* 9am-5.30pm daily. *Oct-Jun* 10am-5.30pm Mon-Fri; Sat, Sun 9.30am-5.30pm. **Admission** £8.35; £6.25 OAPs; £5.25 under-16s; family ticket £21.95 (2 adults, 2 children). *Combined ticket with Planetarium* £11.25; £8.50 OAPs, students; £6.95 under-16s; family ticket £29.45 (2 adults, 2 children). **Credit** A, AmEx, £TC, V.

The hefty admission price proves that this is one of the most popular of all the tourist attractions, and one of the best for children. The premise should be familiar to all by now: life-sized waxwork dummies of the famous and infamous, many of them bearing only a fleeting resemblance to the original.

Well, John Major's good, of course, and Joan Collins' skin has the right consistency, but most of the interest lies in discovering who the management deem to be sufficiently famous to be included. None of this seems to matter to the merry millions who pack the place out, oohing and aahing over the pop stars, royalty, sports personalities, actors and the Chamber of Horrors. It's in this last bit that you can ogle various psychopaths and their victims, frozen for ever in the last moments of terror and pain – children love it. *Café. Disabled: access by prior arrangement. Group discount.*

Museums & Collections

The **Natural History Museum** is the most popular with children, especially the *Jurassic Park*-style robotic monsters in the Dinosaur Section. The **Science Museum**, next door, has Launch Pad, with dozens of do-it-yourself experiments for tots to teenagers; they also organise Science Nights, when children can explore the museum after dark (book ahead). The **Museum of the Moving Image (MOMI)** is another favourite, where kids can watch film clips, audition on a film set, see themselves read the news and get close to a Dalek. The **Museum of London** holds workshops for children and adults. The **National Maritime Museum** has exciting exhibitions, plus a Pirate Playground for younger children. The **British Museum** has an excellent children's guide *Inside the British Museum* (£2.50 in the bookshop).

The all-new **London Toy & Model Museum** is splendidly hands-on and practically indestructible; by contrast, the dolls' houses and back copies of *The Beano* at the **Bethnal Green Museum of Childhood** are strictly hands-off and for older children and adults only. One of the quirkiest of London's museums (a magnificent mish-mash of musical instruments, newts and a stuffed walrus) is the **Horniman Museum**. For details of these and many more, *see chapter* **Museums**.

Cabaret Mechanical Theatre

33 The Market, Covent Garden Piazza, WC2 (0171 379 7961). Covent Garden tube. **Open** *Easter-Sept* 10am-7pm daily. *Oct-Easter* noon-6.30pm Mon; 10am-6.30pm Tue-Sun. **Admission** £1.95; £1.20 under-16s, OAPs, students, UB40s; under-5s free; £4.95 family (2 adults, 3 children). **Credit** A, AmEx, DC, £TC, V.

More than 40 push-button machines and automata make up the collection. There are enough levers and buttons to keep even the most hyperactive child busy, but most spectacular is the life-size barman dispensing an endless flow of Scotch. *Group discount. Shop.*

Pollock's Toy Museum

1 Scala Street (entrance 41 Whitfield Street), W1 (0171 636 3452). Goodge Street tube. **Open** 10am-5.30pm Mon-Sat. **Admission** £2; 75p under-18s (free Sat).

'If you love art, folly, or the bright eyes of children, speed to Pollock's,' proclaimed Robert Louis Stephenson, and he was right. Benjamin Pollock was a maker of toy theatres. Downstairs is a theatrical print shop and a number of toys, puppets and miniature theatres for sale; upstairs, rambling over two small rooms, is the main museum, crammed with dolls, toys, board games and theatrical artefacts. Recommended age range is 7-12, but we find younger children love it.

Bethnal Green Museum of Childhood, *E2.*

Activities & Sports

See chapter **Sport & Fitness** *for swimming pools, go-karting, boating, tennis and ten-pin bowling. See chapter* **Sightseeing** *for the* **Trocadero**.

Brass Rubbing Centre
Crypt of St Martin-in-the-Fields Church, Trafalgar Square, WC2 (0171 930 9306). Charing Cross tube/BR. **Open** 10am-6pm Mon-Sat; noon-6pm Sun. **Admission** free. **Brass rubbings** according to size £1.50-£11.50. **Credit** *shop* A, AmEx, £TC, V.
Housed in one of London's most famous churches. Children can rub replicas of medieval church brasses and so follow a tradition that has been popular in Britain for generations. Steer them towards the smaller exhibits; you pay by size. *Gift shop.*

Central YMCA
112 Great Russell Street, WC1 (0171 637 8131). Tottenham Court Road tube. **Open** children's sessions 10am-noon Sat. **Admission** £1.50 non-members.
Saturday morning supervised sessions for juniors (8-14 years) include badminton, basketball, climbing, fitness training, table tennis, trampolining, and swimming in the beautiful dark-blue pool, plus arts and crafts.

Discovery Zone
First Floor, Clapham Junction Shopping Centre, SW11 (0171 223 1717). Clapham Junction BR. **Open** 10am-8pm daily. **Admission** (2-12s) £3.99 weekdays; £4.99 weekends.
Parents and children can bounce about, climb rope ladders, crawl through tunnels and explore this exciting indoor adventure playground. It's quite small, so go early.

Water Palace
619 Purley Way, Croydon (0181 688 2090). East Croydon BR then bus 194. **Open** 10am-9pm (last adm 8pm) daily. **Admission** *varies according to time* £3.50-£5; £2.50-£4 under-16s; free under-3s free.
This south London Mecca for webbed-footed youngsters boasts six flumes, a wave pool, fun pool, 180-metre lazy river ride where the current takes you round in large inflatable rings, full catering facilities and a licensed bar.

Shopping

These are London's best shops for toys, games and magic. Not listed here, but worth checking out, are the toy departments at **Harrods** (87-135 Brompton Road, SW1/*0171 730 1234*) and **John Lewis** (278-306 Oxford Street, W1/*0171 629 7711*).

5-12
Bentall Centre, Wood Street, Kingston, Surrey (0181 974 8900). Kingston BR. **Open** 9am-6pm Mon-Wed, Fri, Sat; 9am-9pm Thur. **Credit** A, V.
Non-violent and non-addictive computer games. All the displays are at children's eye-level, and the shop is on one floor. *Play area.*

Baby Gap/Gap Kids
146 Regent Street, W1 (0171 287 5095). Oxford Circus tube. **Open** 9.30am-7pm Mon-Wed, Fri, Sat; 9.30am-8pm Thur; noon-6pm Sun. **Credit** A, AmEx, EC, V.
Clothes are strong on denim and very pleasing to the eye. A Gap hat is the well-dressed baby's trademark.

Bananas
7 Clarendon Cross, W11 (0171 727 1011). Holland Park tube. **Open** 9.30am-5.30pm Mon-Fri; 10.30am-4.30pm Sat. **Credit** A, V.
First-clothes for baby and fashionable gear for children up to 12. It also has wooden and traditional nursery toys.

Buckle My Shoe
19 St Christopher's Place, W1 (0171 935 5589). Bond Street tube. **Open** 10am-6pm Mon-Wed, Fri, Sat; 10am-7pm Thur. **Credit** A, AmEx, DC, JCB, V.
Multiple award-winning shoe designs and a chic clothing department (Oilily, Chipie, Blu Kid, Paul Smith).

Children's Bookshop
29 Fortis Green Road, N10 (0181 444 5500). East Finchley tube. **Open** 9.15am-5.45pm Mon-Sat. **Credit** A, AmEx, V.
Over 20,000 titles, including science tomes, atlases, a wonderful range of fiction, plus plenty for the pre-school brigade. There are Saturday-morning and school-holiday events.

The Computer Exchange
32 Rathbone Place, W1 (0171 636 2666). Tottenham Court Road tube. **Open** 10am-7pm Mon-Sat; noon-5pm Sun. **Credit** A, V.
Popular, funky outlet for new and secondhand video games and consoles and ideal if you want to swop well-played games for new ones, see the latest imports or just hang out. *Mail order.*

Davenport's Magic Shop
7 Charing Cross Underground Shopping Concourse, Strand, WC2 (0171 836 0408). Charing Cross tube/BR. **Open** 10.15am-5.30pm Mon-Fri; 10.15am-4pm Sat. **Credit** A, V.
A family business whose staff are keen to encourage newcomers to get into magic, suggesting a beginners' range of coin and card tricks. Also a wide range of stage equipment. *Catalogue. Mail order.*

Disney Store
140 Regent Street, W1 (0171 287 6558). Oxford Circus tube. **Open** 9.30am-8pm Mon-Sat; noon-6pm Sun. **Credit** A, AmEx, JCB, V.
Snow White, Lion King, 101 Dalmations – whichever Disney is in at the moment, all the plastic to buy in its honour is here.

Early Learning Centre
Putney Exchange Shopping Centre, Putney High Street, SW15 (0181 780 1074). Putney BR. **Open** 9am-6pm Mon-Sat. **Credit** A, V.
A flourishing chain of shops with large stocks of brightly coloured, chunky toys. As well as their own well-priced toys, stores carry the full Duplo and Brio ranges. ELC was one of the first toy chains to set up a play area for children. *Baby-changing facilities. Free catalogue. Toilet.*
Branches are too numerous to list here. Check the phone book for your nearest.

Games & Puzzles

65 The West Yard, Camden Lock, NW1 (0171 267 8220). Camden Town tube. **Open** 10am-5.30pm Tue-Sun. **Credit** A, £TC, V.

Traditional games – chess, mah-jong, Go! – plus books on games and a fine selection of wooden puzzles.
Mail order.

Hamleys

188-196 Regent Street, W1 (0171 734 3161). Oxford Circus tube. **Open** 10am-6.30pm Mon-Wed; 10am-8pm Thur; 10am-7pm Fri; 9.30am-7pm Sat; noon-6pm Sun. **Credit** A, AmEx, DC, JCB, V.

Five floors of noise, colour, beaming staff in red T-shirts, crazed children and harassed parents. Hamleys has all the toys that have ever passed a safety test: games, soft toys, ride-on toys, crafts, videos and more. London's biggest selection of board games is on the fourth floor. If the idea doesn't fill you with a nameless dread, you can always visit Sega Dome in the basement, a high-tech games zone with the very latest in arcade equipment.
Baby-changing facilities. Café. Catalogue. Mail order

HMV

150 Oxford Street, W1 (0171 631 3423). Oxford Circus tube. **Open** 9.30am-7pm Mon-Wed, Fri, Sat; 9.30am-8pm Thur. **Credit** A, AmEx, DC, £TC, V.

Half of the first floor is devoted to Nintendo, Sega, 3DO, Philips CD-i, PC and Mac software, consoles and add-ons.
Mail order.
Branches: 363 Oxford Street, W1 (0171 629 1240); 4 Trocadero, Coventry Street, W1 (0171 439 0447).

Toys 'R' Us

Trojan Way, off Purley Way, Croydon, Surrey (0181 686 3133). Waddon BR. **Open** 9am-8pm Mon-Thur, Sat; 9am-9pm Fri; 11am-5pm Sun. **Credit** A, AmEx, V.

Fatuous name, but TRU is unsurpassed for value, if you're after big-name brands. Come without the children, because they're not allowed to play with the toys on the shelves.
Branches: Tilling Road, NW2 (0181 209 0019); 76-78 High Road, N22 (0181 881 6636).

Tridias

25 Bute Street, SW7 (0171 584 2330). South Kensington tube. **Open** 9.30am-6pm Mon-Fri; 10am-6pm Sat. **Credit** A, V.

Original, reasonably priced equipment: a particularly good place to look for rainy-day activity toys, scientific toys and dressing-up gear. The catalogue is inspirational.
Catalogue. Mail order.

Virgin Megastore

14-30 Oxford Street, W1 (0171 631 1234). Tottenham Court Road tube. **Open** 9.30am-8pm Mon, Wed-Sat; 10am-8pm Tue; noon-6pm Sun. **Credit** A, AmEx, £TC, V.

The refurbishment and expansion is complete, so the Megastore can now claim to be the biggest entertainment outlet in Britain. Apart from every CD under the sun, the Megastore has a serviceable games department, with sections devoted to PC and Macintosh software, as well as plenty of stuff for CD-i, Nintendo, 3DO and Sega. On the first floor there is a fantasy role-playing and war games section.
Disabled: access. Export scheme. Mail order.

Warner Brothers Studio Store

178-182 Regent Street, W1 (0171 434 3334). Oxford Circus tube. **Open** 10am-7pm Mon- Fri; 9.30am-8pm Sat; noon-6pm Sun. **Credit** A, AmEx, DC, V.

A retailing shrine to the animated stars of Warner Bros: Daffy, Bugs, Tweetie Pie, Sylvester and so on. Upstairs, young visitors can have a go on the computer painting game, Paint Shack, and muck around in the model space rocket.

Entertainment

Barbican Children's Cinema Club

Barbican Centre (cinema 1), EC2 (0171 638 8891). Barbican tube/BR/Moorgate tube/BR. **Admission** £3; £2.50 under-15s. **Membership** £3 per year. **Credit** A, AmEx, £TC, V.

Films generally start at 2.30pm on Saturdays.

Little Angel Marionette Theatre

14 Dagmar Passage, off Cross Street, N1 (0171 226 1787). Angel tube/Highbury & Islington tube/BR. **Performances** 11am, 3pm Sat, Sun (closed 17 July-2 Sept). **Admission** £4-£5. **No credit cards.**

The Little Angel is London's only permanent puppet theatre, founded in 1961, with seating for 110. It's a delightful place, with regular weekend shows by the resident company as well as visiting puppeteers. There is a minimum age limit of 3; 3-6-year-olds may be admitted to morning performances (telephone to check).
Disabled: access; induction loop for the hard of hearing.

Lyric Theatre Hammersmith

King Street, W6 (0181 741 2311). Hammersmith tube. **Performance** 11am, 1pm Sat. **Admission** £3. **Credit** A, AmEx, DC, £TC, V.

Children's entertainment, from plays and puppets to clowns and workshops, is put on every Saturday.
Disabled: access by prior arrangement.

National Film Theatre

South Bank, SE1 (0171 928 3232). Waterloo tube/BR. **Admission** £4.35 adults; £2.75 under-16s. **Credit** A, AmEx, £TC, V.

Matinées for children on Saturday and Sunday at 4pm.

Nomad Puppet Studio

37 Upper Tooting Road, SW17 (0181 767 4005). Tooting Bec tube. **Performances** 11.30am, 2.30pm, Sun; closed for six weeks mid July-Sept. Private parties by arrangement. **Admission** £2.50.

A small, friendly theatre which provides excellent entertainment in the form of short puppet stories for ages 3-8. Squash and biscuits are provided.

Polka Theatre for Children

240 The Broadway, SW19 (0181 543 0363/4888). Wimbledon South tube/Wimbledon BR. **Admission** £3.30-£5.50. **No credit cards.**

A beautiful purpose-built complex for the under-13s, with a 300-seat theatre, an Adventure Room for under-5s, a delightful playground, a train café and two shops. It's a thriving company with a well-deserved reputation and several award-winning shows. Closed in September.
Café. Disabled: access; induction loop for the hard of hearing.

Rio Cinema

107 Kingsland High Street, E8 (0171 249 2722/0171 254 6677). Dalston/Kingsland BR. **Admission** £2.50; £1.50 under-15s. **No credit cards.**

The Rio Cinema Club takes place on Saturdays at 11am — you can drop your children off and collect them after the film.

Unicorn Theatre for Children

6 Great Newport Street, WC2 (0171 836 3334). Leicester Square tube. **Performances** *term-time* 10.15am, 1.30pm Tue-Fri; 11am, 2.30pm Sat; 2.30pm Sun; *school holidays* phone to confirm. **Admission** £4.50-£8.50 plus 20p. **Credit** A, £TC, V.

Founded in 1948, this is London's oldest professional children's theatre. It puts on an adventurous programme of commissioned plays and other entertainment (puppets, magic, music) for 4-12-year-olds.

Annual Events

For **Changing the Guard** and **Trooping the Colour**, *see chapters* **Sightseeing** *and* **London By Season** respectively.

Teddy Bears' Picnic
Battersea Park, SW11 (0181 871 8107). Battersea Park BR/49 bus. **Date** Usually 1st Friday afternoon in August. **Admission** free.
An annual picnic is held for thousands of children plus their furry friends. Accompanying activities range from face painting to donkey rides.

Summer in the City
Barbican Centre, Silk Street, EC2 (0171 638 4141). Barbican tube/BR. **Date** first week in August. **Admission** £1; £4.50 under-16s.
One of London's major arts centres holds this annual jamboree of events for 2-10-year-olds. It takes place both indoors and outdoors – the Barbican has a lovely waterside terrace and café – with performances of music, comedy and theatre specifically for the under-11s. Phone for details.

Eating Out

Gone are the days when a restaurant that welcomed children was rarer than a clean bib. High chairs, crayons, paint books and children's menus are all now part of the London scene. Of course, the city is over-stuffed with fast food outlets and there's nothing like an infusion of salted E numbers to placate your offspring; but if you want something that's going to keep you all happy, try the following.

There are more places in *chapter* **Restaurants**. In particular, you're assured a warm welcome at Asian, Italian and American restaurants (don't forget the **Hard Rock Café** and **Planet Hollywood**). If you're after ice cream, consult *chapter* **Cafés & Brasseries**.

The Chicago Pizza Pie Factory
17 Hanover Square, W1 (0171 629 2552). Oxford Circus tube. **Open** 11.45am-11.30pm Mon-Sat; noon-10.30pm Sun. **Sunday lunch** £10; £6 children. **Credit** A, AmEx, £TC, V.
Children can share a pizza with their parents any day of the week, but Sundays are Fundays (noon-5pm), with a children's disco, story telling, face painting and entertainment from the Arts Theatre Workshop.

PJ's Grill
30 Wellington Street, WC2 (0171 240 7529). Covent Garden tube. **Open** noon-1am Mon-Sat; noon-4pm Sun. **Average** £12. **Credit** A, AmEx, DC, £TC, V.
Uncle PJ's fun club provides a special menu, toys, entertainers, high chairs and other delights for children who lunch here with their parents on Saturdays and Sundays.

Holland Park Café
Ilchester Place, Holland Park, W14 (0171 602 2216). Holland Park or Kensington High Street tube. **Open** 10am-8pm daily. **Average** £4.50; £2 children. **No credit cards.**
This delightful café in the middle of the beautiful Holland Park has plenty of outside seating. Wholesome Italian food, such as soup, pasta, pizza and ice-cream, is on the menu at very reasonable prices.

Oshobasho Café
Highgate Wood, Muswell Hill Road, N10 (0181 444 1505). Highgate tube. **Open** 8.30am-6.30pm Tue-Sun. **Average** £10. **No credit cards.**
Stroll through the beautiful, restful Highgate Wood, taking in the playground (near the Muswell Hill Road entrance), then arrive at this wonderful Italian café, overlooking the cricket pitch.

Smollensky's Balloon
1 Dover Street, W1 (0171 491 1199). Green Park tube. **Open** noon-midnight Mon-Sat; noon-10.30pm Sun. **Family lunches** noon-3pm Sat, Sun. **Average** £16; £7 children. **Credit** A, AmEx, DC, V.
The popular family lunches are on Saturdays and Sundays. The children's menu costs from £3.95 and there's a magic show, video games, balloons, a raffle and toys to keep the mites amused. Essential to book.
Branch: 105 Strand, WC2.

Sol E Luna
in Thomas Neal's Centre, 22 Shorts Gardens, WC2 (0171 379 3336). Covent Garden tube. **Open** noon-midnight Mon-Sat; noon-10.30pm Sun. **Credit** A, AmEx, DC, V.
Spacious, modern Italian restaurant. The children's menu gives a choice of pasta or pizza, an ice cream and a drink. Children are welcome any time but are amply catered for on Sundays, when Spotty Dotty the Clown presides over face painting, magic and balloon mayhem from 1-3pm *High chairs, crayons and colouring paper.*

Taking a Break

Childminders
9 Paddington Street, W1 (0171 935 3000/2049). Baker Street tube. **Open** 9am-5.30pm Mon-Fri; 9am-4.30pm Sat.
A large agency with more than 1,000 babysitters, mainly nurses and infant teachers (all with references), who live all over London and the suburbs.

Pippa Pop-ins
430 Fulham Road, SW6 (0171 385 2458). Parsons Green tube. **Open** by appointment. **Fees** £25 per morning or afternoon; £30 all day. **Credit** A, AmEx, £TC, V.
A crèche, nursery school, children's hotel and babysitting service run by NNEB and Montessori-trained nursery teachers and nannies in a large, bright, specially adapted house and garden. For children aged 2-12.

Universal Aunts
(childminding during the day 0171 738 8937/evening babysitting 0171 386 5900). **Open** 9.30am-5.30pm Mon-Fri.
An agency which provides reliable people to babysit, meet children from trains, planes and boats, or take them for a day's sightseeing.

Information

Circusline
(0891 343341). **Open** 24 hours daily.
Recorded information on circuses around the country.

Kidsline
(0171 222 8070). **Open** *term-time* 2-6pm Mon-Fri.
Information on films, shows, attractions and activities.

LTB Children's Information
(0839 123 404). **Open** 24 hours daily.
London Tourist Board's recorded service.

Gay & Lesbian

There's a lot more to London's gay and lesbian scene than coffee on Old Compton Street – there's bonhomie in Brixton, boyz in Brompton and babes in The Box.

London's gay and lesbian scene is bigger and brighter than it's ever been and much of it is as accessible to visitors as it is to the city's residents. To see gay London life at its most visible, just take a trip to Soho's Old Compton Street, where busy queer bars, restaurants and shops line the road. Here, though, as in many clubs, youth and beauty have the edge, and if you're less enchanted by fit bodies shoe-horned into Dolce & Gabbana, you might want to look further afield.

Information is easy to come by from the large amount of free press that you can pick up at most of the cafés and bars listed below. The *Pink Paper* and *Capital Gay* provide weekly news and listings; *Thud* and *QX* are geared to the club and entertainment scene; *Boyz* offers up hard bodies for its readers. Buyable options are the fashion-led *Attitude*, the long-running *Gay Times* and the monthly lesbian magazine *Diva*.

While there are bars and clubs that cater to very specific tastes and operate seriously observed dress codes, from uniforms to underwear, most are open to all comers. However, in the majority of mixed places women are hugely outnumbered by men. So it's great news that the lesbian scene is bursting out all over with successful women-only one-nighters springing up in every part of town. There are also plenty of events where you can take the boys along too (if they promise not to look more gorgeous than you do).

The Clubs

Some clubs just go on and on, but many don't. We'd like to think this is a reliable list, but it's best to check what is happening before setting out. Check the Gay section of *Time Out* magazine for up-to-date information.

Ace of Clubs
52 Piccadilly, W1 (0171 408 4457). Green Park tube. **Open** 9.30pm-4am Sat. **Admission** £2 before 10.30pm, £5 after.
The old-fashioned Ace has been bringing in an enthusiastic dyke crowd for the longest time. Butches, femmes and top of the pops tunes.

The Anvil
The Shipwright Arms, 88 Tooley Street, SE1 (0171 407 0371). London Bridge tube/BR/N47, N70, N89 night bus. **Open** 8.30pm-1am Mon-Wed; 8.30pm-2am Thur-Sat; 7.30pm-11pm Sun. **No credit cards**.
A late-night bar-cum-club for Real Men. Décor: corrugated iron netting. Atmosphere: less sleazy than it used to be.

Attitude
The Trafalgar, Junction of Trafalgar Avenue and Sumner Road, SE15 (0171 701 2175). **Open** 7-11pm Mon-Fri; noon-5pm, 7-11pm, Sat; noon-3pm, 7-10.30pm, Sun. **Admission** members free; £2 non-members before 9pm, £3 after.
This year-old men-only pub has already gained a panting city-wide following for its hot and heavy underwear-only nights. Bearing in mind the unlikely location, we'd advise getting a cab.

The Backstreet
Wentworth Mews, Burdett Road, E3 (0181 980 8557). Mile End tube/N76, N98 night bus. **Open** 10pm-2.30am Thur; 10pm-3am Fri, Sat; 9pm-1am Sun.
The Backstreet is supposedly Europe's largest rubber and black leather club for men, with a rigid dress code and a dark designer-macho interior. Students and those aged under 24 get in free.

Benjy's
562A Mile End Road, E3 (0181 980 6427). Mile End tube/N76, N98 night bus. **Open** 9pm-1am Sun. **Admission** £2.
The hairdressers' revenge. Chrome and plush sets the scene for this absolutely not West End, unashamedly commercial disco session. Mostly boys.

Bromptons Nite Club
294 Old Brompton Road, Earls Court, SW5 (0171 370 1344). Earls Court tube. **Open** 5pm-2am Mon-Fri; 6pm-2am Sat; 2pm-midnight Sun. **Admission** free until 11pm (10.30pm Sun); £2 after 11pm Mon-Wed, Sun; £3 after 11pm Thur-Sat.
Recently revamped as a club, Bromptons now offers mainstream disco music, plus male strippers and entertainers on some nights.

DTPM
Bar Rumba, 36 Shaftsbury Avenue (0171 287 2715). Piccadilly Circus tube. **Open** 2-10.30pm Sun. **Admission** £5 members; £7 non-members.
The post-club Sunday outing for those who just can't get enough. Boys and a few girls pack it out weekly. Pumping music, shiny happy people, very friendly.

The Fridge
Town Hall Parade, Brixton Hill, SW2 (0171 326 5100). Brixton tube/N2, N3, N78, N69 night bus. **Open** 9pm-4am Thur; 10pm-5am Fri; 10pm-6am Sat. **Admission** £7-£10, depending on night.
Busy venue with undersized cloakroom. The bare-chested boys at Love Muscle – and the go-go dancers – have been working it on a Saturday night for a good few years. Check press for other nights.

Gay bars, restaurants, shops and businesses now line Old Compton Street in Soho, W1.

The Garage

Holloway Road, N1 (0171 607 1818). Highbury Corner tube. **Open** varies. **Admission** varies.
Not the loveliest of venues, but it currently hosts Friday's casual and friendly indie night Vaseline Upstairs at the Garage (11pm-3am, £3.50, £2 concs) and Sunday's wonderful Tea Dance (5pm-midnight, £3.50) – formation and partner dancing for all camp comers.

GAY at LA2

157 Charing Cross Road, WC2 (0171 734 6963). Tottenham Court Road tube. **Open** 10.30pm-4am Mon, Thur; 10.30pm-5am Sat. **Admission** £1-£3.
With a real disco atsmosphere, real disco dollies and camp PAs on Saturdays, GAY is always packed to the rafters with boys and their girlie (but rarely lesbian) friends. On Saturday nights GAY has moved next door to LA1 (Astoria).

Heaven

Under the Arches, Villiers Street, WC2 (0171 839 3852). Embankment tube or Charing Cross tube/BR. **Open** 10.30pm-3am Wed-Sat; 9pm-1am Sun.
Admission £5-£8.
Don't be put off by the queue that snakes towards Charing Cross Station. Heaven will have you if you can wait. Once inside, find your own paradise: on the hard techno entrance floor; upstairs in the funky Star Bar; or up another floor still in the quieter but eminently groovy Dakota Bar. Wherever you are, you'll be rubbing shoulders with the best mix of fashion girls, boys and drag queens in town, to some of the best music. To make your evening even better, here's some advice: don't be tempted to buy drugs here – one, because it's illegal, and two, because they're all rubbish. Enjoy.

The Lowdown

Falconberg Mews, W1 (0956 400139). Tottenham Court Road tube. **Open** varies. **Admission** varies.
Silks on a Friday night at The Lowdown (11pm-4am; £3

before midnight, £5 after) brings together an attitude-free, totally mixed crowd – black, white, men, women, gay, straight – who just love the funky dance music.

Mars

12 Sutton Row, W1 (no phone). Tottenham Court Road tube. **Open** 10pm-3am Mon; 10.30pm-3am Wed; 10.30pm-4am Fri, Sat. **Admission** £5 Mon; £6 Wed; £10 Fri, Sat.
This small but sweet venue hosts some gay one-nighters. At the time of writing, it's is where fashion dykes (and their gay men friends) flock for Friday's fabulous Kitty Lips, while Fierce Child provides mixed after-club clubbing on Saturday nights (£5 before 11pm).

Turnmills

63B Clerkenwell Road, EC2 (0171 250 3409). Farringdon tube/N83 night bus. **Open** 10pm-7.30am Fri, Sat. **Admission** £10.
The home of Trade (Sun, 4am-noon) where ecstatic sweaty bodies jam the hard-house and techno-laden dance floor. Bare-chested muscle queens outnumber women (who sometimes have their own pre-Trade party here – check listings), but who are all these straight boys we've seen creeping in lately? Sunday's ff (10pm-6am) is trancier, sexier and strictly gay. Expect queues and unnecessary grief from the bouncers. Also check out REW (Thur, 10pm-6am), Gallery (Fri, 10pm-6am), both mixed, and Slip It To Me (Sat, 9pm-3am) which is for women only.

WayOut

143 Knightsbridge, SW1 (0181 363 0948). Knightsbridge tube. **Open** 8.30pm-1am Sat. **Admission** £4.50; £6 non-members after 10pm.
A ritzy Knightsbridge address for a dressed-up Saturday affair for TVs, TSs and their theatrical companions. It's a place to mingle, with some unpredictable cabaret thrown in. Better still, there are changing facilities.

Eating & Drinking

Most of the places listed below are open to gay men and lesbians unless specified, but we've tried to make clear which ones have rather less to offer female customers

79CXR
79 Charing Cross Road, W1 (0171 734 0769). Leicester Square tube. **Open** 1pm-1am Mon-Sat; 7pm-10.30pm Sun.
A popular unpretentious bar with a dark and cruisey feel, cheap prices, lots of boys and men, and late opening.

The Angel
65 Graham Street, N1 (no phone). Angel tube. **Open** noon-midnight Mon-Sat; noon-11.30pm Sun. **No credit cards.**
A pleasant café-bar with good (mostly vegetarian) food, inexpensive drinks and, for once, a 50-50 mix of women and men.

Balans
60 Old Compton Street, W1 (0171 437 5212). Tottenham Court Road tube. **Open** 8am-4am Mon-Thur; 8am-5am Fri, Sat; 8am-1am Sun. **Credit** A, £TC, V.
Incredibly popular café/restaurant in spite of its unpredictability: food and service range from miserable to passable.

The Black Cap
171 Camden High Street, NW1 (0171 485 1742). Camden Town tube. **Open** 1pm-2am Mon-Thur; 1pm-3am Fri, Sat; noon-3pm, 7pm-midnight, Sun. **Admission** free Mon, Sun; £2 Tue-Thur; £3 Fri, Sat.
A drag act institution, although the quality of the entertainment is variable. After the show (around midnight) you can cruise, dance to disco, or hit the late-opening pub-style bar.

The Box
32-34 Monmouth Street, WC2 (0171 240 5828). Covent Garden tube. **Open** 11am-11pm Mon-Sat; noon-6pm, 7-10.30pm, Sun. **Credit** A, AmEx, £TC, V.
A popular rendezvous for good food, coffee and drinks. On Sunday nights (7pm-late) the babe-only Girl Bar fills both floors with gorgeous twentysomethings.

Central Station
37 Wharfdale Road, N1 (0171 278 3294). King's Cross tube/BR. **Open** 5pm-2am Mon-Wed; 5pm-3am Thur; 5pm-5am Fri; noon-5am Sat; noon-midnight Sun. **Admission** free Mon-Thur, Sun, before 10.30pm Fri, Sat; £3 10.30pm-midnight, £4 after midnight, Fri, Sat.
A friendly, busy local male-orientated bar. Expect a variety of themes – sexual and sartorial – in the basement club on different nights. The ground and first floor have also been opened recently.

The Coleherne
261 Old Brompton Road, SW5 (0171 373 9859). Earl's Court tube. **Open** noon-11pm Mon-Sat; noon-3pm, 7-10.30pm, Sun.
London's most famous men's leather-scene bar.

Comptons Of Soho
53 Old Compton Street, W1 (0171 437 4445). Leicester Square or Piccadilly Circus tube. **Open** noon-11pm Mon-Sat; noon-3pm, 7-10.30pm, Sun.
It might have retained its traditional pub décor, but Comptons is once again a major place to be for young gay men.

Old Compton Café
34 Old Compton Street, W1 (0171 439 3309). Tottenham Court Road tube. **Open** 24 hours.
This round-the-clock sandwich bar has become an essential queer stop-off especially for that 5am post-club cappuccino.

Drill Hall Arts Centre
16 Chenies Street, WC1 (0171 637 8270). Goodge Street tube. **Open** 10am-11pm Mon-Sat.
The Drill Hall puts on gay and lesbian theatre and runs a busy women-only bar on Monday nights.

The Duke of Clarence
140 Rotherfield Street, N1 (0171 226 6526). Angel tube then 73, 171, 171A bus. **Open** noon-3.30pm, 5.30-11pm, Mon-Fri; 7-11pm Sat; noon-3.30pm, 7-10.30pm, Sun.
A friendly local for dressed-down dykes. Put your name down for the pool table on arrival.

Earls
180 Earl's Court Road, SW5 (0171 835 1826). Earl's Court tube. **Open** 4pm-midnight Mon-Sat; noon-midnight Sun; *Club 180* 10pm-2am Mon-Sat.
Upstairs drinking, dancing downstairs at Club 180, a pool table and 100 per cent cruising attract a mixed male crowd.

The Edge
11 Soho Square, W1 (0171 439 1313). Tottenham Court Road tube. **Open** noon-1am Mon-Sat; noon-10.30pm Sun. **Credit** A, AmEx, DC, V.
This mixed (gay/straight) café-bar offers trendy food to its hip clientèle.

Father Redcap
319 Camberwell Road, SE5 (0171 708 4474). Elephant & Castle tube, then 35 bus. **Open** noon-midnight Mon-Thur; noon-1am Fri, Sat; noon-3pm, 7-11pm, Sun. **Admission** £1 Fri, Sat.
A large traditional local pub with drag nights, the inexpensive Candlelit Restaurant upstairs and a mixed clientèle. Cabaret on Fridays and Saturdays.

Soho Athletic Club – *for men and women.*

First Out
*52 St Giles High Street, WC2 (0171 240
8042). Tottenham Court Road tube.* **Open**
10am-11pm Mon-Sat; noon-10.30pm Sun. **Average** £5.
No credit cards.
London's original vegetarian gay café is a welcome oasis in
the frantic West End during the day and runs a busy bar by
night. Check the press for women-only evenings.

Freedom
*60-66 Wardour Street, W1 (0171 734 0071).
Tottenham Court Road tube.* **Open** 9am-11pm Mon-Sat;
11am-10.30pm Sun. **Credit** A, AmEx, £TC, V.
Noisy and fashionable, Freedom draws a massive crowd of
young and fabulous pre-clubbers at weekends – lesbians,
gays and switched-on straights.

The Gloucester
1 King William Walk, SE10 (0181 858 2666). **Open**
noon-11pm Mon-Sat; noon-3pm, 7-10.30pm, Sun.
A friendly Greenwich pub.

King Edward VI
25 Bromfield Street, N1 (0171 704 0745). Angel tube.
Open noon-midnight Mon-Sat; noon-11pm Sun.
Pleasant local bar with a decent upstairs restaurant and a
tiny garden (with barbecues on Sundays). Mostly men.

King William IV
*75 Hampstead High Street, NW3 (0171 435 5747).
Hampstead tube.* **Open** noon-11pm Mon-Sat; noon-3pm,
7-10.30pm, Sun.
A long-established traditional pub, the King William IV has
a garden out back and a faithful male clientèle (with more
women at lunchtimes).

King's Arms
*23 Poland Street, W1 (0171 734 5907). Oxford
Circus tube.* **Open** 11am-11pm Mon-Sat; noon-3pm,
7-10.30pm, Sun.
A gay men's pub for a cloney older crowd.

Kudos
*10 Adelaide Street, WC2 (0171 379 4573). Charing
Cross tube/BR.* **Open** 11am-11pm Mon-Sat; 11am-
10.30pm Sun. **Credit** A, AmEx, £TC, V.
Kudos is where the West End guppies go. The light, airy
café upstairs combines awkwardly with the cruisey basement for the boys.

La Rue's Café Bar
*17 Manette Street, W1 (0171 437 5002). Tottenham
Court Road tube.* **Open** 8pm-4am Tue-Sat. **Admission**
£2 after 11pm Tue-Thur; £2.50 Fri, Sat.
Maybe Danny La Rue has opened this kitsch mirrored bar
to brighten up his later years. The drinks are cheap and the
clientèle a bohemian mix.

London Apprentice
*333 Old Street, EC1 (0171 739 5949). Old Street
tube/N83 night bus.* **Open** 9pm-3am Mon-Thur; 9pm-5am
Fri, Sat; 7pm-1am Sun.
A very popular men's bar on two levels with a basement
disco. Smoky and cruisey, with a high quotient of skinheads.
The upper bar has been re-opened.

Madame Jo Jo
*8-10 Brewer Street, W1 (0171 287 1414). Piccadilly
Circus tube.* **Open** 10pm-3am Mon; 9pm-2am Tue;
10.30pm-3am Wed; 10pm-3am Thur-Sat. **Credit** A,
AmEx, £TC, V.
After a few years in the doldrums, a smartened-up Madame
Jo Jo's is back on the map, and making full use of its strip-
tease licence for its queer cabaret.

Market Tavern
*Market Towers, 1 Nine Elms Lane, SW8 (0171 622
5655). Vauxhall tube/BR/N2, N68, N79, N87, N88 night
bus.* **Open** 9pm-2am Mon-Thur; 9pm-3am Fri, Sat; 1-7pm,
9pm-midnight, Sun. **No credit cards.**
This very busy disco bar draws a loyal, local, cloney crowd.
Pub prices, late opening. The Sunday afternoon tea dance
(men only) is an institution, as is lunch with Adrelle at the
Vauxhall across the road.

Royal Oak
*623 Glenthorne Road, W6 (0181 748 2781).
Hammersmith tube.* **Open** 7pm-2am Mon-Sat; noon-
midnight Sun. **Admission** £3 after 10pm Wed-Sat.
Younger lesbians and gay locals gather at the Royal Oak,
the only late-opening venue in the area. There's often cabaret.

Royal Vauxhall Tavern
*372 Kennington Lane, SE11 (0171 582 0833). Vauxhall
tube/BR/N2, N68, N79, N87, N88 night bus.* **Open** 9pm-
1am Mon-Thur; 9pm-2am Fri, Sat; noon-3pm, 7-10.30pm,
Sun.* **Admission** £1-£3.
South London's drag-scene institution. Currently, Friday
nights are women-only.

Substation
*Falconberg Court, W1 (0171 287 9608). Leicester
Square tube.* **Open** 9.30pm-3am Mon-Thur; 9.30pm-4pm
Fri; 10.30pm-6am Sat; 7pm-1am Sun. **Admission** £1-£4
for non-members. **Membership** £4.
A late-night cruise bar that's strictly men-only on Saturdays.
It has little to offer women on any night, except when Betty's
takes over, an infrequent women's Sunday nighter for Tank
Girls and pool players. Check press.
Branch: 9 Brighton Terrace, SW9 (0171 737 2095).

Village
*81 Wardour Street, W1 (0171 434 2124). Leicester
Square tube.* **Open** noon-11pm Mon-Sat; 4-10.30pm Sun.
Credit A, AmEx, V.
Good-time boys gather here in large numbers. The Yard,
with its large open-air courtyard, caters to a more sedate,
mixed clientèle.
Branch: The Yard 57 Rupert Street (0171 437 2652).

Wilde About Oscar
*30-31 Philbeach Gardens, SW5 (0171 835 1858). Earl's
Court tube.* **Open** 7pm-midnight daily. **Average** £18.
Credit A, AmEx, £$TC, V.
Probably the best gay restaurant in town, with professional
service and a small, classic French and Italian menu. There's
a garden if the weather's any good.

Wow Bar
*Michel's, 122-126 Wardour Street, W1 (info 0956 514
574). Leicester Square tube.* **Open** 8pm-midnight
(women only). **Admission** £1 before 9pm, £1.50 after.
A Saturday night women-only bar for slightly to deeply fashionable dykes. Always packed and cruisey. It's also open the
rest of the week for all-comers.

Sport

The **YMCA** might be losing its grip on the muscle queens, but you'll still find yourself in good
company at the young and clubby **Jubilee Hall**
gym, while the **Oasis** sports centre is where theatrical types gather on the sundeck (*see chapter
Sport & Fitness*). On summer days, combine an
invigorating freshwater swim with well-oiled tal-
ent-spotting at the beautiful **Hampstead Ponds**

Yeah, like you're going to ask – **Zipper Store.**

where men and women are thoughtfully catered for separately. Check *Time Out* listings for various swimming clubs and women's football groups.

Soho Athletic Club
10-14 Macklin Street, WC2 (0171 242 1290). Covent Garden tube. **Open** 7am-10pm Mon-Fri; 10am-6pm Sat. **Admission** *men* £480 per year; *women* £430 per year.
A beautifully appointed 8,000 sq ft gym full of beautifully appointed bodies plus a few ordinary blokes who can dream. There are excellent cardio-vascular and resistance machines and no need to fight for the free weights. It's not men only, but we've yet to see a babe on the pec-deck. It's due to start opening on Sundays.

The Wheel
London Women's Centre, Wesley House, 4 Wild Court (off Kingsway), WC2 (0171 831 6946). **Open** 8am-9pm Mon-Fri; noon-6pm Sat. **Admission** £370 per year; £45 per month, £25 per month concs.
What this women-only, primarily lesbian, gym lacks in facilities (the cardio-vascular equipment could be better), it makes up for in the helpfulness and commitment of its staff. Classes, sauna and Jacuzzi also available.

Shopping & Services

Clone Zone
64 Old Compton Street, W1 (0171 287 3530). Leicester Square or Piccadilly Circus tube. **Open** 11am-11pm Mon-Sat; 1-7pm Sun. **Credit** A, AmEx, V.
A multi-level store with a range of sex toys, clothing and books, plus a rack of club flyers and information cards. **Branch:** 1 Hogarth Road, SW5 (0171 373 0598).

Covent Garden Health Spa
29 Endell Street, WC2 (0171 836 2236). Covent Garden tube. **Open** 11am-11pm daily. **Admission** £13.50; £7 students (before 4pm). **Credit** A, £TC, V.
You can't miss the Technicolor doorway of this relaxed, strictly no-sex, men-only health spa. Sunday's Friez (£8.50) offers a special post-club come-down. All towels and toiletries are provided. Beauty treatments available.

Earth
49 Frith Street, W1 (0171 734 3426). Leicester Square or Tottenham Court Road tube. **Open** 9.30am-6pm Mon-Fri. **Credit** A, AmEx, DC, V.
An ABTA-bonded gay travel agency, Earth is full of good advice for those going away.

Detainer
2 Hoxton Street, N1 (0171 739 2199). Old Street tube/BR. **Open** 10.30am-6pm Mon-Sat. **Credit** A, EC, JCB, £TC, V.
If your idea of dressing up is getting tied up then Detainer is an essential port of call. There are no videos, poppers or nudie mags stocked – just some of the best bespoke leather and latex clothing this side of Amsterdam. *Mail order.*

Fare Deal Cabs
(0171 737 4300). **Open** 24 hours daily.
A south London-based lesbian and gay cab company

Freedom Cars
60-62 Old Compton Street, W1 (0171 734 1313). Leicester Square or Tottenham Court Road tube. **Open** 24 hours daily.
Queer and central. Prices are okay.

Gay's The Word
66 Marchmont Street, WC1 (0171 278 7654). Russell Square tube. **Open** 10am-6pm Mon-Wed, Fri, Sat; 10am-7pm Thur; 2-6pm Sun. **Credit** A, AmEx, DC, £TC, V.
London's best selection of gay and lesbian books, magazines and videos.

Shh!
22 Coronet Street, EC1 (0171 613 5458). Old Street tube. **Open** 11.30am-6.30pm Mon, Wed, Sat. **No credit cards.**
A well-stocked sex shop for women, Shh! offers lots of friendly chat and advice.

Silver Moon Women's Bookshop
68 Charing Cross Road, WC2 (0171 836 7906). Leicester Square tube. **Open** 10am-6.30pm Mon-Wed, Fri, Sat; 10am-8pm Thur. **Credit** A, AmEx, EC, £TC, V.
An excellent bookshop with a wide range of stock, a useful noticeboard and polite, helpful staff.

Soho Men
Clone Zone, 64 Old Compton Street, W1 (0171 287 3334). Leicester Square or Piccadilly Circus tube. **Open** 11am-8pm Mon-Sat.
This male beauty salon provides all the usual manicures, waxings and facials.

Zipper Store
283 Camden High Street, NW1 (0171 267 7665). Camden Town tube. **Open** 10am-6.30pm Mon-Thur; 10am-7pm Fri; 10am-6.30pm Sat; noon-5pm Sun. **Credit** A, AmEx, £TC, V.
London's only licensed gay sex store stocks a large variety of goods, including books and clothing.

Health

Audre Lorde Clinic
Ambrose King Centre, The Royal London Hospital, E1 (0171 377 7312). Whitechapel tube. **Open** Fri.
Weekly lesbian health clinic. Appointments necessary.

East 1 Clinic
Ambrose King Centre, The Royal London Hospital, E1 (0171 377 7312). **Open** Thur eves.
Weekly gay men's health clinic.

Mortimer Market Centre
Mortimer Market, off Capper Street, WC1 (0171 380 8880). Warren Street tube. **Open** 9am-6pm Mon, Wed; 9am-7pm Tue; 9am-3pm Fri by appointment.
There are three clinics here: a women's clinic, men's clinic and an HIV clinic. Young gay men (under 26) get special attention 7-10pm on Thursdays.

Sandra Bernhard Clinic
Charing Cross Hospital, Fulham Palace Road, entrance St Dunstan's Road, W6 (0181 846 1577). Barons Court or Hammersmith tube. **Open** 2-5pm Wed.
A clinic for bisexual women and lesbians with STDs.

Accommodation

No 7 Guest House
7 Josephine Avenue, SW2 (0181 674 1880). Brixton tube. **Rates** (incl breakfast and VAT) *single* £35; *double* £55; *deluxe double* £60; *triple* £75. **Credit** A, V.
A gay-run guest house. Ensuite bathrooms, TV and phone.

Philbeach Hotel
30/31 Philbeach Gardens, SW5 (0171 373 1244/4544). Earl's Court tube. **Rates** (incl breakfast and VAT) *single* £40-£45; *double* £50-£60; *suite* £65. **Credit** A, AmEx, DC, £TC, V, US$.
It's particularly favoured by transvestites, but the Philbeach Hotel is open to all gay men and lesbians. It has a good late-opening bar and a restaurant, **Wilde About Oscar** (*see above*).

Reeves
48 Shepherd's Bush Green, W12 (0181 740 1158). Shepherd's Bush tube. **Rates** (incl breakfast and VAT) *single* £25, *with bath* £35; *twin* £45; *double with bath* £55. **Credit** A, V.
A women-only hotel, rather than a strictly lesbian venture. Clean and comfortable.

Information

Bisexual Helpline
(0181 569 7500). **Open** 7.30-9.30pm Tue, Thur.

Black Lesbian & Gay Helpline
(0171 837 5364). **Open** 24 hours daily.
Advice, information and news for black lesbians and gay men. If you need an information pack, write to PR LLGS, PO Box 7324, London N1 9AS.

Body Positive Helpline
(0171 373 9124). **Open** 7-10pm Mon-Fri; 4-10pm Sat, Sun.
Support for HIV-positive people.

Out and Proud

It's the last Saturday in June and you wake up to a sunny London morning. If you're not planning to head off to Lesbian and Gay Pride, then think again. For tens of thousands of Londoners, as well as people from all over Britain and beyond, this is one of the major events of the year. Something that started a couple of decades ago as a gathering for just a few hundred homos has grown into a massive march and festival that now attracts over 150,000 gay people, their friends and families.

The action begins in Hyde Park at midday where marchers gather to follow the glamorous (or just plain ridiculous) floats on their route through the centre of London: you, along with a huge crew of banner-bearing groups, drag queens on rollerskates, SM dykes, sunbed boys, slogan chanters and thousands of others, can be responsible for the reorganisation of the entire traffic system of the West End. Then it's on to luscious park lawns from 3pm onwards to get on with the revelling that lasts until ten at night. Some bring elaborate picnics, others wear elaborate costumes, many simply consume elaborate cocktails throughout the day. Name bands, disco tents, bars, food stalls and, thankfully, Portaloos abound, and all your exes are terrifyingly gathered in one place. While the objective of the march has to be visibility, the objective of the festival is definitely pleasure.

There is, of course, huge debate around the time of Pride as to what it's really about. Among certain contingents it's seen as being too political and among others as not political enough. But one thing is certain, that it is about being proud to be lesbian or gay.

With increasing media attention and ever larger numbers of interested straights coming along to observe or join in, things are inevitably beginning to change. The festival is now being distressingly described as the largest free music festival in Europe.

Don't stop the music, but please don't forget who Lesbian and Gay Pride is really for. And above all, don't miss it.

In 1995 the festival took place in Victoria Park, E9 (Bethnal Green tube) and will probably do so again, but you should check. Disabled facilities are good, free wheelchairs are available and helpful stewards are around at all times.

GALOP (Gay London Policing Group)

(0171 233 0854). **Open** 10am-6pm Mon-Fri.
Where to come if you have been attacked or arrested. Galop offers an advice and counselling referral service.

Gilad (Gay & Lesbian Legal Advice)

(0171 976 0840). **Open** 7-9.30pm Mon-Fri.
Free legal advice offered to gay men and lesbians.

Lesbian Artists Network

PO Box 2DL, London W1A 2DL.
A networking group for lesbian artists.

Lesbian Line

(0171 251 6911). **Open** 7-10pm Mon-Thur; 2-10pm Fri.
Counselling, information and advice.

Lesbian and Gay
Accommodation Switchboard

(flatseekers 0171 704 1302/1303; landlords 0171 354 4182). **Open** 11am-9pm Mon-Sat.

Lesbian & Gay Switchboard

(0171 837 7324).
A 24-hour advice and general information service, with minicom facility for the deaf *(0181 660 2208 evenings)*. Persistence is required as it can be very hard to get through.

London Friend

(0171 837 3337). **Open** 7.30-10pm daily.

London Friend offers counselling for gay men and women. A women-only service is available on 0171 837 2782, 7.30-10pm Tue-Thur.

London Women's Centre

Wesley House, 4 Wild Court (off Kingsway), WC2 (0171 831 6946). **Open** 8am-10pm Mon-Fri; 8.30am-10pm Sat.
This women-only resource centre includes a computer centre, video-editing suite, gym *(see Sport above)*, nursery facilities and the Kulcha Café which is also open to men. It also provides a phone referral service and is the headquarters for various campaigning women's organisations.

Outrage

5 Peter Street, W1 (071 439 2381). **Open** 24-hour answermachine.
Outrage is the pressure group behind the kiss-ins, the condoms in **Westminster Cathedral** and other controversial but successful direct action events that keep issues around homosexuality in the spotlight.

Stonewall

2 Greycoat Place, SW1 (0171 222 9007).
The polite end of pressure. Sir Ian McKellen et al try to win queer ground by taking tea with dignitaries and being nice.

Terrence Higgins Trust

(0171 242 1010). **Open** noon-10pm daily.
Advice and information on HIV and AIDS.

Gay's The Word – *friendly bookshop with a good selection of fiction, non-fiction and mags.*

Students

It may seem an expensive place to live, but there is no more exciting city in which to be a student – especially when you know where and how to pay less and get more.

The first stone of University College was set in place in 1827, but it wasn't until 1836 that a charter was granted. Known as 'the godless college in Gower Street', without the prestige of Oxford or Cambridge, it was set up to provide education for non-Anglicans barred from existing institutions and has retained a commitment to 'all classes and denominations'. London University was the first to admit female students and female professors.

In 1839 the Royal Polytechnic Institution was founded for the study of sciences and technology. It was followed by the Polytechnic of Central London which became the University of Westminster when Polytechnics and Institutes of Higher Education were renamed in the early 1990s.

Universities

City University *Northampton Square, EC1 (general 0171 477 8000/SU 0171 250 0955). Angel/Barbican tube.*
Guildhall University *2 Goulston Street, E1 (general 0171 320 1000/ U 0171 247 1441). Aldgate East tube.*
South Bank University *Borough Rd, SE1 (general 0171 928 8989/SU 0171 815 6060). Elephant & Castle tube.*
University of East London *Stratford Campus, Romford Road, E15 (general 0181 590 7722/SU 0181 311 8268). Stratford tube/BR.*
University of Greenwich *Wellington Street, SE18 (General 0181 316 8000/SU 0181 311 8268). Woolwich Arsenal BR.*
University of Kingston *Penrhyn Road, Kingston, Surrey (general 0181 547 2000/SU 0181 549 9961). Kingston BR.*
University of Middlesex *Trent Park, Bramley Road, N14 (general 0181 362 5000/SU 0181 362 6450). Cockfosters or Oakwood tube.*
University of North London *166-220 Holloway Road, N7 (general 0171 607 2789/SU 0171 609 1212). Holloway Road tube.*
University of Westminster *104-108 Bolsover Street, W1 (general 0171 911 5000/SU 0171 636 6271). Great Portland Street tube.*

University of London

The University consists of 34 colleges, six of which are listed. There are now a total of 77,000 students.
Goldsmiths' College *Lewisham Way, SE14 (general 0181 919 7171/SU 0181 692 1406). New Cross/New Cross Gate tube/BR.*
Imperial College *Prince Consort Road, SW7 (general 0171 589 5111/SU 0171 594 8060). South Kensington tube.*

King's College *The Strand, WC2 (general 0171 836 5454/SU 0171 836 7132). Temple tube.*
London School of Economics (LSE) *Page Building, Houghton Street, WC2 (general 0171 405 7696/SU 0171 955 7158). Holborn tube.*
Queen Mary & Westfield College (QMW) *Mile End Road, E1 (general 0171 975 5555/SU 0171 975 5390). Mile End or Stepney Green tube.*
University College London (UCL) *Gower Street, WC1 (general 0171 387 7050/SU 0171 387 3611). Euston, Goodge Street or Warren Street tube.*

Specialist Libraries

British Architectural Library
66 Portland Place, W1 (0171 580 5533). Great Portland Street tube. **Open** 1.30-5pm Mon; 10am-8pm Tue; 10am-5pm Wed-Fri; 10am-1.30pm Sat. **Day pass** £10; £5 concs (Tue & Sat £5; £2.50 concs).
Covers all aspects of architecture, building and planning.

British Film Institute Library
21 Stephen Street, WC1 (0171 255 1444). Tottenham Court Road tube. **Open** 10.30am-5.30pm Mon, Fri; 10.30am-8pm Tue, Thur; 1-8pm Wed. **Day pass** £5.
All aspects of world cinema and UK television.

British Library Business Information Centre
25 Southampton Buildings, Chancery Lane, WC2 (0171 323 7454). **Open** 9.30am-9pm Mon-Fri; 10am-1pm Sat.
All the gen on markets, products and companies.

British Library National Sound Archive
29 Exhibition Road, SW7 (0171 412 7430). South Kensington tube. **Open** 10am-5pm Mon-Wed, Fri; 10am-9pm Thur.
Music, spoken word, animal noises and sound-effects.

Feminist Library
5 Westminster Bridge Road, SE1 (0171 928 7789). Lambeth North or Waterloo tube. **Open** 11am-8pm Tue; 2-5pm Sat, Sun. **Women only.**
Fiction and non-fiction, journals and research papers.

Poetry Library
Royal Festival Hall, South Bank Centre, SE1 (0171 921 0664). Embankment tube/Waterloo tube/BR. **Open** 11am-8pm daily.
The emphasis is on twentieth-century poetry in English.

Money Savers

NUS cards will not automatically get students vast discounts. Culture vultures can buy a Stage Pass, available to anyone aged 14-29; it costs £15 a year and will get you and a friend up to 50 per cent off selected programmes at certain venues (details on 0171 379 6722). International Student Identity Cards (ISIC) are available from NUS and student travel centres; they are good for cheap flights.

London Transport Travel Information
(0171 222 1234). Lines open 24 hours. Most night buses depart from Trafalgar Square.

International Students House
229 Great Portland Street, W1 (0171 631 3223). Great Portland Street tube. Subsidised bar.

Student Theatreline
(0171 379 8900). Provides notice of standby tickets.

Helplines

Adult Dyslexia Organisation *336 Brixton Road, SW9 (0171 924 9559).* **Open** 10.30am-4.30pm Tue-Thur.
Advisory Service for Squatters *2 St Paul's Road, N1 (0171 359 8814).* **Open** 2-6pm Mon-Fri.
London Nightline *(0171 436 5561).* **Open** 6pm-8am.
National Debtline *(0121 359 8501).* **Open** 10am-4pm Mon, Thur; 2-7pm Tue, Wed.
Samaritans *(0171 734 2800).* **Open** 24 hours daily.

Helpful Organisations

British Council *10 Spring Gardens, SW1 (0171 930 8466). Charing Cross tube/BR.* **Open** 9.30am-5pm Mon-Fri. Information on language schools; help for overseas students.
Student Travel Centre *24 Rupert Street, W1 (0171 434 1306). Piccadilly Circus tube.* **Open** 9am-6pm Mon-Fri; 10am-2pm Sat. Reduced fares to a variety of destinations.
Citizens' Advice Bureau *15 Henrietta Street, WC2 (0171 379 6595). Covent Garden tube.* **Drop-ins** 11am-1pm Mon, Tue, Fri; 3-5.30pm Wed. **Lines open** 2-4pm Mon, Tue, Thur, Fri. Advice to anyone on anything.
National Bureau for Students with Disabilities *366 Brixton Road, SW9 (0171 274 0565).* **Lines open** 1.30-4.30pm Mon-Fri. Information on education for people with disabilities.

Accommodation

Shack provides information on hostels and cheap accommodation for students. They have two telephone lines. Ring 0171 404 2614 if single or a couple. Ring 0171 404 6929 if married with children.

Friends International Centre
Courtauld House, Torrington Place, WC1 (0171 387 5648). Goodge Street tube. **Rates** *single* £28; *shared* £18. Stay for one night or several months.

International Students House
229 Great Portland Street, W1 (0171 631 3223). Great Portland Street tube. **Rates** *single* £23.40; *double* £19.75; *dormitory* £9.99.
Year-round accommodation with 450 beds for full-time and part-time foreign and British students.

London Student House
Friendship House, 1 St Nicholas Glebe, Rectory Lane, SW17 (0181 672 2262). Tooting tube/BR. **Rates** £72 per week.

Breakfast and dinner included. There are 87 single rooms for students over 18. Available at £15 a night in the holidays.

YWCA
Park House, 227 Earl's Court Road, SW5 (0171 373 2851). Earl's Court tube. **Rates** *single* £65 per week.
A self-catering abode for women aged 18-25. With 117 beds, six months is the minimum stay allowed.

YMCA
40-46 Stockwell Road, SW9 (0171 501 9795). Stockwell tube. **Rates** £110 per week.
Single and shared rooms for men and women aged 18-35. Minimum stay is three months; prices include meals.

Eating & Drinking

Gallery Restaurant
University of London Union, Malet Street, WC1 (0171 580 9551). Goodge Street tube. **Open** 10am-7.30pm Mon-Thur; 10am-midnight Fri; noon-midnight Sat.
This airy canteen/bar has replaced what was Palms. Choose from a variety of burgers, potatoes, omelettes and vegetarian meals for about £2.50. *See also page 283* **Union Bars**.

The Great Dining Hall
London House, Mecklenburgh Square, WC1 (0171 837 8888). Russell Square tube. **Open** 7.30-10am, 12.30-2.30pm, 6-8pm, Mon-Fri; 8-10am, 12.30-2.30pm, 6-8pm, Sat; 9-11am, 12.30-2.30pm, 6-8pm, Sun.
Three-course meal with salad and veggie options for a fiver.

Malaysia Hall Dining Room
46 Byanston Square, W1 (0171 723 9484). Marble Arch tube. **Open** 8-10am, noon-3pm, 5-9pm, daily.
Breakfast can mean coconut rice or squid; £2 evening meal.

Pierre Victoire
6 Panton Street, SW1 (0171 930 6463). Leicester Square or Piccadilly Circus tube. **Open** noon-4pm, 5.30-11pm, daily.
Bargain three-course lunch is around a fiver.

The Stockpot
40 Panton Street, SW1 (0171 839 5142). Leicester Square or Piccadilly Circus tube. **Open** 8am-11.15pm Mon-Sat; 11.45am-9.45pm Sun.
Panton Street strikes again. There are few places where you can spend so little and eat so heartily. Friendly service.

Viva Zapata
7 Pond Street, NW3 (0171 431 9134). Hampstead tube. **Open** noon-midnight daily.
All-you-can-eat buffet for around a fiver.

Media

London Student
(0171 580 9551).
Free fortnightly newspaper available at ULU and other London University colleges. Student news updates, arts information and details of student societies and sports.

Student Pages
(0171 498 4663).
The first edition of this free directory will be distributed on campuses in 1995. Events, venues, discount vouchers.

Time Out Student Guide
(0171 813 3000).
Features, listings and offers from London's best-selling guide team. Not that we're biased. Free at freshers' fairs.

Union Bars

School of Oriental and African Studies

Thornhaugh Street, WC1 (0171 637 2388). Goodge Street or Russell Square tube.

SOAS is similar to a sixth-form common room conceived by a student committee with funds that fall short of their ideas – it looks loved but drooping. The African prints and window plants are offset by bar pies and a sauce table. More laid back and welcoming than most.

University of London Union (ULU)

Malet Street, WC1 (0171 580 9551). Goodge Street or Russell Square tube.

Two bars sit opposite one another. The Club House is a windowless vacuum of wood and dark terracotta walls with arcade games and a gig area at one end. The Deli Bar is located here, selling individually prepared wok food, a good idea but the queues are long and the food badly cooked. Its alter ego, the Gallery Bar and Diner, is by contrast almost one big window with glass walls and tunnel-shaped roof. Floors and chairs are bright blue or green and plants abound.

University of Westminster

Marylebone Road site, W1 (0171 636 6271). Baker Street tube.

Stark. From the wire sculpture ceiling and spot bulbs to the plastic fleck floor, benches and stools. Glass panels and a small terrace reveal nothing more than grey buildings and concrete courtyards, but there's a choice between stools and easy chairs. The actual bar surface is the highlight, a transparent laminate plastic, embedded with kitsch and utililitarian culture, from plastic gorillas to clocks' insides.

Imperial College

Beit Quad, Prince Consort Road, SW7 (0171 589 4870). South Kensington tube.

No pass checks here, just stroll through the pleasant grass quad straight to Da Vinci's. A bit like an airport lounge without the departures screens, it's nevertheless quite likable, with plush carpeting, essential dim lighting and a raised seating space with comfy bench sofas. A large MTV screen dominates one wall but the bar soundtrack comes direct from the jukebox. There's another bar next door modelled on a spit and sawdust pub and ample space outdoors for summer revision/guilt alcohol sessions.

King's College

Macadam Building, Surrey Street, WC2 (0171 836 7132). Temple tube.

The Waterfront has little to recommend it, bar (ho ho) the spectacular views. Two walls are glass-panelled and you can see a good stretch of the Thames with **Tower Bridge** in the distance to the left and the **South Bank Centre** directly opposite. The dark green carpeting and ceiling give this oblong box some distinction but it's packed and there's a constant roar of chat from the table-to-table huddles.

City University

Northampton Square, EC1 (0171 250 0955). Angel tube/Barbican tube/BR.

A new union building is underway. Artist's impressions reveal two new bar spaces. One, a spacey blue and purple affair with minimal furniture and clever lighting, the other an imitation of a medieval inn, all wooden with green and red trimmings and candle-flicker lighting.

University College London

25 Gordon Street, WC1 (0171 387 3611). Warren Street tube/Euston tube/BR.

The largest collection of bars within any one union (and stringent pass-check bouncers to match), UCL is always busy. Thursday nights are worth missing unless you enjoy queues. Ground-floor Gordons has pint-sized primary-school chairs, dull grey walls and an absence of aesthetic pleasures or atmosphere. The large second-floor bar apes a sawdust pub with wooden floors and the tang of stale fags and booze. A London Underground theme is created with old and new tube posters, Monopoly boards and other symbols on the walls and ceiling. The G Spot next door is a pool haven/rave space with natty DJ booth. The third-floor Phineas bar is a pub-like area but cosier than downstairs with carpeting, cushioned seats and love corners.

Royal College of Art (RCA)

Kensington Gore, SW7 (0171 584 5020). South Kensington tube.

A lot to live up to and it doesn't quite cut it. Reminiscent of a small club, with grey walls and a gold star motif; the blue church pews probably sounded like a good idea. Perhaps the canvas was kept plain the better to highlight the artists themselves. Like temporary installations.

Royal Academy of Dramatic Arts (RADA)

62 Gower Street, WC1 (0171 580 1809). Goodge Street tube.

Only open during show times at the end of each term, but as you walk under the watchful stone figures over the portico you feel the weight of all those household names who have passed before you. It's a small traditional bar, for cosy luvvy talk over plain round wooden tables. (NUS gives you automatic membership of the theatre club, shows are £5.)

Da Vinci's – *see, they're perfectly steady.*

Women's London

From feminist libraries to single-sex saunas, and Queen's Corsetieres to Lady Cabs Hackney, London is a girl's best friend.

Britain is known as a nation of shopkeepers but there's more to the stereotype than a rotund-bellied male with a striped apron. Women have been running retail businesses for a good while now, although it hasn't always been an easy ride.

Take Elizabeth Calvert, who inherited a bookselling business in the seventeenth century when her husband Giles died. She ran the business in the City but was often in prison for distributing books which the government thought were a tad radical. Anne Dodd had the same problem at her bookselling establishment near the Strand in the 1720s.

Women were also more than happy to get their hands dirty. There was Eleanor Coade who founded a factory to produce Coade stone, the most weatherproof stone ever produced, which builders have since tried unsuccessfully to replicate. Unfortunately the blueprint was lost when the factory burned down in 1840 but the lion near **Westminster Bridge** provides a solid reminder.

Louisa Courtauld ran a silversmith business at the Crown, Cornhill in the eighteenth century and her work can be seen at the **Victoria & Albert Museum** and the **Museum of London**. And then there was Angela Burdett Coutts who built Columbia Market Square in Bethnal Green, and Holly Village, a middle-class housing estate in Highgate, in the late nineteenth century (but not with her own hands and more out of charity than a wish to make money – she already had millions of her own).

Emma Cons was an entrepreneur. In the 1850s she and a few friends opened a watch-engraving business in Clerkenwell. Male engravers sabotaged the shop, so she re-opened the Royal Victoria coffee music hall in 1880 and founded the Old Vic theatre. Her niece Lilian Baylis took over in 1912 and in 1931 went on to take over **Sadler's Wells**.

The Amazonian contingent have continued to hold their own in the capital this century with women-owned outfits blossoming in the free thinking 1960s. Angela Flowers opened her own art gallery. In 1969 Prue Leith started Leith's, a restaurant on Kensington Park Road which has recently received a long-deserved Michelin star. Leith

also runs a cookery school, students of which can be found catering for ski parties on continental slopes. Then, of course, there's Vivienne Westwood, now 53 with an OBE, who set up the infamous Sex shop on the King's Road with Malcolm McLaren and went on to design some of the most outrageous fashions ever glimpsed.

Carmen Callil was probably the biggest success of the 1970s, launching a new concept in the dusty world of books – Virago, a publishing house for women writers run by women. It all started on her kitchen table. Lynne Franks didn't do too badly either – she set up a PR agency which is still going strong even without her participation. Franks is reportedly the model for Jennifer Saunders' Edina in the riotous TV series *Absolutely Fabulous*.

The 1980s saw Ruth Rogers and Rose Gray open the hugely successful (and pricey) **River Café** in Hammersmith. Rumour has it that the initiative came from Ruth's hubby Richard (better known for his contributions to architecture than cuisine) who wanted somewhere special to eat at lunchtime (the site, designed by him, is part of his Riverside offices). This decade also found one of London's most charismatic entrepreneurs Fiona Cartledge sowing the seeds for success in the 1990s. **Sign Of The Times** began as a stall on **Kensington Market** and is now one of the hippest clothes shops around, frequented by Paula Yates, Naomi Campbell, Kate Moss and the like. Cartledge also runs off-the-wall party nights, and her New Year bashes are the stuff of legend.

You can find more information about health in *chapter* **Survival** and places to relax in *chapters* **Shopping & Services** *and* **Sport & Fitness**.

Helplines

London Rape Crisis Centre
(0171 837 1600). **Open** 10am-10pm.
Free and confidential counselling service.

London Women's Aid
(0171 251 6537). **Open** 10am-4.45pm. Answerphone after hours gives alternative numbers for immediate help. Refuge referral for women experiencing domestic violence.

Feminist Library – *weekly discussion groups.*

National Childbirth Trust
(0181 992 8637). **Open** 9am-5pm Mon-Fri.
Independent charity offering information and support to women in pregnancy, childbirth and early parenthood.

Refuge Crisis Line
(0181 995 4430). **Open** 24 hours.
For women experiencing domestic violence.

Groups & Networks

Business & Professional Women UK Ltd
23 Ansdell Street, W8 (0171 938 1729).
A national group of over 4,000 working women set up for networking, training and lobbying purposes. The London group meets monthly and membership (£120 annually) automatically makes you an associate of European and international groups in over 100 countries.

Reel Women
(0181 678 7404).
An organisation for women involved with film and television, whether working in the industry itself, education, experimental work or just plain interested. Screenings and workshops are planned in addition to monthly meetings. Membership (£15 a year) also offers a monthly newsletter.

Women's Theatre Workshops
Isleworth Public Hall, South Street, Isleworth, Middlesex (0181 749 6905).
An organisation which runs courses at different venues around London from September until April. Their programme caters for beginners and professionals in areas of stage and screen scriptwriting and directing.

Women in Publishing
Publishers' Association, 19 Bedford Square, WC1 (0171 281 5180).
WIP holds monthly events with speakers from publishing and other spheres. A lively debate always follows and seasonal parties offer networking opportunities. A monthly newsletter supplied with membership (£15 a year, £10 concs; non-members £1.50 per meeting) details events and job vacancies. There are 400-500 members in London.

Women into Management
64 Marryat Road, SW19 (0181 944 6332).
A network of 1,300 women nationwide who encourage women wanting to move into management and support those who already are. The London group meets monthly.

Women Writers Network
(0171 837 9959).
A group of over 300 women based in and around London. Their monthly meetings feature a panel which give advice

on writing for different markets. Panel guests are drawn from publishing, the women's magazine sector and TV, and are a combination of freelancers and employees. WWN also runs special events such as writing weekends. Annual membership costs £25 (£30 non-EC members) but non-members are welcomed at all events.

Courses & Centres

Drill Hall
16 Chenies Street, WC1 (0171 631 1353). Goodge Street tube. **Open** 10.30am-11pm Mon-Sat.
This centre, comprising a theatre, vegetarian restaurant and bar, also runs 40 classes and workshops on a ten-week term basis. Women-only classes include self-defence, Egyptian dance, photography and drama. The bar becomes a women-only space on Monday nights from 5.30-11pm.

Feminist Library
5 Westminster Bridge Road, SE1 (0171 928 7789). Lambeth North tube or Waterloo tube/BR. **Open** 11am-8pm Tue; 2-5pm Sat, Sun.
This small, friendly, women-only library is staffed by volunteers and holds fiction and non-fiction, results of research papers and a large journal collection. There's a cosy room where visitors can read in comfort and help themselves to tea or coffee for 10p. They also offer information on women's events. A Feminist Discussion Group is held 6-8pm on Tuesdays when a different subject is considered each week.

Irish Women's Centre
59 Church Street, N16 (0171 249 7318). Stoke Newington BR, bus 73. **Open** 10am-1pm, 2-5pm, Tue-Thur.
This centre offers free publications and drop-in advice on housing and welfare, as well as free counselling and legal advice concerning family and domestic law problems. It runs an outreach service for Irish women around London and hopes to establish a regular drop-in for older Irish women.

Jackson's Lane Centre
269A Archway Road, N6 (0181 340 5226). Highgate tube. **Open** 10am-11pm daily.
This community centre has a lot going on besides its entertainment programme and there's a bar and vegetarian café to add fizz to the general atmosphere. Regular courses for women include self-defence classes – £33, £23 concs for six weeks; assertiveness training – £52 for four weeks; and weekly Exerdance aerobics – £3.30, £2.30 concs per session. One-off courses such as First Time Mothers Support Group and Slimnastics Support Group also feature.

Heather's Bistro – *cheering up Deptford.*

King's Cross Women's Centre
*71 Tonbridge Street, WC1 (0171 837 7509). King's
Cross tube/BR.* **Open** 11am-5pm Tue-Thur; *phone lines*
11am-5pm Mon-Fri.
Various women's organisations are based here, such as
Black Women for Wages for Housework, Campaign Against
the Child Support Act, English Collective of Prostitutes,
Wages Due Lesbians, Wages For Housework Campaign,
WinVisible and Women Against Rape.

London Personal Development Centre
2 Thayer Street, W1 (0171 935 8935). Bond Street tube.
Open *phone lines* 9am-6pm Mon-Fri.
The centre has a range of regular intensive one-day workshops concentrating on management and general business
skills. Various aspects of personal development are another
focus; one of the quirkier courses, Think Yourself Young
Again, involves sending messages of rejuvenation to your
cells, a system which has had a high rate of success in the
US. Workshops are led by skilled experts from relevant fields
and cost from £69-£135 per day.

The Wheel
*(formerly the Women's Centre) 4 Wild Court, WC2 (0171
831 6946). Holborn tube.*
A cultural centre which hires out rooms and a theatre space
to various women-led organisations. There's a fitness gym
(8am-9pm Mon-Fri, noon-6pm Sat) and a café/bar (11am-
11pm Mon-Sat, men allowed as women's guests). Women-
only nights are Tue, Thur and Sat from 6pm. Also home to
the Women's Computer Centre *(0171 430 0012).*

Women Artists' Slide Library
*Fulham Palace, Bishops Avenue, SW6 (0171 731 7618)
Putney Bridge tube.* **Open** 10am-4.30pm Tue-Fri.
Admission £1 to non members.
This high-ceilinged room within a listed building is home to
reference books and over 30,000 slides of contemporary and
historical art by women.

Women's Writing Workshops
*Camden People's Theatre, Hampstead Road, NW1 (0171
916 5878). Warren Street tube.*
Informal weekly sessions exploring short story, poetry and
drama writing skills. Expect set exercises and readings for
group feedback. The group makes occasional public readings and works towards publishing an anthology. Workshops run throughout the year with breaks for Christmas,
Easter and summer. It costs £4, £2 concs, per time.

Accommodation

Hotels increasingly recognise the needs of lone
women travellers. You can often get your room
upgraded, but at the very least should be made to
feel welcome in the restaurant. The Athenaeum,
116 Piccadilly, W1 *(0171 499 3464)* recently carried out a survey among hundreds of business
women and knows what's expected. Unfortunately, rooms cost from £160 single. *See chapter*
Accommodation for other likely candidates, but
if you're stuck with nowhere to go, contact:

Women's Link
*1A Snow Hill Court, EC1 (advice 0171 248 1200/lettings
0171 248 1600).* **Open** *phone lines* 10am-4pm Mon-
Thur; 1-4pm Fri. Daytime drop-in by appointment only.
Free advice for women needing emergency, temporary or
permanent accommodation. They have information on flat-
shares in the private rented sector, hostel accommodation
and more. A yearly booklet *Hostels in London* costs £2.50.

Eating & Drinking

London has an overwhelming number of restaurants, bars and pubs. Unfortunately, finding places
where you're not going to be hassled by the other
customers (or indeed by Italian waiters wielding
outsized pepper pots) is slightly more difficult.

As a general rule, vegetarian restaurants, cafés
and the brasserie chains such as **Prêt à Manger**,
the **Dôme** and **Café Rouge** are trouble-free zones.
As well as the vegetarian restaurants listed in
chapter **Restaurants**, Heather's Café/Bistro at
190 Trundleys Road, SE8 *(0181 691 6665)* is
worth the long haul to Deptford. Pasta and pizza
chains are also soothing venues (the excellent
Pizza Express in particular). The cluster of
restaurants and cafés in Neal's Yard, WC2 exude
a mellow vibe.

Finding a pub which doesn't draw a clientèle of
lager-stuffed leerers is slightly harder work. The
Puzzle Pubs (Prince's Puzzle, 151 St John's Hill,
SW11 and the Dragon Puzzle, 72 High Road,
Balham, SE12) have made an effort to be more
appealing to women, but they're rather far from
central London. Consult the *chapters* **Restaurants**, **Cafés & Brasseries** *and* **Pubs & Bars**
and try a few places: Soho is probably the best
place to start.

Of course, if male attention is exactly what
you're looking for, then we're reliably informed
that **Smollensky's on the Strand** is your place.

Lotte Berk Exercise Studio – *women only.*

*Formerly of Jazz FM, Diana Luke brings her mellow tones to **Viva!**, broadcasting 24 hours.*

Health

Brook Advisory Service

*233 Tottenham Court Road, W1 (0171 580 2991).
Tottenham Court Road tube.* **Open** *appointments*
9.30am-7.30pm Mon-Thur; 9am-4pm Fri. *Clinics* noon-
6.30pm Mon-Thur; 9.30am-2.30pm Fri; noon-2pm Sat.
There are 16 centres in London which offer free contraceptives and counselling for women under 25. At this centre
only the free service is restricted to women of 21 and under,
but they offer a Women's Well Being Clinic for ages 21-30 at
£14 per visit.

Pregnancy Advisory Service

*11-13 Charlotte Street, W1 (0171 637 8962). Goodge
Street tube.* **Open** *telephone enquiries* 8.30am-6pm Mon-
Fri. *Personal callers* 9am-5.30pm Mon-Fri; 9.30am-
12.30pm Sat (pregnancy tests only).
This non-profit-making registered charity deals mainly with
termination but also performs cervical smears and gives
advice on contraception. Pregnancy testing costs £7, cervical smears £20, morning-after pill £20, consultation for
termination £45.

St James's Centre
for Health and Healing

*St James's, 197 Piccadilly (entrance in Church Place), W1
(0171 437 7118). Piccadilly Circus tube.* **Open** for
appointments 10am-5pm Mon-Fri.
Women can choose from female practitioners and therapists
at this centre, as treatment is by appointment only. Treatments include Alexander Technique, Homeopathy, Aromatherapy, Shiatsu, Psychotherapy, Reflexology and Indian
Head Massage.

Lotte Berk Excercise Studio

*465 Fulham Road, SW6 (0171 385 2477). West
Brompton tube.* **Open** Fri-Sun; call for times of classes.
Fee £6 per hour.

A women-only studio with classes concentrating on toning
and stretching and conditioning.

The Sanctuary

*12 Floral Street, WC2 (0171 240 9635/gym 0171 240
0695). Covent Garden tube.* **Open** 10am-6pm Mon, Tue,
Sat, Sun; 10am-10pm Wed-Fri. **Admission** £39.50 per
day. *Gym only* £12.50; £5.50 members. **Membership**
£135 per year.
The Sanctuary is one of London's favourite health clubs. It's
kitted out with a Jacuzzi, sauna, team room, sunbeds and a
swimming pool and has 50 treatments to choose from including aromatherapy, massage, facials and bodywraps. The
gym is a women-only space and has the usual treadmill
equipment plus aerobics classes.

The Women's Gym

*Michael Sobell Sports Centre, Hornsey Road, N7 (0171
700 1141). Holloway Road tube.* **Open** 10am-8pm Mon-
Fri; 10am-1pm Sat; occasional classes Sun. **Membership**
£27 per month; £16 concs.
Membership of this women-only gym allows one class per
day and use of facilities during open hours. Classes include
yoga, weight training, circuit training, steps, fitness, African
rhythm and Salsa. The gym also runs regular six-week self-
defence courses.

Transport

Mini-cabs firms using women-only drivers are one
of the safest ways to travel alone.

Baroness Cars for Women

34 Baker Street, W1 (0171 935 8494). **Open** 24 hours
daily. To any destination in London.

Before & After Dark Croydon

(0181 665 0861). **Open** daytime and evening services.

Lady Cabs Highgate/Lady Cabs Hackney

(Highgate 0171 281 4803/Hackney 0171 254 3314).
Open 7.30am-12.30am Mon-Thur; 7.30am-1am Fri;
7.30am-2am Sat.

Women's Safe Transport

46 Kapler Road, SW4 (0171 274 4641). **Open** 6.30am-
11pm Mon-Fri.
Hallsville Road, E16 (0171 473 6100). **Open** 5.30-
11.30pm Wed-Fri.

Media

In addition to the glossy mags and crochet and
egg-beating monthlies, there is some meatier
material available to the discerning woman. There
are plenty of bookshops in *chapter* **Shopping &
Services**. The **Silver Moon Women's Bookshop** is one of the best.

Every Woman

9 St Albans Place, London N1 (0171 704 8440).
A monthly magazine (£1.95) which reflects the acceptable
(radical but not strident) side of feminism. It explores issues
and exposes personalities with a sense of humour and a
wide-ranging brief. The Arts Diary focuses on London; the
March issue gives details of National Women's Day events.

Top Women

44 Grays Inn Road, WC1 (0171 242 3595).
A bi-monthly mag (£1.95) which caters for the 'professional' woman with stories on medicine, law, education, finance,
health, training and more, all slanted to a female perspective.

Viva!

*963 MW. Women's Radio Group, 90 De Beauvoir Road,
N1 (0171 298 7200).*
Launched on 3 July 1995, Viva! comes from the same stable
as **JFM** and is targeted at women aged 25-49 throughout
the Greater London area. Broadcast around the clock, presenters include Steve Allen and Diana Luke and programmes
are a combination of music, children's projects and aspects
of London life.

Golden Girls

There are two ways to enjoy London. As it is
and as it was.

Blue plaques attached to houses mark previous residents of note. To qualify for an English
Heritage blue plaque a person has to have been
dead for 20 years and there must be reasonable
grounds for believing that they are regarded as
eminent by their own profession.

Out of the following writers, Elizabeth Barrett
Browning, George Eliot, Elizabeth Gaskell,
Christina Rossetti and Virginia Woolf have
already been honoured with blue plaques. Doris
Lessing is ruled out by dint of being still alive.
Enid Bagnold and Daphne Du Maurier have not
been dead long enough. Agatha Christie is sure-
ly due a plaque in 1996 and tomorrow would not
be too soon to raise plaques in honour of Dorothy
L Sayers, Mary Shelley and Edith Sitwell.

Enid Bagnold (1889-1981)

29 Hyde Park Gate, SW7.
A novelist, dramatist and poet who lived to a ripe-to-the-
point-of-rancid old age. *National Velvet* was her biggest
claim to fame, as well as being the story which changed
Elizabeth Taylor's fortunes by giving *her* fame *and* a
permanent bad back.

Elizabeth Barrett Browning (1806-61)

99 Gloucester Place, W1; 50 Wimpole Street, W1.
Her over-protective father published her first epic verse
when she was 14 and reportedly locked her away from
the outside world using Elizabeth's bad health as an
excuse. No wonder Robert Browning managed to woo
her with poetry and romance to a secret marriage in
Marylebone Church and thence Florence where she spent
much of her remaining life. Her works include *Aurora
Leigh* and *The Cry of the Children*; she was pipped at the
Poet Laureate post by Tennyson.

Agatha Christie (1890-1976)

58 Sheffield Terrace, W8.
Her portly Poirot, one of Britain's best-known fictional
detectives alongside Miss Marple and Sherlock Holmes,
was apparently based on Cannon Mortlocke who presided
over St Vidas church in Foster Lane, EC2.

Daphne Du Maurier (1907-89)

Cannon Hall, Cannon Place, NW3.
Came from a family of actor/writer types. Her father
Gerald specialised in playing gentleman villains and
Daphne herself liked a bit of adventure in her art. She
wrote *Rebecca, Jamaica Inn, My Cousin Rachel* and *The
House on the Strand.*

George Eliot (1819-80)

4 Cheyne Walk, SW3; 21 North Bank, NW8.
George Eliot was the pseudonym of Marian Evans, who
began writing novels when she was ostracised by polite
society for having a live-in affair with the already married
George Henry Lewes. Jolly good job she made of it too...
her novels include *The Mill on the Floss, Silas Marner* and
Middlemarch.

Elizabeth Gaskell (1810-65)

93 Cheyne Walk, SW10.
More commonly referred to as Mrs Gaskell, this writer
was a close friend of the doomed Charlotte Brontë and, on
Pop Bronte's request, she wrote *The Life of Charlotte
Brontë.* Much time was spent flitting between solitude in
London and elsewhere and staying with her husband and
daughters who were based in Manchester. *North and
South* is her best-known novel.

Doris Lessing (b 1919)

*1960s 60 Carrington Street, W1. 1970s 58 Warwick
Road, South Kensington, SW5.*
Still very much alive, Doris Lessing spent her childhood
in Zimbabwe but has lived here for much of her life. You
can find out more about London according to Doris
Lessing in her recently published *London Observed:
Stories and Sketches* (Flamingo).

Services

For more services, including beauty salons and hairdressers, *see chapter* **Shopping & Services**.

Bare Necessities

(0171 435 6789). **Lines open** 24 hours daily.

The Bare Necessities home-shopping service goes from strength to strength. It specialises in big bulky items that split plastic carrier bags and stretch arms: detergents, household cleaners, pet goods, mineral water, soft drinks and beers, washing and dishwashing products, loo roll, toiletries, nappies and baby food. A useful service for those without cars, anyone who's frantically busy or just dead lazy. All leading brands are available. Delivery is free.

Fashionizer

Unit 10, The Old Power Station, 121 Mortlake High Street, SW14 (0181 878 8212). **Open** by appointment only. **Fee** £150 plus VAT.

Fashionizer was set up by image consultant Debbie Leon to overhaul professional women's images, and to train them to dress correctly for different occasions. The basic consultancy focuses on clothes but advice about hair and other aspects of appearance is also available.

Rigby & Peller

2 Hans Road, Knightsbridge, SW3 (0171 589 9293). Knightsbridge tube. **Open** 9am-6pm Mon, Tue, Thur, Fri; 9am-7pm Wed; 9.30am-6pm Sat.

Anyone who has had a made-to-measure bra from Rigby & Peller will (given half a chance) rave about the experience and (even more so) the results for hours. Rigby & Peller hold the Royal Warrant of Appointment as Corsetieres to the Queen and Queen Mother; the younger (female) royals are also regular customers.

Travel Companions

110 High Mount, Station Road, NW4 (0181 202 8478). **Open** (phone lines) 10am-5pm Mon-Fri; no personal callers.

A service which caters particularly for women wanting to travel in Britain and abroad who don't want to go it alone. A £40 fee will fix you up with a suitable companion, who you'll meet before your trip.

Christina Rossetti (1830-94)

Born *110 Hallam Street, W1.* **Family life** *38 Arlington Road, NW1* **and** *166 Albany Street, NW1;* **also** *30 Torrington Square, WC1.*

A devout Anglican, Rossetti ditched one suitor because he was Catholic and another for being a free thinker. Instead her passion was ploughed into poetry, where the object of her desire was reputedly a married man by the name of Scott; God later took his place. Her contribution to poetry is celebrated in an altar piece painting by pre-Raphaelite artist Sir Edwin Burne Jones in Christ Church, Woburn Square, WC1. Her corpse has lain in Highgate Cemetery for just over a hundred years.

Dorothy L Sayers (1893-1957)

24 Great James Street, WC1.

Wrote detective novels with a take on romantic relationships more sensitive than was usual in the genre. Harriet Vane and Lord Peter Wimsey were favourite characters with her considerable readership. But Dorothy bemoaned the fact that her academic endeavours weren't given deserved credit because of her marked success in the sleuth story department.

Mary Shelley (1797-1851)

5 Bartholomew Road, NW5; 36 North Bank, NW8. **Died** *24 Chester Square, SW1.*

A bit of a wild gal by all accounts, Ms Shelley was the second wife of Percy Bysshe Shelley, who hung out with Byron and co. The Shelleys were married in St Mildred's Church, Blackfriars, the tower of which is the only thing left standing. The Shelleys, Lord Byron and Caroline Lamb had some scandalously decadent times together. Shelley's most famous novel is *Frankenstein.*

Edith Sitwell (1887-1964)

Pembridge Mansions, near Pembridge Square, W2.

A lanky giant with features to match and an Elizabeth I complex. Sitwell wasn't always praised for her innovation – one recital given in London was parodied by Noël Coward in a sketch and volume of slim verse called *Chelsea Buns* by one Hernia Whittlebot.

Virginia Woolf (1882-1941)

Born *22 Hyde Park Gate, SW7.* **Family life** *37 & 39 then 46,* **then** *50 Gordon Square, WC1;* **with Leonard** *52 Tavistock Square, WC1.*

Few would disagree that Virginia Woolf's life was far more interesting than her writing (with the exception of selected essays). A fragile woman mentally and physically, Woolf had nervous breakdowns, an eating disorder, an aversion to sex (except perhaps when it came to Vita Sackville-West) and a flirtatious pash for her sister's husband Clive Bell – not surprisingly there were suicide attempts (ultimately successful). She was enormously celebrated among the literati/arty circles and the Bloomsbury set was largely instigated by the gatherings at Gordon Square. She and hubby Leonard founded the Hogarth Press in Brunswick Square, WC1 and her novels include *To The Lighthouse, Mrs Dalloway* and *Orlando.*

Doris Lessing – *alive and well in London.*

Whipsnade
WILD ANIMAL PARK

Over 2,500 animals in 600 acres of beautiful parkland

Its A Wild Day Out!

Coach Driver Benefits:

FREE entry to Whipsnade
FREE meal voucher
FREE gift voucher
FREE coach parking

FREE daily demonstrations:
Birds of the World
Californian Sealions
Elephant Encounters

EASY methods of booking & payment
FULL facilities for the disabled

Themed Events :
Easter Egg Hunt,
Steam Weekend
Teddy 95
Medieval Weekend
Fun Weekend

Open daily from 10am -6pm
Earlier closing in the winter

EASY to reach via main roads.
Just 20 minutes from M25.

For further information call:
(01582) 872 171

Whipsnade Wild Animal Park
Dunstable, Bedfordshire LU6 2LF

Open every day

W. H. Auden
Christ Church

Margaret Thatcher
Somerville College

Rowan Atkinson
The Queen's College

OXFORD UNIVERSITY'S OWN STORY

The Oxford Story is a lively, informative review of Oxford's past.

A highlight of the visit is a ride through scenes from the early University.

Adult, child and foreign language commentaries are available.

THE OXFORD STORY
EXHIBITION

6 Broad Street
Oxford OX1 3AJ
Tel: (01865) 790055
Fax: (01865) 791716

Trips Out of Town

Trips Out of Town

Should you wish to flee London for a time, the list of worthwhile destinations is virtually endless – we've room only for our nearest and dearest.

Paddington BR, where these InterCity 125s are champing at the bit, serves the south-west.

Against the advice of the former heads of British Rail and InterCity, among others, the Government is pressing ahead with the fragmentation of the country's rail network for privatisation. Services are likely to be reduced and some cut altogether. Chances are it's going to be increasingly difficult and expensive to escape from the big smoke.

But it is always going to be worth the effort and the expense. Britain is a small country, most parts easily accessible from London and offering the tourist a wealth of landscapes and varied opportunities for city breaks.

The best place to start is at the **British Travel Centre** (*see below*). Here you can get guide books, free leaflets and advice on any destination, you can book rail, bus, air or car travel, reserve tours, theatre tickets and accommodation; there's even a bureau de change. Queues may be long in summer, so the earlier you turn up the better.

The Tourist Boards for Scotland, Wales and Northern Ireland provide similar services for their own countries. At your destination, head for the local Tourist Information Centre, where you can pick up free maps and guides. Always check opening times beforehand if you're going

to see a specific sight: some venues are shut on Sundays; many close over the Christmas and New Year Bank Holidays. Museums are often closed all winter.

British Travel Centre

12 Lower Regent Street, SW1 (no phone). Piccadilly Circus tube. **Open** *May-Sept* 9am-6.30pm Mon-Fri; 9am-5pm Sat; 10am-4pm Sun. *Oct-Apr* 9am-6.30pm Mon-Fri; 10am-4pm Sat, Sun. **Credit** A, AmEx, V. Personal callers only.

All Ireland Information Bureau

12 Lower Regent Street, SW1 (0171 839 8416/8417). Piccadilly Circus tube. **Open** *May-Sept* 9am-6.30pm Mon-Fri; 9am-5pm Sat; 10am-4pm Sun. *Oct-Apr* 9am-6.30pm Mon-Fri; 10am-4pm Sat, Sun. **Credit** A, V. Personal callers only.

Scottish Tourist Board

19 Cockspur Street, SW1 (0171 930 8661). Piccadilly Circus or Charing Cross tube/BR. **Open** *May-Sept* 9.30am-5.30pm Mon-Fri; 10am-4pm Sat, phone to confirm. *Oct-Apr* 9.30am-5.30pm Mon-Fri. **Credit** A, V.

Wales Information Bureau

12 Lower Regent Street, SW1 (0171 409 0969). Piccadilly Circus tube. **Open** *May-Sept* 9am-6.30pm Mon-Fri; 9am-5pm Sat; 10am-4pm Sun. *Oct-Apr* 9am-6.30pm Mon-Fri; 10am-4pm Sat, Sun. **No credit cards**.

Rail Travel

Despite the best efforts of the Government, the railway network remains an excellent way to explore the country, with little-known local lines branching off from InterCity routes. A few of these cross breathtaking Victorian viaducts and pass through areas of spectacular beauty, often where no roads exist. This is especially true in Scotland, but as we went to press, the fate of one of our rail network's most romantic services was shrouded in Scotch mist. Roger Salmon, franchising director of the Office of Passenger and Rail Franchising (OPRAF) pronounced the sleeper service to Fort William 'disproportionately uneconomic'. Unless someone, ideally the Government, subsidises the service, it'll most likely be for the chop. So don't hang about.

Unless you book Apex or Super Advance tickets (ask at stations for details), rail tickets are expensive. If, say, there are three or four of you, it may pay to hire a car (ask at the **British Travel Centre**, *see above*, or *see chapter* **Getting Around**). If travelling by rail, try to avoid rush hours when trains get very full.

Train Information

Call the number corresponding to your destination. If it is constantly engaged, try one of the other numbers and you should be able to get the same information. So if you want to go to Swindon, for example (and some one must want to), and the Paddington number is engaged, call Euston.

King's Cross *(0171 278 2477)*. **Open** *phone lines* 7am-10.30pm daily. Serves West Yorkshire, the north-east and eastern Scotland.
Euston/St Pancras *(0171 387 7070)*. **Open** *phone lines* 24 hours daily. Serves the Midlands, West Midlands, north Wales, the north-west and western Scotland.
Paddington *(0171 262 6767)*. **Open** *phone lines* 24 hours daily. Serves the west country and south Wales.
Waterloo/Charing Cross/Victoria/Liverpool Street *(0171 928 5100)*. **Open** *phone lines* 24 hours daily. Serves the south east, Essex and East Anglia.

Rail Travel Centres

Rail Travel Centres offer information on services and local facilities; you can book train tickets there. The main-line stations listed *above* all have Travel Centres, and there are other offices at Heathrow and Gatwick Airports and inside the British Travel Centre – personal callers only, no telephone enquiries. All accept Access, AmEx and Visa.

Tickets & Fares

Rail tickets can be bought right up until the moment of departure, but for InterCity routes at peak times it's wise to reserve a seat at least two hours in advance – otherwise you may end up standing. Reservations can be made when buying the ticket, and usually cost £1 extra. Tickets can be bought from stations and Rail Travel Centres (*see above*) or by phone with Access, AmEx or Visa from the relevant terminus. Return tickets don't cost that much more than single tickets, so it makes sense to buy a return. Full-price Standard Return tickets can be used at any time of day; most people buy the off-peak Super Saver Return, which has certain restrictions (no travel on Friday or Saturday) but is almost half the price. For Friday or Saturday travel, you'll need an ordinary Saver, more expensive than a Super Saver; both are valid for return within one month.

For day trips, Cheap Day Returns are the best value. Family Railcards and Young Person's Railcards offer discounted travel; Travel Centres can advise you.

First Class is so expensive you might as well buy your own Lear jet. Avoid Fridays unless you want to mingle with the entire population of the Greater London area, and on Sundays there's a chance you'll be delayed by engineering works.

Coach Travel

Going by coach is cheaper, but motorway traffic moves slowly at times (Friday pm, for example) and crying on the hard shoulder is no way to see the English countryside. Long-distance routes, however, offer 'luxury' services with videos and refreshments for a bit of extra cash.

National Express (*0171 730 0202*) has routes to all parts of the country, coaches departing from Victoria Coach Station, Buckingham Palace Road, SW1, five minutes' walk from Victoria BR. Green Line Buses (*0181 668 7261*) has routes within Greater London: its major departure point is from Eccleston Bridge, off Buckingham Palace Road, SW1, behind Victoria BR. In these days of cut-throat competition in bus travel there may be competing services to your destination. National Express offers Rover Tickets which can make travel even cheaper.

Cycling & Walking

We're not suggesting you should cycle to Scotland, though no doubt someone is doing that very thing as you read this, but there can be fewer healthier and more enjoyable ways of moving about the towns and countryside of Britain than by bike or on foot.

Sustrans

35 King Street, Bristol BS1 4DZ (0117 926 8893).
Sustrans are embarked on the mammoth task of building a nationwide network consisting of 6,000 miles of cycle routes by the year 2005. They have a claim in with the Millennium Fund for £37 million. The intended network will pass within ten minutes' bike ride of 20 million people, taking in virtually every major centre of population in Britain. Write or phone for further information.

Country Lanes

9 Shaftesbury Street, Fordingbridge, Hampshire SP6 1JF (01425 655022).
Take the train from London and be met at your destination by representatives from Country Lanes who will then lead you on cycling or walking tours of the New Forest, the Cotswolds (*see page 304*), Dorset and other selected areas. There are day-trips, short breaks and six-day tours. Write or phone for a brochure.

Ramblers' Association

1/5 Wandsworth Road, SW8 2XX (0171 582 6878/fax 0171 587 3799).
The Ramblers' Association is a registered charity which 'protects rights of way, campaigns for access to open country and defends the beauty of the countryside'. The RA provides its members (105,000) with a quarterly magazine, *Rambling Today,* membership of a local walking club and the right to borrow Ordnance Survey maps from the RA library.

Hitching

Hitching may be the cheapest form of travel, but judging from the displays of reckless driving on Britain's motorways there are probably more homicidal maniacs behind the wheel than hanging round motorway services sticking out a thumb. It's a risky business and not advisable for single women or, indeed, anyone. You're unlikely to get a lift within London except at the start of major roads and motorways. For a list of useful starting points *see chapter* **Getting Around**.

Finding Accommodation

No one likes sleeping in railway stations, at least not in our climate. So book a room in advance, at least for the first day. The **British Travel Centre** has a Room Centre which, for a small booking fee and deposit, reserves accommodation anywhere in Britain. The **Wales Information Bureau**, **All Ireland Information Bureau** and the **Scottish Tourist Board** offer the same service within their respective countries. If you do turn up somewhere without a room, make for the local Tourist Information Centre – they'll do their best to find you a bed. Most also provide a 'Book a Bed Ahead' service, which means you can book the next night's hotel in another area. All these services are available to personal callers only.

Town & City Breaks
Brighton

Suddenly coming across the Royal Pavilion can be a shock to the system, especially at night when it's floodlit quite spectacularly. Its bizarre blend of architectural styles notwithstanding – Indian, Chinese, Russian, Gothic – the Royal Pavilion was built by an Englishman, John Nash, in 1823 for the Prince Regent (later George IV). If you approach from St James Street and first glimpse the Pavilion shimmering through the trees across

Brighton's **Palace Pier** *– wonderfully gaudy.*

the A23 you can't help but do a double take. It's worth a return ticket from London for this alone.

But even if it weren't, Brighton has much else to offer the visitor. The English Channel for a start: it may be freezing cold most of the year and the beach pebbly rather than sandy, but it's still the sea – partaking of it was once recommended for sufferers of glandular disease. The gaudy Palace Pier has everything from slot machines to a helter-skelter, plus a view along the shore of the derelict West Pier's severed arm. Inland, away from the amusement arcades, conference centre and Grand Hotel where an IRA bomb missed its presumed target and crippled Mrs Norman Tebbit, you'll find The Lanes. Tucked in between West Street, North Street, the A23 and the sea, this warren of winding alleys disorientates in the manner of Venice – just keep your eye on the tiny red-hooded figure ahead. The antiques, jewellery and clothes shops you'll find here are expensive but worth investigation. More interesting are the myriad second-hand shops for books, records and clothes north of North Street and south of the rail station.

Brighton's main attraction, however, is neither a single splendid building, nor the range of shopping opportunites – nor is it the shark-infested Sea-Life Centre (*0273 604234*) in Madeira Drive – people flock to Brighton for its atmosphere. That peculiar peeling charm of the seaside resort, yes, but mainly the air of liberality: the alternative lifestyles, the large, unintimidated gay community, the clubs – start at Zanzibar, 129 St James Street (*01273 622100*) and go on from there.

But there's no getting away from it: we do, oh we do like to be beside the seaside. So why not catch an antique train on Britain's first public electric railway, Volk's Seafront Railway, from the Marina to the Palace Pier. Then promenade west along the seafront to Hove, Brighton's sister town (hence Brighton and Hove Albion FC, currently languishing in the Endsleigh League Division 2), nip into The Card Centre, 39 George Street, and send a postcard home – British Telecom may go on and on about phoning home, but a postcard's something to keep.

Further Information

Getting there *by train* from Victoria, 55 minutes; *by bus* from Victoria, two hours; *by car* A23, M23, A23; *local buses* Brighton and Hove Bus Co (01273 206666).
Eating and drinking The Lanes is good for pubs, seafood restaurants and teashops. For vegetarian fare, *Terre à Terre* at 7 Pool Valley (01273 729051) is excellent, while *Food For Friends* on Prince Albert Street (01273 202310) is certainly above average. *Al Duomos*, Pavilion Gardens (01273 326741), is a cheap Italian that's popular with locals. The *Black Chapati* at 12 Circus Parade, New England Road (01273 699011) offers a variety of extremely enticing Indian dishes, at a price. Good pubs include the *Frock and Jacket* on Prince Albert Street, *The Great Eastern* on Trafalgar Street (cosy, wooden and book-lined) and the *Sussex Yeoman* on Guildford Road, which offers real ales and 32 types of sausage.
Events The *Brighton Festival* (01273 709709) is a feast of literature, debate, music, theatre and comedy second only to the Edinburgh Festival, occupying the first three weeks in May. *Mini Owners' Club Rally* May; *London to Brighton Bike Ride* June; *London to Brighton Veteran Car Run*, first Sunday in November. Also see *The Punter*, a listings magazine available in shops and pubs. The *Escape* and *Zap* clubs are still going in Marine Parade.
If you want to stay The *Adelaide* (01273 205286) is old, four-star and mid-priced; the *Hotel Brunswick* (01273 733326) is a Regency building at the same sort of price; the *Norfolk* (01273 738201) is more expensive. *The Twenty One* (01273 686450) offers a friendly welcome, a double or twin for single occupancy and a tasty breakfast for £35; while *Marina House* (01273 605349) offers bed and breakfast from £19.

Tourist Information Centres

10 Bartholomew Square, Brighton, East Sussex (01273 323755). **Open** 9am-5pm Mon-Fri; 10am-5pm Sat; 10am-4pm Sun.
Hove Town Hall, Church Road, Hove, East Sussex (01273 778087). **Open** 9am-5pm Mon-Fri; 9.30am-1pm Sat.

Bath

Looking at the elegant eighteenth-century terraces of golden stone which fill the Avon Valley and climb the enclosing hills, it's easy to see why Bath is renowned for its glorious Georgian architecture. Yet Britain's only World Heritage City owes its existence to a leprous swineherd and his equally diseased pigs. The story may be apocryphal, but it is believed that in 860 BC Prince Bladud was banished from his father's court after he developed leprosy. He became a swineherd and noticed that his pigs' skin complaints were cured after they wallowed in the mud around a hot spring. He followed them in and was cured likewise. A settlement grew up by the spring and a shrine was established to the Celtic goddess Sulis. The Romans, who invaded Britain in 43 AD, soon realised the value of the healing water and built a series of baths. They called the place Aquae Sulis and it flourished until the departure of the legions, after which it fell into decay for a time.

The Roman baths were buried under medieval buildings but were rediscovered in the eighteenth and nineteenth centuries. They are considered the most impressive non-military Roman remains in Britain, and the Roman Baths Museum is one of the country's most visited historic sites. The hot spring water still gushes up from the earth (250,000 gallons a day at 46.5C) and there's a fascinating collection of Roman artefacts. You can taste the mineral water – if you dare – in the Pump Room, but a pot of Earl Grey might go down better. Immortalised by Jane Austen, the Pump Room is still redolent of a more gracious era, and is an atmospheric place for a bite to eat.

Bath has 18 museums altogether, several of which are of compelling interest; the British Folk Art Collection, for instance, which you'll find in the Countess of Huntingdon Chapel at The Vineyards, or its neighbour The Building of Bath Museum, the highlight of which is a spectacular model of the city. The American Museum at Claverton Manor is well worth the short trip out of town (bus 18).

But Bath's main attraction is simply its streets, the grandest of which is the Royal Crescent, a breathtaking sweep of 30 houses designed by John Wood the Younger in 1767. Number One is furnished in authentic period style and is open to the public. Nearby is the magnificent Circus, composed of three crescents forming a circle, and designed by the elder John Wood.

Not all of Bath's streets are so imposing; there's a delightful tangle of narrow alleyways crammed with wonderful architectural details and tempting

Fifteenth-century **Bath Abbey** *on a Saxon site.*

Cambridge's **Queens' College**, *founded for the first time in 1446, then twice refounded.*

shops. Look for these in the area to the north of Abbey Churchyard, an open space popular with street entertainers. Bath Abbey is a fifteenth-century rebuilding of an earlier Norman structure, itself built on the site of a Saxon church where Edgar, the first king of a united England, was crowned in 973.

The River Avon adds to the appeal of the city and is spanned by Pulteney Bridge, an Italianate masterpiece designed by Robert Adam. There are pleasant walks beside the river and the adjacent Kennet and Avon Canal. Boats may be hired in summer from the Boating Station on Forester Road.

Bath is one of the main shopping centres in the west of England and a good place to find that unusual gift or souvenir, whatever your budget. Enjoy the small specialist shops, check out the Great Western Antique Centre on Bartlett Street, and visit Walcot Reclamation, a fascinating architectural salvage yard, on Walcot Street. The Guildhall Market is worth a look, particularly for food and secondhand books.

Further Information

Getting there *by train* from Paddington; *by coach* National Express from Victoria; *by car* M4 to J18 then A46, use park 'n' ride; *local buses* excellent services from Badgerline (01225 464446).

Eating and drinking *Sally Lunn's Refreshment House and Museum* in North Parade Passage is the oldest house in Bath and you can sample the famous buns made fashionable by Sally Lunn in the 1680s. *Scoffs* in Kingsmead Square is a great bakery/café/takeaway. *Huckleberry's* on Broad Street provides vegetarian meals

while the nearby *Moon and Sixpence* is a popular bistro. The *Walrus and Carpenter* near the Theatre Royal is enjoyable and inexpensive. The *Royal Crescent Hotel* serves classic dishes with prices to match. Popular pubs include the *Coeur de Lion* in Northumberland Place and the *Boater* on Argyle Street (by the river).

Events *Festival of Literature* in February; *International Music Festival* in May/June; *Royal Bath & West Show* in May/June (agricultural show); for details of a year-round programme of cultural events call 01225 462231.

If you want to stay *The Royal Crescent Hotel* (01225 319090) is all that you might expect it to be; *Dukes Hotel* (01225 463512) on Great Pulteney Street is a bit cheaper but still very elegant; *Holly Villa* (01225 310331) in Pulteney Gardens is a good B&B; so is *Bathurst Guest House* (01225 421884) on Walcot Parade; *Bath Youth Hostel* (01225 465674) on Bathwick Hill, is an Italianate mansion with a panoramic view of the city (bus 18).

Tourist Information Centre

Abbey Chambers, Abbey Churchyard, Bath (01225 462831). **Open** *Jun-Sept* 9.30am-6pm Mon-Sat, 10am-4pm Sun; *Oct-May* 9.30am-5pm Mon-Sat; phone for details of Sunday opening.

Cambridge

Though the university is the dominant theme in Cambridge, the city's history began many centuries before the first students arrived. Germinating as a Celtic settlement, Cambridge flourished successively as a Roman fort and trading centre, a Saxon market town, a Danish army base and a Norman regional centre and military stronghold.

It was in the early thirteenth century that scholars began arriving, fleeing from riot-torn Oxford. By 1231 Cambridge had been officially recognised as a seat of learning, but it was not until 1284 that the first proper college was founded. By the end of the fourteenth century the university was already dominating local life, and the character of present-day Cambridge had been established.

The oldest college is Peterhouse on Trumpington Street, endowed in 1284. The original hall still survives, though most of the present buildings are nineteenth century. Just up the road is Corpus Christi, founded in 1352. Its Old Court dates from that time and is linked by a gallery to the eleventh-century St Bene't's Church, the oldest building in Cambridge. Just across the road is Queens', founded originally by Andrew Dokett, Rector of St Botolph's, in 1446, but refounded twice; first by Queen Margaret of Anjou in 1448, then by Queen Elizabeth Woodville in 1475. Most of the original buildings survive and the inner courts are wonderfully picturesque.

Next to Queens' is King's, founded by Henry VI in 1441, and renowned for its chapel, built 1446-1515 and considered one of the greatest Gothic buildings in Europe. The interior is breathtaking and the original stained glass still survives. To the north is Trinity, founded 1336 by Edward III and refounded by Henry VIII in 1546. Its fine collection of Tudor buildings surrounds the Great Court where, tradition has it, Lord Byron used to bathe naked in the fountain with his pet bear (the university wouldn't allow him to keep a dog).

Behind the main group of colleges is The Backs, a series of beautiful gardens and lawns bordering the willow-shaded River Cam, which is spanned by several noteworthy footbridges. The Backs are perfect for summer strolling or you can hire a punt and drift lazily along the river. Bike hire is also an idea if you want to explore the peripheral areas of Cambridge – try Geoff's on Devonshire Road or Mike's Bikes on Mill Road.

Though the colleges are Cambridge's principal attraction, it has much more to offer: visit the Fitzwilliam Museum in Trumpington Street for its outstanding collections of antiquities and Old Masters; climb the tower of Great St Mary's Church on King's Parade for far-reaching views; and wander along picturesque streets lined with period buildings and full of tempting shops. Unsurprisingly, it's a good place to buy books, whether new, secondhand or antiquarian.

Further Information

Getting there *by train* from Liverpool Street or King's Cross; *by coach* National Express from Victoria; *by car* on M11 to exit 11 or 12; *local buses* Cambus 01223 423554.
Eating and drinking Good cafés include *Fitzbillies* on Trumpington Street and *Clowns* on King Street, where newspapers are provided with your cappuccino. *Brown's* (01223 461655) on Trumpington Street is a lively and moderately priced restaurant; *King's Pantry* (01223 321551) on King's Parade is Cambridge's only vegetarian restaurant; *La Margherita* (01223 315232) on Magdalen Street is a good Italian, while *Castle Tandoori* (01223 312569) on Castle Street is one of the best Indian restaurants. For upmarket French cuisine go to

Midsummer House (01223 369299) on Midsummer Common. There are lots of good pubs to choose from, including the venerable *Eagle* on Bene't Street or the *Zebra* on Maid's Causeway (good for food). Students tend to hang out at the *Baron of Beef* on Bridge Street, while the *Free Press* on Prospect Row is usually crammed with boaties.
Events *May Week* – not one week and not in May – boat races (the May Bumps), balls and open-air theatre in the first two weeks of June; *Strawberry Fair*, a variety of entertainments on Midsummer Common in late June; *Cambridge Folk Festival* in July.
If you want to stay Advance booking is advisable in summer. *Hamilton Hotel* (01223 65664) and *Arundel House Hotel* (01223 67701), both on Chesterton Road, are reasonably priced; *Garden House Hotel* (01223 63421) on Mill Lane, and *University Arms Hotel* (01223 351241) on Regent Street are much pricier. Guest houses are plentiful, especially on Tenison Road, Cherry Hinton Road and Chesterton Road, where *Netley Lodge* (01223 247539) has a good riverside position. The youth hostel (01223 354601) is on Tenison Road, near the rail station.

Tourist Information Centre

The Old Library, Wheeler Street, Cambridge (01223 322640). **Open** *Nov-Mar* 9am-5.30pm Mon-Fri, 9am-5pm Sat; *Apr-Oct* 9am-6pm Mon-Fri, 9am-5pm Sat; *Easter-Sept* 10.30am-3.30pm Sun and Bank Holiday Monday (9.30am opening on Wed only throughout year).

Oxford

Founded by the Saxons, Oxford began its development in the early eighth century around a priory established by St Frideswide on the site where Christ Church now stands. Its slow but steady growth in importance and influence received the Royal seal of approval when Henry I built his Palace of Beaumont there in the early twelfth century, at much the same time as the first students were beginning to gather. Their numbers were boosted in 1167 when Paris University was closed to the English, and by the end of the century Oxford was firmly established as England's first university town. Today, the university comprises a federation of 41 independent colleges and halls, mostly occupying the sort of buildings which lend substance to Oxford's claim to be 'one of the great architectural centres of the world'.

Most are usually open to the public, and a short-list of the finest might include Christ Church, with its famous Tom Tower, and a chapel so grand that it serves as Oxford's cathedral. Nearby Merton, founded in 1264, boasts a marvellous medieval library, but University College was Oxford's first college, endowed in 1249. Magdalen (pronounced Maudlin) is often said to be the loveliest college. Its extensive grounds include a deer park and a meadow where the rare snakeshead fritillary still blooms every April.

Other centres of academia include the Ashmolean Museum in Beaumont Street, and the Bodleian Library off Broad Street, whose collection of five million books was begun in 1598. The elegant Radcliffe Camera is England's earliest example of a round reading room (1737).

But Oxford is as much town as gown, and there's more to see than just centres of learning. Even the shops are worthwhile, with the attractive High Street retaining far more individuality than most. Little Clarendon Street and the new development at Gloucester Green offer some interesting specialist shops. Best of all is the classy Covered Market, linking High Street and Market Street. Opened in 1774, it's a foodie's delight, but vegetarians will flinch at some of the displays. If shopping for antiques you should investigate Park End Street between the bus and railway stations, and for bookshop browsing you can't beat Blackwell's on Broad Street.

The countryside pushes green fingers into the heart of the town, with the Oxford Canal, the River Thames (sometimes called the Isis, from the Latin Thamesis) and the River Cherwell (pronounced Charwell) providing opportunities for strolling and punting. Boats may be hired from Folly Bridge, Magdalen Bridge and Cherwell Boathouse on Bardwell Road. There are large areas of meadow, common and parkland to wander over, while for the classic view of Matthew Arnold's 'dreaming spires' you must climb Boar's Hill three miles to the south-west. If that's too far to walk you can hire a bike from Pennyfarthing on George Street (*01865 24936*).

Further Information

Getting there *by train* from Paddington, then use your rail ticket for a free ride into the town centre on one of Oxford's pioneering electric buses (every ten minutes); *by coach* from several London departure points, with coaches providing a fast, cheap and comfortable service 24 hours a day, every day, departures every ten minutes at peak times; details from Thames Transit (01865 772250) or Oxford Bus Company (01865 711312/0181 668 7261); *by car* on M40 then use one of the four park 'n' rides.

Eating and drinking *The Eagle and Child* on St Giles was a favourite watering hole of CS Lewis and JRR Tolkien, *The Bear* on Alfred Street is one of Oxford's oldest buildings, the *Turf Tavern* in Bath Place is always popular. Pleasant riverside pubs a short walk from town include *The Isis* at Iffley Lock, *The Perch* at Binsey and *The Trout* at Wolvercote. Of the restaurants *Brown's* (01865 511995) on Woodstock Road is stylish and very popular, *Nosebag* (01865 721033) on St Michael's is justly famous for its cakes, and the *Hi-Lo Jamaican Eating House* (01865 725984) on Cowley Road is splendidly unconventional. For serious foodies with well-stuffed wallets there is always Raymond Blanc's internationally renowned *Le Manoir Aux Quat' Saisons* (01844 278881) at Great Milton.

Events *The Torpids* (rowing races) in February; *Eights Week* (inter-collegiate rowing races) in May/June; *Encaenia* (honorary degree presentation and procession) in May or June; *Oxford Regatta* in August; *St Giles Fair* in September.

If you want to stay the *Old Parsonage Hotel* (01865 310210) on Banbury Road is well-placed and classy; *St Michael's Guest House* (01865 242101) on St Michael's Street is a central B&B, and *Windrush Guest House* (01865 247933) on Iffley Road is simple and friendly; *Oxford Youth Hostel* (01865 62997) is a fine Victorian house on Jack Straw's Lane. Out of town, *Westwood Country Hotel* (01865 735408) is beautifully set and *The Bear* at Woodstock (01993 811511) is a renowned old coaching inn.

*View of **Oxford** from Carfax Tower – students started gathering in the early twelfth century.*

Tourist Information Centre
*The Old School, Gloucester Green, Oxford (01865
726871).* **Open** 9.30am-5pm Mon-Sat; 10.30am-1pm and
1.30-3.30pm Sun and Bank Holidays only in summer.

Salisbury & Stonehenge

In its first incarnation Salisbury was an Iron Age
hillfort which was taken over by the Romans,
the Saxons and finally the Normans. They called
it Sarum and built a castle and cathedral, but the
site wasn't big enough for both to co-exist happily
and in 1220 the bishop embarked on the building
of a new cathedral two miles to the south. The
settlement that grew up around it became New
Sarum, now Salisbury.

The cathedral took only 38 years to complete,
so it's unusually consistent in style, except for
the spire, the tallest in Britain, which was added
in 1334. The cathedral library contains one of
only four original copies of Magna Carta (1215)
and in the north aisle you can see the country's
(possibly the world's) oldest working clock (1386).
The Cathedral Close is the finest of its kind in
Britain, a haven of peace where beautiful houses
and lawns soothe the eye. Many of the houses
are thirteenth century but with Georgian façades.
Two of the finest are Malmesbury House and
Mompesson House (1701), both of which are open
to the public.

The town centre is a jumble of jettied, gabled,
timber-framed buildings overhanging narrow
streets. Names such as Butcher Row, Fish Row
and Poultry Cross hint at Salisbury's true character as a regional trading centre, and it really comes
alive on market days (Tuesdays and Saturdays),
as it has for the past 400 years.

For all its considerable charms, it seems that
most visitors to Salisbury are just stopping off on
their way to Stonehenge, a World Heritage Site
about ten miles to the north, near Amesbury. In its
way, Stonehenge is one of the most controversial
structures in Britain. On the one hand, there are
the conflicting academic arguments about its
original purpose; on the other hand, there is the
obsession of the authorities about protecting it
from New Age travellers, while officially sanc-
tioned vandalism has surrounded it with roads, car
parks, facilities and fencing.

There is talk of re-routing the road system. In
the meantime, visitors have to work hard to capture the appropriate atmosphere. It's worth the
effort, for it is undeniably one of the most mind-
blowing monuments in the world.

Why they built it we don't know, and never will.
How they built it is staggering enough. It's believed that construction began around 3000 BC
and continued intermittently over a period of 1,500
years. The main components are an outer bank
and ditch surrounding two stone circles. The first
stone circle to be raised consists of bluestones from

Salisbury Cathedral – *Britain's tallest spire.*

Pembrokeshire, while the later circle is of sarsens
hewn from Marlborough Downs.

The stones were transported over land and
water using sledges and rafts. It has been estimated that each of the largest stones would have
required 500 men to pull the sledge, and 100 more
to lay rollers in front of it. We can't begin to imagine what it was that compelled men to undertake
such a task. And it's worth remembering that what
remains today is only a small part of the original
complex (which was plundered over the centuries
for building stone) and that Stonehenge is only one
of over 500 known prehistoric sites in an area of
just ten square miles.

Further Information
Getting there (Salisbury) *by train* from Waterloo; *by
coach* National Express from Victoria; *by car* on M3 to J8
then A303 and A338; *local buses* Wilts & Dorset (01722
336855) is the main operator and runs daily services to
Stonehenge from Salisbury bus and rail stations.
Eating and drinking For drinks, snacks and light
lunches try *Hob Nob Coffee Shop* in The Close, or any of
the cafés in St Thomas' Square. For traditional dinners
Harper's (01722 333118) in Market Square is good value,
while *Crustaceans* (01722 333948) on Ivy Street
specialises in seafood. The fourteenth-century *Haunch of
Venison* on Minster Street is the city's oldest pub; the
King's Arms on St John Street is not much younger.
Events *St George's Spring Festival* (Easter services at
the cathedral) Apr; *Salisbury Festival* (arts) May;
Salisbury Charter Fair (funfair) Oct; *Christmas services* at
the cathedral, Dec.

If you want to stay *The Old Bell* (01722 327958) on St
Ann Street is nicely situated near the cathedral; so is the
more upmarket *Grasmere House Hotel* (01722 338388) on
Harnham Road; the *White Hart* (01722 327476) on St John
Street and the *Rose and Crown* (01722 327908) on
Harnham Road are reasonably priced and popular; the
excellent youth hostel (01722 327572) is on Milford Hill.

Tourist Information Centre

Fish Row, Salisbury, Wiltshire (01722 334956).
Open *Oct-Apr* 9.30am-5pm Mon-Sat; *May* 9.30am-5pm
Mon-Sat, 11am-4pm Sun; *June & Sept* 9.30am-6pm Mon-
Sat, 11am-4pm Sun; *July & Aug* 9.30am-7pm Mon-Sat,
11am-5pm Sun.

Stratford-upon-Avon

William Shakespeare was born in Stratford in
1564, and died there in 1616. His birthplace soon
became a place of literary pilgrimage, but it was
not until 1769 that the phenomenon which is
Stratford tourism really began. It was in this year
that the actor David Garrick persuaded Stratford
to stage a festival in honour of its most famous son.
This proved to be the catalyst which transformed
an attractive but unremarkable market town into
a tourist honeypot second only to London. Top of
the list for most visitors are the Shakespeare properties, five picturesque Tudor houses which function as museums and are worth visiting in their
own right. There are three in the town centre: the
Bard's birthplace on Henley Street; Hall's Croft,
home of his daughter Susanna, in Old Town; and
Nash's House, on Chapel Street, which belonged
to the first husband of his grand-daughter. Its
garden contains the foundations of New Place,
Shakespeare's last home, demolished in 1759.

A mile and a half away at Shottery, and accessible by public footpath, is Anne Hathaway's
Cottage, where Shakespeare's wife lived before her
marriage. The girlhood home of his mother, Mary
Arden's House, is at Wilmcote, a pleasant 3.5-mile
(5.6-km) stroll along the towpath of the Stratford
Canal. Both may also be reached by bus, and there
are trains to Wilmcote.

Shakespeare was educated at Stratford Gram-
mar School, which you can see on Church Street,
and he was buried in Holy Trinity Church, which
has a fine riverside setting. It'll cost you 50p if
you want to see his tomb. The dramatist's most
meaningful memorials are the plays he bequeathed
us, and the Royal Shakespeare Theatre is the place
to see them. Tickets sell out fast but it's always
worth a try. The adjoining Swan Theatre stages
a variety of classics, while The Other Place is
for modern and experimental work. For bookings
call 01789 295623. If you can't get a ticket you
will have to make do with a backstage tour or a
visit to the RSC Collection, a museum of props
and costumes.

Relief from all things Shakespearian is easily
achieved. Stratford has been a market town since
1169 and, in a way, that's still what it does best.
See it on a Friday, when the blue and white
awnings go up over the stalls at the top of Wood
Street, and local people flock in from the outlying
villages. And wander round the town centre,

*A narrowboat entering the canal basin at **Stratford-upon-Avon**, Shakespeare's birthplace.*

which still maintains its medieval grid pattern. Many fine old buildings survive, among them Harvard House on High Street, which dates from 1596. It was the home of Katharine Rogers who married Robert Harvard of London. It was their son John who founded Harvard University.

The town's charms are enhanced by the presence of the River Avon and the Stratford Canal. The canal basin is usually crammed with colourful narrowboats and there are pleasant walks beside both waterways. Stratford is also a good touring centre, with two highlights being the medieval castles at Warwick and Kenilworth, both easily reached by local buses.

Further Information

Getting there *by train* from Paddington (direct), also from Euston or Marylebone, changing at Leamington or Birmingham, or at Coventry for a bus link; *by coach* National Express from Victoria or Guide Friday from Euston; *by car* M40 to J15 then A46; *local buses* Stratford Blue and Midland Red (South), call Busline on 01788 535555 or Warwickshire Traveline on 01926 414140, also Guide Friday (tours and open-top buses) 01789 294466.

Eating and drinking *The Black Swan* (aka the Dirty Duck), by the Avon, is where most of the actors hang out, though some prefer the heavily beamed *Garrick* on High Street. Attractive restaurants and bistros abound – try *Lamb's* or *The Vintner*, both on Sheep Street, or Fatty Arbuckle's on Chapel Street; for Indian food go to *Hussain's*, also on Chapel Street. The Antiques Centre on Ely Street has a tiny, enjoyable café, *The Dealers' Den*.

Events *Shakespeare's Birthday Celebrations* in April; *Raft Race and Regatta* in June; *Stratford Festival* in July; *Vintage Car Run* in September; *Mop Fair* in October.

If you want to stay The sixteenth-century *Falcon Hotel* (01789 205777) on Chapel Street has bags of character; the nearby *Shakespeare Hotel* (01789 294771) is also popular. Guest houses are abundant, especially on Alcester Road, Grove Road and Evesham Place. The *Youth Hostel* (01789 297093) is just out of town (bus 18) at Alveston. *Pear Tree Cottage* (01789 205889) is an attractive B&B next to Mary Arden's House at Wilmcote.

Tourist Information Centre

Bridgefoot, Stratford-upon-Avon, Warwickshire (01789 293127). **Open** *Apr-Oct* 9am-6pm Mon-Sat, 11am-5pm Sun; *Nov-Mar* 9am-5pm Mon-Sat.

Windsor

Situated by the Thames, Windsor is a pretty town which gets swamped by tourists during the summer season. William the Conqueror chose the site of Windsor for a royal castle as it was high on a hill overlooking the Thames, on the edge of a Saxon hunting ground, and a day's march from the Tower of London. The Changing of the Guard takes place every day at 11am, or every day when the Queen is in residence – you can tell if she's there by the Royal Standard which is raised above the Castle. Rebuilding work is still going on after the fire of 1992, but you can visit the State Apartments and the beautiful St George's Chapel, where Henry VIII is buried. The highlight of any tour around Windsor Castle is Queen Mary's Doll's House, a huge, magnificent model which took more than three years to make.

Other attractions in the town include the Crown Jewels of the World exhibition in Peascod Street, the main shopping drag, and the royal carriages and gifts collection, which displays some of the many presents the royal family have received over the years.

Near the Thames is Eton College, founded by Henry VI in 1440 originally for 70 'poor and worthy scholars'. How times change. You can visit the college buildings and the Museum of Eton Life in the afternoons. Eton boys are easily recognisable by the tailcoats which they are required to wear.

Also around the area, accessible either by boat trips or walking through the Great Park or Long Walk, is Runnymede, the site where the Magna Carta was sealed in 1215. It's also home to the John F Kennedy Memorial and the Air Force Memorial – a tribute to 20,000 airmen and women with no known graves. Off the dead-straight and precisely three-mile Long Walk, is where Queen Victoria had Frogmore House built for her beloved Prince Albert. They are both buried there, in Frogmore Mausoleum. Further down the Thames is Cliveden House. Built in 1851 by Sir Charles Barry, this is the third house on the site and was once the home of Nancy and Lady Astor. It's now let as a hotel, though you can tour the grounds (375 acres of garden and woodland) and three rooms of the house.

A guided tour by bus operated by Guide Friday (*01865 790522*) takes in Windsor, Eton and Datchet (where Jerome K Jerome wrote *Three Men in a Boat*). Tickets are valid all day and you can hop on and off the buses as much as you like (£6; £4 OAPs, students; £1.50 under-12s).

Further Information

Getting there *by train* from Paddington to Windsor and Eton Central, change at Slough, 35 minutes, or from Waterloo to Windsor and Eton Riverside, 50 minutes; *by bus* Green Line, 1 hour; *by car* M25, exit 13, then A308 or M4 exit 6; *local buses* Beeeline Buses (01344 424938).

Eating and drinking The *Dome*, Thames Street, is a French café serving meals, drinks and snacks all day; the *Cockpit* in Eton High Street is a pricey bet, but it's situated in a lovely building dating back to 1420, with one of just four working postboxes in the country left from Victoria's reign.

Events *Royal Windsor Show* May; *Henley Regatta* June; *Rose Show* June; *Knowle Hill Steam & Country Show* August; *Windsor Festival* late Sept/Oct.

If you want to stay the *Harte & Garter*, facing the Castle, has the best views in town (01753 863426); *Sir Christopher Wren's House Hotel* (01753 861354, and yes, it is his old house), overlooking the Thames, is a more expensive option; the *Netherton Hotel*, slightly out of the centre (01753 855508) is more reasonably priced.

Tourist Information Centre

Windsor & Eton Central Station, Windsor (01753 852010). **Open** *May-Sept* 9.30am-5.30pm Mon-Fri, 9.30am-6pm Sat, 10am-6pm Sun; *Oct-Mar* times vary, phone to check.

Country House Gardens

You don't have to travel far to experience the full glory of English country gardens. Elizabethan mazes, the eighteenth-century obsession with landscape lookalikes, or the perennial cottage look – none are much more than an hour away.

Groombridge Place Gardens

Groombridge, Tunbridge Wells, Kent (01892 863999). **Getting there** by train Charing Cross to Tunbridge Wells, then connecting bus; by car 4 miles SW of Tunbridge Wells; A264 2 miles towards East Grinstead, then B2110. **Open** *1 Apr-31 Oct* 10am-6pm daily. **Admission** £3.50; £2.25 under-16s; free under-6s.

It comes as little surprise that this medieval site, surrounded by parkland, has inspired artists and writers over the centuries (including film-maker Peter Greenaway and Sir Arthur Conan Doyle for *The Valley of Fear*). With a listed walled garden set against a seventeenth-century moated mansion, walks through an 'enchanted forest', spring-fed pools and waterfalls giving way to dramatic views over the Weald, the possibilities for waxing lyrical seem endless.

Hever Castle

Edenbridge, Kent (01732 865224). **Getting there** by train Victoria to Edenbridge Town (then taxi), or Hever (then 1-mile walk); by car to Junction 5 or 6 on M25, then B2026, 3 miles SE of Edenbridge. **Open** *grounds* 11am-6pm daily; *castle* noon-6pm (last admission 5pm); *after 29 Oct* 11am-5pm (last admission 4pm). **Admission** *castle & gardens* £5.70; £2.90 5-16s; £14.30 family (2 adults, 2 children); *gardens* £4.30; £2.50 5-16s; £11.10 family.

It was in the magnificent grounds of this double-moated, thirteenth-century castle that Henry VIII was said to have courted Anne Boleyn, 1,000 days before she lost her head. Much has changed since, and these 30 acres now boast splendid Italianate gardens with loggia, classical sculpture and colonnaded piazza (no expense spared by the Astor family under whose auspices these changes took place). A large lake, rose garden, topiary and maze all add to the romance of this treasured estate.

Nymans Garden

(National Trust) Handcross, near Haywards Heath, West Sussex (01444 400321). **Getting there** by car M23, A23, 4m S Crawley on the B2114; by train Victoria to Crawley. **Open** *Mar-end Oct* 11am-dusk or 7pm Wed-Sun (last admission 1 hour before closing). **Admission** £3.80.

Nymans is set high on the edge of the Sussex Weald. From the south aspect, the South Downs gently undulate across the horizon. Looking inwardly to the garden, the National Trust has created a showpiece of rare shrubs and trees.

Parham

Parham Park, Nr Pulborough, West Sussex (01903 744888). **Getting there** by train Victoria to Pulborough, then taxi; by car off the A283 Storrington to Pulborough road. **Open** *16 Apr-1 Oct house* 2-5pm; *garden* 1-5pm, Wed, Thur, Sun. **Admission** *house & garden* £4.25; £2.50 5-15s; *garden* £3; £1.50 5-15s.

A near perfect Elizabethan house in a near perfect English country setting, beneath the rolling South Downs. There's

an Elizabethan long gallery, portraits and rare needlework, but it's the way these are set off that gives paying visitors a sense of belonging, with fresh flowers and plants making the least piece of small furniture a joy to behold. In the gardens, a lake, statuary, maze and chapel complete the idyll.

Polesden Lacey

Nr Dorking, Surrey (01372 458203). **Getting there** by car 3m NW of Dorking; reached via Great Bookham (A246), then road leading S (12m); by train Waterloo to Box Hill, then 2-mile walk; to Leatherhead then taxi to Bookham. **Open** *house 29 Mar-end Oct* 1.30-5.30pm Wed-Sun; *Nov-28 Mar* 1.30-4.30pm Sat, Sun; *garden* 11am-dusk or 6pm daily. **Admission** *house* £3; *grounds* £2.50; *both* half-price 5-17s; free under 5s.

This Regency Surrey villa was the honeymooning ground for the Queen Mother and late George VI more than 70 years ago. Tucked into the folds of the North Downs, the house and grounds give way to views over woodland and commons. Within the grounds, tree-lined walks, walled rose gardens and a charming thatched bridge over a typical Surrey sunken lane, connecting the grounds to a glorious spring meadow, all make for a right royal day trip.

Sheffield Park Garden

Uckfield, East Sussex (01825 790655). **Getting there** by car midway between East Grinstead and Lewes on the A275; 5m NW of Uckfield; by train Victoria to Haywards Heath or Uckfield. **Open** *Apr-end Oct* 11am-6pm Tue-Sun. **Admission** from £3.70; £1.80 children.

Created by the master himself, Capability Brown, in the eighteenth century, the gardens were modified in the early twentieth century but still retain that grand landscape feel. There are five lakes connected with cascades and waterfalls in the early spring, fine specimens of azalea and rhododendron in early summer, and awesome autumn hues from myriad trees. The Bluebell Railway Museum is adjacent, with Pullman steam trains running at weekends pulling dining cars *(0825 722370)*.

Sissinghurst Castle Gardens

Sissinghurst, nr Cranbrook, Kent (01580 712850/ 715330). **Getting there** by car 2m NE of Cranbrook (A21); by train Charing Cross to Staplehurst (1 hour), then bus or taxi to Sissinghurst village. **Open** *1 Apr-15 Oct* 1-6.30pm Tue-Fri; 10am-5.30pm Sat, Sun. **Admission** £5.

If Kent is the garden of England, then Sissinghurst is the breath-taking flowerbed within that garden. Here Vita Sackville-West and her husband Harold Nicholson transformed a ruined sixteenth-century mansion and grounds into a paradise of colour and fragrance. Her planting schemes were informal within the formal constraints of separate smaller themed gardens – white, herb and cottage. The results have been inspirational to gardeners ever since, with a resulting tide of visitors which ebbs and flows throughout the year, but is obviously at its height at weekends during the summer months. Visit early on a weekday.

Tucked into the folds of the North Downs, the house and grounds of Surrey's **Polesden Lacey** *give way to tranquil views.*

York

'The history of York,' said King George VI, 'is the history of England.' Definitely an overstatement, but an understandable one, reflecting the significance of this former Roman fort which became a Viking capital, then the commercial, administrative and religious centre of the north. For centuries it was England's second city. Many Yorkshiremen would say it still is.

The city is dominated by its Minster; the seat of the Archbishop of York, it is the fourth cathedral on this site and was built over a period of 250 years, from 1220 to 1470. Britain's largest Gothic building, it contains 128 medieval stained glass windows, amounting to about half the medieval stained glass in existence. Most famous is the glorious East Window which dates from 1405 and is the largest of its kind in the world. If you can tear yourself away from the windows, the best way to get a real sense of the Minster's antiquity is to descend into the crypt and the foundations. It's also worth climbing the huge central tower for the view over the Vale of York.

Roughly contemporary with the Minster are the city walls, though they include fragments of their Norman predecessors and partially follow the line of the original Roman ramparts. The full circuit of the walls, nearly 3 miles (5 km), makes a superb walk. If you just want to sample a short stretch take a ten-minute stroll from Monk Bar to Bootham Bar, two of the four surviving gateways. The others are Walmgate, which is the most complete, and Micklegate, on which used to be displayed the severed heads of traitors.

Enclosed by these walls are some of the finest medieval streets in Europe. Don't miss Stonegate, Goodramgate, Petergate or the Shambles, to mention just four. The narrow, picturesque streets are connected by a web of even narrower alleys known as snickleways. Individual buildings of particular note include the magnificent fourteenth-century Merchant Adventurers' Hall; the fifteenth-century Guildhall, skilfully rebuilt following bomb damage in the last war; and the elegant seventeenth-century Treasurer's House, set in tranquil gardens near the Minster. Older than these is Clifford's Tower, the keep of a Norman castle built 1245-60.

York has an impressive selection of museums, including the award-winning National Railway Museum on Leeman Street. You don't have to be in love with trains to enjoy this, but if you're not when you go in, you probably will be when you come out. It's superb.

Equally enjoyable is Castle Museum, a former prison which is bursting at the seams with a vast and varied collection, as well as a much-praised reconstruction of a Victorian street, authentic in every detail. More offbeat, but another award winner, is The Arc, an archaeological resource centre and museum housed in a former church on St Saviourgate.

Further Information

Getting there *by train* from King's Cross; *by coach* National Express from Victoria; *by car* M1 or A1 to Leeds followed by A64 then use park 'n' ride; *local buses* Rider York (01904 624161).

Eating and drinking Atmospheric pubs include the *Black Swan* at Peasholme Green, *Ye Olde Starre Inne* on Stonegate and the riverside *King's Arms* by Ouse Bridge. Tea shops are everywhere, but *Betty's*, in St Helen's Square, is renowned; *Taylor's* on Stonegate is good too. *Oscar's Wine Bar* on Little Stonegate and *Plunket's* on High Petergate are stylish and serve good food. The restaurant known simply as *No 19 Grape Lane* is highly thought of (01904 636366). There's a good vegetarian café and bakery at *Miller's Yard* on Gillygate.

Events *Jorvik Viking Festival* (culminates in a torchlight procession and the burning of a longboat on the Ouse) in February; *York Early Music Festival* in July; *Guy Fawkes Celebrations* (he was a local lad) in November; *St Nicholas Fayre* in December.

If you want to stay *The Royal York Hotel* (01904 653681) on Station Road is a recently refurbished Victorian hotel of great splendour; *Lady Anne Middleton's Hotel* (01904 613043) on Skeldergate is a historic building near the river; *Middlethorpe Hall* (01904 641241) on Bishopthorpe Road is a country house hotel set in parkland. Lower down the price range are numerous pleasant guest houses and B&Bs, such as *Alban House* (01904 658461) on Moorland Road or *Regency House* (01904 633053) an elegant Georgian building on cobbled Blossom Street, and great value too. The *youth hostel* (01904 653147) is at Water End, Clifton, a short riverside walk from the station.

Tourist Information Centre

De Grey Rooms, Exhibition Square, York (01904 621756). **Open** *Jan-May* 9am-5pm Mon-Sat; *June-July 23* 9am-5pm Mon-Sat, 10am-1pm Sun; *July 24-Aug 29* 9am-6pm Mon-Sat, 10am-1pm Sun; *Aug 30-Dec 31* 9am-5pm Mon-Sat.

English Countryside
The Cotswolds

Stone, sheep and the hand of man are the three elements that have shaped the Cotswolds. The stone lies close to the surface, making it easily quarried and producing thin soils more suited to sheep than cereals. So Stone Age man was able to make his mark on the landscape by building some of the finest chambered stone tombs in England, and, centuries later, medieval merchants grew fat on the wool trade. They repaid their debt by building the enchanting stone villages and incomparable 'wool churches' which characterise the Cotswolds still. Routinely described as 'honey-coloured' the stone is actually extremely variable, yet its ubiquitous use helps to unify a region which sprawls over six counties. Nowhere else in England is there such a harmonious relationship between buildings and landscape, and it is this that makes the Cotswolds unique.

The Cotswolds *is blessed with a unique relationship between buildings and landscape.*

Parts of the region suffer horrible congestion on summer weekends, but it's always localised. While crowds buzz around the honeypots of Bourton and Bibury, equally charming villages such as Stanton and Stanway slumber gently on, almost undisturbed. The small Cotswold towns are often even more memorable than the villages. Places such as Stow-on-the-Wold, whose elegant seventeenth-century houses look down on The Square, where huge sheep markets and horse fairs were once held; Winchcombe, with its gargoyle-encrusted church and its wonderful setting; Broadway, where cottage gardens of wisteria, clematis and old roses spill out on to the High Street; and, best of all, Chipping Campden, with its 600-year-old houses and glorious wool church.

Chipping Campden is also the starting-point of the Cotswold Way, a long-distance footpath which ends 100 miles away outside Bath Abbey, another masterpiece in Cotswold stone. Fortunately, Cotswold footpaths are as suitable for Sunday strollers as hardened hikers. Well-maintained and waymarked by voluntary wardens, they converge on every town and village.

For more sedentary pleasures take a trip to the Cotswold Wildlife Park at Burford or the Cotswold Farm Park at Guiting Power. The world-renowned Westonbirt Arboretum near Tetbury demands a visit – but avoid October Sundays.

Also worth exploring are the large towns on the Cotswold fringe: Bath and Oxford, of course (*see above*); but also Cheltenham, the epitome of

urban elegance; and Gloucester, more downmarket and brutally violated in the 1960s, but fighting back with the masterly refurbishment of its historic docks, while above it all still soars the stunning fourteenth-century tower of the cathedral, the birthplace of Perpendicular Architecture in this country.

Further Information

Getting there *by train* from Paddington to Moreton-in-Marsh or Cheltenham; *by National Express* from Victoria to Moreton-in-Marsh, Cheltenham, Broadway or Stow-on-the-Wold; *by car* on M40 then A40 or M4 then A419, two hours; *local buses* operate throughout the Cotswolds and are cheap and reliable – most comprehensive are Castleways (01242 602949), Pulhams (01451 820369), Barrys (01608 650876) and Stagecoach (01242 522021); information is also provided by the relevant county councils, eg Gloucestershire (01452 425543). Buses are environmentally friendly, bikes are even more so; hire one from Crabtrees of Cheltenham (01242 515291).

Eating and drinking Characterful pubs, tea shops and restaurants abound; try the *Corner Cupboard Inn* at Winchcombe, the *Fleece Inn* (National Trust) at Bretforton, the *Woolpack* at Slad (Laurie Lee's village) or *Lady Northwick's Tearoom* (with devastating cakes) at Blockley. The *Golden Pheasant Hotel and Restaurant* (01993 823223) at Burford and the *White Hart Royal Hotel* (01608 650731) at Moreton-in-Marsh serve good food in comfortable, historic surroundings.

Events *National Hunt Festival* (includes Gold Cup) at Cheltenham in March; *Cheese-rolling* at Brockworth in May (locals chase a Double Gloucester down Cooper's Hill – it's rarely caught and minor injuries are almost obligatory); *Cotswold Olympicks* at Dover's Hill, Chipping Campden in May/June (includes the noble sport of shin-kicking); *International Festival of Music* at Cheltenham in July; *Festival of Literature* at Cheltenham in October.

If you want to stay, and have cash to splash, the *Lygon Arms* (01386 852255) at Broadway is world-renowned, and previous guests have included Charles I and Cromwell (though not on the same night); much cheaper, and claiming to be England's oldest inn (founded 947 AD) is the *Royalist Hotel* (01451 830670) at Stow-on-the-Wold; there are youth hostels at Stow, Cleeve Hill, Charlbury and Duntisbourne Abbots – for details call YHA on 01722 337494.

Tourist Information Centres

77 Promenade, Cheltenham (01242 522878). **Open** *May-Sept* 9.30am-6pm Mon-Fri, 9.30am-5pm Sat, 10am-4pm Sun; *Oct-Apr* 9.30am-5pm Mon-Sat.
Woolstaplers' Hall, High Street, Chipping Campden (01386 840289). **Open** *Easter-Oct* 11am-6pm daily.
Hollis House, The Square, Stow-on-the-Wold (01451 831082). **Open** *Apr-Oct* 10am-5.30pm Mon-Sat; *Nov-Mar* 9.30am-4.30pm Mon-Sat.

The North Downs

The extraordinary thing about south-east England is how much of it remains rural and unspoilt despite its proximity to London. True, there are areas of hideous urban sprawl, but you can still escape into a patchwork countryside of fields and copses, orchards and hops, where narrow lanes wind through charming villages snugly set in the enfolding hills.

The bones of the landscape are the Downs – North and South – long chalk ridges facing each other across the Weald. The South Downs are more spectacular, but the North Downs are closer to London; so close that you can enjoy some of the south-east's best views little more than 20 miles (32 km) from the heart of town.

A long-distance footpath, the North Downs Way, runs for 140 miles (224 km) from Farnham in Surrey to the White Cliffs of Dover. Opportunities for shorter walks are plentiful, and the ancient market town of Dorking is a good centre. There's easy access from here to Box Hill, which has been a popular picnic spot since the days of Charles II – avoid weekends if you can. Not far away is Ranmore Common, which offers good walks on the south slopes of the Downs.

Further east, between Ashford and Canterbury, the Wye National Nature Reserve takes in some of the finest stretches of chalk grassland in the Downs, with wonderful views and the memorable dry valley known as the Devil's Kneadingtrough.

If your preference is for gardens, stately homes, churches and castles your only problem will be choosing from the cornucopia on offer. But nobody should miss Knole, near Sevenoaks. It's one of the largest houses in England, reputedly with 365 rooms, and was built in 1456. Surrounding it is a huge park, well-wooded and populated by tame fallow deer.

Leeds Castle, near Maidstone, is just as spectacular. Surrounded by a lake, it's built on two islands linked by a bridge. Its origins lie in the year 857AD, though it was rebuilt by the Normans.

Canterbury Cathedral, which still towers over its city centre today on the north edge of the North Downs, was built just after the Norman Conquest. The Mother Church for Anglicans worldwide, it has impressive stained glass and a fascinating crypt which together attract large numbers of sightseers who are now charged an entry fee of £2.

On a more human scale are the picturesque timber-framed farmhouses and cottages which are found throughout the region. Some of the loveliest villages include Chilham and Charing in Kent, and Friday Street in Surrey. Westerham is another attractive Kent village, and it's close to Chartwell, the home for many years of Sir Winston Churchill, and now owned by the National Trust.

Further Information

Getting there *by train* from Blackfriars, Cannon Street, Charing Cross, London Bridge, Victoria or Waterloo to dozens of stations including Ashford, Canterbury, Dorking, Farnham, Guildford and Maidstone; *by coach* National Express from Victoria; *local buses* details from Kent County Council's information line (freefone 0800 696996) or Guildford bus station (01483 575226).
Eating and drinking Upmarket venues include *Skippers* (01227 830788) on the High Street at Bridge and the *Royal Oak Hotel* (01732 451109) on Upper High Street, Sevenoaks; picturesque and historic pubs, many offering food and accommodation, are everywhere – examples include the fourteenth-century *White Horse Inn* at Shere, the fifteenth-century *White Horse* at Chilham, the *Angel Hotel* in Guildford, where the thirteenth-century cellar has been turned into a bar, and *The Little Gem* at Aylesford, which was built in 1250 and claims to be the smallest pub in Kent.
Events *Guildford International Music Festival* in March; *Chaucer Festival* at Canterbury in April; *River Festival* at Maidstone in July; *English Hop Festival* at Faversham in September; *Canterbury Festival* in October; events at Leeds Castle throughout the year.
If you want to stay For something a little out of the ordinary there's *The Friars* (01622 717272), a former Carmelite monastery at Aylesford; also unusual, but more luxurious and expensive, is *Goldhill Mill* (01732 851626), a converted watermill near Tonbridge; other upmarket hotels include the *Royal Oak* (*see above*) and *Sevenoaks Park* (01732 454245); ancient pubs well worth considering are the *New Flying Horse Inn* (01233 812297) at Wye, the *Woolpack* (01227 730208) at Chilham and the *Dog and Bear* (01622 858219) at Lenham; rural peace and B&B are on offer at a fifteenth-century farmhouse, *Leaveland Court* (01233 740596), near Faversham; there are youth hostels at Canterbury (01227 462911), Dover (01304 201314), Hindhead (01428 604285), Holmbury St Mary (01306 730777), Kemsing (01732 761341) and Tanners Hatch (01372 452528).

Tourist Information Centres

34 St Margaret's Street, Canterbury, Kent (01227 766567). **Open** *Apr-Oct* 9.30am-5.30pm daily; *Nov-Mar* 9.30am-5pm daily.
72 High Street, Guildford, Surrey (01483 444007). **Open** *all year* 9am-5.30pm Mon-Sat; *May-Sept* also 10am-5pm Sun.
Old Palace Gardens, Mill Street, Maidstone, Kent (01622 673581/602169). **Open** 9am-5pm Mon-Sat; 10am-4pm Sun.
Buckhurst Lane, Sevenoaks, Kent (01732 450305). **Open** *all year* 10am-5pm Mon-Sat; *July-Aug* also 10am-1pm Sun.

Survival

Survival

London life doesn't come without its fair share of headaches. Here's your best bet for fast, effective relief.

Emergencies

Open 24 hours daily. *See also below* **Health**.
Ambulance (*999*).
Fire Service (*999*).
Police (*999*).

Emergency Repairs

Electrical

If you have an electrical emergency, day or night, there are two numbers to call, supplying customers north and south of the river.
North (*0171 251 5161*).
South (*0171 733 5611*).

Gas

The following numbers can be phoned at any time. The number to ring depends on your postcode.
Postcode
E1, E2, E5, E6, E8, E13, E14, N16 (**0171 511 3296**).
E4, E10, E17, E18 (**0181 478 2244**).
N9, N13, N14, N17, N18, N20, N21 (**0181 447 1777**).
N1-N8, N10, N12, NW4, NW7, NW11 (**0181 346 9191**).
NW2, NW3, NW6, NW8, NW9, NW10 (**0181 423 4490**).
W1, W2, W9, WC1, WC2, EC1-EC4, SE1, SE5, SE8, SE11, SE15, SE17 (**0171 828 3299**).
SW2, SW4, SW9, SW12, SW16, SE21, SE22, SE24 (**0171 277 5500**).
SW15, SW18, SW19, SW20 (**0181 687 0747**).
SE2, SE3, SE6, SE7, SE9, SE10, SE12, SE13, SE18, SE19, SE20, SE25, SE26, SE27 (**0181 659 9599**).
SW3, SW6, SW7, SW10, W6, W8, W14 (**0171 828 3262**).
W3, W4, W5, W7, W12, W13 (**0181 878 7501**).
NB Although these numbers are operative at the moment, British Gas aim to introduce a simpler scheme soon.

Glaziers

Lloyd's
(0181 871 4020/0181 760 0760). **Open** 24 hours daily.
Credit A, V. Reacts to most calls within one hour.

Locksmiths

Barry Bros
121-123 Praed Street, W2 (0171 734 1001/0171 262 9009). **Open** 8am-6pm Mon-Sat. 24-hour emergency call-out service. **Credit** A, AmEx, V.
Barry Bros will repair broken locks and doors and almost anything else to do with security, including car ignition keys. Minimum call-out fee is £45, which increases after 6pm to £60, and after midnight to £75.

Chiswick Security
4 Denbigh Street, SW1 (0171 630 6500/0917). **Open** 8.30am-5.30pm Mon-Fri; 9am-5pm Sat. 24-hour emergency call-out service. **Credit** A, V.
The call-out charge depends on the area and the work to be done. The minimum charge is £40 plus VAT in central London; £45 plus VAT in the City; £35 incl VAT in SW1.

North London Locksmiths
79 Grand Parade, Green Lanes, N4 (0181 800 6041/3792/0181 361 8614). **Open** 9am-5.30pm Mon-Sat. 24-hour emergency call-out service. **Credit** A, V.
Before 5.30pm, the call-out fee for a local (anywhere with a north London postcode) incident is between £25-£30. After 5.30pm the fee is £30-£35; after midnight it goes up to £40, plus parts.

Plumbers

The Institute of Plumbing
64 Station Lane, Hornchurch, Essex RM12 6NB (01708 472791). **Open** 9am-5pm Mon-Fri. Answerphone after office hours.
Phone or write for details of approved members in your area.

Thames Water
(0645 200800). 24-hour support.
Phone this number for Thames Water's emergency plumbing service and customer relations.

Embassies

Not all embassies, consulates and High Commissions can be listed below. Check in the phone book and in *Yellow Pages* under Embassies. Most are closed on public holidays.

American Embassy
24 Grosvenor Square, W1 (0171 499 9000/Visa section 0891 200290). Daily 24-hour phone line for emergency help. Bond Street or Marble Arch tube. **Open** 8.30am-5.30pm Mon-Fri.

Australian High Commission
Australia House, The Strand, WC2 (0171 379 4334/Visa information 0891 600333). Holborn or Temple tube. **Open** 9.30am-3.30pm Mon-Fri.

Chinese Embassy
49-61 Portland Place, W1 (0171 636 0380). Oxford Circus or Regent's Park tube. **Open** 9am-noon, 1.30-5pm, Mon-Fri. Visa section: 31 Portland Place, W1 (0891 880808). Regent's Park or Oxford Circus tube.* **Open** 9am-noon Mon-Fri.

French Embassy
58 Knightsbridge, SW1 (0171 201 1000). Knightsbridge tube. **Open** 9am-6pm Mon-Fri. **Consulate General** *21 Cromwell Road, SW7 (0171 838 2000). South*

Kensington tube. **Open** 8.45-11.45am Mon, Fri; 9am-noon, 1.30-3.30pm, Tue-Thur. *Visa section: 6A Cromwell Place, SW7 (0171 838 2050/0891 887733).* **Open** 9-11.30am Mon-Fri; visa collection 4-5pm Mon-Fri.

German Embassy
23 Belgrave Square, SW1 (0171 235 5033/Visa information 0891 331166). Hyde Park Corner or Knightsbridge tube. **Open** 9am-noon Mon-Fri.

Russian Embassy
13 Kensington Palace Gardens, W8 (0171 229 3628). High Street Kensington or Notting Hill Gate tube. **Open** 8.30am-12.30pm, 2-6pm, Mon-Fri. **Consulate** *5 Kensington Palace Gardens, W8 (0171 229 8027/Visa information 0891 171271). High Street Kensington or Notting Hill Gate tube.* **Open** 10am-12.30pm Mon, Tue, Thur, Fri. Telephone enquiries 10am-6pm Mon-Fri.

Health

Free medical treatment under the National Health Service is available to:
- EC Nationals – citizens of Belgium, Denmark, France, Germany, Greece, Italy, Irish Republic, Luxembourg, Netherlands, Portugal and Spain.
- Nationals of the following countries, on production of a passport: Austria, Bulgaria, Finland, Gibraltar, Hungary, Malta, New Zealand, Norway, Sweden.
- Residents of the following countries: Anguilla, Australia, British Virgin Islands, Channel Islands, Czech Republic, Slovakia, CIS, Falkland Islands, Hong Kong, Iceland, Isle of Man, Montserrat, Poland, Romania, St Helena, Turks and Caicos Islands, NATO personnel.
- Anyone who at the time of receiving treatment has been in the UK for the previous 12 months.
- Students and trainees whose course requires them to spend more than 12 weeks in employment during their first year. Students and others living in the UK for a settled purpose for more than six months may be accepted as ordinarily resident and not liable to charges.

People with HIV/AIDS at a special clinic for the treatment of sexually transmitted diseases. Treatment is limited to a diagnostic test and counselling associated with that test.
There are no NHS charges for district nursing, midwifery or health visiting; for ambulance transport; or for family-planning services.

Casualties: NHS
There are 24-hour casualty departments at:
Central Middlesex Hospital *Acton Lane, NW10 (0181 965 5733). North Acton tube.*
Charing Cross Hospital *Fulham Palace Road (entrance St Dunstan's Road), W6 (0181 846 1234). Baron's Court or Hammersmith tube.*
Greenwich District Hospital *Vanbrugh Hill, SE10 (0181 858 8141). Maze Hill BR.*
Guy's Hospital *St Thomas Street (entrance in Weston Street), SE1 (0171 955 5000). London Bridge tube/BR.*
Hackney and Homerton Hospital *Homerton Row, E9 (0181 919 5555). Homerton BR/22B bus.*

Hammersmith Hospital *150 Du Cane Road, W12 (0181 743 2030). East Acton tube.*
King's College Hospital *Denmark Hill (entrance in Bessemer Road), SE5 (0171 737 4000). Denmark Hill BR.*
Lewisham Hospital *Lewisham High Street, SE13 (0181 333 3000). Ladywell or Lewisham BR.*
London Hospital *Whitechapel Road, E1 (0171 377 7000). Whitechapel tube.*
Royal Free Hospital *Pond Street, NW3 (0171 794 0500). Belsize Park tube/Hampstead Heath BR.*
North Middlesex Hospital *Stirling Way, Edmonton, N18 (0181 887 2000). Silver Street BR.*
St George's Hospital *Blackshaw Road, SW17 (0181 672 1255). Tooting Broadway tube.*
St Thomas' Hospital *Lambeth Palace Road, SE1 (0171 928 9292). Westminster tube.*
University College Hospital *Gower Street (entrance Grafton Way), WC1 (0171 387 9300). Euston Square or Warren Street tube.*
Whittington Hospital *St Mary's Wing, Highgate Hill, N19 (0171 272 3070). Archway tube.*

Chemists: Late-Opening
If you have a prescription that needs to be made up outside normal shopping hours, head for one of the following chemists:

Bliss Chemist
5-6 Marble Arch, W1 (0171 723 6116). Marble Arch tube. **Open** 9am-midnight daily. **Credit** A, AmEx, DC, £TC, V.

Boots
75 Queensway, W2 (0171 229 9266). Bayswater tube. **Open** 9am-10pm Mon-Sat; 5-10pm Sun. **Credit** AmEx, MC, V.

Contraception/Abortion
Family planning advice, contraceptive supplies and abortions are free to British citizens on the NHS. This also applies to EC residents and foreign nationals living, working and studying in Britain. According to the 1967 Abortion Act, two doctors must agree to a woman having an abortion, whether on the NHS or not. If you decide to go private, contact one of the organisations listed below.

British Pregnancy Advisory Service
7 Belgrave Road, SW1 (0171 828 2484). Victoria tube/BR. **Open** *office* 9am-5pm Mon, Wed, Thur, Fri; 9am-7pm Tue; 9am-2pm Sat.
Phone lines are open 8am-8pm every day. Contraception advice, contraceptives and the morning-after pill are available. The service carries out pregnancy tests and makes referrals to BPAS nursing homes for private abortions.

Brook Advisory Centres
233 Tottenham Court Road, W1 (0171 323 1522). Tottenham Court Road tube. **Open** 9.30am-7.30pm Mon-Fri; noon-7pm Sat.
Call to find your nearest Brook Advisory family planning clinic. Advice is given on contraception, sexual problems and abortion with referral to NHS or a private clinic.

If you lose something on a train, you can either phone or go to the mainline station, where you're assured of a friendly welcome.

Family Planning Association

27-35 Mortimer Street, W1 (0171 636 7866). Oxford Circus tube. **Open** 9am-5pm Mon-Thur; 9am-4.30pm Fri. There are more than 1,800 NHS-run Family Planning Clinics in Britain. Phone the FPA to find your nearest.

Marie Stopes Clinics

Family Planning Clinic *108 Whitfield Street, W1 (0171 388 0662/0171 388 2585 for family planning/0171 388 5554 for sterilisation). Warren Street tube.* **Open** 9am-8pm Mon-Wed; 9am-5pm Thur, Fri; 9.30am-5pm Sat.

Contraceptives, treatment and advice for gynaecological complaints, counselling for sexual problems and referral for abortion. Fees vary; check with the clinic first.

Pregnancy Advisory Service

11-13 Charlotte Street, W1 (0171 637 8962). Tottenham Court Road tube. **Open** *for appointments* 9am-3.30pm Mon, Wed, Fri; 9am-12.15pm Tue, Thur. Phone lines open 8.30am-6pm Mon-Fri; 9am-12.30pm Sat. (Appointments necessary except in an emergency.)

A registered charity that provides the following: pregnancy counselling; pregnancy tests; abortion advice and help; artificial insemination by donor; morning-after contraception; sterilisation; cervical smears; and post-abortion counselling.

Dental Services

Dental care is only free to British citizens who are receiving supplementary benefit. All other patients, whether National Health Service (NHS) or private, must pay. To find a dentist, get in touch with the local **Citizens' Advice Bureau** (*see below* **Help & Information**) or **Family Practitioner Committee** (*see below* **Doctors**). Prices vary enormously, starting at about £14 for a filling on the NHS. Private dentists can charge whatever they like. We list emergency services below.

Dental Emergency Care Service

(0171 955 2186). **Open** 8.30am-3.30pm Mon-Fri. A separate service runs at the weekend. Call for details. Callers are referred to a surgery open for treatment, whether it's private or NHS.

Eastman Dental Hospital

256 Gray's Inn Road, WC1 (0171 837 3646). Chancery Lane or King's Cross tube/BR. **Open** 9am-4pm Mon-Fri. A free walk-in emergency dental hospital for anyone without a dentist in London. No appointment needed.

Guy's Hospital Dental School

St Thomas' Street, SE1 (0171 955 4317). London Bridge tube/BR. **Open** 8.45am-3.30pm Mon-Fri. A walk-in dental emergency service. Free treatment, except on Saturdays and Sundays.

Doctors

If you're a British citizen visiting London or working in the city, you can go to any general practitioner (GP). You may have to show your medical card or fill in a Lost Medical Card form. Overseas students can register with an NHS doctor.

Great Chapel Street Medical Centre

13 Great Chapel Street, W1 (0171 437 9360). Tottenham Court Road tube. **Open** 11am-12.30pm Mon, Tue, Thur; 2-4pm Mon-Fri.

A walk-in NHS surgery for anyone with no doctor. A psychiatrist, chiropodist and social worker also attend throughout the week. Call for available times.

Family Practitioner Committees

The various London boroughs provide lists of GPs, chemists, opticians and dentists. The telephone number of the borough committee and lists of local NHS doctors are available in libraries and post offices.

Medical Information

Healthline

(0345 678444). **Open** 10am-5pm Mon-Fri. A free telephone information service (except for the cost of the call). Ask to listen to any of the 400 health-related tapes. These give details of symptoms and contact names of groups involved with treatment or support for sufferers. Health advice can also be gleaned from staff during office hours.

Medical Advisory Service

(0181 994 9874). **Open** 2-10pm Mon-Fri. Health advice over the phone.

Medication

Many drugs cannot be bought over the counter. A pharmacist will dispense medicines on receipt of a prescription from a doctor. An NHS prescription costs £5.25 at present. If you are not eligible to see an NHS doctor you will be charged cost price for medicines prescribed by a private doctor.

Medicine: Complementary

The British Acupuncture Association and Register

34 Alderney Street, SW1 (0171 834 1012). Victoria tube/BR. **Open** 9am-5.30pm Mon-Sat. Phone for your local registered specialist. The Association will provide lists of practitioners. A list and handbook are also available, price £2.50 plus p&p.

British Homoeopathic Association

27A Devonshire Street, W1 (0171 935 2163). Baker Street or Great Portland Street tube. **Open** 9.30am-4.30pm Mon-Fri.

The BHA will give you the address of your nearest homoeopathic chemist and doctor (send a stamped addressed envelope for a list). The Association also provides a booklist of helpful information and has a library on the premises.

Mental/Emotional Health

Just Ask

46 Bishopsgate, EC2 (0171 628 3380). Liverpool Street tube/BR. **Open** 10am-9pm Mon-Thur; 9am-5pm Fri. Closed for counselling during August. 24-hour answerphone.

Make an appointment either by calling in or phoning. Counselling is targeted at people aged 35 or under who are homeless, unemployed or on a low income, but advice will be given to anyone with a personal problem.

Mind

Granta House, 15-19 Broadway, E15 (0171 637 0741). Stratford tube/BR. **Open** 9.15am-5.15pm Mon-Fri; *information line* 10am-12.30pm, 2-4.30pm, Mon-Fri.

Callers will be referred to one of 34 London groups. Their legal service advises on maltreatment, wrongful detention and sectioning (involuntary hospitalisation).

National Association of Victims Support Schemes

Cranmer House, 39 Brixton Road, SW9 (0171 735 9166 answerphone out of office hours). Oval tube. **Open** 9am-5.30pm Mon-Fri.
The Association helps victims of crime. Callers are put in touch with a volunteer who visits as soon as possible after the event to provide emotional and practical support.

Samaritans

(24-hour helpline 0171 734 2800).
The Samaritans will listen to anyone with emotional problems. It's a popular service and you may have to phone several times before you get through.

Opticians

Eye Care Information Bureau

(0171 357 7730). **Open** 9am-5pm Mon-Fri.
This service gives you information on the different kinds of eye-care specialists.

Physiotherapy

Chartered Society of Physiotherapy

14 Bedford Row, WC1 (0171 242 1941). Chancery Lane or Holborn tube. **Open** 9am-5pm Mon-Fri.
This is the professional body of physiotherapists. The Society can check whether any practitioner is a qualified member.

Sexually Transmitted Diseases (VD)/AIDS/HIV

NHS Special Clinics listed below are affiliated to major hospitals. They specialise in genito-urinary conditions, treating sexually transmitted diseases (STDs) and non-sex-related problems (thrush and cystitis). They can conduct a confidential blood test to determine HIV status. The Government pamphlets 'AIDS: The Facts'; 'Safer Sex and the Condom' and 'AIDS: The Test' are available from clinics and, with a stamped addressed envelope, by post from: The Health Education Authority, Hamilton House, Mabledon Place, WC1.

AIDS Telephone Helpline

(0800 567123). **Open** 24 hours daily.
A free and confidential help and information service for anybody worried or concerned about HIV/AIDS and safer sex. The helpline caters for many minority languages including Gujarati, Punjabi and Welsh. There is also a minicom service for the hard of hearing. Call to find out availability.

Body Positive

51B Philbeach Gardens, SW5 (0171 835 1045/1046). Earl's Court tube. **Open** 9.30am-5.30pm Mon-Fri.
Run by and for people who are HIV positive, this is a drop-in centre. It also offers a helpline service (0171 373 9124) between 7-10pm Mon-Fri; 4-10pm Sat, Sun.

Terrence Higgins Trust

52-54 Gray's Inn Road, WC1 (helpline 0171 242 1010/legal line 0171 405 2381, 7-10pm Wed). **Open** noon-10pm daily for general advice.
The Trust advises and counsels those with HIV/AIDS, their relatives, lovers and friends. Free leaflets about AIDS are available. The Trust also gives advice about safer sex. Lines are constantly busy, so keep trying.

St Mary's Hospital Special Clinic

Praed Street, W2 (0171 725 1697). Paddington tube/BR. **Open** 8.45am-7pm Mon; 8.45am-6pm Tue; 10.45am-6pm Wed; 8am-6pm Thur; 8.45am-6pm Fri; 9.50am-noon Sat (new patients should arrive at least 30 mins before closing on all days).
Walk-in clinic; free and confidential.

University College Hospital Special Clinic

Gower Street, WC1 (0171 388 8880). Euston Square or Warren Street tube. **Open** 9am-6pm Mon, Wed, Thur; 9-11.15am, 3-7pm Tue; 9am-2.45pm Fri.
Appointment needed.

Help & Information

Capital Helpline

(0171 388 7575). **Open** 10am-10pm Mon-Fri; 8am-8pm Sat; 10am-4pm Sun.
Run in conjunction with Capital Radio, this helpline tackles queries about anything. If the staff can't answer your query themselves, they'll put you in touch with someone who can help. The line is always busy, so keep trying. They have an answerphone after the lines close and will call you back.

Citizens' Advice Bureaux

Greater London Office, 136-144 City Road, EC1 (0171 251 2000). **Open** 9am-5.15pm Mon-Fri.
Citizens' Advice Bureaux are run by local councils and offer free advice on legal, financial and personal matters.

Consumer Problems

Statutory rights protect the consumer, and when you buy a large or expensive piece of equipment it should be guaranteed by the vendor. The **Office of Fair Trading** (*see below*) publishes free leaflets on all aspects of consumer purchase, covering goods and services. They can also be obtained at **Citizens' Advice Bureaux** (*see above* **Help & Information**). Staff at the CAB should be able to advise you of your rights under the law. The Consumers' Association (*0171 486 5544*) publishes many magazines under the *Which?* aegis – worth a read before making a purchase.

Office of Fair Trading

Field House, 15-25 Bream's Buildings, EC4 (0171 242 2858). **Open** 8.30am-5.30pm Mon-Fri.

Financial Advice

Visitors from abroad who run into financial difficulties should, in the first instance, contact their embassies for help (*see above* **Embassies**). But people on long-term stays should seek advice from **Citizens' Advice Bureaux** (*see above* **Help & Information**).

Legal & Immigration

You never know when you're going to need a lawyer or a solicitor. Contact your embassy, go to a **Citizens' Advice Bureau** (*see above* **Help & Information**) or get in touch with one of the organisations listed below. Ask about Legal Aid eligibility. For a leaflet explaining how the system works write to **Legal Aid** (*see below*).

Amnesty International
British Section, 99-119 Rosebery Avenue, EC1 (0171 814 6200). Farringdon or Angel tube. **Open** 9am-6pm Mon-Fri.
Amnesty is a worldwide human rights movement working for the release of prisoners of conscience. Staff can advise those seeking asylum.

Commission for Racial Equality
Elliot House, 10-12 Allington Street, SW1 (0171 828 7022). Victoria tube/BR. **Open** 9am-5.45pm Mon-Thur; 9am-5.30pm Fri.
Established by the 1966 Race Relations Act to work towards eliminating discrimination and promoting equality of opportunity. It offers free advice.

Law Centres Federation
(0171 387 8570). **Open** 10am-6pm Mon-Fri.
There are about 25 Law Centres in London and this organisation will put you in touch with one of them. Centres offer free help concerning all aspects of the law to people who cannot afford to pay for legal advice.

Legal Aid
29-37 Red Lion Street, WC1 (0171 405 6991). Russell Square tube. **Open** 9am-5pm Mon-Fri.
Ask for the Customer Services Department who will provide names and addresses of solicitors who subscribe to the Legal Aid scheme. Staff will advise you on how to proceed.

Joint Council for the Welfare of Immigrants (JCWI)
115 Old Street, EC1 (0171 251 8706). Old Street tube/BR. **Open** *personal callers* 10am-12.30pm; *telephone enquiries* 2-5.30pm, Mon, Tue, Thur.
The JCWI provides advice on immigration, takes up cases of people subject to deportation orders and helps with legal representation. Phone for an appointment.

Release
388 Old Street, EC1 (0171 729 9904). Old Street tube. **Open** 10am-6pm Mon-Fri.
Release offers free legal advice to anyone who has been arrested. They are particularly helpful in cases involving illicit drugs, and provide confidential counselling and referrals. They run a 24-hour helpline (*0171 603 8654*) but contact their daytime number during office hours.

Reference Libraries

Guildhall Reference Library
Aldermanbury, EC2 (0171 606 3030). Bank, Mansion House, St Paul's or Moorgate tube/6, 8, 9, 11, 25, 22B bus. **Open** 9.30am-5pm Mon-Sat. **Admission** free.
Most of the material kept here deals with the history of London. On the ground floor are printed books and on the first floor is a collection of maps, prints and manuscripts. There is also a bookshop (*0171 332 1858*), selling material relevant to the library and the Guildhall Art Gallery. This, along with the first floor, is closed on Saturdays.
Disabled: limited access.

Westminster Central Reference Library
35 St Martin's Street, WC2 (0171 798 2034). Leicester Square or Charing Cross tube/BR. **Open** 10am-7pm Mon-Fri; 10am-5pm Sat. **Admission** free.
A public reference library, with Government publications, international telephone directories and business on the ground floor, performing arts and maps on the first floor and a large Art & Design collection on the second floor.

Gatwick Airport *(01293 56990).* **Office open** North terminal 6am-10pm daily; South terminal 4am-midnight daily. **Rates** up to 24 hours, £3 per item; £15 per item per week.
Heathrow Airport *(0181 759 4321).* **Office open** Terminal 1 *(0181 745 5301)* 6am-11pm daily, Terminal 2 *(0181 745 6100/4599)* 6am-11.30pm daily; Terminal 3 *(0181 759 3344)* 5.30am-10.30pm daily; Terminal 4 *(0181 745 7460)* 6am-10pm daily. **Rates** £3 per item, per day.
London City Airport *(0171 474 5555).* **Office open** 7am-9pm daily. **Rates** up to 12 hours, £1.50 per item up to 24 hours, £2 per item; £2 per item on subsequent days.
Euston Station *(0171 928 5151).* **Office open** 24 hours daily. **Rates** £2 small, £3 large per day.
Paddington Station *(0171 262 6767/0171 922 6773).* **Office open** 7am-midnight Mon-Sat; 8am-midnight Sun. **Rates** £2 small, £2.75 large per day.
Victoria Station *(0171 928 5151).* **Office open** 7am-10.15pm daily. **Rates** £3 per day. Also a locker service; rates range from £2.50-£5 depending on size of locker. There is a 24-hour limit on this facility.
Waterloo Station *(0171 928 2424).* **Office open** 8am-10pm daily. **Rates** £2 per item up to 24 hours; £3 per item on subsequent days.

Always inform the police if you lose anything (to validate insurance claims). Go to the nearest police station. Only dial the emergency number (*999*) if violence has occurred. A lost passport should be reported to the police and to your embassy.

Airports

Gatwick Airport
(01293 503162). **Open** 7.30am-5.30pm daily.
Dealing with property lost in the airport only, the Lost Property Office is located in Zone C on the ground floor. For property lost on the plane, contact the airline or handling agents dealing with your flight.

Heathrow Airport
(0181 745 7727). **Open** 9am-4pm daily.
The Lost Property Office is situated on the ground floor of Terminal 2 car park. It's for property lost in the airport only. For property lost on the plane, contact the airline by using the above number.

London City Airport
(0171 474 5555). **Open** 6am-10pm daily.
The Lost Property Office is situated at the Information Desk for property lost in the airport only. For property lost on the plane, contact the airline on the same number.

Luton Airport
(01582 405100). **Open** 24 hours daily.
Report to the Airport Duty Manager's Office (directions from the Information Desk) for property lost in the airport only. For property lost on the plane, contact the relevant airline via the same number.

British Rail

If it takes you as long to get through to the lost property offices as it did our researcher, claim on your insurance and buy new goods.

Charing Cross Station *(0171 922 6061* answerphone*).* **Open** 7.50am-9.50pm daily. Lost property is deposited in the Information Office for seven days, after which it goes to Waterloo Lost Property *(see below).*
Euston Station *(0171 922 6477).* **Open** 8.30am-6pm Mon-Fri; 8.30am-4pm Sat; 11am-7pm Sun.
King's Cross Station *(0171 922 9081).* **Open** 9am-4.45pm Mon-Fri.
Liverpool Street Station *(0171 928 5100).* **Open** 7.30am-9pm daily.
London Bridge Station *(0171 928 5100).* **Open** 7am-7pm Mon-Fri.
Marylebone Station *(0171 262 6767).* **Open** 6.20am-8pm Mon-Fri; 6.20am-1pm Sat.
Paddington Station *(0171 922 6773).* **Open** 7am-10pm daily.
St Pancras Station *(0171 922 6478).* **Open** 7am-10.15pm Mon-Fri.
Victoria Station *(0171 922 9887).* **Open** 9am-5pm Mon-Sat; 8am-4pm Sun.
Waterloo Station *(0171 922 6135 answerphone).* **Open** 24 hours daily. Leave your address, and staff will write to you if your property is found. Personal calls can be made to the office, situated below the station, 8.15am-1pm Mon-Fri.

Bus & Tube

London Regional Transport

Lost Property Office, 200 Baker Street, NW1 (0171 486 2496 recorded information). Baker Street tube. **Open** 9.30am-2pm Mon-Fri.
Allow two days from the time of loss. If you lose something on a bus, call 0171 222 1234 and ask for the phone numbers of the depots at either end of the route. You can pick up a lost property claim form from any tube station.

Taxis

Taxi Lost Property

15 Penton Street, N1 (0171 833 0996). Angel tube. **Open** 9am-4pm Mon-Fri.
This office deals only with property found in registered black cabs. For items lost in a minicab you will have to contact the office you hired the car from.

Lost/Stolen Credit Cards

Report lost or stolen credit cards to the police and the 24-hour services listed below. Inform your bank by phone and in writing.
Access *(Nat West 0113 277 8899/Lloyd's 0800 585300).*
American Express *(Personal Card 01273 696933/ Corporate Card 01273 689955/enquiries 0171 222 9633).*
Barclaycard/Visa *(01604 230230).*
Co-operative Bank/Visa *(01695 26621).*
Diners Club/Diners Club International *(General Enquiries 01252 516261/Emergency 01252 513500).*
MasterCard/Eurocard *(01702 362988).*
Midland Gold MasterCard *(01702 352244).*
Bank of Scotland Visa *(01383 738866).*

Police & Security

Practically the only public service that wasn't drained of resources during the Thatcher years was the police force. It's still fairly uncommon to encounter 'your friendly local bobby' patrolling his or her beat; more often they're roaring around in patrol cars chasing joy-riders *(aka* car thieves) and making high-speed arrests. Nevertheless, the police are a good source of information about the locality and are used to helping visitors find their way. If you've been robbed, assaulted or involved in an infringement of the law, look under Police in the telephone directory for the nearest police station, or call directory enquiries (free only if you phone from a call box) on 192.

If you have a complaint to make about the police, there are several things you can do. Always make sure that you take the offending police officer's identifying number, which should be prominently displayed on his or her shoulder lapel. You can then register a complaint with the **Police Complaints Authority**, 10 Great George Street, SW1P 3AE *(0171 273 6450).* Alternatively, contact any police station or, if you'd rather not deal directly with the police, visit a solicitor or a law centre. Only dial 999 in an emergency.

You can feel relatively safe in London, but it's unwise to take any risks, especially as robbery and mugging (robbery with violence) have increased over the past decade. Thieves and pickpockets lurk in crowded places. Follow these basic rules:
* **Keep** your wallet and purse out of sight. Do not wear a wrist wallet (they are easily snatched). Keep your handbag securely closed.
* **Don't** leave a handbag, briefcase, bag or coat unattended, especially in pubs, cinemas, department stores or fast-food shops, on public transport, at railway stations and airports, or in crowds.
* **Don't** leave your bag or coat beside, under or on the back of your chair. Hook the handle of your bag around the leg of the chair on which you're sitting.
* **Don't** put your bag on the floor near the door of a public toilet.
* **Don't** wear expensive jewellery or watches that can be easily snatched.
* **Late** at night, travel in groups of three or more. Avoid parks and commons after dark.
* **Don't** put your purse down on the table in a restaurant or on a shop counter while you scrutinise the bill.
* **Don't** carry a wallet in your back pocket.
* **Don't** flash your money or credit cards around.

Post Offices

You can buy stamps and have letters weighed at all post offices, but stamps are also widely available at newsagents. Current **stamp prices** are 19p for second-class letters (inland only) and 25p for first-class letters to all EC countries and these have been frozen until at least March 1996 to compete with the threat from telephones and faxes. Charges for other letters and parcels vary according to the weight and destination. Courier services are listed in *chapter* **Business**; packaging and shipping in *chapter* **Shopping & Services**.

Letters sent to you Poste Restante, London, can be collected from the Post Office, 24-28 William IV

Street, London WC2N 4DL. Bring your passport or ID card. Post office opening hours are normally 9am-5.30pm Mon-Fri; 9am-noon Sat, though they do vary; we list the one that opens late.

Trafalgar Square Post Office
24-88 William IV Street, WC2 (0171 930 9580). Charing Cross tube/BR. **Open** 8am-8pm Mon-Sat.

Public Toilets & Baths

Many public swimming pools have bathrooms for hire, together with soap and a towel.

Kentish Town Pools
Prince of Wales Road, NW5 (0171 267 9341). Kentish Town tube. **Open** 7.30am-9pm Mon-Fri; 9.30am-5pm Sat, Sun. **Admission** £2.15.

The Oasis Sports Centre
32 Endell Street, WC2 (0171 831 1804). Covent Garden tube. **Open** *indoor pool* 7.30am-6.45pm; *outdoor pool* 7.30am-8.30pm; *both pools* 9.30am-5pm Sat, Sun. **Admission** £2.50 adults; 85p under-15s.

Religion

Baptist

Bloomsbury Central Baptist Church
235 Shaftesbury Avenue, WC2 (0171 836 6843/0171 240 0544). Tottenham Court Road tube. **Open** *office* 9am-6.30pm daily; *Friendship Centre* (closed Aug, Sept) 11.30am-2.30pm Tue; 6-8.30pm Wed; 10.30am-8.30pm Sun. **Services** 11am, 6.30pm, Sun.

Buddhist

Buddhapadipa Temple
14 Calonne Road, SW19 (0181 946 1357). Wimbledon Park tube. **Open** 1-6pm Sat; 8.30-10.30am, 12.30-6pm, Sun.
A new meditating class is available to the public.

Catholic

Brompton Oratory
Brompton Road, SW7 (0171 589 4811 enquiries). South Kensington tube. **Open** 6.30am-8pm daily. **Services** 7am, 7.30am, 8am (Latin mass), 10am, 12.30am, 6pm, Mon-Fri; 7am, 7.30am, 8am, 10am, 6pm, Sat; 7am, 8am, 9am, 10am (Tridentine), 11am (sung Latin), 12.30pm, 3.30pm (Vespers and Benediction), 4.30pm, 7pm, Sun.

Westminster Cathedral
Victoria Street, SW1 (0171 798 9055). Victoria tube/BR. **Open** 7am-8pm daily. **Services** eight daily masses Mon-Fri; seven daily masses Sat; 7am, 8am, 9am, 10.30am, noon, 5.30pm, 7pm, Sun.

Christian Scientist

Eleventh Church of Christ Scientist
1 Nutford Place, W1 (0171 723 4572). Marble Arch tube. **Open** for services only. **Services** 11am, 7pm first Sun in month. **Testimony meetings** 7pm Wed.
Public Reading Room *80 Baker Street, W1 (0171 486 0759). Baker Street tube.* **Open** 9.30am-6.30pm Mon, Tue, Thur-Sat; 9.30am-6.30pm Wed; 2.30-6.30pm Sun.

Church of England

St Paul's Cathedral
EC4 (0171 248 2705). St Paul's tube. **Open** 7.30am-6pm daily; *galleries* 9.45am-6pm daily; *services* 8am, 12.30pm (not Friday), 5pm (evensong), Mon-Fri; 8am, 10am (choral), 12.30pm, 5pm (choral), Sat; 8am, 10.30am (choral), 11.30am (choral), 3.15pm (evensong), Sun. Times vary because of special events, phone first to check.

Westminster Abbey
Dean's Yard, SW1 (0171 222 5152). St James's Park or Westminster tube. **Open** *Royal Chapels* 9am-4pm Mon-Fri; 6-7.45pm Wed; 9am-2pm, 3-5pm, Sat. *Chapter House, Pyx Chamber, Abbey Museum* 10am-4pm daily. *Brass Rubbing Centre (0171 222 2085)* 9am-5pm Mon-Sat. **Admission** *Royal Chapels* £3 adults; £1 under-16s; £1.50 students, OAPs. **Guided tours** £6 (including Royal Chapels, bookable on 0171 222 7110). Services 7.30am, 8am (Holy Communion), 12.30am, 5pm (choral evensong, except Wed), Mon-Fri; 8am, 9.20am, 3pm (evensong), Sat; 8am, 10am (sung matins), 11.15am (abbey eucharist), 3pm (evensong), 4.45pm organ recital, 6.30pm (evening service), Sun.

Evangelical

All Souls Church
Langham Place, 2 All Souls Place, W1 (0171 580 3522/6029). Oxford Circus tube. **Open** 9.30am-6pm Mon-Fri; 9am-9pm Sun. **Services** 9am Holy Communion, 11am, 6.30pm, Sun.

Islamic

London Central Mosque
146 Park Road, NW8 (0171 724 3363). Baker Street tube/74 bus. **Open** dawn-dusk daily. **Services** 3.18am, 1.06pm, 5.28pm, 9.22pm, 10.52pm (times vary, so phone to confirm).

East London Mosque
84-98 Whitechapel Road, E1 (0171 247 1357). Aldgate East or Whitechapel tube. **Open** 8.30am-10.30pm daily. **Service** *Friday prayer* 1.25pm (1.10pm in winter).

Jewish

Liberal Jewish Synagogue
28 St John's Wood Road, NW8 (0171 286 5181). St John's Wood tube. **Open** *enquiries* 9am-5pm Mon-Thur; 9am-3pm Fri. **Services** 6.45pm Fri; 11am Sat.

West Central Liberal Synagogue
109 Whitfield Street, SW1 (0171 636 7627). Warren Street tube. **Open** 3pm Sat service.

Methodist

Central Church of World Methodism
Westminster Central Hall, Storeys Gate, SW1 (0171 222 8010). St James's Park tube. **Open** *Chapel* 9am-5pm Mon-Fri. **Services** 11am, 6.30pm, Sun.

Pentecostal

Assemblies of God, Pentecostal Church
141 Harrow Road, W2 (0171 286 9261). Edgware Road tube. **Open** for services only. **Services** prayer meetings and Bible study 7.30pm Wed; Young People's Service 5.30pm Sat; 11am, 6.30pm, Sun.

Presbyterian Church of Scotland

Crown Court Church of Scotland

Russell Street, WC2 (0171 836 5643). Covent Garden tube. **Open** *to visitors Jun-Aug* 11.30am-2.30pm Tue-Thur. **Services** 1.10-1.30pm Thur throughout the year; 11.15am, 6.30pm, Sun.

Quakers

Religious Society of Friends (Quakers)

Friends House, 173-177 Euston Road, NW1 (0171 387 3601). Euston tube/BR. **Open** 9am-5pm Mon-Fri. **Meeting** 11am Sun.

Unitarian Church

Rosslyn Hill Unitarian Chapel

Rosslyn Hill, NW3 (0171 435 3506). Hampstead tube. **Open** for services only. **Service** 11am, 6pm, Sun.

United Reformed Church

United Reformed Church

Central Office, 86 Tavistock Place, WC1 (0171 916 2020). Russell Square tube or King's Cross tube/BR. **Open** 9am-5pm Mon-Fri.

Telephones

The red telephone call box is a famous symbol of Britain, but they are now rare. Always easy to find, Giles Gilbert Scott's much-loved red boxes have almost all been replaced. The new smoke-grey cubicles are cleaner but invisible when you need one. Public call boxes are usually cheaper to use than phones in hotel rooms, the charges for which are added to your bill. Call boxes display instructions for use. There are two types, one accepts money and the other only accepts a Phonecard (*see below*). Scattered throughout London you may see blue and grey Mercury phone booths, although these are in the process of being removed as Mercury quits the public sector (*see below*). In emergencies, dial 999 for police, fire or ambulance.

Here's a phonetic guide to UK telephone sounds. A steady *brrrrrr* when you lift the receiver means go ahead and dial. A higher *brrr-brrr* pause *brrr-brrr* pause, etc means the number's ringing. Quick, evenly spaced *boop-boop-boop* means it's engaged (busy); a solid *woooo* means unobtainable.

Telecom Phonecards

Cards available from post offices and larger newsagents. **Cost** 10p per unit; cards available in units of £1 to £20. **Credit** phones in some stations accept credit cards: A, AmEx, DC, V.
Call boxes with the Phonecard symbol take prepaid cards. A notice in the call box tells you where the nearest stockist is. A digital display shows how many units you have.

Mercury Phonecards

(0171 528 2000). Cards no longer supplied by Mercury to retailers as of December 1994. **Cost** 1p per unit; cards in units of £2, £5 and £10. **Credit** *all phones accept cards* A, AmEx, DC, V.

In order to concentrate its on interests in the business sector, Mercury is in the process of withdrawing its payphones altogether. If you have a Mercury Phonecard, you may still find the odd payphone within the M25 functional up until Jan/Feb 1996, the date by which they expect to have removed all payphones (having started to tackle the London area in August 1995). In 1991, there were 1,550 Mercury phone booths in London and they were up to 20 per cent cheaper than BT calls, partly because they're priced in 1p units: Telecom would charge 20p for an 11p call. Mercury's abandonment of the payphone, therefore, seems to benefit no one apart from Sir Iain Vallance, chairman of BT.

Operator Services

Directory Enquiries

Time was when Directory Enquiries were free. But once BT was privatised, you could bet your life that wouldn't last very long. If you two numbers or fewer, dial **192** and you'll be charged a 12p access charge plus 40p per minute, charged by the second. If you've got a Mercury line rather than a BT line, dial **142** and you can get as many numbers as you like, but you'll be charged a 12p access charge plus an outrageous 50p per minute, charged by the second. Our advice is phone from a public call box, in which case it's free. For how much longer though? There's a BT number for directory enquiries in bulk, **0800 672 192**, but the numbers won't be given to you over the phone. Confused? Join the club.

International Directory Enquiries

More exorbitant charges: dial **153** and pay an access charge of 12p plus 50p per minute. Once again though, it's free from a public call box.

International Operator

Dial **155** if you need to reverse the charges (call collect) or if you can't dial direct. Dial direct if you can, as the service is very expensive.

Operator

Call **100** for the operator in the following circumstances: when you have difficulty in dialling; for an early-morning alarm call; to make a credit card call; for information about the cost of a call; to reverse charges for a call (call collect); and for international person-to-person calls.

International Dialling Codes

Australia *(0061);* **Canada** *(001);* **France** *(0033);* **Eire** *(00353);* **Germany** *(0049);* **Italy** *(0039);* **Netherlands** *(0031);* **New Zealand** *(0064);* **Spain** *(0034);* **USA** *(001).*

International Telegrams/Telemessage

The traditional telegram, sadly, no longer exists in Britain. Instead, by calling **190**, you can phone in your message and it will be delivered by post the next day. There is still a service for overseas telegrams. Call the same number if you urgently need to contact someone abroad.

Telephone Directories

There are three telephone directories for London: two for private numbers (divided into alphabetical fields A-K and L-Z) and one for companies. These are available at post offices and libraries. Hotels have them too and they are issued free to all residents with telephones, as is the *Yellow Pages* directory, listing commercial establishments and services.

Travel & Driving

For public transport and car hire *see also chapter* **Getting Around**. If you're thinking of travelling outside London *see chapter* **Trips out of Town**.

London Regional Transport Travel Information Service

(0171 222 1234). **Open** 24 hours daily.
Phone for information about fares and timetables concerning tube, bus and British Rail travel in Greater London.

Discounts

The Young Person's Railcard

This can be held by anyone aged 16-25 or those in full-time education. It costs £16 for one year, and entitles holders to a discount (usually a third off the off-peak standard fare). Railcards are available from mainline British Rail stations. You'll need identification and a couple of passport-size photographs. Students need a signature from their college.

The Student Coach Card

Costing £7, the Coach Card is for students only. It gives a 33 per cent discount on fares and is valid for a year. The form is available from Victoria Coach Station. Make sure you remember to take a passport-size photo and proof that you are a student.

The Inter-Rail Card

Suitable for all those aged under 26 who are planning a trip to Europe. For up to £249, the pass (available from British Rail stations) entitles holders to unlimited train travel in 26 countries for one month. You can buy more than one (they must run consecutively) and there's a small refund on return of your correctly filled-in card. There's now an Inter-Rail card for those aged over 26, but it doesn't include Spain, Portugal,

Morocco, France, Belgium, Italy or Switzerland. A 15-day card costs £209; a one-month card costs £269. Neither card is valid in the UK (if bought here). A linked insurance which covers loss of travel documents is available and is strongly recommended.

STA Travel

74 & 86 Old Brompton Road, SW7 (Intercontinental 0171 937 9962/European 0171 937 9921). South Kensington tube. **Open** 9am-6pm Mon-Fri; 10am-4pm Sat.
A wide range of low-cost fares across five continents is offered here, with special rates for students, young people and academics. STA also has offices at 117 Euston Road, NW1 and many other colleges throughout London.

Parking

If you've heard that driving in central London is difficult, just wait till you try to find somewhere to park. If you park illegally (check the regulations in the Highway Code, available from newsagents), you'll probably get a £30 parking ticket. If you park illegally in central London your car will probably be immobilised by a yellow triangular wheel-clamp. Vehicles may also be taken away and impounded. To retrieve your vehicle you have to go to a Payment Centre (*see below* **De-clamping & Car Pounds**).

Size conversion chart for clothes

Women's clothes									
British	8	10	12	14	16	•	•	•	•
American	6	8	10	12	14	•	•	•	•
French	36	38	40	42	44	•	•	•	•
Italian	36	38	40	42	44	•	•	•	•
Women's shoes									
British	8	10	12	14	16	•	•	•	•
American	6	8	10	12	14	•	•	•	•
Continental	36	38	40	42	44	•	•	•	•
Men's suits/overcoats									
British	38	40	42	44	46	•	•	•	•
American	38	40	42	44	46	•	•	•	•
Continental	48	50/52	54	56	58/60	•	•	•	•
Men's shirts									
British	14	14.5	15	15.5	16	16.5	17	•	•
American	14	14.5	15	15.5	16	16.5	17	•	•
Continental	35	36/37	38	39/40	41	42/43	44	•	•
Men's shoes									
British	8	9	10	11	12	•	•	•	•
American	9	10	11	12	13	•	•	•	•
Continental	42	43	44	45	46	•	•	•	•
Children's shoes									
British	7	8	9	10	11	12	13	1	2
American	7.5	8.5	9.5	10.5	11.5	12.5	13.5	1.5	2.5
Continental	24	25.5	27	28	29	30	32	33	34

Children's clothes

In all countries, size descriptions vary from make to make, but are usually done by age.

24-Hour Car Parks

Arlington Street, SW1 *(0171 499 3312)*. **Rates**
£8.50 for 3 hours; £29 for 12 hours; £36 up to 24 hours.
Brewer Street, W1 *(0171 734 9497)*. **Rates** £9.50 for
3 hours; £15.80 for 6 hours; £9.50 night rate.
Cambridge Circus, W1 *(0171 434 1896)*. **Rates**
£7.80 for 3 hours; £11.70 for 6 hours; £6.80 night rate.

De-clamping & Car Pounds

The wheel clamp was introduced to deter motorists from ignoring parking tickets. However, it not
only ruins the offender's day, but also guarantees
the road will remain blocked until the car is freed.
If you've been clamped, there will be a label
attached to the car telling you which **Payment
Centre** to phone or visit. Some boroughs let you
pay over the phone with a credit card, others insist
you go to the payment centre. Either way, you'll
have to pay £38 on the spot for de-clamping and
have 28 days in which to pay a £16 parking fine.

The staff at the payment centre promise to de-
clamp your car within the next four hours but can't
tell you exactly when. You are also warned that if
you don't remove your car within one hour of its
being de-clamped they will clamp it again. This
means that you may have to spend quite some time
waiting by your car.

If your car has been hoisted on to the back of a
truck (the size of the crowd of onlookers increases in
direct proportion to the size, or cost, of the car) and
taken to a car pound, you're facing a stiff penalty: a
fee of £105 is levied for removal, plus £12 per day if
you don't collect it immediately. Then a week or so
later, to add insult to injury, you'll probably get a
parking ticket through the post. Do you still think it's
clever to have parked right outside that restaurant?

Privatisation and contracting-out have created terrific confusion in car parking regulations and vehicle recovery, just as they have in telecommunications
(*see above* **Telephones**), but in all cases simply follow the instructions on the label attached to your car.
And if your car's not there, contact the police.

Car Clamp Recovery Club

*PO Box 3, West Wycombe, Kent BR4 9TB (0171 235
9901)*. **Open** 8am-8pm Mon-Sat. **Membership** £30.
Credit A, AmEx, DC, V.
If you're too busy to go through the de-clamp process yourself and want to have the car delivered to your door, pay the
fine plus the membership fee for the first clamp; and an additional £10 for the second clamp.

Camden Car Pound & Payment Centre

*Arcade Motors, Berlin Bank, York Way, NW1 (0171 747
4747)*. *King's Cross tube/BR.* **Open** 24 hours daily.

Westminster Car Pound & Payment Centre

Vehicle removal: *Bells of Richmond, London Street,
Old Paddington Basin, W2 (0171 747 4747)*. *Paddington
tube/BR.* **Open** 24 hours daily.
Clamping: *Arcade Motors, 55 Charing Cross Road,
WC2 (0171 747 4747)*. *Leicester Square tube.* **Open**
8.30am-midnight Mon-Sat.

It's not worth it – park legally or go by tube.

Hammersmith & Fulham Car Pound & Payment Centre

*Arcade Motors, Sopwith Way, off Queenstown Road,
SW8 (0171 747 4747)*. *Battersea Park BR.* **Open** 24
hours daily.

24-Hour Petrol Stations

There are over 100 24-hour petrol stations through-
out Greater London. Here are four of them.
North: Elf Service Station, 109 York Way, N7 (0171 267
5862).
South: Old Kent Road Filling Station, 420-432 Old Kent
Road, SE1 (0171 232 2957).
East: City Road Service Station, 309 City Road, EC1
(0171 253 4059).
West: Star Service Station, 7 Pembridge Villas, W11
(0171 229 6626).

Car Breakdown

The well-prepared visitor never travels without his
or her membership card of a motoring organisation. But we're not all so well prepared.

AA (Automobile Association)

*119-121 Cannon Street, EC4 (information 0990 500
600/freefone breakdown service 0800 887766/shop 0171
626 7260/insurance 0171 626 7787)*. **Open** *office*
8.30am-5.30pm Mon-Fri. **Breakdown service** 24 hours
daily. **Credit** A, V.
You can call the AA if you break down. Become a member
on the spot: it will cost you £10 to join, £35 for the first year's
membership, £25 for the relay service, £17.50 for homestart.

National Breakdown

(Head Office 0113 293434/Breakdown 0800 400 600/Membership 0113 2393666). **Open** 24 hours daily.
A non-member calling National Breakdown pays a call-out fee of £32, mileage of 60p per mile plus labour and parts. To become a member, telephone for details; degrees of cover vary from total protection (£72.50) to recovery (£24). National Breakdown will 'rescue' single women (non-members) and take them to the nearest recovery centre for safety.

RAC (Royal Automobile Club)

RAC House, M1 Cross, Brent Terrace, NW2 (general enquiries 0181 452 8000). **Open** office 9am-5pm Mon-Fri; 9am-12.30pm Sat. **Breakdown service** 24 hours daily. **Credit** A, AmEx, DC, V.
Ring the general enquiries number and ask for the Rescue Service. Membership costs from £29 for basic cover to £139 for the most comprehensive. Describe your mechanical failure to the controller. An engineer will then be sent out to repair your car on the roadside or, if necessary, tow it away. A non-member calling breakdown services also pays a £30 surcharge and must then join.

Spare Parts

Barnet Brake & Clutch Services

120 Myddleton Road, N22 (0181 881 0847). Bounds Green or Wood Green tube/N2, N21 Night bus. **Open** 24 hours daily. **Credit** A, V.
If you know what the problem is and just need parts, contact this 24-hour car spare parts shop.

Visitors with Disabilities

Things are improving (slowly) for disabled visitors to London. Many tourist venues now have wheelchair access; some councils are doing their best to improve the situation further. There are books and organisations which give useful information specifically for disabled people. **London Tourist Board** publishes a leaflet, 'London For All', which covers transport, tours and hotels. It's available from **Tourist Information Centres** (*see chapter* **Essential Information**). For information about public transport, get a free copy of 'Access to the Underground' from Tourist Information Centres, ticket offices or by post from the Unit for Disabled Passengers, 55 Broadway, SW1 (0171 918 3312).

Artsline

54 Chalton Street, NW1 (0171 388 2227). Euston tube/BR. **Open** 9.30am-5.30pm Mon-Fri.
An organisation for disabled people which gives free information on arts and entertainment events in London and on adapted facilities at venues such as cinemas, art galleries and theatres. It produces a monthly publication.

British Sports Association for the Disabled

Solecast House, 13-27 Brunswick Place, N1 (0171 490 4919). Old Street tube/BR. **Open** 9.30am-4pm Mon-Fri.
People with disabilities who are interested in watching or participating in sports should contact the BSAD, a national organisation which puts people in touch with local sports groups and centres. The address is that of the Greater London regional office; contact them for a list of regional branches throughout the country.

Greater London Association for Disabled People (GLAD)

336 Brixton Road, SW9 (0171 274 0107). Brixton tube. **Open** 9am-5pm Mon-Fri.
The *London Disability Guide*, published by GLAD, is a comprehensive resource book covering subjects from education for disabled people to pregnancy and parenthood. It's available free by post, send an SAE.

Handicapped Helpline

Community Links, Canning Town Public Hall, 105 Barking Road, E16 (0171 473 2270). Canning Town BR. **Open** 9am-12.30pm Mon-Thur.
Run by and for disabled people, the Handicapped Helpline gives information and advice on a variety of subjects and counselling on careers. It can put you in touch with other relevant organisations or specific associations and it offers a drop-in service.

Royal Association For Disability and Rehabilitation (RADAR)

25 Mortimer Street, W1 (0171 250 3222). Oxford Circus tube. **Open** 10am-4pm Mon-Fri.
The central organisation for disabled voluntary groups. Through it you can get advice on virtually any aspect of life. The Association publishes *Contact*, a quarterly magazine which has features on disabled issues, and *Bulletin*, a monthly newsletter, which has articles on more news-orientated subjects such as housing, education and Acts of Parliament.

Tripscope

The Courtyard, Evelyn Road, W4 (0181 994 9294). Chiswick Park tube/South Acton BR.
Jim Bennett's advice service for the elderly and disabled can help with all aspects of getting around London and the UK. It's chiefly an enquiry line, but you can write in or visit by appointment if you have difficulty with the telephone.

Working in London

Finding a summer job in London, or temporary employment if you're on a working holiday, is a full-time job in itself. Despite frequent reports that the recession is over, there is precious little evidence of an increase in job vacancies.

But providing you can speak English well, are an EC citizen or have a valid work permit (*see below* **Work Permits**), you should be able to get work doing catering jobs, labouring, bar/pub or shop work. Graduates with either English or a foreign language degree could try teaching. There's also despatch riding (bike messengers need their own bike, a courageous disposition and possibly a death wish) or distributing free magazines. Also try summer work in tourist spots; local councils sometimes take on summer staff such as playgroup leaders or swimming pool attendants. More ideas can be found in *Summer Jobs in Britain* published by Vacation Work, 9 Park End Street, Oxford (£7.95 by post). Central Bureau for Educational Visits and Exchanges (*see below* **Useful Addresses**) has other publications.

To find work, look in the *Evening Standard*, local or national papers, newsagents' windows or Jobcentres. For office work, sign on with temp agencies. If you have good shorthand, typing (40 words per minute upwards) or word-processing

(WP) skills, and dress the part, agencies might find you well-paid office work.

If you're desperate, try a fast-food chain. You'll probably have to wear a hideous uniform and endure hyped-up competition to see who is the fastest burger-maker, but these places are always looking for staff (and no wonder).

Work for Foreign Visitors

With few exceptions, citizens of non-EC countries will need a work permit before they can legally get a job in the UK (*see below* **Work Permits**).

One of the advantages of working here is the opportunity to meet people. But for any work, it's essential that you can speak some English. Try catering – there's a **Jobcentre** at 3 Denmark Street, W1 (full-time work 0171 497 2047/part-time work 33-35 Mortimer Street, W1, 0171 323 9190) dealing in hotel and catering work. For office work you need a high standard of English and skills.

Au-pair work is a possibility. Try an agency in your own country or look in the *Yellow Pages* under Employment Agencies. Try *The Lady* magazine, which advertises au-pair and nanny jobs. The best thing about au-pairing is that you get free accommodation, but wages are often low.

Voluntary work in youth hostels will pay board and lodging and some pocket money. Work can also be found in shops, pubs and bars (*see above* **Working in London** for where to look).

Useful Addresses

Aliens Registration Office

10 Lamb's Conduit Street, WC1 (0171 230 1208). Holborn tube. **Open** 9am-4.45pm Mon-Fri.
It costs £30 to be registered, if you have a work permit.

Central Bureau for Educational Visits & Exchanges

10 Spring Gardens, SW1 (0171 486 5101). Bond Street or Marble Arch tube. **Open** 9.15am-5.30pm Mon-Fri.
Funded by the Department for Education, this office deals with organising visits outside the UK. But contact it anyway for copies of their useful publications.

Department of Employment

Caxton House, Tothill Street, SW1 (0171 273 3000). St James's Park tube. **Open** 9am-5pm Mon-Fri.
The Overseas Labour Section can help with work permit enquiries (*0171 273 5336*).

Home Office

Immigration and Nationality Department, Lunar House, Wellesley Road, Croydon, CR2 (0181 686 0688). East Croydon BR. **Open** 8.30am-4pm Mon-Fri.
The immigration department of the Home Office deals with queries about immigration, visas and work permits for Commonwealth citizens.

Jobcentre

195 Wardour Street, W1 (0171 439 4541). Oxford Circus tube. **Open** 9am-12.30pm, 1.30-5pm, Mon-Thur; 10am-12.30pm, 1.30-5pm, Fri.
Employers advertise job vacancies on noticeboards here and there's often temporary and unskilled work available. Most districts of London have a Jobcentre – they're bright orange so you can't miss them – and they're listed under Manpower Services Commission in the phone book.

Work permits

EC citizens, residents of Gibraltar and certain categories of other overseas visitors don't need a work permit. No other visitors may work in the UK legally without one. Three government departments deal with work permits. Try any Jobcentre, where you can get an application form (form OW1), before going to the Department of Employment or the Home Office (*see above* **Useful Addresses**). In most cases, you will need a UK employer to apply on your behalf and he/she must prove that no UK resident can do the work better. However, there is a 'training and work experience' scheme operated by the Department of Employment for 18- to 35-year-olds. This enables you to gain work experience or training in a certain field for a limited period. A permit must be obtained by a UK employer on your behalf before you enter the UK.

Citizens of Commonwealth countries aged between 17-27 years can get a passport stamp as a Working Holiday Maker which allows you to do part-time work without a work permit

or up to two years. Contact the British High Commission or Consulate in your country to obtain the stamp before entering this country. If applying for a visa extension while in Britain, you might convince the Home Office Immigration Department (*0181 686 0688*) or the Overseas Labour Section at the Department of Employment that you need part-time work and are not looking for full-time employment.

Visiting students from the USA can get a blue card enabling them to work for a maximum of six months. This is not difficult to obtain, but you must get it before entering the country. Contact the Work in Britain department of the Council on International Educational Exchange, 205 East 42nd Street, New York, NY 10017 (*001 212 661 1414*) for details. Alternatively, call BUNAC, 16 Bowling Green Lane, EC1 (*0171 251 3472*), which is a non-profit-making student club that organises work exchange programmes for students from the United States of America, Canada, Australia and Jamaica.

Further Reading

Fiction

Peter Ackroyd: *Hawksmoor*
Tales from the crypt.
Margery Allingham: *The Tiger In The Smoke*
Vivid detective mystery in fogbound London.
Martin Amis: *London Fields*
Murder, millennial terror and darts. Hateful characters.
Clive Barker: *The Books of Blood*
Comfortless creatures in Crouch End.
Jonathan Coe: *The Dwarves of Death*
Mystery, music, mirth and malevolence in Coe's third novel.
Jonathan Coe: *What A Carve Up!*
Award-winning peerless political and social satire.
Charles Dickens: *Oliver Twist*
Classic tale of a waif and stray.
Charles Dickens: *Bleak House*
Unforgettable evocation of foggy London life.
Charles Dickens: *Little Dorrit*
Debt and daughterly love on the South Bank.
Sir Arthur Conan Doyle: *Complete Sherlock Holmes*
Reassuring sleuthing shenanigans with world's greatest tec.
Nell Dunn: *Up The Junction*
Classic Clapham 1960s low life.
George Gissing: *New Grub Street*
Vivid account of trials and tribulations of hack writers.
Graham Greene: *The End Of The Affair*
Adultery, Catholicism and Clapham Common.
Graham Greene: *England Made Me*
Minor public school misfit struggles to make ends meet.
Patrick Hamilton: *Hangover Square*
Love and death in darkest Earl's Court.
Patrick Hamilton: *The Slaves of Solitude*
Hamilton's rancid evocation of boarding-house life.
Patrick Hamilton: *Twenty Thousand Streets Under the Sky*
Yearning romantic trilogy set amid Soho sleaze.
M John Harrison: *The Course of the Heart*
Black magic in Bloomsbury the lure of the Coeur.
M John Harrison: *The Ice Monkey*
The dark spiritual heart of Camden Town (and other tales).
Alan Hollinghurst: *The Swimming Pool Library*
Shimmering evocation of gay life around Russell Square.
Robert Irwin: *Exquisite Corpse*
London as it was in the time of the Surrealists. Fish.
Doris Lessing: *London Observed: Stories and Sketches*
Ms Lessing proclaims her love for the metropolis.
Maria Lexton (ed): *The Time Out Book of London Short Stories*
London-based short story writers pay homage to the city.
Colin MacInnes: *Visions of London*
Glittering coffee bar set of 1950s London in trilogy form.
Wolf Mankowitz: *A Kid For Two Farthings*
Boy meets goat in East End market.
Derek Marlowe: *A Dandy in Aspic*
Cold war espionage in London and Berlin.
Michael Moorcock: *Mother London*
Love-letter to London; genuine characters, broad canvas.
Oscar Moore: *A Matter Of Life And Sex*
Moving tale of love, sex and cottaging in AIDS-hit London.
Iris Murdoch: *Under the Net*
Picaresque adventures of a talented wastrel writer.
Kim Newman: *The Quorum*
Web of intrigue surrounds Docklands-based media magnate.
Kim Newman: *The Original Dr Shade & Other Stories*
London-based satirist embarks on London-set horror-fest.

Pulp Faction: *Skin*
Radical short fiction by London-based writers.
Pulp Faction: *Technopagan*
Editor Elaine Palmer unleashes another bizarre collection.
Derek Raymond: *The Devil's Home on Leave*
The late Robin Cook's view of the underworld's underbelly.
Derek Raymond: *How The Dead Live*
Cookie cooks up more grisly crime.
Derek Raymond: *I Was Dora Suarez*
Blackest London noir.
Alan Ross (ed): *London Magazine*
Essential bi-monthly mix of fiction, reviews, poetry, articles.
Christopher Petit: *Robinson*
Personality disintegration within a personified Soho.
William Sansom: *Selected Short Stories*
Lyrical tales of Londoners at large.
Will Self: *The Quantity Theory of Insanity*
Methods of madness in first award-winning collection.
Will Self: *Grey Area*
'There are only eight people in London…' More stories.
Will Self: *My Idea of Fun*
Ours too. Enid Blyton on acid let loose in London.
Iain Sinclair: *White Chappell, Scarlet Tracings*
Unsettling fusion of Ripper murders and bookdealers.
Iain Sinclair: *Downriver*
The Thames' own *Heart of Darkness* by London's laureate.
Iain Sinclair: *Radon Daughters*
William Hope Hodgson homage via the London Hospital.
Tobias Smollett: *Humphrey Clinker*
Assault on eighteenth-century sensibilities and strawberries.
Muriel Spark: *The Ballad of Peckham Rye*
The devil incarnate spreads mayhem in Peckham.
Muriel Spark: *The Bachelors*
A sinister spiritualist preys on London's vulnerable single set.
Muriel Spark: *A Far Cry From Kensington*
Autobiographical account of Kensington bedsitland.
Virginia Woolf: *Mrs Dalloway*
Ulysses transposed to 1920s London, with female lead.

Non-fiction

Janet Bonthron: *Days Out With Kids*
Easy trips to farms, castles, gardens, theme parks and zoos.
Russell Davies (ed): *Kenneth Williams's Diaries*
Forty-six years' worth of camp, grace and tragedy.
Andrew Duncan: *Secret London*
A series of strolls through the London undergrowth.
Samantha Hardingham: *London: A Guide To Recent Architecture*
Pocket-sized guide to the latest buildings.
John Lahr (ed): *Joe Orton's Diaries*
Graphic accounts of unquenchable sexual thirst.
George Orwell: *Down and Out in Paris And London*
Grim autobiographical account of waitering and starving.
Samuel Pepys: *Diaries*
Fires, plagues, bordellos: Sam saw it all.
Roy Porter: *London – A Social History*
Exhaustive, all-encompassing history of London.
Richard Trench: *London Under London*
Literally that: investigation of the subterranean city.
AN Wilson (ed): *The Faber Book of London*
Metropolitan smorgasbord.
Ben Weinreb/Christopher Hibbert (eds): *Encyclopaedia of London*
Everything you never thought you needed to know.

Index

Note: *italics indicate illustrations.*

Abney Park Cemetery 55, 119-120
accommodation 13-24
    emergency 24, 286
    gay and lesbian 279
    outside London 294-306
    student 22-23, 282
Adam, Robert 58, 180
aerobics classes 248
AIDS counselling 279, 313
airports 6, 7
    left luggage/lost property 314
Albert Bridge 63, *96*, 100, 102
Aldgate 110
Alexandra Park 25, 54
Aliens Registration 321
ambulances 309
American football 248, 250
Amnesty International 314
apartments *see* flats
archaeological remains 66-67
archery 243
architecture 48-49, 56-61, 87, 109, 281
    tours 46
art scene 179-180
    see also galleries, art
Ascot, Royal 28, 250
Athenaeum 49
athletics events 250
athletics tracks 51, 52, 54, 243
auctioneers 174

baby-changing facilities 150, 151
babysitters 273
Baden-Powell Museum 198
badminton 247, 250
bagels 111, 115, *260*, 260
banger racing 251
Bank Holidays 52, 54, 98
Bank of England 37, 59, 74, 76, 95
    Museum 204
banks 5, 262
Bankside 74, 105-105, 147
    Power Station 74, 105, *105*
    see also Globe Theatre; Southwark
Banqueting House 33, 58, 74
Barbican Centre 61, 182, 228, 255, 272, 273
Barker, Clive 119, 223
bars *see* pubs and bars
baseball 243
basketball 247, 248, 250
Bath 295, *295*, 296

bathrooms (for hire) 316
Battersea 102, 147
Battersea Bridge 63, 102
Battersea Park 25, 26, 52, 100, 102, 268, 269
Battersea Power Station 60, *102*, 102
Bazalgette, Sir Joseph 59, 63
BBC 49, 80, 82, 83
Beating the Retreat 26
Beatles 46, 84
beauty salons 15, 17, 150
Bedlam 78
beer festival 27
Belfast, HMS 82, 45
Belgravia 98
Bermondsey 105, 107, 172
Bethlehem Royal Hospital 78
Bethnal Green 115
    Museum of Childhood 196
Big Ben 31
birdwatching 53
Blackfriars Bridge 63, 75
blacksmiths 168
Blakelock, Keith 120
Bloomsbury 41, 93-94
Boadicea 98
Boat Race, Varsity 26, 63, 250
boating lakes 51, 52, 54, 101
Bonfire Night 30, 54, 74, 117
Borough 104-105
boules 51, 52
bowling alleys 246-7
bowling greens 52, 54, 120
boxing 248
brass rubbing 271
Brentford 202, 204, 220, 223
Brick Lane 111, 258, 260
bridges 63, 68, 75, 76
    see also individual bridges
Brighton 294-295
British Council 282
British Film Institute 281
British Library 262, 281
    new building 61, 93, 94
British Museum 59, 66, 67, 93-94, 195
    Reading Room 78, 93
Brixton 103-104, 147, 172
Brixton Academy 236
Brompton Cemetery 55
Brompton Oratory 41, 100, 316
Brook Advisory Centres 310
Brown, Capability 54, 302
BT Tower 61, *86*
Buckingham Palace 51, 92, 31
    Queen's Gallery 182
bungee jumping 243, *248*

Bunhill Fields 55
bureaux de change 5, 150, 151
Burton, Decimus 49, 54, 59
buses 7, 8-9, 101, 103, 110
    sightseeing tours 46
Business Design Centre 120, 262
business services 176, 262-265
    women's 285
Butler's Wharf 61, 126, 151

Cabaret Mechanical Theatre 270
Cabinet War Rooms 82
cabs *see* taxis
Café Royal 79
cafés and brasseries 91, 94, 97, 101, 104, 116, 119, 139-143, 148
    late-night 259-260
    see also restaurants; tea, afternoon
cakes (to order) 150, 153
Cambridge *296*, 296-297
Camden Arts Centre 182
Camden Lock 64, 71
Camden Market 85, 111, 173
Camden Passage *see under* Islington
Camden Town 116, *117*, 143, 148, 258
Camley Street reserve 53, *53*
campsites 23-24
Canary Wharf 95, 148
    Tower 49, 61, *61*, 85, 87, 114, *114*
Canute (Cnut), King 67, *67*
Capital Radio 24, 208
    helpline 313
Carlyle's House 199
cars
    Chelsea Cruise 63
    hire 11
    garages/services 319-320
    parking/clamping 318-319
    veteran car run 30
catering 152
cemeteries 54-55
Cenotaph *28*, 30, 47, 79, 82, 92
ceremonies 25-26, 28, 30, 31
Chambers of Commerce 262, 263
Changing of the Guard 31
Channel Tunnel 7, 88
Charing Cross 8, 69
Charles I *72*, 74, 90
Charlton 109
Chaucer, Geoffrey 28, 69
Chelsea 41, 51, 52, 99-100, 129
    King's Road 84, 99
    Royal Hospital 49, 52, 58, 100
Chelsea Cruise 63

restorers 170, 171, 174
RIBA gallery 184
Richmond 19, 64, 101-102, 142, 147, 148, 258
  Ham House 44, 50
  museum 204
  Park 50, 53, 102, 244
riding stables 53, 245
riots 70, 76, 84, 85, 85, 103, 113
Ritz Hotel 15, 79, 80, 92, 143
river trips 63-64
Riverside Studios 184, 210-211, 218
roads 8, 87
  Westway *10*, 99, *99*
Rock Circus 37
Rogers, Richard 61, 114
rollerskating 245-246, 247
Ronnie Scott's club 83
Rosetti, Dante Gabriel 99-100
Rotherhithe 106, 107
rowing 247, 250
Royal Academy of Arts 26, 61, 76, 179, 184
Royal Air Force Museum 79, 81
Royal Albert Hall 229, 242
Royal Botanic Gardens *see under* Kew
Royal Courts of Justice 45,59, 95
Royal Exchange 41, 59, 73, *74*, 74, 95, 127
Royal Festival Hall 61, 104
  restaurant 125, *125*
Royal Free Hospital 117, 222
Royal Hospital, Chelsea 49, 52, 58, 100
Royal Institute of British Architects 184
Royal Mews 34
Royal Naval College 52, 58, 108
Royal Navy 72
royal occasions 26
Royal Opera House 90, 218, 229
Royal Tournament 28
rugby league 250, 251
rugby union 250, 251
  museum 203
running *see* athletics
Russell Square 93
Russia Dock Woodland 106

S

Saatchi Collection 180, *181*, 182
Sadler's Wells Theatre 219
sailing 247
St Katharine's Dock 47, 112, 113-114
St James's 92
St James's Palace 34, 72, 92
St James's Park 51, 92
St John's Smith Square 229
St Pancras Station 49, 59, 222
St Patrick's Day 26
St Paul's Cathedral 32, *35*, 58, 67, 73, 74, 76, 82, 95
St Thomas' Old Operating Theatre 204
Salisbury *299*, 299-300
Samaritans 282, 313

Savoy Hotel 17, 80, 82, 143, 144
Schofield, Simon *184*
Science Museum 77, 100, 190, *191*
Scottish Tourist Board 292
Selfridges 6, 60, 79, 151
Serpentine Gallery 51, 180, 185
Shakespeare, William 48, 300
Shambles 70, *70*
shelters 24
Shepherd's Bush Empire *235*, 237
Sherlock Holmes Museum 37
Shooters Hill 109
shops 150-176
  antiques 98, 99, 102, 118, 120, 170-172, 173, 174; clothes 161; jewellery 162; twentieth century 171, 174
  books 97, 111, 164-167, 180
  ceramics 103; antique 171
  children's 167, 271-272
  clothes/accessories 92, 150-151, 154-164
  department stores 150-151
  equipment: arts/crafts 167-168; electrical 167; musical 168-169; office 176; photographic 169; sports 170
  food/drink 151-153
  gifts 176
  health/beauty 153-154
  home shopping 289
  house/garden 174-176
  late-night 260
  local shopping: Battersea 102; Chelsea 99; Clapham 103; Covent Garden 90; Kensington 98; Knightsbridge 96; Muswell Hill 120; Oval 104; Woolwich 109
  Oxfam: No Logo *157*, 161
  opening times 5
  records/tapes/CDs 116,169-170
  secondhand 116, 160-161, 165-167, 168, 169, 170, 174-175
  sex/gay/lesbian 278
  Turkish 119
  underwear 161, 289
  see also markets
Silverstone Circuit 250
skateboarding 245-246, 247
skating *see* ice rinks; roller skating
Smithfield Market 49, 59, 69, 70, 73, 94, 144
snooker tournament 250
Soane, Sir John 59, 180
  museum 76, 201
social reform 75, 77, 78, 80, 83, 84
softball 51, 246
Soho 27, 83, 90-91, *92*, 92, 172
  Chinese festivals 28, 30
  Hazlitt's 17, *20*
Sotheby's 174
South Bank 104
  County Hall 79, 84
  see also Bankside; Butler's Wharf

South Bank Centre 61, 83, 104, 219, 229, 242
Southall 137, 152
Southwark
  Bridge 63
  George Inn 57, 104, 147
  The Clink Exhibition 45
  see also Bankside; Globe Theatre
Southwark Cathedral 43, 57, 105
Speakers' Corner 51
Spencer House 44
Spitalfields 48, 110-112, 231
  Market 111, 173, 188
sports
  centres 247-248
  equipment shops 170
  major events 250
  park facilities 51, 52, 54
  participation 243-251
  spectator 248-251
  stadia 251
  see also individual sports
squash courts 52, 247
squatters' advice 24
stately homes 44-45
stations *see* railways; Underground
statues and monuments 47-48
  Boadicea 66
  Burghers of Calais (cast) 51
  Charles I *72*
  Emmeline Pankhurst 51
  John Stow 73
  The Monument 47, 95
  Nelson's Column 48
  Peter Pan 51
  Queen Anne 74
  Victoria Memorial 60
  war memorials 79
  Wolfe Monument 52-53
  see also Cenotaph
Stave Hill 106
stock car racing 251
Stockwell 103-104
Stoke Newington 118-120, 143, 148
Stonehenge 25, 299
Stow, John 73, 114
Strand 69
  Savoy Palace 70
  Somerset House 59
Stratford-upon-Avon 300, *300*, 301
street names 69, 70, 95, 115
street performers 27
students' London 281-283
  educational visits &
    exchanges 321
  travel discounts 316
Suffragettes 51, 54, 80
Surrey 302, 306
Sussex 302
Sutton House 44, 115
swimming pools 54, 153, 246, 247-248, 271, 316
synagogues 120, 316
Syon Park 44, 50, 268

London Guide
Advertisers Index
Please refer to the relevant sections for addresses/telephone numbers

Maps

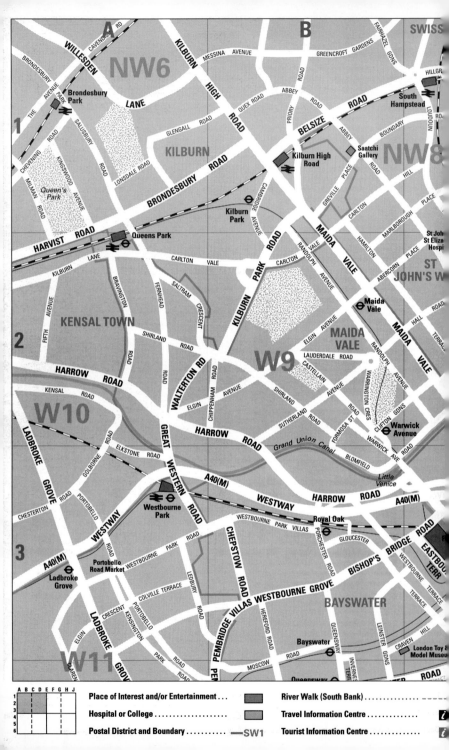

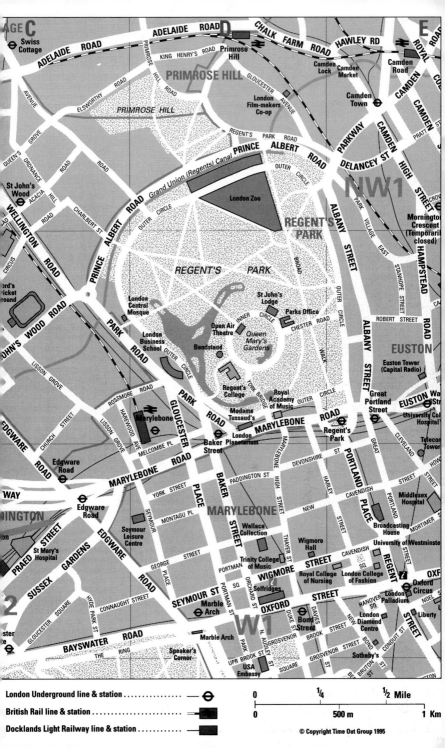

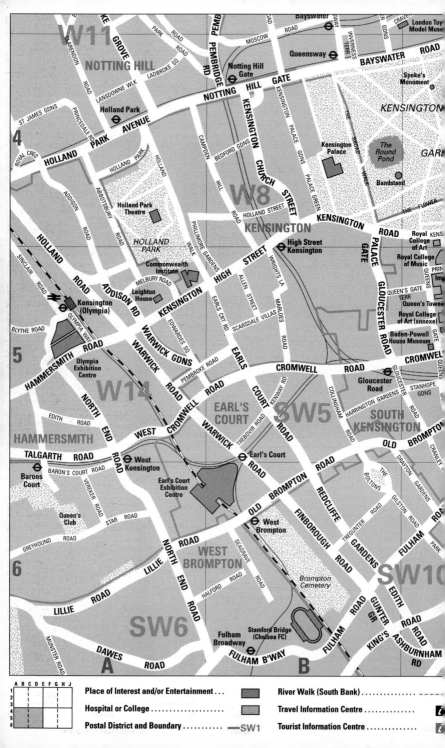

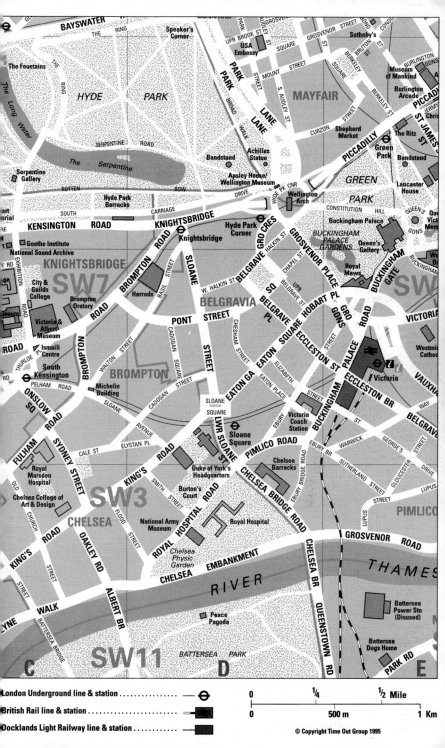

London Underground line & station .... —⊖

British Rail line & station .... —

Docklands Light Railway line & station .... —

| 0 | ¼ | ½ Mile |
| 0 | 500 m | 1 Km |

© Copyright Time Out Group 1995

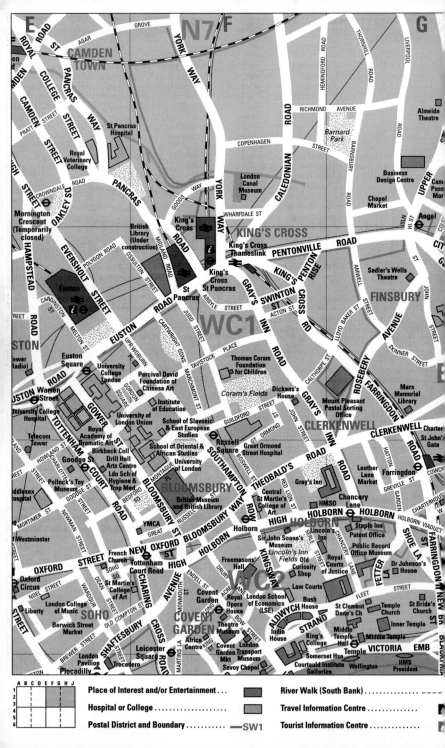

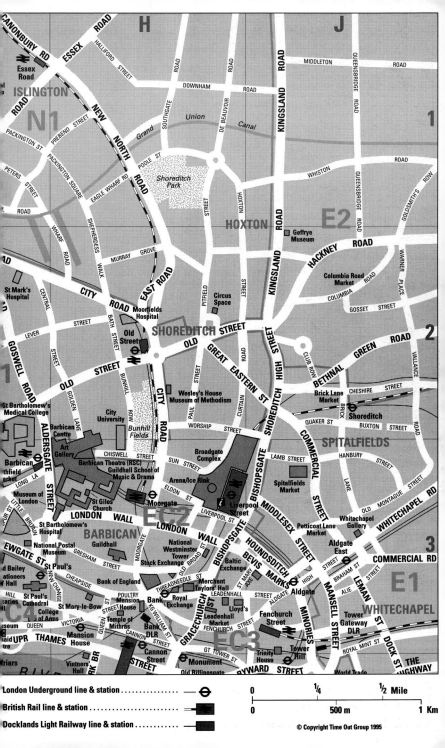

London Underground line & station .... — ⊖
British Rail line & station .... — ■
Docklands Light Railway line & station .... — ■

| 0 | ¼ | ½ Mile |
| 0 | 500 m | 1 Km |

© Copyright Time Out Group 1995

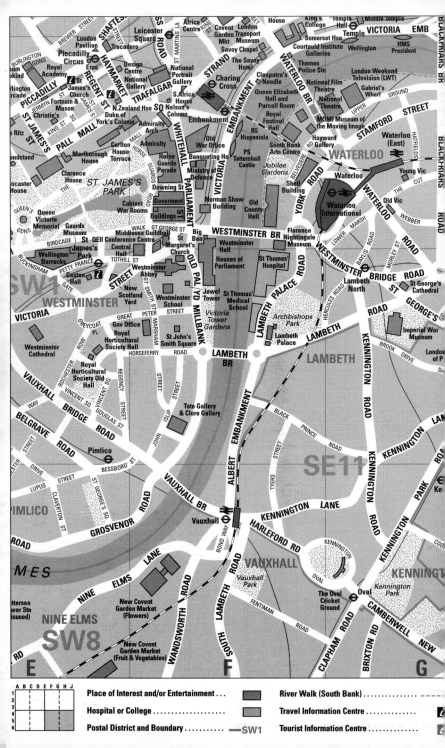

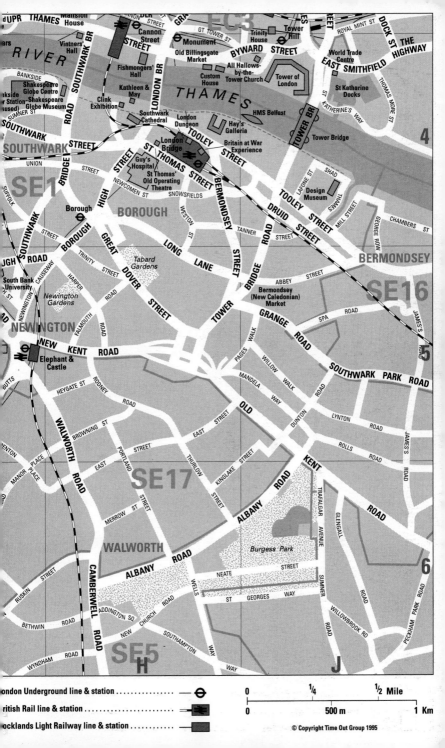

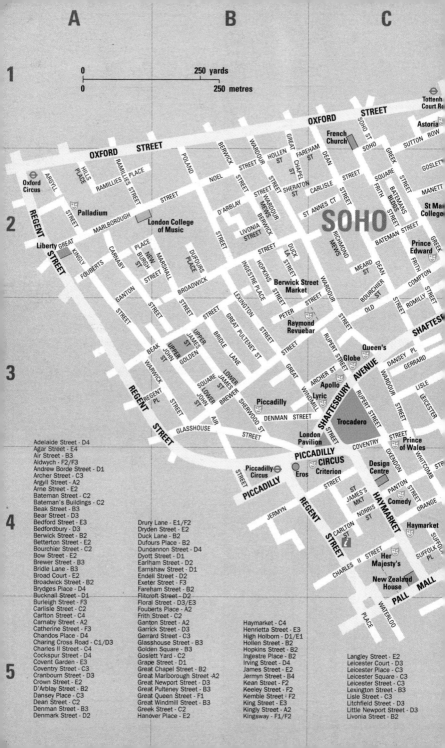

250 yards
250 metres

Adelaide Street - D4
Agar Street - E4
Air Street - B3
Aldwych - F2/F3
Andrew Borde Street - D1
Archer Street - C3
Argyll Street - A2
Arne Street - E2
Bateman Street - C2
Bateman's Buildings - C2
Beak Street - B3
Bear Street - D3
Bedford Street - E3
Bedfordbury - D3
Berwick Street - B2
Betterton Street - E2
Bourchier Street - C2
Bow Street - E2
Brewer Street - B3
Bridle Lane - B3
Broad Court - E2
Broadwick Street - B2
Brydges Place - D4
Bucknall Street - D1
Burleigh Street - F3
Carlisle Street - C2
Carlton Street - C4
Carnaby Street - A2
Catherine Street - F3
Chandos Place - D4
Charing Cross Road - C1/D3
Charles II Street - C4
Cockspur Street - D4
Covent Garden - E3
Coventry Street - C3
Cranbourn Street - D3
Crown Street - E2
D'Arblay Street - B2
Dansey Place - C3
Dean Street - C2
Denman Street - B3
Denmark Street - D2

Drury Lane - E1/F2
Dryden Street - E2
Duck Lane - B2
Dufours Place - B2
Duncannon Street - D4
Dyott Street - D1
Earlham Street - D2
Earnshaw Street - D1
Endell Street - E2
Exeter Street - F3
Fareham Street - B2
Flitcroft Street - D2
Floral Street - D3/E3
Foubert's Place - A2
Frith Street - C2
Ganton Street - A2
Garrick Street - D3
Gerrard Street - C3
Glasshouse Street - B3
Golden Square - B3
Goslett Yard - C2
Grape Street - D1
Great Chapel Street - B2
Great Marlborough Street -A2
Great Newport Street - D3
Great Pulteney Street - B3
Great Queen Street - F1
Great Windmill Street - B3
Greek Street - C2
Hanover Place - E2

Haymarket - C4
Henrietta Street - E3
High Holborn - D1/E1
Hollen Street - B2
Hopkins Street - B2
Ingestre Place - B2
Irving Street - D4
James Street - E2
Jermyn Street - B4
Kean Street - F2
Keeley Street - F2
Kemble Street - F2
King Street - B3
Kingly Street - A2
Kingsway - F1/F2

Langley Street - E2
Leicester Court - C3
Leicester Place - C3
Leicester Square - C3
Leicester Street - C3
Lexington Street - B3
Lisle Street - C3
Litchfield Street - D3
Little Newport Street - D3
Livonia Street - B2

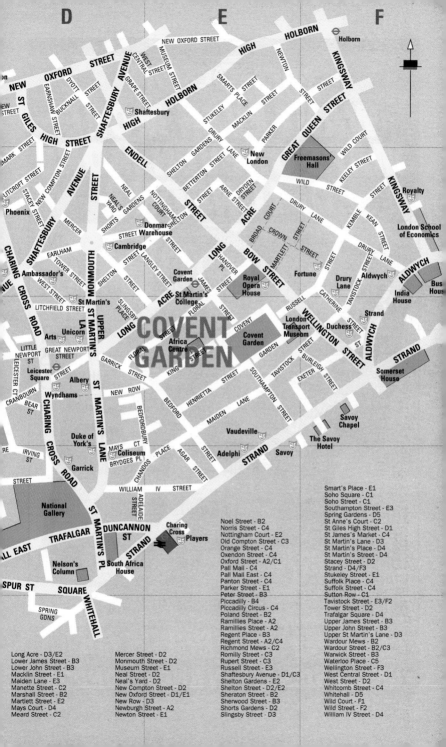

COVENT
GARDEN

London: Underground

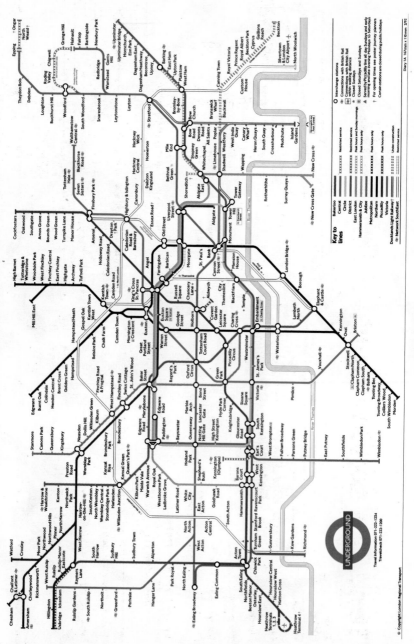

Time Out London Guide Reader's Report

Name:
Address:

Telephone:

Age: up to 19 ☐ 20-24 ☐ 25-29 ☐ 30-34 ☐ 35-44 ☐ 45+ ☐

Nationality:

Occupation:

Did you travel to London:

Alone? ☐	With partner? ☐		
As part of a group? ☐	With children? ☐		

How long is your trip to London?

Less than 3 days ☐	3 days-one week ☐
One week-two weeks ☐	Over two weeks (please specify) ☐

Are you a *Time Out* magazine reader? Yes ☐ No ☐

Have you bought other *Time Out* guides? If so, which ones?

Paris Guide ☐	Prague Guide ☐
Rome Guide ☐	Berlin Guide ☐
New York Guide ☐	Amsterdam Guide ☐

Madrid Guide ☐ Shopping & Services Guide ☐
London Visitors' Guide ☐ Eating & Drinking in London Guide ☐

Would you like to receive information about new titles? Yes ☐ No ☐

How useful did you find the following sections:

	Very?	Useful?	Fairly?	Not very?
Accommodation	☐	☐	☐	☐
Sightseeing	☐	☐	☐	☐
London by Area	☐	☐	☐	☐
History	☐	☐	☐	☐
On the Town	☐	☐	☐	☐
Galleries & Museums	☐	☐	☐	☐
Arts & Entertainment	☐	☐	☐	☐
In Focus	☐	☐	☐	☐
Survival	☐	☐	☐	☐
Trips Out Of Town	☐	☐	☐	☐

Is there anything you'd like us to cover in greater depth?

Please use the space below to tell us about places that you think should be included in the Guide:

AFFIX
STAMP
HERE

Time Out Magazine
Universal House
251 Tottenham Court Road
London
United Kingdom
W1P 0AB